ESSENTIALS OF MARKETING COMMUNICATIONS

CHRIS FILL

Financial Times
Prentice Hall
is an imprint of

PEARSON

Harlow, England • London • New York • Boston • San Francisco • Toronto • Sydney • Singapore • Hong Kong
Tokyo • Seoul • Taipei • New Delhi • Cape Town • Madrid • Mexico City • Amsterdam • Munich • Paris • Milan

Pearson Education Limited
Edinburgh Gate
Harlow
Essex CM20 2JE
England

and Associated Companies throughout the world

Visit us on the World Wide Web at:
www.pearsoned.co.uk

First published 2011

ISBN: 978-0-273-73844-2

British Library Cataloguing-in-Publication Data
A catalogue record for this book is available from the British Library

Library of Congress Cataloging-in-Publication Data
Fill, Chris.
    Essentials of marketing communications / Chris Fill.
       p.   cm.
    ISBN 978-0-273-73844-2 (pbk.)
1. Communication in marketing.   I. Title.
    HF5415.123.F547 2011
    658.8'02–dc22

                                            2011001700

10   9   8   7   6   5
14   13

Typeset in 10/12pt Minion by 35
Printed and bound in the UK by CPI

ESSENTIALS OF MARKETING COMMUNICATIONS

Learning Resource Centre
Tel: 01793 498381

NOT TO BE TAKEN AWAY

Brief contents

Contents

Supporting resources

Visit www.pearsoned.co.uk/fill to find valuable online resources:

Companion Website for students

- Podcasts on the key concepts of marketing communications
- Multiple-choice questions to test your learning
- An online glossary to explain key terms
- Flashcards to test your understanding of key terms

For instructors

- Complete, downloadable Instructor's Manual
- PowerPoint slides that can be downloaded and used for presentations

Also: The Companion Website provides the following features:

- Search tool to help locate specific items of content
- E-mail results and profile tools to send results of quizzes to instructors
- Online help and support to assist with website usage and troubleshooting

For more information please contact your local Pearson Education sales representative or visit www.pearsoned.co.uk/fill

Guided tour

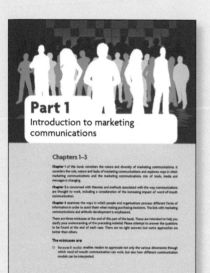

Part openers summarise the key points in each chapter and also give a summary of the MiniCases.

Aims and objectives enable you to focus on what you should have achieved by the end of the chapter.

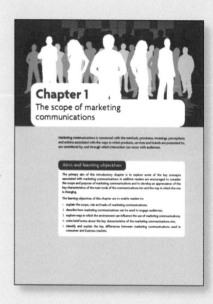

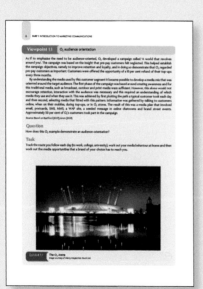

Snappy ViewPoints boxes improve your understanding by providing different perspectives. Each one ends with a question and task.

Great colour photography from actual high-profile marketing campaigns is used throughout the book.

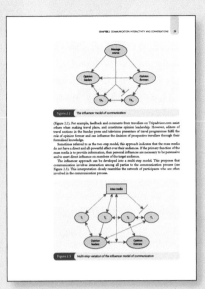

Figures and tables illustrate key points, concepts and processes visually to reinforce your learning.

Each Part concludes with a number of **Minicases** which encourage stimulating debates and class discussion.

Each Minicase is accompanied by **Questions** which will help you apply what you have read in the case study to marketing communications theory.

Summaries clinch the important concepts that have just been presented, to reinforce the chapter.

Every chapter ends with **Review questions** which test your understanding and help you to track your progress.

Each chapter is supported by a list of **References** directing your independent study to a variety of sources.

Guided tour of the companion website

Visit the companion website:
www.pearsoned.co.uk/fill for
a comprehensive collection
of material to help you take
your knowledge of marketing
communications to a higher level.

The **Multiple choice questions**
enable you to test your knowledge
and understanding of each chapter.

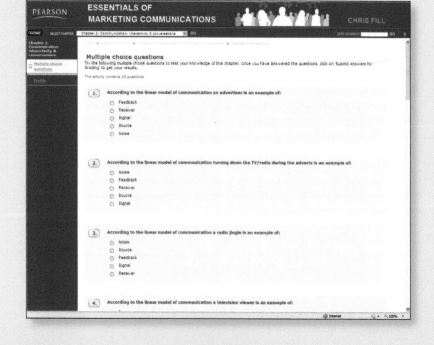

The **Glossary** is a useful quick explanation of key terms.

Test your understanding of key terms with these handy **Flashcards**.

Preface

This book has been written for people who want to know more about marketing communications. If that applies to you then thank you for choosing to read my book. I feel we will get along together.

The book is intended to support a range of people. These include university and college students who are studying marketing communications, advertising or perhaps media studies. Some people may be studying for professional qualifications, such as those offered by the Chartered Institute of Marketing, CAM and the Institute of Direct Marketing. This book is also relevant to them. You may not fall into these categories and have other reasons to learn more about marketing communications. For example, students reading for dissertations, commercial and business people preparing reports and presentations, public service professionals seeking explanations and of course there are people who are just inquisitive. Whoever you are, and whatever your motivation, I hope you find this text accessible and that you find the answers to your questions.

The changing world of marketing communications

Marketing communications is a complex subject and draws on a variety of disciplines. It is evolving very quickly, to the point that some practitioner aspects are changing almost constantly.

This book has been written with a view to disentangling some of the complexity. It has been written largely, but not entirely, from an academic perspective, not a technical or practitioner aspect. The aim therefore is provide an insight into why marketing communications works in particular ways, and of course, why it does not work in other ways. The aim is for you to enjoy the subject, be stimulated to want to know more and to engage further with the exciting and fast-changing world of marketing communications.

All organisations, large and small, commercial, government, charities, educational and other not-for-profit ones need to communicate with a range of stakeholders. This may be in order to get materials and services to undertake their business activities or to collaborate and coordinate with others to secure suitable distribution of their goods and services. In addition, there are consumers, you and me, people who are free to choose among the many hundreds and thousands of product and service offerings. Marketing communications provides a core activity so that all interested parties can understand the intentions of others and appreciate the value of the goods and services offered.

Traditionally, there are five main marketing communication tools: advertising, sales promotion, personal selling, public relations and direct marketing. In addition, there are media in which time and space can be bought or used to deliver messages to target audiences. For a long time the appropriate mix of these tools and the choice of media have, to some extent, been largely predictable. Distinct mixes could be identified for business-to-consumer (b2c) and business-to-business (b2b) audiences. There were variations reflecting particular brand circumstances, but essentially in the b2c market, advertising was used to build brand values, sales promotions were used to encourage customer action and public relations sought to generate goodwill and interest in the company.

Personal selling was regarded as the primary tool in b2b markets, but it also had a role to play in retail environments, for example, selling consumer durables. In the 1990s direct marketing became a more prominent tool in the mix because technology had enabled a form of communication by appealing personally and directly to the target customer. This change introduced new media formats and the subsequent development of the Internet and related digital technologies has accelerated change in the marketing communications industry. There are now a myriad of opportunities to reach audiences, with the Internet now a core communication channel.

Just as these changes were taking place, so the media world has splintered into many different parts, media fragmentation. Simultaneously, audiences have more varied ways to spend their leisure time than they used to and as a result have become less attached to what was a narrow band of conventional media. This is referred to as audience fragmentation. Some of those who choose to incorporate the media as part of their relaxation now have hundreds of television channels, all have access to an increasing number of general and specific interest magazines and a multitude of new cinema complexes. Of course the Internet offers a seemingly endless source of rich information, opportunities to buy online, and global entertainment. Social media and social networking, in particular, have driven huge growth in interacting, creating and sharing consumer generated content which is changing the way in which brands communicate with audiences. The world of marketing communications is bright, exciting, sometimes unpredictable, yet always challenging and evolving.

Managers are now not only required to find new ways to communicate, but many are operating on reduced budgets for which they are accountable. The development of long-term relationships with customers, whether in b2b or b2c markets, is now an essential aspect of marketing policy. Customer retention is crucial today and various devices, such as loyalty schemes, are used to shape long-term customer behaviour. Organisations now accept that the tools of the communications mix are not the only way brands communicate. All parts of the marketing mix communicate: the behaviour of employees and the performance of products, the actions of competitors all serve to influence the way in which each customer perceives a brand.

The recent recession has impacted on clients, agencies and of course consumers and business customers. Marketing communication agencies are trying to realign themselves structurally and in terms of the value they offer clients. Clients are revaluating the way they communicate with customers and how exactly they can use social media, and networking in particular, to their advantage. Customers are more involved with brands and their associated communications. This involvement is through word of mouth communications and increasingly through different forms of user generated content.

Where does this all lead? It leads to a new form and role for marketing communications. It brings into focus an even more urgent need for a redefined and workable approach to integrated marketing communications. Traditionally, an organisation's marketing communications should be planned, coherent and consistent. The need for this approach is still evident, but there is also a need for an increasing element to accommodate the unplanned and spontaneous communications driven by customers. This has ramifications for structure, content, budgets, measurement and strategy.

This book introduces you to this changing world of marketing communications and allows you to appreciate some of the issues associated with marketing communications, and related aspects of integration, coordination and interaction with audiences. There are examples of the practical application of marketing communications and illustrations that demonstrate the application of theory in practice.

Overview of the book

A key topic in this book is engagement. Effective marketing communications enables audiences to engage with products, services, brands and organisations. Through engagement relationships can develop and this enables customers, stakeholders and organisations to achieve their various goals. The degree to which engagement occurs reflects audience perception, interpretation and meaning of the messages delivered. Through engagement brand value and equity can be developed or reduced. Engagement, therefore, encompasses a range of marketing communication activities and is referred to throughout the text.

This book seeks to provide a consistent appraisal of the ever-expanding world of marketing communications. This book also seeks to stimulate thought and consideration about a wide range of interrelated issues. To help achieve these aims a number of theories and models are advanced. Some of these theories reflect marketing practice, while others are offered as suggestions for moving the subject forward. Many of the theories are abstractions of actual practice, some are based on empirical research and others are pure conceptualisation. All seek to enrich the subject, but not all need carry the same weight of contribution. Readers should form their own opinions based upon their reading, experience and judgement.

There are a number of themes running through the text, but perhaps the two main ones concern relationship marketing and integrated communications. It is my view that organisations will in the future perceive communications as a core strategic activity, central to strategic management and thought. Corporate and marketing communications will inevitably move closer together, and provide a stronger force for integration. The need to build and sustain relationships with a variety of stakeholders inside and outside the organisation will become paramount and communications will be a vital source in making it all work.

So, this book uses some core academic materials to explore how some organisations use marketing communications in practice. It is therefore a blend of theory and practice. The book uses examples drawn largely from European and North American organisations to illustrate how organisations use marketing communications.

Structure of this text

There are three main parts to this book.

Part 1   Introduction to marketing communications

Part 1 introduces fundamental ideas and concepts associated with marketing communications. Readers are introduced to the subject from a general perspective before seeking to establish some core information about communication theory and the importance of people and technology on the way in which communication is considered to work. The part closes with important underpinning material about how people and organisations process different forms of information in order to assist them when making purchasing decisions.

There are three chapters in Part 1:

- Chapter 1   The scope of marketing communications
- Chapter 2   Communication: interactivity and conversations
- Chapter 3   Audiences: attitudes, behaviour and decision-making

Part 2   Managing marketing communications

Part 2 is concerned with the management of marketing communications. This part of the book considers some of the key issues management must address in order that an organisation's marketing communications are effective. These involve determining and establishing marketing communications strategy, including segmentation, the identification of target markets and the positioning necessary to establish a strong position in the market.

Ideas associated with integration and the planning of marketing communication activities follow. Other important topics covered in this part concern branding, budgeting and the evaluation of marketing communications events. Other subjects include the role and operations of communication agencies and the regulations concerning the way organisations and agencies communicate with target audiences. Issues concerning international marketing communications are also covered.

The final chapter examines relationship marketing and the crucial underpinning this provides for the way we should manage marketing communication activities.

There are five chapters in Part 2:

- Chapter 4   Strategies, objectives and positioning
- Chapter 5   Integration and planning
- Chapter 6   Branding, budgeting and evaluation
- Chapter 7   Agencies: practice, regulation and international communications
- Chapter 8   Shaping relationships with marketing communications

Part 3   The marketing communications mix

Part 3 focuses on the marketing communications mix, the means by which organisations communicate with their audiences. Several chapters are given over to examining the principal tools; advertising, sales and trade promotions, public relations, direct marketing and personal selling. Consideration is also given to exhibitions, sponsorship and product placement.

The characteristics of conventional and digital media are then examined followed by an exploration of the techniques and processes associated with interactive marketing communications. The final chapter considers the format, style and presentation of messages.

The key aim of this part of the book is to enable readers to understand the different parts of the marketing communications mix and to appreciate the issues associated with bringing them together in order to communicate effectively with target audiences.

There are seven chapters in Part 3:

- Chapter 9   Advertising
- Chapter 10   Public relations and sponsorship
- Chapter 11   Direct marketing and personal selling
- Chapter 12   Sales promotion, exhibitions and product placement
- Chapter 13   Media: conventional and digital
- Chapter 14   Interactive marketing communications
- Chapter 15   Content: credibility, messages and creative approaches

Design features and presentation

In addition to the three-part structure of the book, there are a number of features that are intended to help readers navigate the material.

Chapter objectives

Each chapter opens with both the aims of what is to be covered and a list of (learning) objectives. This helps to signal the primary topics that are covered in the chapter and so guide the learning experience.

Visual supports

This book is produced in four colour and throughout the text there are numerous colour and black and white exhibits, figures (diagrams) and tables of information, which serve to highlight, illustrate and bring life to the written word. The pictures used either serve to illustrate particular points by demonstrating theory in practice or they are used to complement individual examples. The examples are normally highlighted in the text as Viewpoints. These examples are easily distinguishable through the colour contrasts and serve to demonstrate how a particular aspect of marketing communications has been used by an organisation in a particular context. I hope you enjoy these Viewpoints of marketing communication practice.

Summaries and minicases

At the end of each chapter there is a summary and a series of review and discussion questions. Readers are encouraged to test their own understanding of the content of each chapter by considering some or all of the discussion questions. In this sense the questions support self-study but tutors might wish to use some of these as part of a seminar or workshop programme.

In addition, each part of the book opens with a synopsis of the coverage. Each part closes with several minicases and supportive questions, designed to help readers apply some of the content explored in each particular part. These short cases can be used in class for discussion purposes and to explore some of the salient issues that have been raised. Students working alone can use the minicases to test their own understanding and to consolidate their understanding.

Support materials

Students and lecturers who adopt this text have a range of support materials and facilities to help them.

Readers are invited to visit the companion website for the book at **www.pearsoned.co.uk/fill**. Here students have access to further minicases. For lecturers and tutors there is an Instructor's Manual containing a range of teaching schemes, accessible via a password-protected section of the companion website. From this site a range of PowerPoint slides is also available for lecturer use. A test bank of multiple-choice questions has also been developed for use by students and lecturers.

Student resources

- Additional learning materials including podcasts
- Full online glossary
- Multiple-choice questions
- Additional cases and examples

Lecturer resources

- Instructor's guide
- PowerPoint slides for each chapter
- Additional case studies

Chris Fill

www.fillassociates.co.uk
chris@fillassociates.co.uk

Acknowledgements

This book could not have been written without the support of a wide range of brilliant people. Contributions range from those who provided information and permissions, those who wrote minicases, answered questions and those who tolerated my persistent nagging, sending through photographs, answering phone calls and emails and those who simply liaised with others. Finally, there are those who have read, reviewed drafts, made constructive comments and provided moral support and encouragement.

The list of individuals and organisations involved with this book is extensive. My thanks are offered to all of you, including my gratitude for the time and expertise of the Part end Minicase authors. I have tried to list everyone involved with the book but if anyone has been omitted then I offer my apologies.

Jill Brown – University of Portsmouth
Bruce Bowhill – University of Portsmouth
Richard Godfrey – University of Leicester (author of Minicase 1.2, on p. 83)
Mick Hayes – University of Portsmouth
Graham Hughes – formerly with Leeds Metropolitan University
Nigel Markwick – littlebigfish
Lorna Stevens – University of Ulster (author of Minicase 3.1, on p. 401)
Lynn Sudbury – Liverpool John Moores University (author of Minicase 1.1, on p. 82)
Andrew Turnbull – Robert Gordon University (author of Minicase 2.1, on p. 216)
Debra Weatherley – Findphoto

Above all perhaps are the various individuals at Pearson and their associates who have taken my manuscript, managed it and published it in this form. In particular I should like to thank my editor, Rachel Gear. She has been supremely professional, enthusiastic, supportive and patient. In much the same way Emma Violet continues to provide the materials and resources which all help me to get things done. In addition I should like to thank Philippa Fiszzon, Kelly Miller, Linda Dhondy and Jonathon Price for transforming the manuscript into the final product. Thank you all.

Finally, I would like to take this opportunity to once again thank my wife Karen. Her continued support during the writing process, amid the chaos of everyday life, is fantastic, much appreciated, if unspoken, and simply brilliant.

Publisher's Acknowledgements

We are grateful to the following for permission to reproduce copyright material:

Figures

Figure 1.1 from Redefining the nature and format of the marketing communications mix, *The Marketing Review*, 7(1), pp. 45–57 (Hughes, G. and Fill, C. 2007); Figure 2.5 from *Diffusion of*

Innovations, 3rd ed., New York: Free Press (Rogers, Everett M.) Copyright © 1962, 1971, 1983 by The Free Press, all rights reserved, reprinted with the permission of The Free Press, a Division of Simon & Schuster, Inc.; Figure 2.6 from *Consumer Behaviour: Implications for Marketing Strategy*, 4th ed., Homewood, IL: Richard D. Irwin (Hawkins, D.I., Best, R.J. and Coney, K.A. 1989), reproduced with permission of The McGraw-Hill Companies; Figure 8.2 from The commitment-trust theory of relationship marketing, *Journal of Marketing*, 58 (July), pp. 20–38 (Morgan, R.M. and Hunt, S.D. 1994), used with kind permission of the American Marketing Association; Figure 8.3 from *Relationship Marketing: Creating Stakeholder Value*, Oxford: Butterworth Heinemann (Christopher, M., Payne, A. and Ballantyne, D. 2002) Copyright Elsevier; Figure 8.4 from Is your loyalty programme really building loyalty? Why increasing emotional attachment, not just repeat buying, is key to maximizing programme success, *Journal of Targeting, Measurement and Analysis for Marketing*, 12(3), pp. 231–41 (Hallberg, G. 2004), Copyright © 2004 published by Palgrave Macmillan, reprinted by permission from Macmillan Publishers Ltd.; Figure 9.1 from Does it pay to shock? Reactions to shocking and nonshocking advertising content among university students, *Journal of Advertising Research*, 43(3), pp. 268–81 (Dahl, D.W., Frankenberger, K.D. and Manchanda, R.V. 2003); Figure 9.3 adapted from Attitude toward the ad as a mediator of advertising effectiveness: determinants and consequences, *Advances in Consumer Research*, 10, pp. 532–539 (Lutz, J., Mackenzie, S.B. and Belch, G.E. 1983); Figure 10.1 from *Managing Public Relations*, New York: Holt, Rineholt & Winston (Grunig, J. and Hunt, T. 1984), reprinted by permission of James E. Grunig; Figure 10.3 after A new framework for evaluating sponsorship opportunities, *International Journal of Advertising*, 25(4), pp. 471–87 (Poon, D.T.Y. and Prendergast, G. 2006); Figure 11.3 after Evaluating multiple channel strategies, *Journal of Business and Industrial Marketing*, 6(3/4), pp. 37–48 (Cravens, D.W., Ingram, T.N. and LaForge, R.W. 1991), © Emerald Group Publishing Limited, all rights reserved; Figure 12.2 from Branded entertainment: a new advertising technique or product placement in disguise?, *Journal of Marketing Management*, 22(5/6), pp. 489–504 (Hudson, S. and Hudson, D. 2006), Copyright © Westburn Publishers Ltd., reprinted by permission of (Taylor & Francis Ltd., http://www.tandf.co.uk/journals) on behalf of Westburn Publishers Ltd., and with permission of the authors; Figure 14.1 from Internet community bonding: the case of macnews.de., *European Journal of Marketing*, 38(5/6), pp. 626–40 (Szmigin, I. and Reppel, A.E. 2004), © Emerald Group Publishing Limited, all rights reserved; Figures 15.1, 15.2, 15.3, 15.4 after *Advertising Communications & Promotion Management*, 2nd ed. (Rossiter, J.R. and Percy, L. 1997) New York: McGraw-Hill, reprinted by permission of John R. Rossiter.

Tables

Table 2.1 after Dialogue and its role in the development of relationship specific knowledge, *Journal of Business and Industrial Marketing*, 19(2), pp. 114–23 (Ballantyne, D. 2004), © Emerald Group Publishing Limited, all rights reserved; Table 6.4 from Conceptualization and measurement of multidimensionality of integrated marketing communications, *Journal of Advertising Research*, 47(3), pp. 222–236 (Lee, D.H. and Park, C.W. 2007); Table 8.2 from Marketing relationships in Brazil: trends in value strategies and capabilities, *Journal of Business and Industrial Marketing*, 24(5/6), pp. 449–459 (Ribeiro, A.H.P., Brashear, T.G., Monteiro, P.R.R. and Damázio, L.F. 2009), © Emerald Group Publishing Limited, all rights reserved; Table 12.7 from An exploratory study of attendee activities at a business trade show, *Journal of Business and Industrial Marketing*, 25(4), pp. 241–248 (Gopalakrishna, S., Roster, C.A. and Sridhar, S. 2010), © Emerald Group Publishing Limited, all rights reserved; Table 13.5 adapted from Recency planning, *Admap*, February, pp. 32–4 (Ephron, E. 1997), www.admapmagazine.com; Table 14.2 from UK on-line community, *Durlacher Quarterly Internet Report*, Quarter 3, pp. 7–11 (Durlacher 1999).

Photographs

(**Key:** b – bottom; c – centre; l – left; r – right; t – top)

Alamy Images: 333, Ace Stock Ltd. 6, B.L. Images Ltd. 135, Paul Mogford 394r, John Warburton-Lee Photography 267; **Birds Eye Ltd:** 63; **B & Q:** 98; **Google, Inc.:** 356; **Land Rover:** 329; **Danone:** 394l; **Dell:** 287; **E.ON UK plc:** 361; **Fabergé** : 205; **Freud Communications:** Iain Lewis 192; **Getty Images:** Ryan Anson/AFP 382, Feng Li 313, Leon Neal/AFP 381l, Jim Smeal/WireImage 381r, Brent Stirton 254; **Green & Black's, image courtesy of Brave:** 13; **The Advertising Archives:** 36, 49, 60l, 60r, 100, 120, 145, 157, 183, 228, 229, 242t, 243b, 355, 363, 378, 379; **MARK/BBDO in the Czech republic:** Heinz Tomato Ketchup Company (for Heinz) Czech Republic 61; **Nikon:** 230; **Nissan:** 122; **Press Association Images:** PA Wire 261; **Pretty Polly:** 332; **Red Bull Photofiles:** John Gibson 20; **Ronseal Ltd:** 40; **Three Sixty:** 244; © 2010 TNT N.V.:** 209; **Toshiba:** 110, 258–259; **Viking Direct:** 199–200; **Vue Entertainment:** 335.

In some instances we have been unable to trace the owners of copyright material, and we would appreciate any information that would enable us to do so.

Part 1
Introduction to marketing communications

Chapters 1–3

Chapter 1 of this book considers the nature and diversity of marketing communications. It considers the role, nature and tasks of marketing communications and explores ways in which marketing communications and the marketing communications mix of tools, media and messages is changing.

Chapter 2 is concerned with theories and methods associated with the way communications are thought to work, including a consideration of the increasing impact of word-of-mouth communication.

Chapter 3 examines the ways in which people and organisations process different forms of information in order to assist them when making purchasing decisions. The link with marketing communications and attitude development is emphasised.

There are three minicases at the end of this part of the book. These are intended to help you clarify your understanding of the preceding material. Please attempt to answer the questions to be found at the end of each case. There are no right answers but some approaches are better than others.

The minicases are:

1.1 **Because it works!:** enables readers to appreciate not only the various dimensions through which word-of-mouth communication can work, but also how different communication models can be interpreted.

1.2 **Unlocking the secrets of the male shopper:** provides an interesting insight into some of the issues associated with reaching this particular market. Of these, marketing communications is an important matter. The importance of understanding the way in which different segments process information and think and behave is emphasised.

1.3 **Helping Hands:** is an important minicase if only because it depicts the use of marketing communications in a charity context. The case enables readers to consider how engagement can be encouraged through marketing communications and it also enables them to apply the DRIP framework.

Chapter 1
The scope of marketing communications

Marketing communications is concerned with the methods, processes, meanings, perceptions and actions associated with the ways in which products, services and brands are presented to, are considered by, and through which interaction can occur with audiences.

Aims and learning objectives

The primary aim of this introductory chapter is to explore some of the key concepts associated with marketing communications. In addition readers are encouraged to consider the scope and purpose of marketing communications and to develop an appreciation of the key characteristics of the main tools of the communications mix and the way in which the mix is changing.

The learning objectives of this chapter are to enable readers to:

1. explain the scope, role and tasks of marketing communications;
2. describe how marketing communications can be used to engage audiences;
3. explore ways in which the environment can influence the use of marketing communications;
4. write brief notes about the key characteristics of the marketing communications mix;
5. identify and explain the key differences between marketing communications used in consumer and business markets.

Introduction

Organisations such as Apple, O$_2$, Tesco, Santander, Haier, Nokia, BBC, Gillette, Microsoft, Chanel, Boeing, Oxfam and Petrobras all operate across a number of sectors, markets and countries and all use a variety of marketing communications tools, media and messages to communicate with their various audiences. These audiences consist not only of people who buy their products and services but also of people and organisations who might be able to influence them, who might help and support them by providing, for example, labour, finance, manufacturing facilities, distribution outlets and legal advice, or who are interested because of their impact on parts of society or the business sector in particular.

There is no universally agreed definition of marketing communications and there are many interpretations of the subject. The origin of many definitions rests with a promotional outlook where the purpose was to use communications to persuade people to buy products and services. The focus was on products, one-way communications, and the perspective was short term. The expression 'marketing communications' emerged as a wider range of tools and media evolved and as the scope of the tasks these communications activities were expected to accomplish expanded.

In addition to awareness and persuasion, new goals such as developing understanding and preference, and reminding and reassuring customers, became recognised as important aspects of the communications effort. Direct marketing activities heralded a new approach as one-to-one and two-way communications began to shift the focus from mass to personal communications. Now a number of definitions refer to an integrated perspective. This view has gathered momentum since the mid-1990s and has become an essential part of the marketing communications vocabulary. With the integrative perspective a stronger strategic and long-term orientation has developed, although the basis for many marketing communication strategies appears to still rest with a promotional mix orientation.

The key issue is that marketing communications has the potential to provide added value, and it achieves this through the development of appropriate customer relationships. Marketing communications can enable organisations to share understanding, and some would argue that it creates opportunities for value creation (Vargo and Lusch, 2004). Above all else, marketing communications should be an audience-centred activity.

> Marketing communications is an audience centred activity which attempts to encourage engagement between participants and provoke conversations.

This definition has two key points. The first concerns the notion that marketing communications is audience-centred. Traditionally marketing communications has been used to convey product-related information to customer audiences. Today, marketing communications needs to connect with a range of stakeholders who have links and relationships with the organisation, each of varying dimensions. In a customer centric world, marketing communications should seek to provide value for the target audience, based on their needs. Marketing communications should be an audience-centred activity. In that sense, it is important that messages be based on an understanding of both the needs and environment of the audience. To be successful, marketing communications should be grounded in the behaviour and information-processing needs and style of the target audience; an outside-in approach.

Viewpoint 1.1 O_2 audience orientation

As if to emphasise the need to be audience-oriented, O_2 developed a campaign called 'A world that revolves around you'. The campaign was based on the insight that pre-pay customers felt neglected. This helped establish the campaign objectives, namely to improve retention and loyalty, and in doing so demonstrate that O_2 regarded pre-pay customers as important. Customers were offered the opportunity of a 10 per cent refund of their top-ups every three months.

By understanding the media used by this customer segment it became possible to develop a media mix that was oriented around the target audience. The first phase of the campaign was based around creating awareness and for this traditional media, such as broadcast, outdoor and print media were sufficient. However, this alone would not encourage retention, interaction with the audience was necessary and this required an understanding of which media they use and when they use it. This was achieved by first plotting the path a typical customer took each day and then second, selecting media that fitted with this pattern. Information was gathered by talking to customers online, when on their mobiles, during top-ups, or in O_2 stores. The result of this was a media plan that involved email, postcards, SMS, MMS, a WAP site, a seeded message in online chatrooms and brand street events. Approximately 50 per cent of O_2's customers took part in the campaign.

Source: Based on Bashford (2007); Anon (2009)

Question

How does this O_2 example demonstrate an audience orientation?

Task

Track the route you follow each day (to work, college, university), work out your media behaviour at home and then work out the media opportunities that a brand of your choice has to reach you.

Exhibit 1.1   The O_2 Arena
Image courtesy of Alamy Images/Ace Stock Ltd.

The second key point concerns the word *engagement*, or the nature of the communication that can occur between people and between people and machines. Engagement refers to audience captivation, a moment achieved through the use of communication tools, media and people to deliver messages that are relevant, meaningful, of interest and which arouse curiosity. Such captivation may last seconds, such as at the impact of a stunning ad, the sight of a beautiful person or the emotion a piece of music might bring to an individual. Alternatively, engagement may be protracted and last hours, days, weeks, months or years, depending on the context and the level of enjoyment or loyalty felt towards the event, object or person. Whatever the duration engagement enables the communication of messages that are understood, are rich in information or emotional content and which have meaning for the participants. In turn these messages provoke people to talk about their experiences. These conversations may be conducted through face-to-face, ear-to-ear or various electronic formats.

Marketing communications is a complex activity and is used by organisations with varying degrees of sophistication and success. The issue of engagement is examined in greater depth later in this chapter.

The scope of marketing communications

At a basic level, marketing communications, or promotion as it was originally known, is used to communicate elements of an organisation's offering to a target audience. Marketing communications can carry a brand's promise to customers. This promise might refer to the attributes and features of a product/service, its performance characteristics. It might however, focus on the benefits, the functional and emotional feelings and experiences that customers can enjoy through purchase and consumption. Sometimes marketing communications are used to promise on both elements.

Duncan and Moriarty (1997) and Grönroos (2004) suggest that the scope of marketing communications should incorporate four main dimensions. The first of these is that organisations develop a set of **planned** communication events, which are developed through research, resourced, timed and delivered to targeted audiences. These are largely controlled communications unlike those arising from **unplanned** or unintended customer experiences. These might occur through empty stock shelves, accidents or word-of-mouth communications. In addition to these there are marketing communications experienced by audiences relating to both their experience from **using products** (how tasty is this smoothie?) or **the consumption of services** (just how good was the service in that hotel, restaurant or at the airport?). These dimensions of marketing communications are represented at Figure 1.1 (Hughes and Fill, 2007).

Figure 1.1 helps demonstrate the breadth of the subject and the inherent complexity associated with managing communication with audiences and the way they engage with a brand. Although useful in terms of providing an overview, this framework requires elaboration in order to appreciate the detail associated with each of the elements, especially planned marketing communications. This book builds on this framework and in particular considers issues associated with both planned and unplanned aspects of marketing communications.

Planned or formalised marketing communications incorporates three key elements: tools, media and messages, known collectively as the marketing communications mix. The main communication tools are advertising, sales promotion, public relations, direct marketing, personal selling and added-value approaches such as sponsorship, a subpart of public relations. Messages can be primarily informative or emotional but are usually a subtle blend of both dimensions reflecting the preferences and needs of the target audience. To help get these messages through to their audiences, organisations use two main types of media. One type refers to traditional media such as print and broadcast, cinema and outdoor. The other refers to the increasing use of digital media, and the Internet in particular, in order to listen to, interact and converse with audiences.

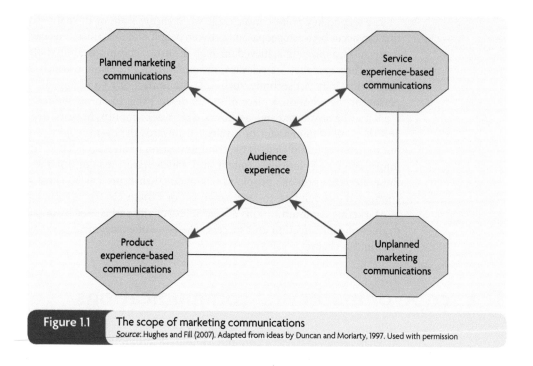

Figure 1.1	The scope of marketing communications

Source: Hughes and Fill (2007). Adapted from ideas by Duncan and Moriarty, 1997. Used with permission

Unplanned marketing communications involve communications that have not been anticipated and hence are relatively uncontrollable. These may be both positive and negative but here the emphasis is more on how the organisation reacts to and manages the meanings attributed by audiences to these messages. For example, unsolicited comments by third-party experts, changes in legislation or regulations by a government, the actions of competitors, failures in the production or distribution processes or perhaps the most potent of all communications, word-of-mouth comments between customers, all impact on the way in which organisations and brands are perceived and the images and reputations that are developed. Many reports, for example JMW (2010), have reported the relative effectiveness of these approaches and that the vast majority find that people use word of mouth recommendation when making purchasing decisions, rather than advertising, preferring to see others using the product. Not surprisingly, many leading organisations recognise the power and influence of word-of-mouth communication and actively seek to shape the nature, timing and speed with which it occurs. In other words, they attempt to control the uncontrollable and the planned and the unplanned begin to merge.

When considering the scope of marketing communications it is important to consider the broad industry context in which marketing communication events occur. Figure 1.2 illustrates the industry context, setting it out within an audience perspective. Planned marketing communications are developed and delivered through the five principal tools mentioned earlier. The media play an increasingly influential role in marketing communications activities and provide an important contextual dimension. What is communicated, the content of the message, is also important. Organisations invest heavily in trying to understand their audiences and to develop messages that resonate with them. These three elements are examined later in this chapter and again in Part 3. The final contextual element concerns people, processes and systems. Most marketing communications require people to establish, maintain and intervene in communication processes and often these are enabled through the use of technology. Indeed, digital technology has been pivotal in shaping the current marketing communications environment, whether it be through mobile phones, webpages, or call centres they are used extensively by organisations to provide customer support.

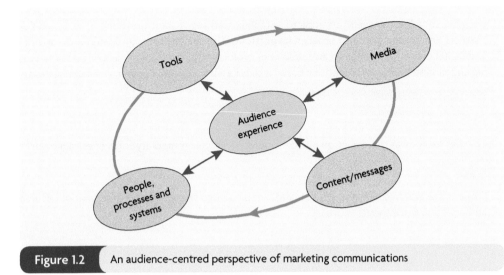

| Figure 1.2 | An audience-centred perspective of marketing communications |

The role of marketing communications

Organisations communicate with a variety of audiences in order to pursue their marketing and business objectives. Marketing communications can be used to engage with a variety of audiences and in such a way that meet the needs of the audience. Messages should encourage individual members of target audiences to respond to the focus organisation (or product/brand). This response can be immediate through, for example, purchase behaviour or use of customer care lines, or it can be deferred as information is assimilated and considered for future use. Even if the information is discarded at a later date, the communication will have attracted attention and consideration of the message.

| Viewpoint 1.2 | Iced apples or will it be pears? |

The campaign used by Magners during the summer of 2006 to roll out their brand of cider across the UK was based primarily on observational consumer research. The basis for the campaign was to position the drink as 'naturally refreshing' by showing it poured over ice, in an apple orchard and in a pint bottle.

One of the first tasks undertaken on the Bulmer's brand in the early 1990s was to elevate cider out of the 'embarrassed-to-be-seen-drinking' category and to do this C&C, the owner, repositioned Bulmer's closer to beer by adding long-neck bottles and cans to its on tap offering. C&C then observed 40- and 50-something golfers choosing Bulmer's to quench their thirst. This led to campaigns that helped to encourage drinkers to consider cider as a refreshing drink. Magners contains a high level of natural apple juice content and a lower alcohol content than other ciders, so it is much easier to make refreshment the key point of differentiation. These elements were critical when repositioning Magners as a quality, refreshing drink rather than a cheap intoxicant, which was how cider was largely viewed in the UK.

In 1997 C&C noticed consumers were adding ice to Bulmer's draught to cool it down. This use of ice was then adopted in Magners' campaigns. By showing consumers how to serve and drink the product it helped to create a clear point of difference for the brand. It was the first cider brand to do this and its success has led to competitive responses such as Sirrus from Scottish & Newcastle, especially formulated to be poured over ice.

The Magners' cider brand struggled to sustain its initial success, partly due to poor summer weather and competitor reactions. The 'over-ice' positioning was copied easily by competitors, and those that had big marketing budgets, squashed Magners' attempt to establish a strong market position. In 2009 the C&C Group launched Magners Pear in an attempt to broaden its portfolio. The launch campaign featured the use of television, outdoor and digital media. The campaign also used sales promotion in the form of sampling activity to encourage trial tasting and familiarity plus a competition based around a Magners 'pub finder' mobile application.

Source: Based on Baker (2006); Simm (2008); Alarcon (2009)

Question

To what extent was the depiction of cider poured over ice a temporary form of engagement?

Task

Observe the way five different drinks brands are presented to audiences. What point of differentiation do they use and how similar are they?

The reason for using marketing communications will vary according to the prevailing situation or context but the essential goal is to provoke an audience response. This response might be geared to developing brand values and the positive thoughts an individual might have about a brand. This is grounded in a 'thinking and feeling orientation', a combination of both cognitive thoughts and emotional feelings about a brand. Another type of response might be one that stimulates the audience to act in particular ways. Referred to as a behavioural or sometimes brand response, the goal is to 'encourage particular behaviours'. For example, these might include sampling a piece of cheese in a supermarket, encouraging visits to a website, placing orders and paying for goods and services, sharing information with a friend, registering on a network, opening letters, signing a petition or telephoning a number. See Figure 1.3 for a list of the factors that can drive engagement opportunities.

Apart from generating cash flows, the underlying purpose of these responses can be considered to be a strategic function of developing relationships with particular audiences and or from (re)positioning brands. For example, LV=, an insurance brand, moved from a behavioural strategy based on daytime direct response tv advertising, to one based on developing brand values. The goal was to boost awareness of its mutual status (rather than a plc) and so reposition the brand as a premium insurer (Brownsell, 2010a).

Engagement therefore can be considered to be a function of two forms of response. The quality of engagement cannot be determined but it can be argued that marketing communications

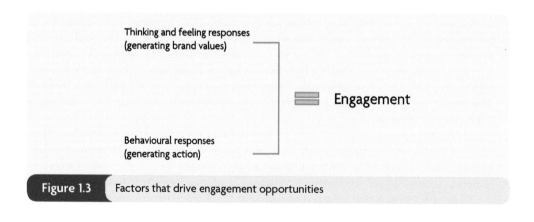

| Figure 1.3 | Factors that drive engagement opportunities |

should be based on driving a particular type of response that captivates an individual. For example, Sarah Copley, Sales and Marketing Director for Virgin Trains explained that for several years the company spent time developing and building the brand values particularly at a time when the product was not complete. However, now Virgin Trains have a focus on growing passenger numbers (Brownsell, 2010b), a behavioural strategy that requires a complementary communications approach.

From this it can be concluded that the primary role of marketing communication is to engage audiences. Where engagement occurs an individual might be said to have been positively captivated, and as a result opportunities for activity should increase. Engagement acts as a bridge, the mechanism through which brands and organisations link with target audiences and through which the goals of both parties can be achieved: mutual value.

Engagement suggests that understanding and meaning has been conveyed effectively. At one level, engagement through one way communication enables target audiences to understand product and service offers, to the extent that the audience is sufficiently engaged to want to enter into further communication activity. At another level, engagement through two-way or interactive communication enables information that is relationship specific (Ballantyne, 2004) to be exchanged. The greater the frequency of information exchange the more likely collaborative relationships will develop. So, the role of marketing communications is to engage audiences.

The tasks of marketing communications

Bowersox and Morash (1989) demonstrated that communication plays an important part in the process through which information flows as it can help accomplish one or more key tasks:

First, marketing communications can act as a differentiator, particularly in markets where there is little to separate competing products and brands. Mineral water products, such as Perrier and Highland Spring, are largely similar: it is the communications surrounding the products that have created various brand images, enabling consumers to make purchasing decisions. In these cases it is the images created by marketing communications that enable people to differentiate one brand from another and position them so that consumers' purchasing confidence and positive attitudes are developed.

Second, communications can also be used to reinforce experiences and beliefs. This may take the form of reminding people of a need they might have or reminding them of the benefits of past transactions with a view to convincing them that they should enter into a similar exchange. In addition, it is possible to provide reassurance or comfort either immediately prior to an exchange or, more commonly, post-purchase. This is important as it helps to retain current customers and improve profitability, an approach to business that is much more cost-effective than constantly striving to lure new customers. Brands are often refreshed, in order that they maintain currency among the target audience and remain competitive.

The third task identified was that communication can inform and make potential customers aware of an organisation's offering. No purchase can be made without prior awareness. Sometimes audiences need to be educated, shown how to use a product or service or advised about why a product might be helpful. The fourth and final task is to use communication to persuade current and potential customers of the desirability of either trialling a product, buying a product or to enter into a relationship.

Therefore, communication can build images about a brand; that is differentiate it, reinforce memories and understanding, inform and make audiences aware of a brand's presence and finally persuade an individual to buy and consume a product or service. To put it another way: DRIP (Fill, 2002). See Table 1.1 for an example.

Table 1.1	DRIP elements of marketing communications
DRIP element	**Examples**
Differentiate	Cravendale milk is better for us than ordinary milk because it is finely filtered, making it purer for a fresher taste.
Reinforce	McCain used communications to reassure consumers about the nutritional content of its products.
Inform/make aware	The Environment Agency and Flood Action Week inform various organisations, such as the Met Office, local media and the general public of the new flood warning codes.
Persuade	Cillit Bang . . . bang and the dirt is gone

At a higher level, the communication process not only supports the transaction, by informing, persuading, reinforcing or differentiating, but it also offers a means of exchange itself. Communications involve intangible benefits, such as the psychological satisfactions associated with, for example, the entertainment value of television advertisements or the experiences within a sponsored part of a social network.

Communications can also be seen as a means of perpetuating and transferring values and culture to different parts of society or networks. For example, it is argued that the way women are portrayed in the media and stereotypical images of very thin or 'size zero' women are dysfunctional in that they set up inappropriate role models. The form and characteristics of the communication process adopted by some organisations (both the deliberate and the unintentional use of signs and symbols used to convey meaning) help to provide stability and continuity.

Other examples of intangible satisfactions can be seen in the social and psychological transactions involved increasingly with the work of the National Health Service (NHS), charities, educational institutions and other not-for-profit organisations, such as housing associations. Not only do these organisations recognise the need to communicate with various audiences,

Viewpoint 1.3   Chocolate DRIPs

Green & Black's is a very successful premium organic brand of chocolate. Their use of marketing communications might be to:

- differentiate it from other chocolate brands;
- remind/reassure customers of the taste and experience of the brand;
- inform and educate the market about the ethics and economics of Fairtrade and the nutritional benefits of chocolate;
- persuade potential consumers and retailers to purchase and distribute Green & Black's respectively.

Question

Which of these tasks are the most important? Justify your view.

Task

Think of a campaign for a brand of your choice and consider how the DRIP model can be applied.

NEW BAR OPENING

Get in line for the smoothest, creamiest, most indulgent milk chocolate imaginable.

CREATED WITHOUT COMPROMISE

www.greenandblacks.com

Exhibit 1.2 Green and Black's 'Creamy Milk' chocolate
Image courtesy of Brave

but also they perceive value in being seen to be 'of value' to their customers. There is also evidence that some brands are trying to meet the emerging needs of some consumers who want to know the track record of manufacturers with respect to their environmental policies and actions. For example, the growth in 'Fairtrade' products, designed to provide fairer and more balanced trading arrangements with producers and growers in emerging parts of the world, has influenced Kraft that they should engage with this form of commercial activity. Sainsbury's claim that all of their bananas are Fairtrade, while Typhoo have claimed for some time on their packaging, 'care for tea and our tea pickers'.

The notion of value can be addressed in a different way. All organisations have the opportunity to develop their communications to a point where the value of their messages represents a competitive advantage. This value can be seen in the consistency, timing, volume or expression of the message. Heinonen and Strandvik (2005) argue that there are four elements that constitute communication value. These are the message content, how the information is presented, where the communication occurs and its timing. In other words, the all-important context within which a communication event occurs. These elements are embedded within marketing communications and are referred to throughout this book.

Environmental influences

The management of marketing communications is a complex and highly uncertain activity. This is due in part to the nature of the marketing communication variables, including the influence of the environment. The environment can be considered in many different ways, but for the purposes of this opening chapter, three categories are considered; the internal, external and market environments. The constituents of each of these are set out in Figure 1.4.

Internal influences

The internal environment refers primarily to the organisation and the way it works, what its values are and how it wants to develop. Here various forces seek to influence an organisation's marketing communications. The overall strategy that an organisation adopts should have a huge impact. For example, how the organisation wishes to differentiate itself within its target markets will influence the messages and media used and, of course, the overarching positioning and reputation of the company. Brand strategies will influence such things as the way in which brands are named, the extent to which sales promotions are an integral part of the

Figure 1.4   The environmental influences that shape marketing communications

communication mix and how they are positioned. The prevailing organisational culture can also be extremely influential. For a long time the hierarchical management structure and power culture at Procter and Gamble led to the establishment of a pattern of behaviour whereby the marketing communication messages were largely product benefit oriented rather than emotionally driven, as at their arch rivals Unilever.

The amount of money available to the marketing communication budget will influence the media mix or the size of the sales force used to deliver messages. Apart from the quality and motivation of the people employed, the level of preferences and marketing skills deployed can impact on the form of the messages, the choice of media, and the use of agencies and support services. Finally, the socio-political climate of the firm shapes not only who climbs the career ladder fastest, but how and to which brands scarce marketing resources are distributed.

Marketing communications is regarded as one of the elements of the marketing mix and is primarily responsible for the communication of the marketing offer and the brand promise, sometimes referred to as the brand proposition. Although recognising that there is implicit and important communication through the other elements of the marketing mix (through a high price, for example, symbolic of high quality), it is the task of a planned and integrated set of communication activities to communicate effectively with each of an organisation's stakeholder groups.

Marketing communications is sometimes perceived as only dealing with communications that are external to the organisation. It should be recognised that good communications with internal stakeholders, such as employees, are also vital if, in the long term, successful favourable images, perceptions and attitudes are to be established. Influences through the work force and the marketing plan can be both positive and effective. For example, staff used in B&Q and Halifax advertising are intended to project internal values that should reflect positively upon the respective brands.

Market influences

Market influences are characterised by partial levels of control and typified by the impact of competitors. Competitors occupy particular positions in the market and this shapes what others claim about their own products, the media they use, the geographic coverage of the sales force and their own positioning. Intermediaries influence the nature of business-to-business marketing communications. The frequency, intensity, quality and overall willingness to share information with one another are significant forces. Of course, the various agencies an organisation uses can also be very influential. Marketing research agencies (inform about market perception, attitudes, and behaviour), communication agencies (determine what is said and then design how it is said, what is communicated) and media houses (recommend media mixes and when it is said) all have considerable potential to influence marketing communications.

However, perhaps the biggest single market group consists of the organisation's customers and network of stakeholders. Their attitudes, perceptions and buying preferences and behaviours, although not directly controllable, (should) have a far reaching influence on the marketing communications used by an organisation.

External influences

As mentioned earlier, the external group of influencers are characterised by the organisations' near lack of control. The well known PEST framework is a useful way of considering these forces. Political forces, which can encompass both legal and ethical issues, shape their use of marketing communication through legislation, voluntary controls and individual company attitudes towards issues of right and wrong, consequences and duties and the formal and informal communications an organisation uses. Indeed, increasing attention has been placed upon ethics and corporate responsibility to the extent that in some cases a name and shame culture might be identified.

Economic forces, which include demographics, geographics and geodemographics, can determine the positioning of brands in terms of perceived value. For example, if the government raise interest rates then consumers are more inclined not to spend money, especially on non-staple products and services. This may mean that marketing communications needs to convey stronger messages about value and to send out strident calls-to-action.

Social forces are concerned with the values, beliefs and norms that a society enshrines. Issues to do with core values within a society are often difficult to change. For example, the American gun culture or the once prevalent me-orientation with respect to self-fulfilment, set up a string of values that marketing communications can use to harness, magnify and align brands. The current social pressures with regard to obesity and healthier eating habits have forced fast-food companies such as McDonald's to introduce new menus and healthier food options. As a result, marketing communications not only has to inform and make audiences aware of the new menus but also convey messages about differentiation and positioning plus provide a reason to visit the restaurant.

Technological forces have had an immense impact on marketing communications. New technology has revolutionised traditional forms of marketing communications and led to more personalised, targeted, customised and responsive forms of communication. What was once predominantly one-way communications based upon a model of information provision and persuasion, has given way to a two-way model in which integration with audiences and where sharing and reasoning behaviours are enabled by digital technology, is now used frequently with appropriate target audiences.

New forms of marketing communications have been developed in response to changing environmental conditions. For example, public relations are now seen by some to have both a marketing and corporate dimension. Direct marketing is now recognised as an important way of developing relationships with buyers, both consumer and organisational, while new and innovative forms of communication through sponsorship, floor advertising, video screens on supermarket trolleys and checkout coupon dispensers, plus Internet and associated technologies, mean that effective communication requires the selection and integration of an increasing variety of communication tools and media.

The marketing communications mix

Successful marketing communications involves integrating three elements into combinations that have the potential to engage target audiences. The elements that need to be mixed are the tools, media and messages and, collectively these are referred to as the marketing communications mix.

As stated earlier, there are five principal marketing communications tools: advertising, sales promotion, public relations, direct marketing and personal selling. In addition to these tools or methods of communication, there are the media, or the means by which advertising and other marketing communications messages are conveyed. Tools and media should not be confused as they have different characteristics and seek to achieve different goals. Also, just in case you were thinking something is missing, the Internet is a medium not a tool.

To complete the trilogy, messages need to be conveyed to the target audience. Whereas organisations were primarily responsible for the content of messages, today an increasing number of messages are developed by consumers, and shared with other consumers. This last point is referred to as word-of-mouth communication.

In the past decade there have been some major changes in the communications environment and in the way organisations communicate with their target audiences. Digital technology has given rise to a raft of different media at the same time that people have developed a variety of ways to spend their leisure time. This is referred to as media and audience fragmentation respectively, and organisations have developed fresh combinations of the communications mix in order to reach their audiences effectively. For example, there has been a dramatic rise in the use of direct-response media as direct marketing has become a key part of many campaigns. The Internet and digital technologies have enabled new interactive forms of communication, where the receiver has greater responsibility for their part in the communication process. An increasing number of organisations are using public relations to communicate messages about the organisation (corporate public relations) and also messages about their brands (marketing public relations).

The traditional mix has evolved dramatically. Originally brands were developed through the use of advertising to generate 'above-the-line' mass communication campaigns. The strategy was based around buying space in newspapers and magazines, or advertising time (called spots) in major television programmes that were watched by huge audiences (20+ million people in the UK). This strategy required media owners to create programmes (content) that would attract brand owners because of the huge, relatively passive audiences. By interrupting the audience's entertainment, brand owners could talk to (or at) their markets in order to sell their brands.

However, since the days of just two commercial television stations there has been a proliferation of media. Audiences no longer use the television as their main form of information or entertainment and newspaper readership has fallen steadily in recent years. It has been suggested that consumers now use media to satisfy four additional needs:

- to discover;
- to participate;
- to share;
- to express themselves.

Rather than passive media involvement, these motivations, as they are referred to, require active engagement with media. Consumers now have a choice of media and leisure activities, they decide how and when to consume information and entertainment. Consumers are now motivated and able to develop their own content, be it through text, music or video and consider topics that they can share with friends on virtual networks. Thus, media and messages are the key to reaching consumers today, not the tools. More direct and highly targeted, personalised communication activities using direct marketing and the other tools of the mix now predominate. (See Figure 1.5.)

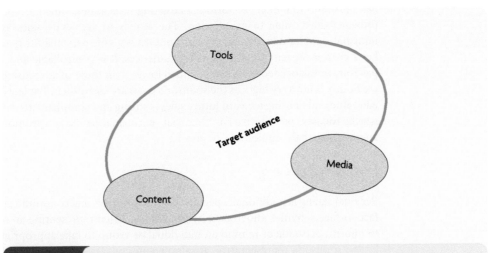

| Figure 1.5 | The marketing communications mix |

Philips and Cooper (2008) refer to the digital reworking in 2008, of the iconic 1990s 'Hello Boys' ad for Wonderbra. The original ad was delivered through posters and PR which required audiences to 'spectate'. The contemporary version involves video content developed online and conversations stimulated through a variety of digital seedings. See www.edelman.co.uk/case-studies/wonderbra-dita-von-teese for more detail about this case and the extraordinary campaign results. These included an immediate product sell-out and, at the time, the most watched YouTube video on launch day. Here content, conversation and engagement are demonstrated wonderfully.

The new mix represents a shift in approach. The conventional format represents an *intervention*-based approach to marketing communications, one based on seeking the attention of a customer who might not necessarily be interested. The shift is towards *conversation*-based marketing communications, where the focus is on communications with and between members of an audience who may have contributed content to the campaign. This has a particular impact on direct marketing, interactive communications and, to some extent, personal selling.

The tools of the MCs mix

Advertising

Advertising is a non-personal form of mass communication that offers a high degree of control for those responsible for the design and delivery of advertising messages. However, the ability of advertising to persuade the target audience to behave in a particular way is suspect. Furthermore, the effect on sales is extremely hard to measure. Advertising also suffers from low credibility in that audiences are less likely to believe messages delivered through advertising than they are messages received through some other tools and word-of-mouth communication.

The flexibility of this tool is good because it can be used to communicate with a national audience or a particular specialised segment. Although the costs can be extremely high, a vast number of people can be reached with a message, so the cost per contact can be the lowest of all the tools in the mix. Advertising is explored in Chapter 9.

Sales promotion

Sales promotion comprises various marketing techniques, which are often used tactically to provide added value to an offering. The aim is to accelerate sales and gather marketing information. Like advertising, sales promotion is a non-personal form of communication but has a greater capacity to target smaller audiences. It is controllable and, although it has to be paid for, the associated costs can be much lower than those of advertising. As a generalisation, credibility is not very high, as the sponsor's goals are easily identifiable. However, the ability to add value and to bring forward future sales is strong and complements a macroeconomic need, which focuses on short-term financial performance. Sales promotion techniques and approaches are the subject of Chapter 12.

Personal selling

Personal selling is traditionally perceived as an interpersonal communication tool that involves face-to-face activities undertaken by individuals, often representing an organisation, in order to inform, persuade or remind an individual or group to take appropriate action, as required by the sponsor's representative. A salesperson engages in communication on a one-to-one basis where instantaneous feedback is possible. The costs associated with interpersonal communication are normally very high.

This tool, considered in Chapter 11, differs from the previous two in that, while still lacking in relative credibility and control, the degree of control is potentially lower, because the salesperson is free at the point of contact to deliver a message other than that intended (Lloyd, 1997). Indeed, many different messages can be delivered by a single salesperson. Some of these messages may enhance the prospect of the salesperson's objectives being reached (making the sale), or they may retard the process and so incur more time and hence costs. Whichever way it is viewed, control is lower than with advertising.

Public relations

Public relations is concerned with establishing and maintaining relationships with various stakeholders and with enhancing the reputation of the organisation. This indicates that public relations should be a part of the wider perspective of corporate strategy. The increasing use of public relations, and in particular publicity, is a reflection of the high credibility attached to messages conveyed through this form of communication.

Publicity involves the dissemination of messages through third-party media, such as magazines, newspapers or news programmes. There is no charge for the media space or time but there are costs incurred in the production of the material. There is a wide range of other tools used by public relations, such as event management, public affairs, sponsorship and lobbying. It is difficult to control a message once it is placed in the media channels, but the endorsement offered by a third party can be very influential and have a far greater impact on the target audience than any of the other tools in the marketing communications mix.

Viewpoint 1.4	Associating with extreme Red Bulls

The energy drink Red Bull was first launched in the mid 1980s but its development in Britain continues to be strong, with sales steadily increasing year on year and maintaining a near 30 per cent market share. There are several factors contributing to this performance, not least of them being the quality of the product and the perceived value consumers derive from drinking the brand.

The brand makes use of a wide range of marketing communications tools and media, with a message that is based around the distinctive, slim silver can, that it is cool to drink Red Bull. The brand uses television, print and cinema as key media channels to reach their 14–19-year-old target audience, and to build brand awareness. However, this is not enough to sustain contemporary brands and so they use other activities to build a brand experience for users, based around excitement, adrenalin, danger and youth culture. To achieve this Red Bull associate themselves with extreme sports (e.g. Formula 1, the Red Bull Air Race World Series, street culture and music events). This builds credibility that in turn fosters word-of-mouth communication.

Source: Based on Turner (2008), www.redbull.com

Question

To what extent is the brand experience a more important driver of sales than the quality of the product and its various attributes?

Task

Make a list of five events with which Red Bull might associate themselves.

Exhibit 1.3	A Red Bull event: Red Bull Rampage, Virgin, Utah 2010
	Image © John Gibson/Red Bull Photofiles

This non-personal form of communication offers organisations a different way to communicate, not only with consumers but also with many other stakeholders.

Direct marketing

The four elements of the communications mix discussed so far have a number of strengths and weaknesses. As a response to some of the weaknesses that revolve around costs and effectiveness, direct marketing emerged in the 1990s as a new and effective way of building relationships with customers over the long term.

Direct marketing represents a shift in focus from mass to personalised communications. In particular, the use of direct mail, telemarketing and the fast-developing area of interactive marketing communications, represents 'through-the-line' communications. By removing the face-to-face aspect of personal selling and replacing it with an email communication, a telephone conversation or a direct mail letter, many facets of the traditional salespersons' tasks can be removed, freeing them to concentrate on their key skill areas.

Direct marketing seeks to target individual customers with the intention of delivering personalised messages and building a relationship with them based on their responses to the direct communications. In contrast to conventional approaches, direct marketing attempts to build a one-to-one relationship, a partnership with each customer, by communicating with the customers on a direct and personal basis. If an organisation chooses to use direct marketing then it has to incorporate the approach within a marketing plan. This is because distribution is different and changes in the competitive environment may mean that prices need to change. For example, charges for packing and delivery need to be incorporated. The product may also need to be altered or adapted to the market. For example, some electrical products are marketed through different countries on home shopping channels and websites. The electrical requirements of each country or region need to be incorporated within the product specification of each country's offering. In addition to these changes, the promotion component is also different, simply because communication is required directly with each targeted individual. To do this, direct-response media must be used.

In many cases, direct-response media are a derivative of advertising, such as direct mail, magazine inserts and television and print advertisements that use telephone numbers and web addresses to encourage a direct response. However, direct response can also be incorporated within personal selling through telemarketing and sales promotions with competitions to build market knowledge and develop the database, which is the key to the direct marketing approach.

This text regards direct marketing as a management process associated with building mutually satisfying customer relationships through personal and intermediary-free interaction and dialogue. Direct-response media are the primary forms of communication when direct marketing is an integral part of the marketing plan.

The Internet is both a distribution channel and communication medium, one that enables consumers and organisations to communicate in radically different ways. It allows for interactivity and is possibly the best medium to enable dialogue. Communication is two-way, often interactive, and very fast, allowing businesses and individuals to find information and enter exchange transactions in such a way that some traditional communication practices and shopping patterns are being reconfigured.

The key characteristics of the communication tools

Each of the tools of the communication mix performs a different role and can accomplish different tasks. This reflects their different capabilities, their various attributes and key characteristics. These are the extent to which each of the tools is controllable, whether it is paid for by the sponsor and whether communication is through mass media or undertaken personally. One additional characteristic concerns the receiver's perception of the credibility of the source of the message. If the credibility factor is high then there is a greater likelihood that a message from that source will be accepted by receivers.

The 4Cs framework set out at Table 1.2, depicts the key characteristics and shows the relative effectiveness of the communication tools across a number of different characteristics. These are the ability of each to communicate, the credibility they bestow on messages, the costs involved and the control that each tool can maintain.

Media and the MCs mix

There is a huge and expanding variety of media used to convey messages to target audiences. For ease of understanding it is helpful to categorise these into six main classes. These consist of broadcast, print, outdoor, digital, in-store and other media classes. Of these the digital class is growing the most and is the most influential. These classes can be broken down into types and vehicles, all of which are explored in greater detail in Chapter 13.

There is a trend to move resources from traditional media to digital media. Each of these classes have particular characteristics that makes the decision to use particular combinations of media, referred to as the media mix, a complex and challenging marketing decision.

Key differences between traditional and digital media

A comparison of traditional and digital media provides an interesting insight into the capabilities of the two main forms of media. These are set out in Table 1.3. Space (or time) within

Table 1.2   The 4Cs framework – a summary of the key characteristics of the tools of marketing communications

	Advertising	Sales promotion	Public relations	Personal selling	Direct marketing
Communications					
Ability to deliver a personal message	Low	Low	Low	High	High
Ability to reach a large audience	High	Medium	Medium	Low	Medium
Level of interaction	Low	Medium	Low	High	High
Credibility					
Given by the target audience	Low	Medium	High	Medium	Medium
Costs					
Absolute costs	High	Medium	Low	High	Medium
Cost per contact	Low	Medium	Low	High	High
Wastage	High	Medium	High	Low	Low
Size of investment	High	Medium	Low	High	Medium
Control					
Ability to target particular audiences	Medium	High	Low	Medium	High
Management's ability to adjust the deployment of the tool as circumstances change	Medium	High	Low	Medium	High

Table 1.3   Comparison of traditional and digital media

Traditional media	Digital media
One-to-many	One-to-one and many-to-many
Greater monologue	Greater dialogue
Active provision	Passive provision
Mass marketing	Individualised marketing
General need	Personalised
Branding	Information
Segmentation	Communities

traditional media is limited and costs rise as demand for the limited space/time increases. Internet space is unlimited so absolute costs remain very low and static, while relative costs plummet as more visitors are recorded as having been to a site. Another aspect concerns the focus of the advertising message. Traditionally, advertisers tend to emphasise the emotional rather than information aspect, particularly within low-involvement categories. Digital media allow focus on the provision of information and so the emotional aspect of advertising messages tends to have a lower significance. As branding becomes a more important aspect of Internet activity, it is probable that there will be a greater use of emotions, especially when the goal is to keep people at a website, rather than driving them to it.

Digital media allow focus on the provision of information and so the emotional aspect of online advertising messages tends to have a lower significance. Apart from the obvious factor that digital media, and the Internet in particular, provide interactive opportunities that traditional media cannot provide, it is important to remember that opportunities-to-see are generally driven by customers rather than by the advertiser that interrupts viewing or reading activities. People drive the interaction at a speed that is convenient to them; they are not driven by others.

Management control over some Internet-based marketing communications is relatively high, as not only are there greater opportunities to control the position and placement of advertisements, promotions and press releases, but it is also possible to change the content of these activities much more quickly than is possible with traditional media. The goals outlined above indicate the framework within which advertising needs to be managed.

Messages and the MCs mix

Brand related messages have two main sources. One is the organisation itself in terms of how it chooses to present their organisation or brand, a planned aspect of marketing communications. What organisations say and how they say it needs careful consideration. The other source involves audiences and the brand messages that customers create and communicate, both positive and negative. These messages may be directed to the brand or shared with one another. In an age of interaction, individual consumers can create and share content with others, and these are largely unstructured and unplanned communications.

What is common to both the planned and unplanned messages is that they both contain two elements, information and emotion. Ensuring that the right balance of information and emotions is achieved and that the presentation of the message is appropriate for the target audience represents a critical part of the planned communication process for agencies, clients and individuals.

Messages should reflect a balance between the need for information and the need for pleasure or enjoyment in consuming the message. Messages can be product oriented and rational or customer-oriented and based on feelings and emotions. All messages contain information and emotional content, it is the balance between the two that needs to be managed according to the task and context.

Messages where there is high-involvement require an emphasis on the information content, in particular the key attributes and the associated benefits. This style is often factual and product oriented. Where there is low-involvement the message should contain a high proportion of emotional content and seek to develop brand values through imagery and associations. These issues are discussed in Chapter 15.

Messages should be developed that enable recipients to not only respond to the source but to also encourage them to talk to others through conversation, offline or online. For example, when Toyota launched the up-rated Prius, social media was an important element of the campaign. Woods (2009) reports that use was made of organic search in order to increase visibility of information about the Prius, but in addition model previews, news stories, videos and other influential content was seeded across relevant websites, all in an attempt to provoke conversation about the brand.

In addition to considering the attributes of both traditional and digital media, it is also worth considering the content of the information that each is capable of delivering. These are set out in Table 1.4.

Table 1.4	Comparison of content

Websites/Internet	Traditional media
Good at providing rational, product-based information	Better at conveying emotional brand values
More efficient as costs do not increase in proportion to the size of the target audience	Costs are related to usage
Better at prompting customer action	Less effective for calling to action except point-of-purchase and telemarketing
Effective for short-term, product-oriented brand action goals and long-term corporate identity objectives	Normally associated with building long-term values
Average at generating awareness and attention	Strong builders of awareness
Measures of effectiveness weak and/or in the process of development	Established methodologies, some misleading or superficial (mass media); direct marketing techniques are superior
Dominant orientation – cognition	Dominant orientation – emotion

As mentioned earlier, digital media are superior at providing rational, product-based informa-tion whereas traditional media are much better at conveying emotional brand values. The former have a dominant cognition orientation and the latter an emotional one. There are other differences, but the predominant message is that these types of media are, to a large extent, complementary, suggesting that they should be used together, not one independently of the other.

Criteria when selecting the mix

Using the key characteristics it is possible to determine the significant criteria organisations should consider when selecting communication tools (see Table 1.5 on p. 26). These are as follows:

- the degree of control required over the delivery of the message;
- the financial resources available to pay a third party to transmit messages;
- the level of credibility that each tool bestows on the organisation;
- the size and geographic dispersion of the target audiences;
- the communication tasks each tool is best at satisfying.

Control

Control over the message, particularly in traditional mass media communication, is necessary to ensure that the intended message is transmitted to and received by the target audience. Furthermore, this message must be capable of being understood in order that the receiver can act appropriately. Message control is complicated by interference or negative 'noise' that can corrupt and distort messages. For example, the media spotlight shone brightly on Eurostar when a number of trains broke down in the channel tunnel during the 2009 Christmas period. The disruption for thousands of passengers, many stranded for hours in the tunnel, generated negative media comments about the company. All advertising and campaign work was stopped immediately by Eurostar and only resumed six months later (Clark, 2010).

Advertising and sales promotions can allow for a high level of control over the message, from design to transmission. Interestingly, they afford only partial control or influence over the feedback associated with the original message.

Control can also be an important factor when considering online and digital-based communications. For example, the ability to place banner ads, to bid for sponsored links and determine keyword rankings in search engines requires control and deliberation. However, it should be noted that message control is an ambiguous term. Brand owners desire control over message placement and seeding but they also want people to talk about their brands. In this context owners sacrifice control over what is said about a brand, who says it and in which context. Engagement is about provoking conversations and that implies that there is virtually no control over this aspect. Planned marketing communications carries a high level of control, whilst unplanned word-of-mouth conversations carry little control.

Financial resources

Control is also a function of financial power. In other words, if an organisation is prepared to pay a third party to transmit the message, then long-term control will rest with the sponsor for as long as the financial leverage continues. However, short-term message corruption can exist if management control over the process is less than vigilant. For example, if the design of the message differs from that originally agreed, then partial control has already been lost. This can happen when the working relationship between an advertising agency and the client is less than efficient and the process for signing off work in progress fails to prevent the design and release of inappropriate creative work.

Advertising and sales promotion are tools that allow for a high level of control by the sponsor, whereas public relations, and publicity in particular, is weak in this aspect because the voluntary services of a third party are normally required for the message to be transmitted.

There is a great variety of media available to advertisers. Each media type (for example television, radio, newspapers, magazines, posters and the Internet) carries a particular cost, and the financial resources of the organisation may not be available to use particular types of media, even if such use would be appropriate on other grounds.

Credibility

Public relations is highly credible because receivers perceive the third party as unbiased and endorsing the offering. They view the third party's comments as objective and trustworthy in the context of the media in which the comments appear.

At a broad level, advertising, sales promotion and, to a slightly lesser extent, personal selling are tools that can lack credibility, as perceived by a target audience. Because of this, organisations often use celebrities and 'experts' to endorse their offerings. The credibility of the spokesperson is intended to distract the receiver from the sponsor's prime objective, which is to sell the offering. Credibility, as we see shall later, is an important aspect of the communication process and of marketing communications.

Dispersion – size and geography

The size and geographic dispersion of the target audience can be a significant influence on the choice of tools. A national consumer audience can only be reached effectively if tools of mass communication are used, such as advertising and sales promotion. Similarly, various specialist businesses require personal attention to explain, design, demonstrate, install and service complex equipment. In these circumstances personal selling – one-to-one contact – is of greater significance. The tools of marketing communications can enable an organisation to speak to vast national and international audiences through advertising and satellite technology, or to single persons or small groups through personal selling and the assistance of word-of-mouth recommendation.

Table 1.5	Key selection criteria for the tools of the marketing communications mix				
	Advertising	Sales promotion	Public relations	Direct marketing	Personal selling
Level of control	Medium	High	Low	High	Medium
Level of cost	High	Medium	Low	Medium	High
Level of credibility	Low	Medium	High	Medium	Medium
Level of dispersion *High*	Low	Medium	High	High	Medium
Low	Medium	High	High	Medium	High
Primary tasks	Differentiating Informing	Persuading	Differentiating Informing	Persuading Reinforcing	Persuading

Source: Baines *et al.* (2011)

Communication tasks

Each communication tool has particular strengths therefore the selected mix of tools should be based on a combination of tools designed to accomplish particular DRIP tasks. One of the reasons direct marketing has become so successful is that it delivers a call-to-action and is therefore a very good persuasive tool as well as being good at reinforcing messages. Advertising on the other hand is much better at differentiating offerings and informing audiences about key features and benefits.

At this point it is worth consolidating our understanding about the role, the tasks and the marketing communications mix. The role is to engage audiences, the tasks are to DRIP and through the selection and deployment of the elements of the mix, organisations seek to engage audiences and achieve their goals (DRIP). The marketing communications universe portrays this visually (see Figure 1.6).

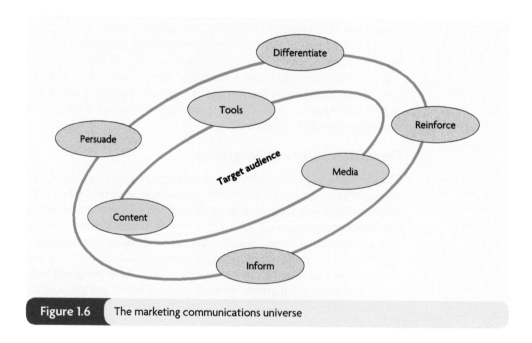

Figure 1.6	The marketing communications universe

Communication differences

Having identified the need to communicate with a number of different audiences, it seems appropriate to conclude this opening chapter by examining the differences between communications used by and targeted at two very different and specific audiences. These are organisations (commonly referred to as business-to-business) and those aimed at consumer markets. Some writers (Brougaletta, 1985; Gilliland and Johnston, 1997) have documented a variety of differences between consumer and business-to-business markets. The following is intended to set out some of the more salient differences (see also Table 1.6).

Message reception

The contextual conditions in which messages are received and ascribed meanings are very different. In the organisational setting the context is much more formal, and as the funding for the purchase is to be derived from company sources (as opposed to personal sources for consumer market purchases) there may be a lower orientation to the price as a significant variable in the purchase decision. The item is intended for company usage, whereas products bought in a consumer context are normally intended for personal consumption.

Table 1.6   Differences between consumer and business-to-business marketing communications

	Consumer-oriented markets	Business-to-business markets
Message reception	Informal	Formal
Number of decision-makers	Single or few	Many
Balance of the promotional mix	Advertising and sales promotions dominate	Personal selling dominates
Specificity and integration	Broad use of communications mix with a move towards integrated mixes	Specificity use of below-the-line tools but with a high level of integration
Message content	Greater use of emotions and imagery	Greater use of rational, logic and information-based messages although there is evidence of a move towards the use of imagery
Message origin	Increasing use of user-generated content	Limited use of user-generated materials
Length of decision time	Normally short	Longer and more involved
Negative communications	Limited to people close to the purchaser/user	Potentially an array of people in the organisation and beyond
Target marketing and research	Great use of sophisticated targeting and communication approaches	Limited but increasing use of targeting and segmentation approaches
Budget allocation	Majority of budget allocated to brand management	Majority of budget allocated to sales management
Evaluation and measurement	Great variety of techniques and approaches used	Limited number of techniques and approaches used

Number of decision-makers

In consumer markets a single person very often makes the decision. In organisational markets decisions are made by many people within a buying centre. This means that the interactions of the participants should be considered. In addition, a variety of different individuals need to be reached and influenced and this may involve the use of different media and message strategies.

The balance of the communications mix

The role of advertising and sales promotions in business-to-business communications is primarily to support the personal selling effort. This contrasts with the mix that predominates in consumer markets. Personal selling plays a relatively minor role and is only significant at the point of purchase in some product categories where involvement is high (cars, white goods and financial services), reflecting high levels of perceived risk. However, the increasing use of direct marketing in consumer markets suggests that personal communications are becoming more prevalent and in some ways increasingly similar to the overall direction of business-to-business communications.

The constituent tools of the marketing communications mix

Business-to-business markets have traditionally been quite specific in terms of the tools and media used to target audiences. While the use of advertising literature is very important, there has been a tendency to use a greater proportion of 'below-the-line' activities. This compares with consumer markets, where a greater proportion of funds have been allocated to 'above-the-line' activities. It is interesting that the communications in the consumer market are moving towards a more integrated format, more similar in form to the business-to-business model than was previously considered appropriate.

Message content

Generally, there is high involvement in many business-to-business purchase decisions, so communications tend to be much more rational and information-based than in consumer markets. However, there are signs that businesses are making increased use of imagery and emotions in the messages.

Message origin

Increasingly, consumers are taking a more active role in the creation of content. Blogging for example, is important in both consumer and business markets, but the development of user-generated-content and word-of-mouth communication is becoming a significant part of consumer-based marketing communications activities.

Length of purchase decision time

The length of time taken to reach a decision is much greater in the organisation market. This means that the intensity of any media plan can be dissipated more easily in the organisational market.

Negative communications

The number of people affected by a dissatisfied consumer, and hence negative marketing communication messages, is limited. The implications of a poor purchase decision in an organisational environment may be far-reaching, including those associated with the use of the product, the career of participants close to the locus of the decision and, depending on the size and spread, perhaps the whole organisation.

Target marketing and research

The use of target marketing processes in the consumer market is more advanced and sophisticated than in the organisational market. This impacts on the quality of the marketing communications used to reach the target audience. However, there is much evidence that the business-to-business markets organisations are becoming increasingly aware and sophisticated in their approach to segmentation techniques and processes.

Budget allocation

The sales department receives the bulk of the marketing budget in the organisation market and little is spent on research in comparison with the consumer market.

Measurement and evaluation

The consumer market employs a variety of techniques to evaluate the effectiveness of communications. In the organisation market, sales volume, value, number of enquiries and market share are the predominant measures of effectiveness.

There can be no doubt that there are a number of major differences between consumer and organisational communications. These reflect the nature of the environments, the tasks involved and the overall need of the recipients for particular types of information. Information need, therefore, can be seen as a primary reason for the differences in the way communication mixes are configured. Advertising in organisational markets has to provide a greater level of information and is geared to generating leads that can be followed up with personal selling, which is traditionally the primary tool in the promotional mix. In consumer markets, advertising used to play the primary role with support from the other tools of the promotional mix. This is not always true today as organisations use other tools such as public relations, combined with digital media, to reach particular audiences. Interestingly, digital media are helping to reconfigure the marketing communications mix and perhaps reduce the gulf and distinction between the mix used in business-to-business and consumer markets. Throughout this book, reference will be made to the characteristics, concepts and processes associated with marketing communications in each of these two main sectors.

Summary

In order to help consolidate your understanding about this introduction to marketing communications, here are the key points summarised against each of the learning objectives:

1 Explain the scope, role and tasks of marketing communications

The scope of marketing communications embraces an audience-centred perspective of planned, unplanned, product and service experiences. The role of marketing communications is to engage audiences with a view to provoking relevant conversations. The tasks of marketing communications are based within a need to differentiate, reinforce, inform and persuade audiences to think and behave in particular ways.

2 Describe how marketing communications can be used to engage audiences

Engagement is a function of two elements. The first is the degree to which a message encourages thinking and feeling about a brand, the development of brand values. The second is about the degree to which a message stimulates behaviour or action. Engagement may last a second, a minute, an hour, a day or even longer.

3 Explore ways in which the environment can influence the use of marketing communications

The internal, market and external environments all influence the use of marketing communications. The internal environment refers to employees, the culture, the financial resources and the marketing skills available to organisations. The market environment refers principally to the actions of competitors and the perceptions and attitudes held by customers towards an organisation or its brands.

The external environment can be considered in terms of the PEST framework. The influence of anyone of these elements on marketing communications can be significant, although the impact is usually generic and affects all organisations rather than any single band or organisation.

4 Write brief notes about the key characteristics of the marketing communications mix

The marketing communication mix consists of the tools, media and messages used to reach, engage and provoke audience-centred conversations. The five tools, six classes of media and two broad types of message can be configured in different ways to meet the needs of the target audience.

5 Identify and explain the key differences between marketing communications used in consumer and business markets

The way in which the marketing communication mix is configured for consumer markets is very different from the mix used for business markets. The tools, media and messages used are all different as the general contexts in which they operate require different approaches. Business markets favour personal selling, consumer markets, advertising. Both make increasing use of digital media whilst rational messages are predominant in business markets, and emotional based messages tend to prevail in consumer markets.

Review questions

1. Prepare brief notes about the scope of marketing communications, including a definition.
2. What is the role of marketing communications and identify the key tasks that it is required to undertake?
3. Name the three main elements that make up the marketing communications mix. Which one is critical?
4. How do each of the tools compare across the following criteria: control, communication effectiveness and cost?
5. How does direct marketing differ from the other tools of the mix?
6. How does the external environment influence an organisation's marketing communications?
7. Identify five different advertisements that you think use direct-response media. How effective do you think they might be?
8. How does the content delivered through traditional media differ from that delivered through digital media?
9. What criteria should be used when configuring a marketing communications mix?
10. Explain how marketing communications tools and media might be used differently to reach business rather than consumer markets.

References

Alarcon, C. (2009) Magners pushes Pear variant in marketing drive, *Marketing Week*, Thursday 30 April, retrieved 18 August 2009 from www.marketingweek.co.uk/news/magners-pushes-pear-variant-in-marketing-drive/2065279.article

Anon (2009) Marketing Society – Ledge Edge Award Winner – O₂, *Marketing*, 10 June, 7.

Baines, P., Fill, C. and Page, K. (2011) *Marketing*, 2nd edn, Oxford: Oxford University Press.

Baker, A. (2006), 'Cider brand rules', *Brand Republic*, 9 August, retrieved 5 December 2007 from www.brandrepublic.com/news/search/article/576158/cider-brand-rules/

Ballantyne, D. (2004) Dialogue and its role in the development of relationship specific Knowledge, *Journal of Business and Industrial Marketing*, 19(2), 114–123.

Bashford, S. (2007) Collaboration is imperative, *Marketing*, 13 December, 4–5.

Bowersox, D. and Morash, E. (1989) The integration of marketing flows in channels of distribution, *European Journal of Marketing*, 23(2), 58–67.

Brougaletta, Y. (1985) What business-to-business advertisers can learn from consumer advertisers. *Journal of Advertising Research*, 25(3), 8–9.

Brownsell, A. (2010a) LV = flags mutual status with primetime activity, *Marketing*, 31 March, 9.

Brownsell, A. (2010b) Keeping Virgin firmly on track, *Marketing*, 10 February, 22–23.

Clark, N. (2010) Eurostar plots mag to boost customer loyalty, *Marketing*, 17 February, 4.

Duncan, T.R. and Moriarty, S. (1997) *Driving Brand Value*, New York: McGraw Hill.

Fill, C. (2002) *Marketing Communications*, 3rd edn. Harrow: Financial Times Prentice-Hall.

Gilliland, D.I. and Johnston, W.J. (1997) Toward a model of business-to-business marketing communications effects. *Industrial Marketing Management*, 26, 15–29.

Grönroos, C. (2004) The relationship marketing process: communication, interaction, dialogue, value. *Journal of Business and Industrial Marketing*, 19(2), 99–113.

Heinonen, K. and Strandvik, T. (2005) Communication as a element of service value. *International Journal of Service Industry Management*, 16(2), 186–98.

Hughes, G. and Fill, C. (2007), Redefining the nature and format of the marketing communications mix. *The Marketing Review*, 7(1), 45–57.

JMW (2010) Jack Morgan Worldwide, Experience brands and the new engagement model, retrieved 13 June 2010 from http://www.jackmorton.com/takeaway/downloads/files/New_Engagement_Model_Exp_Brands.pdf

Lloyd, J. (1997) Cut your rep free, *Pharmaceutical Marketing* (September), 30–32.

Philips, R. and Cooper, J. (2008) PR Essays: Conversation with content, *Marketing*, 26 November, 15.

Simms, J. (2008) Here today, gone tomorrow? *Marketing*, 13 March, 17.

Turner, C. (2008) How Red Bull invented the 'cool' factor, *UTALK Marketing*. Retrieved 12 February 2008 from www.utalkmarketing.com/pages/article

Vargo, S.L. and Lusch, R.F. (2004) Evolving to a new dominant logic for marketing, *Journal of Marketing*, 68 (January), 1–17.

Woods, A. (2009) Searching in social circles, *Marketing*, 2 December, 39–41.

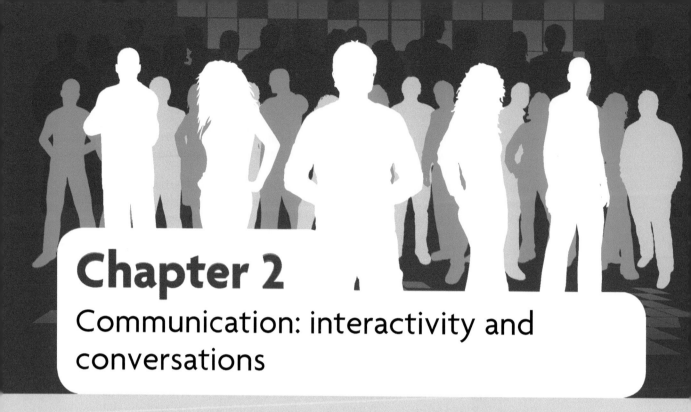

Chapter 2
Communication: interactivity and conversations

Communication is concerned with interpreting messages and sharing meaning. Only by using messages that reduce levels of ambiguity and which share meaning with audiences, can it be hoped to stimulate meaningful interaction and dialogue. To create and sustain valued conversations the support of significant others is often required. These may be people who are experts, those who share common interests, those who have relevant knowledge or have access to appropriate media channels.

Aims and learning objectives

The aims of this chapter are to introduce communication theory and to set it in the context of marketing communications.

The learning objectives of this chapter are to:

1. understand the linear model of communication and appreciate how the various elements link together and contribute to successful communication;

2. examine the impact of the media and personal and influences on the communication process;

3. demonstrate the characteristics of the influencer and interactional forms of communication;

4. explain the characteristics associated with opinion leaders, formers and followers;

5. examine the nature and characteristics associated with word-of-mouth communication;

6. describe the processes of adoption and diffusion as related to marketing communications.

Introduction

It was established in the previous chapter that marketing communications is partly an attempt by an organisation/brand to create and sustain a dialogue with its various audiences. It is also important to encourage members of these audiences to talk amongst themselves about a brand. As communication is the process by which individuals share meaning, each participant in the communication process needs to be able to interpret the meaning embedded in the messages, and be able to respond in an appropriate way.

For this overall process to work, information needs to be transmitted to, from and among participants. It is important, therefore, that those involved with marketing communications understand the complexity of the process. Through knowledge and understanding of the communications process, participants are more likely to achieve their objective of sharing meaning with each member of their target audiences and so have an opportunity to enter into a dialogue.

This chapter examines several models of the communication process. It considers the characteristics associated with word-of-mouth communications and looks at the way products and ideas are adopted by individuals and markets.

A linear model of communication

Wilbur Schramm (1955) developed what is now accepted as the basic model of mass communications (Figure 2.1). The components of the linear model of communication are:

Source: the individual or organisation sending the message.
Encoding: transferring the intended message into a symbolic style that can be transmitted.
Signal: the transmission of the message using particular media.
Decoding: understanding the symbolic style of the message in order to understand the message.

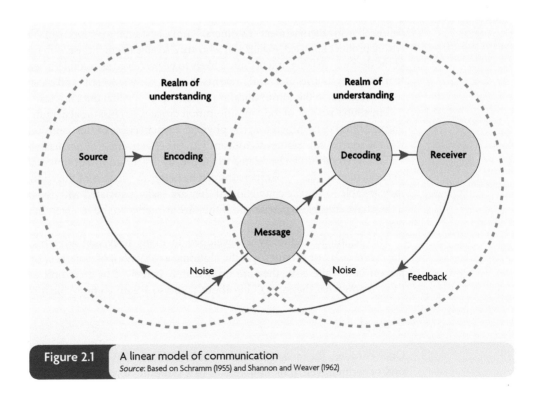

Figure 2.1	A linear model of communication

Source: Based on Schramm (1955) and Shannon and Weaver (1962)

Receiver: the individual or organisation receiving the message.

Feedback: the receiver's communication back to the source on receipt of the message.

Noise: distortion of the communication process, making it difficult for the receiver to interpret the message as intended by the source.

This is a linear model that emphasises the 'transmission of information, ideas, attitudes, or emotion from one person or group to another (or others), primarily through symbols' (Theodorson and Theodorson, 1969). The model and its components are straightforward, but it is the quality of the linkages between the various elements in the process that determine whether a communication event will be successful.

Source/encoding

The source, an individual or organisation, identifies a need to transmit a message and then selects a combination of appropriate words, pictures, symbols and music to represent the message to be transmitted. This is called encoding. The purpose is to create a message that is capable of being understood by the receiver.

There are a number of reasons why the source/encoding link might break down. For example, the source may fail to diagnose a particular situation accurately. By not fully understanding a stakeholder's problem or level of knowledge, inappropriate information may be included in the message, which, when transmitted, may lead to misunderstanding and misinterpretation by the receiver. By failing to appreciate the level of education of the target receiver, a message might be encoded in words and symbols that are beyond the comprehension of the receiver.

Some organisations spend a great deal of time and expense on marketing research, trying to develop their understanding of their target audience. The source of a message is an important factor in the communication process. A receiver who perceives a source lacking conviction, authority, trust or expertise is likely to discount any message received from that source, until such time as credibility is established.

Most organisations spend a great deal of time and expense recruiting sales representatives. The risk involved in selecting the wrong people can be extremely large. Many high-tech organisations require their new sales staff to spend over a year receiving both product and sales training before allowing them to meet customers. From a customer's perspective, salespersons who display strong product knowledge skills and who are also able to empathise with the individual members of the decision-making unit are more likely to be perceived as credible. Therefore, an organisation that prepares its sales staff and presents them as knowledgeable and trustworthy is more likely to be successful in the communication process than one that does not take the same level of care.

The source is a part of the communication process, not just the generator of detached messages. Patzer (1983) determined that the physical attractiveness of the communicator, particularly if it is the source, contributes significantly to the effectiveness of persuasive communications.

This observation can be related to the use, by organisations, of spokespersons and celebrities to endorse products. Spokespersons can be better facilitators of the communication process if they are able to convey conviction, if they are easily associated with the object of the message, if they have credible expertise and if they are attractive to the receiver, in the wider sense of the word.

This legitimate authority is developed in many television advertisements by the use of the 'white coat', or product-specific clothing, as a symbol of expertise. By dressing the spokesperson in a white coat, they are immediately perceived as a credible source of information ('they know what they are talking about'), and so are much more likely to be believed.

Signal

Once encoded, the message must be put into a form that is capable of transmission. It may be oral or written, verbal or non-verbal, in a symbolic form or in a sign. Whatever the format chosen, the source must be sure that what is being put into the message is what is required to be decoded by the receiver.

The channel is the means by which the message is transmitted from the source to the receiver. These channels may be personal or non-personal. The former involves face-to-face contact and word-of-mouth communications, which can be extremely influential. Non-personal channels are characterised by mass media advertising, which can reach large audiences.

Information received directly from personal influence channels is generally more persuasive than information received through mass media. This may be a statement of the obvious, but the reasons for this need to be understood. First, the individual approach permits greater flexibility in the delivery of the message. The timing and power with which a message is delivered can be adjusted to suit the immediate 'selling' environment. Second, a message can be adapted to meet the needs of the customer as the sales call progresses. This flexibility is not possible with mass media messages, as these have to be designed and produced well in advance of transmission and often without direct customer input.

Viewpoint 2.1   Is this what you really meant?

When developing names or taglines for global brands it is important to choose a name that translates appropriately into all the languages. The encoding process, the name of the car, cleaner, biscuit or fashion accessory should be well researched and capable of being decoded by the target audience in such a way that there is meaning, sense and value. The following are examples where the encoding process had not been properly considered:

- When the European hardware store chain 'Götzen' opened in Istanbul they had to change the name as 'Göt' means 'ass' in Turkish.
- 'Traficante' is an Italian brand of mineral water. In Spanish, it means drug dealer.
- Clairol's 'Mist Stick', curling iron had problems when launched in Germany because 'Mist' is slang for manure.
- A mainstream UK bank informed audiences in a recent advertising campaign that to show the soles of your feet in Thailand is a very rude gesture and, to give the thumbs up sign in Turkey, has quite the opposite meaning to its symbolism of cool acceptance here in Britain.
- Finally, workers in an African port saw a consignment with the international symbol for 'fragile' (a wine glass with snapped stem) on the side. They assumed it meant that they had been sent a cargo of broken glass and immediately pitched all the cases overboard into the harbour.

Sources: Based on: www.i18nguy.com/translations and www.sourceuk.net/indexf.html?03590

Question

To what extent should the encoding process be researched?

Task

Search the web and find your own examples of communications where different meanings have emerged.

Decoding/receiver

Decoding is the process of transforming and interpreting a message into thought. This process is influenced by the receiver's realm of understanding, which encompasses the experiences, perceptions, attitudes and values of both the source and the receiver. The more the receiver understands about the source and the greater their experience in decoding the source's messages, the more able the receiver will be to decode the message successfully.

Exhibit 2.1	Decoding Guinness
	Here decoding requires an understanding of two different interpretations of the word 'head'. The 'head' of the beer and the 'head' of a spy organisation. Humour is generated through the suggestion that the beer (Guinness) is intelligent. Image courtesy of The Advertising Archives

Feedback/response

The set of reactions a receiver has after seeing, hearing or reading the message is known as the response. These reactions may vary from the extreme of calling an enquiry telephone number, returning or downloading a coupon or even buying the product, to storing information in long-term memory for future use. Feedback is that part of the response that is sent back to the sender, and it is essential for successful communication. The need to understand not just whether the message has been received but also which message has been received is vital. For example, the receiver may have decoded the message incorrectly and a completely different set of responses may have been elicited. If a suitable feedback system is not in place then the source will be unaware that the communication has been unsuccessful and is liable to continue wasting resources. This represents inefficient and ineffective marketing communications.

The evaluation of feedback is vital if effective communications are to be developed. Only through evaluation can the success of any communication be judged. Feedback through personal selling can be instantaneous, through overt means such as questioning, raising objections or signing an order form. Other means, such as the use of gestures and body language, are less overt, and the decoding of the feedback needs to be accurate if an appropriate response is to be given. For the advertiser, the process is much more vague and prone to misinterpretation and error.

Feedback through mass media channels is generally much more difficult to obtain, mainly because of the inherent time delay involved in the feedback process. There are some exceptions, namely the overnight ratings provided by the Broadcasters' Audience Research Board to the television contractors, but as a rule feedback is normally delayed and not as fast. Some commentators argue that the only meaningful indicator of communication success is sales. However, there are many other influences that affect the level of sales, such as price, the effect of previous communications, the recommendations of opinion leaders or friends, poor competitor actions or any number of government or regulatory developments. Except in circumstances such as direct marketing, where immediate and direct feedback can be determined, organisations should use other methods to gauge the success of their communication activities, for example, the level and quality of customer enquiries, the number and frequency of store visits, the degree of attitude change and the ability to recognise or recall an advertisement. All of these represent feedback, but, as a rough distinction, the evaluation of feedback for mass communications is much more difficult to judge than the evaluation of interpersonal communications.

Noise

A complicating factor, which may influence the quality of the reception and the feedback, is noise. Noise, according to Mallen (1977), is 'the omission and distortion of information', and there will always be some noise present in all communications. Management's role is to ensure that levels of noise are kept to a minimum, wherever it is able to exert influence.

Noise occurs when a receiver is prevented from receiving all or part of a message in full. This may be because of either cognitive or physical factors. For example, a cognitive factor may be that the encoding of the message was inappropriate, thereby making it difficult for the receiver to decode the message. In this circumstance it is said that the realms of understanding of the source and the receiver were not matched. Another reason noise may enter the system is that the receiver may have been physically prevented from decoding the message accurately because the receiver was distracted. Examples of distraction are that the telephone rang, or someone in the room asked a question or coughed. A further reason could be that competing messages screened out the targeted message.

Some sales promotion practitioners are using the word 'noise' to refer to the ambience and publicity surrounding a particular sales promotion event. In other words, the word is being used as a positive, advantageous element in the communication process. This approach is not adopted in this text.

Realms of understanding

The concept of the 'realm of understanding' was introduced earlier. It is an important element in the communication process because it is a recognition that successful communications are more likely to be achieved if the source and the receiver understand each other. This understanding concerns attitudes, perceptions, behaviour and experience: the values of both parties to the communication process. Therefore, effective communication is more likely when there is some common ground – a realm of understanding between the source and receiver.

Some organisations, especially those in the private sector, spend a huge amount of money researching their target markets and testing their advertisements to ensure that their messages can be decoded and understood. The more organisations understand their receivers, the more confident they become in constructing and transmitting messages to them. Repetition and learning are important elements in marketing communications. Learning is a function of knowledge and the more we know, the more likely we are to understand.

Factors that influence the communication process

The linear, sequential interpretation of the communication process fails to accurately represent all forms of communication. It was developed at a time when broadcast media dominated commercial communication and can be argued to no longer provide an accurate representation of contemporary communication processes. Issues concerning media and audience fragmentation, the need to consider social and relational dimensions of communication and the impact of interactive communication have reduced the overall applicability of the linear model.

However, there are two particular influences on the communication process that need to be considered. First, the media used to convey information, and second, the influence of people on the communication process. These are considered in turn.

The influence of the media

The dialogue that marketing communications seeks to generate with audiences is partially constrained by an inherent time delay based on the speed at which responses are generated by the participants in the communication process. Technological advances now allow participants to conduct marketing communication-based 'conversations' at electronic speeds. The essence of this speed attribute is that it allows for real-time interactively based communications, where enquiries are responded to more or less instantly.

New, digital-based technologies and the Internet in particular, provide an opportunity for interaction and dialogue with customers. With traditional media the tendency is for monologue or at best delayed and inferred dialogue. One of the first points to be made about these new, media-based communications is that the context within which marketing communications occurs is redefined. Traditionally, dialogue occurs in a (relatively) familiar context, which is driven by providers who deliberately present their messages through a variety of communication devices into the environments that they expect their audiences may well pass or recognise. Providers implant their messages into the various environments of their targets. Yuan *et al.* (1998) refer to advertising messages being 'unbundled', such as direct marketing, which has no other content, or 'bundled' and embedded with other news content such as television, radio and webpages with banner ads. Perhaps more pertinently, they refer to direct and indirect online advertising. Direct advertising is concerned with advertising messages delivered to the customer (email) while indirect advertising is concerned with messages that are made available for a customer to access at their leisure (websites).

Digital media-based communications tend to make providers relatively passive. Their messages are presented in an environment that requires targets to use specific equipment to actively search them out. The roles are reversed, so that the drivers in the new context are active information seekers, represented by a target audience (members of the public and other information providers such as organisations), not just the information providing organisations.

The influence of people

The traditional view of communication holds that the process consists essentially of one step. Information is directed and shot at prospective audiences, rather like a bullet is propelled from a gun. The decision of each member of the audience to act on the message or not is the result of a passive role or participation in the process. Organisations can communicate with different target audiences simply by varying the message and the type and frequency of channels used.

The linear model has been criticised for its oversimplification, and it certainly ignores the effect of personal influences on the communication process and potential for information deviance. To accommodate these influences two further models are introduced, the influencer model and the interactional model of communication.

The influencer model of communication

The influencer model depicts information flowing via media channels to particular types of people (opinion leaders and opinion formers; see pp. 45–46) to whom other members of the audience refer for information and guidance. Through interpersonal networks, opinion leaders not only reach members of the target audience who may not have been exposed to the message, but may reinforce the impact of the message for those members who did receive the message

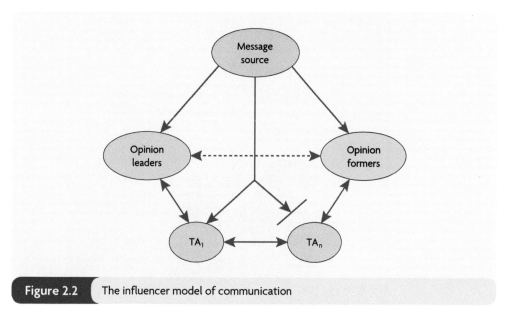

| Figure 2.2 | The influencer model of communication |

(Figure 2.2). For example, feedback and comments from travellers on Tripadvisor.com assist others when making travel plans, and constitutes opinion leadership. However, editors of travel sections in the Sunday press and television presenters of travel programmes fulfil the role of opinion former and can influence the decision of prospective travellers through their formalised knowledge.

Sometimes referred to as the two-step model, this approach indicates that the mass media do not have a direct and all-powerful effect over their audiences. If the primary function of the mass media is to provide information, then personal influences are necessary to be persuasive and to exert direct influence on members of the target audience.

The influencer approach can be developed into a multi-step model. This proposes that communication involves interaction among all parties to the communication process (see Figure 2.3). This interpretation closely resembles the network of participants who are often involved in the communication process.

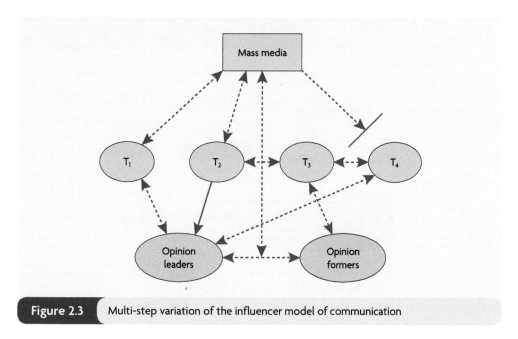

| Figure 2.3 | Multi-step variation of the influencer model of communication |

"I wanted a beautiful natural wax finish, so naturally I used Ronseal Quick & Easy Brushing Wax."

After

Before

Ronseal Quick & Easy Brushing Wax is the quick and easy way to create a beautiful natural wax finish.

It's so simple, just brush it on, leave to dry for 10-20 minutes, then buff off to provide natural colour and protection for interior wood.

Find out more online with colours and step-by-step guides at www.brushingwax.co.uk

 RONSEAL® DOES EXACTLY WHAT IT SAYS ON THE TIN®

Exhibit 2.2   Brushing Wax print ad

This ad uses the principles of opinion leadership (a representative of the target audience) to convey the product benefits

Image courtesy of Ronseal Ltd.

Interactional model of communication

The models and frameworks used to explain the communication process so far should be considered as a simplification of reality and not a true reflection of communication in practice. The linear model is unidirectional, and it suggests that the receiver plays a passive role in the process. The influencer model attempts to account for an individual's participation in the communication process. These models emphasise individual behaviour but exclude any social behaviour implicit in the process.

The interactional model of communication attempts to assimilate the variety of influences acting upon the communication process. This includes the responses people give to communications received from people and machines. Increasingly communication is characterised by attributing meaning to messages that are shared, updated and a response to other messages. These 'conversations' can be termed interactional and are an integral part of society. Figure 2.4 depicts the complexity associated with this form of communication.

Interaction is about actions that lead to a response. The development of direct marketing helped make significant inroads in the transition from what is essentially one-way to two-way and then interactive-based communication. Digital technology has further enabled this interaction process. However, interaction alone is not a sufficient goal simply because the content of the interaction could be about a radical disagreement of views, an exchange of opinion or a social encounter.

Ballantyne refers to two-way communication with audiences in two ways. First, as a 'with' experience, as manifest in face-to-face encounters and contact centres. He also distinguishes a higher order of two-way communication based on communication 'between' parties. It is this latter stage that embodies true dialogue where trust, listening and adaptive behaviour are typical. These are represented diagrammatically in Table 2.1.

A key question emerges, what is interaction and what are its key characteristics? If we can understand the dynamics and dimensions of interactivity then it should be possible to develop more effective marketing communications. In the context of marketing communications,

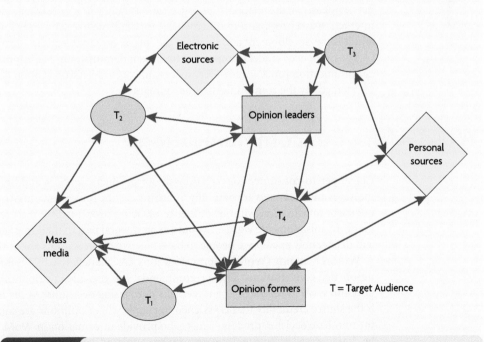

Figure 2.4   The interactional model of communication

Table 2.1	Communication matrix		
Direction	**Mass markets**	**Portfolio/mass-customised**	**Networks**
One-way Planned communications designed to inform and persuade Medium to high wastage	Communication 'to' Planned persuasive messages aimed at securing brand awareness and loyalty; e.g. communication of USPs and ESPs	Communication 'for' Planned persuasive messages with augmented offerings for target markets; e.g. communicating targeted lifecycle products, guarantees, loyalty programmes	
Two-way Formal and informal with a view to listening and learning Minimal wastage		Communication 'with' Integrated mix of planned and interactively shared knowledge; e.g. face to face, direct (database), contact centres, interactive b2b Internet portals	Communication 'between' Dialogue between participants based on trust, learning and adaptation with co-created outcomes; e.g. key account liaison, expansion of communities, staff teamwork

Source: Ballantyne (2004), Emerald Group Publishing Ltd. Used with permission

interactivity can be considered from one of two perspectives. One is the technology, tools and features (e.g. multimedia, www, online gaming) that provide for interaction. The second, according to Johnson *et al.* (2006) is the added value that interactivity is perceived to bring to the communication process.

Arising out of interaction is dialogue. This occurs through mutual understanding and a reasoning approach to interactions, one based on listening and adaptive behaviour. Dialogue is concerned with the development of knowledge that is specific to the relationship of the parties involved. Ballantyne refers to this as 'learning together' (Ballantyne, 2004: 119).

The adoption of dialogue as the basis for communication changes an organisation's perspective of its audiences. Being willing and able to enter into a dialogue indicates that there is a new emphasis on the relationships organisations hold with their stakeholders. Dialogue requires interaction as a precursor. In other words, for dialogue to occur there must first be interaction and it is the development and depth of the interaction that leads to meaningful dialogue.

The influencer model is important because it demonstrates the importance of people in the communication process. However, successful communication is often determined by the level of interactivity the communication encourages.

Word-of-mouth communications

Consumer-to-consumer conversations about products, services and brand related marketing messages and meanings are naturally occurring events. Buyers, potential buyers and non-buyers exchange information without influence or being prompted by the brand owner. However, many organisations use word-of-mouth as an integral part of their marketing communications and deliberately encourage people to have positive conversations about their particular brand.

Word-of-mouth (WoM) communications are characterised as informal, unplanned and unsolicited conversations. These recommendations provide information and purchasing support and serve to reinforce an individual's purchasing decisions. At the heart of this approach is the source credibility that is assigned to people whose opinions are sought after and used in the purchase decision process. Those who provide information in WoM communications can be characterised as informal experts who are unbiased, trustworthy and who can be considered to be objective. Personal influence is important and can enrich the communication process.

Unlike advertising, where messages are primarily linear and unidirectional, WoM communication is interactive and bidirectional.

Definition and motives

Arndt (1967: 66) sets out word-of-mouth as 'an oral, person-to-person communication between a receiver and a communicator whom the receiver perceives as non-commercial, regarding a brand, product, or service'. Put in more simple terms, word of mouth concerns the sharing of an opinion among people independent from the company or its agents (Santo, 2006: 29).

Stokes and Lomax (2002) define word-of-mouth communication as 'interpersonal communication regarding products or services where the receiver regards the communicator as impartial'. This simple definition was developed from some of the more established interpretations that failed to accommodate contemporary media and the restrictions concerning the perceived independence of the communicator.

People like to talk about their product (service) experiences for a variety of reasons that are explored in the next section. However, by talking with a neighbour or colleague about the good experiences associated with a holiday, for example, the first-hand 'this has actually happened to someone I know' effect will be instrumental in the same views being passed on to other colleagues, irrespective of their validity or overall representation of similar vacations. Mazzarol *et al.* (2007) identify the 'richness of the message' and the 'strength of the implied or explicit advocacy' as important triggers for WoM. Palmer (2009) brings these together and refers to WoM as information people can trust as it comes from people just like them and it helps them make better decisions.

Helm and Schlei (1998: 42) refer to WoM as 'verbal communications (either positive or negative) between groups such as the product provider, independent experts, family, friends and the actual or personal consumer'. However, as discussed later, organisations now use electronic WoM techniques in a commercial context in order to generate brand based conversations based around a point of differentiation. Indeed, an important point is that WoM is transmitted person-to-person through a variety of media (Lam, *et al.*, 2009).

One important question that arises is, why do people want to discuss products or advertising messages? Bone (1995) cited by Stokes and Lomax (2002) refers to three elements of WoM (see Table 2.2).

Dichter (1966) determined that there were four main categories of output WoM.

1 *Product involvement*

People, he found, have a high propensity to discuss matters that are either distinctly pleasurable or unpleasurable. Such discussion serves to provide an opportunity for the experience to be relived, whether it be the 'looking for' or the 'use' experience, or both. This reflects the product and service experience elements of marketing communications, identified as part of the scope of the topic, in Chapter 1.

Table 2.2	Elements of word-of-mouth communication	
Element of WoM		**Explanation**
Direction	Input WoM	Customers seeking recommendation prior to purchase
	Output WoM	Expression of feelings as a result of the purchase experience
Valence		The positive or negative feelings resulting from the experience
Volume		The number of people to which the message is conveyed

Source: After Bone (1995)

2 Self-involvement

Discussion offers a means for ownership to be established and signals aspects of prestige and levels of status to the receiver. More importantly, perhaps, dissonance can be reduced as the purchaser seeks reassurance about the decision.

3 Other involvement

Products can assist motivations to help others and to express feelings of love, friendship and caring. These feelings can be released through a sense of sharing the variety of benefits that products can bestow.

4 Message involvement

The final motivation to discuss products is derived, according to Dichter, from the messages that surround the product itself, in particular the advertising messages and, in the business-to-business market, seminars, exhibitions and the trade press, which provide the means to provoke conversation and so stimulate word-of-mouth recommendation.

Marketing communications can be used to stimulate conversations, by using these motivations as the anchor for the messages.

People who identify very closely with a brand and who might be termed brand advocates often engage in word-of-mouth communications. Advocacy can be demonstrated not only through word-of-mouth communications but also through behaviour, for example, by wearing branded clothing or using tools and equipment. The issue of advocacy is explored further in Chapter 8 in the section on loyalty and retention schemes.

Viewpoint 2.2	Spreading the word about Hovis

Founded in 1888, Hovis has become an established household name in the UK bread market. Hovis uses WoM in its attempt to regain the market leadership, both deliberately, and perhaps as a secondary aspect of its branded communications. The planned approach seeks to drive awareness by recruiting 800 advocates to help support the launch of their Hearty Oats brand. Referred to as a 'marketing advocacy campaign', women over 35 were identified as the best opinion leaders (advocates), partly because of their interest in health issues, social networking and a tendency to be early adopters of emerging trends. Selected advocates, as Hovis refers to them, were sent samples and they were encouraged to feedback comments and exchange recipes. The expectation is that they will talk amongst their friends and acquaintances, both off and online, about their positive feelings towards the Hearty Oats (and Hovis) brand.

The secondary approach borrows on Dichter's ideas about why people talk about products and services. When Hovis recognised the difficulties their brand was facing (declining quality, poor packaging and ineffective communications), research was undertaken amongst typical consumers. This revealed that the consumers differentiated between good bread and bad bread, and an increasing proportion aligned Hovis with bad bread. The relaunch campaign revived a famous Hovis ad that featured a small lad on a bike. This time the lad travelled through time, featuring significant world events. The 122 second ad was voted campaign of the year by the BBC and won the best marketing communications prize by the Marketing Society. The point of this story is that the ad was so well made, so memorable and so good that people like to talk about these quality communications. In Dichter's terms, this is message involvement, and is a potent source of word-of-mouth communication.

Source: Based on Reynolds (2010); Smith (2010)

Question

If WoM communication is so important why is it not a core activity within marketing communications for all brands?

Task

When you next visit a leisure or entertainment complex make a mental note of the ways in which the brand owner encourages visitors to talk about the complex.

These motivations to discuss products and their associative experiences vary between individuals and with the intensity of the motivation at any one particular moment. There are two main persons involved in this process of word-of-mouth communications: a sender and receiver. Research indicates that the receiver's evaluation of a message is far from stable over time and accuracy of recall decays (expectedly) through time. What this means for marketing communications is that those people who have a positive product experience, especially in the service sector, should be encouraged to talk as soon as possible after the event (Christiansen and Tax, 2000). For example, Pepsi Raw was launched in pubs and bars in order to reach young affluent consumers. The goal was to encourage this target audience to talk about the brand and in doing so imbue the brand with social group associations and then roll the brand out across supermarkets (Simms, 2007). Goldsmith and Horowitz (2006) found that risk reduction, popularity, reduced costs, access to easy information, and even inspiration from offline sources such as cinema, tv and radio were some of the primary reasons why people seek the opinions of others online.

According to Reichheld (2003) cited by Mazur (2004) organisations should measure word-of-mouth communication because those who speak up about a brand are risking their own reputation when they recommend a brand. Looking at the financial services sector, Reichheld argues that measures based on customer satisfaction or retention rates can mask real growth potential because they are measures of defection, and switching barriers may induce inertia. He found three particular groups based on their type of word-of-mouth endorsement: promoters, passively satisfied and detractors. In particular he identified a strong correlation between an organisation's growth rate and the percentage of customers who are active promoters.

Opinion leaders

Katz and Lazerfeld (1955) first identified individuals who were predisposed to receiving information and then reprocessing it to influence others. Their studies of American voting and purchase behaviour led to their conclusion that those individuals who could exert such influence were more persuasive than information received directly from the mass media. These opinion leaders, according to Rogers (1962), tend 'to be of the same social class as non-leaders, but may enjoy a higher social status within the group'. Williams (1990) uses the work of Reynolds and Darden (1971) to suggest that they are more gregarious and more self-confident than non-leaders. In addition, they have a greater exposure to relevant mass media (print) and as a result have more knowledge/familiarity and involvement with the product class, are more innovative and more confident of their role as influencer (leader) and appear to be less dogmatic than non-leaders (Chan and Misra, 1990).

Opinion leadership can be simulated in advertising by the use of product testimonials. Using ordinary people to express positive comments about a product to each other is a very well-used advertising technique.

The importance of opinion leaders in the design and implementation of communication plans should not be underestimated. Midgley and Dowling (1993) refer to *innovator communicators*: those who are receptive to new ideas and who make innovation-based purchase decisions without reference to or from other people. However, while the importance of these individuals is not doubted, a major difficulty exists in trying to identify just who these opinion leaders and innovator communicators are. While they sometimes display some distinctive characteristics, such as reading specialist media vehicles, often being first to return coupons, enjoying attending exhibitions or just involving themselves with new, innovative techniques or products, they are by their very nature invisible outside their work, family and social groups.

Viewpoint 2.3   Digital influencers

When Sony wanted to launch its BRAVIA LCD television it was a faced with an audience that was essentially cynical towards advertising and promotional messages and hard to reach with telling branded messages. The success of the launch was partly due to its use of a key part of the audience, digital influencers.

Digital influencers are people who understand, appreciate and enjoy technology. They are effectively digital opinion leaders and they represent an important target audience. The key for Sony was to encourage these influencers to spread the word about BRAVIA to the early majority and reach the mass market.

The original BRAVIA television ad was based round 250,000 coloured balls fired out of a cannon in San Francisco. During filming, local residents shot their own video footage. This found its way onto the Internet, which in turn provoked significant comment and interest. Quite transparently, Sony started to feed the digital influencers with blogging 'blog fodder', and they in turn used the material to develop conversations with other much broader audiences. Sony also slowly released official film that helped to create links from the Sony site to the original amateur images posted on Flickr. As the mainstream audiences, who are less technologically able than influencers, tuned into the BRAVIA interest so simpler content was made available, for example, screensavers and mobile phone wallpapers.

Source: Based on Whitton and Ryan (2006)

Question

Do you believe the increasing use of opinion leaders is due to cost cutting or because it is superior form of communication?

Task

Think about buying a new laptop, make a note of who or what you would consult prior to purchase.

Opinion formers

Opinion formers are individuals who are able to exert personal influence because of their authority, education or status associated with the object of the communication process. Like opinion leaders, they are acknowledged and sought out by others to provide information and advice, but this is because of the formal expertise that opinion formers are adjudged to have. For example, community pharmacists are often consulted about symptoms and medicines, and film critics carry such conviction in their reviews that they can make or break a new production.

Popular television programmes, such as *EastEnders*, *Casualty* and *Coronation Street*, all of which attract huge audiences, have been used as vehicles to draw attention to and open up debates about many controversial social issues, such as contraception, abortion, drug use and abuse, and serious illness and mental health concerns.

The influence of opinion formers can be great. For example, the editor of a journal or newspaper may be a recognised source of expertise, and any offering referred to by the editor in the media vehicle is endowed with great credibility. In this sense the editor acts as a gate-keeper, and it is the task of the marketing communicator to ensure that all relevant opinion formers are identified and sent appropriate messages.

However, the credibility of opinion formers is vital for communication effectiveness. If there is a suspicion or doubt about the impartiality of the opinion former, then the objectivity of their views and comments are likely to be perceived as tainted and not believed so that damage may be caused to the reputation of the brand and those involved.

Many organisations constantly lobby key members of parliament in an effort to persuade them to pursue 'favourable' policies. Opinion formers are relatively easy to identify, as they need to be seen shaping the opinion of others, usually opinion followers.

Opinion followers

The vast majority of consumers can be said to be opinion followers. The messages they receive via the mass media are tempered by the opinions of the two groups of personal influencers just discussed. Some people actively seek information from those they believe are well informed, while others prefer to use the mass media for information and guidance (Robinson, 1976). However, this should not detract from the point that, although followers, they still process information independently and use a variety of inputs when sifting information and responding to marketing stimuli.

Ethical drug manufacturers normally launch new drugs by enlisting the support of particular doctors who have specialised in the therapy area and who are recognised by other doctors as experts. These opinion formers are invited to lead symposia and associated events to build credibility and activity around the new product. At the same time, public relations agencies prepare press releases with the aim that the information will be used by the mass media (opinion formers) for editorial purposes and create exposure for the product across the target audience, which, depending upon the product and/or the media vehicle, may be GPs, hospital doctors, patients or the general public. All these people, whether they be opinion leaders or formers, are active influencers or talkers (Kingdom, 1970).

Developing brands with word-of-mouth communication

So far in this chapter word-of-mouth communication (WoM) has been examined as naturally occurring, unplanned conversations. This is not necessarily correct as many organisations deliberately attempt to reach their audiences using WoM principles. The term word-of-mouth marketing (WoMM) refers to the electronic version of the spoken endorsement of a product or service, where messages are targeted at key individuals who then voluntarily pass the message to friends and colleagues. In doing so they bestow, endorse and provide the message with a measure of credibility. WoMM is a planned, intentional attempt to influence consumer-to-consumer communications using professional marketing methods and technologies (Kozinets et al., 2010) to prompt WoM conversations.

From this it can be assumed that there are a variety of methods that organisations use to influence their audiences, all in the name of WoM. Of these, three main forms of WoM can be identified; voluntary, prompted and managed.

- **Voluntary** WoM can be considered to be the most natural form of interpersonal conversation, free from any external influence, coercion or intent. This still occurs among genuine opinion leaders, formers and followers for reasons considered earlier.

- **Prompted** WoM occurs when organisations convey information to opinion leaders and formers, with a view to deliberately encouraging them to forward and share the information with their followers. The goal is to prompt conversations among followers based around the credibility bestowed on the opinion leader. This outward perspective can be counter-balanced by an inward view. For example, some organisations use various elements of social media, for example, blogs, online communities and forums, to prompt consumer-to-consumer conversations and to then listen, observe and revise their approaches to the market.

- **Managed** WoM occurs when organisations target, incentivise and reward opinion leaders for recommending their offerings to their networks of followers. In these situations opinion leaders lose their independence and objectivity within the communication process, and become paid representatives of a brand. As a result the credibility normally attached to these influencers diminishes and the essence of freely expressed opinions about products and brands is removed.

There is evidence that organisational use of contemporary marketing communications seeks to drive voluntary conversations, stimulated by positive product and service experiences. The prompted approach is used extensively and enables organisations to retain credibility and a sense of responsibility. PQ Media reported in 2010 that the managed approach is increasing as clients seek to move their communication budgets closer to where target audiences spend their time online. They expect this sector to grow very quickly. The organisations that exploit their audiences through managed WoM conversations are not acting illegally, but may be guilty of transgressing ethical boundaries and demonstrating disrespect for their audiences. Not a position for long term strength.

Traditionally brands were built partly through offline communications directed to opinion leaders, when they could be identified, and through opinion formers. Sporting and entertainment celebrities have been used as brand ambassadors for a long time. They are used to enable audiences to develop positive associations between the personality of the ambassador and a brand. McCracken (1989) believes that celebrity endorsement works through the theory of meaning transfer. Consumers make an overall assessment of what a celebrity 'represents' to them, based on their perception and interpretation of the celebrity's identity cues. These cues relate to their behaviour, comments, ability, and attributes that are of particular interest to the consumer. McCracken (1989: 315) refers to their public image as demonstrated in 'television, movies, military, athletics, and other careers'.

The meaning assigned to a celebrity is transferred from the celebrity endorser to the product when the two are paired in a commercial message. Gwinner and Eaton (1999) argue that when a consumer acquires/consumes the product, the meaning is transferred to the user and the process is complete.

Contemporary brand development now incorporates the use of social media, and bloggers in particular, who play an increasingly critical role in the dissemination of brand related information. More detailed information about these elements can be found in Chapter 14, but here it is important to establish the way in which brands can be developed through word-of-mouth marketing/communication.

Opinion formers such as journalists, receive information about brands through press releases. They then relay the information, after editing and reformatting, to their readers and viewers through their particular media. So, brands target brand-related information at journalists, with the intention that their messages would be forwarded to their end user audience.

Bloggers are now an important and influential channel of communication. However, they do not share the same characteristics as journalists. For example, the number of bloggers in any one market can be counted in terms of tens of thousands of people (Clark, 2010), in contrast to the relatively small, select number of opinion formers. The majority of bloggers have an informal interest in a subject, whereas opinion formers are deemed to have formal expertise. Bloggers however, are not tied to formal processes or indeed an editor. As a result bloggers do not have to be objective in their comments and are not constrained by any advertising messages. Most importantly, bloggers conduct conversations among themselves and their followers, whereas journalists receive little feedback. More information about blogging can be found in Chapter 14.

Viewpoint 2.4   Fashionable bloggers

In January 2010, fashion blogger Tavi Gevinson, aged 14, sat in the front row at the Christian Dior couture show in Paris, and in front of the *Grazia* journalist. Clark (2010) observes this as a reflection of the way key influencers are changing the branding process. No longer are glossy magazines the primary vehicle to reach consumers. Now it is word of mouth through social media, and blogging in particular, that is shaping the way the fashion industry operates. This change in emphasis is even recognised by many of the leading fashion magazines who have run features about fashion blogs. For example, Clark reports that WhatKatieWore.com has been featured in the *Sunday Times Style* magazine, *Marie Claire* and *Grazia*.

In an attempt to promote the island and reduce the average age of visitors, the Barbados Tourism Authority harnessed the power of bloggers and their propensity to communicate their experiences through social media and their networks. The initiative was supported by airlines and hotels who service the island.

Eight entrepreneurs were taken on a three-week tour to experience not only the holiday dimension but also both the business activities and opportunities.

There was no formal requirement to inform others but it was inevitable that the trip would trigger conversations. In addition to email and general comments, the entrepreneurs blogged regularly, made videos and posted these and their comments on various sites, including Facebook. The cost of the trip, the reach of these influencers and the credibility of their messages was deemed to be superior than a single ad in a national newspaper.

Source: Based on Clark (2010); Roberts (2010)

Question

To what extent is blogging a means of self expression or something else?

Task

Find three different blogs in fashion, travel and sport. Make a list of their similarities and differences.

Process of adoption

An interesting extension to the concept of opinion followers and the discussion on WoM communications is the process by which individuals become committed to the use of a new product. Rogers (1983) has identified this as the process of adoption and the stages of his innovation decision process are represented in Figure 2.5 on page 51. These stages in the adoption process are sequential and are characterised by the different factors that are involved at each stage (e.g. the media used by each individual).

Exhibit 2.3	A 1970's magazine ad for Mane, a hair loss treatment

Image courtesy of The Advertising Archives

1 *Knowledge*

The innovation becomes known to consumers, but they have little information and no well-founded attitudes. Information must be provided through mass media to institutions and people whom active seekers of information are likely to contact. Information for passive seekers should be supplied through the media and channels that this group habitually uses to look for other kinds of information (Windahl *et al.*, 1992).

> Bill washes his hair regularly, but he is beginning to notice tufts of hair on his comb. He becomes aware of an advertisement for Mane in a magazine.

2 *Persuasion*

The consumer becomes aware that the innovation may be of use in solving known and potential problems. Information from those who have experience of the product becomes very important.

> Bill notices that the makers of Mane claim that not only does their brand reduce the amount of hair loss but also aids hair gain. Mane has also been recommended to him by someone he met in the pub last week. Modelling behaviour predominates.

3 *Decision*

An attitude may develop and may be either favourable or unfavourable, but as a result a decision is reached whether to trial the offering or not. Communications need to assist this part of the process by continual prompting.

> Bill is prepared to believe (or not to believe) the messages and the claims made on behalf of Mane. He thinks that Mane is potentially a very good brand (or not). He intends trying Mane because he was given a free sample (or because it was on a special price deal).

4 *Implementation*

For the adoption to proceed in the absence of a sales promotion, buyers must know where to get it and how to use it. The product is then tested in a limited way. Communications must provide this information in order that the trial experience be developed.

> Bill buys 'Mane' and tests it.

5 *Confirmation*

The innovation is accepted or rejected on the basis of the experience during trial. Planned communications play an important role in maintaining the new behaviour by dispelling negative thoughts and positively reaffirming the original 'correct' decision. McGuire, as reported in Windahl *et al.* (1992), refers to this as post-behavioural consolidation.

> It works, Bill's hair stops falling out as it used to before he started using 'Mane'. He reads an article that reports that large numbers of people are using these types of products satisfactorily. Bill resolves to buy 'Mane' next time.

This process can be terminated at any stage (see Figure 2.5) and, of course, a number of competing brands may vie for consumers' attention simultaneously, so adding to the complexity and levels of noise in the process. Generally, mass communications are seen to be more effective in the earlier phases of the adoption process for products that buyers are actively interested in, and more interpersonal forms are more appropriate at the later stages, especially trial and adoption. This model assumes that the stages occur in a predictable sequence, but this clearly

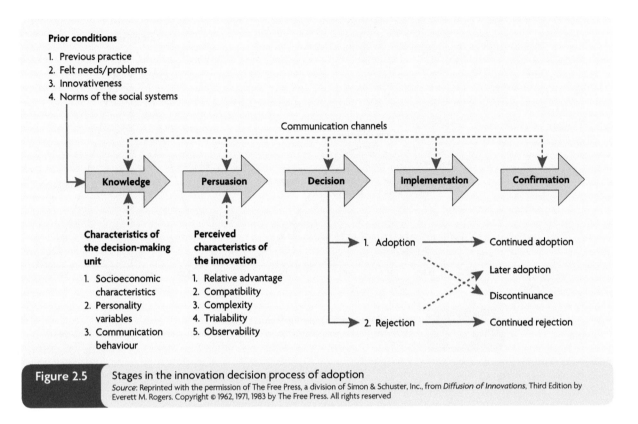

Prior conditions

1. Previous practice
2. Felt needs/problems
3. Innovativeness
4. Norms of the social systems

| Figure 2.5 | Stages in the innovation decision process of adoption |

Source: Reprinted with the permission of The Free Press, a division of Simon & Schuster, Inc., from *Diffusion of Innovations*, Third Edition by Everett M. Rogers. Copyright © 1962, 1971, 1983 by The Free Press.

does not happen in all purchase activity, as some information that is to be used later in the trial stage may be omitted, which often happens when loyalty to a brand is high or where the buyer has experience in the marketplace.

Process of diffusion

The process of adoption in aggregate form, over time, is diffusion. According to Rogers (1983), diffusion is the process by which an innovation is communicated through certain channels over a period of time among the members of a social system. This is a group process and Rogers again identified five categories of adopters. Figure 2.6 shows how diffusion may be fast or slow and that there is no set speed at which the process occurs. The five categories are as follows:

1 *Innovators*

These groups like new ideas and have a large disposable income. This means they are more likely to take risks associated with new products.

2 *Early adopters*

Research has established that this group contains a large proportion of opinion leaders and they are, therefore, important in speeding the diffusion process. Early adopters tend to be younger than any other group and above average in education. Internet activity and use of publications is probably high as they actively seek information. A high proportion of early adopters are active bloggers. This group is important to the marketing communications process because they can determine the speed at which diffusion occurs.

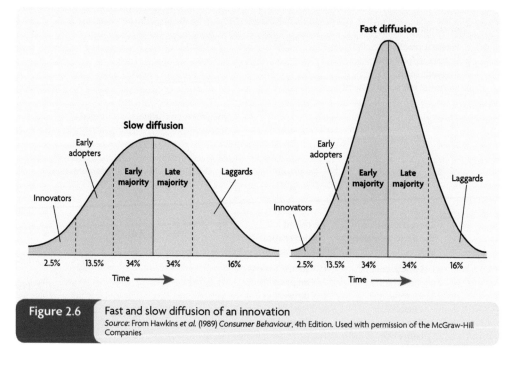

Figure 2.6	Fast and slow diffusion of an innovation

Source: From Hawkins *et al.* (1989) *Consumer Behaviour*, 4th Edition. Used with permission of the McGraw-Hill Companies

3 *Early majority*

The early majority are usually composed of opinion followers who are a little above average in age, education, social status and income. Although not capable of substantiation, it is probable that web usage is high and they rely on informal sources of information and take fewer publications than the previous two groups.

4 *Late majority*

This group of people is sceptical of new ideas and only adopts new products because of social or economic factors. They take few publications and are below average in education, social status and income. Their web usage may be below average.

5 *Laggards*

This group of people is suspicious of all new ideas and is set in their opinions. Lowest of all the groups in terms of income, social status and education, this group takes a long time to adopt an innovation.

This framework suggests that, at the innovation stage, messages should be targeted at relatively young people in the target group, with a high level of income, education and social status. This will speed word-of-mouth recommendation and the diffusion process. Mahajan *et al.* (1990) observe that the personal influence of word-of-mouth communications does not work in isolation from the other communication tools and media. Early adopters are more likely to adopt an innovation in response to 'external influences' and only through time will the effect of 'internal influences' become significant. In other words, mass media communications need time to work before word-of-mouth communications can begin to build effectiveness. However, digital developments circumnavigate the need to use mass media, which means that viral communications and social networks alone can lead to substantial WOM penetration.

Gatignon and Robertson (1985) suggest that there are three elements to the diffusion process, which need to be taken into account, particularly for the fast-moving consumer goods sector

1. the rate of diffusion or speed at which sales occur;
2. the pattern of diffusion or shape of the curve;
3. the potential penetration level or size of the market.

Care should be taken to ensure that all three of these elements are considered when attempting to understand the diffusion process. It can be concluded that if a campaign is targeted at innovators and the early majority, and is geared to stimulating word-of-mouth communications, then the diffusion process is more likely to be successful than if these elements are ignored.

Summary

In order to help consolidate your understanding of communication theory, here are the key points summarised against each of the learning objectives:

1 Understand the linear model of communication and appreciate how the various elements link together and contribute to successful communication

The linear or one-way communication process suggests that messages are developed by a source, encoded, transmitted, decoded and meaning applied to the message by a receiver. Noise in the system may prevent the true meaning of the messages from being conveyed, whilst feedback to the source is limited. The effectiveness of this communication process is determined by the strengths of the linkages between the different components.

2 Examine the impact of the media and personal influences on the communication process

There are two particular influences on the communication process that need to be considered. First, the media used to convey information has fragmented drastically as a raft of new media have emerged. Second, people influence the communication process considerably, either as opinion leaders, formers or as participants in the word-of-mouth process.

3 Demonstrate the characteristics of the influencer and interactional forms of communication

The influencer model depicts information flowing via media channels to particular types of people (opinion leaders and opinion formers; see pp 45–46) to whom other members of the audience refer for information and guidance. Through interpersonal networks, opinion leaders not only reach members of the target audience who may not have been exposed to the message, but may reinforce the impact of the message for those members who did receive the message.

Increasingly communication is characterised by attributing meaning to messages that are shared, updated and a response to other messages. These 'conversations' can be termed interactional and are an integral part of society. The interactional model of communication attempts to assimilate the variety of influences acting upon the communication process and account for the responses (interactions) people give to messages received from people and machines.

4 Explain the characteristics associated with opinion leaders, formers and followers

Opinion leaders are members of a peer group who have informal expertise and knowledge about a specific topic. Opinion formers have formal expertise bestowed upon them by virtue of their qualifications, experience and careers. Opinion followers value and use information from these sources in their decision-making processes. Marketing communications should therefore target leaders and formers as they can speed the overall communication process.

5 Examine the nature and characteristics associated with word-of-mouth communication

Word-of-mouth communication (WoM) is 'interpersonal communication regarding products or services where the receiver regards the communicator as impartial'. WoM is an increasingly important form of effective communication, one which is relatively cost free yet very credible.

6 Describe the processes of adoption and diffusion as related to marketing communications

The process of adoption in aggregate form, over time, is diffusion. It is a group process by which an innovation is communicated through certain channels over a period of time among the members of a social system. Five particular groups each with distinct characteristics can be identified.

The process of adoption in aggregate form, over time, is diffusion. According to Rogers (1983), diffusion is the process by which an innovation is communicated through certain channels over a period of time among the members of a social system.

Review questions

1. Name the elements of the linear model of communication and briefly describe the role of each element.
2. Make brief notes explaining why the linear interpretation of the communication process is not entirely satisfactory.
3. Draw the influencer model of communication.
4. Discuss the differences between the linear, influencer and interactional models of communications.
5. How do opinion leaders differ from opinion formers and opinion followers?
6. Why is word-of-mouth communication so important to marketing communications?
7. What are the three elements of word-of-mouth communication identified by Bone?
8. If voluntary is one form of WoM, what are the other two and how do they differ?
9. Using a product of your choice show how the stages in the process of adoption can be depicted.
10. Draw a graph to show the difference between fast and slow diffusion.

References

Arndt, J. (1967) Role of Product-Related Conversations in the Diffusion of a New Product, *Journal of Marketing Research*, 4 (August), 291–295.

Ballantyne, D. (2004) Dialogue and its role in the development of relationship specific knowledge, *Journal of Business and Industrial Marketing*, 19(2), 114–123.

Bone, P.F. (1995) Word of mouth effects on short-term and long term product judgments, *Journal of Business Research*, 21(3), 213–223.

Chan, K.K. and Misra, S. (1990) Characteristics of the opinion leader: a new dimension, *Journal of Advertising*, 19(3), 53–60.

Christiansen, T. and Tax, S.S. (2000) Measuring word of mouth: the questions of who and when, *Journal of Marketing Communications*, 6, 185–199.

Clark, N. (2010) How brands can reach bloggers, *Marketing*, 3 March, 24–26.

Dichter, E. (1966) How word-of-mouth advertising works, *Harvard Business Review*, 44 (November/December), 147–166.

Gatignon, H. and Robertson, T. (1985) A propositional inventory for new diffusion research, *Journal of Consumer Research*, 11, 849–867.

Goldsmith, R.E. and Horowitz, D. (2006) Measuring motivations for online opinion seeking, *Journal of Interactive Advertising*, 6(2), (Spring), 3–14. Retrieved 5 April 2010 from http://www.jiad.org/article76

Gwinner K.P. and Eaton, J. (1999) Building Brand Image Through Event Sponsorship: The Role of Image Transfer, *Journal of Advertising*, 28(4), (Winter), 47–57.

Hawkins, D.I., Best, R.J. and Coney, K.A. (1989) *Consumer Behaviour: Implications for Marketing Strategy*, Homewood, IL: Richard D. Irwin.

Helm, S. and Schlei, J. (1998) Referral potential – potential referrals: An investigation into customers' communication in service markets, Proceedings from 27th EMAC Conference, *Marketing Research and Practice*, 41–56.

Johnson, G.J., Bruner II, G.C. and Kumar, A. (2006) Interactivity and its facets revisited, *Journal of Advertising*, 35(4), (Winter), 35–52.

Katz, E. and Lazarfeld, P.F. (1955) *Personal Influence*. Glencoe, IL: Free Press.

Kingdom, J.W. (1970) Opinion leaders in the electorate, *Public Opinion Quarterly*, 34, 256–261.

Kozinets, R.V., de Valck, K., Wojnicki, A.C. and Wilner, S.J.S. (2010) Networked Narratives: understanding word-of-mouth marketing in online communities, *Journal of Marketing*, 74 (March), 71–89.

Lam, D., Lee, A. and Mizerski, R. (2009) The Effects of Cultural Values in Word-of-Mouth Communication, *Journal of International Marketing*, 17(3), 55–70.

Mahajan, V., Muller, E. and Bass, F.M. (1990) New product diffusion models in marketing, *Journal of Marketing*, 54 (January), 1–26.

Mallen, B. (1977) *Principles of Marketing Channel Management*. Lexington, MA: Lexington Books.

Mazur, L. (2004) Keep it simple, *Marketing Business* (March), 17.

Mazzarol, T., Sweeney, J.C. and Soutar, G.N. (2007) Conceptualising word-of-mouth activity, triggers and conditions: an exploratory study, *European Journal of Marketing*, 41(11/12), 1475–1494.

McCracken, G. (1989) Who is the Celebrity Endorser? Cultural Foundations of the Endorsement Process, *Journal of Consumer Research*, 16(3), 310–321.

Midgley, D. and Dowling, G. (1993) Longitudinal study of product form innovation: the interaction between predispositions and social messages, *Journal of Consumer Research*, 19 (March), 611–625.

Palmer, I. (2009) WoM is about empowering consumers in shaping your brand, *Admap*, 504 (April), retrieved 2 June 2010 from www.warc.com/admap

Patzer, G.L. (1983) Source credibility as a function of communicator physical attractiveness, *Journal of Business Research*, 11, 229–241.

PQ Media (2010) More brands start paid conversations online, *Warc News*, retrieved 17 May 2010 from www.warc.com/news/

Reichheld, F.F. (2003) The one number you need to grow, *Harvard Business Review* (December), 47–54.

Reynolds, J. (2010) Hovis embarks on first 'buzz marketing' drive, *Marketing*, 2 June, 3.

Reynolds, F.D. and Darden, W.R. (1971) Mutually adaptive effects of interpersonal communication, *Journal of Marketing Research*, 8 (November), 449–454.

Roberts, J. (2010) Mobilise the people to shape your brand, *Marketing Week*, 4 February, retrieved 23 June 2010 from www.marketingweek.co.uk/in-depth-analysis/cover-stories/mobilise-the-people-to-shape-your-brand/3009483.article

Robinson, J.P. (1976) Interpersonal influence in election campaigns: two step flow hypothesis, *Public Opinion Quarterly*, 40, 304–319.

Rogers, E.M. (1962) *Diffusion of Innovations*, 1st edn, New York: Free Press.

Rogers, E.M. (1983) *Diffusion of Innovations*, 3rd edn, New York: Free Press.

Santo, B (2006) Have you heard about *word of mouth?*, *Multichannel Merchant*, 2(2), (February), 28–30.

Schramm, W. (1955) How communication works, in *The Process and Effects of Mass Communications* (ed. W. Schramm), 3–26, Urbana, IL: University of Illinois Press.

Shannon, C. and Weaver, W. (1962) *The Mathematical Theory of Communication*. Urbana, IL: University of Illinois Press.

Simms, J. (2007) Bridging the gap, *Marketing*, 12 December 2007, 26–28.

Smith, N. (2010) Hovis: Marketing Society Award for Excellence, *Marketing*, 9 June, 15.

Stokes, D. and Lomax, W. (2002) Taking control of word of mouth marketing: the case of an entrepreneurial hotelier, *Journal of Small Business and Enterprise Development*, 9(4), 349–357.

Theodorson, S.A. and Theodorson, G.R. (1969) *A Modern Dictionary of Sociology*. New York: Cromwell.

Williams, K. (1990) *Behavioural Aspects of Marketing*. Oxford: Heinemann.

Windahl, S., Signitzer, B. and Olson, J.T. (1992) *Using Communication Theory*, London: Sage.

Whitton, F. and Ryan, L. (2006) Sony BRAVIA LCD TV-Balls, *IPA Effectiveness Awards*, Institute of Practitioners in Advertising, Retrieved 18 January 2008 from www.warc.com/ArticleCentre,/Default.asp?CType=A&AID=WORDSEARCH82662&Tab=A

Yuan, Y., Caulkins, J.P. and Roehrig, S. (1998) The relationship between advertising and content provision on the Internet, *European Journal of Marketing*, 32(7/8), 667–687.

Chapter 3
Audiences: attitudes, behaviour and decision-making

Understanding the way in which customers perceive their world, the way they learn, develop attitudes and respond to marketing communication stimuli is fundamental if effective communications are to be developed. In the same way, understanding the ways in which buyers make decisions and the factors that impact upon the decision process can affect the effectiveness of marketing communications.

Aims and learning objectives

The aims of this chapter are to first consider some of the ways information is processed by people and second to examine the key issues associated with purchase decision-making and their impact on marketing communications.

The learning objectives are to enable readers to:

1. explain the nature of perception and describe how marketing communications can be used to influence the way people perceive and position brands;

2. describe the key components of attitudes and explain ways in which marketing communications can be used to influence attitudes;

3. set out ideas concerning the nature of perceived risk and to relate ways in which marketing communications can be used to alleviate such uncertainty;

4. appreciate the nature of involvement and to explain how marketing communications can be used to reflect high and low involvement situations;

5. explain how marketing communications can be used to complement the purchase decision-making processes adopted by organisations.

Introduction

Marketing is about many things, but one of its central themes is the management of behaviour. Marketing communications is about making promises and so it makes sense therefore, to understand buyer behaviour, in order that these promises be realistic and effective. Understanding the ways in which buyers make decisions and the factors that impact upon the decision process can affect the effectiveness of marketing communications. In particular, it can influence message structure, content and scheduling. In this chapter, and indeed the book, reference is made to both buyers and audiences. This is because although all buyers constitute an audience, not all audiences are buyers.

Information processing

Marketing communications is an audience-centred activity so it is vitally important to understand the way in which audiences' process information prior to, during and after making product/service purchase decisions. Here three main information processing issues are considered; awareness, perception and attitudes.

Awareness

Awareness of the existence and availability of a product/service or an organisation is necessary before information can be processed and purchase behaviour expected. Much of marketing communications activity is directed towards getting the attention of the target audience, simply because of the vast number of competing messages and 'noise' in the marketplace. Many different techniques and approaches have been developed, first through advertising and now in most aspects of marketing communications. The goal is to get the undivided attention of the audience, to create awareness of the key messages and induce engagement opportunities. Awareness, therefore, needs to be created, developed, refined or sustained, according to the characteristics of the market and the particular situation facing an organisation at any one point in time (see Figure 3.1).

In situations where the audience experiences high involvement and is fully aware of a product's existence, attention and awareness levels need only be sustained, and efforts need to be applied to other communication tasks, which may be best left to the other elements of the communications mix. For example, sales promotion and personal selling are more effective at informing, persuading and provoking purchase of a new car once advertising has created the necessary levels of awareness.

Where low levels of awareness are found, getting attention needs to be a prime objective so that awareness can be developed in the target audience. Where low involvement exists, the decision-making process is relatively straightforward. With levels of risk minimised, buyers with sufficient levels of awareness may be prompted into purchase with little assistance of the other elements of the mix. Recognition and recall of brand names and corporate images are felt by some (Rossiter and Percy, 1987) to be sufficient triggers to stimulate a behavioural response. The requirement in this situation would be to refine and strengthen the level of awareness in order that it provokes interest and stimulates a higher level of involvement during recall or recognition.

Where low levels of awareness are matched by low involvement, the prime objective has to be to create awareness of the product in association with the product class. It is not surprising that organisations use awareness campaigns and invest a large amount of their resources in establishing their brand or corporate name. Many brands seek to establish 'top of mind awareness' as one of their primary objectives for their advertising spend. For example,

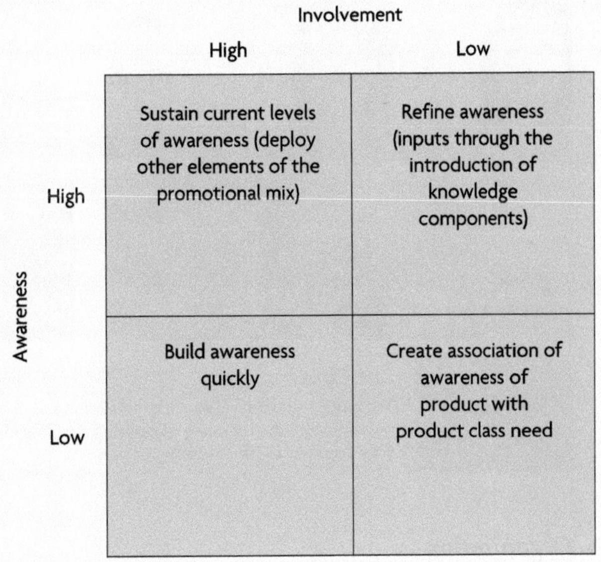

Involvement

	High	Low
High	Sustain current levels of awareness (deploy other elements of the promotional mix)	Refine awareness (inputs through the introduction of knowledge components)
Low	Build awareness quickly	Create association of awareness of product with product class need

(Awareness axis labelled on left: High at top, Low at bottom)

Figure 3.1 An awareness grid

Comparethemarket.com, a price comparison car insurance website, decided to differentiate themselves in an intensely competitive market. They decided to change the way their name was perceived because name familiarity is key (and their name was unmemorable), and their identity and name were very similar to their nearest competitor (gocompare). By adopting the name 'meerkat' and developing the comparethemeerkat.com site, brand name awareness rose considerably (Jukes, 2009).

Once awareness has been created in the target audience, it should not be neglected. If there is neglect, the audience may become distracted by competing messages and the level of awareness of the focus product or organisation may decline.

Perception

Perception is concerned with how individuals see and make sense of their environment. It is about how individuals select, organise and interpret stimuli, so that they can understand their world.

Selection

Individuals are exposed, each day, to a tremendous number of stimuli. De Chernatony (1993) suggested that each consumer is exposed to over 550 advertisements per day, while Lasn (1999) estimated that this should be 3,000 advertisements per day (cited by Dahl *et al.*, 2003). In addition there are thousands of other non-commercial stimuli that each individual encounters. To cope with this bombardment, our sensory organs select those stimuli to which attention is given. The nature of the stimuli, or external factors such as the intensity and size, position, contrast, novelty, repetition and movement, are factors that have been developed and refined by marketing communicators to attract attention. Animation is used to attract attention when the product class is perceived as bland and uninteresting, such as margarine or teabags. Unexpected camera angles and the use of music can be strong methods of gaining the attention of the target audience, as used successfully in the Bacardi Breezer and Renault commercials. Sexual attraction can be a powerful means of capturing the attention of audiences, and when associated with a brand's values can be a very effective method of getting attention (for example, the Diet Coke advertisement, see Exhibit 3.1).

Exhibit 3.1	Diet Coke
	The hugely successful Diet Coke television ads depict office workers timing their work break to coincide with the presence of certain attractive males.
	Images courtesy of The Advertising Archives

Organisation

These selected stimuli are organised in order to make them comprehensible and are then given meaning. Stimuli therefore need to be presented in ways that we can understand or create meaning. The use of contour (e.g. the Coke bottle), and grouping objects to convey meaning by association enable easier organisation of stimuli. For example, some products are shown next to fruit or vegetables so that we transfer the healthy association to the promoted product.

Interpretation

Once stimuli are organised they need to be interpreted so that meaning can be attributed. As Cohen and Basu (1987) state, by using existing categories meanings can be given to stimuli. These categories are determined from the individual's past experiences and they shape what the individual expects to see. These expectations, when combined with the strength and clarity of the stimulus and the motives at the time perception occurs, mould the pattern of the perceived stimuli. Stimuli, therefore, are selected, organised and interpreted.

Marketing communication and perception

The way in which individuals perceive, organise and interpret stimuli is a reflection of their past experiences and the classifications used to understand the different situations each individual frames every day. Individuals seek to frame or provide a context within which their role becomes clearer. Shoppers expect to find products in particular situations, such as rows, shelves or display bins of similar goods. They also develop meanings and associations with some grocery products because of the utility and trust/emotional satisfaction certain pack types evoke. The likelihood that a sale will be made is improved if the context in which a purchase transaction is undertaken does not contradict a shopper's expectations.

Marketing communications should attempt to present products (objects) in a frame or 'mental presence' (Moran, 1990) that is recognised by a buyer, such as a consumption or purchase situation. A product has a much greater chance of entering an individual's evoked set if the situation in which it is presented is one that is expected and relevant. However, a new pack design can provide differentiation and provoke people into reassessing their expectations of what constitutes appropriate packaging in a product category.

Javalgi et al. (1992) point out that perception is important to product evaluation and product selection. Consumers try to evaluate a product's attributes by the physical cues of taste, smell, size and shape. Sometimes no difference can be distinguished, so the consumer has to make a judgement on factors other than the physical characteristics of the product. This is the basis of branding activity, where a personality is developed for the product that enables it to be

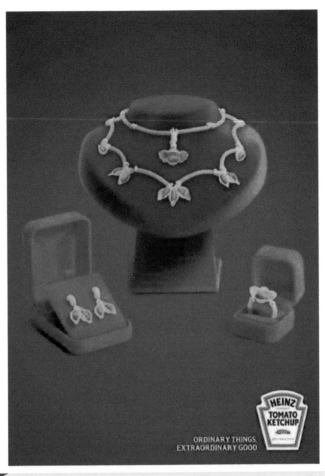

Exhibit 3.2	Heinz seek to position their tomato ketchup as a refinement in the Czech Republic
	Image used with permission from MARK/BBDO in the Czech Republic

perceived differently from its competitors. The individual may also set up a separate category or evoked set in order to make sense of new stimuli or satisfactory experiences. Consumer perception of salon- and shop-based haircare products shows important differences and indicates the different roles that marketing communication needs to play: see Figure 3.2. Within each of these sectors many brands are developed that are targeted at different segments based upon demographic, benefit and psychographic factors.

Finally, individuals carry a set of enduring perceptions or images. These relate to themselves, to products and to organisations. The concept of positioning the product in the mind of the consumer is fundamental to marketing strategy and is a topic that will be examined in greater depth in Chapter 4. The image an individual has of an organisation is becoming recognised as increasingly important, judging by the proportion of communication budgets being given over to public relations activities and corporate advertising in particular.

Organisations develop multiple images to meet the positioning requirements of their end-user markets and stakeholders. They need to monitor and adjust their identities constantly in respect of the perceptions and expectations held by the other organisations in their various networks. For example, the level of channel coordination and control can be a function of the different perceptions of channel members. These concern the perception of the channel depth, processes of control and the roles each member is expected to fulfil. Furthermore, the perception of an organisation's product quality and its associated image (reputation) is becoming increasingly important.

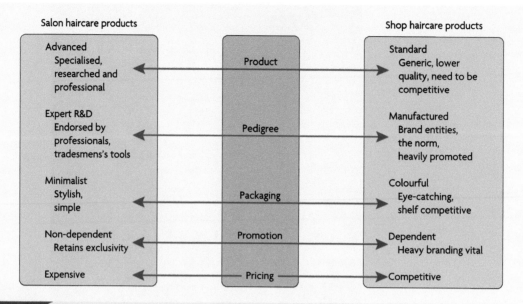

Salon haircare products		**Shop haircare products**

<table>
<tr><td>Advanced
  Specialised,
  researched and
  professional</td><td>Product</td><td>Standard
  Generic, lower
  quality, need to be
  competitive</td></tr>
<tr><td>Expert R&D
  Endorsed by
  professionals,
  tradesmens's tools</td><td>Pedigree</td><td>Manufactured
  Brand entities,
  the norm,
  heavily promoted</td></tr>
<tr><td>Minimalist
  Stylish,
  simple</td><td>Packaging</td><td>Colourful
  Eye-catching,
  shelf competitive</td></tr>
<tr><td>Non-dependent
  Retains exclusivity</td><td>Promotion</td><td>Dependent
  Heavy branding vital</td></tr>
<tr><td>Expensive</td><td>Pricing</td><td>Competitive</td></tr>
</table>

Figure 3.2   A comparison of the different perceptions and beliefs of salon and shop haircare brands

Attitudes

Attitudes relate to an individual's predispositions, shaped through experience, to respond in an anticipated way to an object or situation. Attitudes are learned through past experiences and serve as a link between thoughts and behaviour. These experiences may relate to the product itself, to the messages transmitted by the different members of the channel network (normally mass media communications) and to the information supplied by opinion leaders, formers and followers.

Attitudes tend to be consistent within each individual: they are usually clustered and very often interrelated. This categorisation leads to the formation of stereotypes, which is extremely useful for the design of messages as stereotyping allows for the transmission of a lot of information in a short time period (30 seconds) without impeding learning or the focal part of the message.

Attitude components

Attitudes are hypothetical constructs, and they are considered to consist of three components: a cognitive or learning component, an affective or feeling element and a conative or action component (see Figure 3.3).

1 Cognitive component (learn)

This component refers to the level of knowledge and beliefs held by individuals about a product and/or the beliefs about specific attributes of the offering. This represents the learning aspect of attitude formation. Marketing communications are used to create attention and awareness, to provide information and to help audiences learn and understand the features and benefits a particular product/service offers.

2 Affective component (feel)

By referring to the feelings held about a product – good, bad, pleasant or unpleasant – an evaluation is made of the object. This is the component that is concerned with feelings, sentiments, moods and emotions about an object. Marketing communications are used to induce feelings about the product/service such that it becomes a preferred brand. This preference may

Exhibit 3.3	An ad by Birds Eye to change the way frozen food was perceived by consumers
	At a time when chiller sales were exceeding frozen foods, Bird's Eye launched a campaign where one of the messages was that Bird's Eye fish was frozen as soon as it was caught, unlike some wet fish sales where the fish can be up to 10 days old.
	Image courtesy of Birds Eye Ltd.

be based on emotional attachment to a brand, conferred status through ownership, past experiences and longevity of brand usage or any one of a number of ways in which people can become emotionally involved with a brand.

3 Conative component (do)

This is the action component of the attitude construct and refers to the individual's disposition or intention to behave in a certain way. Some researchers go so far as to suggest that this component refers to observable behaviour. Marketing communications therefore, should be used to encourage audiences to do something. For example, visit a website, phone a telephone number, take a coupon, book a visit, press red (on a remote control unit) for interactivity through digital television.

This three-component approach to attitudes is based upon attitudes towards an object, person or organisation. The sequence of attitude formation is learn, feel and do. This approach to attitude formation is limited in that the components are seen to be of equal strength.

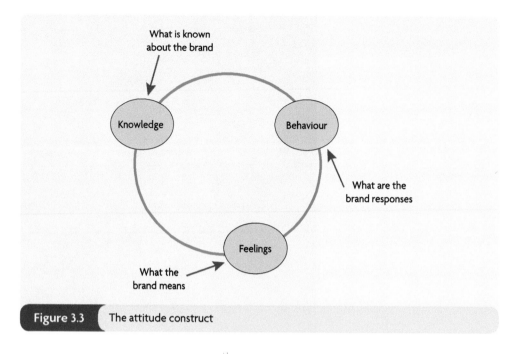

Figure 3.3   The attitude construct

A single-component model has been developed where the attitude only consists of the individual's overall feeling towards an object. In other words, the affective component is the only significant component.

Changing attitudes with marketing communications

Marketing communications is important to either maintain or change attitudes held by stakeholders. It is not the only way as product and service elements, pricing and channel decisions all play an important part in shaping the attitudes held. However, marketing communications has a pivotal role in conveying each of these aspects to the target audience. Branding (Chapter 6) is a means by which attitudes can be established and maintained in a consistent way and it is through the use of the tools of the communication mix that brand positions can be sustained. The final point that needs to be made is that there is a common thread between attributes, attitudes and positioning (Chapter 4). Attributes provide a means of differentiation and positions are shaped as a consequence of the attitudes that result from the way people interpret the associated marketing communications.

Viewpoint 3.1   Changing attitudes towards Weetabix

Weetabix is a premier brand among breakfast cereals. Many people have experienced the brand as a child, often as a baby, as the biscuit reduces to a mush when soaked with milk and becomes an ideal food for weaning. Weetabix is well established and market penetration rates of 40 per cent mean there is little room for growth and development. However, attitudes towards the brand were at best neutral, the biscuit being perceived to be bland. In addition, the breakfast market was experiencing change in the period 2003–05 and the blander products such as Cornflakes and Shredded Wheat were starting to lose share.

Weetabix commissioned qualitative research and asked a group of lapsed users to eat the brand for a week and keep a diary. Two of the more startling results were that many of the group soon reported health benefits (no snacking before lunch). In addition, others had started to add 'things' to the cereal to overcome the monotony of its blandness. Here lay the foundation for the advertising campaign, to reveal the variety, interest and added value by using different toppings. A 'Weetabix Week' advertising campaign was devised, which provided the basis for an event designed to stimulate and motivate people to use the brand. One of the goals was to change perceptions of the brand by encouraging consumers to experiment with different toppings. This was achieved by showing them ways other people topped off their daily Weetabix. The second goal was to motivate people to try the brand for three or four days, so that they started to feel the health benefits, before switching to their regular brand.

Television was the critical media because it allowed the audience to see the different toppings the participants used to decorate their Weetabix. The second benefit was that television enabled the audience to see 'real people' trying the Weetabix Week. These testimonials provided source credibility and opportunities to link consumption into lifestyle (e.g. children at breakfast, students late at night).

Source: Based on Okin and Robothan-Jones (2007)

Question

What might have been the impact had celebrities been used rather than normal consumers?

Task

Make a list of ideas that could be used to help consumers perceive the Weetabix brand differently.

Environmental influences on the attitudes people hold towards particular products and services are a result of many elements. First they are a reflection of the way different people interpret the marketing communications surrounding them. Second, they are a result of their direct experience of using them and third, a result of the informal messages received from family, friends and other highly credible sources of information. These all contribute to the way people perceive (and position) products and services and the feelings they have to them and to competing products. Managing attitudes (towards a brand) is therefore very important and marketing communications can play an important part in changing or maintaining attitudes. There are a number of ways in which attitudinal change can be implemented.

Change the physical product or service element

At a fundamental level, attitudes might be so ingrained that it is necessary to change the product or service. This may involve a radical redesign or the introduction of a significant new attribute. Only once these changes have been made should marketing communications be used to communicate the new or revised object. When VW bought Skoda it redesigned the total product offering before relaunch.

Change misunderstanding

In some circumstances people might misunderstand the benefits of a particularly important attribute and marketing communications is required to correct the beliefs held. This can be achieved through product demonstration of functionally based communications. Packaging and even the name of the product may need to be revised.

Build credibility

Attitudes towards a brand might be superficial and lack sufficient conviction to prompt conative behaviour. This can be corrected through the use of an informative strategy, designed to build credibility. Product demonstration and hands-on experience (e.g. through sampling) are effective strategies. Skoda supports a rally team to convey durability, speed and performance.

Change performance beliefs

Beliefs held about the object and the performance qualities of the object can be adjusted through appropriate marketing communications. For example, by changing the perceptions held about the attributes, it is possible to change the attitudes about the object.

Change attribute priorities

By changing the relative importance of the different attributes and ratings it is possible to change attitudes. Therefore, a strategy to emphasise a different attribute can change the attitude not only towards a brand but also to a product category. By stressing the importance of travel times, the importance of this attribute might be emphasised in the minds of potential holiday-makers. Dyson changed attitudes to carpet cleaning equipment by stressing the efficiency of its new cyclone technology rather than the ease of use, aesthetic design or generic name (Hoover) associations used previously.

Introduce a new attribute

Opportunities might exist to introduce a radically different and new (or previously unused) attribute. This provides a means for clear differentiation until competitors imitate and catch up. For example, by making prominent new service levels which are coupled with guaranteed refunds in the event of performance failure, this new attribute may lead to greater success.

Change perception of competitor products

By changing the way competitor products are perceived it is possible to differentiate your own brand. This could be achieved by using messages that distance a competitor's brand from your own. For example, an airline could highlight a key competitor's punctuality record, and this might help change the way its own performance level is perceived. In much the same way, Thomson Holidays used this approach when it used copy that read, 'We go there, we don't stay there'.

Change or introduce new brand associations

By using celebrities or spokespersons with whom the target audience can identify, it might be possible to change the way in which a brand is perceived. For example, a bread producer might use a well known athlete to represent their brand as a healthy food. Alternatively it may use children in its marketing communications to suggest that it is fun to eat and that all children love the brand.

Use corporate branding

By altering the significance of the parent brand relative to the product brand, it is possible to alter beliefs about brands and their overall value. In some situations there is little to differentiate competitive brands and little credible scope to develop attribute-based attitudes. By using the stature of the parent company it is possible to develop a level of credibility and brand values that other brands cannot copy, although they can imitate by using their parent brand. Procter & Gamble has introduced its name to the packs of many of its brands.

Change the number of attributes used

Many brands still rely on a single attribute as a means of providing a point of differentiation. This was popularly referred to as a unique selling proposition at a time when attribute and information based communications reflected a feature-dominated understanding of branding. Today, two or even three attributes are often combined with strong emotional associations in order to provide a point of differentiation and a set of benefit-oriented brand values.

Viewpoint 3.2	Branching out as NatWest change attitudes

The banking system is a classic example of market inertia. Customers see little reason to move or change their banks unless provoked by gross inefficiency or their accounts are mishandled. At the same time that many banks have closed a large proportion of their UK branch network and moved their call centres off shore to reduce costs, they have moved away from a human approach to customer service to one based on mechanics. There has since been a 'consumer backlash against foreign call centres [that] has led some companies to return operations to the UK' (Winterman, 2007).

When the Royal Bank of Scotland bought NatWest in 2000 it reversed the strategy of closing branches and using overseas call centres. A policy of refurbishing all the branches has since been implemented, new branches opened and all call centre operations are now UK-based.

As a result, NatWest have used this initiative as the backbone of their communication strategy. By positioning themselves against an attribute that had been discarded by competitors, NatWest have been able to establish a clear point of differentiation. By focusing their marketing and communications on their branch network in order to provide customers the opportunity for personal contact by just walking into a local branch, they have been able to add considerable value to the brand and given inert customers a reason to change to NatWest.

Source: Based on Winterman (2007); www.natwest.com/

Question

As all banks provide a service, how feasible is it for them to use service as a basis for differentiation?

Task

Find two other banks and determine the attributes they use for differentiation.

Decision-making

Much of marketing communication activity has been oriented towards decision-making, and knowledge of a buyer's decision-making processes is vital if the correct type of information is to be transmitted at the right time and in the right or appropriate manner. There are two broad types of buyer: consumers and organisational buyers. First, consideration will be given to a general decision-making process and then an insight into the characteristics of the decision-making processes for consumers and organisational buyers will be presented. Figure 3.4 shows that there are five stages in the general process whereby buyers make purchase decisions and implement them. Marketing communications can impact upon any or all of these stages with varying levels of potential effectiveness.

Problem recognition

Problem recognition occurs when there is a perceived difference between an individual's current position and their ideal state. Marketing communications can be used to encourage 'problem recognition' by suggesting that the current state is not desirable, by demonstrating how consumers can tell whether they have a similar problem (e.g. 'Is your hair dull and lifeless?') or by suggesting that their current brand is inferior.

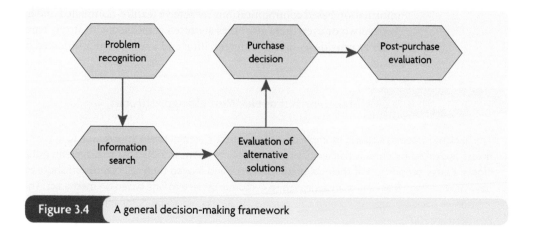

| Figure 3.4 | A general decision-making framework |

Information search

Having identified a problem a prospective buyer will search for information in an attempt to resolve it. There are two main areas of search activity. The internal search involves a memory scan to recall experiences and knowledge, utilising the perceptual processes to see whether there is an 'off-the-shelf' solution. If there is no 'off-the-shelf' solution, the prospective buyer will resort to an external search. This will involve family and friends, reference sources and commercial guides and advertising.

Alternative evaluation

Potential solutions need to be evaluated in order that the optimum choice be made. Products considered feasible constitute the *preference set*, and it is from these seven or eight products that a smaller group of products is normally assembled. This is referred to as the *evoked set* (or repertoire) and it is from this that consumers make a choice. Attributes used to determine the sets are referred to as evaluative criteria. Very often these attributes are both objective and subjective in nature.

Purchase decision

Having evaluated various solutions, the buyer may develop a predisposition to make a purchase. This will involve matching motives and evaluative criteria with product attributes. This necessitates the use of the processes of learning and attitude formation.

Post-purchase evaluation

Direct experience of the product is an important part of the decision process. Feedback from use helps learning and attitude development and is the main contributor to long-run behaviour. Communication activity must continue to provide satisfaction and prevent the onset of cognitive dissonance. This is a state where, after the purchase decision has been made, a buyer might feel tension about a past decision either because the product fails to reach expectations or because the consumer becomes aware of a superior alternative.

Marketing communications, at this stage, should be aimed at reinforcing past decisions by stressing the positive features of the product, the emotional enhancement usage brings or by providing more information to assist its use and application. For example, much of the advertising undertaken by car manufacturers seeks to prevent the onset of tension and purchase dissatisfaction.

Types of consumer decision-making

Buyers do not follow the general decision sequence at all times. The procedure may vary depending upon the time available, levels of perceived risk and the degree of involvement a buyer has with the type of product. Perceived risk and involvement are issues that will be covered later. At this point three types of problem-solving behaviour (extended problem-solving, limited problem-solving and routinised response) will be considered.

Extended problem-solving (EPS)

Consumers considering the purchase of a car or house undertake a great deal of external search activity and spend a lot of time reaching a solution that satisfies, as closely as possible, the evaluative criteria previously set. This activity is usually associated with products that are unfamiliar, where direct experience and hence knowledge are weak, and where there is considerable financial risk.

Marketing communications should aim to provide a lot of information to assist the decision process. The provision of information through sales literature, such as brochures and leaflets, websites for determining product and purchase criteria in product categories where there is little experience, access to salespersons and demonstrations and advertisements, are just some of the ways in which information can be provided.

Limited problem-solving (LPS)

Having experience of a product means that greater use can be made of internal memory-based search routines and the external search can be limited to obtaining up-to-date information or to ensuring that the finer points of the decision have been investigated.

Marketing communications should attempt to provide information about any product modification or new attributes and convey messages that highlight those key attributes known to be important to buyers. By differentiating the product, marketing communications provides the buyer with a reason to select that particular product.

Routinised response behaviour (RRB)

For a great number of products the decision process will consist only of an internal search. This is primarily because the buyer has made a number of purchases and has accumulated a great deal of experience. Therefore, only an internal search is necessary, so little time or effort will be spent on external search activities. Low-value items that are frequently purchased fall into this category, for example toothpaste, soap, tinned foods and confectionery.

Some outlets are perceived as suitable for what are regarded as distress purchases. Tesco Express and many petrol stations position themselves as convenience stores for distress purchases (for example, a pint of milk at 10 o'clock at night). Many garages have positioned themselves as convenience stores suitable for meeting the needs of RRB purchases. In doing so they are moving themselves away from the perception of being only a distress purchase outlet.

Communicators should focus upon keeping the product within the evoked set or getting it into the set. Learning can be enhanced through repetition of messages, but repetition can also be used to maintain attention and awareness.

Perceived risk

An important factor associated with the purchase decision process is the level of risk perceived by buyers. This risk concerns the uncertainty of the consequences arising from a decision to purchase a particular brand.

Risk is perceived because the buyer has little or no experience of the performance of the product or the decision process associated with the purchase. Risk is related to not only brand-based decisions but also to product categories, an especially important aspect when launching new technology products, for example. The level of risk an individual experiences varies through time, across products, and is often a reflection of an individual's propensity to manage risk. Settle and Alreck (1989) suggest that there are five main forms of risk that can be identified; the purchase of a laptop demonstrates each element. These are set out in Table 3.1 with respect to the purchase of such a laptop.

A sixth element, time, is also considered to be a risk factor (Stone and Gronhaug, 1993):

> Using the laptop example, will purchase of the computer lead to an inefficient use of my time? Or can I afford the time to search for a good laptop so that I will not waste my money?

What constitutes risk is a function of the contextual characteristics of each situation, the individuals involved and the product under consideration.

A major task of marketing communications is to reduce levels of perceived risk. By providing extensive and relevant information a buyer's risks can be reduced substantially. Mass media, word-of-mouth, websites and sales representatives for example are popular ways to set out the likely outcomes from purchase and so reduce the levels of risk. Brand loyalty can also be instrumental in reducing risk when launching new products. The use of guarantees, third-party endorsements, money-back offers (some car manufacturers offer the opportunity to return a car within 30 days or exchange it for a different model) and trial samples (as used by many haircare products) are also well-used devices to reduce risk.

Many direct response magazine ads seek to reduce a number of different types of risk. Companies offering wine for direct home delivery, for example, try to reduce performance risk by providing information about each wine being offered. Financial risk is reduced by comparing their 'special' prices with those in the high street, social risk is approached by developing the brand name associations trying to improve credibility and time risk is reduced through the convenience of home delivery.

Table 3.1	Types of perceived risk
Type of perceived risk	**Explanation**
Performance	Will the unit reproduce my music clearly?
Financial	Can I afford that much or should I buy a less expensive version?
Physical	Will the unit damage my other systems or endanger me in any way?
Social	Will my friends and colleagues be impressed?
Ego	Will I feel as good as I want to feel when listening to or talking about my unit?

| Viewpoint 3.3 | Appealing to thoughtful car buyers |

In 2006 Hyundai had set a goal to sell 500,000 cars in the USA in 2009. Then the recession broke and changed the context and market conditions for selling cars. The cars had been made and were being shipped to the States. The only reasonable variable open to Hyundai to shift the cars out of the dealerships, was to revisit the marketing communications.

The goals for the programme remained tough. The aim was to increase the brand based communications for the previous Jan–Feb results by 2 per cent, to maintain the previous period's number of shoppers (352,000) and to match the previous Jan–Feb's sales performance figures. In a market where only 9 per cent of consumers were looking to buy a new car, these were ambitious targets.

Rather than focus on the car the campaign sought to focus on the consumer and their perceived risks, mainly financial. This was to be achieved by assuring consumer confidence by removing the financial risk from buying a new car.

Research in 2007 found that there was a significant gap between the surprising truth of the cars' quality and the negative perceptions held by many individuals. Also, current Hyundai owners were more likely to be analytical, thoughtful decision-makers. Retail sales events followed the thoughtful theme, using a promotion that provided potential buyers access to investment experts who advised individuals about what to do with the money saved by buying a Hyundai.

Research also showed that consumers would be worried about their ability to maintain the payments for a new car, if the economy got worse. This was overcome when an insurance company agreed to indemnify and protect the credit of any new Hyundai consumer.

The transparent, upfront, matter-of-fact tone of the 'Assurance' campaign was thought to be important in order to be seen as sincere and understanding of the consumers' predicament. TV was used in order to be salient and reach as many people in the target market as quickly as possible. Large events such as the Super Bowl were used, as these stimulated both media and individual conversations.

The results were startling. Sales at Chrysler, GM, Ford and Toyota each fell by anything from 32 per cent to 55 per cent. At Hyundai they were up 14 per cent. Not only did Hyundai reduce financial risk, they led a change in the way car companies communicated with their audiences.

Source: Based on Anon (2010)

Question

What other risks might a car buyer have experienced when considering Hyundai? How might the Assurance campaign have helped overcome them?

Task

Flip through a newspaper or magazine, select three ads and determine whether there has been an attempt to reduce risk. If so how?

Involvement theory

Purchase decisions made by consumers vary considerably, and one of the factors thought to be key to brand choice decisions is the level of involvement (in terms of individual importance and relevance) a consumer has with either the product or the purchase process.

Involvement is about the degree of personal relevance and risk perceived by consumers when making a particular purchase decision (Rossiter *et al.*, 1991). This implies that the level of involvement may vary through time as each member of the target market becomes more (or less) familiar with the purchase and associated communications. At the point of decision-making involvement is high or low, not some point on a sliding scale or a point on a continuum between two extremes.

High involvement

High involvement occurs when a consumer perceives an expected purchase that is not only of high personal relevance but also represents a high level of perceived risk. Cars, washing machines, houses and insurance policies are seen as 'big ticket' items, infrequent purchases that promote a great deal of involvement. The risk described is financial but, as we saw earlier, risk can take other forms. Therefore the choice of perfume, suit, dress or jewellery may also represent high involvement, with social risk dominating the purchase decision. The consumer, therefore, devotes a great deal of time to researching the intended purchase and collecting as much information as possible in order to reduce, as far as possible, levels of perceived risk.

Low involvement

A *low-involvement* state of mind regarding a purchase suggests little threat or risk to the consumer. Low-priced items such as washing powder, baked beans and breakfast cereals are bought frequently, and past experience of the product class and the brand cues the consumer into a purchase that requires little information or support. Items such as alcoholic and soft drinks, and chocolate are also normally seen as low involvement, but they induce a strong sense of ego risk associated with the self-gratification that is attached to the consumption of these products.

Two approaches to decision-making

From this understanding of general decision-making processes, perceived risk and involvement theory, it is possible to identify two main approaches to consumer decision-making.

High-involvement decision-making

If an individual is highly involved with the initial purchase of a product, EPS is the appropriate decision sequence, as information is considered to be processed in a rational, logical order. Individuals who are highly involved in a purchase are thought to move through the process shown in Figure 3.5. When high-involvement decision-making is present individuals perceive a high level of risk and are concerned about the intended purchase. The essential element in this sequence is that a great deal of information is sought initially and an attitude is developed before a commitment or intention to trial is determined.

Information search is an important part of the high-involvement decision-making process. Because individuals are highly motivated, information is actively sought, processed and

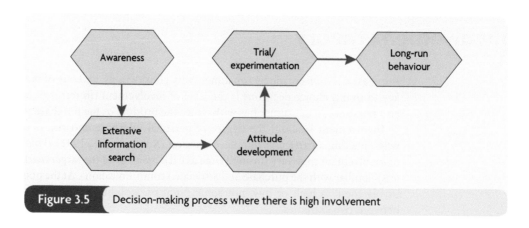

Figure 3.5   Decision-making process where there is high involvement

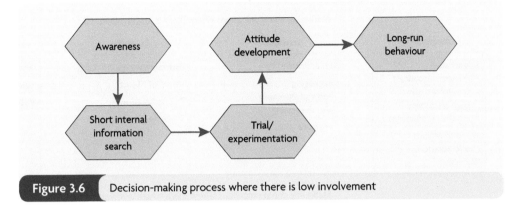

Figure 3.6   Decision-making process where there is low involvement

evaluated. Many media sources are explored, including the mass media, word-of-mouth communications, websites, and point-of-sale communications. As individuals require a lot of information, print media used to be the primary media where high involvement was identified. Today, websites are the primary source of large volumes of detailed information. Unlike print these sites can also be updated quickly but both types enable visitors to search and process information at a speed they can control.

Low-involvement decision-making

If an individual has little involvement with an initial purchase of a product, LPS is the appropriate decision process. Information is processed cognitively but in a passive, involuntary way. Processing occurs using right-brain thinking so information is stored as it is received, in sections, and this means that information is stored as a brand association (Heath, 2000). An advertisement for Andrex toilet tissue featuring the puppy is stored as the 'Andrex Puppy' without any overt thinking or reasoning. Because of the low personal relevance and perceived risk associated with this type of processing, message repetition is necessary to define brands and create meaningful brand associations. Individuals who have a low involvement with a purchase decision choose not to search for information and are thought to move through the process shown in Figure 3.6.

Communications can assist the development of awareness in the low-involvement decision-making process. However, as individuals assume a passive problem-solving role, messages need to be shorter than in the high-involvement process and should contain less information. Broadcast media are preferred as they complement the passive learning posture adopted by individuals. Repetition is important because the receiver has little or no motivation to retain information, and his or her perceptual selection processes filter out unimportant information. Learning develops through exposure to repeated messages, but attitudes do not develop at this part of the process (Harris, 1987).

Where low involvement is present, each individual relies upon internal, rather than external, search mechanisms, often prompted by point-of-purchase displays.

Impact on communications

Involvement theory is central to our understanding of the way in which information is processed and the way in which people make decisions about product purchases. We have established in the preceding section that there are two main types of involvement, high and low. These two types lead directly to two different uses of marketing communications. In decisions where there is high involvement, attitude precedes trial behaviour. In low-involvement cases this position is reversed.

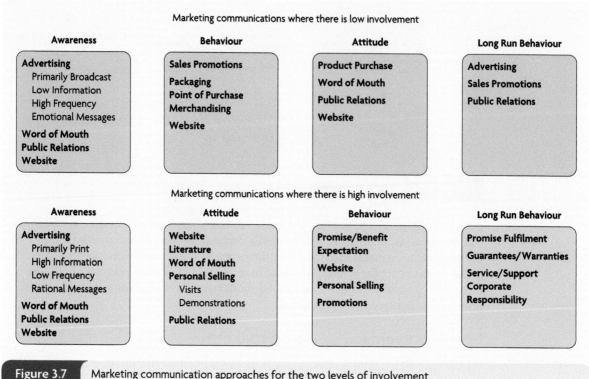

Figure 3.7 Marketing communication approaches for the two levels of involvement

Where there is high involvement, consumers seek out information because they are concerned about the decision processes and outcomes. This can be because of the levels of uncertainty associated with the high costs of purchase and usage, inexperience of the product (category) often brought about due to the infrequency of purchases, the complexity of product and doubts about its operational usefulness. Because they have these concerns, people develop an attitude prior to behaviour. Informational ads that require cognitive processing are recommended.

Where there is low involvement, consumers are content to select any one of a number of acceptable products and often rely on those that are in the individual's evoked set. Low involvement is thought to be a comfortable state, because there are too many other decisions in life to have to make decisions about each one of them, so an opportunity not to have to seek information and make other decisions is welcome. See Figure 3.7 which indicates the marketing communication strategies best suited for each level within both involvement sequences. Emotional or transformational ads are recommended.

Planning communications based on involvement is not as straightforward as the preceding material might suggest. Various factors might influence the outcomes. For example, some individuals who are cognitively capable of processing information, may not always be able to process information in informational based ads because they are overloaded. In these circumstances they are more likely to develop positive attitudes towards affective or transformational based ads. Ranjbariyan and Mahmoodi (2009) also found that people under time pressure are more prone to use transformational ads as they will pick up visual cues to help their decision-making.

The material presented so far in this section is based on classical research, theoretical development and is supported by research. However, much of the knowledge has been developed in a non digital era and that raises questions about the depth of its validity in the contemporary world. Foley *et al.* (2009) undertook research that showed that people organise product categories according to the level of risk associated with brand choice decisions and the level of reward, the enjoyment people derive from the decisions they make. They also found that the types of categories people organise leads to different patterns of decision-making. Four main product categories were identified:

- **Routine** In this category people perceive low risk and low reward. Brand choice decision-making therefore characterised by inertia and decision-making is robotic.
- **Burden** People perceive high risk and low reward. Search is extensive and decision-making improved if someone can assist.
- **Passion** Risk is high and reward is high because people are emotionally engaged with these types of products and services. The symbolism and meaning attached to brands in the category is high, reflected in high ego and social risks.
- **Entertainment** People use this category where risk is low but reward can be high. This means that decision-making can be a pleasant, if brief experience.

Each of these categories has implications for the communications strategies necessary to reach people and be effective. For example, consideration of the type of website that best suits each of these categories provides immediate insight into how having an understanding or insight into the target audience can shape marketing communications.

Organisational buying decision processes

Organisational buying, according to Webster and Wind (1972), is 'the decision-making process by which formal organisations establish the need for purchased products and services and identify, evaluate and choose among alternative brands and suppliers'. Of particular significance is the relationship that develops between organisations involved as buyers or sellers.

One way of examining the context is to compare organisational decisions with those made in consumer markets. There are far fewer buyers in the organisational context than in the consumer market, although there can be a number of people associated with a buying decision in an organisation. Orders are invariably larger and the frequency with which they are placed is much lower. It is quite common for agreements to be made between organisations for the supply of materials over a number of years. Similarly, depending upon the complexity of the product (photocopying paper or a one-off satellite), the negotiation process may also take a long time.

Viewpoint 3.4   Healthy buying decisions

The purchase of medical supplies and equipment by hospitals is an important decision, if only because of the implications of the decisions made with regard to patient welfare. However, the wide variety of people involved in the process can lead to buying decisions becoming overly complex, sometimes over budget and delayed. For example, purchasing decisions regarding infusion pumps are influenced by various stakeholder groups including medical experts (such as doctors and consultants), administrators (such as general managers and purchasing administrators), those with financial responsibilities, purchasing agents and of course certain direct government representatives, primary care trusts and other influential stakeholders.

Question

What are the implications for manufacturers and suppliers in order that they communicate effectively with this range of influencers?

Task

Draw up a list of communication tools and media that you might use to communicate your infusion pumps. Prioritise them and justify your decisions.

Many of the characteristics associated with consumer decision-making processes can be observed in the organisational context. However, organisational buyers make decisions that ultimately contribute to the achievement of corporate objectives. To make the necessary decisions a high volume of pertinent information is often required. This information needs to be relatively detailed and is normally presented in a rational and logical style. The needs of the buyers are many and complex and some may be personal. Goals, such as promotion and career advancement within the organisation, coupled with ego and employee satisfaction, combine to make organisational buying an important and complex task, one that requires professional training and the development of expertise if the role is to be performed optimally.

Buyclasses

Organisational buyers make decisions that vary with each buying situation and buyclass. Buyclasses, according to Robinson *et al.* (1967), comprise three types: new task, modified rebuy and straight rebuy (Table 3.2).

New task

As the name implies, the organisation is faced with a first-time buying situation. Risk is inevitably high at this point, and partly as a consequence there are a large number of decision participants. Each participant requires a lot of information and a relatively long period of time is required for the information to be assimilated and a decision to be made.

Modified rebuy

Having purchased a product, the organisation may request through its buyer that certain modifications be made to future purchases, for example adjustments to the specification of the product, further negotiation on price levels or perhaps the arrangement for alternative delivery patterns. Fewer people are involved in the decision process than in the new task situation.

Straight rebuy

In this situation, the purchasing department reorders on a routine basis, very often working from an approved list of suppliers. No other people are involved with the exercise until different suppliers attempt to change the environment in which the decision is made. For example, they may interrupt the procedure with a potentially better offer.

Readers may have noticed the strong resemblance to the extended, limited and routinised response identified earlier with respect to the consumer market.

Table 3.2	Main characteristics of the buyclasses		
Buyclass	**Degree of familiarity with the problem**	**Information requirements**	**Alternative solutions**
New buy	The problem is fresh to the decision-makers	A great deal of information is required	Alternative solutions are unknown, all are considered new
Modified rebuy	The requirement is not new but is different from previous situations	More information is required but past experience is of use	Buying decision needs new solutions
Rebuy	The problem is identical to previous experiences	Little or no information is required	Alternative solutions not sought or required

Reference has been made on a number of occasions to organisational buyers, as if these people are the only representatives of an organisation to be involved with the purchase decision process. This is not the case, as very often a large number of people are involved in the purchase decision. This group is referred to as either the decision-making unit (DMU) or the buying centre.

Buying centres vary in size and composition in accordance with the nature of each individual task. Webster and Wind (1972) identified a number of people who make up the buying centre.

Users are people who not only initiate the purchase process but will use the product, once it has been acquired, and evaluate its performance. *Influencers* very often help set the technical specifications for the proposed purchase and assist the evaluation of alternative offerings by potential suppliers. *Deciders* are those who make purchasing decisions. In repeat buying activities the buyer may well also be the decider. However, it is normal practice to require that expenditure decisions involving sums over a certain financial limit be authorised by other, often senior, managers. *Buyers* (purchasing managers) select suppliers and manage the process whereby the required products are procured. As identified previously, buyers may not decide which product is to be purchased but they influence the framework within which the decision is made. *Gatekeepers* have the potential to control the type and flow of information to the organisation and the members of the buying centre. These gatekeepers may be technical personnel, secretaries or telephone switchboard operators.

The size and form of the buying centre is not static. It can vary according to the complexity of the product being considered and the degree of risk each decision is perceived to carry for the organisation. Different roles are required and adopted as the nature of the buying task changes with each new purchase situation (Bonoma, 1982). It is vital for seller organisations to identify members of the buying centre and to target and refine their messages to meet the needs of each member of the centre.

The task of the marketing communications manager and the corresponding sales team is to decide which key participants have to be reached, with which type of message, with what frequency and to what depth contact should be made. Just as with individual consumers, each member of the buying centre is an active problem-solver and processes information so that personal and organisational goals are achieved.

Buyphases

The organisational buying decision process consists of several stages or buyphases (Robinson *et al.*, 1967). The following sequence of six phases or events is particular to the new task buyclass. Many of these buyphases are ignored or compressed when either of the other two buyclasses are encountered.

Need/problem recognition

Products or services are purchased because of two main events (Cravens and Woodruff, 1983). Difficulties may be encountered first as a result of a need to solve problems, such as a stock-out or new government regulations, and, secondly, as a response to opportunities to improve performance or enter new markets. Essentially, the need/recognition phase is the identification of a gap. This is the gap between the benefits an organisation has now and the benefits it would like to have. For example, when a photocopier breaks down or fails to meet the needs of the organisation, the communication benefits the copier offers are missed by the users. This gap can be bridged by getting the machine mended, by using a different machine on a temporary basis or by buying a new machine that provides the range of benefits required.

Product specification

As a result of identifying a problem and the size of the gap, influencers and users can determine the desired characteristics of the product needed to resolve the problem. This may take the form of a general description or may require a much more detailed analysis and the creation of a specification for a particular product. What sort of photocopier is required? What is it expected to achieve? How many documents should it copy per minute? Is a collator or tray required? This is an important part of the process, because if it is executed properly it will narrow the supplier search and save on the costs associated with evaluation prior to a final decision.

Supplier and product search

At this stage the buyer actively seeks organisations who can supply the necessary product. There are two main issues at this point. Will the product reach the required performance standards and will it match the specification? Secondly, will the potential supplier meet the other organisational requirements? In most circumstances organisations review the market and their internal sources of information and arrive at a decision that is based on rational criteria.

Organisations work wherever possible to reduce uncertainty and complexity. By working with others who are known, of whom the organisation has direct experience and who can be trusted, risk and uncertainty can be reduced substantially. This highlights another reason why many organisations seek relational exchanges and operate within established networks and seek to support each other.

The quest for suppliers and products may be a short task for the buyer; however, if the established network cannot provide a solution, the buying organisation has to seek new suppliers, and hence new networks, to be able to identify and short-list appropriate supplier organisations.

Evaluation of proposals

Depending upon the complexity and value of the potential order(s), the proposal is a vital part of the communication plan and should be prepared professionally. The proposals of the short-listed organisations are reviewed in the context of two main criteria: the product specification and the evaluation of the supplying organisation. If the organisation is already a part of the network, little search and review time need be allocated. If the proposed supplier is new to the organisation a review may be necessary to establish whether it will be appropriate (in terms of price, delivery and service) and whether there is the potential for a long-term relationship or whether this is a single purchase that is unlikely to be repeated.

Supplier selection

The buying centre will undertake a supplier analysis and use a variety of criteria depending upon the particular type of item sought. This selection process takes place in the light of the comments made in the previous section. A further useful perspective is to view supplier organisations as a continuum, from reliance on a single source to the use of a wide variety of suppliers of the same product.

Jackson (1985) proposed that organisations might buy a product from a range of different suppliers, in other words a range of multiple sources are maintained (a practice of many government departments). She labelled this approach 'always a share', as several suppliers are given the opportunity to share the business available to the buying centre. The major disadvantage is that this approach fails to drive cost as low as possible, as the discounts derived from volume sales are not achieved. The advantage to the buying centre is that a relatively small investment is required and little risk is entailed in following such a strategy.

At the other end of the continuum are organisations that only use a single-source supplier. All purchases are made from the single source until circumstances change to such a degree that the buyer's needs are no longer being satisfied. Jackson referred to these organisations as 'lost for good', because once a relationship with a new organisation has been developed, they are lost for good to the original supplier. An increasing number of organisations are choosing to enter alliances with a limited number or even single-source suppliers. The objective is to build a long-term relationship, work together to build quality and help each other achieve their goals. Outsourcing manufacturing activities for non-core activities has increased, and this has moved the focus of communications from an internal to an external perspective.

Evaluation

The order is written against the selected supplier and immediately the supplier is monitored and performance is evaluated against such diverse criteria as responsiveness to enquiries and modifications to the specification and timing of delivery. When the product is delivered it may reach the stated specification but fail to satisfy the original need. This is a case where the specification needs to be rewritten before any future orders are placed.

Organisational buying has shifted from a one-to-one dyadic encounter, salesperson to buyer, to a position where a buying team meets a selling team. The skills associated with this process are different and are becoming much more sophisticated, and the demands on both buyers and sellers are more pronounced. The processes of buying and selling are complex and interactive.

Readers are referred to the section at the end of Chapter 1 in which the differences between consumer and organisational marketing communications was highlighted. These differences reflect the various contextual issues that frame both the consumer and organisational environments. The nature of the environments, the tasks involved and the overall need of the recipients for particular types of information are some of the principal contextual issues.

Summary

In order to help consolidate your understanding of attitudes, behaviour and decision-making behaviour, here are the key points summarised against each of the learning objectives:

1 Explain the nature of perception and describe how marketing communications can be used to influence the way people perceive and position brands

Perception is concerned with how individuals see and make sense of their environment. It is about the selection, organisation and interpretation of stimuli by individuals so that they can understand their world. The effectiveness of marketing communications can be improved substantially if the elements of the marketing communications mix are designed to empathise with the perceptive view of buyers.

2 Describe the key components of attitudes and explain ways in which marketing communications can be used to influence attitudes

Attitudes are predispositions, shaped through experience, to respond in an anticipated way to an object or situation. Attitudes are learned through past experiences and serve as a link between thoughts and behaviour. Attitudes are hypothetical constructs, and they are considered to consist of three components: a cognitive or learning component, an affective or feeling element and a conative or action component.

Attitudes can be changed by using marketing communications to influence one or more of the three components.

3 Set out ideas concerning the nature of perceived risk and to relate ways in which marketing communications can be used to alleviate such uncertainty

Risk is perceived because the buyer has little or no experience of the performance of the product or the decision process associated with the purchase. Five main types of risk are normally observed, all which vary in intensity according to the individual, the product category and context. These are performance, social, ego, financial and functional risks.

A major task of marketing communications is to reduce levels of perceived risk. By providing extensive and relevant information a buyer's risks can be reduced substantially.

4 Appreciate the nature of involvement and to explain how marketing communications can be used to reflect high and low involvement situations

Involvement is about the degree of personal relevance and risk perceived by consumers when making a particular purchase decision. Involvement is about the way in which information is processed and the way in which people make decisions about product purchases. We have established in the preceding section that there are two main types of involvement, high and low. These two types lead directly to two different uses of marketing communications. In decisions where there is high involvement, attitude precedes trial behaviour. In low-involvement cases this position is reversed.

5 Explain how marketing communications can be used to complement the purchase decision-making processes adopted by organisations

Organisations can be observed to make purchase decisions in different ways, according to experience and product complexity. With many different people involved in organisational purchase decisions, a seller's marketing communications need to be adapted to suit the needs of the different participants and the experience the organisation has of purchasing in the product category.

Review questions

1. Name the dimensions of the awareness grid.
2. What are the three elements of perception used for processing stimuli?
3. Make brief notes about the characteristics of each of the attitude components.
4. Explain how marketing communications can be used to change attitudes.
5. What are buyclasses and buying centres?
6. What are EPS, LPS and RRB?
7. Describe the elements that constitute perceived risk.
8. Describe the high- and low-involvement decision-making processes.
9. Explain how marketing communications works with regard to attitude development in low and high involvement situations.
10. How might a salesperson utilise knowledge about the buying centre?

References

Anon (2010) North America Effies: Hyundai – Assurance, *Effie Worldwide*, retrieved 10 July 2010 from www.effie.org

Bonoma, T.V. (1982) Major sales: who really does the buying? *Harvard Business Review* (May/ June), 113.

Cohen, J. and Basu, K. (1987) Alternative models of categorisation, *Journal of Consumer Research* (March), 455–472.

Cravens, D. and Woodruff, R. (1983) *Marketing*. Reading, MA: Addison-Wesley.

de Chernatony L. (1993) The seven building blocks of brands, *Management Today* (March), 66–67.

Dahl, D.W., Frankenberger, D. and Manchanda, R.V. (2003) Does it pay to shock? *Journal of Advertising Research*, 43(3), September, 268–280.

Foley, C., Greene, J. and Cultra, M. (2009) Effective ads in a digital age, *Admap*, 503 (March), retrieved 2 June 2010 from www.warc.com/articlecentre

Harris, G. (1987) The implications of low involvement theory for advertising effectiveness, *International Journal of Advertising*, 6, 207–221.

Heath, R. (2000) Low-involvement processing, *Admap* (March), 14–13.

Jackson, B. (1985) Build customer relationships that last, *Harvard Business Review*, 33(3), 120–128.

Javalgi, R., Thomas, E. and Rao, S. (1992) US travellers' perception of selected European destinations, *European Journal of Marketing*, 26(7), 45–64.

Jukes, M. (2009) Creative review: Comparethemarket.com *revolutionmagazine.com*, 26 February 2009, retrieved 3 November 2010 from www.brandrepublic.com/features/888761/ Creative-review-Comparethemarketcom/?DCMP=ILC-SEARCH

Lasn, K. (1999) *Culture Jam: The Uncooling of America*. New York: Eagle Brook.

Moran, W. (1990) Brand preference and the perceptual frame, *Journal of Advertising Research* (October/November), 9–16.

Okin, G. and Robothan-Jones, R. (2007) Weetabix – The Weetabix Week: turning a barrier into a benefit, IPA Effectiveness Awards, 2007, retrieved 3 November 2010 from www.warc.com/ ArticleCenter/Default.asp?CType=A&AID=WORDSEARCH86130&Tab=A

Ranjbariyan, B. and Mahmoodi, S. (2009) The Influencing Factors in Ad Processing: Cognitive vs. Affective Appeals, *Journal of International Marketing and Marketing Research*, 34(3), 129–140.

Robinson, P.J., Faris, C.W. and Wind, Y. (1967) *Industrial Buying and Creative Marketing*. Boston, MA: Allyn & Bacon.

Rossiter, J.R. and Percy, L. (1997) *Advertising Communications & Promotion Management*, 2nd edn. New York: McGraw-Hill.

Rossiter, J.R., Percy, L. and Donovan, R.J. (1991) A better advertising planning grid, *Journal of Advertising Research* (October/November), 11–21.

Settle, R.B. and Alreck, P. (1989) Reducing buyers' sense of risk, *Marketing Communications* (January), 34–40.

Stone, R.N. and Gronhaug, K. (1993) Perceived risk: further considerations for the marketing discipline, *European Journal of Marketing*, 27(3), 39–50.

Webster, F.E. and Wind, Y. (1972) *Organizational Buying Behavior*. Englewood Cliffs, NJ: Prentice-Hall.

Winterman, D. (2007) Just returning your call … to the UK, *BBC News Magazine* Wednesday, 14 February 2007. Retrieved 15 January 2008 from http://news.bbc.co.uk/1/hi/magazine/ 6353491.stm

Minicase 1.1   Because it works!

Lynn Sudbury: Liverpool John Moores University

The array of beauty lotions and potions that claim to ward off wrinkles and other signs of ageing that women – and increasingly men – can choose from, is extensive. Indeed, in an overall industry reputed to be worth £25 billion world-wide and £6.2bn in Britain, Boots N°7 'Protect & Perfect' serum, retailing at £16.75 for 30ml and being on the shelves for three years already, was an unlikely contender for the title 'Magic Cream' that was to spark a wave of near hysteria that reached as far as the USA and Australia. Yet, that's exactly what happened after the product was featured on BBC's science programme *Horizon*.

The *Horizon* programme featured Lesley Regan, a 50-year-old professor of obstetrics and gynaecology at St Mary's Hospital in London, who went in search of 'The Holy Grail' – otherwise known as an anti-ageing product that scientifically worked. Her search led her to the cream perfected by scientist Steve Barton and his team in Nottingham. Mr Barton has been using the serum for several years, and had conducted his own trials with what he described as 'fantastic' results. However, it was only when the product was examined by a team of expert dermatologists at Manchester University that the claims became more believable. Professor Chris Griffiths, who heads the team at Manchester, explained that although they were initially sceptical, their independent research spanning 10 months and investigating a range of anti-ageing creams – many of which retail for far more than £17 – scientifically proved that N°7's Protect & Perfect actually worked. The cream was found to contain protecting and renewing agents associated with the production of collagen and elastin, as well as silicone and antioxidants, and was compared to prescription drugs used to treat severe acne and sun damage to skin. Professor Griffiths was reported to say 'At both basic science and clinical levels Boots N°7 Protect & Perfect has been shown scientifically to repair photo-aged skin and improve the fine wrinkles associated with photo-ageing.'

Boots had expected demand to rise once the programme had aired, and had prepared by shipping in 21 weeks supply of the product prior to the *Horizon* programme. Yet, despite the fact that the serum was only shown on camera for a few seconds, within 24 hours of the programme being aired, sales rose by 2,000 per cent, the shelves in Boots up and down the country were empty, waiting lists reportedly comprising four figures were opened, Boots' web store received 4,000 requests in one evening, and within days the product was being traded on eBay for up to £100. Some stores reported women charging behind counters, convinced that there would be hidden supplies there, others raced each other down aisles to get to the 'Magic Cream', and one store reported a near-riot when a single customer bought up their entire stock.

These events were only the beginning of the frenzy, however. While Boots switched most of their production to the Protect & Perfect line in an effort to cope with demand, the shortage fuelled further demand, as the news of the cream spread and more and more people wanted to buy it. The serum was a major conversation topic among mums outside schools and between friends. When stores received stock, they would telephone customers on the waiting lists telling them to be quick, and these customers would tell their friends, so stocks continued to disappear from shelves almost as fast as they could be filled, despite the product then being limited to one purchase per customer. Media reports of queues developing in the early hours outside Boots stores when stocks were expected fuelled even more demand. Many men also waited outside stores from 5a.m., some of them claiming to be under strict instructions from females to get their hand on the cream. Others, however, admitted to wanting to try the cream for themselves. Young girls queued up, some of them to buy for their mothers who had been trying to get hold of the cream for some time; others because they had heard from older friends that it actually worked.

Protect & Perfect was also big news on the web. Blogging gave individuals an outlet to share their thoughts, while an extraordinary number of online beauty forums such as 'Hey, Dollface!' focused on the serum. The 'Beauty Community Forum' of the magazine *Good Housekeeping*, for example, which has almost 44,000 members and can have many non-member guests online at any one time as well, contained entries from scores of women sharing their experiences, beliefs and knowledge about the product. Many asked for advice on how to get hold of the cream, and the magazine's Beauty Director was asking women to share their results with the forum after using the product for at least 8 weeks – the time she believed it took to see results. The product even featured on plastic surgery blogs, and on-line discussions about the brand could be found from doctors in Australia to beauty editors in America.

Not all communication about the brand was positive. Both the *Guardian* and the *Independent on Sunday* contained pieces from journalists pouring scorn on the women who queued half the night for the product, labelling their reaction as 'madness' and 'a case study of human perversity ... another instance of the growing phenomenon we might call hysteria marketing'. Others, of course, might just call it word-of-mouth.

Questions

1. Discuss the reasons why in the first instance the *Horizon* programme caused such a reaction among consumers.

2. Identify the opinion formers and opinion leaders in the case.

3. Discuss the variables that influenced the word-of-mouth communications around *Protect & Perfect*.

Minicase 1.2   Unlocking the secrets of the male shopper

Richard Godfrey: School of Management, University of Leicester

Men have been a marketing afterthought for more than a century. Starting in the late 1800s, when *Good Housekeeping* and *Cosmopolitan* began teaching generations of women how to be Type A wives and mothers, brand managers painted a giant bull's-eye on the female consumer. They have taken relentless aim ever since. 'He makes. She buys.' That's the calculation that turned women into shoppers and men into providers.

(Byrne, 2006)

All this began to change following the Second World War, and has quickened apace in the last 30 years. Men are now actively forced/encouraged into a way of being in which they too have become increasingly objectified, measured through their own practices of consumption: by what they wear; their body image; their material possessions etc. This can be seen through the emergence and spread of men's magazines, High Street stores and forms of popular entertainment that encourage men to take greater interest in their appearance, to adopt consumption-led lifestyles.

The importance of men as (a market of) consumers has been marked by numerous attempts at classification and careful targeting by marketers. A recent issue of *Business Week* (4 September 2006) ran with the cover story 'Secrets of the Male Shopper' in which Nanette Byrne attempted to categorise male shopping habits into five distinct groups, based on a range of shared traits, attitudes and consuming behaviours. The first, the 'Metrosexual', who might be conceived of as the successor to the 1980s yuppie, is the quintessential 'feminised' male consumer. For him, consumption is all about style and the completion of self through designer brands and services. Against this she situates the 'Retrosexual', rejecting all things feminine, and reasserting a notion of masculinity through consumption

of alcohol, sports (viewing) and junk food. There is also 'Modern Man', called by others 'New Man', who sits at something of a halfway point between the metro- and retrosexual. He has a vested interest in his appearance but does not subscribe to some of the vanity practices of the metrosexual: 'Moisturizer and hair gel are perfectly ordinary to him; a manicure is a tougher call' (Byrne, 2006). Then there is the 'Maturiteen' – the current cohort of teenagers – far more sophisticated in their consumption habits than previous teen generations and, thanks to their literacy with the Internet and other forms of telecommunications, far more influential over family decision-making than their predecessors. Finally, there is the 'Dad', for the most part something of a marketing undesirable but with new-found interest in fatherhood, increasingly the target of marketing communications. Byrne cites the example of the Bugaboo baby stroller, with its black and chrome frame, front and rear suspension and off-road wheels, as indicative of the targeted offerings now made towards such men.

Despite differences among these trait-based typologies, these men share a number of consuming habits. Perhaps one of the most significant of these is the increased attention paid to physical appearance. Most notably this occurs in relation to increased care and attention paid to one's body in terms of grooming, body modification and in the selection of clothing and accessories (of course, through these processes and practices, such body routines become 'masculinised'; that is to say, they become legitimate forms of masculine behaviour).

This changing attitude towards and among men has resulted in the rapid growth of a range of 'self-presentation' industries including fashion, cosmetic surgery and, markedly, in the market for men's grooming products, which was estimated to be worth more than £780 million in 2006. This market is now saturated with offerings all vying for a slice of this lucrative pie. Reflecting prevailing trends in the female grooming markets, many of the competitors in this industry position and communicate their brands using common (masculine) themes, such as use of sex appeal (especially at the higher end of the market), aspirational celebratory endorsers (such as Gillette's use, since 2004, of David Beckham), and, in the packaging of their goods, through the use of masculine colours and materials such as strong blues, black, red and brushed steel or silver. This makes for a cramped and, at times, undifferentiated drugstore shelf.

However, against this trend a number of competitors, recognising that not all men are alike, have started to move away from such standardised positioning in order to reflect the increasingly fragmented male audience. Lynx, for example, has focused on the social benefits of its brand. By combining sex with humour, campaigns over the last few years, such as the highly successful 'Pulse' campaign have sought to almost parody the communications activities of more exclusive brands. The Pulse ad demonstrated that even a 'nerdy' guy, with little going for him, can ooze sex appeal and get the girls, thanks to the 'Lynx effect'! The tongue-in-cheek ad, which sought to break down some of the established norms of communicating in this industry, not only proved a commercial success but also spawned a new dance craze and saw the track 'Make Luv', which was used in the ad, re-enter the singles chart at number one. The spread of the ad into popular culture was invaluable in helping to reposition a brand that had come to be associated, primarily, with the declining 'lad' culture of the 1990s.

Elsewhere, 'King of Shaves' has attempted to side-step many of the brands that adopt a more aspirational appeal by focusing on the functional (or technical) value of the brand. Playing on male traits that turn around the control and mastery of technology it deploys overt masculine language in its branding such as in the use of the slogan: 'The World's Best shaving and skincare "software"'. It offers brands such as the XCD Defender, where XCD stands for 'Enhance', 'Camouflage', 'Defend' and also offers a website offering 'expert' shaving tips and techniques.

A new entrant, Bulldog, launched in 2007, perhaps going after the 'Modern Man' or 'Dad's offers a range of grooming products using all natural ingredients but at supermarket prices. As noted in a recent edition of *Marketing Week*:

> They decided that they would not pitch their brand at an exclusive, niche market but instead aim Bulldog at mainstream consumers, giving them, they claim, a natural choice at a reasonable price for the first time. They gave the brand a strong masculine identity, taking a risk with the potentially polarising name Bulldog. Clean, white packaging with a bold typeface was chosen to make the range look markedly different from the market leaders such as Lynx, Nivea, Gillette and L'Oréal.
>
> (Jack, 2008)

With the spread of the tweenager phenomenon and boys as young as 10 or 12 now using grooming products, these consuming behaviours look set to continue well into the future.

References

Byrne, N. (2006) 'Secrets of the Male Shopper', *Business Week*, 4 September 2006. Last accessed on 14 March 2008.

Jack, L. (2008) 'Analysis: Bulldog aims to see off men's skincare competition', *Marketing Week*, 13 March 2008. Last accessed on 14 March 2008.

Questions

1. Identify the social and cultural changes that have led to the rise of the male shopper.

2. How might an understanding of 'perception theory' be used in the targeting of male consumers?

3. Identify the different male consumer typologies outlined in the case. What are their key personality traits? How could a marketing communicator use this information in order to position a brand?

Minicase 1.3   Helping Hands

Charities such as Oxfam, Action Aid and Save the Children all provide aid on an international basis. Their mission is to provide a range of support services in areas that do not have sufficient resources, or where natural disasters such as floods and earthquakes cause large-scale poverty and starvation. All these charities rely mostly on voluntary donations to fund their activities.

Helping Hands is a worldwide charity (based in the UK) to promote the wellbeing of communities through education programmes about hygiene and diet. Helping Hands also aims to improve the lives and prospects of its beneficiaries through environmental development programmes.

In 2009–10, Helping Hands' voluntary income was £72.5 million. This was made up of money from the following sources:

Source of voluntary income	£m value
Emergency appeals	23.0
Donations/gifts	20.1
Government and other grants	13.3
Helping Hand Week	10.6
Legacies*	4.3
Other income	1.2
Total	£72.5m

* Money received from people after they have died.

Out of every £1 donated, approximately 20 per cent is spent driving fresh donations, with 10 per cent spent on administration and the remaining 70 per cent distributed across the various projects that are supported by the charity. Inevitably there are some tensions and negative attitudes between donors and charity managers concerning the distribution of the funds raised. The primary concern is that too much is spent on administration rather than supporting good causes.

Traditional charity supporters tend to be high-income women aged over 65, but there are indications that charity-giving has reached saturation. This is due partly to the demands arising from single disaster appeals, and partly to the need to support on-going projects around the world. Interestingly, there is a significant problem in encouraging younger people to donate regularly to charitable causes.

Charity-based marketing communications need to fulfil several goals, but two of the more important concern the maintenance of brand awareness (and associated brand values) and encouraging people to make donations.

Creating brand awareness

Maintaining brand awareness can be a problem, especially for a charity such as Helping Hands. The name suggests to some people, wrongly, that donations are spent on medical aid and equipment, or that aid only goes to poorer regions. To help overcome such misconceptions, the well-established annual event Helping Hands Week is used. This mass-market appeal is targeted at everyone in the UK and aims to raise awareness about Helping Hands and explain the work it does, as well as to collect donations.

Public relations and advertising are important parts of the charity's communications mix during this period. In 2009, Helping Hands spent over £2 million on media advertising. A well-known bank provided additional supportive press advertising. Helping Hands provides an online TV channel via their website, whilst celebrities are used to attract attention and provide publicity about overseas projects. Advertising messages are carefully designed to deliver key propositions, and television, press, radio and the Internet are the key media used to convey these messages to mass audiences, as well as to predetermined segments such as the youth market.

Driving donations

To drive donations, three main methods have traditionally been used: direct marketing, door-drops and street fund-raising. Income is also raised by selling branded merchandise such as bags, T-shirts, mugs, books, and other resource materials. These are promoted via a catalogue and can be purchased over the telephone or through the Helping Hands website.

Direct marketing, using direct mail and telemarketing, has been at the forefront of fund-raising activities. However, research by Nielsen in 2006 shows that 30 per cent of direct mail sent by charities is never opened, compared with the direct mail industry average of 22 per cent. An increasing number of people in the UK are signing up to the Mailing Preference Service in order to avoid receiving unsolicited direct mail. Some people are closing their letter boxes so that they cannot receive door-drops, whilst there appears to be growing public resistance to people waving collecting tins in the high street. Consumer resistance to the overuse of these techniques has become a problem, and because of the increasing number of charity appeals and demands made on individuals, 'compassion fatigue', a reluctance to make a charitable donation, is now quite common.

Emotionally based advertising appeals, based on guilt or humour, are well-used message approaches in many charity campaigns, but these can also have a negative effect on the target audience, however worthy the cause may be. In particular, younger audiences tend to switch off and disengage from charity-based communications. As a result of these developments, charities have been forced to consider fresh approaches to encourage donations.

One of the new and very successful initiatives is referred to as *ethical gift-giving*. This involves buying animals or farming equipment from a catalogue for a villager in a developing country, in the name of a friend or family member. One of the most popular charity Christmas gifts is a goat from the *Oxfam Unwrapped* catalogue and website. The *Lifetime Gift* scheme run by Helping Hands raised £1 million in 2004, £3 million in 2007 and over £3.5 million in 2009, at a time of recession and increasing hardship.

Activities that members of the youth market *do* like to support are major events such as music concerts supporting LIVE 8, and more recently, the Make Poverty History campaigns. These events represent 'added value' in the sense that those attending are being 'entertained' as well as supporting the charities or causes involved. This segment is also willing to engage with cause-related marketing, that is, making product or service purchases where a percentage of the payment goes to charity.

Sources: The above data has been based on a real-life organisation, but details have been changed for assessment purposes and do not reflect current management practices.

Questions

1. How might an understanding of engagement impact on any charity's marketing communications?

2. Using the DRIP framework, explain how charities such as Helping Hands, use marketing communications to carry out different communication tasks.

3. How can Helping Hands use marketing communications to try to change the attitudes of people who currently do not donate money to the charity?

Part 2
Managing marketing communications

Chapters 4–8

This part of the book is concerned with issues associated with the management of marketing communications.

Chapters 4 and 5 are concerned with strategy and planning. They are important chapters as they provide a context for much of the content that follows in subsequent chapters. Strategy, objectives and positioning are core activities for successful marketing communications. Ideas about integration and planning for marketing communications campaigns can be found in Chapter 5.

Chapter 6 examines three interrelated topics. The first is how marketing communications can be used to develop brands. The second examines the main methods used by organisations to develop budgets to support brands. The third and final section considers methods and issues associated with measuring and evaluating marketing communications and their impact on brands.

Chapter 7 also considers three co-related topics. The first examines the main methods used by communication agencies to manage a client's marketing communications activities. From this point the important aspect of regulations and controls necessary to sustain a viable and socially acceptable communications industry, including aspects of ethics is presented. The final element considers some of the core issues associated with developing international marketing communications.

Chapter 8 explores the nature and characteristics of relationships and then reviews the impact marketing communications can have on relationship marketing and its development. This provides a platform for the way in which the rest of the book is developed.

There are three minicases at the end of this part of the book. These are intended to help you clarify your understanding of the preceding material. Please attempt to answer the questions to be found at the end of each case. There are no right answers but some approaches are better than others.

The minicases are:

2.1 'Get on your bike!': is set in the Cairngorms National Park, is concerned with mountain biking and considers strategy and segmentation issues. There are some interesting questions concerning the role of regulations, controls and ethics with the scenario developed in this case.

2.2 **The Thoroughly Delicious Ice Cream Company:** this minicase focuses on the relationships that arise between a franchise holder and the franchisee. It is also a good means of examining ideas about branding and marketing communications. The minicase can also be used to consider the strategic issues concerning communications to support national and local campaigns. Some readers might wish to return to this case once they have read the final part of the book.

2.3 **Seaport Communications:** this is a b2b case and requires readers to consider ideas related to strategy, objectives and positioning. Ideas about integration, regulations, controls and international issues can be explored.

Chapter 4
Strategies, objectives and positioning

A marketing communications strategy refers to an organisation's overall positioning orientation and their preferred approach to communicating with customers and stakeholders. Marketing communications strategies are used to achieve specific objectives and to position brands in the minds of the target audiences.

Aims and learning objectives

The aims of this chapter are to explore the nature of strategy and marketing communications strategies in particular. The goal is to enable readers to appreciate the elements and concepts associated with marketing communication strategy and to introduce ideas concerning the role of objectives and the nature of positioning.

The learning objectives of this chapter are to:

1. consider the issues associated with the nature and characteristics of the strategy concept;
2. explain the STP process and its significance to marketing communications;
3. establish the key characteristics associated with marketing communications strategy;
4. explain the three main marketing communication strategies: pull, push and profile;
5. introduce ideas concerning the role and use of marketing communication objectives;
6. understand how to write SMART objectives;
7. discuss various ways in which brands might be positioned in the minds of target audiences.

Introduction

It is assumed by many that marketing communication strategy is simply the combination of tools of the communications mix. In other words, strategy is about the degree of direct marketing, personal selling, advertising, sales promotion and public relations that is incorporated within a planned set of communication activities. This is important but this is tactical perspective, and is not the essence of marketing communications strategy. This view fails to account for the media or the messages used in a communication activity.

From a strategic perspective, key decisions concern the overall direction of the programme and target audiences, the fit with marketing and corporate strategy, the key message and desired positioning the brand is to occupy in the market, and the resources necessary to deliver the position and satisfy the overall goals.

This chapter begins with a consideration of strategy generally and the relationship between marketing communications strategy and other higher level strategies. Time is then spent exploring the segmentation, targeting and positioning (STP) process. This provides a foundation to develop ideas about the characteristics of marketing communications strategy, including the different types of marketing communications objectives that can be used to assist the delivery of the marketing communication strategy. The chapter concludes with an exploration of the nature and types of positioning strategies.

Understanding strategy

In order to appreciate the role and nature of communication strategy it is necessary to appreciate the dimensions of the strategy concept. Chaffee (1985) identifies that there is general agreement in the literature that strategy is about two key elements. The first is that strategy is used by organisations as a means of adjusting to changing environmental conditions and the second is that strategy is concerned with decision-making, actions and implementation.

Two main strategy schools of thought can be identified, namely the planning and the emergent approaches. The planning school is the pre-eminent paradigm and is based on strategy development and implementation, which is explicit, rational and planned as a sequence of logical steps. Andrews (1987) comments that strategy is concerned with a company's objectives, purpose and policies and its plans to satisfy the goals using particular resources with respect to a range of internal and external stakeholders. The organisation interacts with and attempts to shape its environment in pursuit of its goals. This perspective of strategy was first formulated in the 1950s and 1960s when the operating environments of most organisations were simple, stable and thus predictable. However, these conditions rarely exist in the twenty-first century and the validity of the rational model of strategy has been questioned.

The emergent school of thought considers strategy to develop incrementally, step-by-step, as organisations learn, sometimes through simple actions of trial and error. The core belief is that strategy is comprised of a stream of organisational activities that are continuously being formulated, implemented, tested, evaluated and updated. Chaffee suggests that strategy should be considered in terms of a linear, adaptive or interpretive approach, each one reflecting a progressively sophisticated perspective. While the linear approach reflects the more traditional and deliberate approach to strategy (Ansoff, 1965; Andrews, 1987), the adaptive strategy is important because it reflects the view that organisations flex and adjust to changing environments. The interpretive or higher-order point of view considers strategy to be a reflection of the influence of social order on strategic decision-making.

Views on strategy have evolved and it is generally agreed that strategy is not just about a deliberate, planned approach to business development, although it can be at the functional and competitive levels. Strategy is about the means, speed and methods by which organisations adapt to and influence their environments in order that they achieve their goals. What is also clear is that the demarcation between an organisation and its environment is less clear than it used to be. An imaginary line was once used to refer to a border between an organisation and its environment. This line is no longer deemed valid as organisations are now viewed as boundary-free. The implications of this borderless concept for marketing communications are potentially enormous. Not only do contemporary views of strategy amplify the significance of the interaction between strategy and an organisation's environment but they also stress the importance for strategy, at whatever level, to be contextually oriented and determined.

Although there is debate about what strategy is and what it is not, the one main area wherein most authors find agreement concerns the hierarchical nature of strategy within organisations (Kay, 1993; Mintzberg and Ghoshal, 2003; Johnson *et al.*, 2010). This refers to the notion that there are three main levels of organisational strategy; corporate, competitive and functional. Corporate strategy is considered to be directional and sets out the broad, overarching parameters and means through which the organisation operates in order to realise its objectives. Strategies at the functional level, for example, marketing, finance and production, should be integrated in such a way that they contribute to the satisfaction of the higher-level competitive strategies, which in turn should satisfy the overall corporate goals. Competitive-level strategies are important because not only do they set out the way in which the organisation will compete and use resources, but they should also provide clear messages about the way in which the organisation seeks to manage its environment.

From this it becomes clear that marketing strategy should support an organisation's competitive strategy and complement the corporate strategy. In the same way the marketing communications strategy should support the marketing strategy by delivering the marketing promise to targeted customer groups. Figure 4.1 sets out the inter-relationships between the different levels of strategy hierarchies.

Segmentation, targeting and positioning

One of the elements central to most marketing strategies is the market segmentation, target marketing and positioning process. This STP approach is a sequence of activities that

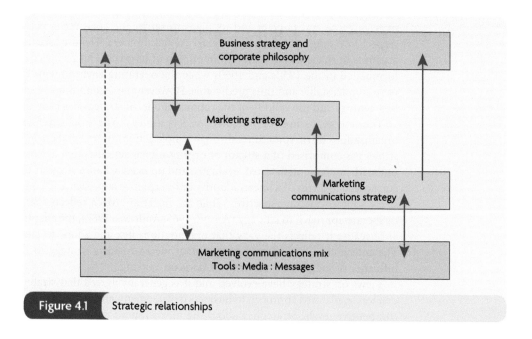

Figure 4.1   Strategic relationships

constitutes a core part of marketing strategy because it involves several key strategic activities, namely; how is the market segmented, which segments are to be targeted and how are we to be positioned within the selected target markets?

The process of market analysis and evaluation leading to planned strategies designed to meet prescribed and measurable goals is well established. It is argued that this approach enables finite resources to be used more efficiently as they can be directed towards markets which hold, potentially, greater value than other markets. Wastage of resources is reduced and, more importantly, the STP process enables organisations to define the broad context within which their strategic business units (SBUs) and products are offered.

Viewpoint 4.1   Segments galore

United Airlines

United Airlines segments its global markets using psychographic data about its customers. Among its categories are:

- **Schedule optimisers**: must reach their destination by a certain time and select their flights accordingly.
- **Mile accumulators**: go out of their way to take flights that will build up their air miles entitlement.
- **Quality vacationers**: treat the travel as part of the holiday experience and so fly with carriers that provide superior services.
- **Frugal flyers**: seek out the lowest-cost carriers, but still expect their flight experience to be a good one.

Source: Based on http://www.thetimes100.co.uk/case_study

T-Mobile

According to T-Mobile's website it targets four key market segments: **personal, small businesses, medium businesses and corporates**.

The segments identified for a women's portal include the following groups:

- **Pillars**: characterised by their family orientation, high income and broad range of interests.
- **Explorers**: notable for being single, 30-something, outgoing and more social than career oriented.
- **Free spirits**: the youngest segment, typically unmarried, Internet savvy, and not yet committed to careers or raising a family.

Source: Based on www.debmcdonald.com/

Question

How might these segment characteristics inform the marketing communications to be used by United and T-Mobile?

Task

Choose an industry and find out how it has been segmented by the principal brands.

Market segmentation is the division of a mass market into identifiable and distinct groups or segments, each of which have common characteristics and needs and display similar responses to marketing actions. Through this process specific target segments can be selected and marketing plans developed to satisfy the individual needs of the potential buyers in these chosen segments. The development, or rather identification, of segments can be perceived as opportunities and, as Beane and Ennis (1987) suggest, 'A company with limited resources needs to pick only the best opportunities to pursue'. The most common bases upon which markets can be segmented are set out in Table 4.1.

Table 4.1	Bases for segmenting markets

Segmentation base	Explanation
Demographic	Key variables concern age, sex, occupation, level of education, religion, social class and income characteristics, many of which determine, to a large extent, a potential buyer's ability to enter into an exchange relationship or transaction.
Geographic	In many situations the needs of potential customers in one geographic area are different from those in another area. For example, it is often said that Scottish beer drinkers prefer heavy bitters, Northerners in England prefer mild, drinkers in the West prefer cider, and in the South lager is the preferred drink.
Geodemographic	This type of segmentation is based on the assumption that there is a relationship between the type of housing people live in and their purchasing behaviours. At the root of this approach is the ability to use postcodes to send similar messages to similar groups of households, on the basis that where we live determines how we live. The most well-known commercial applications are Acorn (a classification of residential neighbourhoods), Mosaic and Pinpoint.
Psychographic	Through an analysis of consumers' activities, interests and opinions (AIO) it is possible to determine lifestyles or patterns of behaviour. These are a synthesis of the motivations, personality and core values held by individuals. These AIO patterns are reflected in the buying behaviour and decision-making processes of individuals. By identifying and clustering common lifestyles, a correlation with a consumer's product and/or media usage patterns becomes possible.
Behaviouristic	Usage and lifestage segments are derived from analysing markets on the basis of customer behaviour. Usage of soft drinks can be considered in terms of purchase patterns (two bottles per week), usage situations (parties, picnics or as an alcohol substitute) or purchase location (supermarket, convenience store or wine merchant). Lifestage analysis is based on the principle that people have varying amounts of disposable income and different needs at different stages in their lives. Their priorities for spending change at different trigger points and these points or lifestages do not occur at the same time.

This process of segmentation is necessary because a single product is unlikely to meet the needs of all customers in a mass market. If it did, then a single type of toothpaste, chocolate bar or car would meet all of our needs. This is not so, and there are a host of products and brands seeking to satisfy particular buyer needs. For example, ask yourself the question, 'Why do I use toothpaste?' The answer, most probably, is one of the following:

- You want dental hygiene.
- You like fresh breath and you don't want to offend others.
- You want white, shining teeth.
- You like the fresh oral sensation.
- Other products (e.g. water, soap) do not taste very good.

Whatever the reason, it is unlikely that given a choice everyone would choose the same product. In what is now regarded as a classic study, Russell Haley (1968) undertook some pioneering research in this field and from it established four distinct types of customer. Over 40 years later this typology remains a potent practical example of market segmentation: those who bought toothpaste for white teeth (sociables), those who wished to prevent decay (worriers), those who liked the taste and refreshment properties (sensors) and finally those who bought on a price basis (independents). Each of these groups has particular demographic, behaviouristic and psychographic characteristics.

It is not surprising that a range of toothpaste products has been developed that attempts to satisfy the needs of different buyers, for example Macleans for fresh breath, Crest for dental hygiene, Sensodyne for those sensitive to hot and cold drinks and numerous others promoted on special offers for those independent buyers looking for a low price. There are others who are not very interested in the product and have continued using a brand that others in their current or past households are comfortable with. Therefore, target segments constitute the environment and the context for the marketing communications strategy and activities. It is the characteristics of the target segment therefore that are the focus of an audience-centred marketing communications strategy.

Targeting

The next task is to decide which, if any, of the segments discovered should be the focus of the marketing programme. The following criteria need to be present:

- All segments should be *measurable* – is the segment easy to identify and measure?
- All segments should be *substantial* – is the segment sufficiently large to provide a stream of profits?
- All segments should be *accessible* – can the buyers be reached with promotional programmes?
- All segments should be *differentiable* – is each segment clearly different from other segments so that different marketing mixes are necessary?
- All segments should be *actionable* – has the organisation the capability to reach the segment?

Decisions need to be made about whether a single product is to be offered to a range of segments, whether a range of products should be offered to multiple segments or a single segment or whether one product should be offered to a single segment. Whatever the decision, a marketing mix should be developed to meet the needs of the segment and reflect the organisation's available resources.

Positioning

Within each of the selected target markets decisions need to be made concerning how the brand is to be presented to customers in each market. This requires presenting the brand in such a way that customers understand what the brand represents, what the brand promise is, how it is different to competitor brands and what the value is to customers. This is known as positioning and is developed later in this chapter.

It has also been established earlier that marketing communications should be an audience-centred rather than product-centred activity. From this it can be concluded that marketing communications strategy is essentially about helping audiences understand how a brand is positioned. For new products and services, marketing communications needs to engage target audiences so that they can understand what the brand means, how it differs from similar offerings and as a result position it clearly in their minds. For the vast majority of products and services that are already established, marketing communications strategy should be concerned with either maintaining a strong position or repositioning it in the minds of the target audiences.

Marketing communications strategy

Marketing communications strategy should articulate the theme established through higher level strategies. For example, the corporate strategy might embody core values that stress the importance of care and respect for all stakeholders. The marketing strategy might complement this by developing customer service and customer retention strategies. The marketing communications strategy might then echo this approach by focusing messages on customer service and support, customer relationship management systems (CRM), carelines and loyalty programmes.

Marketing communications strategy is concerned with two key dynamics. The first dynamic is concerned with whom, in broad terms, is the target audience? End-user customers need to derive particular benefits based on their perceived value, generated from the communication process. These benefits are very different from those that intermediaries expect to derive, or indeed any other stakeholder who does not consume the product or service.

The second dynamic concerns the way in which an audience understands the offering they are experiencing either through use or through communications. The way in which people interpret messages and frame objects in their mind is concerned with positioning. Marketing communications strategy therefore, is concerned with both audiences and positioning.

Audiences

The prevailing approach to marketing communications (advertising) strategy has traditionally been founded upon the configuration of the 'promotional' mix. Strategy was an interpretation of the mix and hence the resources an organisation deployed. This represents a production rather than market orientation to marketing communications and is intrinsically misplaced. This inside-out form of strategy is essentially resource-driven. However, a market orientation to strategy requires a consideration of the needs of the audience first and then a determination of the various messages, media and disciplines to accomplish the strategy, an outside-in approach.

Consumer purchase decisions are characterised by a single-person buying centre whereas organisational buying decisions can involve a large number of different people, all fulfilling different roles and all requiring different marketing communication messages. It follows from this that the approach to communicating with these two very different target sectors should be radically different, especially in terms of what, where, when and how a message is communicated. However, communication strategy should be developed once communication objectives have been established.

Communication objectives that are focused on consumer markets require a different strategy from those formulated to satisfy the objectives that are focused on organisational customers. In addition, there are circumstances and reasons to focus communications on the development of the organisation with a corporate brand and range of other stakeholders. Often, these corporate brands need to work closely with the development of product brands.

Positioning

As noted in the earlier section about the STP process, positioning is an integral concept, and for some, the essence of strategy. Jewell (2007) cites Wind (1990) who stated quite clearly that positioning is the key strategic framework for an organisation's brand-based communications. All products and all organisations have a position in the minds of audiences. The task, therefore, is to actively manage the way in which audiences perceive brands. This means that marketing communications strategy should be concerned with achieving effective and viable positions so that the target audience understands what the brand does, what it means (to them) and can ascribe value to it. This is particularly important in markets that are very competitive and where mobility barriers (ease of entry into and exit from a market, e.g. plant and production costs) are relatively low.

Positioning is about distinguishing a brand and providing visibility and recognition of what a product/service/organisation represents to a buyer. In markets where the intensity of rivalry and competition is increasing and buyers have greater choice, identification and understanding of a product's intrinsic values become critical. Channel members have limited capacities, whether this is the level or range of stock they can carry or for retailers, the amount of available shelf space that can be allocated. An offering with a clear identity and orientation to a particular target segment's needs will not only be stocked and purchased, but can warrant a larger margin through increased added value.

The 3Ps of marketing communications strategy

As a result of understanding the broad nature of the target audience and the way we want them to position the offering in their minds, it is possible to identify three main marketing communication strategies by bringing these elements together:

- Pull-positioning strategies – these are intended to influence end-user customers (consumers and b2b).
- Push-positioning strategies – these are intended to influence marketing (trade) channel buyers.
- Profile-positioning strategies – these are intended to influence a wide range of stakeholders, not just customers and intermediaries.

These are referred to as the 3Ps of marketing communications strategy. Push and pull relate to the direction of the communication flow, relative to the marketing channel: pushing communications down through the marketing channel or pulling consumers/buyers into the channel via retailers, as a result of receiving the communications. They do not relate to the intensity of communication and only refer to the overall approach.

Profile refers to the presentation of the organisation as a whole and therefore the identity is said to be 'profiled' to various other target stakeholder audiences, which may well include consumers, trade buyers b2b customers and a range of other influential stakeholders. Normally, profile strategies do not contain or make reference to specific products or services that the organisation offers (see Table 4.2). In many large organisations, profile strategies are managed by a corporate communication team and are not the direct concern of the marketing team. However, in many small and medium sized enterprises where resources for communications are tight, a profile strategy is run instead of a product oriented campaign.

The demarcation of the pull/profile and push/profile strategies may be blurred, especially where the name of a company is the name of its primary (only) product, as is often the case with many retail brands. For example, messages about B&Q are very often designed to convey meaning about the quality and prices of its consumer products and services. However, they often reflect on the organisation itself, especially when its advertising shows members of staff in workwear, doing their work and very often providing customer service. Exhibit 4.1 provides an example of staff being used in B&Q's advertising.

Table 4.2	Marketing communications strategy options		
Strategy	**Target audience**	**Message focus**	**Communication goal**
Pull	Consumers	Product/service	Purchase
	End-user b2b customers	Product/service	Purchase
Push	Channel intermediaries	Product/service	Developing relationships and distribution network
Profile	All relevant stakeholders	The organisation	Building reputation

Exhibit 4.1	B&Q staff use in their advertising
	B&Q use their staff in advertising campaigns as brand ambassadors. The intention is to communicate brand values and to recognise the value of staff to the marketing programme.
	Image courtesy of B&Q

All three of these strategies are intended to position the offering, in particular ways, in the minds of the target audience. Within each of these overall strategies, individual approaches should be formulated to reflect the needs of each particular case. So, for example, the launch of a new shampoo product will involve a push-positioning strategy to get the product on the shelves of the appropriate retailers. The strategy would be to gain retailer acceptance and to position it as a profitable new brand to gain consumer interest. Personal selling supported by trade sales promotions will be the main marketing communications tools. A pull-positioning strategy to develop awareness about the brand will need to be created, accompanied by appropriate public relations work. The next step will be to create particular brand associations and thereby position the brand in the minds of the target audience. Messages may be primarily functional or expressive but they will endeavour to convey a brand promise. This may be accompanied or followed by the use of incentives to encourage consumers to trial the product. To support the brand, carelines and a website will need to be put in place to provide credibility as well as a buyer reference point and an opportunity to interact with the brand.

A pull-positioning strategy

If messages designed to position a brand are to be directed at targeted, end-user customers, then the intention is invariably to generate increased levels of awareness, change and/or reinforce attitudes, reduce risk, encourage involvement and ultimately provoke a motivation within the target group. This motivation is to stimulate action so that the target audience expects the offering to be available to them when they decide to enquire, experiment or make a repeat purchase. This approach is a *pull-(positioning)* strategy and is aimed at encouraging customers to 'pull' products through the channel network (see Figure 4.2). This usually means that consumers go into retail outlets (shops) to enquire about a particular product and/or buy it, or to enter a similar transaction direct with the manufacturer or intermediary through direct mail or the Internet. B2B customers are encouraged to buy from dealers and distributors while both groups of consumers and b2b customers have opportunities to buy through direct marketing channels where there is no intermediary.

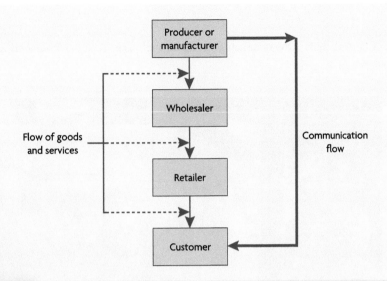

| Figure 4.2 | Primary communication flow in a pull-positioning strategy |

To accomplish and deliver a pull-positioning strategy, the traditional approach has been to deliver mass media advertising supported by below-the-line communications, most notably sales promotions. There has been greater use of direct marketing in non-fast-moving consumer goods sectors and use of the Internet presents opportunities to reach audiences in new ways, thereby reducing any reliance on the old formulaic approach to pull-based strategies. The decision to use a pull-positioning strategy has to be supported by a core message proposition. This will vary according to the outcomes of the context analysis and the needs of the target audience. However, it is probable that the core message will seek to differentiate (position), remind or reassure, inform or persuade the audience to think, feel or behave in a particular way. Agencies and clients have their own approach to this labelling activity.

Viewpoint 4.2   Probably the best pull strategy in the world

Carlsberg just like many other consumer brands, are competing in a Western European market characterised by a proliferation of channels, media and customer segments. They use a wide communication mix, incorporating a full range of tools and media. For example, their consumer advertising uses television, outdoor, in-store, digital and print media. In addition, they use public relations, sponsorship and product placement, and they support local events and festivals to gain visibility.

As 10 per cent of their brands drive 80 per cent of their profits (that is one power brand in each of the 10 European markets), so they have started to focus more of their resources on a reduced number of brands.

Pull-positioning strategies are configured around developing relationships with customers and Carlsberg refer to this development process as a 'funnel'. When building awareness they use sponsorship, festivals and events. When building on the awareness to generate increased loyalty they use media such as television as they believe they can communicate their messages more effectively this way. The final stage in the funnel process is to provide visibility in pubs and restaurants, and to activate brands in-store. This seemingly simple process can be complex because of the timing, costs and effectiveness associated with the move from one stage to another.

Source: Based on Riiber Knudsen (2007)

Question

How do Carlsberg position their brand?

Task

Find three drinks brands in the same category (e.g. alcohol, juice, water or carbonated) and determine how they want to be perceived.

Exhibit 4.2	'Carlsberg don't do pub teams . . . but if they did it would probably be the best pub football team in the world.'

This still from a Carlsberg TV ad ran during the 2006 World Cup. It features many English World Cup stars from 1966 and other well-known players. Not only does it use the humour associated with the past great players, but it also draws on the name of the pub (The Lion) and the unofficial name of the English national team, 'the Lions', three of which are emblazoned on all-English team shirts.

Image courtesy of The Advertising Archives

ASDA has developed a strong market share in the United Kingdom based mainly on price competition or on what is referred to as everyday low pricing (pull/price). Tesco runs everyday low pricing but uses sales promotions as a form of complementary positioning (pull/price/ promotions). In their wake, Sainsbury's and Morrisons have used differing pull strategies to try and regain share, increase profitability and stave off takeover threats.

Although Sainsbury's uses EDLP (everyday low pricing) on 1,000 selected lines, it has adopted a classic branding campaign, based around the celebrity chef Jamie Oliver. Making heavy use of television, the brand is positioned around a quality proposition emphasised by the personality and the associated redesign of major stores.

The level and degree of audience involvement has some implications for pull strategies. Marketing communication messages can be considered to be a stimulus that in some situations will have a strong impact on the level of involvement enjoyed by the target audience. A strategic response to this would be to adapt marketing communication messages so that they are effective at different levels of involvement, a form of differentiation.

Another approach would be to turn low-involvement decisions into high-involvement ones that, through communications, encourage members of the target audience to reconsider their perception of a brand or of the competition. Again, this represents a form of differentiation. A third approach is to segment the market in terms of the level of involvement experienced by each group and according to situational or personality factors, and then shape the marketing communication messages to suit each group.

A pull strategy therefore, refers to marketing communications (the use of tools, media and messages) designed to position an offering in the minds of particular end-user customer audience(s).

A push-positioning strategy

A second group or type of target audience can be identified, based first on their contribution to the marketing channel, and second because these organisations do not consume the products and services they buy, but add value before selling the product on to others in the demand chain. The previous strategy was targeted at customers who make purchase decisions related largely to their personal (or organisational) consumption of products and services. This second group buys products and services, performs some added-value activity and moves the product through the marketing channel network.

Trade channel organisations, and indeed all b2b organisations, are actively involved in the development and maintenance of interorganisational relationships. The degree of cooperation between organisations will vary and part of the role of marketing communications is to develop and support the relationships that exist.

The 'trade' channel has received increased attention in recent years as the strategic value of intermediaries has become both more visible and questioned in the light of the Internet. As the channel networks have developed, so has their complexity, which impacts upon the marketing communications strategies and tools used to help reach marketing goals. The expectations of buyers in these networks have risen in parallel with the significance attached to them by manu-facturers. The power of multiple retailers, such as Tesco, Sainsbury's, Morrisons, Waitrose and Asda, is such that they are able to dictate terms (including the marketing communications) to many manufacturers of branded goods.

A *push-positioning* communication strategy involves the presentation of information in order to influence other trade channel organisations and, as a result, encourage them to take stock, to allocate resources (e.g. shelf space) and to help them to become fully aware of the key attributes and benefits associated with each product with a view to adding value prior to further channel transactions. This strategy is designed to encourage resale to other members of the network and contribute to the achievement of their own objectives. This approach is known as a *push* strategy, as it is aimed at pushing the product down through the channel towards the end-users for consumption (see Figure 4.3).

The channel network consists of those organisations with whom others must cooperate directly to achieve their own objectives. By accepting that there is interdependence, usually dispersed unequally throughout the network, it is possible to identify organisations that have a stronger/weaker position within a network. Communication must travel not only between the different levels of dependence and role ('up and down' in a channel context) and so represent bidirectional flows, but also across similar levels of dependence and role, that is horizontal flows. For example, these may be from retailer to retailer or wholesaler to wholesaler.

Marketing communications targeted at people involved in organisational buying decisions are characterised by an emphasis on personal selling. Trade advertising, trade sales promotions and public relations all have an important yet secondary role to play. Direct marketing has become increasingly important and the development of the Internet has had a profound impact on b2b communications and interorganisational relationships. However, personal selling has traditionally been the most significant part of the communication mix where a push strategy has been instigated.

Finally, just as it was suggested that the essence of a pull strategy could be articulated in brief format, a push strategy could be treated in a similar way. The need to consider the core message is paramount, as it conveys information about the essence of the strategy. Push/inform, push/position or push/key accounts/discount might be examples of possible terminology. Whether

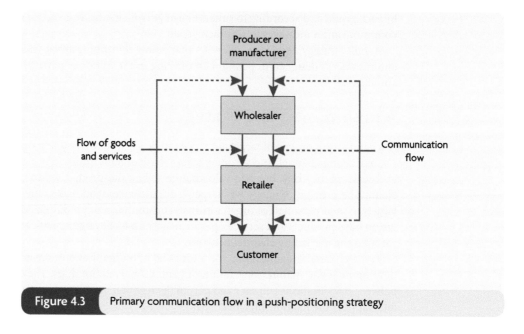

Figure 4.3 Primary communication flow in a push-positioning strategy

or not this form of expression is used, it is important that marketing communication strategy be referred to more than just push; what is to be achieved also needs to be understood.

A profile-positioning strategy

The strategies considered so far concern the need for dialogue with customers (pull) and trade channel intermediaries (push). However, there is a whole range of other stakeholders, many of whom need to know about and understand the organisation rather than actually purchase its products and services (see Figure 4.4). This group of stakeholders may include financial

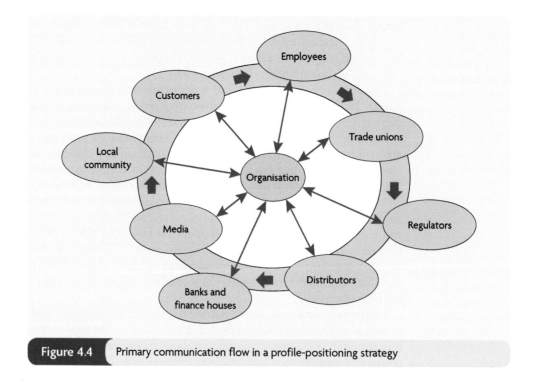

Figure 4.4 Primary communication flow in a profile-positioning strategy

analysts, trade unions, government bodies, employees or the local community. It should be easy to understand that these different stakeholder groups can influence the organisation in different ways and, in doing so, need to receive (and respond to) different types of messages. Thus, the financial analysts need to know about financial and trading performance and expectations, and the local community may be interested in employment and the impact of the organisation on the local environment, whereas the government may be interested in the way the organisation applies health and safety regulations and pays corporation, VAT and other taxes.

Traditionally these organisational-oriented activities have been referred to as corporate communication, as they deal more or less exclusively with the corporate entity or organisation. Products, services and other offerings are not normally the focus of these communications. It is the organisation and its role in the context of the particular stakeholders' activities that is important. However, it should be noted that as more corporate brands appear, the distinction between corporate and marketing communications begins to become much less clear. Indeed, when considered in the light of the development and interest in internal marketing (and communications), it may be of greater advantage to consider corporate communications as an organisation's umbrella communications approach, with marketing communications activities a subpart of corporate communications.

The awareness, perception and attitudes held by stakeholders towards an organisation need to be understood, shaped and acted upon. This can be accomplished through continual dialogue, which will normally lead to the development of trust and commitment and enable relationships to grow. This is necessary in order that stakeholders act favourably towards an organisation and enable strategies to flourish and objectives be achieved.

Viewpoint 4.3   So, who are we?

Organisations need to raise their profile for different reasons and at different times. These might reflect changing market conditions, trading circumstances, poor trading results, threat of takeover or a general repositioning.

G4S had to raise its profile because of a series of takeovers and mergers, which required the company to restructure, rebrand and reposition itself. Group 4 merged with Danish Falck in 2000, it in turn merged with Securicor in 2004, and then rebranded as G4S in 2006.

The first part of the rebranding incorporated staff. Through the use of a relaunch event day, 15,000 contracted staff were given information about the new company name, structure, board composition, new uniforms and livery. In addition, internal staff received information through desk drops, magazines, new letters and question–answer sessions.

Externally oriented communications revolved around the new logo. Fresh, clean and a break from the previous visual identity.

Source: Based on Anon (2008)

Question

What do you believe are the main differences between rebranding and raising profile?

Task

Make a list of all the reasons an organisation might choose to deliberately raise its profile.

A *profile-positioning* strategy focuses an organisation's communications upon the development of stakeholder relationships, corporate image and reputation, whether that be just internally, just externally or both. To accomplish and deliver a profile-positioning strategy, public relations, including sponsorship and corporate advertising, become the pivotal tools of the marketing communications mix. Personal selling may remain a vital element delivering both product/service and corporate messages.

Strategic balance

While the pull, push and profile strategies are important, it should be remembered that they are not mutually exclusive. Indeed, in most organisations it is possible to identify an element of each strategy at any one time. In reality, most organisations are structured in such a way that those responsible for communications with each of these three main audiences do so without reference to or coordination with each other. This is an example of how integrated marketing communications, which is examined in the following chapter, needs to have one senior person responsible for all the organisational communications. Only through a single point of reference is it realistically possible to develop and communicate a set of brand values that are consistent and credible.

The 3Ps should be considered as part of a total communication approach. Figure 4.5 depicts how the emphasis of a total communication strategy can shift according to changing contextual elements. For example, the needs of the various target audiences, resources and wider elements such as the environment and the competition. The marketing communications eclipse provides a visual interpretation of the balance between the three strategic dimensions. The more that is revealed of any one single strategy, the greater its role in any single campaign. Conversely, the less that is revealed, the smaller the contribution. In any one campaign, one or two of the three strategies might be used in preference to another and will often reflect branding approaches. For example, a brand manager's use of a profile strategy at Procter and Gamble or Mars will be virtually zero and will almost certainly be entirely pull or push in order to support the marketing channel or trade customers.

Strategy needs to be understood in terms of the answers given in response to several critical questions. First, how are the communication goals that have been set going to be achieved? Second, how they are going to be accomplished in terms of complementing the business and marketing strategies? Third, can current resources and opportunities support the strategy and do they encourage target audiences to respond to the communications?

Answers to these questions are not always easy to find and very often there will be conflicting proposals from different coalitions of internal stakeholders. In other words, there is a political element that needs to be considered and there may also be a strong overriding culture that directs the communication strategy and which may hinder innovation or the development of alternative methods of communication. Everyone who is involved with the development of marketing communications campaigns (internally and externally) should agree and prioritise necessary activities. The development of a marketing communications plan facilitates this process and enables the strategy to be articulated in such a way that the goals are achieved in a timely, efficient and effective manner.

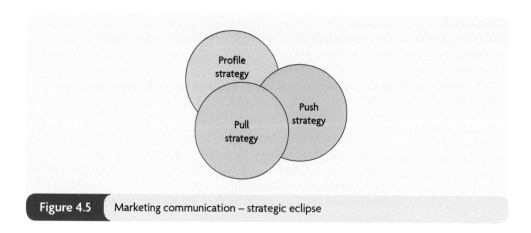

| Figure 4.5 | Marketing communication – strategic eclipse |

Marketing communication objectives

Having established the target segments to be approached the next key task is to formulate and establish the campaign objectives. Marketing communication objectives are an important and often neglected part of marketing communication activities.

The most common communication objectives set by managers are sales related. These include increases in market share, return on investment, sales volume increases and improvements in the value of sales made after accounting for the rate of inflation. Such a general perspective ignores the influence of the other elements of the marketing mix and implicitly places the entire responsibility for sales performance with the communications mix. This is not an accurate reflection of the way in which businesses and organisations work. In addition, because sales tests are too general, they would be an insufficiently rigorous test of promotional activity and there would be no real evaluation of communications activities. Sales volumes vary for a wide variety of reasons:

- Competitors change their prices.
- Buyers' needs change.
- Changes in legislation may favour the strategies of particular organisations.
- Favourable third-party communications become known to significant buyers.
- General economic conditions change.
- Technological advances facilitate improved production processes, economies of scale, experience effects and, for some organisations, the opportunity to reduce costs.
- The entry and exit of different competitors.

These are a few of the many reasons why sales might increase and conversely why sales might decrease. Therefore, the notion that marketing communications is entirely responsible for the sales of an offering is clearly unacceptable, unrealistic and incorrect.

Marketing communication objectives should consist of three main components. The first component concerns issues relating to sales volume, market share, profitability and revenue. The second concerns issues relating to the communication impact on the target audience whilst the third stream relates to the image, reputation and preferences, which other stakeholders have towards the organisation (see Figure 4.6).

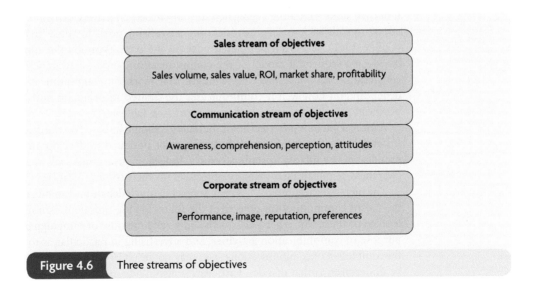

Sales stream of objectives

Sales volume, sales value, ROI, market share, profitability

Communication stream of objectives

Awareness, comprehension, perception, attitudes

Corporate stream of objectives

Performance, image, reputation, preferences

Figure 4.6   Three streams of objectives

The sales school

Many managers see sales as the only meaningful objective for marketing communication activities. Their view is that the only reason an organisation spends money on such communication is to sell its product or service. Therefore, the only meaningful measure of the effectiveness of the communication spend is in the sales results.

These results can be measured in a number of different ways. Sales turnover is the first and most obvious factor, particularly in business-to-business markets. In consumer markets and the fast-moving consumer goods sector, market share movement is measured regularly and is used as a more sensitive barometer of performance. Over the longer term, return on investment measures can be used to calculate success and failure. In some sectors the number of products (or cases) sold, or volume of product shifted, relative to other periods of activity, is a common measure.

Those who favour the use of sales in this way advocate the measure on the grounds of simplicity. Any manager can utilise the tool, and senior management does not wish to be concerned with information that is complex or unfamiliar, especially when working to short lead times and accounting periods. It is a self-consistent theory, but one that may misrepresent consumer behaviour and the purchase process (perhaps unintentionally), and to that extent may result in less than optimal expenditure on marketing communications.

There are some issues with this approach, namely that sales result from a variety of influences, such as the other marketing mix elements, competitor actions and wider environmental effects, for example the strength of the currency, changing social preferences or the level of interest rates. A second difficulty rests with the concept of adstock or carryover. The impact of promotional expenditure may not be immediately apparent, as message receivers may not enter the market until some later date, but the effects of the communications programme may influence the eventual purchase decision. This means that, when measuring the effectiveness of a campaign, sales results will not always reflect its full impact.

The communications school

There are many situations, however, where the aim of a communications campaign is to enhance the image or reputation of an organisation or product. Sales are not regarded as the only goal. Consequently, communication efforts are seen as communication tasks, such as the creation of awareness or positive attitudes towards the organisation or product. To facilitate this process, receivers have to be given relevant information before the appropriate decision processes can develop and purchase activities established as a long-run behaviour.

Various models have been developed to assist our understanding about how these promotional tasks should be segregated and organised effectively. AIDA and other hierarchy of effects models such as Dagmar (defining advertising goals for measured advertising results) (Colley, 1961) have been popular models in the past. Typically the communications task is based on a sequential model of the communications process: awareness – comprehension – conviction – action. It was once thought that marketing communications succeeds or fails depending on how well it communicates the desired information and attitudes to the right people at the right time and at the right cost (see Table 4.3).

A more contemporary view holds that success should be based on the degree to which audience (brand) behaviour is influenced but campaigns designed to develop awareness and establish brand name familiarity are still necessary. Indeed, many brands seek to establish 'top of mind awareness' as one of their primary objectives for their communications (advertising) spend.

The hierarchical approach has been subject to much debate and among the arguments against the use of communication objectives the following are prevalent. Among them are criticism levelled by those who regard sales as the only valid measure of campaign effectiveness. The sole purpose of communication activities, and advertising in particular, is to generate sales. So, as the completion of communications tasks may not result in purchases, the only measure that need be undertaken is that of sales. Criticism is also made in terms of the loss of creative flair as

Table 4.3	Hierarchy of communications (after Colley)

Stage	Explanation
Awareness	Awareness of the existence of a product or brand is necessary before any purchase will be made.
Comprehension	Audiences need information and knowledge about the product and its specific attributes. Often the audience needs to be educated and shown either how to use the product or how changes (in attributes) might affect their use of the product.
Conviction	By developing beliefs that a product is superior to others in a category or can confer particular rewards through use, audiences can be convinced to trial the product at the next purchase opportunity.
Action	Potential buyers need help and encouragement to transfer thoughts into behaviour. Providing call-free numbers, website addresses, reply cards, coupons and sales people helps people act upon their convictions.

Source: Based on Colley (1961)

attention passes from looking for the big idea to concentration upon the numbers game, of focusing on measures of recall, attitude change and awareness. The third reason cited here concerns the impracticality of targeted communications effects. Management and associated agencies are required to account for their performance and with accounting periods being reduced to as little as 12 weeks, there is too little time for all of the communication tasks to be progressed or completed. Sales measures present a much more readily digestible benchmark of performance.

From a practical perspective, it should be appreciated that most successful marketing organisations do not see the sales and communications schools as mutually exclusive. They incorporate both views and weight them according to the needs of the current task, their overall experience, the culture and style of the organisation and the agencies with whom they operate.

Marketing communication objectives need to be set which reflect the communication and sales tasks that the product or organisation needs to accomplish. It should be appreciated that these objectives are vitally important, as they provide the basis for a string of decisions that are to be taken at subsequent stages in the development of the communication plan. This is examined in the next chapter.

SMART objectives

To assist managers in their need to develop suitable objectives, a set of guidelines has been developed, commonly referred to as SMART objectives. This acronym stands for specific, measurable, achievable, relevant, targeted and timed.

The process of making objectives SMART requires management to consider exactly what is to be achieved, when, where, and with which audience. This clarifies thinking, sorts out the logic of the proposed activities and provides a clear measure for evaluation at the end of the campaign.

Specific

What is the actual variable that is to be influenced in the campaign? Is it awareness, perception, attitudes, or some other element that is to be influenced? Whatever the variable, it must be clearly defined and must enable precise outcomes to be determined.

Measurable

Set a measure of activity against which performance can be assessed; this may be a percentage level of desired prompted awareness in the target audience.

Achievable

Objectives need to be attainable, otherwise those responsible for their achievement will lack motivation and a desire to succeed.

Realistic

The actions must be founded in reality and be relevant to the brand and the context in which they are set.

Targeted and timed

Which target audience is the campaign targeted at, how precisely is the audience defined and over what period are the results to be generated?

Having determined what levels of awareness, comprehension or preference are necessary or how attitudes need to be developed, the establishment or positioning of these objectives as a task for the organisation to accomplish should be seen as a primary communication objective. The attitude held or what individuals in the target market perceive, comprehend or prefer is a focus for campaign activity and subsequent evaluation.

Positioning

Having established the target markets, strategy and objectives the final part of the overall marketing communications strategy development process is to formulate the desired position for the product/service offering. In many cases this may just be a confirmation and reinforcement of the current positioning. In others, it may be a matter of repositioning. Before considering some of the more common positioning strategies it is necessary to establish what positioning means.

Ries and Trout (1972) were the first to claim, that it is not the physical nature of the product that is important for positioning, but how the product is perceived by others that matters. This is why a consideration of perception and attitudes and the way stakeholders see and regard brands and organisations is necessary. Of course, this may not be the same as the way brand managers intend their brands to be seen or how they believe the brand is perceived. If there is a disparity between the way the brand manager intended the brand to be seen and the way it is actually perceived, then this positioning gap needs to be closed. This can be achieved by either making changes to the product/service offering or by changing the communication strategy.

In the consumer market, established brands from washing powders (Ariel, Daz, Persil) and hair shampoos (such as Wash & Go, Timotei), to cars (for example, Peugeot, Ford, Nissan) and grocery multiples (Sainsbury's, Morrisons, Tesco) each carry consistent communications that enable audiences to position them in their respective markets. The process of positioning might also enable audiences to confer a level of perceived value on a brand, following a communication activity. The perceived value might be revised, up or down, for an established brand, should the positioning change.

The positioning concept is not the sole preserve of branded or consumer-oriented offerings or indeed those of the business-to-business market. Organisations are also positioned relative to one another, mainly as a consequence of their corporate identities, whether they are deliberately managed or not. The position an organisation takes in the mind of stakeholders may be the only means of differentiating one product from another. Given the advancement in technology, the high level of physical and functional similarity of products in the same class, and the increasing emphasis on ethical, corporate and social responsibilities, it is not surprising that many consumers make purchase decisions on their assessment of the company they are dealing with. Therefore, it is important to position organisations as brands in the minds of actual and potential customers.

The positioning concept

All products and all organisations have a position. The position held by each stakeholder can be managed or it can be allowed to drift. An increasing number of organisations are trying to manage the positions occupied by their brands and are using positioning strategies to move to new positions in buyers' minds and so generate an advantage over their competitors. This is particularly important in markets that are very competitive and where mobility barriers (ease of entry and exit to a market, e.g. plant and production costs) are relatively low.

Positioning, therefore, is the natural conclusion to the sequence of activities that constitute a core part of the marketing strategy. Market segmentation and target marketing are prerequisites to successful positioning. From the research data and the marketing strategy, it is necessary to formulate a positioning statement that is in tune with the promotional objectives.

One of the roles of marketing communications is to convey information so that the target audience can understand what a brand stands for and differentiate it from other competitor brands. Clear, consistent positioning is an important aspect of integrated marketing communications. So the way in which a brand is presented to its audience determines the way it is going to be perceived. Therefore, accepting that there are extraneous reasons why a brand's perception might not be the same as that intended, it seems important that managers approach the task of positioning in an attentive and considered manner.

Generally there are two main ways in which a brand can be positioned: functionally and expressively (or symbolic). Functionally positioned brands stress the features and benefits, and expressive brands emphasise the ego, social and hedonic satisfactions that a brand can bring. Both approaches make a promise, a promise to deliver a whiter, cleaner and brighter soap powder (functional) or clothes that we are confident to hang on the washing line (for all to see), dress our children in and send to school and not feel guilty, or dress ourselves and complete a major business deal (symbolic).

Viewpoint 4.4   Sticky, yet functional positioning

Marketing communications in the adhesives market place heavy reliance on demonstrating the performance of each the individual brands. Solvite, for example, present a man glued to a board and suspended in dangerous situations (above sharks, towed into the sky and at a theme park on a 'vertical drop ride').

Another brand, 'No More Nails', uses a similar functional approach. One execution shows a man sitting on a chair that has been glued half-way up a wall inside a house.

Adhesives provoke low-involvement decision-making and there is generally little consumer interest in the properties of each brand. The essential information that consumers require is that the brand has strong performance characteristics. This sets up umbrella brand credibility so that sub-brands for different types of glue are perceived to have the same properties as the umbrella brand and will do the 'job'.

Advertising needs to have dramatic qualities in order to attract attention and to build up a store of images that enable people to recall a brand of adhesives which do actually stick.

Question

To what extent is the success of a functional position dependent on the quality of the attribute rather than the communications used to convey it?

Task

Determine the key functions associated with a product category and then find communications that reflect those key functions.

Viewpoint 4.5 | Sit tight – it's expressive positioning

The range of expressive positioning opportunities can vary from the subtle suggestion that a brand of hair colourant can change not only a person's ego and the way they feel they are perceived, to a more extreme, sometimes bizarre and remote expression of a brand's identity.

For example, much of Toshiba's communications have been product led, partly a result of the dominant Japanese culture. Recent management changes in the UK operation have seen a move towards advertising and a position that hardly features the company's products. The award winning 'Space Chair' ad takes viewers, seated on an ordinary living room chair, on a breathtaking journey to the edge of space. The goal was to communicate the amazing quality of the Toshiba viewing experience, delivered through sharper, smoother images that crisply define every cloud and every star. This form of ad not only helped Toshiba break away from its past, but also symbolised Toshiba's brand philosophy and positioning as a leader in innovation.

Filmed in the Nevada desert, a Helium balloon was used to take the purpose made, lightweight chair and Toshiba cameras, to 98,268 feet above the earth. After 83 minutes, the rig broke up and the chair took 24 minutes to crash back to earth.

Source: Based on Tylee (2010); Ball (2009)

Question

What are the advantages and disadvantages of using this type of expressive form of communication to position a brand?

Task

Go to page 258 to see the Press Release relating to this piece.

Exhibit 4.3	Still from Toshiba 'Space Chair' ad
	Image courtesy of Toshiba

Positioning strategies

Positioning is the communications element of the segmentation process and is concerned with influencing the way target audiences perceive a product or brand. This should be achieved through communication which presents the product so that it occupies a particular position in

Table 4.4	Common positioning strategies

Positioning strategy	Explanation
Product features	The brand is set apart from the competition on the basis of the attributes, features or benefits that the brand has relative to the competition. For example, Red Bull gives you energy and Weetabix contains all the vitamins needed each day.
Price/quality	The price/quality appeal is used by many brands including M&S where quality is worth every penny.
Use	Used to inform buyers about when or how a product can be used. For example, Milky Way, 'The sweet you can eat between meals', informs just when it is permissible to eat chocolate; and After Eight chocolate mints clearly indicate when they should be eaten.
Product class dissociation	Some markets are essentially uninteresting and others have no obvious available positions as they have been adopted by competitors. For example, the moisturising bar Dove is positioned as 'not a soap'.
User	This approach enables the target user to be clearly identified. Flora margarine was for men, and then it became 'for all the family'. Some hotels position themselves as places for weekend breaks, as leisure centres or as conference centres.
Competitor	By associating directly with a competitor it becomes possible to create a perceived advantage. Virgin Atlantic challenge British Airways, and famously, Avis performed very successfully 'trying even harder' against Hertz, the industry number one.
Benefit	Here, proclaiming the benefits of usage, a superior position can be established. Sensodyne toothpaste appeals to all those who suffer from sensitive teeth, and a vast number of pain relief formulations claim to smooth away headaches or relieve aching limbs, sore throats or some offending part of the anatomy.
Heritage or cultural symbol	Used to convey quality, experience and knowledge, appeals to cultural heritage and tradition are often symbolised by age, particular heraldic devices or visual cues. For example, Kronenbourg 1664, 'Established since 1803', and the use of coats of arms by many universities to represent depth of experience and a sense of permanence.

the mind of each (potential) buyer, relative to the offerings of competitive products. In essence, the position adopted is a statement about what the brand is, what it stands for and the values and beliefs that customers (hopefully) will come to associate with the particular brand. The visual images or the position statement represented in the strapline may be a significant trigger that buyers use to recall images and associations of the brand.

There are a number of overall positioning strategies that can be implemented. The list in Table 4.4 is not intended to be comprehensive or to convey the opinion that these strategies are discrete. They are presented here as means of conveying the strategic style, but in reality a number of hybrid strategies are often used.

There are occasions when offerings need to be repositioned in the minds of customers. This may be due to market opportunities and development, mergers and acquisitions or changing buyer preferences, which may be manifested in declining sales. Research may reveal that the current position is either inappropriate or superseded by a competitor, or that attitudes have changed or preferences been surpassed; whatever the reason, repositioning is required if past success is to be maintained. However, repositioning is difficult to accomplish, often because of the entrenched perceptions and attitudes held by buyers towards brands and the vast (media) resources required to make the changes. Google began to reposition itself as a collaborative, technology brand, rather than a media company focused on aggregating and distributing content (Boyd, 2010).

Summary

In order to help consolidate your understanding of marketing communications strategy, here are the key points summarised against each of the learning objectives:

1 Consider issues associated with the nature and characteristics of the strategy concept

Strategy is used by organisations as a means of adjusting to changing environmental conditions. It is about the means, speed and methods by which organisations adapt to and influence their environments in order that they achieve their goals. Strategy is also concerned with decision-making, actions and implementation.

There are two main strategy schools of thought, the planning and the emergent approaches. There is also agreement that there are three main levels of strategy; corporate, competitive and functional.

2 Explain the STP process and its significance to marketing communications

Most marketing strategies utilise the market segmentation, target marketing and positioning process. This STP process requires that organisations consider how a market can be effectively segmented, and which segments are to be targeted. The third and final element concerns how a brand is to be positioned within the selected target markets. Marketing communications delivers the positioning element, promising customers a certain perceived value, which the prevailing marketing strategy and plans have to fulfil.

3 Establish the key characteristics associated with marketing communications strategy

Marketing communications strategy should develop messages than are themed around a consistent story, idea or promise. Marketing communications strategy is concerned with two key dynamics. The first concerns the target audience and associated brand promises. The second dynamic concerns the way in which an audience positions a brand. Positioning is a function of the way in which an organisation presents itself or its brands.

4 Explain the three main marketing communication strategies: pull, push and profile

Pull-positioning strategies are intended to influence end-user customers (consumers and b2b). Push-positioning strategies are intended to influence marketing (trade) channel buyers. Both of these strategies are product/service led and create audience expectations concerning the value inherent in the offerings.

Profile-positioning strategies are intended to influence a wide range of stakeholders, not just customers and intermediaries. These messages are oriented to the organisation, its values, actions and responsibilities.

5 Introduce ideas concerning the role and use of marketing communication objectives

Marketing communication objectives should reflect both the communication and sales tasks that need to be accomplished through a campaign. Communication objectives refer to levels of awareness, understanding, preference or conviction about a brand. Sales objectives refer to sales volumes, market share or return on investment. However, care is needed as there are many variables that influence sales, not just marketing communications. Setting objectives is important because they provide a means of measuring the effectiveness and success of a campaign.

6 Understand how to write SMART objectives

Managers need to develop a suitable set of objectives, a set of guidelines that provide a framework for measuring results. Campaign objectives should be written so that they are specific, measurable, achievable, relevant, targeted and timed. These are commonly referred to as SMART objectives.

The process of making objectives SMART requires management to consider exactly what is to be achieved, when, where, and with which audience. This clarifies thinking, sorts out the logic of the proposed activities and provides a clear measure for evaluation at the end of the campaign.

7 Discuss various ways in which brands might be positioned in the minds of target audiences

There are two main ways in which a brand can be positioned: functionally and expressively (or symbolic). Functionally positioned brands stress the features and benefits, and expressively positioned brands emphasise the ego, social and hedonic satisfactions that a brand can bring. Both approaches make a promise, a promise to deliver a whiter, cleaner and brighter soap powder (functional) or clothes that we are confident to hang on the washing line (for all to see), dress our children in and send to school and not feel guilty, or dress ourselves and complete a major business deal (symbolic). There are a variety of positioning strategies ranging from a focus on product features and price/quality dimensions to its use, who uses it, and the benefits arising through use.

Review questions

1. Write brief notes explaining what strategy is.
2. Explain the role of strategy in marketing communications.
3. What does STP stand for and how does it assist marketing communications?
4. What are the 3Ps of marketing communications strategy? Explain the differences between each of them and use the marketing communications eclipse to support your answer.
5. Explain the key characteristics associated with a pull-positioning strategy.
6. Draw two diagrams depicting the direction of communications in both the push- and the pull-positioning strategies.
7. Why should organisations write campaign objectives?
8. What does SMART stand for?
9. Brands can be positioned functionally and expressively. What do these terms mean and find examples to illustrate each of them.
10. Find examples to illustrate any four of the positioning strategies.

References

Andrews, K. (1987) *The Concept of Corporate Strategy*. Homewood, IL: Richard D. Irwin.

Anon (2008) Guarding her patch, *themarketer*, February, 27–9.

Ansoff, H.I. (1965) *Corporate Strategy*. New York: McGraw-Hill.

Ball, K. (2009) Toshiba premieres new 'Space Chair' ad campaign – Campaign to support Toshiba's SV REGZA LCD TV and Satellite T series laptops, *Toshiba Social Media News Release*, 16 November, retrieved 21 July 2010 from http://socialnews.toshiba.co.uk/?ReleaseID=14262

Beane, T.P. and Ennis, D.M. (1987) Market segmentation: a review, *European Journal of Marketing*, 21(5), 20–42.

Boyd, M. (2010) Google shows adland the new tools of its trade, *Campaign*, 25 June, 11.

Chaffee, E. (1985) 'Three models of strategy', *Academy of Management Review*, 10(1), 89–98.

Colley, R. (1961) *Defining Advertising Goals for Measured Advertising Results*. New York: Association of National Advertisers.

Haley, Russell I. (1968) Benefit segmentation: a decision-oriented research tool, *Journal of Marketing*, 32 (July), 30–35.

Jewell, R.D. (2007) Establishing effective repositioning communications in a competitive marketplace, *Journal of Marketing Communications*, 13(4), 231–241.

Johnson, G., Scholes, K. and Whittingham, R. (2010) *Exploring Corporate Strategy*, 9th edn. Harlow: Pearson Education.

Kay, J. (1993) The structure of strategy, *Business Strategy Review*, 4(2) (Summer), 17–37.

Mintzberg, H. and Ghoshal, S. (2003) *Strategy Process: Concepts, Context and Cases*, global edn. Englewood Cliffs, NJ: Financial Times/Prentice-Hall.

Ries, A. and Trout, J. (1972) The positioning era cometh, *Advertising Age*, 24 April, 35–38.

Riiber Knudsen, T. (2007) Confronting proliferation . . . in beer: An interview with Carlsberg's Alex Myers, *McKinsey Quarterly* (May), retrieved 4 November 2010 from www. mckinseyquarterly.com/Marketing/Management/Confronting_proliferation__in_beer_ An_interview_with_Carlsbergs_Alex_Myers_2009.

Tylee, J. (2010) The man who revealed Toshiba's emotional side, *Campaign*, 14 May, 16.

Wind, Y.J. (1990) Positioning analysis and strategy, in *The Interface of Marketing and Strategy* (eds G. Day, B. Weitz and R. Wensley), Greenwich, CT: JAI Press, 387–412.

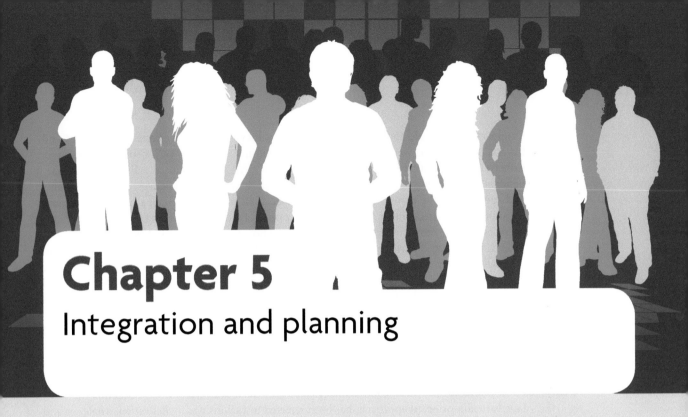

Chapter 5
Integration and planning

Ideas about integrated marketing communications have developed rapidly since the early 1990s. At the heart of the idea is a logical, sound approach to bring all the elements associated with a marketing communications campaign together. However, it can be argued that integrated marketing communications (IMC) is little more than a fancy name for sound commercial practice. Marketing communication plans are concerned with programmes and campaigns designed to articulate an organisation's marketing communication strategy and tactics.

Aims and learning objectives

The aims of this chapter are twofold. The first is to explore the nature and characteristics of integrated marketing communications. The goal is to enable readers to appreciate the arguments for and against the IMC concept. The second is to introduce the elements associated with planning marketing communications activities and to examine the marketing communications planning framework.

The learning objectives of this chapter are to:

1. introduce and explore the concept of IMC and consider what it is that should be integrated;
2. consider the background and reasons for the development and interest in IMC;
3. understand different perspectives of IMC;
4. explore some of the issues associated with managing IMC;
5. examine an incremental approach to the development of IMC;
6. present a planning framework and consider the different elements involved in the development marketing communication plans;
7. highlight the importance of the linkages and interaction between the different elements of the plan.

Introduction

Original thinking held that clients were able to achieve impacts or effects *on* audiences and buyers. These impacts were achieved through the autonomous use of each communication tool. Consequently, clients were required to deal with a variety of functionally different and independent organisations in order to communicate with their various audiences. As a result, clients and suppliers of the promotional tools saw specialisation as the principal means to achieve communication effectiveness. This resulted in a proliferation of advertising and public relations agencies plus the development of sales promotion houses and direct marketing agencies.

IMC has emerged partially as a reaction to these structural inadequacies of the industry and the realisation by clients that their communication needs can (and should) be achieved more efficiently and effectively than previously. In other words, just as power has moved from brand manufacturers to multiple retailers and now to consumers, so power is moving from agencies to clients and among customers.

There has also been a trend away from the use of traditional communication strategies, based largely on mass communications, delivering generalised messages. Now the overall approach is based upon personalised, customer-oriented and technology-driven approaches, referred to as integrated marketing communications. For many, integration is about orchestrating the tools of the marketing communications mix. Indeed Duncan and Everett (1993) recall that this new, largely media-oriented approach, has been referred to variously as *orchestration*, *whole egg* and *seamless communication*. Since this time many authors have expanded upon ideas concerning IMC and most recently Duncan (2002) and Grönroos (2004) have provided valuable insights into this dimension of IMC, one which Kitchen *at al.* (2004) refer to as the 'outside-in' IMC approach. For our purposes the following definition is offered:

> IMC is a strategic approach to the planned management of an organisation's communications. IMC requires that organisations coordinate their various strategies, resources and messages in order that it engage coherently and meaningfully with target audiences. The main purpose is to develop relationships with and provoke conversations among audiences that are of mutual value.

This definition serves to link IMC with business level strategies and the importance of coherence within the organisation wide use of resources and messages. Implicit is the underpinning notion that IMC is necessary for the development of effective relationships and that not all relationships need be collaborative and fully relational, as so often assumed to be in many contemporary interpretations.

Why the interest in IMC?

The explosion of interest in IMC has resulted from a variety of drivers. Generally they can be grouped into three main categories: those drivers (or opportunities) that are market-based, those that arise from changing communications, and those that are driven from opportunities arising from within the organisation itself. These are set out in Table 5.1.

The opportunities offered to organisations that contemplate moving to IMC are considerable and it is somewhat surprising that so few organisations have been either willing or able to embrace the approach. One of the main organisational drivers for IMC is the need to become increasingly efficient. Driving down the cost base enables managers to improve profits and levels of productivity. By seeking synergistic advantages through its communications and associated activities and by expecting managers to be able to account for the way in which they consume marketing communication resources, so integrated marketing communications becomes increasingly attractive. At the same time, organisation structures are changing more frequently and the need to integrate across functional areas reflects the efficiency drive.

From a market perspective, the predominant driver is the developing interest in relationship marketing and the creation of mutual value. By adopting a position designed to enhance

Table 5.1	Drivers for IMC

Organisational drivers for IMC
- Increasing profits through improved efficiency
- Increasing need for greater levels of accountability
- Rapid move towards cross-border marketing and the need for changing structures and communications
- Coordinated brand development and competitive advantage
- Opportunities to utilise management time more productively
- Provide direction and purpose for employees

Market-based drivers for IMC
- Greater levels of audience communications literacy
- Media cost inflation
- Media and audience fragmentation
- Stakeholders' need for increasing amounts and diversity of information
- Greater amounts of message clutter
- Competitor activity and low levels of brand differentiation
- Move towards relationship marketing from transaction-based marketing
- Development of networks, collaboration and alliances

Communication-based drivers for IMC
- Technological advances (Internet, databases, segmentation techniques)
- Increased message effectiveness through consistency and reinforcement of core messages
- More effective triggers for brand and message recall
- More consistent and less confusing brand images
- Need to build brand reputations and to provide clear identity cues

trust and commitment, an organisation's external communications need to be consistent and coordinated, if only to avoid information overload and misunderstanding.

From a communication perspective, the key driver is to provide a series of triggers by which buyers can understand a brand's values and a means by which they can use certain messages to influence their activities within the relationships they wish to develop. By differentiating the marketing communications, often by providing clarity and simplicity, advantages can be attained.

An integrated approach should attempt to provide a uniform or consistent set of messages. These should be relatively easy to interpret and to assign meaning. This enables target audiences to think about and perceive brands within a relational context and so encourage behaviour as expected by the source. Those organisations that try to practise IMC understand that buyers refer to and receive messages about brands and companies from a wide range of information sources. Harnessing this knowledge is a fundamental step towards enhancing marketing communications.

The advantages and disadvantages associated with IMC are set out in Table 5.2. General opinion suggests that the advantages far outweigh the disadvantages and that increasing numbers of organisations are seeking to improve their IMC resource. As stated earlier, database technology and the Internet have provided great impetus for organisations to review their communications and to implement moves to install a more integrated communication strategy.

What is it that should be integrated?

The notion that some aspects of marketing communications should be integrated has received widespread and popular support over the past decade. However, defining what integration actually means and what should be integrated is far from universal agreement, especially as

Table 5.2	Advantages and disadvantages of IMC

Advantages of IMC
Provides opportunities to cut communication costs and/or reassign budgets
Has the potential to produce synergistic and more effective communications
Can deliver competitive advantage through clearer positioning
Encourages coordinated brand development with internal and external participants
Provides for increased employee participation and motivation
Has the potential to cause management to review its communication strategy
Requires a change in culture and fosters a customer focus
Provides a benchmark for the development of communication activities
Can lead to a cut in the number of agencies supporting a brand

Disadvantages of IMC
Encourages centralisation and formal/bureaucratic procedures
Can require increased management time seeking agreement from all involved parties
Suggests uniformity and single message
Tendency to standardisation might negate or dilute creative opportunities
Global brands restricted in terms of local adaptation
Normally requires cultural change from employees and encourages resistance
Has the potential to severely damage a brand's reputation if incorrectly managed
Can lead to mediocrity as no single agency network has access to all sources of communications

there is an absence of any empirical evidence or definitive research in the area. While the origins of IMC might be found in the prevailing structural conditions and the needs of particular industry participants, an understanding of what elements should be integrated in order to achieve IMC needs to be established.

The problem with answering this question is that unless there is an agreement about what IMC is then identifying appropriate elements is far from easy, practical or in anyone's best interests. (Figure 5.1 shows some of the elements that need integrating.) At one level the harmonisation of the elements of the marketing communications mix represents the key integration factors, but as these represent a resource driven view then perhaps a more strategic (audience centred) perspective, one driven by the market and the objectives of the organisation, might be more realistic. Between these two extremes it is possible to identify messages, media, employees (especially in service-based environments), communication planning processes, client/agency relationships and operations, and the elements of the marketing mix all of which need to be involved and be a part of the integration process.

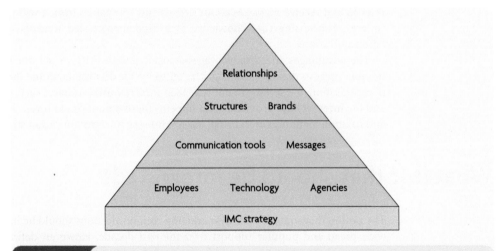

Figure 5.1	Elements to be integrated

However, two issues need to be raised at this point. The first concerns technology and the second concerns branding.

Technology the enabler

The use of technology, and in particular database technologies, has enabled marketing managers to obtain a vastly improved view of customer behaviour, attitudes and feelings towards brands. This has facilitated more precise and insightful communications and the subsequent feedback and measurement facilities have further developed the overall quality of customer communications. However, the mere presence of technology does not result in effective marketing communications. Technology needs to be integrated into not just the overall information systems strategy but also the marketing strategies of organisations. Technology is an enabler and to use it effectively requires integration. The effective use of technology can touch a number of areas within the IMC orbit. For example, technology can be used to develop effective websites, extranets and intranets, customer contact centres, databases, advertising campaigns, fulfilment processes, CRM and sales force automation. If each of these applications are deployed independently of each other, then their impact will be limited. If they are developed within an integrated framework, the potential for marketing and improved levels of customer service can be tremendous.

Associated with the use of technology are issues concerning the measurement and evaluation of IMC activities. One of the criticisms of IMC is that there are very few evaluation systems so the claims made about IMC delivering superior returns cannot be validated (Swain, 2004). Lee and Park (2007) proposed a multidimensional model of IMC based on four key dimensions. These have been drawn from the literature and are; a single message, multiple customer groups, database marketing and the need to use IMC to build customer relationships. Empirical validation of this approach has yet to be established.

Branding

Amongst other things, brands represent the outcome of marketing communications activities, over a period of time. Strong brands represent successful integration activities over a period of time. This means that internally organisations need to be sufficiently coordinated so that the brand is perceived externally as consistent and uniform. However, this proposition is based on the view that a brand is prepared and delivered for a single target audience, but audience and media fragmentation make this task more challenging. Audience sizes are shrinking, which means that in many situations a single audience is no longer economically viable. Brands therefore need to appeal to a number of different audiences (White, 2000) and to do this it is necessary to develop brands that appeal to diverse consumer groups. For example, a top of the range home cinema system may be regarded by the owner, as prestigious and technically superb, by a guest at a party as ostentatiously outrageous and overpriced and by a friend as a product of clever design and marketing. All three might have developed their attitudes through different sources (e.g. different print media, exhibitions, the Internet, retail stores, word of mouth) but all agree that the brand has a common set of values and associations that are important to each of them.

A further dimension of the branding factor concerns the role of corporate brands and issues of corporate communication. Should these be integrated with product brand communications, and if so what are the branding strategies that should be followed?

Once the internal reorientation has begun (but not completed), it is possible to take the message to external audiences. As long as they can see that employees are starting to act in different ways, do care about them as customers and do know what they are talking about in support of the products and services offered, then it is likely that customers (and other stakeholders) will be supportive. IMC should be concerned with blending internal and external messages so that there is clarity, consistency and reinforcement of the organisation's (or brand's) core proposition, and hence derived from corporate strategy. Viewpoint 5.1 provides an example of integrated marketing communications which has been driven from a strategic position.

Viewpoint 5.1   'Try something integrated today'

The development and launch of Sainsbury's highly successful 'Try something new today' campaign, is regarded by many as a good example of a form of integrated marketing communications. The root of the campaign was in the business strategy, one which aimed to boost sales by £2.5 billion by March 2008. At a store level this was translated into getting shoppers to put an extra £1.40 into their shopping baskets on each visit to a Sainsbury's store.

From this strategic goal the communications strategy took shape. From a positioning based on 'Making life taste better' to one which read, 'Try something new today', the £10 million campaign, led by Jamie Oliver, sought to awake shoppers from what Sainsbury's referred to as 'Sleep Shopping', where people tend to buy the same products on a routine basis, to one where they are prepared to experiment a little.

The strength of the basic idea enabled the message to be used in various media, across channels and adapted for different target segments. Not only was the campaign rooted in business strategy but it also encouraged staff participation.

Staff were given two days' training and then provided with various ingredients and recipes so that they could try them out at home. The thinking was that they could pass ideas onto customers and in doing so provide credibility and enhance the in-store experience for shoppers.

When the recession struck in 2008, the idea that Sainsbury's could encourage people to spend a little more on each visit contradicted their desire to spend a little less. A revised approach was required and it needed to change perceptions that shoppers had of Sainsbury's ability to deliver value for money. Rather than resort to price deals that have little impact when changing price perceptions, Sainsbury's decided to challenge perceptions with the statement that they could help shoppers feed their family for just £5. With a campaign called 'Feed your family for a fiver', 30 meal options were developed and made available through recipe cards, branded point-of-sale materials, magazine ads and on the website. A tv campaign fronted by Jamie Oliver was used to drive awareness for a campaign that generated over £203 million in sales.

Sources: Based on Thomas (2009); Brook (2005); Reed (2006); Anon (2009); www.sainsburys.co.uk

Question

Can IMC be achieved without having to incorporate a strategic orientation?

Task

Find out what each of the other main supermarkets regard as IMC.

Exhibit 5.1	Sainsbury's 'Feed your family for a fiver' campaign
	Image courtesy of The Advertising Archives

Perhaps the challenge of integration should focus on two elements, offline and online communications. Research informs that online advertising effectiveness is improved when offline work is used to drive awareness, create brand values and guide site traffic. Online activity consists of display, search, SEO, affiliate plus a range of media channels. As Walmsley (2008) suggests, integrating these media and data activities with offline media is achievable and important so as to enhance customer responses. However, the real integration goal in the future will be to integrate digital media itself, as the web becomes the hub of a consumer's marketing experience.

Content and process perspectives of IMC

Although IMC has yet to become an established marketing theory, the original ideas (Schultz, 1993) inherent in the overall approach are intuitively appealing and appear to be of value. However, what is integration to one person may be coordination to another or just plain commonsense to another. Until there is a theoretical base upon which to build IMC practice the phrase will continue to be misused, misunderstood and used in a haphazard and inconsistent way.

Cornelissen (2003) researched the subject and finds that there are two main interpretations of IMC: a content and a process perspective. The content perspective assumes that traditional view that IMC is about achieving a 'one voice, one look' position. IMC works when there is consistency throughout the various communication materials and messages.

Viewpoint 5.2 | Nissan gets integrated

The Urbanproof campaign designed by Nissan showcased the Qashqai and Murano models in a variety of urban settings. These included 'Play with the city', 'Skateboard', and 'Gangs'. In March 2010 Nissan launched a new campaign under this framework, called Artistic Paintball. This was designed to support the unveiling of the updates to the new Qashqai model. The work started with a teaser campaign designed to encourage the audience to follow the Qashqai's journey to Urbanproof, online.

The next step was a tv commercial which displayed the new shape and the changes made. A print campaign, based on an international competition about urban parking, was used to back the programme, whilst 3D videos were posted online to increase the product experience.

The campaign also featured user generated content. Users designed their own Nissan ads and the winners had their ads shown in cinemas and online, and used as support for the launch of 'Juke', Qashqai's baby brother.

Source: Based on Fernandez (2010)

Question

Are these primarily a process or content perspective of IMC?

Task

Visit the Nissan website and comment on whether you believe the Urbanproof element is a genuine part of an integrated approach.

Model	Vista 1.6 5dr 2WD Man
On the road	£13,499
Deposit	£3,381
Amount of Credit	£10,118
36 months	£199
Guaranteed future value	£4,245.34
APR	5.9%
Total amount payable	£14,790.34

**NEW NISSAN QASHQAI
URBANPROOF
FROM £199 per month**
COMPACT, AGILE, YET TOUGH. THE HATCHBACK REDEFINED.

For more information visit www.nissan-qashqai.co.uk

SHIFT convention

Exhibit 5.2 Nissan Qashqai – an integrated campaign
Image reproduced with permission of Nissan

The second interpretation is the process perspective. Here the emphasis is on a structural realignment of the various communication disciplines within organisations, to the point of collapsing all communications into a single department. Even if this extreme interpretation is not a valid goal for an organisation, cross-functional systems and processes are regarded as necessary to enable integrated marketing communications.

Research suggests that organisations have made little attempt to restructure their marketing communications disciplines and that public relations and marketing remain as a clear divide. What has happened, however, is that there are much closer cross-functional relationships and systems and processes to support them. Some organisations are moving incrementally towards a process perspective of IMC.

Viewpoint 5.3   Integrated smoking

Imperial Tobacco Ltd (ITL) is Canada's largest tobacco manufacturer and its leading brand, Player's has experienced a growth in market share from 37 per cent in 1973 to over 68 per cent in 1998. The brand was targeted at males under 25 years old and used messages set in mountainous or aquatic settings using sports themes.

What is interesting about ITL is that they abandoned the brand management structure and adopted a brand planning process structure. This involves a cross-functional approach that is regarded as a more strategic approach to brand development and brand defence. The company also developed a detailed insight into product and image positioning.

The brand strategy was clearly articulated internally and it was used to provide a platform for a consistent approach to messages and media selection. Consistency across their marketing communications and brand imagery was also achieved through the division head of brand marketing who considered activities across all brands and functional areas.

Source: Based on Dewhirst and Davis (2005)

Question

Is this primarily a process or content perspective of IMC?

Task

Read the paper by Dewhirst and Davis (2005) and learn more about ITL's approach to IMC.

Viewed holistically integration is a strategic concept that strikes at the heart of an organisation's marketing and business orientation. The word integration has been used in various ways and it is the interpretation of the word integration that determines whether integrated marketing communications is real, achievable or even practised. In many ways, reality suggests that the claims many organisations and the communications industry make in the name of IMC are simply a reflection of improved management and coordination of the communication tools.

Managing IMC

The development and establishment of IMC by organisations has not been as widespread as the amount of discussion around the subject. Recent technological advances and the benefits of the Internet and related technologies have meant that organisations have had a reason to reconsider their marketing communications and have re-evaluated their approach. Whatever route taken, the development of IMC requires change, a change in thinking, actions and expectations. The changes required to achieve IMC are large and the barriers are strong. What can be observed in practice are formative approaches to IMC, organisational experiments undertaken within their resource and cultural contexts.

As with many aspects of change, there is nearly always resistance to the incorporation of IMC and, if sanctioned, only partial integration has been achieved. This is not to say that integration is not possible or has not been achieved, but the path to IMC is far from easy and the outcomes are difficult to gauge with great confidence. However, it is the expectation (what level of IMC) that really matters, as it signals the degree of change that is required.

Resistance to integration

Resistance to change is partly a reflection of the experiences and needs of individuals for stability and the understanding of their environments. However, it is also a reflection, again, of the structural conditions in organisations and industry that have helped determine the expectations of managers and employees.

Eagle and Kitchen (2000) set out four principal areas or themes concerned with barriers to IMC programmes:

- power, coordination and control issues;
- client skills, centralisation/organisation and cultural issues;
- agency skills/talent and overall time/resource issues;
- flexibility/modification issues.

While these provide a useful general overview, the following represent some of the more common, more focused reasons for the resistance to the incorporation of IMC.

Financial structures and frameworks

Resistance through finance-led corporate goals, which have dominated industry performance and expectations, has been particularly significant. The parameters set around it and the extent to which marketing communications are often perceived as a cost rather than an investment have provided a corporate environment where the act of preparing for and establishing integrative activities is disapproved of at worst or room for manoeuvre restricted at best. Furthermore, the period in which marketing communication activities are expected to generate returns works against the principles of IMC and the time needed for the effects to take place.

Opposition/reluctance to change

The attitudes and opinions of staff are often predictable, in the sense that any move away from tried and proven methods to areas which are unknown and potentially threatening is usually rejected. Change has for a long time been regarded with hostility and fear, and as such is normally resisted. Our apparent need for stability and general security has been a potent form of resistance to the introduction of IMC. This is changing as change itself becomes a familiar aspect of working life. Any move towards IMC therefore represents a significantly different approach to work, as not only are the expectations of employees changed but so also are the working practices and the associated roles with internal customers and, more importantly, those providing outsourcing facilities.

Traditional hierarchical and brand management structures

Part of the reluctance to change is linked with the structure and systems inherent in many organisations. Traditional hierarchical structures and systems are inflexible and slow to cope with developments in their fast-adapting environments. These structures stifle the use of individual initiative, slow the decision-making process and encourage inertia. The brand management system, so popular and appropriate in the 1970s and early 1980s, focuses upon functional specialism, which is reflected in the horizontally and vertically specialised areas of responsibility. Brands now need to be managed by flexible teams of specialists, who are charged with responsibilities and the resources necessary to coordinate activities across organisations in the name of integration.

Attitudes and structure of suppliers and agencies

One of the principal reasons often cited as a barrier to integration is the relationship that clients have with their agencies, and in particular their advertising agencies. Generally, advertising agencies have maintained their traditional structures and methods of operating, while their clients have begun to adapt and reform themselves. The thinking behind this is that advertising agencies have tried to maintain their dominance of mass media advertising as the principal means of brand development. In doing so they seek to retain the largest proportion of agency fee income, rather than having these fees diluted as work is allocated below-the-line (to other organisations).

The establishment of IMC threatens the current role of the main advertising agencies. This is not to say that all agencies think and act in this way. They do not, as witnessed by the innovative approaches to restructuring and the provision of integrated resources for their clients by agencies such as St Lukes. So, while clients have seen the benefits of integrated marketing communications, their attempts to achieve them have often been thwarted by the structures of the agencies they need to work with and by the attitudes of their main agencies.

Perceived complexity of planning and coordination

The complexity associated with integrating any combination of activities is often cited as a means for delaying or postponing action. Of greater significance are the difficulties associated with coordinating actions across departments and geographic boundaries. IMC requires the cooperation and coordination of internal and external stakeholder groups. Each group has an agenda that contains goals that may well differ from or conflict with those of other participants. For example, an advertising agency might propose the use of mass media to address a client's needs, if only because that is where its specialist skills lie. However, direct marketing might be a more appropriate approach to solving the client's problem, but because there is no established mechanism to coordinate and discuss openly the problem/solution, the lead agency is likely to have its approach adopted in preference to others.

Implementing IMC

The restraints that prevent the development of IMC need to be overcome. Indeed, many organisations that have made significant progress in developing IMC have done so by instigating approaches and measures that aim to reduce or negate the impact of the barriers that people put up to prevent change. The main approaches to overcoming the barriers are as follows.

Adopting a customer-focused philosophy

The adoption of a customer-focused approach is quite well established within marketing departments. However, this approach needs to be adopted as an organisation-wide approach, a philosophy that spans all departments and which results in unified cues to all stakeholders. In many cases, agencies need to adopt a more customer-oriented approach and be able and willing to work with other agencies, including those below-the-line.

Training and staff development programmes

A move towards IMC cannot be made without changes in the expectations held by employees within the client and agency sectors. Some of the key processes that have been identified as important to successful change management need to be used. For example, the involvement and participation of all staff in the process is in itself a step to providing motivation and acceptance of change when it is agreed and delivered.

Appointing change agents

The use of change agents, people who can positively affect the reception and implementation of change programmes, is important. As IMC should span an entire organisation, the change agent should be a senior manager, or preferably director, in order to signal the importance and speed at which the new perspective is to be adopted. Some organisations have experimented with the appointment of a single senior manager who is responsible for all internal and external communications.

Planning to achieve sustainable competitive advantage

In order to develop competitive advantage, some organisations have restructured by removing levels of management, introducing business reprocessing procedures and even setting up outsourcing in order that they achieve cost efficiencies and effectiveness targets. Prior to the implementation of these delayering processes, many organisations were (and many still are) organised hierarchically.

An incremental approach to IMC

Integrated marketing communications means different things to different people. Opportunities to develop IMC appear to vary according to a variety of factors, including organisation size and development. Low (2000) suggests that IMC is more likely to be successful in smaller rather than large organisations. This is because they have fewer brands to be integrated, lower levels of hierarchical complexity and departmental formalisation and are inherently more adaptive. However, Reid (2005) found that large organisations were more likely to adopt IMC principles, suggesting this was due to their more sophisticated planning systems, greater number of formal mechanisms for managing customer data, and the fact that they are already experienced at managing internal functional groups and external agencies. He also found that the greater the level of market orientation within an organisation the more likely IMC practices would be successful. Both Low and Reid appear to agree that IMC is positively related to the intensity of competitive activity experienced by an organisation.

It is clear therefore, that the successful implementation of IMC needs to be founded on an audience-centred (outside-in) orientation. However, IMC also means different things to different organisations and the level of IMC implemented and experienced by organisations is bounded by their context. There is an emerging belief that although organisations should embrace the marketing mix and the communications mix in the name of IMC, they should use cross-functional systems and processes to incorporate internal communications and all those outsourced providers who contribute to the overall marketing communication process. As Figure 5.2 demonstrates, all of these elements should be linked to the overall purpose of the organisation, normally encapsulated and framed in the strategy, philosophy and mission of the organisation.

It seems logical that moves towards the establishment of IMC must be undertaken in steps as it cannot be accomplished overnight, an incremental approach is required (Fill, 2001). Organisations experience an incremental approach to the implementation and establishment of IMC. What they achieve at any one moment is a function of their context, and may be recognised as forms of coordination. Different organisations have coordinated various aspects of their communications activities. Many organisations have focused upon their promotional

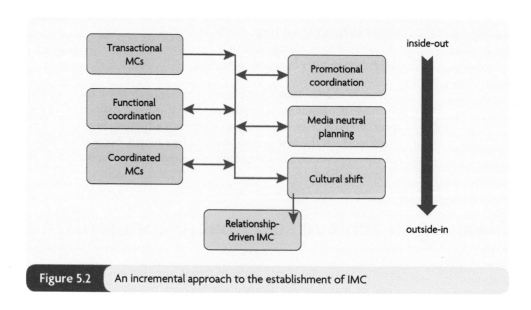

| **Figure 5.2** | An incremental approach to the establishment of IMC |

activities and have tried to bring together their communications to provide consistency and thematic harmonisation. Others have developed more sophisticated systems and procedures to interlink their activities internally.

Stage 1

Therefore, it seems that the starting point in the move towards IMC needs to reflect the context within which exchanges occur. In the majority of cases these will be transactional, where the focus is on product and price. The move from this point will be towards coordinating the tools, media and messages of the mix and this will gradually take place both internally and externally with the organisation's various agencies.

Stage 2

In order to make this work and to move forward, organisations need to create a technology platform necessary to provide a stream of information upon which it is possible to interact coherently with customers. The technology will be used internally to provide an operational tie between the different departments and functional areas. This is an important part of the process as different sections of the organisation are introduced to the ideas of being market-oriented. To support this, the notion that internal marketing relationships and internal marketing communications play an important role in the overall orientation process is also introduced.

Stage 3

Organisations will begin to adopt media-neutral planning principles and/or develop fully coordinated, even integrated marketing communications. This will be characterised by data-driven communications, CRM and meaningful evaluation and measurement techniques. This stage will be complemented by the organisation moving towards a strong(er) customer orientation. This requires a cultural shift of values and beliefs, whereby organisational, brand identity and relationship issues become paramount. This can only be implemented at this stage, as the internal systems, procedures and employee mind set need to be in place if the strategy is to be credible to customers and other stakeholders.

Stage 4

The final IMC stage is reached when planned communications and brand experiences encourage continued interaction, dialogue and relationship development. At this stage all parties involved in IMC derive an enhanced value over and above the value that would have been achieved without the integration.

The final IMC stage is reached when planned communications and brand experiences encourage continued interaction, dialogue and relationship development.

In order for these incremental stages to be undertaken and completed satisfactorily, managers must be clear and agreed about what it is they wish to achieve and communicate their intent to all those it involves, both inside and outside the organisation.

This sequential depiction sets out various incremental stages and does not require that they all be followed in strict order, and nor is it intended that all organisations should or do progress to the end. For many, perhaps small and medium-sized organisations, especially those with many transactional customers, promotional coordination or coordinated marketing communications stages may suffice.

One of the key issues encouraging the establishment of IMC has been the willingness of some public relations practitioners to move closer to the marketing department. When IMC began to emerge, Miller and Rose (1994) commentated that the previously held opposition to integration by public relations practitioners had begun to dissolve as the more enlightened agencies see it as 'a reality and a necessity'. Although this movement has not surged forward, many public relations agencies now proclaim that they provide IMC, particularly web and direct and database marketing services. Apart from this, the marketing communications industry has yet to come together and provide clients with the fully integrated services they desire.

Planning for marketing communications

The complexities associated with understanding, structuring and implementing integrated marketing communications serve to underline two key points. The first concerns the difficulty of planning marketing communications activities and attempting to consolidate the wide, often disparate range of people, systems, events and resources necessary to develop a politically coherent and agreed plan. The second concerns the real need to develop a plan in the light of these complexities. If integration is important then activities need to be managed, and a part of that management process is the development of plans. So, on the one hand integration makes planning difficult yet on the other, planning is a critical activity if integrated marketing communications are to be achieved.

Developing a marketing communications plan

Planning is a necessary management activity but it can be considered to be a detailed, meticulous, time consuming activity, often reflective of a managerially restrictive and hierarchical approach, undertaken in the name of financial awareness. In most cases this approach is not going to work today as plans need to be fluid and demonstrate flexibility in order to be able to react to changing environmental circumstances.

Part of the answer to the planning/integration dilemma is to focus on the level of planning that is required. At one level it is important to bring together and plan for all the overall activities to be undertaken in the name of integrated marketing communications. However, this needs to be accomplished at a broad level, often to consider the resource implications for an organisation or strategic business unit.

At a more focused level, integrated marketing communications should be developed at a brand and/or campaign level. Only at this level is it possible to meet the needs of the audience through a media focused integrated marketing communications schedule. Planning used to be considered a means of controlling events, yet much of contemporary marketing communications is about stimulating and enabling communication among many groups, for example, online brand communities. In these circumstances there is little or no control and so that aspect of planning is redundant.

The context in which a communication event is to occur shapes not only what and how messages are developed and conveyed, but they also influence the interpretation and meaning ascribed to the communication. In other words the intended positioning can be missed if the marketing communication is not entirely effective. The development of marketing communication plans helps to minimise errors and provide for efficiency and effectiveness.

There are a number of contexts that influence or shape marketing communications. All marketing managers (and others) need to understand these contextual elements and appreciate how they contribute and influence the development of marketing communication programmes. In addition, there are a number of other elements and activities that need to be built into a programme in order that it can be implemented. These elements concern the goals, the resources, the communication tools to be used and measures of control and evaluation. Just like the cogs in a clock, these elements need to be linked together, if the plan is to work. The marketing communications planning framework (MCPF) aims to bring together the various elements that constitute marketing communications into a logical sequence of activities. The rationale for communication decisions is built upon information generated at previous levels in the framework. It also provides a checklist of activities that need to be considered.

To help students and managers comprehend the linkages between the elements and to understand how these different components complement each other, the rest of this chapter deals with the development of marketing communication plans. To that extent it will be of direct benefit to managers seeking to build plans for the first time or for those familiar with the activity to reconsider current practices. Secondly, the material should also be of direct benefit to students who are required to understand and perhaps prepare such plans as part fulfilment of an assessment or examination in this subject area.

The MCPF represents a way of understanding the different components in the communication process, of appreciating the way in which they relate to one another and is a means of writing coherent marketing communications plans for work or for examinations, such as those offered by the Chartered Institute of Marketing.

The marketing communications planning framework

It has been established that the principal tasks facing marketing communications managers are to decide:

- Who should receive the messages.
- What the messages should say.
- What image of the organisation/brand receivers are expected to retain.
- How much is to be spent establishing this new established image.
- How the messages are to be delivered.
- What actions the receivers should take.
- How to control the whole process once implemented.
- What was achieved.

Note that more than one message is transmitted and that there is more than one target audience. This is important, as recognition of the need to communicate with multiple audiences and their different information requirements, often simultaneously, lies at the heart of marketing communications. The aim is to generate and transmit messages which present the organisation and their offerings to their various target audiences, encouraging them to enter into a dialogue. These messages must be presented consistently and they must address the points stated above. It is the skill and responsibility of the marketing communications manager to blend the communication tools, media and messages and create a mix that satisfies these elements.

A framework for IMC

To enable managers and students to bring together the various communications elements into a cohesive plan, which can be communicated to others, an overall framework is required. The MCPF (Figure 5.3) seeks to achieve this by bringing together the various elements into a logical sequence of activities where the rationale for marketing communications decisions is built upon information generated at a previous level in the framework. Another advantage of using the MCPF is that it provides a suitable checklist of activities that need to be considered.

The MCPF represents a sequence of decisions that marketing managers undertake when preparing, implementing and evaluating communication strategies and plans. It does not mean that this sequence reflects reality; indeed many marketing decisions are made outside any recognisable framework. However, as a means of understanding the different components, appreciating the way in which they relate to one another and bringing together various aspects

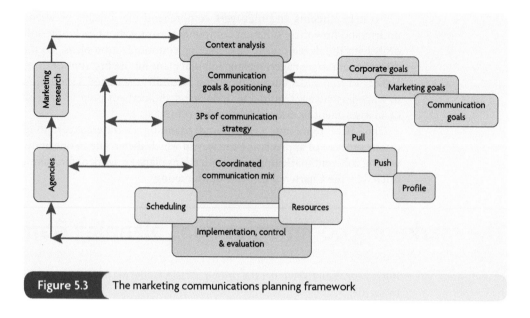

Figure 5.3   The marketing communications planning framework

for work or for answering examination questions such as those offered by the Chartered Institute of Marketing, this approach has many advantages and has been used by a number of local, national and international organisations.

Marketing communications require the satisfaction of communication objectives through the explicit and deliberate development of communication strategy. The MCPF will be used to show first the key elements, second some of the linkages and third the integrated approach that is required.

This framework reflects the deliberate or planned approach to strategy marketing communications. The process of marketing communications, however, is not linear, as depicted in this framework, but integrative and interdependent. To that extent, this approach is a recognition of the value of stakeholder theory and of the requirement to build partnerships with buyers and other organisations networked with the organisation.

The MCPF approach presented here is not intended to solve all the problems associated with the formulation of such plans, but it is robust enough to meet the needs of employers and examiners, and is recommended.

Elements of the plan

Marketing communications plans consist of the following elements. These elements will now be considered in turn.

- context analysis;
- marketing communication objectives;
- marketing communications strategy;
- communication methods;
- scheduling;
- resources (human and financial);
- control and evaluation;
- feedback.

Context analysis

Analysing the context in which marketing communication episodes occur is a necessary, indeed vital first step in the planning process. The purpose is to understand the key market and communication drivers that are likely to influence (or already are influencing) a brand (or organisation) and either help or hinder its progress towards meeting its long-term objectives. This is different from a situation analysis, because the situation analysis considers a range of wider organisational factors, most of which are normally considered in the development of marketing plans (while the communication focus is lost). Duplication is to be avoided, as it is both inefficient and confusing.

The compilation of a Context Analysis (CA) is very important, as it presents information and clues about what the communications plan needs to achieve. Information and market research data about target audiences (their needs, perception, motivation, attitudes and decision-making characteristics), the media and the people they use for information about offerings, the marketing objectives and time-scales, the overall level of financial and other resources that are available, the quality and suitability of agency and other outsourced activities, and the environment in terms of societal, technological, political and economic conditions, both now and at some point in the future, all need to be considered.

At the root of the CA is the marketing plan. This will already have been prepared and contains important information about the target segment, the business and marketing goals, competitors and the time-scales on which the goals are to be achieved.

The rest of the CA seeks to elaborate and build upon this information so as to provide the detail in order that the plan can be developed and justified.

The CA provides the rationale for the plan. It is from the CA that the marketing objectives (from the marketing plan) and the marketing communications objectives are derived. The type, form and style of the message are rooted in the characteristics of the target audience, and the media selected to convey messages will be based upon the nature of the tasks, the media habits of the audience and the resources available. The main components of the context analysis are set out in Table 5.3.

Table 5.3	The main elements of the context analysis
Context element	**Dimensions**
The customer context	Segment characteristics Levels of awareness, perception and attitudes towards the brand/organisation Level of involvement Types of perceived risk DMU characteristics and issues
The business context	Corporate and marketing strategy and plans Brand/organisation analysis Competitor analysis
The internal context	Financial constraints Organisation identity Culture, values and beliefs Marketing expertise Agency availability and suitability
The external context	Who are the key stakeholders and why are they important? What are their communication needs? Social, political, economic and technological restraints and opportunities.

Marketing communication objectives

The role of marketing communication objectives in the planning process is important for a number of reasons. The first is that they provide a balance to the plan and take away the sole emphasis on sales that inevitably arises. Secondly, they indicate positioning issues, thirdly they highlight the required balance of the communications mix, fourthly they provide time parameters for campaigns and finally they provide a crucial means by which particular marketing communication activities are evaluated.

Ideally, marketing communication objectives should consist of three main elements.

Corporate objectives

These are derived from the business or marketing plan. They refer to the mission and the business area that the organisation believes it should be in.

Marketing objectives

These are derived from the marketing plan and are output oriented. Normally these can be considered as sales-related objectives, such as market share, sales revenues, volumes, return on investment (ROI) and profitability indicators.

Communication objectives

These are derived from an understanding of the current context in which a brand exists and the future context in the form of where the brand is expected to be at some point in the future. These will be presented as awareness levels, perception, comprehension/knowledge, attitudes towards and overall degree of preference for the brand. The choice of communication goal depends upon the tasks that need to be accomplished. In addition, most brands need either to maintain their current brand position or reposition themselves in the light of changing contextual conditions.

These three elements constitute the campaign objectives and they all need to be set out in SMART terminology (see the previous chapter for details about SMART objectives). What also emerges is a refinement to the positioning that managers see as important for success. Obviously, not all plans require express attention to positioning (e.g. government information campaigns) but most commercial and brand-oriented communication programmes need to communicate a clear position in their market. So, at this point the positioning intentions are developed and these will be related to the market, the customers or some other dimension. The justification for this will arise from the CA.

Marketing communication strategy

The marketing communication strategy should be customer not method/media oriented. Therefore, the strategy depends upon whether the target audience is a consumer segment, a distributor or dealer network or whether all stakeholders need to be reached. In addition, it is imperative that the strategy be geared to the communication needs of the target audience that is revealed during the customer and business context analyses. This will show what the task is that marketing communications needs to achieve. Having established who the audience is, push-, pull- or profile-dominated strategies can be identified. The next step is to determine the task that needs to be accomplished. This will have been articulated previously in the marketing communications objectives but the approach at this stage is less quantitative and softer.

The DRIP tasks of marketing communications can be used to suggest the strategy being pursued. For example, if a new brand is being launched, the first task will be to inform and differentiate the brand for members of the trade before using a pull strategy to inform and differentiate the brand for the target end-user customers. An organisation wishing to signal a change of strategy and/or a change of name following a merger or acquisition may choose to use a profile strategy and the primary task will be to inform of the name change. An organisation experiencing declining sales may choose to remind customers of a need or it may choose to improve sales through persuasion.

Communication methods

Having formulated, stated and justified the required position, the next step is to present the basic form and style of the key message that is to be conveyed. Is there to be a lot of copy or just a little? Is there to be a rational or emotional approach or some weighting between the two? What should be the tone of the visual messages? It is at this point that those responsible for the development of these plans can be imaginative and try some new ideas. Trying to tie in the message to the strategic orientation is the important part, as the advertising agency will refine and redefine the message and the positioning.

From this the marketing communication mixes need to be considered for each of the strategies proposed, that is, a mix for the consumer strategy, a mix for the trade strategy and a distinct mix for the communications to reach the wider array of stakeholders.

The choice of methods should clearly state the tools and the media to be used. A short paragraph justifying the selection is very important, as the use of media in particular is to a large extent dependent upon the nature of the goals, the target audience and the resources. The key is to provide message consistency and a measure of integration.

Scheduling

The next step is to schedule the deployment of the methods and the media. This is best achieved by the production of a Gantt chart.

Events should be scheduled according to the goals and the strategic thrust. So, if it necessary to communicate with the trade prior to a public launch, those activities tied into the push strategy should be scheduled prior to those calculated to support the pull strategy.

Similarly, if awareness is a goal then, if funds permit, it may be best to use television and posters first before sales promotions (unless sampling is used), direct marketing, point of purchase and personal selling.

Resources

This is a vitally important part of the plan, one that is often avoided or forgotten about. The resources necessary to support the plan need to be determined. These refer not only to the financial issues but also to the quality of available marketing expertise and the time that is available to achieve the required outcomes.

Gantt charts and other project planning aids are best used to support this part of the plan. The cost of the media and methods can either be allocated in a right-hand column of the chart, or a new chart can be prepared. Preferably, actual costs should be assigned, although percentages can be allocated if examination time is at a premium. What is of importance is the relative weighting of the costs and that there is a recognition and understanding of the general costs associated with the proposed individual activities.

It should be understood that a television campaign cannot be run for less than £1.5 million and that the overall cost of the strategy should be in proportion to the size of the client organisation, its (probable) level of profitability and the size and dynamics of the market in which it operates.

Control and evaluation

Unless there is some form of evaluation, there will be no dialogue and no true marketing communications. There are numerous methods to evaluate the individual performance of the tools and the media used, and for examination purposes these should be stated. In addition, and perhaps more meaningfully, the most important measures are the promotional objectives set in the first place. The success of a promotional strategy and the associated plan is the degree to which the objectives set are achieved.

Feedback

The planning process is completed when feedback is provided. Not only should information regarding the overall outcome of a campaign be considered but so should individual aspects of the activity. For example, the performance of the individual tools used within the campaign, whether sufficient resources were invested, the appropriateness of the strategy in the first place, any problems encountered during implementation and the relative ease with which the objectives were accomplished are aspects which need to be fed back to all internal and external parties associated with the planning process.

This feedback is vitally important because it provides information for the next context analysis, which anchors subsequent campaigns. Information fed back in a formal and systematic manner constitutes an opportunity for organisations to learn from their previous campaign activities, a point often overlooked and neglected.

Links and essential points

It was mentioned earlier that there are a number of linkages associated with different parts of the marketing communications plan. It is important to understand the nature of these links as they represent the interconnections between different parts of the plan and the rationale for undertaking the contextual analysis in particular. The contextual analysis (CA) feeds the items shown in Table 5.4. For example, research undertaken by Interbrand for Intercontinental Hotels to find out what influenced the brand experience of hotel guests, discovered that one of the key factors was the hotel concierge. As a result the role of the concierge became a central character in the communication strategy, influencing the campaign goals, positioning and message strategy (Gustafson, 2007). The communication objectives derived from the CA feed decisions concerning strategy, tools and media, scheduling and evaluation.

The marketing communications strategy is derived from an overall appreciation of the needs of the target audience (and stakeholders) regarding the brand and its competitive position in the market. The communication mix is influenced by the previous elements and the budget that follows. However, the nature of the tools and the capacity and characteristics of the media influence scheduling, implementation and evaluation activities.

Table 5.4	Linkages within the MCPF
Objectives	From the marketing plan, from the customer, stakeholder network and competitor analysis and from an internal marketing review
Strategic balance between push, pull and profile	From an understanding of the brand, the needs of the target audiences, including employees and all other stakeholders, and the marketing goals
Brand positioning	From users' and non-users' perceptions, motivations, attitudes and understanding about the brand and its direct and indirect competitors
Message content and style	From an understanding about the level of involvement, perceived risk, DMU analysis, information-processing styles and the positioning intentions
Promotional tools and media	From the target audience analysis of media habits, involvement and preferences, from knowledge about product suitability and media compatibility, from a competitor analysis and from the resource analysis

Viewpoint 5.4   Repeating the storming of Leeds Castle

The 900-year-old Leeds Castle is a picturesque historical, tourist attraction set in the Kent countryside. Typically, people perceive these attractions as a once only event; seen it – done it. Leeds wanted to change this and to encourage frequent annual visits. This was to be achieved by drawing attention to the variety of functions and events held at the castle throughout the year.

Using the theme 'Key to the Castle', one of the first elements to be changed was the ticket structure. Instead of buying a single day pass, visitors bought an 'all year entry pass'. A logo incorporating the established swan emblem with a 3D image of a key, was designed and implemented across campaign materials.

All advertising incorporated the 'Get your Key to the Castle' message. TV, radio, print, PR, literature, and email were used to drive traffic to the new website. Here the database was enhanced and used to remind visitors of the annual pass and the different seasonal events as the year unfolded.

Previously individual event leaflets were distributed but this was replaced by a 24-page, saddle-stitched brochure, in which the whole year's events were set out. Tear-out coupons entitling visitors to discounts to particular events were also included. These were mailed to the 27,000 strong database of addresses, 250,000 door-dropped to Kent addresses and 400,000 were distributed via the Tourist Information Centre, motorway service and hotels in the South East region.

Working with local trains, hotels and coach companies Leeds Castle enabled them to offer 2-4-1 and money off promotions, and so reach a wider audience.

The results are impressive. The number of day visitors has increased by over 40 per cent, the number of unique visitors has doubled, the marketing spend has reduced, whilst the direct marketing cost per visitor has declined drastically from £1.13 to 53p, when the national average for these types of attractions is 63p.

Source: Based on Barda (2010)

Question

To what extent do you think this is a good or poor example of integrated marketing communications?

Task

Prepare a retrospective marketing communications plan using the information provided in this viewpoint. Make assumptions where information is not provided.

Exhibit 5.3   Leeds Castle
Image courtesy of Alamy Images/B.L. Images Ltd.

Summary

In order to help consolidate your understanding of marketing communications strategy, here are the key points summarised against each of the learning objectives.

1 Introduce and explore the concept of IMC and consider what it is that should be integrated

Integrated marketing communications (IMC) is concerned with the development, coordination and implementation of an organisation's various strategies, resources and messages. The role is to enable coherent and meaningful engagement with target audiences. In an age when consumers can touch brands across a range of channels it is important that each contact reinforces previous messages and facilitates the development of valued relationships. While the concept of IMC is attractive, to date the development of the approach in practical terms has not been very encouraging. There has been a great deal of debate about the meaning and value of an integrated approach and some attempt to coordinate the content and delivery of marketing communication messages. Most organisations have yet to achieve totally integrated marketing communications; only partial or coordinated levels of activity have so far been achieved.

A wide range of elements need to be integrated. These include the communication tools, media and messages, plus the elements of the marketing mix, brands, strategy, employees, agencies and technology.

2 Consider the background and reasons for the development and interest in IMC

The interest in IMC has resulted from three main drivers. These include market-based drivers, those that arise from changing communications, and those that are driven from opportunities arising from within the organisation itself.

3 Understand the different perspectives of IMC

Cornelissen identified two main perspectives of IMC running through the literature. He refers to one of these as a predominantly process-oriented concept and the second is that IMC is a content-oriented concept.

The content perspective holds that IMC works when there is a consistency throughout the various materials and messages. The process perspective of IMC is rooted in the belief that real IMC can only be generated through an organisational structure that brings the various communication disciplines together in a single body or unit.

4 Explore some of the issues associated with managing IMC

The management of IMC has been shown to be a challenging task and one that does not always result in a successful outcome. There is much resistance to the development of IMC, again based on a range of factors, some of them found in many situations regardless of what it is that is to be changed. There are several ideas concerning the best way to implement IMC but perhaps the most important point is that IMC can only be achieved by incremental change, not a one-off wholesale change.

5 Examine an incremental approach to the development of IMC

Integrated marketing communications means different things to different people. Opportunities to develop IMC appear to vary according to a variety of factors, including organisation size and development.

The development of IMC appears to best achieved when an incremental approach is adopted. Stage 1 considers the transactional elements and any move forward should be based on coordinating the tools, media and messages of the mix. This will gradually take place both internally and externally with the organisation's various agencies. Stage 2 requires a technology platform necessary to provide a stream of information upon which it is possible to interact coherently with customers. Stage 3 is characterised by data-driven communications, CRM and meaningful evaluation and measurement techniques. This stage is often complemented by a strong(er) customer orientation. This requires a cultural shift of values and beliefs, whereby organisational, brand identity and relationship issues become paramount. Finally, Stage 4 is reached when planned communications and brand experiences encourage continued interaction, dialogue and relationship development.

6 Present a planning framework and consider the different elements involved in the development marketing communication plans

The marketing communications planning framework (MCPF) consists of the following elements:

- context analysis;
- marketing communication objectives;
- marketing communications strategy;
- communication methods;
- scheduling;
- resources (human and financial);
- control and evaluation;
- feedback.

The MCPF aims to bring together the various elements that constitute marketing communications into a logical sequence of activities. The rationale for promotional decisions is built upon information generated at previous levels in the framework. It also provides a checklist of activities that need to be considered.

This framework reflects the deliberate or planned approach to strategic marketing communications. The MCPF represents a way of understanding the different communication components, of appreciating the way in which they relate to one another, and is a means of writing coherent marketing communications plans for work or for assessment.

7 Highlight the importance of the linkages and interaction between the different elements of the plan

Just as the strength of the value chain is in the internal links so the strength of a marketing communication plan is to be found within the various links that bind the components together. It is important to understand the nature of these links as they represent the interconnections between different parts of the plan and the rationale for undertaking the contextual analysis in particular.

Review questions

1. Discuss the main reasons for the development of IMC.
2. Prepare brief notes explaining four different elements that should be part of the integration process.
3. Write a definition of IMC as you understand the concept.

4. What are the reasons for interest in IMC and is it a valid concept?

5. Appraise the main reasons offered for the failure of organisations to develop IMC.

6. What is the incremental approach to establishing IMC?

7. What do the expressions 'outside-in' and 'inside-out' mean?

8. Sketch the marketing communications planning framework – from memory.

9. Make notes about the content and meaning of a context analysis

10. Following on from the previous question, check your version of the MCPF with the original and then prepare some bullet-point notes, highlighting the critical links between the main parts of the framework.

References

Anon (2005) Sainsbury's polishes up its image, 19 September. Retrieved 5 November 2007 from www.news.bbc.co.uk/1/hi/business/4259224.stm

Barda, T. (2010) Key to the Castle, *themarketer*, December/January, 20–22.

Brook, S. (2005) Sainsbury's unveils new slogan, *MediaGuardian*, 19 September. Retrieved 5 November 2007 from http://www.guardian.co.uk/media/2005/sep/19/business.advertising

Cornelissen, J.P. (2003) Change, continuity and progress: the concept of integrated marketing communications and marketing communications practice, *Journal of Strategic Marketing*, 11 (December), 217–234.

Dewhirst, T. and Davis, B. (2005) Brand strategy and integrated marketing communications (IMC): A case study of Player's cigarette brand marketing, *Journal of Advertising*, 34(4) (Winter), 81–92.

Duncan (2002) *IMC: using advertising and promotion to build brand* (international edn.). New York: McGraw-Hill.

Duncan, T. and Everett, S. (1993) Client perceptions of integrated marketing communications, *Journal of Advertising Research*, 3(3), 30–39.

Eagle, L. and Kitchen, P. (2000) IMC, brand communications, and corporate cultures, *European Journal of Marketing*, 34(5/6), 667–686.

Fernandez, J. (2010) Nissan plots integrated campaign for the new Qashqai push, *Marketing Week*, retrieved 30 March 2010 from www.marketing.co.uk/news/

Fill, C. (2001) Essentially a matter of consistency, *Marketing Review*, 1(4) (Summer), 409–425.

Grönroos, C. (2004) The relationship marketing process: communication, interaction, dialogue, value, *Journal of Business and Industrial Marketing*, 19(2), 99–113.

Gustafson, R. (2007) Best of all Worlds, *Marketing: Brands by Design*, 14 November, 11.

Kitchen, P., Brignell, J., Li, T. and Spickett-Jones, G. (2004) The emergence of IMC: a theoretical perspective, *Journal of Advertising Research*, 44 (March), 19–30.

Lee, D.H. and Park, C.W. (2007) Conceptualization and measurement of multidimensionality of integrated marketing communications, *Journal of Advertising Research* (September), 222–236.

Low, G.S. (2000) Correlates of integrated marketing communications, *Journal of Advertising Research*, 40(3), 27–39.

Miller, D.A. and Rose, P.B. (1994) Integrated communications: a look at reality instead of theory, *Public Relations Quarterly* (Spring), 13–16.

Reed, D. (2006) Media rivalry barring integrated path, *Precision Marketing*, 25 August, 6.

Reid, M. (2005) Performance auditing of integrated marketing communication (IMC) actions and outcomes, *Journal of Advertising*, 34(4) (Winter), 41–54.

Schultz, D. (1993) *Integrated Marketing Communications: Putting It Together and Making It Work*. Lincolnwood, IL: NTC Business Books.

Swain, W.N. (2004) Perceptions of IMC after a decade of development: who's at the wheel, and how can we measure success? *Journal of Advertising Research*, 44(1) (March), 46–65.

Thomas, J. (2009) Jamie Oliver and the Try Team encourage people to cook in latest Sainsbury's ad, *Marketing*, retrieved 4 November 2010 from www.marketingmagazine.co.uk/news/915344/Jamie-Oliver-Try-Team-encourage-people-cook-latest-Sainsburys-ad/

Walmsley, A. (2008) The truth about integration, *Marketing*, 24 September, 12.

White, R. (2000) Chameleon brands: tailoring brand messages to consumers, *Admap* (July/August), 8–40.

Chapter 6
Branding, budgeting and evaluation

The images, associations and experiences that customers make with brands, and the brand identities that managers seek to create, need to be closely related if long-run brand purchasing behaviour is to be achieved. To achieve this, resources – in particular finance – are necessary to invest in branding. Once the investment is made, it is necessary to evaluate the success of the campaign.

Aims and learning objectives

The aims of this chapter are to explore the way in which marketing communications assists the branding process, consider ways in which budgets are decided and to examine the principles associated with the ways campaigns can be evaluated.

The learning objectives of this chapter are to:

1. explore the nature and common characteristics of brands;

2. understand the different ways in which marketing communications can be used to build and support brands;

3. explain the role of the communication budget and clarify the benefits of using budgets for communication activities;

4. examine various budgeting techniques, both practical and theoretical;

5. discuss the role of evaluation as part of marketing communications;

6. consider other ways in which the effectiveness of marketing communications can be evaluated;

7. explain ideas associated with measuring the fulfilment of brand promises and brand equity.

Introduction

Brands are promises which set up customer expectations. Successful brands deliver on their promises, by meeting or exceeding expectations, consistently.

Brands which create strong, positive and lasting impressions, deliver something of value to those who consume the brand. Brands are perceived by their customers to be of value to them personally. People perceive brands without having to purchase or have direct experience of them. The elements that make up this impression are numerous, and research by de Chernatony and Dall'Omo Riley (1998a) suggests that there is little close agreement on the definition of a brand. They identified 12 types of definition. Some of the more commonly quoted definitions are presented in Table 6.1.

Indeed, de Chernatony (2009: 101) suggests that from a managerial perspective, there is a 'plethora of interpretations', which can lead to brand management inefficiencies. To support his argument, he identifies a spectrum of brand interpretations, ranging from differentiation through to added value. He suggests a brand might be defined 'as a cluster of values that enables a promise to be made about a unique and welcomed experience' (104).

What these authors have identified is that brands are a product of the work of managers who attempt to augment their products with values and associations that are recognised by, and are meaningful to, their customers. In other words, brands are a composite of two main constructs, the first being an identity that managers wish to portray (the promise and expectation) and the second being images, construed by audiences, of the identities they perceive (the image and realisation of the promise). The development of Web 2.0, social media including user-generated-content in the form of blogs, wikis and social networks have added a new dimension to the managerial-driven perspective of brands. Consumers are assuming a greater role in defining what a brand means to them and are prone to sharing this with their friends, family and contacts rather than with the organisation itself. What this means is that brand managers have reduced levels of influence over the way their brands are perceived and this in turn impacts on the influence they have managing brand reputation.

It is important, therefore to recognise that both managers and customers are involved in the branding process. In the past the emphasis and control of brands rested squarely with brand owners. Today, this influence has shifted to consumers as they redefine what brands mean to them and how they differentiate among similar offerings and associate certain attributes or feelings

Table 6.1	Brand definitions
Author	**Brand definition**
Alexander (1960) **American Marketing Association**	'A name, term, sign, symbol, or design, or a combination of them, intended to identify the goods or services of one seller or group of sellers and to differentiate them from those of competitors'.
Assael (1990)	'. . . name, symbol, packaging and service reputation'.
Schmitt (1999)	'a rich source of sensory, affective, and cognitive associations that result in memorable and rewarding brand experiences'.
Riezebos (2003)	'. . . every sign that is capable of distinguishing the goods or services of a company and that can have a certain meaning for consumers both in material and in immaterial terms'.
Keller (2008)	'. . . something that has actually created a certain amount of awareness, reputation, prominence . . . in the marketplace'.

and emotions with particular brands. Indeed, there is discussion that brands should be considered outside the narrow marketing perspective as they are a construct of a wider realm of influences. For those interested in these issues see Brodie and de Chernatony (2009), and for developments in managerial aspects, see de Chernatony (2009) and de Lencastre and Côrte-Real (2010).

Branding is a task that requires a significant contribution from marketing communications and is a long-term exercise. Organisations that cut their brand advertising in times of recession reduce the significance and power of their brands. The Association of Media Independents claims, not surprisingly, that the weaker brands are those that reduce or cut their advertising when trading conditions deteriorate.

In line with moves towards integrated marketing communications many organisations are moving the balance of their communication mix away from an emphasis on advertising (especially offline) towards the other tools and media. For example, mobile phone companies have used advertising to develop brand awareness and positioning and have then used sales promotion and direct marketing activities to provide a greater focus on loyalty and reward programmes. These companies operate in a market where customer retention is a challenge. Customer loss (or churn rate) used to exceed 30 per cent and there was a strong need to develop marketing and communications strategies to reduce this figure and provide for higher customer satisfaction levels and, from that, improved profitability.

Brand characteristics

The essence of a strong brand is that it is sufficiently differentiated to the extent that it cannot be easily replicated by its competitors. This level of differentiation requires that a brand possess many distinctive characteristics and to achieve this it is important to understand how brands are constructed.

Brands consist of two main types of attributes: intrinsic and extrinsic (Riezebos, 2003). Intrinsic attributes refer to the functional characteristics of the product such as its shape, performance and physical capacity. If any of these intrinsic attributes were changed, it would directly alter the product. Extrinsic attributes refer to those elements that are not intrinsic and if changed do not alter the material functioning and performance of the product itself: devices such as the brand name, marketing communications, packaging, price and mechanisms that enable consumers to form associations that give meaning to the brand. Buyers often use the extrinsic attributes to help them distinguish one brand from another because in certain categories it is virtually impossible for them to make decisions based on the intrinsic attributes alone.

Brand experiences

A more recent approach to brand development work involves creating a brand experience. Tango was an early pioneer of this approach, using road-shows to create indirect brand-related experiences, such as bungee jumping, trampolining and other out-of-the-norm activities. FujiFilm underpin a great deal of their UK marketing communications on events, if only because they provide opportunities to provide direct experiences; in this case of the features and benefits of Fujifilm's brand values. Their events are grouped under three main headings – exhibitions, product launches and sponsorship. The first two of these enable contact with trade customers and consumers, who can handle the products and become immersed in the brand. They can also provide direct feedback. Further material on brand experience is considered later in this chapter.

Kapferer (2004) refers to a brand identity prism and its six facets (see Figure 6.1). The facets to the left represent a brands-outward expression, while Kapferer argues that those to the right are incorporated within the brand, an inner expression or spirit as he refers to it. These facets represent the key dimensions associated with building and maintaining brand identities and are set out in Table 6.2; they are interrelated and define a brand's identity, while also representing the means by which brands can be managed, developed and even extended.

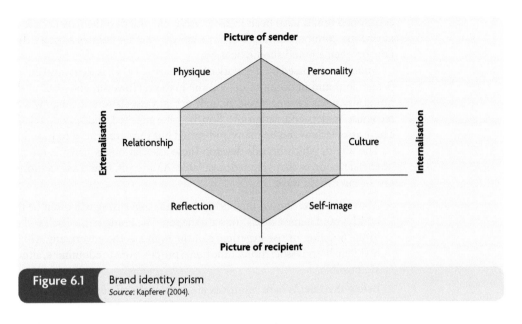

Figure 6.1 Brand identity prism
Source: Kapferer (2004).

Table 6.2 Brand facets

Brand facet	Explanation
Physique	Refers to the main physical strength of the brand and its core added value. What does the brand do and what does it look like (e.g. the Coca-Cola bottle)?
Personality	Those human characteristics that best represent the identity, best understood by the use of celebrity spokespersons who provide an instant personality.
Culture	A set of values that are central to a brand's aspirational power and essential for communication and differentiation.
Relationship	A brand's relationship defines the way it behaves and acts towards others. Apple exudes friendliness, IBM orderliness and Nike provocation. Important in the service sector.
Customer reflection	Refers to the way customers see the brand . . . for old people, for sporty people, clever people, people who want to look younger. This is an outward reflection.
Self-image	Refers to how an individual feels about themselves, relative to the brand. This is an inner reflection.

Source: Adapted from Kapferer (2004)

All brands consist of a mixture of intrinsic and extrinsic attributes and management's task is to decide on the balance between them. Indeed, this decision lies at the heart of branding in the sense that it is the strategy and positioning that lead to strong brands.

The role of marketing communications in branding

Marketing communications plays a vital role in the development of brands and is the means by which products become brands. The way in which marketing communications is used to build brands is determined strategically by the role that the brand is expected to play in achieving an organisation's goals. De Chernatony and Dall'Olmo Riley (1998b) argue that there are several roles that marketing communications can play in relation to brand development. For example, they suggest the role during brand extensions is to show buyers how the benefits from the established brand have been transferred or extended to the new brand. During introduction, marketing communications needs to inform and sometimes educate the audience regarding how or when a brand should be used.

Another role, based on the work of Ehrenberg (1974), is to remind buyers and reinforce their perceptions and in doing so defend the market. However, above all of these marketing communications has a primary role, namely to build associations through which consumers identify, recognise, understand, assign affection, become attached, and develop relationships with a brand. These associations can be many and varied but they are crucial to brand strength and equity.

The way in which brands develop these associations is partly a function of the size of the financial resources that are made available. As a result, brand associations can be developed in one of three main ways.

- **Above-the-line:** Should the budget be high, advertising will often be the main way through which brand name associations are shaped. The brand name itself will not need to be related to the function or use experience of the brand as the advertising will be used to create and maintain brand associations. Emotional propositions predominate, although both approaches are possible.

- **Below-the-line:** Where resources are restricted and advertising is not an option, the brand name needs to be closely related to the function and use experience of the product. In the FMCG sector packaging should also play a significant role in building brand associations. Functional associations tend to predominate.

- **Around-the-line:** Whether resources are tight or available, there are circumstances when the use of a formal mix of brand building tools and media is inappropriate. Here word of mouth communication and brand experience are sufficient to propel a brand's visibility. Emotional propositions predominate, although both approaches are possible.

Each of these is now considered in turn.

Brand building: above the line

When there are sufficient resources, and competitive conditions are intense and margins small, advertising is used to help consumers to make brand associations. Two main approaches can be used: a rational or an emotional approach. When a rational approach is used the functional aspects of a brand are emphasised and the benefit to the consumer is stressed. Very often product performance is the focus of the message and a key attribute is identified and used to position the brand. Typically, unique selling propositions (USPs) were often used to draw attention to a single superior functional advantage that consumers found attractive. For example, a washing powder that washes clothes whiter, drinks that have the highest percentage of fruit juice content and paint that covers more square metres than any other paint.

Many brands now try to present two or even three brand features as the USP has lost ground. For example, when Britvic launched Juice Up into the chilled fruit juice sector to compete with Sunny Delight, it used the higher fruit juice and lower sugar attributes as the main focus of the communication strategy. The rational approach is sometimes referred to as an informative approach (and complements functional positioning).

When an emotional approach is used, advertising should provide emotional selling points (ESPs). These can enable consumers to make positive brand associations based on both psychological and socially acceptable meanings, a psychosocial interpretation. Product performance characteristics are dormant while consumers are encouraged to develop positive feelings and associations with the brand. A further goal can be to create positive attitudes towards the advertising itself, which in turn can be used to make associations with the brand. In other words, the role of likeability, discussed later in this chapter, becomes paramount when using an emotional advertising approach. Therefore, these types of advertisements should be relevant and meaningful, credible, and be of significant value to the consumer. In essence, therefore, emotional advertising is about people enjoying the advertisement (and complements expressive positioning).

Viewpoint 6.1   The Famous Grouse...built above-the-line

The UK whisky market experienced major changes during the 1990s. At one time the blended sector was dominant but the market had been eroded through the growth of own label brands, Irish and American spirits and single malts. These pressures combined to create difficult trading conditions for blended whisky brands. Not only was the market in decline but also many brands such as Famous Grouse, were suffering long-term declining sales, in this case 36 per cent in 16 years. Even Bells, the market leader, had suffered declining volume sales. The question was how could advertising revive a brand in this context?

Some brands for example, Teachers and Grants, withdrew all advertising support and effectively treated their brands as cash cows, draining their residual profits. This was not seen as a strategy that could deliver long-term value so it was decided to invest and build the Famous Grouse brand through advertising. The key was to build a brand that not only consumers could become engaged with, but also one that would enable the brand to stand out and retain on trade distribution. This was achieved through a creative that used the iconic bird depicted on the label. In real life the grouse is a shy and retiring bird. Not so with The Famous Grouse who was used to demonstrate cheekiness, fun and even a slight irreverence.

Over the decade since the advertising campaign began, the strength of the brand has increased considerably. The above-the-line campaign cost £15.4 million between 1996 and 2006 and it is claimed that it has generated an additional £513 million of value. Of the brands in the blended sector, only Bells and Famous Grouse have increased the strength of their brands. It is interesting to note that they were the only two to invest in advertising. The investment in advertising has continued with the introduction of a roguish cousin, The Black Grouse. The intention was to keep the story rolling and add a touch of mystery, with a bird which prefers to appear unorthodox and unpredictable.

Source: Based on Barnett *et al.* (2006); Lovell (2008)

Question

Is it too late for Teachers and Grants to develop their brands and add value?

Task

Try to collect five different ads of the Famous Grouse and identify three strengths and three weaknesses associated with the brand's advertising.

Exhibit 6.1   The Famous Grouse
Image courtesy of The Advertising Archives

Brand building: below-the-line

When the marketing communications budget is limited or where the target audience cannot be reached reasonably or effectively through advertising, then it is necessary to use various other communication tools to develop brand associations.

Direct marketing and public relations are important methods used to build brand values, especially when consumers experience high involvement. The Internet offers opportunities to build new dot.com brands and the financial services sector has tried to harness this method as part of a multichannel distribution policy. What appears to be overridingly important for the development of brands operating with limited resources is the brand name and the merchandising activities, of which packaging, labelling and POP are crucial. In addition, as differentiation between brands becomes more difficult in terms of content and distinct symbolism, the nature of the service encounter is now recognised to have considerable impact on brand association. The development of loyalty schemes and carelines for FMCG, durable and service-based brands is a testimony to the importance of developing and maintaining positive brand associations.

Viewpoint 6.2	Sula Vineyards do it below-the-line

Beer is currently India's preferred alcoholic drink but the rapid growth of the wine industry is threatening to challenge beer's overall supremacy. Sula Vineyards are a typical new winery seeking to establish their brand in the emerging market. Faced with a market where taxes are extremely heavy (except on beer), new entrants need to find a strong point of differentiation.

However, there is one big problem that faces all producers of alcohol, namely that advertising of alcohol is not allowed. Some major global brands are able to create brand awareness using television and outdoor media to promote their names using their other brands such as Kingfisher mineral water and Smirnoff CDs.

The marketing communications used to support brands such as Sula Vineyards therefore need to be below-the-line and closely oriented to help consumers learn and experience their brands. Sula Vineyards use sales promotion (sampling and tastings), experiential marketing (winery tours), public relations (media relations and lobbying) and word-of-mouth recommendation. Sampling is important, especially within the trade. Once restaurant, hotel and bar staff and distributors appreciate the quality of their brand they are in a better position to recommend the brand. Lobbying helps raise the profile of the brand but is also undertaken to get the rules relating to alcohol relaxed and available through supermarkets and accessible to more women, who currently prefer not to frequent traditional liquor shops.

Source: Based on Durston (2008)

Question

Does the ban on advertising alcohol prevent consumers from having full knowledge of brand availability?

Task

How might Sula name their brands to assist brand identification?

The below-the-line route needs to achieve a transfer of image. Apart from the clarity of the brand name, which needs to describe the product functions, it is the packaging and associated labelling that shapes the way a brand is perceived.

Brand building: around-the-line

Although not an entirely contemporary strategy, a further approach involves the development of brands without the use of formal communication tools or conventional media. The key to success is to seed the brand through word-of-mouth communication. Two of the most notable examples are Google and Hotmail. Both are global brands and both have been developed without any advertising, sales promotion or direct marketing. They have used some public relations but their market dominance has been developed through word-of-mouth communication (often viral) and experience through usage strategies.

Digital communications, in particular social networks, email, viral marketing, blogging and in some cases Twitter, have enabled people to pass on news and views about brands. When opinion leaders and formers are targeted with relevant and interesting brand-related material they pass on information and views, usually with an exponential impact. Brand-based conversations among consumers enables the development of brand associations.

Brand experience has become an important factor in both marketing practice and the marketing literature. These experiences are considered to be the 'internal responses (sensations, feelings and thoughts) and behavioural responses evoked by brand-related stimuli that are part of a brand's design and identity, packaging, communications and environments' (Brakus *et al.*, 2009: 53).

Consumers experience brands in a number of ways, but perhaps the most common experiences occur at one of three distinct points. According to Arnould *et al.* (2002), cited by Brakus *et al.* (2009), these are when searching for brands, when they buy brands and when they consume them. Brakus *et al.* (2009) go on to demonstrate that brand experiences consist of four dimensions, all of which vary according to brand type and category. These are sensory, affective, intellectual and behavioural. Therefore, the sound management of these elements and dimensions can have a positive impact on developing the right brand associations.

Viewpoint 6.3   Around the line with books and domes

Waterstone's, the high street book retailer, embarked on a social media and brand experiences campaign, seeking to drive website traffic and boost the Waterstone's brand name. Activities undertaken include use of Twitter to promote Ant and Dec's book, a Flickr activity to find an unpublished illustrator to work with a best-selling book author and several blogger promotions.

Consider the role of The O_2. Once the Millennium Dome was scorned by the population, but O_2 have transformed the structure into a major music venue and branded entertainment experience. The O_2 offers opportunities for brand extensions and added value opportunities for O_2 customer visitors over non-O_2 ones. For example, the Priority Ticket Offer enables O_2 customers to book tickets 48 hours before others. Over 1 million O_2 customers have signed up and over 180,000 priority sales have been made.

Source: Based on Woods (2009); Anon (2009)

Question

Why do you think Waterstone's and O_2 avoided using advertising in their campaigns?

Task

Identify three other brands who have used the around-the-line approach, and write brief notes explaining why they have been successful.

In addition to these three forms of brand development, there are several additional mechanisms through which brand associations can be developed. These include: co-branding, geographical identifiers, the use of ingredient brands, support services and award symbols.

Marketing communications is the means through which products can evolve into brands. People make associations immediately they become aware of a brand name. It is the brand manager's task to ensure that the associations made are appropriate and provide a means of differentiation. By communicating the key strengths and differences of a brand, by explaining how a brand enables a customer to create value for themselves, and by reinforcing and providing consistency in the messages transmitted, a level of integration can be brought to the way a brand is perceived by the target market.

Finally in this section, the importance of branding as a part of integrated marketing communications should not be forgotten, and to do this internal brand education is crucial. The way a brand relates internally to departments and individuals and the way the brand is articulated by senior management are important parts of brand education. Brands are not just external elements – they should form part of the way in which an organisation operates, part of its cultural configuration.

Marketing communication budgets

The role of the marketing communications budget is the same whether the organisation is a multinational, trading from numerous international locations, or a small manufacturing unit on an industrial estate outside a semi-rural community. Both organisations want to ensure that they achieve the greatest efficiency with each pound/dollar/euro they allocate to communication activities. Neither can afford to be profligate with scarce resources, and each is accountable to the owners of the organisation for the decisions it makes.

There are three general levels of decision-making with regard to financial investment in brands. The first concerns how much of the organisation's available financial resources (or relevant part) should be allocated to the company's brand communications over the next period. This is sometimes referred to as the appropriation. The second concerns how much of the total amount should be allocated to each of the individual brands, whilst the third refers to the investment between the tools and media designated to support each brand.

There are four main stakeholder groups that contribute to budgetary decisions. These are the focus organisation, any communication agencies, the media owners and agents whose resources will be used to carry the designated messages and the target audience. It is the ability of these four main stakeholders to collaborate effectively that will impact most upon the communications budget. However, determining the 'appropriate appropriation' is a frustrating exercise for the marketing communications manager. The allocation of scarce resources across a communications budget presents financial and political difficulties, especially where the returns are difficult to identify. The development and significance of technology within marketing can lead to disputes concerning ownership and the control of resources. For example, in many companies management and responsibility for the website rests with the IT department, which understandably take a technological view of issues. Those in marketing, however, see the use of the website from a marketing perspective and need a budget to manage it. Tension between the two can result in different types of website design and effectiveness, and this leads to different levels of customer perception and support.

Readers may have noticed that the terms spend and investment have been used alternatively in this chapter. Conventional terminology refers to adspend, but the word *spend* suggests that communication represents a cost and as such is reflected on the profit and loss account. Increasingly communication is understood to represent an investment and as such should be capable of measurement in terms of the return that the investment generates on the balance sheet.

An interesting observation concerns the way in which the communication mix has been changing over the past 10–15 years. For a long time investment in media advertising dominated the communication budget of most consumer brands. Investment in sponsorship grew consistently but has fallen back considerably during recession. As if to mirror this activity, investment in sales promotion generally picks up during periods of economic hardship as customers choose their purchases more selectively and look for bargains.

However, the mix of these tools has changed over the past few years and now direct marketing and online activities are attracting increasing levels of investment. There are two key drivers for this shift. The first is the increasing attention and accountability that management is attaching to their communication investment/spend. Increasingly, marketing managers are being asked to justify the amounts they spend on their entire budgets, including advertising and sales promotion. Senior managers want to know the return they are getting for their communication investments, in order that they meet their objectives and that scarce resources can be used more effectively in the future. The second reason concerns the emergence of digital technologies and applications which are transforming the marketing communications landscape. For many consumers the web is becoming a hub and their main interface with brands. As a result increasing proportions of budgets are being switched from offline communications, and predominantly advertising, to online advertising and other digital applications.

It is not uncommon in recessionary conditions to find companies slashing their ad investment, if only on a temporary basis, in anticipation of difficult trading conditions. There is an argument that this is not necessarily the correct course of action and that companies that maintain their investment levels do better than those who cut, when conditions improve (Dyson, 2008). For example, both Marks & Spencer and Sainsbury's have experienced difficulties but have either increased or maintained their above-the-line spend. Research by Profit Impact on Market Strategy (PIMS) (Tylee, 1999; Tomkins, 1999) found that companies that maintain or even increase their adspend during a recession are likely to grow three times faster than those companies that cut the adspend when the economy turns round. Dyson reports that PIMS reinforced their view following further research in 2002.

Techniques and approaches

Marginal analysis is the main theoretical approach to setting optimal budgets. This determines the point at which maximum returns are achieved based on an extra unit of investment in promotional activities. The main problem with this approach is that it has little practical application because the data to run the analysis is either non-existent in many organisations or insufficient to withstand the analysis. It is not surprising, therefore, that other more practical approaches have been developed. These are set out in Table 6.3.

Competitive parity

In certain markets, such as the relatively stable fast-moving consumer goods (FMCG) market, many organisations use budgets as a competitive tool. The underlying assumption is that advertising is the only direct variable that influences sales. The argument is based on the point that while there are many factors that impact on sales, these factors are all self-cancelling. Each factor impacts upon all the players in the market. The only effective factor is the amount that is invested in planned communications. As a result, some organisations deliberately spend the same amount on advertising as their competitors spend: competitive parity.

Competitive parity has a major benefit for the participants. As each organisation knows what the others are spending and while there is no attempt to destabilise the market through excessive or minimal promotional spend, the market avoids self-generated turbulence and hostile competitive activity.

There are, however, a number of disadvantages with this simple technique. The first is that, while information is available, there is a problem of comparing like with like. For example, a carpet manufacturer selling a greater proportion of output into the trade will require different levels and styles of advertising and promotion from another manufacturer selling predominantly to the retail market. Furthermore, the first organisation may be diversified, perhaps importing floor tiles. The second may be operating in a totally unrelated market. Such activities make comparisons difficult to establish, and financial decisions based on such analyses are highly dubious.

Table 6.3	Practical approaches to setting promotional budgets

Budgeting approach	Explanation
Arbitrary	This simple method is based on what the boss says or guesses to be the right figure. In practice this is implemented through a succession of decisions as demands for communication resources arrive. There is no reference to strategy.
Inertia	Through this approach, and rather than guess, decisions are based on 'let's keep it the same' as last time. Here all elements of the environment and the costs associated with the tasks facing the organisation are ignored.
Media multiplier	This approach is based on maintaining the same media impact as in the previous year yet recognising the need to increase spend by the rate at which media costs have increased.
Percentage of sales	A popular approach is to set the budget at a level equal to some predetermined percentage of past or expected sales. However, no consideration is given to the sales potential that may exist, so this technique may actually limit performance.
Affordable	This approach is still regarded by many organisations as sophisticated and relatively free of risk. It requires a cost calculation, so that after making an allowance for profit, what is left is to be spent on communications. In other words, what is left is what we can afford to spend.

The competitive parity approach fails to consider the qualitative aspects of the advertising undertaken by the different players. Each attempts to differentiate itself, and very often the promotional messages are one of the more important means of successfully positioning an organisation. It would not be surprising, therefore, to note that there is probably a great range in the quality of the planned communications. Associated with this is the notion that, when attempting to adopt different positions, the tasks and costs will be different and so seeking relative competitive parity may be an inefficient use of resources.

The final point concerns the data used in such a strategy. The data are historical and based on strategies relevant at the time. Competitors may well have embarked upon a new strategy since the data were released. This means that parity would not only be inappropriate for all the reasons previously listed, but also because the strategies are incompatible.

Advertising-to-sales ratio

An interesting extension of the competitive parity principle is the notion of advertising-to-sales (A/S) ratios. Instead of simply seeking to spend a relatively similar amount on promotion as one's main competitors, this approach attempts to account for the market shares held by the different players and to adjust promotional investment accordingly.

If it is accepted that there is a direct relationship between the volume of advertising (referred to as weight) and sales, then it is not unreasonable to conclude that if an organisation invests more on advertising then it will see a proportionate improvement in sales. The underlying principle of the A/S ratio is that, in each industry, it is possible to determine the average advertising spend of all the players and compare it with the value of the market. Therefore, it is possible for each organisation to determine its own A/S ratio and compare it with the industry average. Those organisations with an A/S ratio below the average may conclude either that they have advertising economies of scale working in their favour or that their advertising is working much harder, pound for pound, than some of their competitors. Organisations can also use A/S ratios as a means of controlling expenditure across multiple product areas. Budgets can be set based upon the industry benchmark, and variances quickly spotted and further information requested to determine shifts in competitor spend levels or reasons leading to any atypical performance.

Each business sector has its own characteristics, which in turn influence the size of the advertising expenditure. In 2007 the A/S ratio for cold remedies was 10.71 per cent, baby foods, 10.08 per cent, packet soup 2.54 per cent, facial skincare 15.54 per cent, household smoke alarms, 0.19 per cent and hair loss/scalp treatment, 39.70 per cent (Advertising Association, 2009). It can be seen that the size of the A/S ratio can vary widely. It appears to be higher (that is, a greater proportion of revenue is used to invest in advertising) when the following are present:

- The offering is standardised, not customised.
- There are many end-users.
- The financial risk for the end-user customer is small.
- The marketing channels are short.
- A premium price is charged.
- There is a high gross margin.
- The industry is characterised by surplus capacity.
- Competition is characterised by a high number of new product launches.

A/S ratios provide a useful benchmark for organisations when they are trying to determine the adspend level. These ratios do not set out what the promotional budget should be, but they do provide a valuable indicator around which broad commercial decisions can be developed.

Share of voice

Brand strategy in the FMCG market has traditionally been based upon an approach which uses mass media advertising to drive brand awareness, which in turn allows premium pricing to fund the advertising investment (cost). The alternative approach has been to use price-based promotions to drive market share. The latter approach has often been regarded as a short-term approach which is incapable of sustaining a brand over the longer term.

The concept underlying the A/S ratio can be seen in the context of rival supporters chanting at a football match. If they chant at the same time, at the same decibel rating, then it is difficult to distinguish the two sets of supporters, particularly if they are chanting the same song. Should one set of supporters shout at a lower decibel rating, then the collective voice of the other supporters would be the one that the rest of the crowd, and perhaps any television audience, actually hears and distinguishes.

This principle applies to the concept of share of voice (SOV). Within any market the total of all advertising investments, that is all the advertising by all of the players, can be analysed in the context of the proportions each player has made to the total. Should one advertiser invest more than any other then it will be its messages that are received and stand a better chance of being heard and acted upon. In other words, its SOV is the greater. This implies, of course, that the quality of the message transmitted is not important and that it is the sheer relative weight of ad-investment that is the critical factor.

This concept can be taken further and combined with another, share of market (SOM). When a brand's market share is equal to its share of advertising spend, equilibrium is said to have been reached (SOV = SOM).

Viewpoint 6.4	Gauging the right level of spend

Tiger Beer increased its UK spend up in 2008 from £85,000 to £5.5 million. This was partly because the owner wants to develop the brand away from its Asian origins.

Back in 1987 Nike's marketing president was pitching to the board for a revised advertising budget. The previous year Nike had spent $8 million, and the marketing chief wanted to raise this to $34 million, an astronomical increase, particularly for a company that was just getting going. The CEO, Philip Knight, turned to the marketing man and asked the question: 'How do I know if you are asking for enough?'

One of the (many) problems associated with digital media is that there has been very little activity on which to build knowledge about how to optimise its use.

Brand Gauge is a proprietary tool developed to assist both budgeting and media planning. Incorporating the goals of particular campaigns, this system stores online competitive data regarding particular expenditure on ads and market share across different categories. This enables it to generate share-of-voice and share-of-market calculations.

These data are filtered through reach and effective frequency figures and compute the size of market covered, awareness levels and from this is delivered a figure that is equated to a 'positive brand reaction' score or PBR. The PBR is related to a campaign's objectives and therefore provides a measure of the value a campaign has delivered, whether this be a shift in brand perception, awareness or behaviour.

Of the many benefits of this approach one of the key ones is that wastage is reduced as the system advises when exposure is optimised and budget well spent.

Source: Based on Holmes (2004); Charles (2008); Longhurst (2006)

Question

Why did Tiger Beer settle at a £5.5 million investment? Why not £7 million or £3 million?

Task

Which brand invested the most in advertising last year and were they successful?

West and Prendergast (2009) researched the various levels of sophistication used by organisations to set their advertising and promotions budgets. They found that on average organisations use two methods to determine their communications budgets. Of these, judgemental methods such as 'the affordable' and 'arbitrary' plus the 'objective and task' methods account for over 50 per cent of the methods used. What they also found was that the prevailing organisational culture, as manifest through the 'personalities, organisation, timing, planning; and the nature of the market and access to data' (2009: 1471) underpinned the responses of those interviewed. In other words, culture shapes the nature of risk taking and the size and shape of the budgets, the frame in which financial decisions are made.

The value of brand communications

The ideas and principles associated with the SOV concept provide a foundation upon which to consider the value of marketing communications as an aid to brand development. The importance of brands cannot be understated. Indeed, many organisations have attempted (and succeeded) in valuing the worth of their brands and have had them listed as an asset on their balance sheets. While this has stimulated the accountancy profession into some debate, the concept of a brand's worth to an organisation cannot be refuted. Among other things, when companies buy other companies or brands, they are purchasing the potential income streams that these target brands offer, not just the physical assets of plant, capital and machinery. However, communications are a vital element used to develop these assets and so it is organisationally important to understand the relationship between the required level of investment in communications and the asset value that results from this activity.

Butterfield (1999) argued that marketers are required to account for their activities in terms of the contribution they make to the financial performance of an organisation. This means that markets and customers will be viewed as assets, which in turn will become subject to development, cultivation and leverage. Marketers will also be required to use different measures of performance. Market share, margin and revenues will give way to terms such as return on investment, net present value of future cash flows or just shareholder value. He commented that it will not be just a question of how much your adspend is, but how much you spend relative to your main competitors' market share. Although some of his views have yet to become reality there are signs that this longer-term, strategic value-oriented approach is beginning to become part of the overall marketing communications vocabulary, if not yet part of everyday practice. Ideas concerning shareholder value as a means of developing marketing strategy have become quite common and articulated by an increasing number of authors (Doyle, 2000) since Butterfield first speculated about future techniques.

Although there are exceptional cases, it is generally accepted that stronger brands are more likely to maintain market share in the following year than weaker brands. This means that the revenue streams from stronger brands are more secure and attract lower risk than weaker brands. Farr (2004: 30) refers to the use of brand-related communications as media pressure. He defines media pressure 'as the brand's share of communications spending minus its prior-year market share'. A brand's strength is in (major) part due to the accumulated investments and activities in the past. It follows therefore that these investments in communications should be continued rather than truncated.

Evaluation

All organisations review and evaluate the performance of their various activities. Many undertake formal mechanisms, while others review in an informal, ad hoc manner, but the process of evaluation or reflection is a well-established management process. The objective is to monitor the often diverse activities of the organisation so that management can exercise control. It is through the process of review and evaluation that an organisation has the opportunity to learn and develop. In turn, this enables management to refine its competitive position and to provide for higher levels of customer satisfaction.

The evaluation of planned marketing communications consists of two distinct elements. The first element is concerned with the development and testing of individual messages and the tools used to deliver them. For example, a particular sales promotion (such as a sample pack) has individual characteristics that may or may not meet the objectives of a sales promotion event. An advertising message has to achieve, among other things, a balance of emotion and information in order that the communication objectives and message strategy be achieved. To accomplish this, testing is required to ensure that the intended messages are encoded correctly and are capable of being decoded accurately by the target audience and the intended meaning is ascribed to the message.

The second element concerns the overall impact and effect that a campaign has on a target audience once a communications plan has been released. This post-test factor is critical, as it will either confirm or reject management's judgement about the viability of its communications strategy. The way in which the individual components of the communications mix work together needs to be understood so that strengths can be capitalised on and developed and weaknesses negated.

This final part of the chapter considers the second element, issues related to campaign evaluation. Readers interested in the techniques and methods used to evaluate the performance of individual tools are referred to Fill (2009).

The role of evaluation in planned communications

The evaluation process is a key part of marketing communications. The findings and results of the evaluative process feed back into the next campaign and provide indicators and benchmarks for further management decisions. The primary role of evaluating the performance of a communications strategy is to ensure that the communications objectives have been met and that the strategy has been effective. The secondary role is to ensure that the strategy has been executed efficiently, that the full potential of the individual promotional tools has been extracted and that resources have been used economically.

Research activity is undertaken for two main reasons. The first is guidance and development and the second is prediction and evaluation (Staverley, 1993). Guidance takes the form of shaping future strategies as a result of past experiences. Development is important in the context of determining whether the communications worked as they were intended to.

The prevalence and acceptance of the integrated marketing communications concept suggests that its measurement should be a central aspect when evaluating marketing communications activities. One of the predominant issues surrounding the development of IMC is the difficulty and lack of empirical evidence concerning the measurement of this concept. In an attempt to resolve this Lee and Park (2007) provide one of the first multidimensional-scaled measures of IMC. Their model is based on four key dimensions drawn from the literature. These are set out in Table 6.4.

Each of these dimensions are regarded as separate yet integral elements of IMC. Lee and Park developed an 18-item scale to measure these dimensions. The use of this approach may advance our understanding of IMC and provide a substantial basis on which IMC activities can be measured. It is interesting to note that Lee and Park see IMC as a customer only communication activity and choose to exclude other critical stakeholders from their measurement model.

However, the measurement of a campaign's success is critical and various techniques and methodologies have been proposed. These are invariably method oriented and relate to the impact of advertising rather than the influence of all the tools and media used. Therefore, the only reasonable measure is to consider the extent to which the campaign objectives have been satisfied, within the time frame originally specified, and in the light of the final amount of financial resources invested. This of course emphasises the importance of setting SMART based objectives at the outset.

Table 6.4	Four dimensions of IMC
Dimension of IMC	**Explanation**
Unified communications for consistent messages and images	Activities designed to create a clear, single position, in the target market, delivering a consistent message through multiple channels.
Differentiated communications to multiple customer groups	The need to create different marketing communications campaigns (and positions) targeted at different groups (in the target market) who are at different stages of the buying process. Sequential communication models based on the hierarchy of effects or attitude construct apply.
Database-centred communications	This dimension emphasises the need to generate behavioural responses through direct marketing activities created through information collected and stored in databases.
Relationship fostering communications for existing customers	The importance of retaining customers and developing long-term relationships is a critical element of marketing communications.

Source: Lee and Park (2007). Used with permission of the World Advertising Research Center

Campaign measurement has for a long time attracted minimal interest and resources from organisations. Before the recession there were signs that this was beginning to change. Sales, a market indicator continues to be the primary measure of effectiveness. Ideally a combination of market factors (e.g. market share, return on investment and sales volume) and communication factors (e.g. awareness, attitude, preference), should be considered.

Other tests

In addition to the measurement by objectives route, there is a range of other measures that have been developed in an attempt to understand the effect of campaigns. Among these are tracking studies and financial analyses.

Tracking studies

A tracking study involves interviewing a large number of people on a regular basis, weekly or monthly, with the purpose of collecting data about buyers' perceptions of marketing communication messages, not just advertisements and how these messages might be affecting buyers' perceptions of the brand. By measuring and evaluating the impact of a campaign when it is running, adjustments can be made quickly. The most common elements that are monitored, or tracked, are the awareness levels of an advertisement and the brand, image ratings of the brand and the focus organisation, and attributes and preferences.

Tracking studies can be undertaken on a periodic or continuous basis. The latter is more expensive, but the information generated is more complete and absorbs the effect of competitor's actions, even if the effects are difficult to disaggregate. Sherwood *et al.* (1989) report that in a general sense, continuous tracking appears more appropriate for new products, and periodic tracking more appropriate for established products.

Financial analysis

The vast amount of resources that are directed at planned communications, and in particular advertising, requires that the organisation reviews, on a periodic basis, the amount and the manner in which its financial resources have been used. For some organisations the media spend alone constitutes one of the major items of expenditure. For example, many grocery products incur ingredient, packaging and distribution plus media as the primary costing elements to be managed.

Variance analysis enables a continuous picture of the investment to be developed and acts as an early warning system should unexpected levels of expenditure be incurred. In addition to this and other standard financial controls, the size of the discount obtained from media buying is becoming an important and vital part of the evaluation process.

Increasing levels of accountability and rapidly rising media costs have contributed to the development of centralised media buying. Under this arrangement, the promotion of an organisation's entire portfolio of brands, across all divisions, is contracted to a single media-buying organisation. Part of the reasoning is that the larger the account the greater the buying power an agency has, and this in turn should lead to greater discounts and value of advertising spend.

The point is that advertising economies of scale can be obtained by those organisations that spend a large amount of their resources on the media. To accommodate this, centralised buying has developed, which in turn creates higher entry and exit barriers, not only to and from the market but also from individual agencies.

Measuring the fulfilment of brand promises

Brands are promises and these are communicated in one of two main ways. One is to make loud claims about the brand's attributes and the benefits these deliver to customers. This approach tends to rely on advertising and the strength of the brand to deliver the promise. The alternative is not to shout but whisper and then surprise customers by exceeding their expectations when they experience the brand. This is an under-promise/over-deliver strategy; one which reduces risk and places a far greater emphasis on word of mouth communication, and brand advocacy. This in turn can reduce an organisation's investment in advertising and lead to a redirection of communication effort and resources in order to improve the customer experience.

It follows therefore that there are measurable gaps between the image and perceptions customers have of brands and their actual experiences. Where expectations are exceeded the promise gap is said to be positive. Where customers feel disappointed through experience of a brand, a negative promise gap can be identified. These gaps are reflected in the financial performance of brands.

The Promise Index, reported by Simms (2007), found that although 66 per cent of the brands surveyed had positive promise gaps, only 15 per cent had gaps that impacted significantly on business performance. Other research, by Weber Shandwick, found that the main factor for creating brand advocacy was the ability to 'surprise and delight customers'. This survey of 4,000 European consumers, reported by Simms, found that brand advocacy is five times more likely to prompt purchase than advertising.

A related metric, the Net Promoter Score (NPS), seeks to identify how likely an individual is to recommend a brand. Again, a key outcome is that brand growth is driven principally by surprising and delighting customers.

On the basis that brand advocacy is of major importance, two key marketing communication issues emerge. The first concerns how the marketing communications mix should be reformulated in order to encourage brand advocacy. It appears that advertising and mass media has an important role to play in engaging audiences to create awareness and interest. However, more emphasis needs to be given to the other tools and media in order to enhance each customer's experience of a brand beyond their expectations.

The second issue concerns identifying and communicating with passive rather than active advocates. Encouraging customers to talk about a brand means developing content which gives passive advocates a reason to talk about a brand. This means that the message component of the mix needs to be designed away from product attributes and towards stories and memorable events that can be passed on through all customer contact points. This in turn points to a greater use of public relations, viral and the use of user generated content, networks and communities, and the use of staff in creating brand experiences.

Viewpoint 6.5   Measuring gorillas

For Cadbury the news had not been very good in 2006 and the first part of 2007. A salmonella scare in 2006 had resulted in more than one million bars of chocolate (including Dairy Milk) being removed from shelves accompanied by considerable negative media comment. In February 2007 Cadbury spent £10 million launching the US chewing-gum Trident but then became enmeshed in controversy as the Advertising Standards Authority reprimanded the company for an ad featuring an Afro-Caribbean poet which was perceived to be racially offensive. This was followed by the news that Cadbury Schweppes was having to shed staff in a £300 million cost cutting exercise.

In the autumn however it launched an ad that propelled its reputation in the opposite direction. The ad featured a man in a gorilla suit playing the drums to the Phil Collins hit 'In the Air Tonight'.

The ad caught the public's imagination, if only because there is no reason for a gorilla to play the drums, there is no connection between Cadbury's and a gorilla (at the time) and the ad says nothing about Dairy Milk apart from a shot of the brand name at the end. The ad was relatively inexpensive to produce and was released through a spoof real film production company, A Glass and a Half Full Productions.

The ad featured in a pre-ad teaser campaign in TV listings that resembled a film. The Glass and a Half Full Productions website helped to sustain dialogue with fans while 90-second spots during the Rugby World Cup and Big Brother Finals delivered the ad to huge audiences.

The ad was not part of an integrated campaign and the support might have been stronger. However, it was a one-off masterpiece of creativity that resonated with the nation. Sales rose 7 per cent by the end of October 2007 in value terms, and weekly sales were up 9 per cent year on year during the period 'gorilla' was on air. The ad generated the highest recognition scores ever recorded by Hall & Partners.

Source: Based on various including Campaign (2007)

Question

How should the 'Gorilla' ad be evaluated, and how would you measure its success?

Task

Gorillas featured in other ways for some other brands. Find two other campaigns that featured gorillas.

Exhibit 6.2   The Cadbury gorilla in action
Image courtesy of The Advertising Archives

Brand equity

This chapter has considered the role of marketing communications in brand development, issues concerning budgeting and financial resources to support these brands and concluded by considering ways of evaluating the outcomes of these brand investments. It seems appropriate that the chapter concludes by examining the overall impact of these activities and this is accomplished through brand equity.

The concept of brand equity has arisen from the increasing recognition that brands represent a value to both organisations and shareholders. Brands as assets can impact heavily on the financial well-being of a company. Brand equity is considered important because of the increasing interest in trying to measure the return on promotional investments and pressure by various stakeholders to value brands for balance sheet purposes. A brand with a strong equity is more likely to be able to preserve its customer loyalty and so fend off competitor attacks. Indeed, Pirrie (2006: 40) refers to the evidence that organisations with strong brands 'consistently outperform their markets'.

Brand equity is a measure of the value of a brand. It is an assessment of a brand's wealth and health, sometimes referred to as goodwill. Financially, brands consist of the value of their physical assets plus a sum that represents their reputation or goodwill, with the latter far exceeding the former. So, when Premier Foods, who own Branston sauces and Ambrosia Creamed Rice, paid £1.2 billion to buy Rank Hovis McDougall (RHM), who own Oxo, Hovis, and Mr Kipling cakes, in 2006, they bought the physical assets and the reputation of RHM brands, whose sales at the time amounted to £1.6 billion annually.

According to Ehrenberg (1993), market share is the only appropriate measure of a brand's equity or value and, as a result, all other measures taken individually are of less significance, and collectively they come together as market share. However, this view excludes the composition of brands, the values that consumers place in them and the financial opportunities that arise with brand development and strength.

Lasser *et al.* (1995) identify two main perspectives of brand equity, namely a financial and a marketing standpoint. The financial view is based on a consideration of a brand's value as a definable asset, based on the net present values of discounted future cash flows (Farquahar, 1989). The marketing perspective is grounded in the beliefs, images and core associations consumers have about particular brands. Richards (1997) argues that there are both behavioural and attitudinal elements associated with brands and recognises that these vary between groups and represent fresh segmentation and targeting opportunities. A further component of the marketing view is the degree of loyalty or retention a brand is able to sustain. Measures of market penetration, involvement, attitudes and purchase intervals (frequency) are typical. Feldwick (1996) used a three-part definition to bring these two approaches together. He suggests brand equity is a composite of:

- *brand value*, based on a financial and accounting base;
- *brand strength*, measuring the strength of a consumer's attachment to a brand;
- *brand description*, represented by the specific attitudes customers have towards a brand.

In addition to these, Cooper and Simmons (1997) offer *brand future* as a further dimension. This is a reflection of a brand's ability to grow and remain unhindered by environmental challenges such as changing retail patterns, alterations in consumer buying methods and developments in technological and regulative fields. As if to reduce the increasing complexity of these measures Pirrie (2006) argues that brand value needs to be based on the relationship between customer and brand owner and this has to be grounded in the value experienced by the customer, which is subsequently reflected on the company. For consumers the brand value is about 'reduction'; reducing search time and costs, reducing perceived quality assurance risks, and making brand associations by reducing social and ego risks (see Chapter 3 for more information about perceived risks). For brand owners, the benefits are concerned with 'enablement'. Pirrie refers to enabling brand extensions, premium pricing and loyalty.

Attempts to measure brand equity have to date been varied and have lacked a high level of consensus, although the spirit and ideals behind the concept are virtually the same. Table 6.5 sets out some of the approaches adopted. As a means of synthesising these approaches the following are considered the principal dimensions through which brand equity should be measured:

Table 6.5	Five approaches to measuring brand equity

Source	Factors measured
David Aaker	Awareness, brand associations, perceived quality and market leadership, loyalty, market performance measures.
BrandDynamics, BrandZ (Millward Brown)	Presence, relevance to consumer needs, product performance, competitive advantage, bonding.
Brand asset valuator (Young and Rubicam)	Strength (differentiation and relevance), stature (esteem and knowledge).
Interbrand Global Top 100 (Omnicom)	Intangible future earnings, the role of the brand, brand strength.

Sources: Adapted from Cooper and Simmons (1997); Haigh (1997); Pirrie (2006); http://www.brandassetvaluator.com.au/, www.millwardbrown.com/Sites/; http://www.interbrand.com/best_brands_2006_FAQ.asp

- *brand dominance*: a measure of its market strength and financial performance;
- *brand associations*: a measure of the beliefs held by buyers about what the brand represents;
- *brand prospects*: a measure of its capacity to grow and extend into new areas.

From the BrandZ Top 100 model, Farr (2006) determined that the top brands are characterised by four factors. They are all strong in terms of innovation, great customer experience, clear values and strong sector leadership.

Developing brand equity is a strategy-related issue and whether a financial, marketing or twin approach is adopted, the measurement activity can help focus management activity on brand development. However, there is little agreement about what is measured and how and when it is measured. Ambler and Vakratsas (1998) argue that organisations should not seek a single set of measures simply because of the varying circumstances and contextual factors that impinge on brand performance. In reality, the measures used by most firms share many common elements.

Summary

In order to help consolidate your understanding of branding, budgets and evaluation, here are the key points summarised against each of the learning objectives.

1 Explore the nature and common characteristics of brands

Branding is a strong means by which a product can be identified, understood and appreciated. Brands are a composite of two main constructs: an identity that managers wish to portray, and secondly, images, construed by audiences, of the identities they perceive.

Brands consist of two main types of attributes: intrinsic and extrinsic. Intrinsic attributes refer to the functional characteristics of the product such as its shape, performance and physical capacity. If any of these intrinsic attributes were changed, it would directly alter the product. Extrinsic attributes refer to those elements that are not intrinsic and if changed do not alter the material functioning and performance of the product itself: devices such as the brand name, marketing communications, packaging, price and mechanisms which enable consumers to form associations that give meaning to the brand.

2 Understand the different ways in which marketing communications can be used to build and support brands

Marketing communications has an important role to play in brand development and maintenance. To help customers make associations with brands either a rational, information-based approach might be adopted or alternatively a more emotional relationship might be forged, one based more on imagery and feelings.

Brands can be developed through one of three forms of marketing communications. The first concerns the use of above-the-line (advertising) techniques, the second involves below-the-line approaches to promote functional associations through the brand name. The third approach concerns around-the-line approaches which involve word-of-mouth communications and brand experience.

3 Explain the role of the communication budget and clarify the benefits of using budgets for communication activities

The role of the communication budget is to ensure that the organisation achieves the greatest efficiency with each euro/dollar/pound/rouble allocated to communication activities. Managers cannot be profligate with scarce resources, and they are accountable to the owners of the organisation for the decisions made. The budgeting process provides for internal coordination and helps ensure that communications support the marketing strategy.

Setting budgets serves to focus people's attention on the costs and benefits of undertaking the communication activities. The act of quantifying the means by which the marketing plan will be communicated to target audiences instils a management discipline necessary to ensure that the objectives of the plan are achievable. The process facilitates cross-function coordination and forces managers to ensure that the planned communications are integrated and mutually supportive. The process provides a means by which campaigns can be monitored, evaluated and management control asserted.

4 Examine various budgeting techniques, both practical and theoretical

Marginal analysis provides a theoretical basis to determine the 'right' budget. However, this approach is impractical so organisations use a variety of practical approaches. These range from guesswork, a percentage of sales, what is affordable, inertia and objective and task. The last is considered to be the most appropriate.

5 Discuss the role of evaluation as part of marketing communications

Evaluation provides a potentially rich source of material for the next campaign and the ongoing communications that all organisations operate, either intentionally or not. The evaluation of planned marketing communications consists of two distinct elements. The first element is concerned with the development and testing the impact of individual tools, media and messages. The second element concerns the overall impact and effect that a campaign has on a target audience once a communications plan has been released.

6 Consider ways in which the effectiveness of marketing communications can be evaluated

Marketing communication campaigns can be best evaluated by considering the degree to which the campaign objectives have been met. These may be market related (share, ROI, volume) or communication related (awareness, consideration, attitude change, behaviour).

Other methods involve tracking the perceptions, attitudes and meanings attributed to campaign buyers, so that adjustments can be made to campaigns. Measuring the level and timing of the financial resources invested in bands is an important factor for many organisations.

7 Explain ideas associated with measuring the fulfilment of brand promises and brand equity

There are measurable gaps between the image and perceptions customers have of brands and their actual experiences. Where expectations are exceeded the promise gap is said to be positive. Where customers feel disappointed through experience of a brand, a negative promise gap can be identified. These gaps are reflected in the financial performance of brands.

Brand equity is a measure of the value of a brand. It is an assessment of a brand's wealth and health, sometimes referred to as goodwill. Financially, brands consist of the value of their physical assets plus a sum that represents their reputation or goodwill, with the latter far exceeding the former.

Review questions

1. Write brief notes explaining what a brand is and list four ways in which brands assist customers and brand owners.

2. Select five consumer brands and evaluate their characteristics.

3. Find examples to explain above, below and around the line approaches to branding.

4. Explain how business-to-business markets might benefit from adopting a branding approach.

5. If the process is difficult and the outcomes imprecise, why should organisations evaluate and monitor their marketing communications?

6. Many organisations fail to undertake suitable research to measure the success of their campaigns. Why is this and what can be done to change this situation?

7. What are the four dimensions used by Lee and Park to evaluate IMC?

8. Explain the Promise Index and the Net Promoter Score.

9. Comment on the view that, if a method of evaluation and testing lacks objectivity and testing, then the method should not be used.

10. Is brand equity a valid concept when measuring brand development?

References

Advertising Association (2009) *The Advertising Statistics Yearbook 2009*. Advertising Association/ Warc.

Alexander, R.S. (1960) *Marketing Definitions: A Glossary of Marketing Terms*. Chicago, IL: American Marketing Association, 8.

Ambler, T. and Vakratsas, D. (1998) Why not let the agency decide the advertising, *Market Leader*, 1 (Spring), 32–37.

Anon (2009) O_2 – Marketing Society Leading-edge category winner, *Marketing*, 10 June, 7.

Arnould, E.J., Price, L.L. and Zinkhan, G.L. (2002) *Consumers*, 2nd edn. New York: McGraw-Hill/Richard D. Irwin.

Assael, H. (1990) *Marketing: Principles and Strategy*. Orlando, FL: Dryden Press.

Barnett, A., Davidson, M. and Dias, S. (2006) The Famous Grouse, *IPA Advertising Effectiveness Paper*. Institute of Practitioners in Advertising. Retrieved 10 December 2007 from www. warc.com/ArticleCenter/Default.asp?CType=A&AID=WORDSEARCH82620&Tab=A

Brakus, J.J., Scmitt, B.H. and Zarantonello, L. (2009) Brand experience: what is it? How is it measured? Does it affect loyalty? *Journal of Marketing*, 73 (May), 52–68.

Brodie, R.J. and de Chernatony, L. (2009) Towards new conceptualizations of branding: theories of the middle range, *Marketing Theory*, 9(1), 95–100.

Butterfield, L. (1999) *Excellence in Advertising: The IPA Guide to Best Practice*. Oxford: Butterworth Heinemann.

Campaign (2007) Cadbury 'gorilla' wins Campaign of the Year, *Campaign*, 13 December. Retrieved 16 January 2008 from http://www.brandrepublic.com/InDepth/Features/773064/Cadbury-gorilla-wins-Campaign-Year/

Charles, G. (2008) Tiger Beer plans UK spending hike to £5.5m, *Marketing*, 19 March, 5.

Cooper, A. and Simmons, P. (1997) Brand equity lifestage: an entrepreneurial revolution. TBWA Simmons Palmer. Unpublished working paper.

de Chernatony, L. (2009) Towards the holy grail of defining 'brand', *Marketing Theory*, 9(1), 101–105.

de Chernatony, L. and Dall'Omo Riley, F. (1998a) Defining a brand: beyond the literature with experts' interpretations, *Journal of Marketing Management*, 14, 417–443.

de Chernatony, L. and Dall'Omo Riley, F. (1998b) Expert practitioners' views on roles of brands: implications for marketing communications, *Journal of Marketing Communications*, 4, 87–100.

de Lencastre, P. and Côrte-Real, A. (2010) One, two, three: A practical brand anatomy, *Brand Management*, 17(6), 399–412.

Doyle, P. (2000) *Value-based Marketing: Marketing Strategies for Corporate Growth and Shareholder Value*. Chichester: Wiley.

Durston, J. (2008) How to turn Indians into wine drinkers: the case of Sula Vineyards, *WARC. com*, (February). Retrieved 16 March 2008 from www.warc.com.

Dyson, P. (2008) Cutting adspend in a recession delays recovery, Warc Exclusive (March). Retrieved 2 June 2010 from www.warc.com/articlecentre.

Ehrenberg, A.S.C. (1974) Repetitive advertising and the consumer, *Journal of Advertising Research*, 14 (April), 25–34.

Ehrenberg, A.S.C. (1993) If you are so strong why aren't you bigger? *Admap* (October), 13–14.

Farquahar, P. (1989) Managing brand equity, *Marketing Research*, 1(9) (September), 24–33.

Farr, A. (2004) Managing advertising as an investment, Admap, 39(7) (July/August), 29–31.

Farr, A. (2006) Soft measure, hard cash, *Admap*, November, 39–42.

Feldwick, P. (1996) What is brand equity anyway, and how do you measure it? *Journal of Market Research*, 38(2), 85–104.

Fill, C. (2009) *Marketing Communications: interactivity, communities and content*. Harlow: Financial Times/Prentice Hall.

Haigh, D. (1997) Brand valuation: the best thing to ever happen to market research, *Admap* (June), 32–35.

Kapferer, J.-N. (2004) *The New Strategic Brand Management*. London: Kogan Page.

Keller, K.L. (2008) *Strategic Brand Management: Building, Measuring and Managing Brand Equity*. NY: Englewood Cliffs, Pearson Education.

Holmes, S. (2004) What happened to 'just do it'? *Independent on Sunday*, 12 September, 8–9.

Lasser, W., Mittal, B. and Sharma, A. (1995) Measuring customer based brand equity, *Journal of Consumer Marketing*, 12(4), 11–19.

Lee, D.H. and Park, C.W. (2007) Conceptualization and Measurement of multidimensionality of integrated marketing communications, *Journal of Advertising Research*, 47(3) (September), 222–236.

Longhurst, P. (2006) Budgeting for online: is it any different? *Admap* (November), 36–37.

Lovell, C. (2008) The Famous Grouse launches new character in TV spot, Campaign. Retrieved 14 April 2009 from www.campaignlive.co.uk/news/868555/Famous-Grouse-launches-new-character-TV-spot/

Pirrie, A. (2006) What value brands? *Admap* (October), 40–42.

Richards, T. (1997) Measuring the true value of brands, *Admap* (March), 32–36.

Riezebos, R. (2003) *Brand Management*. Harlow: FT/Prentice Hall.

Schmitt, B.H. (1999) *Experiential Marketing*. New York: Free Press.

Sherwood, P.K., Stevens, R.E. and Warren, W.E. (1989) Periodic or continuous tracking studies: matching methodology with objectives, *Market Intelligence and Planning*, 7, 11–13.

Simms, J. (2007) Bridging the Gap, *Marketing*, 12 December, 26–28.

Staverley, N.T. (1993) Is it right . . . will it work? *Admap* (May), 23–26.

Tomkins, R. (1999) If the return is right, keep spending, *Financial Times*, 19 March, 8.

Tylee, J. (1999) Survey warns against adspend cuts, *Campaign*, 12 March, 10.

West, D. and Prendergast, G.P. (2009) Advertising and promotions budgeting and the role of risk, *European Journal of Marketing*, 43(11/12), 1457–1476.

Woods, A. (2009) Searching in social circles, *Marketing*, 2 December, 39–41.

Chapter 7
Agencies: practice, regulation and international communications

Communication agencies provide clients with access to the media, research materials, creative teams and the production facilities necessary for them to communicate with a range of audiences. However, there are certain practices, processes and procedures plus regulations that need to be understood in order for a client's message to be implemented, whether in domestic or international markets.

Aims and learning objectives

The aim of this chapter is to introduce the communications industry, the various organisations involved and some of the issues and practices, including international communications, associated with the operation of the industry.

The learning objectives of this chapter are to:

1. provide an introductory understanding of the communications industry, including the nature and role of the main types of organisations;

2. consider the processes associated with selecting an agency;

3. explore the key operations used by clients and agencies in the development of campaigns;

4. examine the methods of remuneration used to reward agencies;

5. review the regulation, including ethical issues, associated with marketing communications;

6. explain the principal ideas and strategies involved with international marketing communications practice.

Introduction

The marketing communications industry consists of four principal actors. These are the media, the clients, the agencies (historically, the most notable of which are advertising agencies) and finally the thousands of support organisations, such as production companies and fulfilment houses, that enable the whole communication process to function. It is the operations and relationships between these organisations that not only drive the industry but also form an important context within which marketing communications can be understood. Figure 7.1 sets out the main actor organisations in the industry.

There is an argument that organisations should manage and develop their marketing communications 'in-house', that is, do it themselves. This could enable better control and lower costs. However, this argument is now very weak due to the increasing complexity and diversity of communication activities and the restructuring of organisations aimed at de-layering and hollowing out their organisations. It can only be through outsourcing that organisations experience increased levels of flexibility and gain access to the special skills and expertise necessary to engage audiences in competitive environments.

One of the many decisions an organisation has to make is whether to employ people on a permanent basis, recruit temporary workers as demand requires or use specialists on a continuous or ad hoc basis. Most organisations use a mixture of these different types and adjust the balance between them according to trading and other environmental factors.

With regard to marketing communications, organisations can do-it-themselves and develop what is called an in-house facility. This provides a good level of control over the tools, messages and media used, and can improve on the speed of decision-making, compared to using an outside agency. On the other hand it increases fixed costs, reduces flexibility and introduces political dimensions, often around budgets, which tend to deflect from objectivity and creativity. Perhaps the most critical dimension concerns the lack of access to expertise. In an age where integration is a popular concept, it is important to have access to experts in the various communication disciplines. It is extremely unlikely that such experts can be readily found in-house. Having said this, many retail and business-to-business organisations choose to use in-house facilities, if only because of a lack of resources.

An alternative route is to use freelancers or self-employed consultants. Although each individual's skills may have been developed within a particular discipline, such as public relations or advertising, freelancers can provide flexibility and access to some experts through their network of personal contacts. However, it should be remembered that the use of freelancers

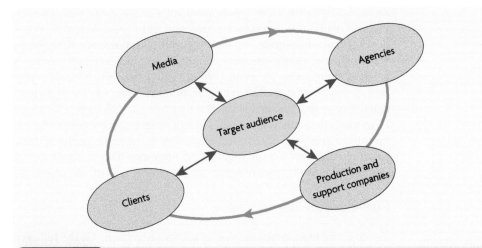

Figure 7.1   Key stakeholders in the marketing communications industry

and in-house facilities requires use of the client organisation's resources, if only to manage the freelancers. Crowdsourcing, the use of the public to generate creative advertising content, is an attempt by clients to circumnavigate the agency sector in order to find new material and cut costs. This form of user generated content is explored in more detail in Chapter 15.

The use of agencies is popular because they can provide objectivity, access to expertise and specialist technologies whilst at the same time allow the client to concentrate on their core business activities. Indeed, this is the route taken by the vast majority of organisations who regard the use of communication agencies in the same way as they do accountants, consultants, lawyers and other professionals. By outsourcing these activities, organisations buy experts whose specialist services can be used as and when required. This flexibility has proved to be both efficient and effective for both client and agency. However, the decision to use an agency leads to further decisions concerning, which type of agency and what do we want them to do, how many agencies should we use and what role should the client play in the relationship with the agency?

These may sound to be strange questions but consider the question of strategy. Should the client decide on the marketing communications, branding and positioning strategies or is this a part of the agency's tasks? Different client organisations will adopt different positions depending upon their experience, size and the nature of the task that needs to be undertaken. Another question concerns whether a single agency is required to deliver integrated marketing communication activities, whether a single agency should manage the integration process and subcontract tasks to other specialist or group-based agencies (and in doing so act as lead agency) or should a series of specialist agencies be appointed, each reporting to the client?

Agency types and structures

The marketing communications industry consists of a number of different types of organisations whose purpose is to enable clients to communicate effectively and efficiently with their target audiences. Essentially, clients appoint agents to develop and implement campaigns on their behalf. To accomplish this advertising agencies buy media time and space from media owners, public relations agencies place stories with the media for their client's representation, and other agencies undertake a range of other communications activities on behalf of their clients.

Originally, advertising agents undertook two main roles, creative message design and media planning and buying. The media component has subsequently been spun off to specialist agencies. However, the interest and drive towards integrated marketing communications has helped agents assume new, more independent roles in the communications industry. The development of digital media has had a profound impact on the public relations industry and the development of integrated marketing communications. For example, agencies that can form teams of specialists who can work across different audiences, yet provide an integrated approach are much sought after by clients (Wilson, 2009). Ideally these teams should consist of 12 members. Too many and ineffectiveness becomes an issue, too few and creativity is sacrificed. The real difficulty that Wilson identifies is how to ensure all 12 are client focused.

In addition to this White (2007) identifies several pressures working on agencies. These are the growth in importance of direct marketing, the increasing range of media and the need among large organisations for quasi-global ad networks. The result of this development is that a number of different types of agencies have emerged, all of which seek to fulfil particular roles.

Full-service agencies

The first and most common type of agency (advertising) is the full-service agency. This type of organisation offers the full range of services that a client requires in order to advertise its products and services. Agencies such as J. Walter Thompson and Leo Burnett offer a full service consisting of strategic planning, research, creative development, production, interactive and media planning and buying. Very often these services are offered on a global basis but this does not mean a full service agency needs to be large, employing thousands of people. Some mid-size agencies employing a couple of dozen people can offer a full service. Whatever the size, some of these activities may be subcontracted, but overall responsibility rests with the full-service agency.

Boutiques

A derivative of this type of agency is the boutique or creative shop, which often forms when creative personnel (teams) leave full service agencies to set up their own business. Boutiques provide specialist or niche services for clients such as copyrighting, developing creative content and other artistic services. These agencies provide clients with an alternative source of ideas, new ways of thinking about a problem, issue or product. Clients choose to use them because they either wish to use particular styles and approaches for their creative work or they want to generate a raft of creative ideas.

Viewpoint 7.1   It's not advertising, it's communication

Many aspects of the marketing communications industry have changed and are continuing to change. Some of these concern the nature and size of agencies with many large dominant groups emerging. For example, four major organisations pitched for Samsung's worldwide branding account; Interpublic (using its Fraftfcb operation), Omnicom (using BBDO agency), WPP (using J. Walter Thompson and Red Cell) and Publicis Groupe (using Leo Burnett and Saatchi & Saatchi).

The fact that WPP won the account is not the point. These organisations evolve as advertising agencies but now they have transformed themselves into 'communication partners'. This reflects the increasing attention given to relationship marketing, the development of integrated marketing communications and the relative decline in the dominance of advertising within the communications mix. Organisations now seek to communicate different messages and this involves using a variety of (neutral) media. The term 'communication agencies' or partners, suggests variety and flexibility and reflects a change in core business.

Apart from structural and name change the industry launched Social Professional in September 2007. This is a social network site designed specifically for all people working in the marketing communications industry. The free-to-use site was developed so that the industry had a facility in which to collaborate, network and communicate in a secure, moderated environment.

Among the main features are forums on a wide range of topics, including advertising, direct marketing, branding, sponsorship, reverse chronological ordering of blogs, an option to create an alter ego to encourage more honest debate and an RSS feed service to help users keep up-to-date with market developments.

Source: Based on Donohue (2007) plus various

Question

Is use of the term 'communication partners' disingenuous when advertising continues to be core business?

Task

Visit the website of one of the big four and determine the spread of their business activities.

Media specialists

Similarly, media specialists provide clients with media services expertise. These organisations deliver media strategy and consulting services for both client advertisers as well as agencies.

Their core business however, is focused on the planning, scheduling, buying and monitoring of a client's media schedule. Child (2007) reports that advertisers believe the role of strategic media planning is 50 per cent more important today than it was seven years ago. The key advantage of using a media specialist is that they have the capacity to buy media time and space at rates far lower than a client or advertising agency can procure them. This is because of the sheer volume of business that media specialists buy. Child also believes that there are some indications that clients believe it is more important to have a global media network rather than a global advertising agency.

Two main forms of media specialist have emerged: media independents, where the organisation is owned and run free of the direction and policy requirements of a full service agency, and media dependents, where the organisation is a subsidiary of a creative or full service organisation. The largest dependent in Britain is ZenithOptimedia, owned originally by Saatchi & Saatchi, and the largest independent is Carat.

Digital media

Digital media agencies have developed as a result of the rapid growth of the digital media industry. The growth has come from two main areas. The first concerns the surge of online brands that hit the market full of expectation of transforming the way business is conducted. The second concerns established offline brands seeking to reach customers by adding interactive capabilities to their marketing channels.

The provision of Internet facilities has been the main area of work, mainly communication and business operations activities. This has been followed by WAP technology activity, Web 2.0 and interactive television.

À la carte

Partly in response to the changing needs of clients and consumers, many organisations require greater flexibility in the way their advertising is managed. Consequently these clients prefer to use the services of a range of organisations. So, the planning skills of a full service agency, the creative talent of a particular boutique and the critical mass of a media-buying independent provide an *à la carte* approach. This approach requires the client advertiser to manage the entire marketing communication process, an 'in-house' arrangement. This process enables improved flexibility yet demands strong management coordination and control as the process is more complex and problematic.

Other communication agencies

The agencies and organisations set out so far have their roots and core business firmly set within the advertising part of the communications industry. In addition to these there is a swathe of other agencies, each specialising in a particular aspect of the marketing communications industry. So, there are agencies that provide sales promotion, public relations, sponsorship, field marketing, events, experiential marketing and direct marketing. Their structure and operations reflect the needs of their market specialism but they are based on the principles through which advertising agencies operate.

Direct marketing agencies

Direct marketing has become a significant and influential part of the marketing communications industry. Direct marketing and direct response agencies create and deliver campaigns through direct mail, telemarketing or through a variety of offline and online media, which is referred to as direct response media.

One of the distinguishing elements of a direct marketing agency is the database. These agencies maintain large databases that contain mailing lists. This data can be merged and reconstructed to reflect a client's target market. The agency helps to develop promotional materials and then implements the campaign through the data list. Direct agencies will either own or have access to a fulfilment house. These organisations fulfil customer orders, that is, process the order and take payment resulting from the direct marketing campaign, send out the ordered products and deal with after sales services as necessary.

Selecting an agency

The process of selecting an agency that is set out below appears to be rational and relatively straightforward. Readers should be aware that the reality is that the process is infused with political and personal issues, some of which can be contradictory. Logically the process commences with a *search*, undertaken to develop a list of potential candidates. This is accomplished by referring to publications such as *Campaign Portfolio* and the *Advertising Agency Roster*, together with personal recommendations. The latter is perhaps the most potent and influential of these sources. As many as 10 agencies could be included at this stage although six or seven are to be expected.

Viewpoint 7.2   Better to pitch the relationship

When Rob Murray was appointed as Marketing Director for Wickes, the building and DIY supplies store, he had to appoint an advertising agency to help bring about the changes he had determined needed to happen. In his previous position at Ryvita he had used the agency MWO who had proved successful for all parties.

Murray appointed MWO to the Wickes account, worth £10 million a year, without a pitch, and just a little bit of support from procurement consultants. Based on the successful relationship and the known operations and processes, Murray felt the strength of the relationship was important and was not something that could be replicated by the many other agencies, all of whom could also produce good ads.

Martin Glenn at Birds Eye Iglo is reported to have appointed Abbot Mead Vickers BBDO with whom he worked when at PepsiCo, while Jim Hytner appointed Walker Media when at Channel 5 and Barclays. Agency–client relationships do matter.

Source: Based on Charles (2008)

Question

Should it be mandatory that all agency appointments be made as a result of a fair and equal pitching process?

Task

Pick two brands of your choice, go to their websites and find out how long their current agency has been with the brand.

Next, the client will visit each of the short-listed candidates in what is referred to as a *credentials presentation*. This is a crucial stage in the process, as it is now that the agency is evaluated for its degree of fit with the client's expectations and requirements. Agencies could develop their websites to fulfil this role, which would save time and costs. The agency's track record, resources, areas of expertise and experience can all be made available on the Internet from which it should be possible to short-list three or possibly four agencies for the next stage in the process: the pitch.

In the PR industry agencies are selected to pitch on the basis of the quality and experience of the agency people, its image and reputation and relationships with existing clients. In addition, Pawinska (2000) reports that the track record of the agency and the extent of its geographical coverage are also regarded as important.

To be able to make a suitable bid the agencies are given a brief and then required to make a formal presentation (the *pitch*) to the client some 6–8 weeks later. This presentation is about how the agency would approach the strategic and creative issues and the account is awarded to whichever produces the most suitable proposal. Suitability is a relative term, and a range of factors need to be considered when selecting an organisation to be responsible for a large part of a brand's visibility. A strategic alliance is being formed and therefore a strong understanding of the strategic objectives of both parties is necessary, as is an appreciation of the structure and culture of the two organisations. The selection process is a bringing together of two organisations whose expectations may be different but whose cooperative behaviour is essential for these expectations to have any chance of materialising. For example, agencies must have access to comprehensive and often commercially confidential data about products and markets if they are to operate efficiently. Otherwise, they cannot provide the service that is expected.

However, it should be noted that pitches are not mandatory, and as Jones (2004) reports, nearly one-third of clients move their accounts without involving pitches. One of the reasons for this is the increasing cost involved in running the whole process, as much as £50,000 according to Jones. Indeed Wethey (2006) questions the whole validity and efficacy of the pitching process. He argues that many pitches are a waste of resources (time and money), that too many agencies devote too much of their resources chasing new business, that pitches do not solve client problems and that the whole process is often unrealistic.

The immediate selection process is finalised when terms and conditions are agreed and the winner is announced to the contestants and made public, often through press releases and the use of trade journals such as *Campaign*, *Marketing* and *Marketing Week*.

This formalised process is now being questioned as to its suitability. The arrival of new media firms and their need to develop communication solutions in one rather than eight weeks has meant that new methods have had to be found. In addition, agencies felt that they were having to invest a great deal in a pitch with little or no reward if the pitch failed. Their response has been to ask for payment to pitch which has not been received well by many clients. The tension that arises is that each agency is required to generate creative ideas over which they have little control once a pitch has been lost.

The pitching process also fails to give much insight into the probable working relationships and is very often led by senior managers who will not be involved in the day-to-day operations.

Agency operations

Most communications agencies are generally organised on a functional basis. There have been moves to develop matrix structures utilising a customer orientation, but this is very inefficient and the low margins prohibit such luxuries. There are departments for planning, creative and media functions coordinated on behalf of the client by an account handler or executive.

The account executive fulfils a very important role in that these people are responsible for the flow of communications between the client and the agency. The quality of the communications between the two main parties can be critical to the success of the overall campaign and to the length of the relationship between the two organisations. Acting at the boundary of the agency's operations, the account executive needs to perform several roles, from internal coordinator and negotiator to presenter (of the agency's work), conflict manager and information gatherer. Very often account executives will experience tension as they seek to achieve their clients' needs while trying to balance the needs of their employer and colleagues. These tensions are similar to those experienced by salespersons and need to be managed in a sensitive manner by management.

Viewpoint 7.3	Google tools assist agencies

Google's strategy is very different to that pursued by others in or related to the media industry. For many, innovation is about closed, payment-based systems. In contrast Facebook and Google follow an open, collaborative systems approach. This means that developers can develop innovative applications using the Google platform, without having to pay for the access to the underpinning technology. This helps ensure that the innovations and applications are compatible and based on a common platform.

In another dimension, communication agencies can benefit from the stream of ideas and applications from Google. Boyd (2010) considers the Google Wonder Wheel, a tool which simplifies and arranges search results, similar to a mind map. Sketchup, a new 3D modelling facility, and Google Insight, a tool that enables keyword research, provides trend data on keyword searches and permits the data to be filtered by location. All of these have high potential usage by agencies. Edge (2010) refers to the range of free tools that can be used to track campaign performance, ad development and testing, using YouTube (which is owned by Google). In the same article Rebelo (2010) refers to the power of the Google tools to assist the creativity process and to move the way agencies operate, forward.

Source: Based on Rebelo (2010); Edge (2010); Boyd (2010)

Question

To what extent do these advancements assist marketing communications?

Task

Find out two other recent innovations by Google and make notes about how they might help agencies do a better job for their clients.

Once an account has been signed, a client brief is prepared that provides information about the client organisation. It sets out the nature of the industry it operates in together with data about trends, market shares, customers, competitors and the problem that the agency is required to address. This is used to inform agency personnel. In particular, the account planner will undertake research to determine market, media and audience characteristics and make proposals to the rest of the account team concerning how the client problem is to be resolved.

Briefing is a process that is common across all client–agency relationships in the communication industry. Regardless of whether working in direct marketing, sales promotion, advertising, public relations, media planning and buying or other specialist area, the brief has a special importance in making the process work and the outcomes significant. However, the importance of preparing a brief of suitable quality has for some been underestimated. With agencies having to brief themselves and some briefs insufficiently detailed, a recent joint industry initiative sought to establish common working practices. The outcome of the process was a briefing template intended to be used by all across the communications agencies in the industry. Eight key headings emerged from the report and these can be seen in Figure 7.2.

In addition to the role of account handler, which might be regarded as one of traffic management, is the role undertaken by account planners (or creative planners). The role of the account planner was the subject of a flurry of debate (Collin, 2003; Grant *et al*., 2003; Zambarino and Goodfellow, 2003). The general conclusion of these papers is that the role of account planner, which has been evolving since the beginning of the 1960s, has changed as the communications industry has fragmented and that a new role is emerging in response to integrated marketing communication and media neutral planning initiatives.

The traditional role of the account planner, which began in full-service agencies, was to understand the client's target consumers and develop strategies for the creative and media departments. As media broke away from full-service agencies so the role of the account planner shifted to the creative aspect of the agency work. Media planners assumed the same type of

Project management – Provide basic project details, e.g. timescales, contacts and people, project numbers

Where are we now? – Describe current brand details, e.g. background, position, competitors, key issues

Where do we want to be? – What needs to be achieved in terms of goals, e.g. sales, market share, ROI, shareholder value, awareness, perception, etc.

What are we doing to get there? – What is the context in terms of the marketing strategy, overall communication strategy and campaign strategy?

Who do we need to talk to? – What is understood about the audiences the communications are intended to influence?

How will we know if we have arrived? – What will be measured, by whom, how and when to determine whether the activity has been successful?

Practicalities – Budgets, timings and schedules, creative and media imperatives

Approvals – Who has the authority to sign off the brief and the agency work?

Figure 7.2	Briefing template

work in media companies although their work focused on planning the right media mix to reach the target audience.

Creative teams comprise a copywriter and an art director, supported by a service team. This team is responsible for translating the proposal into an advertisement. In a full-service agency, a media brief will also be generated, informing the media planning and buying department of the media and the type of media vehicles required. However, the vast majority of media planning work is now undertaken by specialist media agencies, media independents, and these will be briefed by the client, with some support from those responsible for the creatives.

In recent years, partly as a response to the growth of new media, a raft of small entrepreneurial agencies has emerged, to exploit the new opportunities arising from the digital revolution. Many of these are run without the control and structures evident in large, centralised agencies. While dedicated teams might theoretically be the best way to manage a client's project, the reality in many cases is the use of project teams comprising expert individuals working on a number of projects simultaneously. This is not a new phenomenon, but as a result many people are multi-tasking and they assume many roles with new titles. For example, the title *Head of Content* has arisen to reflect the significance of content issues in the new media market. Project managers assume responsibility for the implementation phase and the coordination of all aspects of a client's technological facilities. In addition, there are positions such as head of marketing, mobile (increasing focus on WAP technology), production and technology. The result is no hierarchies, flat structures and flexible working practices and similar expectations.

Agency remuneration

There are three main ways in which agencies are paid. These are *commission*, *fees* and *payment by results* (PBR). These are often supplemented by retainers and bonuses (see Figure 7.3). Very rarely is a single method used within a contract.

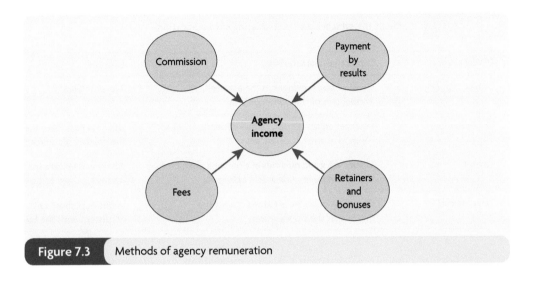

| Figure 7.3 | Methods of agency remuneration |

Traditionally, advertising agencies were paid a commission by media owners for selling space in their publications. A fee of 15 per cent of the value of the media bought emerged as the norm. However, as relationships between agencies and clients strengthened, it seemed only reasonable that the clients should feel that agencies should act for them (and in their best interests), and not for the media owners. A number of questions were raised about whether the agency was actually being rewarded for the work it did and whether it was being objective when recommending media expenditure. As media independents emerged, questions started to be asked about why media agencies received 3 per cent and the creative agency received 12 per cent.

Fees became more popular, and there were some experiments with payment by results. The use of bonuses is widespread but whereas the intention is to reward excellent work, some agencies see bonuses as a means by which fees are reduced and as some clients refuse to pay, the impact on relationships can be far from positive (Child, 2007). Fees have been around for a long time, either in the form of retainers or on a project-by-project basis. Indeed, many agencies charge a fee for services over and above any commission earned from media owners.

For many, payment by results seems a good solution. In 2009 Coca-Cola introduced a new way by which their agencies were to be remunerated. Referred to as a value-based compensation model, Tylee (2010) argues that it extends the PBR model. Agencies are promised profit mark ups of 30 per cent if specific targets are met. If they are not, then only their costs are covered. At the time of writing it is uncertain whether this model will be adopted by other clients. Procter & Gamble have also adopted a similar value based reward programme, and as Williams (2010) indicates, value-based systems can be based on a variety of factors, as long as they are not timesheets based on hours and costs.

However, agencies have no control over the other marketing activities of the client, which might determine the degree of success of the campaign. Indeed, this raises the very thorny question of what 'success' is and how it might be measured. Despite these considerations, it appears that PBR is starting to become an established form of remuneration with over 30 per cent of agency–client contracts containing an element of PBR.

Regulating marketing communications

Just as organisations send messages about their identity through both formal and informal ways, so organisations send messages, partially through marketing communications, about

Table 7.1	Some of the ethical issues in marketing communications	
Ethical theory	**Distinctive characteristic**	**Example**
Duties or principles	Good or bad is evident in the act itself, irrespective of the consequences	'Never tell lies'
Consequences	Whether an act is good or bad depends on what happens as a result of the act	Utilitarianism: 'take the action that results in the greatest good for the greatest number'
Virtues	Virtues are good qualities in a person's character that lie between undesirable extremes	'Study and imitate the behaviours of those who are judged to be good'
Teleological	Goodness or badness judged against the purpose of the organisation	'A business should not do things that are not consistent with the business purpose'

their attitude and stance on ethical issues. As ethical issues are becoming increasingly prominent, so organisations are attempting to become more actively involved in addressing the ethical consequences of their marketing communications (Christy, 2009: 88).[1]

Issues about matters that may be right or wrong are manifest in a wide range of marketing communications activities. The way an organisation attends to its duties and responsibilities, the extent to which it plans and considers the consequences of its actions before acting provides a broad measure of its overall attitude towards to all of its stakeholders and associated environments. This is referred to as corporate and social responsibility (CSR) and is fast becoming a key agenda item for many organisations.

There are three main theoretical approaches to CSR, each of which reflects an organisation's perspective of to whom it is primarily responsible. The shareholder approach suggests that an organisation's actions should be considered in terms of its ability to satisfy shareholders. The stakeholder approach recognises the influence of a wider array of stakeholders or constituencies, whilst the societal approach accepts the role organisations play in the fabric and expectations of society. Whichever of these approaches are adopted, the role of marketing communications within CSR is still wide and its use therefore should be carefully considered (managed) especially in an era of integrated marketing communications. Some of the different ways in which ethical issues can be considered in this context are listed in Table 7.1.

The importance of context

The importance of context in judging ethical behaviour can be seen in the debate in the UK over the problems arising from the selling of private pensions during the 1980s. In many cases customers were persuaded by salespeople to switch out of existing pension schemes into new schemes whose subsequent performance left them worse off. In these cases the complex nature of the services, together with the unfamiliarity of many of the customers with the various types of product and how to choose between them, led them to place an unusually great reliance on the advice provided by the salesperson. Put another way, the extent to which the buyer was foreseeably able to 'beware' in these cases was very limited, which in turn should have placed a greater than normal ethical duty on the salesperson to ensure that the customers were properly informed of the consequences and implications of the switch. The fact that these ethical standards were clearly not met in a large number of cases has caused a great deal of loss, anxiety and inconvenience for the customers who lost out, but also a great deal of difficulty, expense and embarrassment for the pensions industry as a whole.

[1] The author wishes to acknowledge the work of Richard Christy from whose chapter in Fill (2009) much of this material on ethics has been adapted.

Viewpoint 7.4   Pension confusion

Diacon and Ennew (1996) point out that marketing transactions in financial services have greater than normal potential for ethical complications. The unavoidable complexity of many financial services products is heightened by the fact that the evaluation may depend upon individual calculations carried out for the customer by the salesperson; also, risk for the customer may be significant, in that the actual benefits received will often depend upon the performance of the economy over a long period. The authors highlight a number of other ethical issues relevant to insurance selling, including:

- the issue of 'fitness for purpose' in both the design of the products and the way in which they are matched to customer needs;
- the transparency of the price for these products, such that any commissions payable to the intermediary organisation or individual salesperson are clearly visible;
- the need for truth in promotion, not only in terms of strict factual correctness, but also in terms of what the consumer might be expected to understand from a phrase;
- the effect of the sales targeting and reward systems of the selling organisation on the behaviour of salespeople, particularly in view of the important advisory component of this type of selling.

The serious problems arising from personal pension selling during the 1980s provide an example of how important it is for businesses to maintain an active awareness of the likely effects of their actions. It is difficult to escape the conclusion that a more enlightened assessment of the long-term interests of the business on the part of financial service providers would have helped to avert many of the problems, to the great benefit of all involved. This is easy to conclude with hindsight: the effective ethical businesses are those that manage to cultivate this type of foresight.

Source: Based on Diacon and Ennew (1996)

Question

To what extent could the recent failure of the financial services industry and the recession that was triggered, be traced to any of the four items highlighted in this viewpoint?

Task

Choose a financial services company, go to its website and consider the transparency of its communications.

A further critical contextual element concerns the relationship between buyer/seller. In relational exchanges value for all parties is rooted in the maintenance of trust and commitment. So, the communications and associated expectations used in relational exchanges will be different to those used in transactional exchanges. A customer might, for example, feel upset if a car salesperson with whom he had dealt for many years failed to tell him that the model he was buying was about to be superseded, because that would seem to be inconsistent with the trust built up over the years. The same customer might not be at all upset to find the same thing happen with a personal computer bought from a discount store in London, not only because computers are known to date more quickly than models of cars, but also because there was no long-term relationship to be brought into question.

Regulating marketing communications

It should be clear that a range of marketing communications activities have ample opportunity to mislead, offend or, at another level, individuals might be subject to more severe distress such as physical injury, psychological suffering or perhaps financial loss. It is important therefore to have in place a system that provides a measure of control over the industry, one which regulates marketing communications activities in order to protect and serve society in ways in which are regarded as appropriate.

Regulation is managed through a blend of two main approaches. One is based on legislation, that is the use of law to provide a legal boundary on what is and what is not permitted. The second approach is based on a set of voluntary codes and processes, run by members of the marketing industry. Although the voluntary codes are used to manage day-to-day questions, Harker's (1998) review of approaches to regulation in five countries suggests that a combination of both legal and voluntary approaches can work effectively to regulate the marketing communications industry.

In the UK, the Advertising Standards Authority has responsibility for advertising content regulation in both broadcast and non-broadcast advertising (the former by delegation from Ofcom, the general regulator for the communications industry and the latter by continuance of the ASA's former role). The ASA, which is funded by levies from advertising, administers a set of codes of advertising practice for the various types of advertising (see www.asa.org.uk for further details). The system aims to provide clear arrangements for consumers, as well as a consistent structure for dealing with the increasingly diverse range of communications media that has developed in recent years.

Although Ofcom retains backstop powers over the regulations for managing the arrangements for broadcast advertising, the system remains effectively self-regulatory in approach, building on the ASA's experience as the regulator of non-broadcast advertising content. Strictly speaking, the system is co-, rather than self-regulatory, in that Ofcom, with its statutory powers, has delegated the responsibility for maintaining and applying codes of practice approved by the regulator (see www.ofcom.org.uk).

Self-regulation

In the UK, a range of specialised codes have been developed to provide guidance on the production of acceptable marketing communications in particular circumstances. The website of the Advertising Standards Authority (ASA) (http://www.asa.org.uk) provides access to full-text versions of these codes. The ASA's main code for non-broadcast advertising (the Code of Advertising, Sales Promotion and Direct Marketing, published by the Committee of Advertising Practice) begins with a set of general principles. The first two in particular set the tone for the whole code:

> All marketing communications should be legal, decent, honest and truthful. All marketing communications should be prepared with a sense of responsibility to consumers and to society.
> (ASA Code of Advertising, Sales Promotion and Direct Marketing (2003: 6))

The general rules of the Code discuss the requirements of legality, decency, honesty and truthfulness in more detail and also provide guidance on, for example, the protection of privacy, the use of testimonials and endorsements, on competitor comparisons and product availability.

Later sections of the main Code focus on sales promotion (sections 27 to 40) and direct marketing (sections 41 to 45), with guidance on specific issues such as free offers and free trials (section 32) and the increasingly important area of database practice (section 43). The Code also offers detailed guidance on specific marketing communications contexts, such as: alcoholic drinks, children, motoring, health and beauty products and therapies, weight control, financial products and tobacco.

Besides the advice and guidance, it defines the processes through which advertisers should comply with the Code and the sanctions that can be applied. A key aim of the Code is to help those in the industry to produce 'marketing communications that are welcomed and trusted' (p. 3). Since the broadening of its responsibilities in 2004, the ASA also now maintains a range of Codes on broadcast advertising:

- the Radio Advertising Standards Code;
- the TV Advertising Standards Code;
- the Alcohol Advertising Rules;
- Advertising Guidance Notes (concerning, for example, the identification of programmes likely to appeal to children and young people);
- Rules on the Scheduling of Advertising;
- Code for Text Services;
- Guidance on Interactive TV.

As can be seen from this list, the self-regulatory regime is required to encompass the technology-fuelled proliferation of broadcast entertainment and information services. Keeping up to date with this rapid development, as well as remaining sensitive to changes in public sensitivity or taste is a major challenge for any organisation and the ASA's library of advertising codes can be expected to continue to evolve in future.

International marketing communications

The differences between operating within home or domestic markets, compared with overseas or international markets are many and varied. Most of these differences can be considered within an economic, cultural, legal, technological and competitive framework. If the core characteristics of a home market (such as prices, marketing channels, finance, knowledge about customers, legislation, media and competitors) are compared with each of the same factors in the international markets in which an organisation might be operating, the degree of complexity and uncertainty can be easily illuminated. Management might be conversant with the way of doing business at home but, as they move outside the country/regional borders/areas that represent their domain of knowledge, understanding and to some extent security, so levels of control decline and risk increases.

Key variables

There are a large number of variables that can impact on the effectiveness of marketing communications that cross international borders. Many of these are controllable by either local or central management. However, there are a large number that are uncontrollable, and these variables need to be carefully considered before communications are attempted. The following variables (culture and media) are reviewed here because of their immediate and direct impact on organisations and their communication activities.

Culture

The values, beliefs, ideas, customs, actions and symbols that are learned by members of particular societies are referred to as culture. The importance of culture is that it provides individuals with identity and the direction of what is deemed to be acceptable behaviour. Culture is acquired through learning. If it were innate or instinctive, then everyone would behave in the same way. Human beings across the world do not behave uniformly or predictably. Therefore different cultures exist, and from this it is possible to visualise that there must be boundaries within which certain cultures, and hence behaviours and lifestyles, are permissible or even expected. These boundaries are not fixed rigidly, as this would suggest that cultures are static. They evolve and change as members of a society adjust to new technologies, government policies, changing values and demographic changes, to mention but a few dynamic variables. From a marketing communications perspective, the prevailing culture in a region must be respected, otherwise it is likely that a brand and or an organisation will be rejected. For example, the Dove ads in which happy women of all shapes and sizes pose in their underwear have had to be shown in different ways to meet the needs of different cultures. In Brazil the women are depicted hugging each other yet in the United States they stand slightly apart from each other, as body contact in the United States is not part of the culture (Laurance, 2007).

Culture is passed from generation to generation. This is achieved through the family, religion, education and the media. These conduits of social behaviour and beliefs serve to provide consistency, stability and direction. The extent to which the media either move society forward or merely reflect its current values is a debate that reaches beyond the scope of this book. However, there can be no doubt as to the impact that the media have on society and the important part that religion plays in different cultures around the world.

Culture has multiple facets, and those that are of direct relevance to marketing communications are the values and beliefs associated with *symbols*, such as language and aesthetics, *institutions* and *groups*, such as those embracing the family, work, education, media and religion, and finally *values*, which according to Hofstede *et al.* (1990) represent the core of culture. These will be looked at in turn.

Symbols

Language, through both the spoken and the non-spoken word, permits members of a society to enter into dialogue and to share meaning. Aesthetics, in the form of design and colour, forms an integral part of packaging, sales promotions and advertising. Those involved in personal selling must be aware of the symbolic impact of formal and informal dress codes and the impact that overall personal appearances and gestures (for example when greeting or leaving people) may have on people in different cultures. Advertisers need to take care that they do not infringe a culture's aesthetic codes when designing visuals or when translating copy into the local language.

Institutions and groups

The various institutions that help form the fabric of societies and particular cultures provide a means by which culture is communicated and perpetuated through time. These groups provide the mechanisms by which the process of socialisation occurs. Of these groups, the family plays an important role. The form of the *family* is evolving in some Western cultures, such that the traditional family unit is declining and the number of single-parent families is increasing. In many developing economies the extended family, with several generations living together, continues to be a central, stable part of society. Marketing communication messages need to reflect these characteristics. The impact and importance of various decision-makers need to be recognised and the central creative idea needs to be up to date and sensitive to the family unit.

Work patterns vary across regions: not all cultures expect a 9-to-5 routine. This is breaking down in the UK as delayering pressurises employees to work increased hours, while in Asia-Pacific Saturday morning work is the norm.

Literacy levels can impact heavily on the ability of target audiences to understand and to ascribe meanings to marketing communication messages. The balance between visual and non-visual components in messages and the relative complexity of messages should be considered in the light of the education levels that different countries and regions have reached. In addition to these factors, some target audiences in more developed economies have developed a high level of advertising sophistication. The meaning given to messages is in some part a reflection of the degree to which individuals understand commercial messages and what the source seeks to achieve. This high level of interaction with messages or advertising literacy suggests that advertisers need to create a dialogue with their audiences that recognises their cognitive processing abilities and does not seek to deceive or misinform.

Religion has always played an important part in shaping the values and attitudes of society. Links between religion and authority have been attempted based on the highly structured nature of religion and the role that religion can play in the family, forming the gender, decision-making roles and nurturing the child-rearing process. While the results of research are not conclusive, there appears to be agreement that religion plays an important part in consumer buying behaviour and that marketing communications should take into account the level of religious beliefs held by the decision-maker (Delner, 1994).

Similarly, mass communication technologies provide audiences with improved opportunities to understand and appreciate different religious beliefs and their associated rituals and artefacts, so care needs to be taken not to offend these groups with upsetting or misinformed marketing communications.

Values

One of the most important international, culturally oriented research exercises, was undertaken by Hofstede (1980, 1991). Using data gathered from IBM across 53 countries, Hofstede's research has had an important impact on our understanding of culture (Hickson and Pugh, 1995). From this research, several dimensions of culture have been discerned. The first of these concerns the individualist/collectivist dimension. It is suggested that individualistic cultures emphasise individual goals and the need to empower, to progress and to be a good leader. Collectivist cultures emphasise good group membership and participation. Consequently, difficulties can arise when communications between these two types of culture have meanings ascribed to them that are derived from different contexts. To avoid the possible confusion and misunderstanding, an adapted communication strategy is advisable.

In addition to these challenges, comprehension (ascribed meaning) is further complicated by the language context. In high-context languages, information is conveyed through who is speaking and their deportment and mannerisms. Content is inferred on the basis that it is implicit: it is known and does not need to be set out. This is unlike low-context languages, where information has to be detailed and 'spelled out' to avoid misunderstanding. Not surprisingly, therefore, when (marketing) communications occur across these contexts, inexperienced communicators may be either offended at the blunt approach of the other (of the low-context German or French, for example) or intrigued by the lack of overt information being offered from the other (from the high-context Japanese or Asians, for example). Referring to advertising creative strategy, Okazaki and Alonso (2003) assert that the Japanese prefer a more subtle, soft approach. In contrast, North Americans prefer a more direct, hard-sell strategy with direct, explicit messages.

A further cultural dimension concerns the role that authority plays in society. Two broad forms can be identified. In high-power-distance cultures, authority figures are important and guide a high proportion of decisions that are made. In low-power-distance cultures, people prefer to use cognitive processing and make reasoned decisions based on the information available. What might be deduced from this is that expert advice and clear, specific recommendations should be offered to those in high-power-distance cultures, while information provision should be the goal of marketing communications to assist those in low-power-distance cultures (Zandpour and Harich, 1996).

People in different cultures can exhibit characteristics that suggest they feel threatened or destabilised by ambiguous situations or uncertainty. Those cultures that are more reliant on formal rules are said to have high levels of uncertainty avoidance. They need expert advice, so marketing communications that reflect these characteristics and are logical, clear and provide information directly and unambiguously (in order to reduce uncertainty) are likely to be more successful.

From the adaptation/standardisation perspective, this information can be useful in order to determine the form of the most effective advertising messages. Zandpour and Harich used these cultural dimensions, together with an assessment of the advertising industry environment in each target country. The results of their research suggest that different countries are more receptive to messages that have high or low levels of logical, rational and information-based appeals (think). Other countries might be more receptive to psychological and dramatically based appeals (feel).

Research concerning the effectiveness of advertising strategies in the USA and Australia (Frazer and Sheehan, 2002) found that safety appeals were more frequently used in Australia than the USA. This may well reflect varying cultural values regarding concern for safety-related issues, concern for the environment and varying regulatory requirements.

Media

The rate of technological change has had a huge impact on the form and type of media that audiences can access. However, media availability is far from uniform, and the range and types of media vary considerably across countries. These media developments have been accompanied by a number of major structural changes to the industry and the way in which it is regulated. Many organisations (client brands, media and agencies) have attempted to grow through diversification and the development of international networks (organic growth and alliances), and there has been an increase in the level of concentration as a few organisations/individuals have begun to own, and hence control, larger proportions of the media industry. For example, Rupert Murdoch, Ted Turner, Time-Warner, Bertelsmann and Silvio Berlusconi now have substantial cross-ownership holdings of international media. This concentration is partly the result of the decisions of many governments to deregulate their control over the media and to create new trading relationships. As a result, this cross-ownership of the media (television, newspapers, magazines, cable, satellite, film, publishing, advertising, cinema, retailing, recorded music) has created opportunities for client advertisers to have to go to only one media provider, which will then provide access to a raft of media across the globe. For example, the Time-Warner/AOL merger was intended to take the concentration and cross-industry collaboration a stage further as positions for future markets are adopted. This facility, known as one-stop shopping, has been available in North America for some time, and was attempted by Saatchi & Saatchi and WPP in the 1980s from a European base, but it is only since the 1990s that this opportunity has been offered elsewhere. The failure of the Time-Warner/AOL merger is symptomatic of other cultural and business-related problems.

Deregulation has had a profound impact on media provision in nearly all parts of the world. This often manifests itself in terms of the growth in types of the media available and the number of media vehicles.

International communication strategy

The degree to which organisations should adapt their external messages to suit local or regional country requirements has been a source of debate since Levitt (1983) published his seminal work on global branding. The standardisation/adaptation issue is unlikely to be resolved, yet is an intuitively interesting and thought-provoking subject. The cost savings associated with standardisation policies are attractive and, when these are combined with the opportunity to improve message consistency, communication effectiveness and other internally related efficiencies such as staff morale, cohesion and organisational identity, the argument in favour of standardisation seems difficult to renounce. However, in practice there are very few brands that are truly global. Some, such as McDonald's, Coca-Cola and Levi's, are able to capitalise on the identification and inherent brand value that they have been able to establish across cultures. The majority of brands lack this depth of personality, and because individual needs vary across cultures, so enterprises need to retune their messages in order that their reception is as clear and distinct as possible.

Adaptation

The arguments in favour of adapting messages to meet the needs of particular local and/or regional needs are as follows:

- Consumer needs are different and vary in intensity. Assuming there are particular advertising stimuli that can be identified as having universal appeal, it is unlikely that buyers across international borders share similar experiences, abilities and potential either to process information in a standardised way or to ascribe similar sets of meanings to the stimuli they perceive. Ideas and message concepts generated centrally may be inappropriate for local markets.

- The infrastructure necessary to support the conveyance of standardised messages varies considerably, not only across but often within broad country areas.

- Educational levels are far from consistent. This means that buyers' ability to give meaning to messages will vary. Similarly, there will be differing capacities to process information, so that the complexity of message content has to be kept low if universal dissemination is to be successful.

- The means by which marketing communications are controlled in different countries is a reflection of the prevailing local economic, cultural and political conditions. The balance between voluntary controls through self-regulation and state control through legislation is partly a testimony to the degree of economic and political maturity that exists. This means that what might be regarded as acceptable marketing communications activities in one country may be unacceptable in another. For example, cold calling is not permissible in Germany but, although not popular with either sales personnel or buyers, is allowed in the Netherlands and France.

- Local management of the implementation of standardised, centrally determined messages may be jeopardised because of a lack of ownership. Messages crafted by local 'craftsmen' to suit the needs of local markets may receive increased levels of support and motivation.

The localised communication strategy used by McDonald's in India reflects the company's sensitivity to local culture. On entry to the Indian market the global brand values were amended to position McDonald's as supportive of Indian family values. This appeal was targeted at middle class families, designed to encourage the younger generation to perceive McDonald's as a key part of their social identity. Once this had been established communications were used to present the brand as inexpensive and accessible to a wide range of other consumers (Anon, 2010). Coca-Cola recognise that they are a local business and the need to differentiate in India and China is paramount.

Standardisation

Just as the arguments for adaptation appear convincing at first glance, then so do those in favour of standardisation:

- Despite geographical dispersion, buyers in many product categories have a number of similar characteristics. This can be supported by the various psychographic typologies that have been developed by advertising agencies for their clients. As brand images and propositions are capable of universal meaning, there is little reason to develop a myriad of brand messages.

- Many locally driven campaigns are regarded as being of poor quality, if only because of the lack of local resources, experiences and expertise (Harris, 1996). It is better to control the total process and at the same time help exploit the opportunities for competitive advantage through shared competencies.

- As media, technology and international travel opportunities impact on increasing numbers of people, so a standardised message for certain offerings allows for a strong brand image to be developed.

- Just as local management might favour local campaigns, so central management might prefer the ease with which they can implement and control a standardised campaign. This frees local managers to concentrate on managing the campaign and removes from them the responsibility of generating creative ideas and associated issues with local advertising agencies.

● Following on from this point is one of the more enduring and managerially appealing ideas. The economies of scale that can be gained across packaging, media buying and advertising message creation and production can be enormous. In addition, the prospect of message consistency and horizontally integrated campaigns across borders is quite compelling. Buzzell (1968) argued that these economies of scale would also improve levels of profitability.

Fielding (2000) and Hite and Fraser (1988) argue that the evidence indicates that, although organisations pursued standardisation strategies in the 1970s, the trend since then has been towards more local adaptation. Harris (1996) makes the point that, although the operation of a purely standardised programme is considered desirable, there is no evidence to suggest that standardisation actually works. There appears to have been little research to compare the performance of advertising that has been developed and implemented under standardisation policies with that executed under locally derived communications.

However, while a few organisations do operate at either end of the spectrum, the majority prefer a contingency approach. This means that there is a degree of standardisation, where for example creative themes, ideas and campaign planning are centrally driven and other campaign elements such as language, scenes and models are adapted to the needs of the local environment. The cosmetic manufacturer L'Oréal used to distribute its Studio Line of hair care products aimed at 18–35-year-olds, across 50 countries. 'These are the same products with the same formulation with the same attitudinal message of personal choice' (Sennett, in Kaplan, 1994). All the advertisements have the same positioning intentions, which are developed centrally, but the executions (featuring different hairstyles) are produced locally to reflect the different needs of different markets.

It is too easy to consider the internationalisation debate in terms of packaged goods companies when other sectors have approached the task in different ways. Bold (2000) refers to pharmaceutical companies that have generally made the product, as opposed to brands, the centre of their communication strategy. Drugs are launched in different countries using different names and different strategies targeted at the medical professionals. He comments that while this approach was prevalent, the structure of pharmaceutical companies tended to be nation-focused, even to the extent that there would be separate regionalised budgets. The merger and consolidation activity, together with the rapid rise in patient involvement in health care (e.g. AIDS), has resulted in the formation of centralised marketing departments and the development of multinational brands.

The argument for some form of standardisation is twofold. First, there is an increasing need for improved levels of internal efficiency (and accountability) in terms of the use of resources. Second, there is an increasing awareness of the benefits that standardised advertising may have on organisational identity, employee morale and satisfaction. The pressure to make cost savings and to develop internal efficiencies, therefore, appears to override the needs of the market.

However, those who argue in favour of standardisation need to be aware that the information content will often need to be correspondingly low. Mueller (1991) observes that the greater the amount of information the greater the opportunity for buyers to discriminate among alternative purchases. Conversely, the emphasis with uninformative advertising is to use imagery and indirect (peripheral) cues. Multinational organisations prepare individual marketing mixes for individual countries/areas. Products and prices will be different, so comparisons are difficult. Likewise, key attributes will vary across countries/areas, so this means that organisations need to decide whether high levels of standardisation and low levels of information are preferable to adapted campaigns with higher levels of information content.

The criteria by which organisations should decide whether to adapt or standardise their marketing (communications) activities is normally the impact that the different strategies are likely to have on profit performance (Buzzell, 1968). The basis for these financial projections has to be a suitably sensitive segmentation analysis based on a layering of segment information. Country-only or arbitrary regional analysis is unlikely to be suitable. Cross-cultural and psychographic data need to be superimposed to provide the richness upon which to build effective communications.

Organisations rarely decide on a polarised strategy of total adaptation or complete stand-ardisation. In practice, a policy of 'glocalisation' seems to be preferred. Under this approach, organisations develop standard messages centrally, but expect the local country areas to adapt them to meet local cultural needs by adjusting for language and media components. There are, of course, variations on this theme. For example, head office might decide on the strategic direction and thrust of the campaign and leave the local country management to produce its own creatives.

Viewpoint 7.5   Beat the international cravings

Pharmaceutical brands tend to be country-specific due mainly to cultural attitudes towards healthcare, medicine and related activities. Regulations also pose problems as they vary across countries and restrict what messages can and cannot be said. Therefore, the task of converting a pharmaceutical brand into a global entity requires lateral thinking, something that Nicorette undertook in their quest to be a billion dollar brand by 2010.

The answer lay in repositioning Nicorette as a consumer brand, one imbued with emotion rather than one that conveyed rational, information health-dominated messages. This meant that rather than convey messages about how Nicorette could help a smoker give up completely, messages were designed to support smokers through each cigarette not smoked and overcoming the cravings.

The creative instrument used across the campaign was 'Cravings Man'. A 2.5 metre cigarette with a face, legs and arms. Each ad showed a smoker literally beating the craving for a cigarette. This creative idea travelled across all countries as the same underlying feelings are experienced by all smokers (see Exhibit 7.1).

Source: Based on Horry and Miller (2006)

BEAT CIGARETTES ONE AT A TIME.
WHILE KEEPING YOUR WEIGHT UNDER CONTROL.

Exhibit 7.1	Nicorette cravings ad
	Image courtesy of The Advertising Archives

Question

How might 'Cravings Man' be used in other tools and media?

Task

Find one of Nicorette's competitors and compare the basic messages they convey with Nicorette's.

Summary

In order to help consolidate your understanding of the marketing communication industry, here are the key points summarised against each of the learning objectives:

1 Provide an introductory understanding of the communications industry, including the nature and role of the main types of organisations

The structure of the industry is similar in most countries but the relationships and operations will inevitably vary. However, the marketing communication industry in Britain has evolved slowly, with large agencies seeking to bring a range of communication skills and facilities together within a single group. Mid-size and small agencies still maintain a functional orientation (e.g. advertising, promotion, public relations or digital), although there are many attempting to provide an integrated service.

The agencies broker or facilitate the communication needs of clients, while media houses plan, buy and monitor media purchases for their clients. Production facilitators ensure the processes work by making videos, providing fulfilment or staging events. All deliver specific value to the industry and have different roles to play.

2 Consider the processes associated with selecting an agency

The process commences with a *search*, undertaken to develop a list of potential candidates. The client should then visit each of the short-listed candidates in what is referred to as a *credentials presentation*. This is a crucial stage in the process, as it is now that the agency is evaluated for its degree of fit with the client's expectations and requirements.

Selected agencies are given a brief and then required to make a formal presentation (the *pitch*) to the client some 6–8 weeks later. This presentation is about how the agency would approach the strategic and creative issues and the account is awarded to whichever produces the most suitable proposal. The winning agency is invited to discuss terms and conditions, and the winner is announced to the contestants and made public.

3 Explore the key operations used by clients and agencies in the development of campaigns

Once the client–agency relationship is established, the operational procedures are based on briefings, and there are three main ones: the client, creative and media briefs.

4 Examine the methods of remuneration used to reward agencies

Relationships between clients and agencies are of critical importance and part of their trust and commitment is reflected in the remuneration agencies receive for their contribution to their client's business. There are three keys methods: commission, payment by results and fees. These are normally combined within a contract.

5 Review the regulation, including ethical issues, associated with marketing communications

The regulation of marketing communications is generally undertaken through a blend of statutory measures, imposed by a government, or voluntary codes, coordinated and implemented by the industry itself, otherwise referred to as self-regulation.

Ethical issues are becoming increasingly prominent and many organisations are attempting to become more actively involved in addressing the ethical consequences of their marketing communications activities. Concern about telling the truth, their attitude towards vulnerable groups, respect and concern for individual privacy, ensuring all communications are tasteful and decent and that the use of inducements to clients, sales personnel and others are transparent and appropriate are some of the more obvious areas towards which organisations should direct their attention.

6 Explain the principal ideas and strategies involved with international marketing communications practice

There are a large number of variables that need to be carefully considered before communications are attempted in an international or global arena. Two of the more important ones are culture and media availability.

Organisations that operate in an international environment need to consider whether their messages should be adapted to meet the needs of country or regional audiences or whether they should be standardised and use a single message that is delivered to all audiences.

Review questions

1. Who are the main types of organisation that make up the marketing communication industry?
2. Identify some of the issues that prevail in the industry.
3. Write notes for a presentation explaining the different types of agency available to clients.
4. What factors should be taken into consideration and what procedures might be followed when selecting an agency?
5. What are the basic dimensions for the development of good agency–client relationships?
6. Write short notes about the briefing system.
7. Prepare some brief notes explaining how culture impacts on an organisation's marketing communications.
8. Select two countries of your choice. Compare the significance of cultural symbols and provide examples of how these are used.
9. You have been asked to make a presentation to senior managers on the advantages and disadvantages of standardising the marketing messages delivered for your brand throughout the world. Prepare notes for each of the slides you will use.
10. Your client is currently following an adapted strategy, but is considering changing to a standardised approach. What might be the impact of this move on your agency?

References

Anon (2010) McDonald's takes localised approach in India, *Exchange4Media and Warc*. Retrieved 12 May 2010 from www.warc.co./news/

Bold, B. (2000) Unlocking the global market, *PR Week*, 11 August, 13–14.

Boyd, M. (2010) Google shows adland the new tools of its trade, *Campaign*, 25 June, 11.

Buzzell, R. (1968) Can you standardise multinational marketing? *Harvard Business Review*, 46 (November/December), 102–113.

Charles, G. (2008) The buddy system, *Marketing*, 6 February, 16.

Child, L. (2007) How to manage your relationship, *Marketing Agency*, (December), 4–7.

Christy, R. (2009) Ethics in Marketing Communications. In *Marketing Communications: interactivity, communities and content*, 5th edn. (ed. C. Fill) 99–127. Harlow: FT/Prentice Hall.

Collin, W. (2003) The interface between account planning and media planning – a practitioner perspective. *Marketing Intelligence and Planning*, 21(7), 440–445.

Delner, N. (1994) Religious contrast in consumer decision behaviour patterns: their dimensions and marketing implications. *European Journal of Marketing*, 28(5), 36–53.

Diacon, S.R. and Ennew. C.T. (1996) Can Business Ethics Enhance Corporate Governance? Evidence from a Survey of UK Insurance Executives, *Journal of Business Ethics*, 15(6), 623–634.

Donohue, A. (2007) Social networking site for marketing professionals launches. *Brand Republic*, 28 September. Retrieved 8 October 2007 from www.brandrepublic.com/News/741288/Social-networking-site-marketing-professionals-launches/

Edge, M. (2010) Google shows adland the new tools of its trade, *Campaign*, 25 June, 11.

Fielding, S. (2000) Developing global brands in Asia, *Admap* (June), 26–29.

Frazer, C.F. and Sheehan, K.B. (2002) Advertising strategy and effective advertising comparing the USA and Australia, *Journal of Marketing Communications*, 8, 149–164.

Grant, I., Gilmore, C. and Crosier, K. (2003) Account planning: whose role is it anyway? *Marketing Intelligence and Planning*, 21(7), 462–472.

Harris, G. (1996) International advertising: developmental and implementational issues, *Journal of Marketing Management*, 12, 551–560.

Hickson, D.J. and Pugh, D.S. (1995) *Management Worldwide*. London: Penguin.

Hite, R.E. and Fraser, C. (1988) International advertising strategies of multinational corporations. *Journal of Advertising Research*, 28 (August/September), 9–17.

Hofstede, G. (1980) *Culture's Consequences: International Differences in Work Related Values.* Thousand Oaks, CA: Sage.

Hofstede, G. (1991) *Cultures and Organisations*. London: McGraw-Hill.

Hofstede, G., Neuijen, B., Ohayv, D.D. and Sanders, G. (1990) Measuring organisational cultures: a qualitative and quantitative study across twenty cases, *Administrative Science Quarterly*, 35(2), 286–316.

Horry, T. and Miller, J. (2006) Sold not dispensed – the power of consumer brands vs pharmaceutical brands, *Advertising Works,* 15, 333–334. Henley: NTC Publications.

Jones, M. (2004) 10 things agencies need to know about clients, *Admap*, 39(5) (May), 21–23.

Kaplan, R. (1994) Ad agencies take on the world, *International Management* (April), 50–52.

Laurance, B. (2007) Unilever learns to join the dots, *Sunday Times*, 18 March, 11.

Levitt, T. (1983) The globalization of markets, *Harvard Business Review* (May/June), 92–102.

Mueller, B. (1991) An analysis of information content in standardised vs. specialised multinational advertisements, *Journal of International Business Studies* (First Quarter), 23–39.

Okazaki, S. and Alonso, J. (2003) Right messages for the right site: online creative strategies by Japanese multinational corporations, *Journal of Marketing Communications*, 9, 221–239.

Pawinska, M. (2000) The passive pitch, *PR Week*, 12 May, 14–15.

Rebelo, M. (2010) Google shows adland the new tools of its trade, *Campaign*, 25 June, 11.

Tylee, J. (2010) Will others follow Coke's remuneration model?, *Campaign*, 19 February, 17.

Wethey, D. (2006) The shocking truth about the pitch, *The Marketer*, September, 7–8.

White, R. (2007) Structuring the (ad) agency, *Admap*, March, 14–15.

Williams, T. (2010) Why agencies should call time on selling time, *Campaign*, 16 July, 12.

Wilson, S. (2009) The purpose of integration, *PRWeek-Thought Leader* (December), 15.

Zambarino, A. and Goodfellow, J. (2003) Account planning in the new marketing and communications environment (has the Stephen King challenge been met?), *Marketing Intelligence and Planning*, 21(7), 424–434

Zandpour, F. and Harich, K. (1996) Think and feel country clusters: a new approach to international advertising standardization, *International Journal of Advertising*, 15, 325–344

Chapter 8
Shaping relationships with marketing communications

The importance of relationship marketing is now recognised as a central aspect of both consumer and business marketing. The role that marketing communications can play in establishing and nurturing key relationships is pivotal, yet the ways in which marketing communications might best be deployed depend to a large extent on the context in which both the relationship and the communications are configured.

Aims and learning objectives

The aim of this chapter is to explore concepts and ideas concerning marketing relationships and to consider the role marketing communications can play in developing and sustaining relationships with customers, employees and agencies.

The learning objectives of this chapter are to:

1. examine ideas associated with perceived customer value;

2. consider the theoretical concepts underpinning relationship marketing, including marketing exchanges and value creation;

3. explain the concepts of trust and commitment and how they can be used to develop loyalty and retention programmes;

4. consider the customer development cycle and the role of marketing communications in developing customer relationships;

5. appraise the role of marketing communications in the development of employee relationships;

6. examine the characteristics associated with client/agency relationships.

Introduction

Relationship marketing has become a key aspect of both consumer and business marketing. There are a number of dimensions associated with organisational and consumer relationships, many of which encompass established concepts such as trust, commitment and loyalty. The role that marketing communications can play in establishing and nurturing key relationships can be pivotal, yet the ways in which marketing communications might be best deployed depends to a large extent on the context in which both the relationship and the communications are configured.

Value has become an increasingly significant concept, to both marketing practitioners and academics. Indeed, many believe that the only viable marketing strategy should be to deliver improved shareholder value (Doyle, 2000) whilst others believe value creation represents the only viable interpretation about how marketing works (Vargo and Lusch, 2004). However, the importance of providing value for customers is not a new idea. Concepts of differentiation, unique and emotional selling propositions (USPs and ESPs) and positioning are founded on the idea that superior perceived value is of primary significance to customers.

It has been understood for a long time that customers buy benefits not features, that they buy products and services as solutions which enable them to achieve their goals. The majority of women buy lipstick because of a mixture of both tangible and intangible attributes or even features and benefits. They buy particular brands because they feel different as a result of using them. What they buy varies from person to person, but in terms of tangible attributes they prefer to buy colour and smudge-free lips (no 'bleed'), that the lipstick stays on the lips, prevents dryness, is long lasting and smooth (Puth *et al.*, 1999). However, among the intangible attributes are self-confidence, a coordinated fashion accessory, trust, perhaps an alter ego or, as Revlon once claimed, 'hope'.

The same principle applies to organisational marketing. Business customers buy solutions to business problems, not just stand-alone products. These benefits and solutions constitute potential added value for customers, and represent the reason why one offering is selected in preference to another. For both consumers and business customers, value is determined by the net satisfaction derived from a transaction, not the costs incurred to obtain it.

So, if customers seek to satisfy their needs through their purchase of specific products and services then it can be said that the satisfaction of needs is a way of delivering value. Kothandaraman and Wilson (2001) argue that the creation of value is dependent upon an organisation's ability to deliver high performance on the benefits that are important to the customer and this in turn is rooted in their competency in technology and business processes, or core competences. According to Doyle (2000) the creation of customer value is based on three principles:

- Customers will choose between alternative offerings and select the one that (they perceive) will offer them the best value.

- Customers do not want product or service features, they want their needs met.

- It is more profitable to have a long-term relationship between a customer and a company rather than a one-off transaction.

Value is the customer's estimate of the extent to which a product or service can satisfy their needs. However, normally there are costs associated with the derivation of benefits such that a general model of value would identify the worth of the benefits received for the price paid (Anderson and Narus, 1998). Therefore, value is relative to customer expectations and experience of competitive offerings within a category and can be derived from sources other than products, such as the relationships between buyers and sellers (Simpson *et al.*, 2001).

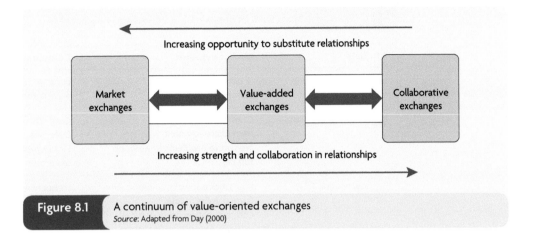

Figure 8.1	A continuum of value-oriented exchanges
	Source: Adapted from Day (2000)

Development of the relationship marketing concept

Interaction between customers and sellers is based around the provision and consumption of perceived value. However, the quality, duration and level of interdependence between customers and sellers can vary considerably. The reasons for this variance are many and wide-ranging but at the core are perceptions of shared values and the strength and permanence, referred to as connectedness, of any relationship that might exist. Relationship value can be visualised as a continuum (see Figure 8.1).

At one end of the continuum are market exchanges, characterised by short-term, product or price oriented exchanges, between buyers and sellers coming together for one-off exchanges independent of any other or subsequent exchanges. Both parties are motivated mainly by self-interest. Movement along the continuum represents the acceptance and desire for increasingly valued relationships. Interactions between parties are closer and stronger. The focus moves from initial attraction to retention and mutual understanding of each other's needs.

At the other end of the continuum are relational exchanges or what Day (2000) refers to as collaborative exchanges. These are characterised by a long-term orientation, where ultimately there is complete integration of systems and processes and where the relationship is motivated by partnership and mutual support. Trust and commitment underpin these relationships and these variables become increasingly important as relational exchanges become established.

Perceived value may take many forms and be rooted in a variety of attributes, combined in different ways to meet segment needs. However, the context in which an exchange occurs between a buyer and a seller provides a strong reflection of the nature of their relationship. If the exchange is focused on the product (and the price) then the exchange is considered to be essentially transactional or market. If the exchange is focused around the needs of the customer and the seller then the exchange is considered to be collaborative, truly relational. The differences between market and collaborative exchanges are set out in Table 8.1 and provide an important starting point in understanding the nature of relationship marketing. The table provides a more comprehensive list of fundamental differences between market and collaborative-based marketing.

Although market exchanges focus on products and prices, there is still a relational component, if only because interaction requires a basic relationship between parties for the transaction to be completed (Macneil, 1980).

Table 8.1	Characteristics of market and collaborative exchanges	
Attribute	**Market exchange**	**Collaborative exchange**
Length of relationship	Short term Abrupt end	Long term A continuous process
Relational expectations	Conflicts of goals Immediate payment No future problems (there is no future)	Conflicts of interest Deferred payment Future problems expected to be overcome by joint commitment
Communication	Low frequency of communication Formal, mass media communication predominates	Frequent communication Informal, personal, interactive communication predominates
Cooperation	No joint cooperation	Joint cooperative projects
Responsibilities	Distinct responsibilities Defined obligations	Shared responsibilities Shared obligations

Viewpoint 8.1　Added value OnAir

As part of its customer development Airbus has developed facilities for airlines to offer a range of consumer communications while in flight. The system enables passengers to use email and text messages, send and receive voice messages and browse the web all through the use of their own phones, laptops and PDAs.

Airbus has identified a major opportunity in the market and believes the system, branded as OnAir, represents significant added value for major premium travel airlines to offer their passengers. It is expected that Boeing will offer a similar system with both manufacturers recognising the need for their customers to offer passengers additional value in what is a highly competitive market.

Question

Consider the view that the speed at which Boeing nullified Airbus' OnAir system suggests that added value has to be protected and, in the long term, be of significance.

Task

Make a note of two ways in which a rail operator might provide added value to attract and retain travellers.

The role of collaboration in relationship marketing is important. However, many organisations maintain a variety of relationships with their different customers and suppliers, some highly collaborative and some market oriented or, as Spekman and Carroway (2006: 10) suggest, 'where they make sense'. Relationship marketing is characterised by the frequency and intensity of the exchanges between customers and sellers. As these exchanges become more frequent and more intense so the strength of the relationships between buyers and sellers improves. It is this that provided the infrastructure for this perspective of marketing, one based on relationships (Spekman, 1988; Rowe and Barnes, 1998), rather than the objects of a transaction, namely products and prices.

Relationships expressed as value creation

Just as ideas about relationships have evolved, so have those associated with perceived value. Rather than consider relationships as a function of exchange, an emerging view, driven by the service-dominant logic (SDL) group (Vargo and Lusch, 2004; Vargo, 2009), is to consider relationships as a function of value, or what is known as, value-in-use.

The conventional view is that sellers create value for their customers who select suppliers on the basis of their perception of the optimal value offered to them. Grönroos (2009) argues that value can only be realised by customers when utilised through the use of their own processes, resources and capabilities. Grönroos considers that value should be considered to consist of two fundamental elements; value propositions and value creation. Suppliers develop *value propositions* and these are essentially suggestions or promises of value that are embedded in their offerings. Customers fulfil *value creation* when they incorporate these products and services into their processes. Suppliers can assist their customers by creating opportunities to engage with their value generating processes. The level of interaction between the parties might vary from zero to full participation, co-creation.

So, an alternative to the spectrum of exchange relationships presented earlier would be a spectrum of value propositions, or more importantly, a spectrum of interaction leading to various forms of value creation. Movement along the relationship continuum can be interpreted as a change in the way value is created. Ribeiro *et al.* (2009) identify four core value strategies. These are exchange (or commodity) value, added value, performance value and value co-creation strategies.

Market exchange relationships are characterised by an exchange of basic resources. Sellers provide a core service but it is buyers who assume full responsibility and resources, to create the value they require out of the essential service resource that is transacted.

The role for marketing communications is to convey brand promises, or value propositions. Communications should be concerned not just with features and benefits associated with their products but with an overall service solution that buyers can incorporate into their own systems to resolve their problems. The promise is to provide buyers with the resources necessary to help them create the value they require. This approach is referred to as an 'added value' strategy and examples include providing training, financial assistance or installation support.

Following these interactions buyers and sellers become stronger and closer, so that the original value perceived in the exchange of products and prices gradually gives way to a focus on the relationship which itself becomes of value. Further along the continuum some organisations provide 'performance value' strategies. Here value is created by the activities of buyers and sellers working together for mutual benefit, but value is still passed from one to another. Examples include joint product development and projects to enhance the buyer's software systems and processes and initiatives designed to improve manufacturing efficiencies.

Viewpoint 8.2   Performance value crisps

A campaign launched in July 2008 by Walkers sought to forge stronger bonds with their customers. By actively integrating them with the campaign not only did the brand get extensive product exposure but also the relationship between consumers and the brand was developed. The campaign, called 'Do Us a Flavour' challenged the public to think up a unique flavour of crisp.

The campaign involved all of Walkers' agencies to work together, as different stages required different contributions. The first stage began with a TV push created by AMV, with the goal of stimulating members of the public to come up with flavour ideas. Simultaneously, a PR drive led by Freud, had the goal of creating excitement among TV hosts and radio presenters. This was achieved partly by Freud devising bespoke flavours for different presenters. For example, the flavour for Chris Moyles was 'meat and two veg'.

The *Sun* newspaper generated a great deal of PR as did a substantial cross-section of the media. Underpinning it all was the drive to encourage people to visit a dedicated website. At the end of this first stage, customers sent in over 1.2 million entries. Stage 2 was about a judging panel, led by chef Heston Blumenthal, picking the top six entries. These were Cajun Squirrel, Crispy Duck & Hoisin, Fish & Chips, Builder's Breakfast, Chilli & Chocolate and Onion Bhaji.

Stage 3 was the period ending May 2009 during which the crisps could be bought individually or in a special multipack containing all six flavours. Votes could be cast on the Walkers website, through Facebook, and through Yahoo!, which hosted a 'do us a flavour' channel. In addition to all the multichannel activity it was the well-established technique of the on-pack promotion that worked well for many contestants, including one of the six finalists.

Builders Breakfast won the most votes and the person behind it won £50,000, in addition to the £10,000 that each finalist was awarded. Better still, the winner was set to receive one per cent of profits from all future sales of their flavour, an estimated £50,000+ a year.

One of the points this campaign illustrates is the way the brand and its customers worked together to create value that both parties enjoyed consuming, either physically or emotionally. Here real performance value emerged through the parties to the relationship working together.

Source: Based on Nettleton (2009); Anon (2009); Angear and Sambles (2009); White *et al.* (2010)

Question

Identify the key elements that support the relationship between Walkers and their customers. Is this form of the relationship sustainable?

Task

Write notes explaining how this example demonstrates trust and commitment in a relationship.

Exhibit 8.1	The finalists in Walkers' 'Do Us a Flavour' campaign

Here are the six finalists, whose recipes were subjected to a public vote. From left to right:
Martyn Wright, Staffordshire – Cajun Squirrel; Vicky Howard, Northwich – Crispy Duck & Hoisin sauce; Jane Hallam, Sheffield – Fish & Chips; Carole Wood, Durham – Onion Bhaji; Catherine Veitch, High Wycombe – Chilli & Chocolate; Emma Rushin, Derbyshire – Builder's Breakfast.
Image courtesy of Freud Communications (Photographer: Iain Lewis)

Table 8.2	Value strategies and defining characteristics

Defining characteristics	Value strategies			
	Commodity	Value added	Performance	Value co-creation
Value-generating drivers	Product quality Delivery performance Market price	Services support Personal interactions Product and service quality	The know-how of others Time to market Performance from both (costs, revenues, productivity)	Joint and radical innovation Leveraging new competencies
Management intention	Attract and satisfy	Customer retention (implicit: profit, satisfaction, loyalty, risk reduction, etc.)	Interactions to establish, develop and facilitate cooperative relationship and mutual benefit	Coordinating relationships among companies in a network to seek new resources and value networks
Duration	Discrete	Continuous, but discrete hiring	Continuous and long-term contracts	Continuous, mutual cooperation contracts
Adaptation	Little or no adaptation	Process adaptations	Process adaptations	Adaptations and business creation
Description of value offering	'We offer good products and competitive prices'	'We offer excellence'	'We customize, we build on order for the customer'	'Our customers, suppliers and other partners got us here and will take us wherever it need be to generate value'
Management structure	Functional hierarchical: mkt., sales, R&D, etc.	Processes and functions like: customer service manager. CRM manager	Customer and market managers/cross-functions and levels	Business managers
Capabilities	Production Delivery Promoting-communicating Process leveraging Relationship Mastery and integration into the customer's business model Radical innovation Setting up networks			

Source: Ribeiro *et al.* (2009), adapted from: Möller and Törrönen (2003); Coviello *et al.* (1997); Ulaga and Eggert (2006); Möller *et al.* (2005); Prahalad and Ramaswamy (2004). Used with permission

Collaborative relationships are characterised by value that is created by both parties as a form of co-production or through 'value co-creation' (Sheth and Uslay, 2007). This is a situation where both organisations work together for mutual benefit, and value is generated together, not traded by a supplier to a buyer, as in performance value. More information about these different value strategies is given in Table 8.2.

Trust, commitment and loyalty

Embedded within these exchange and service ideas and concepts associated with relationship marketing, are three core concepts, trust, commitment and loyalty (and retention). These are considered in turn.

Trust

Many writers contend that one of the crucial factors associated with the development and maintenance of both personal and interorganisational relationships is trust (Morgan and Hunt, 1994; Doney and Cannon, 1997). Trust is an element of personal, intraorganisational and interorganisational relationships, and is both necessary for and results from their perpetuation of others. As Gambetta (1988) argues, trust is a means of reducing uncertainty in order that effective relationships can develop.

Cousins and Stanwix (2001) suggest that, although trust is a term used to explain how relationships work, often it actually refers to ideas concerning risk, power and dependency, and that these propositions are used interchangeably. From their research of vehicle manufacturers it emerges that b2b relationships are about the creation of mutual business advantage and the degree of confidence that one organisation has in another.

Interorganisational trust is based on two main dimensions: credibility and benevolence. Credibility concerns the extent to which one organisation believes (is confident) that another organisation will undertake and complete it's agreed roles and tasks. Benevolence is concerned with goodwill, and that the other organisation will not act opportunistically, even if the conditions for exploitation should arise (Pavlou, 2002). In other words, interorganisational trust involves judgements about another organisation's reliability and integrity.

Institutional trust is clearly vital in b2c markets where online perceived risk is present and known to have prevented many people from purchasing online. In the b2b market, institutional trust is also important but more in terms of the overall reputation of the organisation. The development and establishment of trust is valuable because of the outcomes that can be anticipated. Three major outcomes from the development of trust have been identified by Pavlou, namely satisfaction, perceived risk and continuity.

- **Satisfaction** can reduce conflict and the threat of opportunism and that in turn enhances the probability of buyer satisfaction, an important positive outcome of institutional trust.
- **Perceived risk** is concerned with the expectation of loss and is therefore tied closely with organisational or brand performance. Trust that a seller will not take advantage of the imbalance of information between buyer and seller effectively reduces risk.
- **Continuity** is related to business volumes, necessary in online b2b marketplaces, and the development of both on and offline enduring relationships. Trust is associated with continuity and when present is therefore indicative of long-term relationships. Ryssel *et al.* (2004: 203) recognise that trust (and commitment) have a 'significant impact on the creation of value and conclude that value creation is a function of the atmosphere of a relationship rather than the technology employed'.

Trust within a consumer context is equally important as a means of reducing uncertainty. Brands are an important means of instilling trust mainly because they are a means of condensing and conveying information so that they provide sufficient information for consumers to make calculated purchase decisions in the absence of full knowledge. In a sense consumers transfer their responsibility for brand decision-making, and hence brand performance, to the brand itself. Through extended use of a brand, purchasing habits develop or what is termed routinised response behaviour emerges. This is important not just because complex decision-making is simplified but because the amount of communication necessary to assist and provoke purchase is considerably reduced.

The establishment of trust can be based around the existence of various components. Morrison and Firmstone (2000) identify reputation, familiarity/closeness, performance and accountability as four critical elements. According to Young and Wilkinson (1989) the presence of trust within a relationship is influenced by four other factors. These are the duration of the relationship, the relative power of the players, the presence of cooperation and various environmental factors that may be present at any one moment. Extending these ideas into what is now regarded by many as a seminal paper in the relationship marketing literature,

Morgan and Hunt (1994) argued, and supported with empirical evidence, that the presence of both commitment and trust leads to cooperative behaviour and this in turn is conducive to successful relationship marketing.

Commitment

Morgan and Hunt regard commitment as the desire that a relationship continue (endure) in order that a valued relationship be maintained or strengthened. They postulated that commitment and trust are key mediating variables between five antecedents and five outcomes (see Figure 8.2).

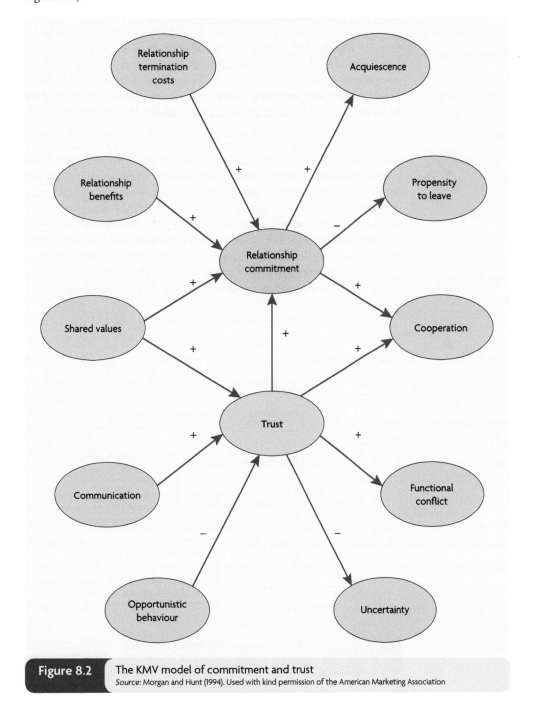

Figure 8.2	The KMV model of commitment and trust

Source: Morgan and Hunt (1994). Used with kind permission of the American Marketing Association

According to the KMV model the greater the losses anticipated through the termination of a relationship the greater the commitment expressed by the exchange partners. Likewise, when these partners share the same values commitment increases. Trust is enhanced when communication is perceived to be of high quality but decreases when one organisation knowingly takes action to seek to benefit from the relationship, which will be to the detriment of the other.

The centrality of the trust and commitment concepts to relationship marketing has thus been established and they are as significant to marketing channel relationships as to other b2b relationships (Achrol, 1991; Goodman and Dion, 2001).

Customer loyalty and retention

Implicit within ideas about customer relationships is the notion that retained customers are loyal. However, this can be misleading as 'loyalty' may actually be a term used to convey convenience or extended utility. Loyalty, however presented, takes different forms, just as there are customers who are more valued than others. Christopher *et al.* (2002) depict the various types of relationships as stages or steps on a ladder, the relationship marketing ladder of loyalty (see Figure 8.3).

A prospect becomes a purchaser, completed through a market or discrete exchange. Clients emerge from several completed transactions but remain ambivalent towards the seller organisation. Supporters, despite being passive about an organisation, are willing and able to enter into regular transactions. Advocates represent the next and penultimate step. They not only support an organisation and its products but actively recommend it to others by positive, word-of-mouth communications. Partners, who represent the top rung of the ladder, trust and support an organisation just as it trusts and supports them. Partnership status is the embodiment of relational exchanges and interorganisational collaboration.

The simplicity of the loyalty ladder concept illustrates the important point that different customers represent different value to sellers. The perceived value (or worth) of a customer

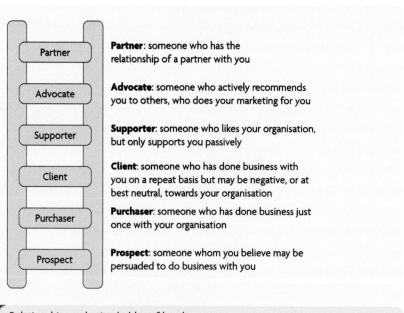

Figure 8.3	Relationship marketing ladder of loyalty

Reprinted from *Relationship Marketing: Creating stakeholder value*, Christopher *et al.* Copyright (2002), with permission from Elsevier

Table 8.3	Types of loyalty
Emotional loyalty	This is a true form of loyalty and is driven by personal identification with real or perceived values and benefits.
Price loyalty	This type of loyalty is driven by rational economic behaviour and the main motivations are cautious management of money or financial necessity.
Incentivised loyalty	This refers to promiscuous buyers: those with no one favourite brand who demonstrate through repeat experience the value of becoming loyal.
Monopoly loyalty	This class of loyalty arises where a consumer has no purchase choice owing to a national monopoly. This, therefore, is not a true form of loyalty.

may or may not always be fully reciprocated, understood or recognised, so it is not surprising that that there is a wide variety and complexity of relationships. What the ladder does not reveal is the dynamic nature of relationships.

Types and levels of loyalty

In addition to the popularity of the loyalty concept shown by organisations, manifest in the increasing number of loyalty based schemes, the term loyalty has attracted much research attention. As a result there are a variety of interpretations, definitions and depictions of the concept. According to Oliver (1997: 392) loyalty is a deeply held sense of commitment to continue buying a preferred product or service on a consistent basis for the foreseeable future. As Evanschitzky and Wunderlich (2006) phrase it, 'thereby causing repetitive same-brand or same brand-set purchasing, despite situational influences and marketing efforts that have the potential to cause switching behavior'.

Table 8.3 represents some of the more general types of loyalty that can be observed.

These hierarchical schemes suggest that consumers are capable of varying degrees of loyalty. Loyalty at one level can be seen to be about increasing sales volume, or fostering loyal purchase behaviour. High levels of repeat purchase, however, are not necessarily an adequate measure of loyalty, as there may be a number of situational factors determining purchase behaviour, such as brand availability (Dick and Basu, 1994).

At another level, loyalty can be regarded as an attitudinal disposition. O'Malley (1998) suggests that customer satisfaction has become a surrogate measure of loyalty. However, she points out that there is plenty of evidence to show that many satisfied customers buy a variety of brands and that polygamous loyalty, as suggested by Dowling and Uncles (1997), may be a better reflection of reality.

At whichever level of loyalty, customer retention is paramount and neither behavioural nor attitudinal measures alone are adequate indicators of true loyalty. O'Malley suggests that a combination of the two is of greater use and that the twin parameters, relative attitudes (to alternatives) and patronage behaviour (the recency, frequency and monetary model), as suggested by Dick and Basu, when used together offer more accurate indicators of loyalty.

Principles of retention

Reference to customer retention is a central concept to relationship marketing, whether considered a function of exchange or service value. Marketing has been characterised by its potential to influence and attract customers. Indeed, early ideas considered marketing to be a social anathema due to the perception that it persuaded and manipulated people into purchasing goods and services they did not want. While these fears and misgivings have generally been overcome, a further fallacy concerned the notion that all customers are good customers. As most commercial organisations will now agree, some customers are far more attractive than other customers, on the grounds that some are very profitable, others are marginally profitable but offer great potential and others offer little and/or incur losses.

Through the use of relationship cost theory it was possible to identify the benefits associated with stable and mutually rewarding relationships. Such customers avoid costly switching costs that are associated with finding new suppliers, while suppliers experience reduced quality costs incurred when adapting to the needs of new customers. Reichheld and Sasser (1990) identified an important association between a small (e.g. 5 per cent) increase in customer retention and a large (e.g. 60 per cent) improvement in profitability. Therefore, a long-term relationship leads to lower relationship costs and higher profits. Since this early work there has been general acceptance that customers who are loyal not only improve an organisation's profits but also strengthen its competitive position (Day, 2000) because competitors have to work harder to dislodge or destabilise their loyalty. It should be noted that some authors suggest the link between loyalty and profitability is not that simple (Dowling and Uncles, 1997), while others argue that much more information and understanding is required about the association between profitability and loyalty, especially when there may be high costs associated with customer acquisition (Reinartz and Kumar, 2002).

By undertaking a customer profitability analysis it is possible to identify those segments that are worth developing, and hence build a portfolio of relationships, each of varying dimensions and potential. These relationships provide mutually rewarding benefits and offer a third dimension of the customer dynamic, namely customer development.

Loyalty and retention programmes

Dowling and Uncles (1997) developed a conceptual framework in which they identified the primary characteristics of loyalty programmes. They highlighted three main dimensions, each with bipolar elements; the type of rewards (direct versus indirect), the timing of the rewards (immediate or delayed) and the tangibility of rewards (tangible versus intangible). So, where there is low involvement decision-making, as in the purchase of grocery products, the key rewards preferred by customers were identified as direct, immediate and tangible.

Despite questions about the nature and meaning of the term loyalty, the growth of loyalty programmes has been a significant development in recent years. Often developed inappropriately in the name of relationship marketing, loyalty schemes have received a great deal of attention. One of the more visible and successful schemes has been the Clubcard offered by Tesco. This has been partly responsible for Tesco dominating the UK retail market.

The use of loyalty schemes was encouraged through the use of swipe cards. Users are rewarded with points each time a purchase is made. This is referred to as a 'points accrual programme', whereby loyal users are able to build up the necessary points, which are stored (often) on a card, and 'cashed in' at a later date for gifts or merchandise. The benefit for the company supporting the scheme is that the promised rewards motivate customers to accrue more points and in doing so increase their switching costs, effectively locking them into the loyalty programme and preventing them from moving to a competitor brand. Swipe cards were then developed technologically into smart cards (a card that has a small microprocessor attached) which can record enormous amounts of information, and is updated each time a purchase is made. The applications for this are much greater and of increased benefit to customers.

Some frequent flyer loyalty schemes, such as BA Executive Club and Virgin Freeway, have been very successful (Brownsell, 2009) and the cards are also used to track individual travellers. Airlines are able to offer cardholders particular services, such as special airport lounges and magazines; the card through its links to a database also enables a traveller's favourite seat and dietary requirements to be offered. In addition, the regular accumulation of air miles fosters continuity and hence loyalty, through which business travellers reward themselves with leisure

Viewpoint 8.3 | Cantrell retains customers

The office products division of the Cantrell Corporation had been an important part of the company's overall performance with 40 per cent of its revenue derived online. However, office products customers rely on flawless ecommerce performance from their suppliers to help reduce their administrative overheads, and as a result competition within this sector is strong.

One of the challenges facing Cantrell was that their website was not integrated with customer account information, so customers with questions about order status or account balances flooded the call centres. Costs were rising, customers were leaving and performance targets were being missed with increased regularity. Cantrell resolved to

Exhibit 8.2 | Viking Direct – an office supplies company

Using an offline catalogue and online store in combination, Viking Direct drive traffic and provide business customers with different channels to access and buy their office supplies. See www.viking-direct.co.uk/
Images courtesy of Viking Direct

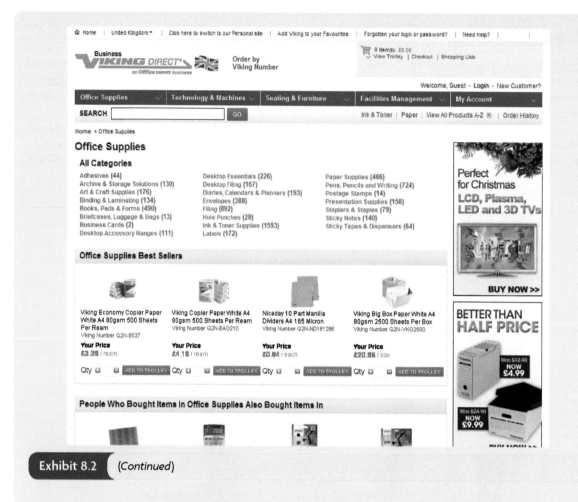

Exhibit 8.2   (Continued)

reassert their prominence in the market. To do this they had to create a world-class shopping experience, with CRM capabilities, automatic fulfilment and integration with their largest customers. The company developed a new website and as a result customers are now able to research their questions online, and the company no longer needs to fund an additional call centre.

Customers can now shop online for office supplies, order online training courses and read online newsletters that are customised for them. They can quickly and efficiently find the items they need in the online catalogue, order them and check stock. Cantrell's order fulfilment system now reads web orders just as if they had been generated from the call centre, and fulfils them automatically. As a result, instead of customers leaving, new accounts are being registered at record levels, order fulfilment cycles have been reduced and costs lowered, all in the name of using technology to improve customer management and retention.

Question

To what extent do you believe customer retention is function of the trade-off between trust and the switching costs associated with finding and establishing a relationship with a different supplier?

Task

List and prioritise the top four attributes you believe the supplier of office equipment must possess.

travel. However, the airlines' desire to develop relationships with their customers might not be fully reciprocated as customers seek only convenience.

Perhaps the attention given to loyalty and retention issues is misplaced because marketing is either about the identification, anticipation and satisfaction of customer needs (profitably), or it is about customer management. Either way, if marketing strategies are successful, it might be reasonable to expect that customers would return anyway, reducing the need for overt 'loyalty' programmes. The absence of any loyalty card at ASDA suggests that they do not see such investment as a suitable (profitable) way of achieving competitive advantage and differentiation. There is an argument that these schemes are important not because of the loyalty aspect but because they allow for the collection of up-to-date customer information and which can be used to make savings in the supply chain. Research indicates strongly that owners of store loyalty cards tend to be more store loyal than those who do not hold a card. Furthermore, when card holders are satisfied with the reward scheme associated with the card programme, they demonstrate greater loyalty and become less price sensitive than card holders who are dissatisfied with the scheme (Demoulin and Zidda, 2008). However, the use of loyalty cards does not appear to influence customer loyalty, for example, by enhancing performance or satisfaction. The one element that loyalty programmes appear to achieve is a strengthening of the relationship between an individual's intention to buy and their actual buying behavior (Evanschitzky and Wunderlich, 2006).

That information has not been updated, but what was one of the main logistical problems concerning the management and analysis of the huge volumes of data collected has largely been overcome. Some organisations use less than half the data they collect and then it was argued that the data actually used can be bought in at a much lower cost than these loyalty schemes cost to run. This may be partly true but vastly improved data-mining and warehousing techniques have led to more effective use of customer data.

There has been a proliferation of loyalty cards, reflecting the increased emphasis upon keeping customers rather than constantly finding new ones and there is evidence that sales lift by about 2 or 3 per cent when a loyalty scheme is launched. Schemes do enable organisations to monitor and manage stock, use direct marketing to cross and up-sell customers, and manage their portfolio in order to consolidate (increase?) customer's spending in a store. Whether loyalty is being developed by encouraging buyers to make repeat purchases or whether the schemes are merely sales promotion techniques that encourage extended and consistent purchasing patterns is debatable. Customer retention is a major issue and a lot of emphasis has been given to loyalty schemes as a means of achieving retention targets.

Hallberg (2004) reports a major study involving in excess of 600,000 in-depth consumer interviews. The study identifies different levels of loyalty and concludes that significant financial returns are gained only when the highest level of loyalty is achieved. These levels of loyalty are set out in Figure 8.4.

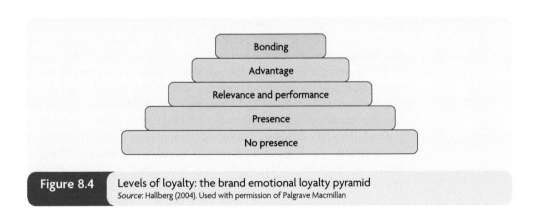

| Figure 8.4 | Levels of loyalty: the brand emotional loyalty pyramid |

Source: Hallberg (2004). Used with permission of Palgrave Macmillan

Hallberg refers to the impact of emotional loyalty, a non-purchase measurement of attachment to a brand:

- At the 'No Presence' level consumers are unaware of a brand and so there is no emotional loyalty.
- At the 'Presence' level there is awareness but emotional loyalty is minimal.
- At the 'Relevance and Performance' level the consumer begins to feel that the brand is acceptable in terms of meeting their needs.
- At the 'Advantage' level consumers should feel that the brand is superior with regard to a particular attribute.
- At the 'Bonding' level emotional loyalty is at its highest because consumers feel the brand has several unique properties. They love the brand.

Loyalty schemes are exponentially effective when the consumers reach the bonding stage. Although sales generally increase the further up the pyramid consumers move it is only at the bonding stage that sales start to reflect the emotional attachment people feel towards the brand. Hallberg refers to the success and market leadership that Tesco has achieved but the principles established through this study should apply to loyalty programmes regardless of category or sector.

The role of marketing communications in relationships

Having considered ideas about relationship marketing and retention, and established its centrality within contemporary marketing thought, it now remains to explore ways in which marketing communications can contribute to relationship marketing. As a general guide, transaction marketing, where the focus is product and price, uses mass, formal based, relatively infrequent communications, where persuasion (promotion) is a central element. With relationship marketing, and its focus on the relationship between the participants, communications are characterised as personal, informal and relatively frequent, which leads to individual communication behaviours that encourage interaction and dialogue. This is compatible with the concepts of integrated marketing communications (IMC).

Grönroos (2004) suggests that although IMC cannot be synonymous with relationship marketing, it is an important aspect. He develops the view that there are two main types of message that customers receive, process and use to determine the extent to which a relationship delivers value. The first of these types is the planned marketing communication message, which is predetermined and delivered through various media and tools of the communication mix. Planned messages set out an organisation's promises. The second are messages generated through the product and service aspects of the interaction that occurs between organisations and their customers. The degree to which these two streams of messages support or counter each other will influence the type of unplanned communications that ensue, and the nature of word-of-mouth communications that arise. (See Figure 1.1 for a graphical representation of these types of marketing communication message.)

The greater the degree that the two sets of messages support or reinforce one another, the more favourable the unplanned communication that should result in positive word-of-mouth communication (Grönroos and Lindberg-Repo, 1998). This can lead to the establishment of two-way communication, an increasing propensity to share information, a process of reasoning and ultimately dialogue. Reasoning is important because it enables a sharing of values and a deeper understanding of the other party's needs and position. Through shared meaning, trust increases. Grönroos (2004) argues that relationship marketing develops not from planned marketing communications, but through the interaction and personal experience of products and services and the degree to which these two sets of messages and meanings complement the

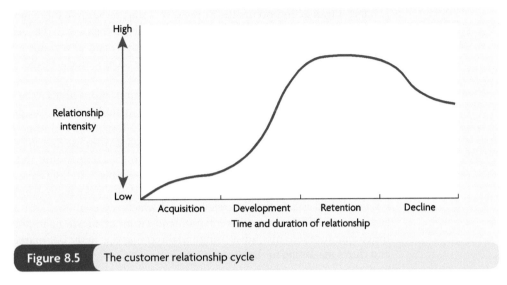

Figure 8.5   The customer relationship cycle

promises and messages transmitted previously. He suggests that when these two processes come together a single communication process emerges. Put precisely he says, 'the two processes merge into a relationship dialogue' (2004: 107).

Marketing communications can play an important role throughout all relationship phases and at all stages of the customer lifecycle. Indeed, marketing communications should be used to engage with audiences according to the audiences' needs, whether transactional and remote or whether relational and close. According to Ryssel *et al.* (2004) the use of information systems and technology, which enables communication to be timely, accurate and direct, has a positive impact on trust.

Customer relationships can be considered in terms of a series of relationship development phases; customer acquisition, development, retention and decline. Collectively these are referred to as the customer lifecycle. The duration and intensity of each relationship phase in the lifecycle will inevitably vary and it should be remembered that this representation is essentially idealistic. A customer relationship cycle is represented in Figure 8.5.

Customer acquisition

The acquisition phase is characterised by three main events: search, initiation and familiarisation (see Table 8.4).

The logical sequence of acquisition activities moves from search and verification through the establishment of credentials. The length of this initiation period will depend partly on the importance of the buying decision and the complexity of the products, and partly upon the nature of the introduction. If the parties are introduced by an established and trusted source then certain initiation rites can be shortened.

Table 8.4   Customer acquisition events

Acquisition event	Explanation
Search	Buyers and sellers search for a suitable pairing
Initiation	Both parties seek out information about the other before any transaction occurs
Familiarisation	The successful completion of the first transaction enables both parties to start revealing more information about themselves

Once a transaction occurs the buyer-sellers start to become more familiar with each other and gradually begin to reveal more information about themselves. The seller receives payment, delivery and handling information about the buyer, and as a result is able to prepare customised outputs. The buyer is able to review the seller's products and experience the service quality of the seller.

During the acquisition phase marketing communications needs to be geared towards creating awareness and providing access to the brand. Included within this period will be the need to help potential customers become familiar with the brand and to help them increase their understanding of the key attributes, possible benefits from use and to know how the brand is different and represents value that is superior to the competition. Indeed, marketing communications has to work during this phase because it needs to fulfil a number of different roles and it needs to be targeted at precise audiences. Perhaps the main overriding task is to create a set of brand values that are relevant and which represent significant value for the target audience. In DRIP terms, differentiation and information will be important and, in terms of the communications mix, advertising and direct marking in the b2c market and personal selling and direct marketing in the b2b market.

Customer development

The development phase is characterised by the seller attempting to reduce buyer risk and enhancing credibility. This is achieved by encouraging cross-selling whereby the buyer consumes other products, by improving the volume of purchases, by engaging the buyer with other added-value services and by varying delivery times and quantities. The buyer's acquiescence is dependent upon their specific needs and the degree to which the buyer wishes to become more involved with the supplier. Indeed, it is during this phase that the buyer is able to determine whether or not it is worth developing deeper relationships with the seller.

The main goals during the development phase are for the sellers to reduce buyer-perceived risk and to simultaneously enhance their own credibility. In order to reduce risk a number of messages will need to be presented through marketing communications. The selection of these elements will depend upon the forms of risk that are present either in the market sector or within individual customers. Marketing communications needs to engage by communicating messages concerning warranties and guarantees, finance schemes, third-party endorsements and satisfied customers, independent testing and favourable product performance reports, awards and the attainment of quality standards, membership of trade associations, delighted customers, growth and market share, new products and alliances and partnerships, all of which seek to reduce risk and improve credibility.

In DRIP terms information and persuasion will be important and in terms of the communications mix, public relations, sales promotion and direct marking in the b2c market and personal selling, public relations and direct marketing in the b2b market.

Viewpoint 8.4	Integrated, luxurious communications by Fabergé

Fabergé's re-entry into the luxury jewellery market is remarkable for many reasons, but of these one stands out, the brand's use of marketing communications to build relationships.

The average price of a piece of Fabergé jewellery is over £100,000, so issues concerning security, access, positioning, and service and support are critical. The traditional channel strategy is to establish a small number of prestigious retail stores where all of these factors can be managed. However, the downside is that this product oriented strategy fails to maximise customer convenience.

Fabergé's solution was to develop customer relationships based on an integrated online/offline strategy. Customers can visit the website and inspect jewellery in their own time, from any part of the world. Using high-quality photography it is possible for customers to see jewellery in greater depth than they can physically in store.

Help is provided by online sales assistants. Using voice, video, and text according to the customer's choice customers are able to refine their preferences. However, purchasing is not carried out online. Once an item is selected, a sales assistant flies out to meet the customer to allow them to see, touch and try on the product, as necessary. Experience suggests that a purchase is made on most occasions once the product is seen physically.

Source: Based on Murphy (2009); www.faberge.com

Question

List the ways the elements of the marketing communications mix have been used to build customer relationships at Fabergé.

Task

Visit the Fabergé website (www.faberge.com/) and find the bell!

Exhibit 8.3	The Poppy Ring – a thing of beauty
	The *Poppy Ring* epitomises Fabergé's positioning in the luxury jewellery market. Image courtesy of Fabergé

Customer retention

The retention phase is the most profitable, where the greatest level of relationship value is experienced. The retention phase will generally last as long as both the buyer and seller are able to meet their individual and joint goals. If the relationship becomes more involved greater levels of trust and commitment between the partners will allow for increased cross-buying and product experimentation and, for b2b relationships, joint projects and product development. However, the very essence of relationship marketing is for organisations to identify a portfolio of customers with whom they wish to develop a range of relationships. This requires the ability to measure levels of retention and also to determine when resources are to be moved from acquisition to retention and back to acquisition.

The length of the retention phase will reflect the degree to which the marketing communications is truly interactional and based on dialogue. Messages need to be relational and reinforcing. Incentive schemes are used extensively in consumer markets as a way of retaining customers and minimising customer loss (or churn, defection or attrition). They are also used to cross-sell products and services and increase a customer's commitment and involvement with the brand. Through the use of an integrated programme of communications value can be enhanced for both parties and relational exchanges are more likely to be maintained. In business markets personal contact and key account management are crucial to maintaining interaction, understanding and mutual support. Electronic communications have the potential to automate many routine transactions and allow for increased focus on one-to-one communications.

In DRIP terms reinforcement and information will be important and, in terms of the communications mix, sales promotion and direct marking in the b2c market and personal selling (and key accounts), public relations and direct marketing in the b2b market.

Customer decline

Customer decline is concerned with the closure of a relationship. Termination may occur suddenly as a result of a serious problem or episode between the parties. The more likely process is that the buying organisation decides to reduce their reliance on the seller because their needs have changed, or an alternative supplier who offers superior value has been found. The buyer either formally notifies the established supplier or begins to reduce the frequency and duration of contact and moves business to other, competitive organisations.

The termination process therefore may be sharp and sudden or slow and protracted. Marketing communications plays a minor role in the former but is more significant in the latter. During an extended termination, marketing communications, especially direct marketing in the form of telemarketing and email, can be used to deliver orders and profits. These forms of communication are beneficial because they allow for continued personal messages but do incur the heavy costs associated with field selling (b2b) or advertising (b2c).

In DRIP terms reinforcement and persuasion will be important and, in terms of the communications mix, direct marketing in both markets and sales promotion in the b2c will be significant.

This cycle of customer attraction (acquisition), development, retention and decline represents a major difference to the four Ps approach. It is, above all else, customer focused and more appropriate to marketing values. The car manufacturer Audi developed the Audi Customer Journey. This is used to chart the ownership cycle and then superimpose optimised brand communications for each owner. This approach is reflected in Audi's loyalty rate which has grown consistently since the Journey was introduced.

However, even this approach is questionable as, although the focus of analysis is no longer the product but the relationship, the focus tends to be oriented towards the 'customer relationship' rather than the relationship per se. In other words there is a degree of asymmetry inherent in the relationship marketing concept.

Employee relationships and marketing communications

Traditionally, external stakeholders (customers, intermediaries and financiers) are the prime focus of marketing communications. However, recognition of the importance of internal stakeholders as a group who should receive marketing attention has increased, and the concept of *internal marketing* emerged in the 1980s.

Today the role of the employee within the branding process, and through their interface with customers and other stakeholders, is recognised as critically important. Now employees are recognised as brand ambassadors (Freeman and Liedtka, 1997 and Hemsley, 1998). This is particularly important in service environments where employees represent the interface between an organisation's internal and external environments and where their actions can have a powerful effect in creating images among customers (Schneider and Bowen, 1985; Balmer and Wilkinson, 1991).

Employees are important to external stakeholders not only because of the tangible aspects of service and production that they provide but also because of the intangible aspects, such as attitude and the way in which the service is provided: 'How much do they really care?' Images are often based more on the intangible than the tangible aspects of employee communications. Toyota's reassurance-based communications following the well publicised safety issues was anchored in its use of employees. Their campaign entitled 'Your Toyota is my Toyota' was used to present the human face of the car manufacturer and involved selected employees pledging their support to customers (Brownsell, 2010).

Management is responsible for the allocation of resources and the process and procedures used to create value. Its actions effectively constrain the activities of the organisation and shape the nature and form of the communications the organisation adopts, either consciously or unconsciously. Each organisation is a major influence upon its own marketing communications and can influence the perception others have of the character and personality of the organisation.

Purpose of internal marketing communications

Research by Foreman and Money (1995) indicates that managers see the main components of internal marketing as falling into three broad areas, namely development, reward and vision for employees. These will inevitably vary in intensity on a situational basis.

All of these three components have communication as a common linkage. Employees and management (members) need to communicate with one another and with a variety of non-members, and do so through an assortment of methods. Communication with members, wherever they are located geographically, needs to be undertaken for a number of reasons. These include the DRIP factors (Chapter 1), but these communications also serve the additional purposes of providing transaction efficiencies and affiliation needs; see Table 8.5.

The values transmitted to customers, suppliers and distributors through external communications need to be reinforced by the values expressed by employees, especially those who interact with these external groups. Internal marketing communications are necessary in order that internal members are motivated and involved with the brand such that they are able to present a consistent and uniform message to various stakeholders. This is an aspect of integrated marketing communications and involves product and organisation centred messages.

Table 8.5	The roles of internal marketing communications
DRIP factors	To provide information To be persuasive To reinforce – reassure/remind To differentiate employees/groups
Transactional	To coordinate actions To promote the efficient use of resources To direct developments
Affiliation	To provide identification To motivate personnel To promote and coordinate activities with non-members

If there is a set of shared values then internal communications are said to blend and balance the external communications. This process whereby employees are encouraged to communicate with customers helps ensure that what is promised by an organisation is realised and delivered, sometimes referred to as 'living the brand'.

Organisational culture

According to Beyer (1981), organisational identity is a subset of the collective beliefs that constitute an organisation's culture. Indeed, internal marketing is shaped by the prevailing culture, as it is the culture that provides the context within which internal marketing practices are to be accomplished.

Corporate culture, defined by Schein (1985), is 'the deeper level of basic assumptions and beliefs that are shared by members of an organisation, that operate unconsciously and define in a basic taken for granted fashion an organisation's view of its self and its environment'. A more common view of organisational culture is 'the way we do things around here'. It is the result of a number of factors, ranging through the type and form of business the organisation is in, its customers and other stakeholders, its geographical position, and its size, age and facilities. These represent the more tangible aspects of corporate culture. There are a host of intangible elements as well. These include the assumptions, values and beliefs that are held and shared by members of the organisation. These factors combine to create a unique environment, one where norms or guides to expected behaviour influence all members, whatever their role or position.

Internal engagement

Ideas about engagement, explored elsewhere in this book, have their roots in employee-based communications. It is generally accepted that employees need to buy-in to their workplace values in order that they be fully motivated and effective (Thomson and Hecker, 2000). This buy-in or process of engagement, consists of two main components; an intellectual and an emotional element (Hardaker and Fill, 2005). The intellectual element is concerned with employees buying-in and aligning themselves with the organisation's strategy, issues and overall direction. The emotional element is concerned with employees taking ownership of their contribution and becoming committed to the achievement of stated goals. Engagement is not passive as Starling (2008) believes, it has learning, understanding and action elements, not all of which need to be implemented at the same time, for all people.

Viewpoint 8.5	Explosive employee engagement at TNT

Most CEOs know how important it is that employees understand the organisation's strategy, mission and values. One of the standard ways of communicating these elements is to cascade the message through levels of management to employees. This is often coupled with question and answer sessions, newsletters and email. However, this sequential process suffers from information loss and deviance as messages are relayed in wave, each successively distanced from the perceived source.

TNT overcame this problem by developing a Virtual CEO office, called 'In Touch with Peter', on the firm's intranet. The site contains the CEO Agenda which details the strategic priorities for the coming year. Every two months there is a 90-minute online chat session, based around one the strategic agenda items. A transcript of the chat is posted and actions arising are also made available. The CEO blogs once every two weeks and his response to the employees' responses are also posted. Participation in the blogging process is often undertaken by those employees who are already engaged. TNT believes that reaching out to the disengaged can be achieved successfully by responding openly and respectfully to negative postings. What is more, those who are engaged can be expected to share their engagement with the disengaged, through dialogue.

Source: Based on van Harmelen (2008)

Question

To what extent are electronic communications between management and employees a poor substitute for face-to-face communication?

Task

Write a list of all the ways managers and employees might communicate with one another. Prioritise this list in terms of the effectiveness of the communication methods.

Exhibit 8.4   Peter Bakker (CEO), who features in the 'In Touch with Peter' interface
Image © 2010 TNT N.V.

Communication strategies should be based on the information processing styles of employees and access to preferred media. Ideally these communications should reflect a suitable balance between the need for rational information to meet intellectual needs, and expressive types of communication to meet the emotional needs of a workforce. It follows that the more effective the communication, the higher the level of engagement.

The development of brands based around employees, can be accomplished effectively and quickly by simply considering the preferred information processing style of an internal audience. By developing messages that reflect the natural processing style and using a diversity of media that best complements the type of message and the needs of each substantial internal target audience, the communication strategy is more likely to be successful.

Client–agency relationships

There are a vast number of relationships that form between various clients and agencies, disciplines, and within individual organisations. The nature of the relationships that exist in the marketing communications industry undoubtedly shapes and influences the strategies and operations of its member organisations. These are of course business-to-business relationships and require marketing communications that reflect the personal, often face-to-face nature of the way these two parties interact.

There are a number of agency–client relationships that have flourished over a very long period of time, and some for several decades. However, these appear to be in the minority, as many relationships appear to founder as clients abandon agencies and search for better, fresher solutions, because a contract expires, the client needs change or because of takeovers and mergers between agencies, which require that they forfeit accounts that cause a conflict of interest.

From a contextual perspective these buyer/seller relationships can be seen to follow a pattern of formation, maintenance and severance, or pre-contract, contracting process and post-contract stages (Davidson and Kapelianis, 1996). Clients and agencies enter into a series of interactions (West and Paliwoda, 1996) or exchanges through which trust and commitment are developed. Hakansson (1982) identified different contexts or atmospheres within which a relationship develops. These contexts had several dimensions: closeness/distance, cooperation/conflict, power/dependence, trustworthiness and expectations. Therefore, the client–agency relationship should be seen in the context of the network of organisations and interactions (or exchanges) that occur in a system. It is through these interactions that the tasks that need to be accomplished are agreed, resources made available, strategies determined and goals achieved.

The quality of an agency/client relationship is a function of trust, which is developed through the exchanges which fosters confidence. As discussed earlier, commitment is derived from a belief that the relationship is worth continuing and that maximum effort is warranted at maintaining the relationship (Morgan and Hunt, 1994). The development of new forms of remuneration, based around payment by results, also signifies a new client focus and a willingness to engage with clients and to be paid according to the success and contribution the agency can provide (Lace and Brocklehurst, 2000).

Poor relationships between agencies and clients are likely to result from a lack of trust and falling commitment. As it appears that communication is a primary element in the formation and substance of relational exchanges, clients might be advised to consider the agencies in their roster as an extended department of the core organisation and to use internal marketing communication procedures to assist the development of identity and sense of belonging.

In many ways agencies are an extension of the internal perspective discussed earlier. If this notion is accepted then it is important to involve, engage and embrace agencies in the same way as employees. However laudable this might be, practice suggests many agencies are kept at a distance and are treated on a need-to-know basis.

Traditionally communications have been based on face-to-face meetings and telephone conversations, supported by contact reports and briefing documents. Increasingly digital media plays a central role in the communications between clients and agencies. Often this can be through a portal and FTP sites through which briefs, contact reports, creative ideas and market knowledge can be shared globally, 24/7.

The agency–client relationship is based on the value clients can generate through the services provided their selected an agency. Therefore, agencies are keen to demonstrate their willingness and potential to generate value as frequently as possible, normally in the way in which the client is serviced. One of the issues that can arise from this client–agency dynamic is the 'over-servicing' that can occur as agencies strive to please their clients. Essentially this involves giving extra time to the client, free of charge, rather than charge lower rates. Blyth (2009) identifies two forms of over-servicing, observed in the PR industry. The first is the *deal-based* over-service, where an agreement between senior managers on both sides to promote a new product, is reached without any planning and costing. The result is that the client rarely gets what they expect, and the agency over works to deliver the desired outcomes and the account loses money.

The second form is *client-induced* over-servicing. This can occur when the client encourages the account team to put in more time and the agency managers fail to prevent the team responding. Again the result can be reduced margins, not only on this account but also on others in the portfolio as the account team's time is spread more thinly.

Summary

In order to help consolidate your understanding of the way marketing communications can shape relationships, here are the key points summarised against each of the learning objectives:

1 Examine ideas associated with perceived customer value

Value is the customer's estimate of the extent to which a product or service can satisfy their needs. According to Doyle (2000) the creation of customer value is based on three principles:

- Customers will choose between alternative offerings and select the one that (they perceive) will offer them the best value.
- Customers do not want product or service features, they want their needs met.
- It is more profitable to have a long-term relationship between a customer and a company rather than a one-off transaction.

2 Consider the theoretical concepts underpinning relationship marketing, including marketing exchanges and value creation

Relationship value can be visualised as a continuum. At one end of the continuum are transactional exchanges, characterised by short-term, product or price oriented exchanges, between buyers and sellers coming together for one-off exchanges. At the other end of the continuum are relational exchanges. These are characterised by a long-term orientation, where ultimately there is complete integration of systems and processes and where the relationship is motivated by partnership and mutual support.

An alternative view considers a spectrum of value propositions, which depict various forms of value creation. Movement along the relationship continuum can be interpreted as a change in the way value is created. Ribeiro *et al.* (2009) identify four core value strategies. These are exchange (or commodity) value, added value, performance value and value co-creation strategies.

3 Explain the concepts of trust and commitment and how they can be used to develop loyalty and retention programmes

Trust is a means of reducing uncertainty in order that effective relationships can develop. Commitment is a desire to continue and strengthen a valued relationship. Loyalty arises from these two concepts and can be considered from a behavioural (increasing sales) and/or an attitudinal (customer satisfaction) perspective. Loyalty is a deeply held sense of commitment to continue buying a preferred product or service on a consistent basis for the foreseeable future.

4 Consider the customer development cycle and the role of marketing communications in developing customer relationships

Customer relationships can be considered in terms of a series of relationship development phases; customer acquisition, development, retention and decline. Collectively these are referred to as the customer lifecycle. The duration and intensity of each relationship phase in the lifecycle will inevitably vary and it should be remembered that this representation is essentially idealistic.

Relationship marketing develops through a combination of planned marketing communications, the interaction and personal experience of products and services and the degree to which these two sets of messages and meanings complement the promises and messages transmitted previously. When these two processes come together a single communication process emerges and a relationship dialogue ensues.

5 Appraise the role of marketing communications in the development of employee relationships

Internal marketing communications are necessary in order that employees, managers and outsourced agencies providing client interfaced activities (e.g. subcontractors, call centres), are sufficiently motivated and involved with the brand such that they are able to present a consistent and uniform message to various stakeholders.

Communication strategies should be based on the information processing styles of employees and their access to preferred media. Ideally these communications should reflect a suitable balance between the need for rational information to meet intellectual needs and expressive types of communication to meet emotional needs of the workforce. It follows that the more effective the communication, the higher the level of engagement.

6 Examine the characteristics associated with client/agency relationships

The quality of an agency/client relationship is a function of trust, which is developed through the exchanges and that fosters confidence and commitment. This is derived from a belief that the relationship is worth continuing and that maximum effort is warranted at maintaining the relationship. Today, the client/agency relationship might be seen in terms of the current and potential value created by the two parties working together.

The development of new forms of remuneration, based around payment by results, plus the use of digital technology to cut production costs, increase communication speed and enhance responsiveness and signifies a willingness by agencies to engage with clients and improve the relationship outcomes.

Review questions

1. Discuss the view that the notion of customer value is too abstract to be of worth to organisations when loyalty is so hard to establish.
2. Identify the three principles Doyle established for the development of customer value.
3. Without looking back, draw the figure depicting the range of value oriented exchanges.
4. Make a list of the main differences between transactional and relationship marketing.
5. What is the link between trust and commitment?
6. Prepare brief notes defining loyalty and then find two different commercial loyalty programmes and consider the marketing communications used to support them.
7. Draw the customer relationship lifecycle and show how marketing communications is used at the different stages.
8. Discuss ways in which marketing communications can be used to develop relationships with customers.
9. What is employee engagement from a communication perspective?
10. Explain the term 'over-servicing' and suggest ways in which it might be managed.

References

Achrol, R.S. (1991) Evolution of the marketing organisation: new forms for turbulent environments. *Journal of Marketing*, 55(4), 77–93.

Anderson, J.C. and Narus, J.A. (1998) Business marketing: understand what customers value, *Harvard Business Review*, 76 (June), 53–65.

Angear, B. and Sambles, M. (2009) How Walkers used co-creation to get the UK to do it a flavour, *Admap*, 508 (September). Retrieved 6 November 2010 from www.warc.com/ArticleCenter/Default.asp?CType=A&AID=WORDSEARCH89872&Tab=A

Anon (2009) Cajun squirrel among crisp flavours tested by Walkers, *The Telegraph*. Retrieved 1 March 2010 from www.telegraph.co.uk/foodanddrink/4206310/Cajun-squirrel-among-crisp-flavours-tested-by-Walkers.html

Balmer, J.M.T. and Wilkinson, A. (1991) Building Societies: change, strategy and corporate identity, *Journal of General Management*, 17(2), 22–33.

Beyer, J.M. (1981) Ideologies, values and decision making in organisations. In *Handbook of Organisational Design* (eds P. Nystrom and W. Swarbruck). London: Oxford University Press.

Blyth, A. (2009) Calling time on over-servicing, *PRWeek-Thought Leader* (December), 4–5.

Brownsell, A. (2009) Not just the ticket, *Marketing*, 9 December, 14.

Brownsell, A. (2010) Toyota's road to recovery, *Marketing*, 12 May, 17.

Christopher, M., Payne, A. and Ballantyne, D. (2002) *Relationship Marketing: Creating Stakeholder Value*. Oxford: Butterworth Heinemann, Elsevier.

Cousins, P. and Stanwix, E. (2001) It's only a matter of confidence! A comparison of relationship management between Japanese and UK non-owned vehicle manufacturers, *International Journal of Operations and Production Management*, 21(9), October, 1160–1180.

Davidson, S. and Kapelianis, D. (1996) Towards an organisational theory of advertising: agency–client relationships in South Africa, *International Journal of Advertising*, 15, 48–60.

Day, G. (2000) Managing market relationships, *Journal of the Academy of Marketing Science*, 28(1), Winter, 24–30.

Demoulin, N.T.M. and Zidda, P. (2008) On the impact of loyalty cards on store loyalty: Does the customers' satisfaction with the reward scheme matter? *Journal of Retailing and Consumer Services*, 15(5) (September), 386–398.

Dick, A.S. and Basu, K. (1994) Customer loyalty: toward an integrated framework, *Journal of the Academy of Marketing Science*, 22(2), 99–113.

Doney, P.M. and Cannon, J.P. (1997) An examination of the nature of trust in buyer–seller relationships, *Journal of Marketing*, 62(2), 1–13.

Dowling, G.R. and Uncles, M. (1997) Do customer loyalty programmes really work?, *Sloan Management Review* (Summer), 71–82.

Doyle, P. (2000) *Value Based Marketing*. Chichester: John Wiley.

Evanschitzky, H. and Wunderlich, M. (2006) An Examination of Moderator Effects in the Four-Stage Loyalty Model, *Journal of Service Research*, 8(4) (May), 330–345.

Foreman, S.K. and Money, A.H. (1995) Internal marketing: concepts, measurements and application, *Journal of Marketing Management*, 11, 755–768.

Freeman, E. and Liedtka, J. (1997) Stakeholder capitalism and the value chain, *European Management Journal*, 15(3), 286–296.

Gambetta, D. (1988) *Trust: Making and Breaking Co-operative Relations*. New York: Blackwell.

Goodman, L.E. and Dion, P.A. (2001) The determinants of commitment in the distributor–manufacturer relationship. *Industrial Marketing Management*, 30(3) (April), 287–300.

Grönroos, C. (2004) The relationship marketing process: communication, interaction, dialogue, value, *Journal of Business and Industrial Marketing*, 19(2), 99–113.

Grönroos, C. (2009), Marketing as promise management: regaining customer management for marketing, *Journal of Business and Industrial Marketing*, 24(5/6), 351–359.

Grönroos, C. and Lindberg-Repo, K. (1998) Integrated marketing communications: the communications aspect of relationship marketing, *The IMC Research Journal*, 4(1), 3–11.

Hakansson, H. (1982) *International Marketing and Purchasing of Industrial Goods: An Interaction Approach*. Chichester: John Wiley.

Hallberg, G. (2004) Is your loyalty programme really building loyalty? Why increasing emotional attachment, not just repeat buying, is key to maximizing programme success, *Journal of Targeting Measurement and Analysis for Marketing*, 12(3), 231–241.

Hardaker, S. and Fill, C. (2005) Corporate Service Brands: the intellectual and emotional engagement of employees, *Corporate Reputation Review: an International Journal*, 7(4) (Winter), 365–376

Hemsley, S. (1998) Internal affairs, *Marketing Week*, 2 April, 49–53.

Kothandaraman, P. and Wilson, D. (2001) The future of competition: value creating networks, *Industrial Marketing Management*, 30(4) (May), 379–389.

Lace, J.M. and Brocklehurst, D. (2000) You both win when you play the same game, *Admap*, October, 40–42.

Macneil, I.R. (1980) *The New Social Contract*. New Haven, CT: Yale University Press.

Morgan, R.M. and Hunt, S.D. (1994) The commitment-trust theory of relationship marketing, *Journal of Marketing*, 58 (July), 20–38.

Morrison, D.E. and Firmstone, J. (2000) The social function of trust and implications of e-commerce, *International Journal of Advertising*, 19, 599–623.

Murphy, D. (2009) Structural Change, *Revolution*, December, 38–39.

Nettleton, K. (2009) Close-Up: Walkers' 'do us a flavour' is engaging the nation, *Campaign*, 23 January, retrieved 1 March 2010 from www.campaignlive.co.uk/news/features/875884/close-up-walkers-do-us-flavour-engaging

Oliver, R.L. (1997) *Satisfaction: A Behavioral Perspective on the Consumer*. New York: McGraw-Hill.

O'Malley, L. (1998) Can loyalty schemes really build loyalty?, *Marketing Intelligence and Planning*, 16(1), 47–55.

Pavlou, P.A. (2002) Institution-based trust in interorganisational exchange relationships: the role of online b2b marketplaces on trust formation, *The Journal of Strategic Information Systems*, 11(3–4) (December), 215–243.

Puth, G., Mostert, P. and Ewing, M. (1999) Consumer perceptions of mentioned product and brand attributes in magazine advertising, *Journal of Product Brand Management*, 8(1), 38–50.

Reichheld, F.F. and Sasser, E.W. (1990) Zero defections: quality comes to services, *Harvard Business Review* (September), 105–111.

Reinartz, W.J. and Kumar, V. (2002) The mismanagement of customer loyalty, *Harvard Business Review* (July), 86–94.

Ribeiro, A.H.P., Brashear, T.G., Monteiro, P.R.R. and Damázio, L.F. (2009) Marketing relationships in Brazil: trends in value strategies and capabilities, *Journal of Business and Industrial Marketing*, 24(5/6), 449–459.

Rowe, W.G. and Barnes, J.G. (1998) Relationship marketing and sustained competitive advantage, *Journal of Market-Focused Management*, 2(3), 281–289.

Ryssel, R., Ritter, T. and Gemunden H.G. (2004) The impact of information technology deployment on trust, commitment and value creation in business relationships, *Journal of Business and Industrial Marketing*, 19(3), 197–207.

Schein, E.H. (1985) *Organisational Culture and Leadership*. San Francisco, CA: Jossey-Bass.

Schneider, B. and Bowen, D. (1985) Employee and customer perceptions of service in banks: replication and extension, *Journal of Applied Psychology*, 70, 423–433.

Sheth, J.N. and Uslay, C. (2007) Implications of the Revised Definition of Marketing: From Exchange to Value Creation, *Journal of Public Policy & Marketing*, 26(2) (Fall) 302–307.

Simpson, P.M., Sigauw, J.A. and Baker, T.L. (2001) A model of value creation; supplier behaviors and their impact on reseller-perceived value, *Industrial Marketing Management*, 30(2)

(February), 119–34.

Spekman, R. (1988) Perceptions of strategic vulnerability among industrial buyers and its effect on information search and supplier evaluation, *Journal of Business Research*, 17, 313–326.

Spekman, R.E. and Carraway, R. (2006) Making the transition to collaborative buyer–seller relationships: An emerging framework, *Industrial Marketing Management*, 35, 10–19.

Starling, J. (2008) Why engagement is no longer enough, *Strategic Communication Management*, 12(1) (December/January), 7.

Thomson, K. and Hecker, L.A. (2000) The business value of buy-in. In *Internal Marketing: Directions for Management* (eds R.J. Varey and B.R. Lewis), 160–172. London: Routledge.

van Harmelen, R. (2008) Inviting TNT's employees into the CEOs virtual office, *Strategic Communication Management*, 12(1) (December/January), 12.

Vargo, S.L. (2009) Toward a transcending conceptualization of relationship: a service-dominant logic perspective, *Journal of Business & Industrial Marketing*, 24(5/6), 373–379.

Vargo , S.L. and Lusch, R.F. (2004) Evolving a New Dominant Logic for Marketing, *Journal of Marketing*, 68 (January), 1–17.

West, D.C. and Paliwoda, S.J. (1996) Advertising client–agency relationships, *European Journal of Marketing*, 30(8), 22–39.

White, T., Wassef, S. and Angear, B. (2010) Walkers – Embracing the unfamiliar: Walkers do us a flavour, *IPA Effectiveness Awards 2010*. Retrieved 6 November from www.warc.com/ArticleCenter/Default.asp?CType=A&AID=WORDSEARCH92547&Tab=A

Young, L.C. and Wilkinson, I.F. (1989) The role of trust and co-operation in marketing channels: a preliminary study, *European Journal of Marketing*, 23(2), 109–122.

| Minicase 2.1 | 'Get on your bike!' Mountain biking tourism in the Cairngorms National Park (CNP) |

Andrew Turnbull: Aberdeen Business School, Robert Gordon University

Interest in mountain biking is currently undergoing rapid growth in Scotland and mountain biking tourism offers a means to use the Scottish landscape to attract several, largely untapped, target audiences, including thrill seekers, mountaineers, mountain bike owners, holidaymakers and families. These groups represent a small but growing proportion of the nearly 20 million visitors each year to Scotland from the UK, as well as those from abroad. The question is, however, how can these audiences, with their differing requirements, be engaged and what communications strategies might be employed to reach them most cost effectively?

Areas in Scotland such as the CNP can potentially benefit significantly from successful diversification and provision of facilities for the sport, but a number of stakeholders will need to be satisfied in the process, not least those concerned about the effects on the environment. Certainly mountain biking fits in well with some of the principal aims of the park, for example to promote understanding and enjoyment of the special qualities of the area and to contribute to the social development of the area's communities. The issue is whether this can be successfully linked to the promotion of sustainable use of the park's natural resources. For the long term, it is critical that any new mountain biking facilities do not have a detrimental impact upon fragile landscapes or rare wildlife.

Before considering how to communicate, profiles of the receivers must be drawn up. The interest groups here can be summarised as users, divided into the sub-segments above, environmentalists, the media and both local authorities and the Scottish Executive. It is not enough simply to communicate with actual and potential customers when considering such a high profile and environmentally sensitive location. A clear conflict in each group's desires and objectives represents a major obstacle to a successful communications plan.

So the strategy put forward, which stems from primary research activity, included a mix of communications tools taking into account potential resources, the complexity of the messages to be conveyed and the diversity of the audiences, as well as the nature, size and location of the market. Above all, it should be realised that mountain biking trails in the Cairngorms are in their infancy, so awareness creation is the key.

To start with however, advertising will be limited, in part because the audiences are geographically spread and

in part because of the expense. Specialist publications such as *Cycling World* and *Men's Health* can be used, however, and other titles will be considered in or immediately pre-season, including local press in the CNP area. Inserts, as a form of direct marketing, also represent an option and information leaflets, including sales promotional offers, will be distributed to all visitor centres, attractions and accommodation outlets, including Guest Houses, B&Bs, hostels and hotels. These can be targeted not just within the CNP area, but in any location within a two-hour drive time.

Cinema, in all the major cities in Scotland, is a medium that has potential when the right films are on screen, as the cost is significantly lower than broadcast media, the impact is high and audiences can be easily matched to the mountain biker user profiles identified above. The disadvantage, of course, is that unlike press ads and leaflets, no direct response is possible, only the inclusion of a web address.

The importance of new media, in particular the Internet, cannot be underestimated given the young, educated and well-off customer profile. Dialogue allows interactivity and feedback can give competitive advantage! Websites (such as http://cycling.visitscotland.com/mountain_biking/mb_centre/mountain_biking_cairngorms) providing maps and giving information regarding the newest facilities, the latest trails and access routes will be vital too, in encouraging word-of-mouth among a close-knit group who will frequently communicate between themselves. Receivers in such a market will be easily influenced by opinion and style leaders.

Inevitably, in a campaign with limited finances, publicity gained through public relations activities are expected to form the central part of the communications strategy involving traditional media. Apart from the use of press releases concerning events such as mountain biking championships, advertorials and competitions will be placed in relevant press titles and stands reserved at selected UK exhibitions. Costs can be shared by entering alliances with bike manufacturers and other joint promotional activities are potentially available with equipment and clothing providers, retail outlets and even the ordnance survey map producers. All these organisations are in a position to help each other and combined activity through the pooling of resources will prove mutually beneficial.

Joining forces with other businesses looking to serve the mountain bike community will also assist with presenting a united front to the environmental lobby and the authorities. A socially responsible, environmentally aware message that nevertheless emphasises the financial benefits to the area, allows the media too to support mountain biking initiatives, rather than seek to find fault and take issue with the influx of new people and new activities that potentially conflict with more traditional pursuits such as hill walking and climbing.

An evaluation focus is always critical when measuring the reaction to initiatives targeted so precisely at niche audiences. As with all communications activities, measurement involves both 'hard' factors, which can be precisely quantified, and 'soft' factors, that must then be interpreted to assess their value.

So, for example, the number of new mountain bike trails is known exactly, the number of visitors using them can be estimated and expenditure associated with each visitor group can also be calculated from market research. The share of visits that mountain bikers represent to the area can also be determined as can uplift of, and response to, leaflets left in accommodation establishments and 'hits' on web sites, together with pages viewed and time spent browsing. Visitors to exhibition stands, as well as numbers leaving contact details, are further measures of success. Where media are utilised, then cover, reach and frequency, as well as a profile of the media user, give a good indication of who has been reached and how often.

Nevertheless, it is not just quantifiable measures that demonstrate effectiveness of a campaign. Qualitative measures, including attitudes towards the messages conveyed, the imagery associated with the creative execution, and values expressed, will all contribute to the overall impact.

The way is clear to allow CNP to diversify into mountain biking tourism. Given a good product, with the establishment of trails and facilities, then a focused communications campaign should overcome conservative values and capitalise on the opportunities this relatively new sport provides. The region's economy will benefit, Scotland's reputation will grow and a country that breathes history will further embrace the modern tourist marketplace.

Questions

1. For any marketing communications programme to work, it is essential that the messages sent reach the target audience(s). Summarise all the audiences identified in the case and consider the segmentation criteria that have been applied.

2. Critically analyse the communications process in the case, in the context of at least two models identified earlier in the text book. For example, the process of adoption model and the original Schramm *et al.* linear model.

3. Identify and critically examine the choice and balance of communications activities and media planned and determine first, the reasons for their selection and second, how well you believe they will work together.

Minicase 2.2   The Thoroughly Delicious Ice Cream Company

Ice cream is made from a mixture of milk, fat and sugar, which is cooled and whipped to create a light, airy texture. Flavours, such as fruit or chocolate, are added before the blend is frozen again and then packaged. Premium and super premium ice creams were developed in the 1980s and 1990s and these contain a much higher concentration of milk and cream.

People consume ice cream at one of two main locations. One of these is 'at home', having purchased the product from a supermarket or other retail outlet. This purchase is often planned, as part of a shopping event. The 'at-home' market is worth approximately 33 per cent of the total ice cream market. The other type of location is at a restaurant or café, or when relaxing on a beach or in the countryside. This is referred to as the 'out-of-home' market and is very often the result of an impulse, or unplanned purchase. This market constitutes approximately 66 per cent of the total. Apart from good distribution, there is one critical success factor that applies to all producers in the ice cream market and that is the need to be innovative and have proven new product development processes.

Unilever and Nestlé are the world's leading ice cream companies with brands that are established in many countries around the world. The UK ice cream market is led by Unilever, with brands such as Magnum, Carte D'Or, and Cornetto. Baskin-Robbins, the US ice cream brand, entered the UK market in 2010 with a range of premium ice cream tubs. Häagen-Dazs and Unilever's Ben & Jerry's have established themselves as the leading brands in the global super premium market.

The ice cream sector is facing a number of interrelated challenges. Consumers are beginning to be concerned with health issues such as obesity and allergies. As a result they are now much more interested in the ingredients of the foods they are eating, with purity and freshness key elements. Related to this are trends towards consuming more locally produced foods in preference to mass-produced factory products. Green issues are also much more prevalent in the sector than they used to be and the rapid development of 'Fairtrade' brands is testimony to the recent success of these brands in some developed economies. Ben & Jerry's have always been positioned on an ethical platform demonstrated by their policy not to use eggs from caged birds. However, their Classic Vanilla brand, launched in August 2006, was the first UK Fairtrade ice cream brand. Another successful brand, Green & Black's ice cream, has been positioned on their pure organic content.

The final major issue concerns the growing trend towards smaller households (one to two people). This means that the traditional family unit is changing and this requires that ice cream producers adapt their 'at home' products to meet the needs of smaller, different family units.

The Thoroughly Delicious Ice Cream company (TDIC) is a medium-sized family owned company and is typical of a growing number of smaller, local, European premium ice cream producers. Their rapid development owes much to the founder's need to diversify away from milk production when government regulations and milk quotas began to make the milk business unprofitable in the mid-1990s. TDIC's extensive range of ice cream products uses fresh milk, double cream and is free of artificial flavourings, preservatives or colours, all of which are to be found in global brands.

Many people choose the TDIC brand because they know where it is made, what goes into it and there is no complicated supply chain. TDIC's product innovation abilities are well established and have drawn substantial media attention. Their range of subtle and bold flavours appeal to different market segments, have widespread appeal and are even used by many top chefs.

Unlike national and global ice cream brands such as Unilever and Nestlé, TDIC differentiates itself by selling its ice cream through its own ice cream stores or parlours. Here customers not only buy their favourite TDIC brands but can also consume them within a specialist ice cream environment, one which is dedicated to indulgence and luxury. TDIC own 12 stores but they have started to franchise an increasing number of retail outlets. These are developed in clusters and located around major towns and cities.

National brands make extensive use of mass media communications and use national advertising to create awareness and emotional brand values. Smaller companies such as TDIC do not have the budget or the necessity to reach such broad audiences. They use regional and local advertising to reach highly targeted audiences. They also make extensive use of public relations, and their press coverage can be found regularly in leading magazines and newspapers. TDIC have also won several awards, often in recognition of their product development and branding. Vanessa Burridge is the Marketing Manager for TDIC and she has established some key relationships with journalists attached to both local and national newspapers. However, she is aware that the new franchise development strategy requires a new approach to TDIC's marketing communications.

Sources: This case is drawn from a number of sources, including those listed below. It is based partly on a real ice cream company, one that has been anonymised. This case is to be used for teaching and learning purposes and is not intended to infer good or bad management practice; www.icecreamprofits.com/articles/ice-cream-franchise-advertising.asp; Cowlett, M. (2010) Don't blame it on the weather, *Marketing*, 25 July, 26–27; Lewis, H. (2006) Market is heating up for premium, natural, convenient and green ice cream, *Just-Food*, 23 November. Retrieved, 18 January 2007 from www.just-food.com/article.aspx?id=96729

Questions

One of tasks facing Vanessa Burridge is to find ways of developing the TDIC brand and at the same time support the emerging franchise network. As a marketing communications expert and friend of the family, she has asked you for advice in response to the following issues.

Having spent some time considering the issues you should prepare a hand-written, formal response outlining your views with regard to the following questions:

1. Explain the key differences between the marketing communications used to support national brands and those used to support local brands of ice cream.

2. Identify the main relationship issues that might concern the TDIC franchisees, and then explain how TDIC might use marketing communications to manage these issues.

3. Explain how an understanding of customer buyer behaviour might influence the marketing communications used by ice cream companies.

4. Examine ways in which online and digital marketing communications might be used by companies such as TDIC.

Minicase 2.3   Seaport Communications

It could be argued that the importance of marketing communications in the development and competitive positioning of seaports around the world has never been as strong as it is now. This is due mainly to advances in technology, alternative forms of transport and changing seaport customer preferences. These have all served to influence the volume, nature and frequency of freight and passenger traffic using seaports, and in recent years often creating excess or under-utilised port capacity.

The role of marketing communications in the seaport context can be understood in the light of stakeholder management theory. All ports have a number of different stakeholders, each of whom derives different benefits from their stake in the port's activities. Typical stakeholders include ferry and cargo operators, logistics and freight handlers, ferry passengers, employees, the local community, financial services providers and local companies who support the port's infrastructure. Many of these stakeholders are interdependent and few operate successfully without the support of others. An example of these stakeholder interdependencies can be seen through the problems faced by a major European port. Having sustained a thriving port business for many years, based partly on the full utilisation of its ferry berths, difficulties arose when one of the two main ferry companies using the port decide to withdraw its services. This was forced upon them by severe competition from low cost airlines. The withdrawal of the ferry operator resulted in excess capacity, an increase in local unemployment, a fall in income to the local government and a subsequent impact on the provision of some of the local community services, due to budget revisions.

Most seaports play a major role in the economic and social environment of their hinterland, or local region that supports the port. Marketing communications can be used to reach different stakeholders, many of whom are to be found in this area. Once identified, it is important to communicate different messages to different stakeholders using different media. Of course, the choice of communications mix depends largely on the goal of each campaign. Port users, such as a ship owners and freight managers are key stakeholders, so as well as seeking new customers, communications targeted at these stakeholders are often geared to operational issues, providing information about port procedures, fees and access.

The local community derives both an economic and social benefit. For example school children can learn about ports, their facilities, commerce, role and relationship with other countries and companies. Very often these marketing communications can be used to reach parents in order to educate and inform them about recent port developments and its overall significance to the local community. Apart from the benefits of social cohesion and local identity, this can be important for example when a port seeks support for development or investment opportunities. Sponsorship and funding of local community projects can also be used to build community relations.

Communications with ferry passengers are also important as these stakeholders often have an opportunity to sail from alternative ports or forms of transport. Public relations and advertising are often used to develop a port's identity and enable passengers to develop favourable images of the seaport and immediate area. This can create opportunities for passengers to stay in the town before the outward trip or after the return journey.

Although all the tools of the communications mix are used by seaports to communicate with various stakeholders, sales promotions are the least used and personal selling is mainly deployed to create contracts with seaport cargo carriers. Word of mouth communications are vitally important, especially as seaports are largely service providers and there is little tangible evidence of the facilities offered. Word of mouth communications between prospective and established seaport customers can be critical. The use of opinion leaders and opinion formers is therefore necessary to stimulate positive comment and develop relationships.

Questions

1. Explain how marketing communications might be used to change the attitudes of international freight and transportation companies, so that they use your local seaport rather than a competitor seaport, 35 miles (55 km) along the coast.

2. Determine a suitable position for the port and then explain how the port's positioning might be communicated to freight carriers.

Part 3
The marketing communications mix

Chapters 9–15

This part of the book is concerned with the nature and characteristics of the elements that make up the marketing communications mix.

Chapter 9 considers advertising, its role, and how it is used to create engagement in both consumer and business markets. Attention is given to USPs, ESPs and the use of emotion in shock advertising. Considerable time is devoted to exploring the different models and concepts used to explain how advertising works.

Chapter 10 explores two main topics, public relations and sponsorship. It considers the role and characteristics of both tools and provides an overview of some of the main tools used by public relations, including media relations, lobbying, corporate advertising and crisis management. The section on sponsorship examines the reasons for using this tool, the types of objectives that might be set and the variety and different forms of sponsorship activities.

Chapter 11 is concerned with direct marketing and personal selling. Apart from understanding the different methods used to implement direct marketing, including the role of the database the essence of the first part of this chapter is to appreciate the significance of direct marketing and how organisations can use this approach in many different ways. The second part considers the different types, roles and tasks of personal selling before touching upon ideas about multichannel marketing.

Chapter 12 examines three particular tools, sales promotion, exhibitions and product placement. Huge amounts are invested in sales promotion each year, partly because promotions are a key driver of behaviour in both consumer and business markets. Attending exhibitions and trade shows (there is a difference), is a critically significant activity for most businesses. Product placement is developing rapidly, partly because of the benefits in avoiding advertising clutter. All of these are explored in this chapter.

Chapter 13 investigates the different media that organisations can use when configuring their mixes. The chapter is used to explain the broad types of available media, presents a classification process and examines their characteristics. A key section is the explanation of the key differences between conventional and digital media. The chapter closes with a consideration of the principles and issues associated with media planning.

Chapter 14 develops some of the ideas introduced in the previous chapter and considers the nature and characteristics of interactive marketing communications. These embrace the conventional tools but also explores contemporary ideas about interactivity as reflected through search engine marketing, email, electronic word-of-mouth communications, viral, podcasting, RSS feeds, weblogs and of course, online communities, social networks and affiliate marketing.

Chapter 15 is the final chapter and is used to consider the third element of the marketing communications mix, the content of the communication activity. Ideas associated with source credibility, user-generated content, message framing and storytelling are considered before examining the characteristics of different types of message appeal.

There are four minicase studies at the end of this part of the book. These are intended to help you clarify your understanding of the preceding material. Please attempt to answer the questions to be found at the end of each case. There are no right answers but some approaches are better than others.

The minicases are:

3.1 **Tapping into a new zeitgeist:** considers issues associated with *Red* magazine's entry into a crowded marketplace. It draws on a range of media issues and demonstrates the importance of content.

3.2 **EasyPack, Easy Comms:** enables readers to explore ideas associated with developing and justifying a marketing communications mix for a furniture manufacturer. It is therefore a helpful case because it draws on all elements in Part 3.

3.3 **ZipZap Channels:** enables readers to consider personal selling and direct marketing as well as examine the role of websites and digital media in a business to business context. In addition, it considers the principles of relationship marketing and challenges readers to consider how marketing communications should be used to counterbalance a buyer's preferred relationship style.

3.4 **Jol Yoghurt – keeping things in proportion:** allows readers to draw on a range of issues, not just those explored in this part of the book. Ideas about strategy and segmentation, and branding, need to be considered before formulating the right communications mix.

Chapter 9
Advertising

The many facets of advertising, with its rich mosaic of perceptions, feelings, emotions, attitudes, information and patterns of behaviour, have been of interest to academics, researchers, authors and marketing professionals for a long time. Any attempt to understand what advertising is, how it might work and how it is developing, should be tempered with an appreciation of its complexity and inherent contradictions.

Aims and learning objectives

The aims of this chapter are to explore different ideas about advertising and to consider the complexities associated with understanding how clients can best use advertising in the marketing communications mix.

The learning objectives of this chapter are to:

1. consider the role advertising plays in influencing and engaging audiences;

2. examine the use of selling propositions in advertising;

3. explain the principles associated with shock advertising;

4. explore various models, concepts and frameworks which have been used to explain how advertising is thought to influence individuals;

5. consider cognitive processing as a means of understanding how advertising works;

6. examine ideas concerning the use of emotion in advertising.

Introduction

For a long time advertising has been considered to be a significant means of communicating with target audiences, because of its potential to influence the way people think or behave. The thinking element may be concerned with the utilitarian or aspirational benefits of product ownership, or simply a matter of memorising the brand and its features for future recall. The behavioural element may be seen in terms of buying an advertised brand, visiting a website to enquire about a product's features or even to share brand related ideas with a friend or colleague.

Whatever the motivation, the content and delivery of messages are derived from an understanding of the variety of contexts in which the messages are to be used. For example, research might reveal a poor brand image relative to the market leader, or audiences might misunderstand when or how to use a product or service. In both cases the messages are going to be different.

This chapter explores two main advertising issues. The first is about the role and use of advertising, and how ideas about selling propositions and emotion can be used in advertising.

The second concerns the way advertising might work. Here consideration is given to some of the principal models and frameworks that have been published to best explain the process by which advertising might influence audiences.

The role of advertising

If the role of marketing communications is to engage audiences then it is not surprising that the principal role of advertising, is also concerned with engagement. Whether it be on an international, national, local or direct basis, advertising can engage audiences by creating awareness, changing perceptions/attitudes and building brand values, or by influencing behaviour, often through calls-to-action.

Advertising has the capacity to reach huge audiences with simple messages. These messages are intended to enable individuals to comprehend what an offering is, appreciate what its primary benefit is and how this might be of value to an individual. Wherever these individuals are located, the prime goals are to build awareness of a product or an organisation in the mind of the audience and engage them. Engagement, as explored in Chapter 1, occurs when audiences are stimulated to either think about or take action about featured products, services, brands and organisations.

Having successfully engaged an audience, advertising can be used to achieve a number of DRIP-based outcomes, again, as set out in Chapter 1. Advertising is excellent at differentiating and positioning brands. It can be used to reinforce brand messages by reminding, reassuring or even refreshing an individual's perception of a brand. Advertising is also excellent at informing audiences, mainly by creating awareness or helping them to learn about a brand or how it works. The one part of the DRIP framework where its ability is challenged is persuasion. Advertising is poor at provoking or changing behaviour and a different marketing communications mix is necessary to stimulate change. In this circumstance sales promotion, direct marketing and personal selling are going to be prominent tools in the mix.

Management's control over advertising messages is strong; indeed, of all the tools in the communications mix, advertising has the greatest level of control. The message, once generated and signed off by the client, can be transmitted in an agreed manner and style and at times that match management's requirements. This means that, should the environment change unexpectedly, advertising messages can be 'pulled' immediately. For example, had a BP global image campaign designed to build the reputation of the company, been planned for May 2010, it would have had to have been 'pulled' (stopped) following the oil rig explosion and consequent leak in the Gulf of Mexico. Difficulties associated with damage to marine life, the coastline and peoples' livelihoods plus the wider debate concerning what caused the problem, and the potential of further 'disruption', would have prevented BP's messages from being received and processed positively. It is more likely that there would have been a negative effect had any planned advertising been allowed to proceed.

Advertising costs can be considered in one of two ways. On the one hand, there are the absolute costs, which are the costs of buying the space in magazines or newspapers, or the time on television, cinema or radio. These costs can be enormous, and they impact directly on cash flow. For example, the rate card cost of a full-page (colour) advertisement in the *Daily Mail* on a Thursday or Friday was £57,204 (July 2010). To show a 30-second ad each day for one week in the 365-seater Screen 6 at the Sheffield Vue Cinema multiplex, costs £175 (April 2008).

On the other hand, there are the relative costs, which are those costs incurred to reach a member of the target audience with the key message. So, if an audience is measured in hundreds of thousands, or even millions on television, the cost of the advertisement spread across each member of the target audience reduces the cost per contact significantly.

Advertising's main tasks are to build awareness and to (re)position brands, by changing either the perception or attitudes of the target audience. The regular use of advertising, in coordination with the other elements of the communication mix, can be important to the creation and maintenance of a brand personality. Indeed, advertising has a significant strategic role to play in the development of competitive advantage. In some consumer markets advertising is a dominant form of promotion. For example, over 80 per cent of Kellogg's communications budget is directed towards advertising.

Advertising can be used as a mobility barrier, deterring exit from and entry to markets. Some organisations are initially attracted to a new market by the potential profits, but a key entry decision factor will be the weight of advertising, that is the investment or 'spend', necessary to generate demand and a sufficient return on the investment. Many people feel that some brands sustain their large market share by sheer weight of advertising; for example, the washing powder brands of Procter & Gamble and Unilever. In many product categories word-of-mouth communications and the use of digital technologies can stimulate strong levels of awareness. Google and Hotmail are prime examples of contemporary brands developed without the use of advertising. However, advertising, both offline and online, is still a key driver of both brand values and directing certain behaviour, most notably driving people to a website.

Advertising can create competitive advantage by providing the communication necessary for target audiences to frame a product or service. By providing a frame or the perceptual space within which to categorise a product, target audiences are able to position an offering relative to their other significant products, much more easily. Therefore, advertising can provide the means for differentiation and sustainable competitive advantage. It should also be appreciated, however, that differentiation may be determined by the quality of the execution of the advertisements, rather than through the content of the messages.

There has also been a shift in focus away from mass communications, towards more personalised messages delivered through different media. This shift has been demonstrated by the increased use of direct marketing and the Internet, by organisations over the past 10 years. It can also be argued that the development of direct marketing is a response to some of the weaknesses, to do with cost and effectiveness of the other tools, most notably advertising.

The marketing communication mix has expanded and become a more complex managerial instrument, but essentially it is now capable of delivering two main solutions. On the one hand it can be used to develop and maintain brand values, and on the other it could be used to change behaviour through the delivery of calls to action. From a strategic perspective, the former is oriented to the long term and the latter to the short term. It is also apparent that the significant rise of the below-the-line and around-the-line approaches within the mix, is partly a result of the demise of the unique selling proposition (USP), but it is also a reflection of the increasing financial pressures experienced by organisations to improve performance and return on investment, and at the same time demonstrate increased accountability.

Organisations therefore, are faced with a dilemma. On the one hand they need to create brands that are perceived to be of value, but on the other they need to prompt or encourage customers into purchase behaviour. To put it another way, marketing communications should be used to encourage buyers along the purchase decision path but how should advertising be involved, what is its contribution, in creating brand values and which and how many of an organisation's other yet scarce communication resources, should be used to prompt behaviour?

Using advertising to engage audiences

Advertising has traditionally been used to inform audiences and to stimulate brand awareness, an informational task. It has also been used to develop brand preference and brand values and associations, an emotional task. However, advertising and communications as a whole have evolved to the point that these identity and value tasks alone, are now insufficient. The growth of direct marketing and one-to-one, preferably interactive, digital based communications, are now regarded as more effective and efficient. As a result marketing budgets have swung towards establishing a call-to-action, a behavioural rather than attitudinal response.

This then begs the question, what is the role for advertising and what strategies should be used? One approach would be to maintain current advertising strategies on the grounds that awareness and perception are always going to be key factors in an individual's decision-making process. The other extreme approach would be to only use advertising for direct-response work. Neither of these two options seems appropriate or viable in the twenty-first century.

In an age where values and response are necessary ingredients for effective overall communication, advertising strategy needs to be based around the notion of engagement. Customers will want to engage with the values offered by a brand that are significant to them individually. However, there will also be a need to engage with them at a behavioural level and to encourage them to want to respond to the advertising. Advertising strategy should therefore reflect a brand's context. This means it should be adjusted according to the required level of engagement regarding the balance between identity and the development of brand values, with the required level of behavioural response.

Viewpoint 9.1   Ding dong: attacking advertising

Following BSkyB's share purchase of 18 per cent of ITV in 2007 a dispute erupted with its arch rival Virgin Media. Virgin claimed it was a move designed to prevent them from buying the organisation. Not long after this Sky and Virgin agreed to disagree about a fee for the Sky Basics TV package, which led to those channels being unavailable to Virgin Media viewers.

The dispute has two sides. Sky claim the dispute is about Virgin's refusal to pay the asking price to continue carrying the channels. Virgin on the other hand believe that Sky is trying to compel Virgin's customers into switching providers by denying them access to the basic channels (BBC).

Since then the two companies entered into a public spat and used advertising to make allegations and claims designed to inform the public of the real situation as each side saw it.

For example, Virgin Media used a print campaign to compare the TV, broadband and phone services of the two companies. Called 'The Real Deal' the campaign sought to show their superior service. However, Sky brought six complaints about the ads, claiming them as misleading or untrue. These were upheld by the Advertising Standards Authority (Sweney, 2007).

In November 2007 Virgin announced that it was to cease its campaign against Sky, after having spent £32 million on the advertising. James Kidd, Managing Director of Marketing at Virgin Media is reported to have said 'There's no point in spending any more time or money whacking the crap out of each other' (Jones, 2007).

Source: Based on BBC (2007); Jones (2007); Sweney (2007)

Question
What value might Virgin have generated from this £32 million spend?

Task
Find two other brands that have been engaged in a public 'spat' and what was the outcome?

Selling propositions

For a very long time in the advertising world, great emphasis was placed upon the use of unique selling propositions, or USPs. Advertising was thought to work most effectively when the message said something about a product that no competitor brand could offer. For example, Olay claim their products offer 'younger looking skin'. USPs are based on product features and are related to particular attributes that differentiate one product from another, as demonstrated by many washing powders that wash 'whiter', presumably than the competition. If this uniqueness was of value to a consumer then the USP alone was thought sufficient to persuade consumers to purchase. However, as Barwise and Meehan (2009:1) point out, 'customers rarely buy a product because its offers something unique', what they want are better products and services, something that delivers real value.

However, the reign of the USP was short lived when technology enabled me-too and own label brands to be brought to market very quickly and product lifecycles became increasingly shorter. The power of the USP was eroded and with it the basis of product differentiation as it was known then. In addition, the power and purpose of advertising's role to differentiate was challenged. It is interesting that many people still refer to a product in terms of its USP. Some companies believe USP refers to a single selling point. In some cases people refer to USPs, as if a product is capable of having several unique qualities. This is unlikely and is essentially a contradiction in terms.

What emerged were emotional selling propositions or ESPs. Advertising's role became more focused on developing brand values, ones that were based on emotion and imagery. This approach to communication helps build brand awareness, desire and aspirational involvement. However, it often fails to provide customers with a rationale or explicit reason to purchase, what is often referred to as a 'call to action'.

Other tools were required to provide customers with an impetus to act and sales promotions, event marketing, road-shows and later, direct marketing evolved to fulfil this need. These tools are known collectively as below-the-line communication tools and their common characteristic is that they are all capable of driving action or creating behavioural change. For example, sales promotions can be used to accelerate customer behaviour by bringing forward sales that might otherwise have been made at some point in the future. Methods such as price deals, premiums and bonus packs are all designed to change behaviour by calling customers into action. This may be in the form of converting or switching users of competitive products, creating trial use of newly introduced products or encouraging existing customers to increase their usage of the product.

Viewpoint 9.2	Moving from oral health care USPs to ESPs

Toothpaste, the biggest part of the oral hygiene market (including dental floss, mouthwashes, dental gum and dental cleaners and fixatives) has experienced declining sales. This is due in part to competitive price deals, bonus packs and the increasing use of electronic toothbrushes that require less toothpaste.

Toothpaste has traditionally been presented on an attribute basis with each brand focusing on a particular USP. For example, Sensodyne for sensitive teeth and gums and Colgate for decay prevention and tartar control. In the 1990s manufacturers started to develop and position brands on whitening agents with cosmetic benefits. The use of USPs in this market was quite common as products are launched for smokers, children and, for people with gum disease. This focus on USPs began to decline, if only because competitors were able to neutralise each others' USPs.

The change to emotional positioning and ESPs was evident in Crest's 'Revitalise'. Targeted at women, Revitalise used celebrities such as Ulrika Jonsson in their advertising. The focus and positioning became lifestyle oriented with demonstrations about how teeth contribute to an individual's overall beauty, appearance and feelings about oneself. Growing interest in the cosmetic benefits of toothpaste has led Crest's owners, Procter & Gamble, to move the brand from the oral care to the beauty division. In 2009 Macleans launched a new brand, called Macleans Confidence. The brand is positioned for those for whom 'social confidence' is important and aims to be based on 'being ready' for unexpected romantic encounters, a strong emotive positioning.

Source: Based on Bainbridge (2004); Jack (2009)

Question

Discuss the notion that to be really effective messages should include both USPs and ESPs.

Task

Find out the USPs or ESPs used in the cosmetics, fruit juice, digital cameras and PDA categories.

Shock advertising

Advertising strategy may also be considered in terms of the overall response a target audience might give on receipt of particular messages. Some organisations choose a consistent theme for their campaigns, one that is often unrelated to their products or services. One such strategy is the use of shock advertising. Shock advertising according to Venkat and Abi-Hanna (1995) 'is generally regarded as one that deliberately, rather than inadvertently, startles and offends its audience'.

Dahl *et al.* (2003) suggest that shock advertising by definition is unexpected and audiences are surprised by the messages because they do not conform to social norms or their expectations. They argue that audiences are offended because there is 'norm violation, encompassing transgressions of law or custom (e.g., indecent sexual references, obscenity), breaches of a moral or social code (e.g., profanity, vulgarity), or things that outrage the moral or physical senses', for example gratuitous violence and disgusting images (2003: 268). The clothing company French Connection's use of the FCUK slogan and the various Benetton campaigns depicting a variety of incongruous situations (for example, a priest and a nun kissing and a man dying of AIDS) are examples of norm violation. Shock advertising is not only used by commercial organisations such as Diesel, Egg and Sony Entertainment but is also used by not-for-profit organisations such as the government (anti-smoking), charities (child abuse), climate change (Greenpeace) and human rights campaigners (Amnesty International). See Exhibits 9.1 and 9.2, and Viewpoint 9.3 for ways in which shock tactics have been used to stop smoking, and to campaign against child poverty.

Viewpoint 9.3   Shocking tactics to stop smokers

The NHS launched a series of public service advertisements as part of an anti-smoking campaign. Television, press, Internet and posters were used to show smokers having a fish hook pulled through their cheeks. This was intended to illustrate how they were 'hooked' on cigarettes, a representation of a smoker's craving for tobacco. The campaign attracted a huge number of complaints with many claiming the pictures would have negative effects on children and that the ads were offensive, frightening and distressing. Despite this the Department of Health claimed that the 'Get Unhooked' campaign was 'highly effective'.

Non-Smokers' Rights Association (NSR) in France also used shock advertising tactics in an attempt to deter teenagers from taking up the habit. The approach they used was to depict young people smoking as if they were performing oral sex. The assertion was that letting children smoke is tantamount to child abuse.

Cigarette companies have been required to display Egraphic images on packaging to shock people into giving up smoking. In April 2010, the Australian government introduced a 25 per cent increase in cigarette tax and then announced that all cigarette packaging would be in plain cartons. The packs are only allowed to depict the brand name and must include a 'graphic photo depicting the gruesome consequences of smoking'. All branding materials, such as logos, slogans, design features, and use of colour have been banned.

Source: Based on Varley (2010); Kamenev (2010); Lichfield (2010)

Question

Do you believe that the use of advertising to shock people into a change of behaviour is morally wrong?

Task

Find an ad that uses shock techniques. What are the elements in the ad that generates the shock impact?

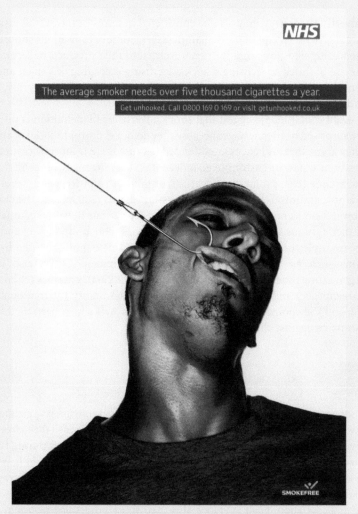

Exhibit 9.1	Fishing to shock smokers – 'hooked' print ad from the NHS
	Image courtesy of The Advertising Archives

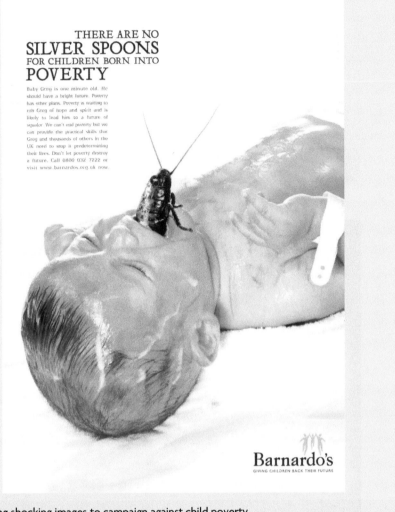

THERE ARE NO
SILVER SPOONS
FOR CHILDREN BORN INTO
POVERTY

Baby Greg is one minute old. He
should have a bright future. Poverty
has other plans. Poverty is waiting to
rob Greg of hope and spirit and is
likely to lead him to a future of
squalor. We can't end poverty but we
can provide the practical skills that
Greg and thousands of others in the
UK need to stop it predetermining
their lives. Don't let poverty destroy
a future. Call 0800 032 7222 or
visit www.barnardos.org.uk now.

Barnardo's
GIVING CHILDREN BACK THEIR FUTURE

Exhibit 9.2   Using shocking images to campaign against child poverty
Image courtesy of The Advertising Archives

The main reason for using a shock advertising strategy is that it is a good way to secure an audience's attention and achieve a longer-lasting impact than through traditional messages and attention-getting devices. The surprise element of these advertisements secures attention, which is followed by an attempt to work out why an individual has been surprised. This usually takes the form of cognitive engagement and message elaboration in order that the message be understood. Through this process a shocking message can be retained and behaviour influenced. This process is depicted in Figure 9.1.

Exhibit 9.3 shows a Nikon billboard in a Seoul tube station (one of the largest stations in Korea, with a daily passing population of five hundred thousand people). The picture on the billboard features the paparazzi fighting to get a shot of the passing celebrities on a red carpet. However, these are no ordinary celebrities, they are just normal people passing by the billboard. The movement of those passing by triggers flashing camera lights and attracts attention to the scene making the passers-by feel like superstars on the red carpet. Meanwhile, the carpet continues through the tube station to a store selling the Nikon D700 (Luke, 2009), and purchase intentions have hopefully been triggered.

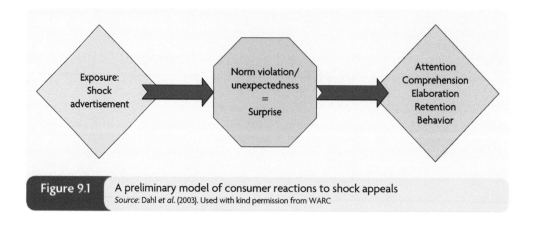

Figure 9.1   A preliminary model of consumer reactions to shock appeals
Source: Dahl *et al.* (2003). Used with kind permission from WARC

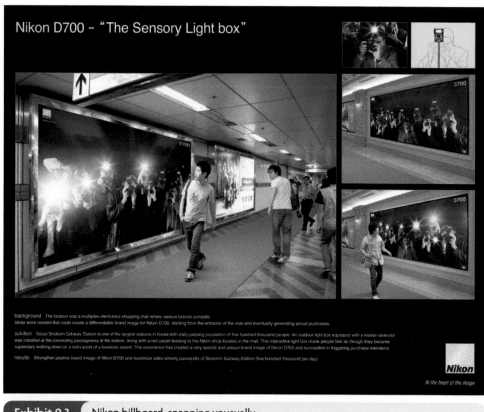

Exhibit 9.3   Nikon billboard, snapping unusually
Image used with permission from Nikon, UK office. This June 2009 ad was produced by the agency Cheil Worldwide

Shocking ads also benefit from word-of-mouth communication as these messages provoke advertisement-related conversations (Dichter, 1966). These can be distributed orally or digitally as virals. The credibility of word-of-mouth communication impacts on others who, if they have not been exposed to the original message, often seek out the message through curiosity. Associated with this pass-along impact is the generation of controversy, which can lead to additional publicity for an organisation and its advertisements. This 'free' publicity, although invariably negative, is considered to be desirable as it leads to increased brand awareness without further exposure and associated costs. This in turn can give the organisation further opportunities to provide more information about the advertising campaign and generate additional media comment.

The use of shock tactics has spread to viral marketing, a topic discussed in more detail in Chapter 14. Virals delivered through email communications have an advantage over paid-for advertising because consumers perceive advertising as an attempt to sell product, whereas virals are perceived as fun, can be opened and viewed (repeatedly) at consumer-determined times. Furthermore, virals are not subject to the same regulations that govern advertising, opening opportunities to convey controversial material. For example, a Volkswagen viral showed a suicide bomber exploding a device inside a car but the vehicle remained in one piece ('small but tough'). Another for Ford Ka showed a cat being decapitated by the sunroof. As Bewick (2006) suggests, joking with terrorism and pets is a sure-fire way of generating shock, and with that comes publicity.

Advertising models and concepts

For many years, a large number of researchers have attempted to determine how advertising works. Finding the answer would bring commercial success. We know that for a message to be communicated successfully it should be meaningful to the recipient. Messages need to be targeted at the right audience, be capable of gaining attention, be understandable, relevant and acceptable.

One approach to answering this question has been to model the advertising process. From the model it should be possible to test the linkages and deduce how advertising works. Unfortunately, despite the effort of many researchers over many years, no single model has attracted widespread agreement. However, from all the work undertaken in this area, a number of views have been prominent. The following sections seek to present some of these more influential perspectives.

Sequential models

Various models have been developed to assist our understanding of how these promotional tasks are segregated and organised effectively. Table 9.1 shows some of the better-known models. These models were developed primarily to explain how advertising worked. However, the principle of these hierarchical models also applies to marketing communications.

AIDA

Developed by Strong (1925), the AIDA model was designed to represent the stages that a salesperson must take a prospect through in the personal selling process. This model shows the prospect passing through successive stages of attention, interest, desire and action. This expression of the process was later adopted, very loosely, as the basic framework to explain how persuasive communication, and advertising in particular, was thought to work.

Hierarchy of effects models

An extension of the progressive, staged approach advocated by Strong emerged in the early 1960s. Developed most notably by Lavidge and Steiner (1961), the hierarchy of effects models represent the process by which advertising was thought to work and assume that there is a series of steps a prospect must pass through, in succession, from unawareness to actual purchase. Advertising, it is assumed, cannot induce immediate behavioural responses; rather, a series of mental effects must occur with fulfilment at each stage necessary before progress to the next stage is possible.

Table 9.1	Sequential models of advertising		
Stage	AIDA[a]	Hierarchy of effects[b]	Information processing[c]
		Awareness	Presentation
			↓
Cognitive			Attention
		↓	↓
	Attention	Knowledge	Comprehension
	↓	↓	↓
	Interest	Liking	Yielding
		↓	
Affective		Preference	
	↓	↓	↓
	Desire	Conviction	Retention
Conative	↓	↓	↓
	Action	Purchase	Behaviour

Source: [a] Strong (1925); [b] Lavidge and Steiner (1961); [c] McGuire (1978)

The information processing model

McGuire (1978) contends that the appropriate view of the receiver of persuasive advertising is as an information processor or cognitive problem solver. This cognitive perspective becomes subsumed as the stages presented reflect similarities with the other hierarchical models, except that McGuire includes a retention stage. This refers to the ability of the receiver to retain and understand information that is valid and relevant. This is important, because it recognises that marketing communication messages are designed to provide information for use by a prospective buyer when a purchase decision is to be made at some time in the future.

Difficulties with the sequential approach

For a long time the sequential approach was accepted as the model upon which advertising was to be developed. However, questions arose about what actually constitute adequate levels of awareness, comprehension and conviction and how it can be determined which stage the majority of the target audience has reached at any one point in time.

The model is based on the logical sequential movement of consumers towards a purchase via specified stages. The major criticism is that it assumes that the consumer moves through the stages in a logical, rational manner: learn, then feel and then do. This is obviously not the case, as anyone who has taken a child into a sweet shop can confirm. There has been a lot of research that attempts to offer an empirical validation for some of the hierarchy propositions, the results of which are inconclusive and at times ambiguous (Barry and Howard, 1990). Among these researchers is Palda (1966), who found that the learn–feel–do sequence cannot be upheld as a reflection of general buying behaviour and provided empirical data to reject the notion of sequential models as an interpretation of the way advertising works. Green (2007) supports this view and dismisses AIDA. He argues that people do not use advertising in a reasoned way, that their behaviour and use of advertising is shaped by feelings.

The sequential approach sees attitude towards the product as a prerequisite to purchase, but, there is evidence that a positive attitude is not necessarily a good predictor of purchase behaviour. What is important, or more relevant, is the relationship between attitude change and an individual's intention to act in a particular way (Ajzen and Fishbein, 1980). Therefore, it seems reasonable to suggest that what is of potentially greater benefit is a specific measure of attitude *towards* purchasing or *intentions* to buy a specific product. Despite measurement difficulties, attitude change is considered a valid objective, particularly in high-involvement situations.

All of these models share the similar view that the purchase decision process is one in which individuals move through a series of sequential stages. Each of the stages from the different models can be grouped in such a way that they are a representation of the three attitude components, these being cognitive (learn), affective (feel) and conative (do) orientations. This could be seen to reflect the various stages in the buying process, especially those that induce high involvement in the decision process but do not reflect the reality of low-involvement decisions.

All sequential models are essentially hierarchy of effects frameworks. The sequential nature of these early interpretations was attractive because they were easy to comprehend, neatly mirrored the purchase decision process and provided a base upon which campaign goals were later assigned (Dagmar). All of these sequential models are based on the notion that attention is a necessary starting point. Work by Heath and Feldwick (2007), and colleagues, suggest that attention is not a necessary precursor for effective advertising, again undermining the validity of the sequential models.

As our knowledge of buyer behaviour has increased and as the significance of the USP has waned, so hierarchy of effects models have declined in terms of our understanding about advertising and how it works. Now they are relatively insignificant and are no longer used as appropriate interpretations of how advertising works.

Eclectic models of advertising

A number of new frameworks and explanations have arisen, all of which claim to reflect practice. In other words these new ideas about how advertising works are a practitioner reflection of the way advertising is considered to work, or at least used, by advertising agencies. The first to be considered here are four main advertising frameworks developed by O'Malley (1991) and Hall (1992). These reflect the idea that there are four keys ways in which advertising works, depending on context and goals. This also says that different advertising works in different ways, there is no one all embracing model. These were updated by Willie (2007) to incorporate the impact of digital media and interactivity. Figure 9.2 depicts the essence of these ideas. The essential point is that advertising cannot be explained by a single interpretation or model.

The sections that follow are divided into two aspects – analogue and digital.

1 The persuasion framework

Analogue

The first framework assumes advertising works rationally, and that a 'brand works harder for you'. This is based on messages that are persuasive, because they offer a rational difference, grounded in unique selling propositions (USPs). Persuasion is affected by gradually moving buyers through a number of sequential steps, as depicted through hierarchy of effects models such as AIDA.

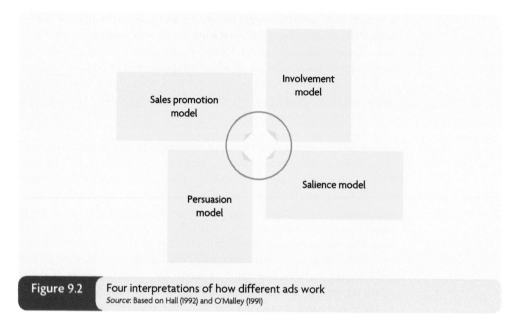

Figure 9.2	Four interpretations of how different ads work

Source: Based on Hall (1992) and O'Malley (1991)

Digital

Digitisation enables persuasion to be extended into opportunities for exploration, as individuals can now be encouraged to search, 'go to', and to find out more. Willie points out, that this is still persuasion, but it is occurs through guided exploration, rather than just telling.

Viewpoint 9.4   **Persuasive mobiles**

The use of advertising to persuade audiences can be key when launching new brands, when the competition becomes intensive or when the audience experiences high involvement.

In 2008 Sony Ericsson implemented a campaign designed to offset the threat of Apple and the iPhone, plus the push from market leaders Nokia. Sony Ericsson used campaigns to support its latest handsets, Cyber-Shot, Walkman, clamshell and touch-screen handsets. Included within this activity was support for their first sub-brand, Xperia and the first handset, SamsungX1 were also experiencing pressure and used a £16 million pan-European awareness campaign to introduce Soul, its key handset for 2008. Motorola meanwhile sought to back its Z10 kick-slider phone using television to demonstrate key attributes.

Source: Based on Jones (2008)

Question

Why did Motorola use television to demonstrate the key attributes of their Z10 brand?

Task

Visit www.sonyericsson.com/x1/?lc=en&cc=gb. Watch the film for X1. Good?

2 The involvement framework

Analogue

Involvement-based advertisements work by drawing the audience into the advertisement and eliciting a largely emotional form of engagement. Involvement with the brand develops because the messages convey that the 'brand means more to you'. As Willie indicates, involvement can be developed through shared values (Dove), aspirational values (American Express) or by personifying a brand, perhaps by using celebrities (adidas).

Digital

Today, digitisation develops the notion of involvement by encouraging people to play. This is about content creation and consumers controlling brands. User-generated content can be seen through ads (crowd sourcing), blogs, wikis, videos and social networking for example.

3 The salience framework

Analogue

This interpretation is based upon the premise that advertising works by standing out, by being different from all other advertisements in the product class (see Exhibit 9.4 later). The ads used by brands such as Cillit Bang, GoCompare.com, Injurylawyers4u, and Sheila's Wheels were deemed by consumers to be irritating, partly because the messages make people think more about the brand, more frequently than they would prefer.

Digital

Contemporary interpretations of salience incorporate ideas about sharing messages about the brand either directly or virally, and getting the brand discussed, mentioned and talked about.

4 The sales promotion framework

Analogue

This view holds that advertising activities are aimed ultimately at shifting product that is, generating sales. Messages are invitations to participate in promotions, sales, and various forms of price deals. This framework, oriented mainly to direct-response work, is based on the premise that the level of sales is the only factor that is worth considering when measuring the effectiveness of an advertising campaign.

Digital

Digitisation has not affected this framework, simply because sales promotion was always a 'do' or behavioural model.

Viewpoint 9.5 | The day Cillit went bang

Cillit Bang is a brand of household cleaner, owned by Reckitt Benckiser and introduced to the market in 2004. Since then the brand has been supported by a heavyweight ad campaign that features a fictional spokesperson, Barry Scott. The message is delivered through demonstration of the power of the brand to clean various surfaces, including a 1p coin dipped into the fluid. 'Members of the public' provide testimonials to the power of the cleaners and Barry Scott constantly repeats the brand name loudly, supported by heavy music, to the point that the message becomes annoying and for many, exceedingly irritating.

These ads are designed as if they are spoofing 1960s commercials. Yet despite the old-fashioned approach the brand became a market leader with a 12 per cent share (Mintel) and the ads have spawned a wave of look-alikes and remixes.

Source: Based on various including Tiltman (2008)

Question

Why has an ad that irritates the audience so much become a market leader?

Task

Use Google to find some of the remixes of the Cillit Bang ads.

Table 9.2	Digital and analogue advertising messages	
Analogue delivered messages say		**Digitally delivered messages encourage**
This is the reason why this brand is different	**Persuasion**	People to explore a brand such as search
Imagine you are associated with the brand	**Involvement**	People to play and create content
Please think about this brand	**Salience**	People to talk and share information about a brand
Act now because you will be rewarded	**Promotion**	People to act now because they will be rewarded

The analogue based frameworks represent communications that induce a thinking, value based response. The digital based frameworks represent a behavioural response that is related to the brand, not the communications. These two fundamentally different types of response can be seen in Table 9.2. Furthermore, the models bring to attention two important points about people and advertising. Advertisements are capable of generating two very clear types of response: a response to the advertisement itself and a response to the featured brand. Both have clear roles to play in advertising strategy.

The strong and the weak theories of advertising

Many of the explanations offered to date are all based on the premise that advertising is a potent marketing force, one that is persuasive and which is done *to* people. More recent views of advertising theory question this fundamental perspective. The second group of eclectic interpretations about how advertising works concerns ideas about advertising as a force for persuasion and as a force for reminding people about brands. Prominent among these theorists are Jones, McDonald and Ehrenberg, some of whose views will now be presented. Jones (1991) presented the new views as the strong theory of advertising and the weak theory of advertising.

The strong theory of advertising

All the models presented so far are assumed to work on the basis that they are capable of affecting a degree of change in the knowledge, attitudes, beliefs and sometimes, the behaviour of audiences. Jones refers to this as the strong theory of advertising, and it appears to have been universally adopted as a foundation for commercial activity.

According to Jones, exponents of this theory hold that advertising can persuade someone to buy a product that they have never previously purchased. Furthermore, continual long-run purchase behaviour can also be generated. Under the strong theory, advertising is believed to be capable of increasing sales at the brand and class levels. These upward shifts are achieved through the use of manipulative and psychological techniques, which are deployed against consumers who are passive, possibly because of apathy, and are generally incapable of processing information intelligently. The most appropriate theory would appear to be the hierarchy of effects model, where sequential steps move buyers forward to a purchase, stimulated by timely and suitable promotional messages.

The weak theory of advertising

Increasing numbers of European writers argue that the strong theory does not reflect practice. Most notable of these writers is Ehrenberg (1988, 1997), who believes that a consumer's pattern of brand purchases is driven more by habit than by exposure to promotional messages. The framework proposed by Ehrenberg is the awareness–trial–reinforcement (ATR) framework. Awareness is required before any purchase can be made, although the elapsed time between awareness and action may be very short or very long. For the few people intrigued enough to want to try a product, a trial purchase constitutes the next phase. This may be stimulated by retail availability as much as by advertising, word-of-mouth or personal selling stimuli. Reinforcement follows to maintain awareness and provide reassurance to help the customer to repeat the pattern of thinking and behaviour and to cement the brand in the repertoire for occasional purchase activity. Advertising's role is to breed brand familiarity and identification (Ehrenberg, 1997).

Following on from the original ATR model (Ehrenberg, 1974), various enhancements have been suggested. However, Ehrenberg added a further stage in 1997, referred to as the nudge. He argues that some consumers can 'be nudged into buying the brand more frequently (still as part of their split-loyalty repertoires) or to favour it more than the other brands in their consideration sets' (1997: 22). Advertising need not be any different from before; it just provides more reinforcement that stimulates particular habitual buyers into more frequent selections of the brand from their repertoire.

According to the weak theory, advertising is capable of improving people's knowledge, and so is in agreement with the strong theory. In contrast, however, consumers are regarded as selective in determining which advertisements they observe and only perceive those that promote products that they either use or have some prior knowledge of. This means that they already have some awareness of the characteristics of the advertised product. It follows that the amount of information actually communicated is limited. Advertising, Jones continues, is not potent enough to convert people who hold reasonably strong beliefs that are counter to those portrayed in an advertisement. The time available (30 seconds in television advertising) is not enough to bring about conversion and, when combined with people's ability to switch off their cognitive involvement, there may be no effective communication. Advertising is employed as a defence, to retain customers and to increase product or brand usage. Advertising is used to reinforce existing attitudes, not necessarily to drastically change them.

Unlike the strong theory, this perspective accepts that when people say that they are not influenced by advertising they are in the main correct. It also assumes that people are not apathetic or even stupid, but capable of high levels of cognitive processing.

In summary, the strong theory suggests that advertising can be persuasive, can generate long-run purchasing behaviour, can increase sales and regards consumers as passive. The weak theory suggests that purchase behaviour is based on habit and that advertising can improve knowledge and reinforce existing attitudes. It views consumers as active problem-solvers.

These two perspectives serve to illustrate the dichotomy of views that has emerged about this subject. They are important because they are both right and they are both wrong. The answer to the question 'How does advertising work?' lies somewhere between the two views and is dependent upon the particular situation facing each advertiser. Where elaboration is likely to be high if advertising is to work, then it is most likely to work under the strong theory. For example, consumer durables and financial products require that advertising urges prospective customers into some form of trial behaviour. This may be a call for more information from a sales representative or perhaps a visit to a showroom. The vast majority of product purchases, however, involve low levels of elaboration, where involvement is low and where people select, often unconsciously, brands from an evoked set.

New products require people to convert or change their purchasing patterns. It is evident that the strong theory must prevail in these circumstances. Where products become established their markets generally mature, so that real growth is non-existent. Under these circumstances, advertising works by protecting the consumer franchise and by allowing users to have their product choices confirmed and reinforced. The other objective of this form of advertising is to increase the rate at which customers reselect and consume products. If the strong theory were the only acceptable approach, then theoretically advertising would be capable of continually increasing the size of each market, until everyone had been converted. There would be no 'stationary' markets.

Considering the vast sums that are allocated to advertising budgets, not only to launch new products but also to pursue market share targets aggressively, the popularity and continued implicit acceptance of the power of advertising suggest that a large proportion of resources are wasted in the pursuit of advertising-driven brand performance. Indeed, it is noticeable that organisations have been switching resources out of advertising into digital, interactive and sales promotion activities. There are many reasons for this, but one of them concerns the failure of advertising to produce the expected levels of performance: to produce market share. The strong theory fails to deliver the expected results, and the weak theory does not apply to all circumstances. Reality is probably a mixture of the two.

Cognitive processing

Reference has been made to whether buyers actively or passively process information. In an attempt to understand how information is used, cognitive processing tries to determine 'how external information is transformed into meanings or patterns of thought and how these meanings are combined to form judgments' (Olsen and Peter, 1987).

By assessing the thoughts (cognitive processes) that occur to people as they read, view or hear a message, an understanding of their interpretation of a message can be useful in campaign development and evaluation (Greenwald, 1968; Wright, 1973). These thoughts are usually measured by asking consumers to write down or verbally report the thoughts they have in response to such a message. The assumption is that thoughts are a reflection of the cognitive processes or responses that receivers experience and they help shape or reject a communication.

Researchers have identified three types of cognitive response and have determined how these relate to attitudes and intentions. Figure 9.3 shows these three types of response, but readers should appreciate that these types are not discrete; they overlap each other and blend together, often invisibly.

Product/message thoughts

These are thoughts that are directed to the product or communication itself. Much attention has been focused on the thoughts that are related to the message content. Two particular types of response have been considered: counter-arguments and support arguments.

A counter-argument occurs when the receiver disagrees with the content of a message. The likelihood of counter-argument is greater when the message makes claims that oppose the beliefs or perceptions held by the receiver. Not surprisingly, the greater the degree of counter-argument, the less likely the message will be accepted. Conversely, support-arguments reflect acceptance and concurrence with a message. Support-arguments, therefore, are positively related to message acceptance.

Source-oriented thoughts

A further set of cognitive responses is aimed at the source of a message. This concept is closely allied to that of source credibility, where, if the source of the message is seen as annoying or distrustful, there is a lower probability of message acceptance. Such a situation is referred to as source derogation; the converse as a source bolster. Those responsible for communications should ensure, during the context analysis, that receivers experience bolster effects to improve the likelihood of message acceptance.

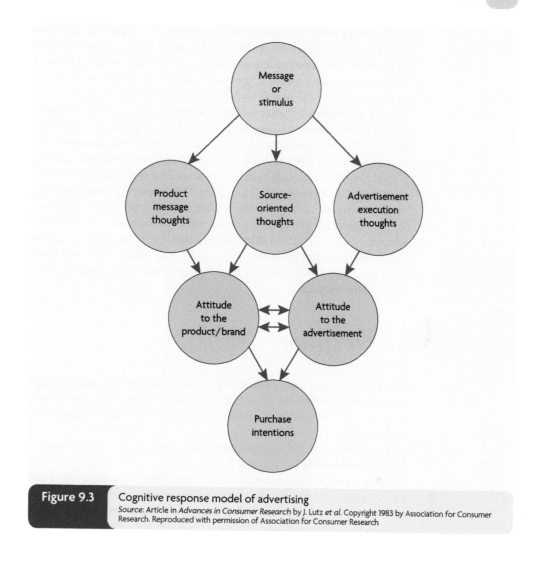

Figure 9.3	Cognitive response model of advertising

Source: Article in *Advances in Consumer Research* by J. Lutz *et al.* Copyright 1983 by Association for Consumer Research. Reproduced with permission of Association for Consumer Research

Message execution thoughts

This relates to the thoughts an individual may have about the overall design and impact of the message. Many of the thoughts that receivers have are not always product-related but are emotionally related towards the message itself. Understanding these feelings and emotions is important because of their impact upon attitudes towards the message, most often an advertisement, and the offering.

Attitudes towards the message

It is clear that people make judgments about the quality of advertisements and the creativity, tone and style in which an advertisement (or website, promotion or direct mail piece) has been executed. As a result of their experiences, perception and degree to which they like an advertisement, they form an attitude towards the advertisement (message) itself. From this base an important stream of thought has developed about cognitive processing. Lutz's work led to the attitude-toward-the-ad concept which has become an important foundation for much of the related marketing communications literature. As Goldsmith and Lafferty (2002: 319) argue, there is a substantial amount of research that clearly indicates that advertising that promotes a 'positive emotional response of liking an ad is positively related to subsequent brand-related cognitions (knowledge), brand attitudes and purchase intentions'. Similar work by Chen and

Wells (1999) shows that this attitude-towards-the-ad concept applies equally well with new media and ecommerce in particular. They refer to an attitude-toward-the-site concept, and similar ideas developed by Bruner and Kumar (2000) conclude that the more a website is liked, the more attitudes improve to the brand and purchase intentions.

It seems highly reasonable therefore, to conclude that attitudes-towards-the-message (and delivery mechanism) impact on brand attitudes, which in turn influences a consumer's propensity to purchase. It is also known that a large proportion of advertisements attempt to appeal to feelings and emotions, simply because many researchers believe that attitudes towards both the advertisement and the product should be encouraged and are positively correlated with purchase intention. Similarly, time and effort is placed with the design of sales promotion instruments, increasing attention is given to the design of packaging in terms of a pack's communication effectiveness and care is taken about the wording in advertorials and press releases. Perhaps above all else, more and more effort is being made to research and develop websites with the goal of designing them so that they are strategically compatible, user-friendly and functional, or to put it another way – liked. Any model developed to explain how marketing communications works should therefore be based around the important concept, attitude-towards-the-message.

Emotion in advertising

The preceding material, if taken at face value, suggests that advertising only works by people responding to advertising in a logical, rational and cognitive manner. It also suggests that people only take out the utilitarian aspect of advertising messages (cleans better, smells fresher). This is obviously not true and there is certainly a strong case for the use of emotion in advertising in order to influence and change attitudes through the affective component of the attitudinal construct, considered in Chapter 3.

Most advertised brands are not normally new to consumers as they have had some experience of the brand, whether that be through use or just through communications. This experience affects their interpretation of advertising as memories have already been formed. The role of feelings in the way ads work suggests a consumerist interpretation of how advertising works rather than the rational, which is much more a researchers' interpretation (Ambler, 1998).

Consumers view advertising in the context of their experience of the category and memories of the brand. Aligned with this approach is the concept of likeability, where the feelings evoked by advertising trigger and shape attitudes to the brand and attitudes to the advertisement (Vakratsas and Ambler, 1999). Feelings and emotions play an important role in advertising especially when advertising is used to build awareness levels and brand strength.

Most of the models presented in this chapter are developed on the principle that individuals are cognitive processors and that ads are understood as a result of information processing. The best examples of these are the sequential models referred to earlier where information is processed step by step. This view is not universally accepted. Researchers such as Krugman (1971), Ehrenberg (1974), Corke and Heath (2004), Heath and Feldwick (2007) and Heath *et al.* (2009) all dispute the importance of information processing, denying that attention is necessary for people to understand ads and that the creativity within an ad is more important, in many circumstances, than the rational message the ad purports to deliver.

The elaboration likelihood model

What should be clear from the preceding sections is that neither the purely cognitive nor the purely emotional interpretation of how advertising works is realistic. In effect, it is probable

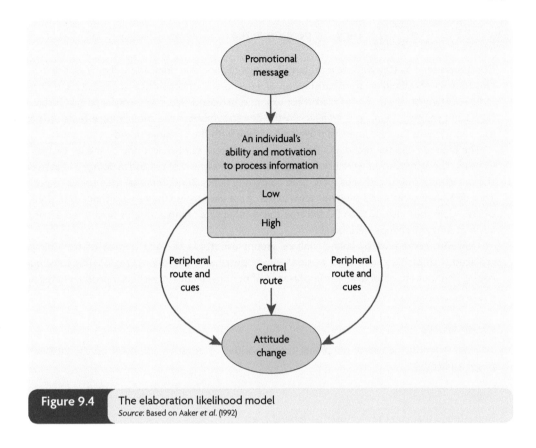

Figure 9.4	The elaboration likelihood model
	Source: Based on Aaker *et al.* (1992)

that both have an important part to play in the way advertising works. However, the degree of emphasis should swing according to the context within which message is expected to work.

One approach that can be used to accommodate both these elements was developed by Petty and Cacioppo (1983). The elaboration likelihood model (ELM) has helped to explain how the use of cognitive processing and emotion can be used to bring about attitude change, when different levels of involvement are present. Elaboration refers to the extent to which an individual needs to develop and refine information necessary for decision-making to occur. If an individual has a high level of motivation or ability to process information, elaboration is said to be high. If an individual's motivation or ability to process information is poor, then their level of elaboration is said to be low. The ELM distinguishes two main cognitive processes, as depicted in Figure 9.4.

Under the central route the receiver is viewed as very active and involved. As the level of cognitive response is high, the ability of the advertisement to persuade will depend on the quality of the argument rather than executional factors. For example, the purchase of a consumer durable such as a car or washing machine normally requires a high level of involvement. Consequently, potential customers would be expected to be highly involved and willing to read brochures and information about the proposed car or washing machine prior to demonstration or purchase. Their decision to act would depend on the arguments used to justify the model as suitable for the individual. For the car purchase these might include the quiet and environmentally friendly engine, the relatively excellent fuel consumption and other safety and performance indicators, together with the comfort of the interior and the effortless driving experience. Whether the car is shown as part of a business executive's essential 'kit' or the commercial is flamboyant and rich will be immaterial for those in the central route.

Viewpoint 9.6	Time for peripheral tea

Consumers tend to stay with their preferred brands of food and drink and will only switch if their preferred brand fails to reach threshold levels of satisfaction or a new brand offers sufficient curiosity and engagement that trial is induced. Many brands in the tea market for example, use peripheral cues in order to get the brand noticed, remembered and enjoyed. Twinings used a Jack-in-the Box to symbolise the stimulating effects of their breakfast tea and as an easy means for customers to make associations with the Twinings brand.

The Brooke Bond tea brand, PG Tips, used chimpanzees in what was one of the longest running ad campaigns, 45 years. The chimpanzees were used to bring humour to a brand of tea and in doing so helped consumers associate the brand with fun. The chimps were used to parody James Bond, removal men trying to get a piano downstairs, Tour de France cyclists and even housewives doing the ironing and they all (pretended) to drink their favourite cup of tea. After their introduction PG became the number one brand and sales fluctuated according to whether the ads featuring the chimps were on air.

However, complaints by animal welfare groups eventually saw the demise of the Chimps. They have been replaced with Monkey, a knitted version, who appears with Al (Johnny Vegas). The subsequent success of this pairing continues to emphasise the importance of peripheral cues in particular product categories.

Source: Based on Blackstock (2002); Carter (2008)

Question

To what extent is the use of peripheral cues a positive or negative comment on the intellectual capacity of the target audience?

Task

Find a brand that you like that uses peripheral cues.

Exhibit 9.4	Use of peripheral cues to advertise tea (1)

PG Tips – chimpanzees perform as peripheral cues
Image courtesy of The Advertising Archives

Exhibit 9.5	Use of peripheral cues to advertise tea (2)

PG Tips now with Monkey as a peripheral cue
Image courtesy of The Advertising Archives

Under the peripheral route, the receiver is seen to lack the ability or motivation to process information and is not likely to engage in cognitive processing. Rather than thinking about and evaluating the message content, the receiver tends to rely on what have been referred to as 'peripheral cues', which may be incidental to the message content. Twinings use peripheral cues to attract attention to their brand (see Exhibit 9.6).

In low-involvement situations, a celebrity may serve to influence attitudes positively. This is based upon the creation of favourable attitudes towards the source rather than engaging the viewer in the processing of the message content. For example, Gary Lineker was the celebrity spokesperson used to endorse Walkers crisps for many years. Gary Lineker, former Tottenham Hotspur and England football hero and now BBC sports presenter, was an important peripheral cue for Walkers crisps (more so than the nature of the product), in eventually persuading consumers to try the brand or retain current users. Think crisps, think Gary Lineker, think Walkers. Where high involvement is present, any celebrity endorsement is of minor significance to the quality of the message claims.

It has long been argued that communication strategy should be based upon the level of cognitive processing that the target audience is expected to engage in and the route taken to affect attitudinal change. If the processing level is low (low motivation and involvement), the peripheral route should dominate and emphasis needs to be placed on the way the messages are executed and on the emotions of the target audience (Heath, 2000). If the central route is expected, the content of the messages should be dominant and the executional aspects need only be adequate.

Exhibit 9.6	Use of peripheral cues to advertise tea (3)
	Through the use of peripheral cues, Twinings have been able to enrich the way their brand is perceived while at the same time improve the level of awareness
	Image courtesy of Three Sixty

Summary

In order to help consolidate your understanding of advertising strategy, here are the key points summarised against each of the learning objectives:

1 Consider the role advertising plays in influencing and engaging audiences

The role of advertising in most marketing communications campaigns is to engage audiences. Engagement is enabled either by informing, changing perceptions and building brand values or by encouraging a change in behaviour.

Advertising can reach huge audiences with simple messages that present opportunities to allow receivers to understand what a product is, what its primary function is and how it relates to all the other similar products. This is the main function of advertising: to communicate with specific audiences. These audiences may be consumer- or organisation-based, but wherever they are located the prime objective is to build or maintain awareness of a product or an organisation.

2 Examine the use of selling propositions in advertising

There are two main forms of selling proposition. Unique selling propositions, or USPs, were considered to be powerful ways of influencing audiences. A message that says something about a product that no competitor brand could offer is said to be a USP. USPs are based on product features and are related to particular attributes that differentiate one product from another. However, there are few genuine USPs as it is easy and quick to copy a competitor's claims.

Emotional selling propositions, or ESPs, emerged as advertising's role became focused on developing brand values, through emotion and imagery. This approach to communication helps build brand awareness, desire and aspirational involvement. However, it often fails to provide customers with a rationale or explicit reason to purchase, what is often referred to as a 'call to action'.

3 Explain the principles associated with shock advertising

Shock advertising can be considered as advertising that deliberately, rather than inadvertently, seeks to startle and offend its audience. They are used to surprise audiences because they do not conform to social norms or their expectations. The main reason for using shock advertising is that the surprise element secures attention, which is followed by an attempt to work out why an individual has been surprised. This usually takes the form of cognitive engagement and message elaboration in order that the message be understood.

4 Explore various models, concepts and frameworks which have been used to explain how advertising is thought to influence individuals

The sequential models (e.g. AIDA), were the first attempts to explain how advertising works. The hierarchical nature of these early interpretations was attractive because they were easy to comprehend, neatly mirrored the purchase decision process and provided a base upon which campaign goals were later assigned (Dagmar). These ideas are no longer accepted as valid reasons or interpretations about how advertising works.

In their place a number of new frameworks and explanations have arisen, many of which claim to reflect practice. These eclectic interpretations about how advertising works are a reflection of those working in advertising agencies and marketing research. One of the most significant of these was developed by O'Malley (1991) and Hall (1992) who suggest that there are four main advertising frameworks: persuasion, sales, salience and involvement. Different advertising models for different advertising. These were updated by Willie (2007) to incorporate digital developments.

The final models to be considered concern the strong and the weak theories of advertising. The strong theory of advertising reflects the persuasion concept, and has high credibility when used with new brands. However, the contrasting view is that advertising should be regarded as a means of defending customers' purchase decisions and for protecting markets, not building them. Reality suggests that both the strong and the weak theories are equally applicable, although not at the same time nor in the same context.

5 Consider cognitive processing as a means of understanding how advertising works

Cognitive processing is an attempt to understand how people utilise information, develop thoughts and respond, in this case, to a brand message. Three types of cognitive thoughts are processed in response to receiving an advertising message. These are thoughts about the product, the source and the way the ad has been executed or designed.

Out of this people develop attitudes towards the brand and attitudes-towards-the-message (or delivery mechanism) and these are considered to impact on brand attitudes, which in turn can influence a consumer's propensity to purchase.

6 Examine ideas concerning the use of emotion in advertising

Most of the models used to explain how advertising works are developed on the principle that individuals are cognitive processors and that ads are understood as a result of information processing. This is not universally agreed and some doubt the importance of information processing on the basis that attention in particular is not always required for individuals to be influenced by ads.

Feelings and emotions play an important role in advertising especially when advertising is used to build awareness levels and brand strength.

The elaboration likelihood model attempts to assimilate the needs for people to process some ads with a great deal of thought and some ads without any thought or appreciation that they are processing a commercial message.

Review questions

1. Find two advertisements and write notes explaining how they depict the roles of advertising.
2. Explain the differences between absolute and relative costs of advertising.
3. Write brief notes outlining the differences between a USP and an ESP.
4. Name the three elements in advertising, identified by Dahl *et al.* (2003), which cause audiences to be offended. Find an example of each.
5. Write brief notes explaining how sequential models can contribute to our understanding of how advertising works.
6. What are the essential differences between the involvement and salience frameworks of advertising? Find four advertisements (other than those described in the text) that are examples of these two approaches.
7. Write a short presentation explaining the differences between the strong and weak theories of advertising.
8. Select an organisation of your choice and find three ads it has used recently. Are the ads predominantly trying to persuade audiences or are they designed to reinforce brand values?
9. Name the elements of the cognitive processing model.
10. Find four ads and write notes explaining how the elaboration likelihood model can be used to interpret how they might work.

References

Aaker, D.A., Batra, R. and Myers, J.G. (1992) *Advertising Management*, 4th edn. Englewood Cliffs, NJ: Prentice-Hall.

Ambler, T. (1998) Myths about the mind: time to end some popular beliefs about how advertising works, *International Journal of Advertising*, 17, 501–509.

Ajzen, I. and Fishbein, M. (1980) *Understanding Attitudes and Predicting Social Behavior*, Englewood Cliffs, NJ: Prentice-Hall.

Bainbridge, J. (2004) Dental diversification, *Marketing*, 12 September, 36–37.

Barry, T. and Howard, D.J. (1990) A review and critique of the hierarchy of effects in advertising, *International Journal of Advertising*, 9, 121–135.

Barwise, P. and Meehan, S. (2009) Differentiation that Matters, *Market Leader*, Quarter 2, retrieved 11 January 2010 from www.warc.com

BBC (2007) *Q&A: Sky and Virgin Media TV row*, 24 May. Retrieved from http://news.bbc.co.uk/1/hi/business/6390655.stm

Blackstock, C. (2002) Tea party over as PG Tips chimps are given the bird, *The Guardian*, 12 January. Retrieved 12 February 2008 from www.monkeyworld.co.uk/press.php?ArticleID=59

Bruner, G.C. and Kumar, A. (2000) Web commercials and advertising hierarchy of effects, *Journal of Advertising Research*, January/April, 35–42.

Bewick, M. (2006) Pushing the boundaries, *The Marketer*, September, 25.

Carter, M. (2008) Monkey Business, *The Independent*, 17 March, 8–9.

Chen, Q. and Wells, W.D. (1999) Attitude toward the site, *Journal of Advertising Research*, September/October, 27–37.

Cohen, A. (2003) Closing the brand/response gap, *Admap* (September), 20–22.

Corke, S. and Heath, R.G. (2004) The hidden power of newspaper advertising. *Media Research Group Conference*, Madrid (November).

Dahl, D.W., Frankenberger, K.D. and Manchanda, R.V. (2003) Does it pay to shock? Reactions to shocking and nonshocking advertising content among university students, *Journal of Advertising Research*, 43(3) (September), 268–281.

Dichter, E. (1966) How word-of-mouth advertising works, *Harvard Business Review*, 44 (November/December), 147–166.

Ehrenberg, A.S.C. (1974) Repetitive advertising and the consumer, *Journal of Advertising Research*, **14** (April), 25–34.

Ehrenberg, A.S.C. (1988) *Repeat Buying*, 2nd edn. London: Charles Griffin.

Ehrenberg, A.S.C. (1997) How do consumers come to buy a new brand? *Admap* (March), 20–24.

Goldsmith, R.E. and Lafferty, B.A. (2002) Consumer response to websites and their influence on advertising effectiveness, *Internet Research: Electronic Networking Applications and Policy*, 12(4), 318–328.

Greenwald, A. (1968) Cognitive learning, cognitive response to persuasion and attitude change. In *Psychological Foundations of Attitudes* (eds A. Greenwald, T.C. Brook and T.W. Ostrom), 197–215. New York: Academic Press.

Green, A. (2007) How many times do people need to see my message before they buy? *Warc Media FAQ* (January). Retrieved 2 June 2010 from www.warc.com/article centre/

Hall, M. (1992) Using advertising frameworks, *Admap* (March), 17–21.

Heath, R. (2000) Low involvement processing, *Admap* (April), 34–36.

Heath, R. and Feldwick, P. (2007) 50 years using the wrong model of TV advertising, *Admap*, (March), 36–38.

Heath, R.G., Nairn, A.C. and Bottomley, P.A. (2009) How Effective is Creativity? Emotive Content in TV Advertising Does Not Increase Attention, *Journal of Advertising Research*, 49(4) (December), 450–463.

Jack, L. (2009) GSK unveils raft of oral care launches to beat back Colgate, *Marketing Week*, 4 February. Retrieved 16 July 2010 from www.marketingweek.co.uk/news/

Jones, G. (2007) Virgin Media pulls ads attacking rival Sky service, *Marketing*, 7 November, 3.

Jones, G. (2008) Handset manufacturers plot response to iPhone, *Marketing*, 13 February, 1.

Jones, J.P. (1991) Over-promise and under-delivery, *Marketing and Research Today* (November), 195–203.

Kamenev, M. (2010) Australian smokers get a rude shock, *GlobalPost*, 10 May. Retrieved 10 August 2010 from www.globalpost.com/dispatch/asia/100508/smoking-australia-law-packaging-tobacco-tax

Krugman, H.E. (1971) Brain wave measurement of media involvement, *Journal of Advertising*, 11(1), 1, 3–9.

Lavidge, R.J. and Steiner, G.A. (1961) A model for predictive measurements of advertising effectiveness, *Journal of Marketing* (October), 59–62.

Lichfield, J. (2010) French in uproar over oral sex anti-smoking posters, *The Independent*, 24 February. Retrieved 10 August 2010 from www.independent.co.uk/news/world/europe/french-in-uproar-over-oral-sex-antismoking-posters-1908559.html

Luke (2009) 10 Guerrilla & Ambient Marketing Examples. Retrieved 7 August 2010 from www.mrlukeabbot.com

McGuire, W.J. (1978) An information processing model of advertising effectiveness. In *Behavioral and Management Science in Marketing* (eds H.L. Davis and A.J. Silk), 156–180. New York: Ronald/Wiley.

Olsen, J.C. and Peter, J.P. (1987) *Consumer Behavior*. Homewood, IL: Irwin.

O'Malley, D. (1991) Sales without salience? *Admap* (September), 36–39.

Palda, K.S. (1966) The hypothesis of a hierarchy of effects: a partial evaluation, *Journal of Marketing Research*, 3, 13–24.

Petty, R.E. and Cacioppo, J.T. (1983) Central and peripheral routes to persuasion: application to advertising. In *Advertising and Consumer Psychology* (eds L. Percy and A. Woodside), 3–23. Lexington, MA: Lexington Books.

Strong, E.K. (1925) *The Psychology of Selling*, New York: McGraw-Hill.

Sweney, M. (2007) Sky wins ad wrangle with Virgin, *The Guardian*, 1 August. Retrieved 4 December 2007 from http://www.guardian.co.uk/media/2007/aug/01/advertising.news

Tiltman, D. (2008) People's choice: most irritating ads of 2007, *Marketing*, 8 January. Available at www.brandrepublic.com/Marketing/News/774978/Peoples-choice-irritating-ads-2007/.

Vakratsas, D. and Ambler, T. (1999) How advertising works: what do we really know? *Journal of Marketing*, 63 (January), 26–43.

Varley, M. (2010) When to use the 'shock' factor and why it works, *Utalk*, 2 March. Retrieved 10 August 2010 from www.utalkmarketing.com/pages/Article.aspx?ArticleID=16945

Venkat, R. and Abi-Hanna, N. (1995) *Effectiveness of Visually Shocking Advertisements: Is it Context Dependent?* Administrative Science Association of Canada Proceedings, 16(3), 139–146.

Willie, T. (2007) New models of communication for the digital age, *Admap*, October, 487. Retrieved 23 July 2010 from www.warc.com

Wright, P.L. (1973) The cognitive processes mediating the acceptance of advertising, *Journal of Marketing Research*, 10 (February), 53–62.

Chapter 10
Public relations and sponsorship

Public relations is a management process that is used to shape the attitudes and opinions held by an organisation's stakeholders. Through interaction and dialogue organisations aim to develop relationships that are of significant value to all parties. Sponsorship is used by organisations, partly to cut through the communications clutter and partly to establish awareness of corporate values and associations.

Aims and learning objectives

The aims of this chapter are to explore the role and characteristics of public relations and sponsorship, and to examine how organisations can use these tools to profile their corporate identity and their products.

The learning objectives of this chapter are to:

1. explain the nature, characteristics and audiences for public relations;

2. consider the issues relating to corporate responsibility and cause-related marketing;

3. provide an overview of some of the main tools used by public relations, including media relations, lobbying, corporate advertising and crisis management;

4. consider reasons for the use of sponsorship and the types of objectives that might be set;

5. appreciate the variety and different forms of sponsorship activities;

6. understand the role of sponsorship in the communications mix.

Introduction

The increasing emphasis given to public relations over recent years is testimony to its power and effectiveness. All organisations in the public, hybrid, not-for-profit and private sectors can use this tool to raise visibility, generate interest and build relationships.

Traditionally, public relations has been perceived as a tool that dealt with the manner and style with which an organisation interacted with its major 'publics'. It sought to influence other organisations and individuals through public relations, projecting an identity that would affect the image that different publics held of the organisation. By spreading information and improving the levels of knowledge that people held about particular issues, organisations use public relations to advance itself in the eyes of those it saw as influential. This approach is reflected in the definition of public relations provided by the Institute of Public Relations: 'Public Relations practice is the planned and sustained effort to establish and maintain goodwill and mutual understanding between an organisation and its publics.' However, Jacques (2009) observes some difficulties associated with defining public relations. First he refers to Harlow, who reported 472 different definitions of public relations, in 1976. Then, at the turn of the century, Cropp and Pincus (2001) state that definitions continue to proliferate.

One such 'new' definition, by Bruning and Ledingham (2000), is important as it serves to change the perspective of public relations. Now it becomes an instrument of relationship management. They say, public relations is the management of relationships between organisations and their stakeholders (publics).

Public relations is concerned with the development and communication of corporate and competitive strategies. Public relations provides visibility for an organisation, and this in turn, it is hoped, allows it to be properly identified, positioned and understood by all of its stakeholders. What some definitions do not emphasise or make apparent is that public relations should also be used by management as a means of understanding issues from a stakeholder perspective. Good relationships are developed by appreciating the views held by others and by 'putting oneself in their shoes'.

Through this approach to planned communication, a dialogue can be developed that is not frustrated by punctuated interruptions (anger, disbelief, ignorance and objections). Public relations is a management activity that attempts to shape the attitudes and opinions held by an organisation's stakeholders. It attempts to identify its policies with the interests of its stakeholders and formulates and executes a programme of action to develop mutual goodwill and understanding, and in turn develop relationships that are in the long-term interests of all parties.

Characteristics of public relations

Public relations should therefore, be a planned activity, one that encompasses a wide range of events. However, there are a number of characteristics that single out this particular tool from the others in the marketing communications mix. For example, the use of public relations does not require the purchase of airtime or space in media vehicles, such as television or magazines. This makes a major saving on a communication budget.

The decision about whether an organisation's public relations messages are communicated or not rests with those charged with managing the media resource, not the source of the message. Messages that are selected are perceived by stakeholders to be endorsements or the views of parties other than management. The outcome is that these messages usually carry greater perceived credibility than those messages transmitted through paid media, such as advertising.

The degree of trust and confidence generated by public relations singles out this tool from others in the marketing communications mix as an important means of reducing buyers' perceived risk. However, while credibility may be high, the amount of control that management is able to bring to the transmission of the public relations message is very low. For example, a press release may have been carefully prepared in-house, but as soon as it is passed to the editor of a magazine or newspaper, a possible opinion former, all control is lost. The release may be destroyed (highly probable), printed as it stands (highly unlikely) or changed to fit the available space in the media vehicle (almost certain, if it is decided to use the material). This means that any changes will not have been agreed by management, so the context and style of the original message may be lost or corrupted.

The costs associated with public relations also make this an important tool in the marketing communications mix. The absolute costs are minimal, except for those organisations that retain an agency, but even then their costs are low compared with those of advertising. The relative costs (the costs associated with reaching each member of a target audience) are also very low. The main costs associated with public relations are the time and opportunity costs associated with the preparation of press releases and associated literature. If these types of activity are organised properly, many small organisations could develop and shape their visibility much more effectively and in a relatively inexpensive way.

A further characteristic of this tool is that it can be used to reach specific audiences in a way that paid media cannot. With increasing media fragmentation and finer segmentation (customisation) of markets, the use of public relations represents a cost-effective way of reaching such markets and audiences.

Viewpoint 10.1 Kittens in need

The KittenAid appeal in 2007, run by the Cats Protection charity, was designed to generate funds from the donors on the charity's database. The number of kittens delivered to the charity was exceptionally large in 2007 due to un-neutered cats breeding in the warm weather.

The campaign was started with a vismail teaser, showing video clips of the charity's kittens and announcing the arrival of kitten season. This was sent to the charity's 18,000 e-subscribers. This activity was then followed by direct mail activity, this time targeted at their 94,000 donors. The mailer was used to tell the story of the recovery of two very ill kittens, now in the care of the charity. The charity's magazine *The Cat* ran the story while their 29 adoption centres and 252 branches actively discussed the story and associated issues with local media.

As a result of this public relations campaign, the appeal generated 40 items of coverage in the media. On the morning of the first broadcast, the KittenAid message reached 1.5 million people and featured on various BBC Radio programmes. After just six weeks the donations reached £244,000, 15 per cent up on the whole of the previous year's fund raising.

Source: Based on Anon. (2007)

Question

What role did the vismail play in generating donations?

Task

Identify the direct marketing and public relations activities in the KittenAid example.

New technology has played a key role in the development and practice of public relations. Gregory (2004) refers to the Internet and electronic communication 'transforming public relations'. With regard to the use of the Internet by public relations practitioners she identifies two main schools. One refers to those who use the Internet as an extension to traditional or pre-Internet forms of communication. The second sees opportunities through the Internet to develop two-way, enhanced communication. There can be little doubt that new technology has assisted communication management in terms of improving the transparency, speed and reach of public relations messages, while at the same time enabling interactive communication between an organisation and its specific audiences. For example, in March 2010, Greenpeace released a viral campaign alleging that Nestlé were planting palm oil trees on land that had been reclaimed from the rain forests and in doing so were endangering the natural habitat of orangutans in Indonesia. Nestlé use palm oil in their KitKat brand and the viral depicted the oil running out of a KitKat as if it was blood. This was a powerful use of digital public relations, one that reached millions, before it was taken down off YouTube (Utalk, 2010).

So, the main characteristics of public relations are that it represents a very cost-effective means of carrying messages to stakeholder audiences, with a high degree of credibility. However, the degree of control that management is able to exert over the transmission of these messages can be limited.

Who are the audiences?

Although stakeholder groups are not static and new groups can emerge in response to changes in the environment, the core groups tend to be the following.

Employees (employee relations)

The employees of an organisation are key stakeholders and represent a major opportunity to use word-of-mouth communications. It has long been established that employees need to be motivated, involved and stimulated to perform their tasks at a high level. Their work as external communicators is less well-established, but they play a critical role providing external cues as part of an organisation's corporate identity.

Financial groups (financial or investor relations)

Shareholders require regular information to maintain their continued confidence in the organisation and to prevent them changing their portfolios and reducing the value of the organisation.

In addition to the shareholders, there are those individuals who are either potential shareholders or who advise shareholders and investors. These represent the wider financial community, but nevertheless have a very strong influence on the stature, strength and value of an organisation. Financial analysts need to be supplied with information in order that they be kept up to date with the activities and performance outcomes of organisations, but also need to be advised of developments within the various markets that the organisation operates.

Organisations attempt to supply financial analysts with current information and materials about the organisation and the markets in which they are operating, to ensure that the potential and value of publicly quoted organisations is reflected in the share price.

Customers (media relations)

The relationships that organisations develop with the media are extremely important in ensuring that their messages reach their current and potential customers. Customers represent a major stakeholder audience and are often the target of public relations activities, because although members of the public may not be current customers the potential they represent is significant. The attitudes and preferences towards the organisation and its products may be unfavourable, in which case it is unlikely that they will wish to purchase the product or speak positively about the organisation. By creating awareness and trust it is possible to create goodwill and interest, which may translate into purchase activity or favourable word-of-mouth communications. This is achieved through media relations.

Of all the media, the press is the most crucial, as it is always interested in newsworthy items and depends to a large extent on information being fed to it by a variety of corporate press officers. Consequently, publicity can be generated for a range of organisational events, activities and developments.

Organisations and communities (corporate public relations)

There are a variety of public, private, commercial and not-for-profit organisations and communities with whom organisations need to communicate and interact on a regular basis. Corporate public relations are used to reach this wide spectrum of audiences and cover a range of activities. Each audience has a particular set of issues and characteristics that lead to individual forms of public relations practice:

- public affairs – government and local authorities;
- community relations – members of local communities;
- industry relations – suppliers, associations and other trade stakeholders;
- issues management – various audiences concerning sensitive industries (e.g. tobacco or pharmaceuticals).

Organisations should seek to work with, rather than against, these stakeholder groups. As a result, public relations should be aimed at informing audiences of their strategic intentions and seeking ways in which the objectives of both parties can be satisfied.

Corporate responsibility

One major reason for the development of public relations in recent years has been the rise in importance of corporate responsibility and the use of cause-related marketing activities. Following increasing interest in sustainability and accountability issues, several high-profile financial disasters (e.g. Enron), technical disasters (e.g. BP) and the irresponsibility demonstrated by some organisations when the financial crisis broke in 2007/08 (e.g. Lehmann Brothers), corporate responsibility is now an important agenda item for a large number of organisations. There is now a need to be perceived as credible, transparent, responsible and ethically sound. This is now seen as an opportunity to differentiate organisations, especially where price, quality and tangible attributes are relatively similar. Being able to present corporate brands as contributors to the wider social framework, a role beyond that of simple profit generators, has enabled many organisations to achieve stronger, more positive market positions.

One of the avenues available to organisations to express their values and attitudes towards their need to be responsible is cause-related marketing. This is a commercial activity through which profit-oriented and not-for-profit organisations form partnerships to exploit, for mutual benefit, their association in the name of a particular cause.

The benefits from a properly planned and constructed cause-related campaign can accrue to all participants. Cause-related marketing helps improve corporate reputation, enables product differentiation and appears to contribute to improved customer retention through enhanced sales. In essence, cause-related marketing is a means by which relationships with stakeholders can be developed. As organisations outsource an increasingly larger part of their business activities and as the stakeholder networks become more complex, so the need to be perceived as (and to be) socially responsible becomes a critically important dimension of an organisation's image.

Viewpoint 10.2   Pouring water on troubled Coke

Although WWF and the Coca-Cola Corporation had been working together for several years on a number of projects to conserve water and address water efficiency in the company's operations, the announcement of a formal agreement between the two organisations marked a critical point for Coke.

The vast amount of water consumed by the Coca-Cola Corporation had led to widespread comment and criticism. In an attempt to change the perception held by the company's stakeholders, the announcement in 2007 that they were pledging to invest $20 million in WWF freshwater schemes, wherever they had a bottling plant, represented a public commitment to change.

Neville Isdell, then Chairman of Coca-Cola, stated:

> Our goal is to replace every drop of water we use in our beverages and their production. For us that means reducing the amount of water used to produce our beverages, recycling water used for manufacturing processes so it can be returned safely to the environment, and replenishing water in communities and nature through locally relevant projects.

As part of the deal WWF provide Coca-Cola with advice on a range of related environmental topics, including water conservation, usage and recycling in manufacturing, how to cut its energy and carbon footprint, and how the organisation can replenish water in local communities. In addition, the agreement involves joint communications programmes and campaigns, framing the relationship under cause for water conservation.

This scheme enables Coca-Cola to be seen as a more environmentally aware and socially responsible company. The scheme helps WWF achieve its goals and move towards encouraging other leading companies to become involved in similar schemes.

Source: Based on Bokaie (2007); Kleinman (2007); WWF Pressroom, www.panda.org/news_facts/newsroom/index.cfm?uNewsID=104940

Question

To what extent is this scheme a cynical ploy to soften Coke's reputation?

Task

Find out how Pepsi are meeting the environmental challenge.

Exhibit 10.1   WWF visual representing the drive to save freshwater ecosystems
Image courtesy of Getty Images/Brent Stirton

A framework of public relations

Communications with such a wide variety of stakeholders need to vary to reflect different environmental conditions, organisational objectives and forms of relationship. Grunig and Hunt (1984) have attempted to capture the diversity of public relations activities through a framework. They set out four models to reflect the different ways in which public relations is, in their opinion, considered to work. These models, based on their experiences as public relations practitioners, constitute a useful approach to understanding the complexity of this form of communication. The four models are set out in Figure 10.1.

The press agentry/publicity model

The essence of this approach is that communication is used as a form of propaganda. That is, the communication flow is essentially one way, and the content is not bound to be strictly truthful as the objective is to convince the receiver of a new idea or offering. This can be observed in the growing proliferation of media events and press releases.

The public information model

Unlike the first model, this approach seeks to disseminate truthful information. While the flow is again one way, there is little focus on persuasion, more on the provision of information. This

	Model			
Characteristic	**Press agentry/publicity**	**Public information**	**Two-way asymmetric**	**Two-way symmetric**
Purpose	Propaganda	Dissemination of information	Scientific persuasion	Mutual understanding
Nature of communication	One way; complete truth not essential	One way; truth important	Two way; imbalanced effects	Two way; balanced effects
Communication model	Source → Rec.*	Source → Rec.*	Source ⇄ Rec.* Feedback	Group ⇄ Group
Nature of research	Little; 'counting house'	Little; readability, readership	Formative; evaluative of attitudes	Formative; evaluative of understanding
Leading historical figures	P.T. Barnum	Ivy Lee	Edward L. Bernays	Bernays, educators, professional leaders
Where practised today	Sports, theatre, product promotion	Government, not-for-profit associations, business	Competitive business, agencies	Regulated business, agencies
Estimated percentage of organisations practising today	15%	50%	20%	15%

* Receiver.

Figure 10.1 Models of public relations
Source: Grunig and Hunt (1984). Used with kind permission

can best be seen through public health campaigns and government advice communications in respect of crime, education and health.

The two-way asymmetric model

Two-way communication is a major element of this model. Feedback from receivers is important, but as power is not equally distributed between the various stakeholders and the organisation, the relationship has to be regarded as asymmetric. The purpose remains to influence attitude and behaviour through persuasion.

The two-way symmetric model

This represents the most acceptable and mutually rewarding form of communication. Power is seen to be dispersed equally between the organisation and its stakeholders and the intent of the communication flow is considered to be reciprocal. The organisation and its respective publics are prepared to adjust their positions (attitudes and behaviours) in the light of the information flow. A true dialogue emerges through this interpretation, unlike any of the other three models, which see an unbalanced flow of information and expectations.

The model has attracted a great deal of attention and has been reviewed and appraised by a number of commentators (Miller, 1989). As a result of this and a search for excellence in public relations, Grunig (1992) revised the model to reflect the dominance of the 'craft' and the 'professional' approaches to public relations practices. That is, those practitioners who utilise public relations merely as a tool to achieve media visibility can be regarded as 'craft'-oriented.

Those organisations whose managers seek to utilise public relations as a means of mediating their relationships with their various stakeholders are seen as 'professional' practitioners. They are considered to be using public relations as a longer term and proactive form of planned communication. The former see public relations as an instrument, the latter as a means of conducting a dialogue.

These models are not intended to suggest that those responsible for communications should choose among them. Their use and interpretation depend upon the circumstances that prevail at any one time. Organisations use a number of these different approaches to manage the communication issues that exist between them and the variety of different stakeholder audiences with whom they interact. However, there is plenty of evidence to suggest that the press/agentry model is the one most used by practitioners and that the two-way symmetrical model is harder to observe in practice.

These models have been subjected to further investigation and Grunig (1997) concluded that these four models are not independent but coexist with one another. Therefore, as Yun (2006) suggested, it is better to characterise public relations as dimensions of communication behaviour.

Public relations: methods and techniques

The range of public relations cues or methods available to organisations is immense. Different organisations use different permutations in order that they can communicate effectively with their various stakeholder audiences. For the purposes of this text a general outline is provided of the more commonly used methods.

The range of public relations activities is diverse and categorisation problematic. The approach adopted here is that public relations consists of a range of communication activities, of which media relations, publicity and event management appear to be the main ones used by practitioners.

Media relations

Media relations consist of a range of activities designed to provide media journalists and editors with information. The intention is that they relay the information, through their media, for consumption by their audiences. Obviously, the original message may be changed and subject to information deviance as it is processed, but audiences perceive much of this information as highly credible simply because opinion formers (Chapter 2) have bestowed their judgement on the item. Of the various forms of media relations, press releases, interviews, press kits and press conferences are most used.

Press releases

The press release is a common form of media relations activity. A one-page written report concerning an event or a change in the organisation is sent to various media houses for inclusion in the media vehicle as an item of news. The media house may cover a national area, but very often a local house will suffice. These written statements concern developments in the organisation, such as promotions, new products, awards, prizes, new contracts and customers. The statement is deliberately short and written in such a style that it attracts the attention of the editor. Further information can be obtained if it is to be included within the next publication or news broadcast. See the Toshiba press release (Exhibit 10.2). One of the characteristics of a good press release is that it is planned restricted in terms of when it can be used by media organisations. An 'embargo time' requires that the item cannot be used until a certain date. This means that instead of a single media house using the material ahead of others, the news opportunity is maximised as several organisations seek to utilise the material at the due time.

Press conferences

Press conferences are used when a major event has occurred and where a press release cannot convey the appropriate tone or detail required by the organisation. Press conferences are mainly used by politicians, but organisations in crisis (e.g. accidents and mergers) and individuals appealing for help (e.g. police requesting assistance from the public with respect to a particular incident) can use this form of communication. Press kits containing a full reproduction of any statements, photographs and relevant background information should always be available.

Interviews

Interviews with representatives of an organisation enable news and the organisation's view of an issue or event to be conveyed. Other forms of media relations concern by-lined articles (articles written by a member of an organisation about an issue related to the company and offered for publication), speeches, letters to the editor, and photographs and captions.

Viewpoint 10.3 **Entertainment PR for TV Wars**

There are two big UK Saturday night television shows, *The X Factor* (XF) and *Strictly Come Dancing* (SCD). These shows command audiences of approximately 11–12 and 7–8 million respectively, and they run head-to-head in the three months leading to Christmas. Public relations is used to support both of them, but in slightly different ways.

SCD is produced by the BBC and all the PR relating to the show is managed in-house. PR agencies are used to create attention but many of the celebrity contestants, one of the judges, and the two presenters have their own

TOSHIBA
Leading Innovation ⟩⟩⟩

Toshiba premieres new 'Space Chair' ad campaign
Campaign to support Toshiba's SV REGZA LCD TV and Satellite T series laptops

London, UK, 16th November 2009 – Toshiba UK continues to lead innovation as it premieres its latest advertising campaign, 'Space Chair'; a piece of film which takes viewers on an awe-inspiring journey to the edge of space.

Created for Toshiba by Grey London, 'Space Chair' builds on the phenomenal success of 2008's record-breaking 'Timesculpture' ad campaign and has once again been filmed using Toshiba cameras. Shot in the wilderness of the Nevada Black Rock desert, the advertisement follows the journey of an ordinary living room chair to the extraordinary heights of the edge of space, lifted to an altitude of 98,268 feet by a simple helium balloon.

The advert is split into two executions, the first playing in 2009 for the **Toshiba REGZA SV LCD TV Series** and 2010 for the new range of **Satellite T Series** of ultra low voltage laptops. The REGZA SV is Toshiba's first ever model to include an LED backlight with local dimming, and is set to redefine the armchair viewing experience by delivering sharper, smoother images that clearly define every cloud and every star. The ultra portable, lightweight Satellite T Series enables users to go further by offering up to eleven hours of battery life – enough to take you to space and back.

The ad was shot by Haris Zambarloukos, the acclaimed cinematographer behind films including 'Enduring Love' and 'Mamma Mia' and was directed by Andy Amadeo, Creative Director at Grey London. The shoot was made possible via the construction of a unique custom-built camera rig engineered by John Powell of JP Aerospace – experts in this field who have successfully sent over 100 balloons into the upper atmosphere. A specially created full-sized model chair made of biodegradable balsa wood; light enough to make the 83 minute journey up towards space was tied to the rig and launched by the team.

Four independent GPS systems were placed on the rig to accurately record its height at any second to within 4 meters in altitude, and within 30cm in longitude and latitude position. This information was transmitted every 15 seconds back to ground control where it was monitored via a computer satellite system to enable the team to locate the rig once it had fallen back to earth.

The film is cinematic, opening with a shot of the solitary chair silhouetted against the Nevada sunrise and taking the viewer on its journey above the desert, into the clouds and beyond.

Matt McDowell, Marketing Director at Toshiba UK comments: 'Our aim was to create a new advertising campaign that would bring to life Toshiba's brand philosophy of leading innovation. We chose to send a chair on the journey as it is central to the user's experience of Toshiba's products; whether they are watching TV or using a laptop.'

'The ad features two exciting new products. The REGZA SV Series is the first-ever Toshiba LCD TV to combine Toshiba's Resolution+ technology and an LED backlight – delivering stunning high quality images that enhances the viewers' armchair experience. Offering the performance and functionality of full-sized laptops with portability and a battery life of up to eleven hours, the Satellite T Series frees users from the shackles of their desks, empowering them to explore new environments.'

Andy Amadeo, Creative Director at Grey London comments: 'Keeping with our tact of being as innovative as the brand, we once again created a mould-breaking commercial with Toshiba. Last year we set a new world record with "Timesculpture" and proved that their domestic camcorders could produce a breathtaking, never before seen piece of film. This time we have used Toshiba HD cameras to produce some of the most stunning footage shot at the edge of space.'

Facts about the shoot:

- The shots were taken at a staggering 98,268 feet above the earth using Toshiba's own cameras
- To reach the altitude required and to conform with Federal Aviation Administration regulations, the weight of the rig had to be carefully managed to a weight of no more than four pounds

Exhibit 10.2	Press release for the launch of the Toshiba Space Chair ad
	Press release courtesy of Toshiba

Press Release

- Tied to the rig was a specially created full-sized model chair made of biodegradable balsa wood – the chair was made by a company called Artem and cost about £2,500
- Launch coordinates of the rig were – 119 degrees, 14 minutes by 40 degrees, 48 minute (12 miles North-East of the town of Gerlach, Nevada)
- The quality of the footage from the Toshiba IK-HR1S cameras was: 1920 × 1080 pixel count; 1080i @ 50hz; 100 Mbps
- The temperature dropped to minus 90 degrees when the chair reached 52,037 feet
- The chair took 83 minutes to reach an altitude of 98,268 feet where it broke and took just 24 minutes to fall back down to earth with the rig.

Notes to Editors
The full 60 second advert premieres on 16 November on ITV1 and runs for three weeks. The ad will then run again in February 2010.

Creative Credits

Creative Agency:	Grey London
Production Company:	Hungry Man LTD
Director:	Andy Amadeo
Editor and editing company:	The Whitehouse / Russell Ike
Post-production company:	The Mill

– Ends –

For more information, interview requests or photography, please contact:
Katy Ball @ Nelson Bostock Communications
E: katy.ball@nelsonbostock.com
T: 020 7792 7489

About Toshiba
Toshiba is a world leader and innovator in pioneering high technology, a diversified manufacturer and marketer of advanced electronic and electrical products spanning information & communications systems; digital consumer products; electronic devices and components; power systems, including nuclear energy; industrial and social infrastructure systems; and home appliances. Toshiba was founded in 1875, and today operates a global network of more than 740 companies, with 199,000 employees worldwide and annual sales surpassing 6.6 trillion yen (US$73 billion). Visit Toshiba's web site at www.toshiba.co.jp/index.html

About Grey London
We are 200 people, drawn from different marketing and media backgrounds, working together in a wonderfully open environment in Holborn, London. We do the lot: multi-channel, integrated, online, offline, above, through and below the line for a wide range of clients including Ryvita, P&G, GlaxoSmithKline, IPC Media, the British Heart Foundation, Dairy Crest and Toshiba.

We don't believe in agency positionings. We do believe in making our clients both successful and happy. We believe we're better than most agencies at listening to what clients really want. Which means we're better at understanding the problem and getting to the most exciting and effective answer.

Exhibit 10.2   *Continued*

personal PR support, all of which is coordinated by the BBC. The show has incurred many issues, varying from affairs between professional dancers and celebrities, the sacking of one of the judges and replacing her with a younger, former winner of the show, and issues concerning the positioning of the show, as a form of entertainment or dance competition. The latter issue is often exposed through the way the public votes to keep certain celebrities in.

XF is produced by ITV but all the judges have their own PR support. ITV's PR is involved but does not coordinate activities in the same way as the BBC. It appears that the central figure driving the show, and various offshoots, is Simon Cowell. When the show launched, his PR team (Max Clifford) drew attention by shaping Cowell's nasty image. Now, with the show well established, PR is used to manage the controversy and issues that emerge as the show moves forward and to cover relevant media stories concerning contestants and their backgrounds.

Interest in SCD is partly driven by providing exclusive information to websites and portals. This is achieved through the use of targeted niche blogs, forums and social networking groups. To increase the audience's experience of the show a new application was used in September 2009 which let online viewers interact with the live show by commenting on the performances and engaging emotionally with electronic 'boos', 'gasps' and 'wows'.

Source: Based on Magee (2009), O'Reilly (2009)

Question

What is the main role of entertainment PR?

Task

Storytelling can be powerful. Find stories that were used about SCD and X Factor.

Media relations can be planned and controlled, to the extent of what is sent to the media and when it is released. However, there is no control over what material is actually used or the perspective adopted through editing.

The quality of the relationship between an organisation and the media will dramatically affect the impact and dissemination of news and stories released by an organisation. The relationships referred to are those between an organisation's public relations manager and the editor and journalists associated with both the press and the broadcast media.

Publicity and events

Control over public relations events is not as strong as that for media relations. Indeed, negative publicity can be generated by other parties, which can impact badly on an organisation by raising doubts about its financial status or perhaps the quality of its products. Three main event activity areas can be distinguished: product, corporate and community events.

Product events

Product-oriented events are normally focused on increasing sales. Cookery demonstrations, celebrities autographing their books and the opening of a new store by the CEO or local MP are events aimed at generating attention, interest and sales of a particular product.

Alternatively events are designed to attract the attention of the media and, through stories and articles presented in the news, are able to reach a wide audience. For example, the public's attention was drawn to the launch of *The Simpsons Movie* in July 2007, by a stunt involving the painting of a giant Homer Simpson next to the 180-foot chalk cut Cerne Abbas giant in Dorset. News coverage of the new work of art, Homer holding a doughnut, was in most national newspapers, on ITV, Sky and BBC television, plus radio coverage (see Exhibit 10.3).

Corporate events

Events designed to develop the corporate profile are often designed to provide some entertainment. These can generate considerable local media coverage, which in turn facilitates awareness,

Exhibit 10.3	Chalky Homer
	A paint line drawing of Homer Simpson next to the chalk cut Cerne Abbas Giant, used to attract media attention prior to the launch of *The Simpsons Movie* in July 2007
	Image courtesy of Press Association Images/PA Wire

goodwill and interest. For example, events such as open days, factory visits and donations of products to local events can be very beneficial.

Community events

These are activities that contribute to the life of the local community. Sponsoring local fun runs and children's play areas, making contributions to local community centres and the disabled are typical activities. The organisation attempts to become more involved with the local community as a good employer and good member of the community. This helps to develop goodwill and awareness in the community.

The choice of events an organisation becomes involved with is critical. The events should have a theme and be chosen to satisfy objectives established earlier in the communications plan.

In addition to these key activities the following are important forms of public relations:

- lobbying (out of personal selling and publicity);
- sponsorship (out of event management and advertising);
- corporate advertising (out of advertising);
- crisis management (out of issues management).

Lobbying

The representation of certain organisations or industries within government is an important form of public relations work. While legislation is being prepared, lobbyists provide a flow of information to their organisations to keep them informed about events (as a means of scanning the environment), but they also ensure that the views of the organisation are heard in order that legislation can be shaped appropriately, limiting any potential damage that new legislation might bring.

Moloney (1997) suggests that lobbying is inside public relations as it focuses on the members of an organisation who seek to persuade and negotiate with its stakeholders in government on matters of opportunity and or threat. He refers to in-house lobbyists (those members of the organisation who try to influence non-members) and hired lobbyists contracted to complete specific tasks.

His view of lobbying is that it is one of monitoring public policy-making for a group interest; building a case in favour of that interest; and putting it privately with varying degrees of pressure to public decision-makers for their acceptance and support through favourable political intervention (1997: 173).

Where local authorities interpret legislation and frame the activities of their citizens and constituent organisations, the government determines legislation and controls the activities of people and organisations across markets. The tobacco industry is well known for its lobbying activities, as are chemical, transport and many other industries.

Corporate advertising

In an attempt to harness the advantages of both advertising and public relations, corporate advertising has been seen by some as a means of communicating more effectively with a range of stakeholders. The credibility of messages transmitted through public relations is high, but the control that management has over the message is limited. Advertising, however, allows management virtually total control over message dispersion, but the credibility of these messages is usually low. Corporate advertising is the combination of the best of advertising and the best of public relations.

Corporate advertising that is, advertising on behalf of an organisation rather than its products or services, has long been associated with public relations rather than the advertising department.

The main purpose of corporate advertising appears to be the provision of cues by which stakeholders can identify and understand an organisation. This is achieved by presenting the personality of the organisation to a wide range of stakeholders, rather than presenting particular functions or products that the organisation markets. Schumann *et al.* (1991) conclude that a number of US studies indicate that the first goal of corporate advertising is to enhance the company's reputation and the second is to provide support for the promotion of products and services. However, research indicates that today the majority of organisations use corporate advertising to promote products and services.

Crisis communications

A growing and important part of the work associated with public relations is crisis communications. Crises can occur because of a simple or minor managerial mistake, an incorrect decision or because of a seemingly distant environmental event. All organisations face the prospect of managing a crisis, indeed, some commentators ominously suggest that all organisations have a crisis just around the corner (Fink, 2000). Jacques (2009) considers the lack of agreement in defining crises management and the various sections or stages through which a crisis proceeds. He suggests the need to identify the phases of the continuum. He offers the view of Mitroff (2004) who suggests that *crisis management* consists of a reactive phase, after a crisis has happened, whereas the preparation phase, before the crisis, should be characterised as *crisis leadership*.

Table 10.1	Common causes of disasters

Origin of crisis	Explanation
Economic	As the Western world currently experiences growth and high levels of employment and countries in the developing world follow a fluctuating path of revitalisation and competition, this has brought some organisations and industries in the West to collapse (e.g. UK shipbuilding).
Managerial	Human error and the pursuit of financial goals by some organisations give rise to the majority of disasters. For example, cutting costs at the expense of safety and repair of systems or deliberate sabotage as in Enron.
Political	Issues concerning war and terrorism have encouraged kidnapping, as well as organisations having to change the locations of their business.
Climate	The climate is changing substantially in certain parts of the world, and this has brought disaster to those who lie in the wake of natural disturbances. For example, the earthquakes in Haiti and Chile in 2010 and unusual rainfall patterns causing flooding in Australia.
Technology	The rate at which technology is advancing has brought about crises such as those associated with transportation systems and aircraft disasters. Human error is also a significant factor, which can be associated with the rate of technological change.
New media	The age of electronic media and instant communication means that information can be disseminated throughout the world within 30 minutes of an event occurring. Corporate blogging and use the use of Twitter can give immediate insight into events.
Consumer groups	The rise of consumer groups (e.g. Amnesty International and Greenpeace) and their ability to investigate and publicise the operations and policies of organisations.

Crises are emerging with greater frequency as a result of a number of factors. Table 10.1 sets out some of the main factors that give rise to crises for organisations.

Figure 10.2 describes organisational crises in the context of two key variables. On the horizontal axis is the degree to which management has control over the origin of the crisis. Is the origin of the crisis outside management's control, such as an earthquake, or is it within its control, such as those crises associated with poor trading results? The vertical axis reflects the potential impact that a crisis might have on an organisation. All crises, by definition, have a potential to inflict damage on an organisation. However, some can be contained, perhaps on a geographic basis, whereas others have the potential to cause tremendous damage to an organisation, such as those experienced through product tampering and environmental pollution.

The increasing occurrence of crises throughout the world has prompted many organisations to review the manner in which they anticipate managing such events, should they be implicated. It is generally assumed that those organisations that take the care to plan in anticipation of disaster will experience more favourable outcomes than those that fail to plan. When British Airways was faced with the prospect of strike action, the airline planned a response that included social media. This included a series of videos posted on YouTube and BA.com. These featured the CEO apologising for the inconvenience to their customers and providing updates on the current strike and operational situation (Kimberley, 2010).

However, when there is poor planning, poor results can be expected. Indeed, organisations that do not plan, experience crises that last over twice as long as those that do plan (Fink, 2000). For example, Eurostar have experienced a series of issues in recent years. In September 2008 a train caught fire, resulting in a 16 hour blaze. Brownsell (2009) reports that a full service was not resumed until February 2009. Later in December that year, trains ground to a halt in freezing weather, for no apparent reason. Passengers were stranded for hours, often in the dark, with no facilities and no support. Eurostar was thrown into crisis, experienced high levels of negative media visibility and was subsequently found not have a suitable crisis plan in position.

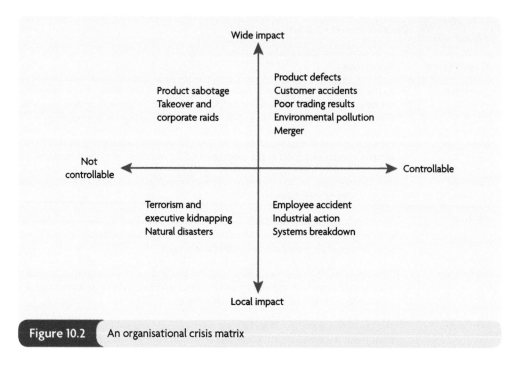

Figure 10.2 An organisational crisis matrix

Crisis planning is about putting into position those elements that can effect speedy outcomes to the disaster sequence. When a crisis strikes, it is the application of contingency based tactics by all those concerned with the event that will determine the strength of the outcome. Crises tend to move through a series of distinct phases. Coombs (2007) proposed three sequential phases:

- pre-crisis (signal detection, prevention, preparation);
- crisis event (recognition, containment);
- post-crisis (evaluation, learning, follow up communication).

Jaques (2007) developed clusters of action, as set out in Table 10.2.

For a long time the key issue associated with crisis communication has been speed. The speed of response has been crucial. However, as Borremans (2010) points out, speed is no longer the issue, as social media has enabled all organisations to respond quickly. The issue now is the impact of what is being communicated.

Social media not only disseminates bad news quickly it can also be used to gather information and to disperse positive news. For example, RSS feeds can be used to replace clipping

Table 10.2 Clusters of crisis management activities (Jacques, 2007)

Crisis stage	Management activities
Crisis preparedness	Planning processes, systems and manuals, documentation, training/simulations
Crisis prevention	Early warning, risk and issue management, social forecasting, environmental scanning, emergency response
Crisis incident management	Recognition, activation, damage mitigation, implementation
Post-crisis management	Recovery/resumption, post-crisis issue impacts, judicial inquiries, evaluation, modification

services and provide near real-time access to what is being said about the organisation at the centre of the crisis and it can do this 24/7. RSS feeds aggregate news items which can be read in one of three main ways. These are through email, an online 'feedreader', or through a 'feedreader application' which is downloaded to a PC.

Wikis can be used at all stages of the crisis, and even organised into the different phases of crisis planning process, from the 'preparedness' to 'post crisis management' stage. At the outset a 'wiki' can be used as a dynamic document, where all parties to the communication plan can input information and ideas to the same page. Draft statements, forms and other documents can be created, reviewed and managed throughout the crisis period, even from remote access.

Sponsorship

Sponsorship has become an increasingly popular element of the mix because of the quality of the communication it generates. It is a mix of advertising, with its capacity for message control, and public relations with its potential for high levels of credibility and message diffusion, directed through or with a third party. In this sense sponsorship lacks the harshness of advertising and the total lack of control that characterises much of the work of public relations. Sponsorship can be defined as a commercial activity, whereby one party permits another an opportunity to exploit an association with a target audience in return for funds, services or resources. In particular sponsorship;

- gives exposure to particular audiences that each event attracts, in order to convey simple awareness-based brand messages;
- suggests to target audiences that there is an association between the sponsored and the sponsor and that by implication this association may be of interest and/or value;
- allows members of the target audiences to perceive the sponsor indirectly through a third party and so diffuse any negative effects associated with traditional mass media and direct persuasion;
- provides sponsors with the opportunity to blend a variety of tools in the communication mix and use resources more efficiently and arguably more effectively.

Normally sponsorship involves two parties, the sponsor and the sponsee, although many sponsors may be assigned to a single sponsee. The degree of fit or congruence between these two parties partly determines the relative effectiveness of the relationship (Cornwell, *et al.*, 2006; Poon and Prendergast, 2006). The degree of fit, or product relevance as proposed by McDonald (1991) cited by Poon and Prendergast, can be considered in terms of two main dimensions. Function-based similarity occurs when the product is used in the event being sponsored. For example, the piano manufacturer *Bösendorfer* sponsoring a Viennese piano recital. The second dimension concerns image-based similarities, which reflects the image of the sponsor in the event. Here *Airbus*'s sponsorship of a major technical or even artistic exhibition serves to bestow prestige on all parties. Poon and Prendergast suggest that rather than treat these as mutually exclusive elements, there can be four interconnected dimensions. Figure 10.3 serves to illustrate their intentions.

Sponsorship, a part of public relations, should be used as part of an integrated approach to an organisation's communications. In other words, sponsorship provides a further tool that, to be used effectively, needs to be harnessed strategically. As Tripodi (2001) comments, the implementation of integrated marketing communications is further encouraged and supported when sponsorship is an integral part of the mix in order to maximise the full impact of this communication tool. For example, many companies and brands originating in south-east Asia and the Pacific regions have used sponsorship as a means of overseas market entry in order to develop name or brand awareness (e.g. Panasonic, JVC and Daihatsu).

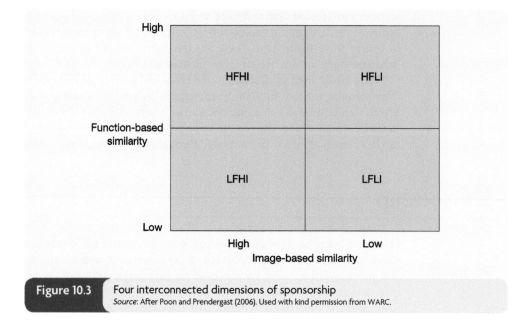

Figure 10.3   Four interconnected dimensions of sponsorship
Source: After Poon and Prendergast (2006). Used with kind permission from WARC.

Coppetti *et al.* (2009) emphasise the value of congruence but also demonstrate that even when there is a lack of fit, the effectiveness of the sponsorship can be enhanced by involving the audience in what they refer to as 'attractive sponsor activities'. This suggests that by building in experiences for the audience and encouraging their participation, and by using advertising before and after the sponsorship event, such integration can serve to increase the value of the communication programme.

Sponsorship objectives

There are both primary and secondary objectives associated with using sponsorship. The primary reasons are to build awareness, developing customer loyalty and improving the perception (image) held about the brand or organisation. Secondary reasons are more contentious, but generally they can be seen to be to attract new users, to support dealers and other intermediaries and to act as a form of staff motivation and morale building (Reed, 1994).

Sponsorship is normally regarded as a communications tool used to reach external stakeholders. However, if chosen appropriately sponsorship can also be used effectively to reach internal audiences. Care is required because different audiences transfer diverse values (Grimes and Meenaghan, 1998). According to Harverson (1998), one of the main reasons IT companies sponsor sports events is that this form of involvement provides opportunities to 'showcase' their products and technologies, in context. Through application in an appropriate working environment, the efficacy of a sponsor's products can be demonstrated. The relationship between sports organisers and IT companies becomes reciprocal as the organisers of sports events need technology in order for the events to run. Corporate hospitality opportunities are often taken in addition to the brand exposure that the media coverage provides. EDS claims that it uses sponsorship to reach two main audiences, customers (and potential customers) and potential future employees. The message it uses is that the EDS involvement in sport is sexy and exciting.

A further important characteristic concerns the impact of repeat attendance on brand image. Work by Lacey *et al.* (2007) found that a car manufacturer's image improved modestly by sponsoring a sporting event. However, through repeat attendance positive opinion scores towards the sponsor improved. The obvious implication for marketing is that it is important to attract attendees back to sporting events.

Viewpoint 10.4   Sponsoring the geegees

The Cheltenham Festival is a major event in the horse racing calendar and with attendances and interest in all forms of the sport increasing, despite the recession, sponsorship remains an attractive from of marketing communications for many organisations. It was estimated that sponsorship was worth £1.68 million in 2010. Thomas Pink (the quality fashion retailer), Spinal Research (a charity) and Ryanair (the low cost airline) all sponsored events at the festival for the first time in 2010.

Thomas Pink sponsored the prestigious Leading Rider and Trainer Awards and so associated themselves with a sport and some of its most talented individuals, with their own heritage.

Cenkos Securities plc funded the Spinal Research Supreme Novices' Hurdle and so gave visibility to an important and racing related charity, as many involved in horse racing suffer spinal injury.

Sponsors can provide financial support for individual races and in return generate brand awareness and local visibility. In addition, the event provides a focus for the sponsor to provide corporate hospitality for selected customers and other stakeholders. The race also attracts media coverage and a certain level of word of mouth communication generated by spectators.

Source: Based on Turner (2010); www.cheltenhamfestival.net/New-sponsorship-of-Festival-awards.php
www.southwestbusiness.co.uk/news/Cheltenham-Festival-win/article-1918458-detail/article.html

Exhibit 10.4   Thomas Pink
Image courtesy of Alamy Images/John Warburton-Lee Photography

Following on from this is the issue about whether sponsorship is being used to support a product or the organisation. Corporate sponsorships, according to Thwaites (1994), are intended to focus on developing community involvement, public awareness, image, goodwill and staff relations. Product- or brand-based sponsorship activity is aimed at developing media coverage, sales leads, sales/market share, target market awareness and guest hospitality.

Types of sponsorship

It is possible to identify particular areas within which sponsorship has been used. These areas are sports, programme/broadcast, the arts and others that encompass activities such as wildlife/conservation and education. Of all of these, sport has attracted most attention and sponsorship money.

Sports sponsorship

Sports activities have been very attractive to sponsors, partly because of the high media coverage they attract. Sport is the leading type of sponsorship, mainly for the following reasons:

- Sport has the propensity to attract large audiences, not only at each event but more importantly through the media that attach themselves to these activities.
- Sport provides a simplistic measure of segmentation, so that as audiences fragment generally, sport provides an opportunity to identify and reach often large numbers of people who share particular characteristics.
- Visibility opportunities for the sponsor are high in a number of sporting events because of the duration of each event (e.g. the Olympics or the FIFA World Cup).

Barclaycard's sponsorship of the football Premier League and Coca-Cola's sponsorship of the football championship have been motivated partly by the attraction of large and specific target audiences with whom a degree of fit is considered to exist. The constant media attention enables the sponsors' names to be disseminated to distant audiences, many of them overseas. Marshall and Cook (1992) found that event sponsorship (e.g. the Olympics or the Ideal Home Exhibition) is the most popular form of sponsorship activity undertaken by organisations. This was followed by team, league and individual support.

Vodafone sponsored Manchester United in order to boost global awareness. Then the company bought Mannesmann and found it then sponsored Benfica, Porto, Olympiakos and teams in La Liga in Spain and the Bundesliga in Germany. Rationalisation was necessary and wanting to maintain an association with football, it then became a Champions League sponsor (Murphy, 2007). AIG became United's next shirt sponsor in an attempt to fuel AIG's expansion out of North America and reach new markets, principally Asia, where a high percentage of the target market are football, and Manchester United fans. AIG have pulled out due to the financial crisis.

Golf has attracted a great deal of sponsorship money, mainly because it has a global upmarket appeal and generates good television and press coverage. Golf clubs are also well suited for corporate entertainment and offer the chance of playing as well as watching. Volvo sponsored the European Golf Championship for the period 1996–2000 for £20 million. Johnnie Walker continues to sponsor major golfing championships. Toyota used to support the World Matchplay Championship at Wentworth each year because the tournament fitted into a much wider promotion programme. Toyota dealers sponsored competitions at their local courses, with qualifiers going through to a final at Wentworth. The winner of that played in the pro-am before the World Matchplay. Toyota incorporated the tournament into a range of incentive and promotional programmes and flew in top distributors and fleet customers from around the world. In addition, the environment was used to build customer relationships. This championship is now supported by HSBC.

Programme sponsorship

Television programme sponsorship began to receive serious attention in Britain in the late 1990s. The market has grown, as reflected in TV sponsorship revenues, from £81.2 million in 2000 to nearly £200 million in 2009. This growth has occurred partly because of a relaxation in the regulations. For example, the visibility that each sponsor is allowed was strictly controlled to certain times, and before, during the break and after each programme with the credits. This was changed so that while sponsors are not allowed to influence the content or scheduling of a programme so as to affect the editorial independence and responsibility of the broadcaster, it is now permissible to allow the sponsor's product to be seen along with the sponsor's name in bumper credits and to allow greater flexibility in terms of the use of straplines. There is a requirement on the broadcaster to ensure that the sponsored credit is depicted in such a way that it cannot be mistaken as a spot advertisement. So, Hedburg (2000) gives the example of Nescafé sponsoring *Friends* showing a group of people sitting on a sofa and drinking coffee and of *Coronation Street* and former sponsor Cadbury's, which presented a whole chocolate street and set of chocolate characters.

Masthead programming, where the publisher of a magazine such as *Amateur Photographer* sponsors a programme in a related area, such as *Photography for Beginners*, is generally not permitted, although the regulations surrounding this type of activity are being relaxed. There are a number of reasons why programme sponsorship is appealing. First, it allows clients to avoid the clutter associated with spot advertising. In that sense it creates a space, or mini-world, in which the sponsor can create awareness and provide brand identity cues unhindered by other brands. Second, it represents a cost-effective medium when compared with spot advertising. Although the cost of programme sponsorship has increased as the value of this type of communication has appreciated, it does not command the high rates required for spot advertising. Third, the use of credits around a programme offers opportunities for the target audience to make associations between the sponsor and the programme.

Research by the Bloxam Group suggests that for a sponsorship to work there needs to be a linkage between the product and the programme. Links that are spurious, illogical or inappropriate are very often rejected by viewers. For example, a branded soft drink might work well with a youth-oriented programme, but a financial services brand supporting a sports programme or film series would not have a strong or logical linkage.

The line between product placement, brand entertainment and programme sponsorship becomes increasingly blurred. However, programme sponsorship should not be seen as a replacement for advertising. The argument that sponsorship is not a part of advertising is clearly demonstrated by the point that many sponsors continue with their spot advertising when running major sponsorships.

Arts sponsorship

Arts sponsorship, according to Thorncroft (1996), began as a philanthropic exercise, with business giving something back to the community. It was a means of developing corporate image and was used extensively by tobacco companies as they attempted to reach their customer base. It then began to be appreciated for its corporate hospitality opportunities: a cheaper, more civilised alternative to sports sponsorship, and one that appealed more to women.

Many organisations sponsor the arts as a means of enhancing their corporate status and as a means of clarifying their name. Another important reason organisations use sponsorship is to establish and maintain favourable contact with key business people, often at board level, together with other significant public figures. Through related corporate hospitality, companies can reach substantial numbers of their targeted key people.

Most recently, sponsorship has been used to reach specific groups of consumers. Orange sponsors a range of music-related events, one of them being the Glastonbury Festival. One of the key facilities is the 'chill 'n charge' tent. This is a bright orange-coloured tent in which people can use the phone-charging equipment or the Internet facilities to pick up their email and over 50,000 people used the tent at the 2007 festival. Orange see their sponsorship of the festival as a way to develop their brand and purchase consideration, but not as a means of directly acquiring customers (Bartlett, 2007).

The sponsorship of the arts has moved from being a means of supporting the community to a sophisticated means of targeting and positioning brands. Sponsorship, once part of corporate public relations, is now a significant aspect of marketing public relations.

Viewpoint 10.5	Robinsons supports juicy pantos

Robinsons has been involved with many sponsorship events over the years and is probably most associated with the Wimbledon tennis tournament. In 2009 Robinsons sponsored festive pantomimes in conjunction with First Family Entertainment. This is a large theatrical production company who had recruited several celebrities to star in pantomimes around the country. Robinsons wanted to raise awareness of the events and their association without using television, a costly route, one that they use for their Wimbledon work.

The result was a website to help children and parents develop and run their own pantomimes at home. The intention was to provide a way in which families could work together. The website contained information about writing scripts, costumes and promotional posters were all made available online. In order to enrich the experience an iPhone app was developed providing sound effects.

The launch was delivered through an on-pack promotion involving over 41 million bottles of Robinsons soft drinks. PR and promotional activity at pantomime events was also used to publicise the sponsorship. Ads were placed in First Family panto magazines, editorial content was seeded across 100 blog sites associated with mother-hood and parenting, and a Flash game was placed on 25 children oriented game sites.

Source: Based on Anon (2009)

Question

To what extent might Robinson's be overly dependent on their relationship with Wimbledon?

Task

Make a list of the other activities Robinsons could sponsor successfully.

To support their global brand HSBC has a cultural sponsorship programme. In 2008 the bank supported cultural events in China, in 2009 they backed various Indian cultural initiatives and in 2010 they supported 'Festival Brazil'. This event was focused on exhibitions and various artistic performances by Brazilian artists in London at the festival. HSBC also supported events in South America, the Middle East, South-East Asia and the USA. The bank has co-partnered with the *Financial Times* and the Economist Intelligence Unit to advise companies thinking of exporting and setting up in Brazil (Brownsell, 2010).

Other forms of sponsorship

It has been argued that there is little opportunity to control messages delivered through sponsorship, and far less opportunity to encourage the target audiences to enter into a dialogue with sponsors. However, the awareness and image opportunities can be used by supporting either the local community or small-scale schemes. In March 2011 a Climate Week was held, with Aviva, RBS, EDF Energy and Kellogg as some of the first sponsors to sign up. These companies will be able to demonstrate what actions they are taking with regard to climate change as well as assist other organisations to become involved (Thomas, 2010).

Samsung Electronics use sponsorship to link up with a variety of activities. One of these is football and is a partner with Chelsea FC, Inter Milan FC, Palmeiras, Suwon Bluwings, Olympiacos and Feyenoord. The company is also an official sponsor for the Olympic Games, and the Asian Games. However, they feel that the greater the number of sponsors tied to an event the less opportunity there is to leverage the linkage. The one exception to this rule is the Olympics. This event involves all nations and Samsung signed an agreement in 2010 to be a main sponsor of the Olympics until 2016.

The majority of sponsorships, regardless of type, are not the sole promotional activity undertaken by the sponsors. They may be secondary and used to support above-the-line work or they may be used as the primary form of communication but supported by a range of off-screen activities, such as sales promotions and (in particular) competitions. For example, Sony Pictures developed a programme to encourage school pupils to be innovative and to develop their interest in science. Using an animated film, *Cloudy with a Chance of Meatballs*, the unbranded film provides a context for activities, quizzes and competitions (Thomas, 2009). More of a partnership than a straight sponsorship, the relationship furthers Sony's positioning as an innovator.

This section would not be complete without mention of the phenomenon called 'ambush marketing'. This occurs when an organisation deliberately seeks an association with a particular event but does so without paying sponsorship fees. Such hijacking is undertaken with the purpose of influencing the audience to the extent that they believe the ambusher is legitimate. According to Meenaghan (1998), this can be achieved by overstating the organisation's involvement in the event, perhaps through major communication activity using theme-based advertising or by sponsoring the media coverage of the event.

The role of sponsorship in the communications mix

Whether sponsorship is a part of advertising, sales promotion or public relations, has long been a source of debate. It is perhaps more natural and comfortable to align sponsorship with advertising. Since awareness is regarded as the principal objective of using sponsorship, advertising is a more complementary and accommodating part of the mix. Sales promotion from the sponsor's position is harder to justify, although from the perspective of the sponsored the value-added characteristic is interesting. The more traditional home for sponsorship is public relations (Witcher *et al.*, 1991). The sponsored, such as a football team, a racing car manufacturer or a theatre group, may be adjudged to perform the role of opinion former. Indirectly, therefore, messages are conveyed to the target audience with the support of significant participants who endorse and support the sponsor. This is akin to public relations activities.

Hastings (1984) contests that advertising messages can be manipulated and adapted to changing circumstances much more easily than those associated with sponsorship. He suggests that the audience characteristics of both advertising and sponsorship are very different. For advertising there are viewers and non-viewers. For sponsorship there are three groups of people that can be identified. First, there are those who are directly involved with the sponsor or the event, the active participants. The second is a much larger group, consisting of those who attend sponsored events, and these are referred to as personal spectators. The third group is normally the largest, comprising all those who are involved with the event through various media channels; these are regarded as media followers.

As if to demonstrate the potential sizes of these groups, estimates suggest that in excess of 4 million people attend the Formula 1 Grand Prix championship races (active participants) and over half a billion people (media followers) watch the races on television.

Exploratory research undertaken by Hoek *et al.* (1997) suggests that sponsorship is better able to generate awareness and a wider set of product-related attributes than advertising when dealing with non-users of a product, rather than users. There appears to be no discernible difference between the impact that these two promotional tools have with users.

The authors claim that sponsorship and advertising can be considered to work in approximately the same way if the ATR (attention, trial, reinforcement) model developed by Ehrenberg (1974) is adopted (Chapter 9). Through the ATR model, purchase behaviour and beliefs are considered to be reinforced by advertising rather than new behaviour patterns being established. Advertising fulfils a means by which buyers can meaningfully defend their purchase patterns. Hoek *et al.* regard this approach as reasonably analogous to sponsorship. Sponsorship can create awareness and is more likely to confirm past behaviour than prompt new purchase behaviour. The implication, they conclude, is that, while awareness levels can be improved with sponsorship, other communication tools are required to impact upon product experimentation or purchase intentions. Indeed, Smoliannov and Aiyeku (2009) make the point that integrated tv and major event sponsorship appear to work by influencing markets through TV audiences.

It was suggested earlier in this chapter that one of the opportunities that sponsorship offers is the ability to suggest that there is an association between the sponsored and the sponsor which may be of value to the message recipient. This implies that there is an indirect form of influence through sponsorship. This is supported by Crimmins and Horn (1996), who argue that the persuasive impact of sponsorship is determined in terms of the strength of links that are generated between the brand and the event that is sponsored.

These authors claim that sponsorship can have a persuasive impact and that the degree of impact that a sponsorship might bring is as follows:

$$\frac{\text{persuasive}}{\text{impact}} = \frac{\text{strength}}{\text{of link}} \times \frac{\text{duration}}{\text{of the link}} \times \left\{ \frac{\text{gratitude felt}}{\text{due to the link}} + \frac{\text{perceptual change}}{\text{due to the link}} \right\}$$

The strength of the link between the brand and the event is an outcome of the degree to which advertising is used to communicate the sponsorship itself. Sponsors that failed to invest in advertising during the Olympic Games have been shown to be far less successful in building a link with the event than those who chose to invest.

The *duration* of the link is also important. Research based on the Olympic Games shows that those sponsors who undertook integrated marketing communications long before the event itself were far more successful than those who had not. The use of mass media advertising to communicate the involvement of the sponsor, the use of event graphics and logos on packaging, and the creative use of pro-motional tie-ins and in-store, event-related merchandising facilitated the long-term linkage with the sponsorship and added value to the campaign.

Gratitude exists if consumers realise that there is a link between a brand and an event. For example, 60 per cent of US adults said that they 'try to buy a company's product if they support the Olympics'. They also stated that 'I feel I am contributing to the Olympics by buying the brands of Olympic sponsors'.

Perceptual change occurs as a result of consumers being able to understand the relationship (meaning) between a brand and an event. The sponsor needs to make this clear, as passive consumers may need the links laid out before them. The link between a swimwear brand and the Olympics may be obvious, but it is not always the case. Crimmins and Horn (1996) describe how Visa's 15 per cent perceived superiority advantage over MasterCard was stretched to 30 per cent during the 1992 Olympics and then settled at 20 per cent ahead one month after the Games had finished. The perceptual change was achieved through the messages that informed audiences that Visa was the one card that was accepted for the Olympic Games; American Express and MasterCard were not accepted.

This research, while based only upon a single event, indicates that sponsorship may bring advantages if care is taken to invest in communications long before and during the event to communicate the meaning between the brand and the event, which will leverage gratitude from a grateful audience. Finally, as if to confirm the point, Olson and Thjomoe (2009) find that combining television advertising increases the effectiveness of a sponsorship activity.

Summary

In order to help consolidate your understanding of public relations and sponsorship, here are the key points summarised against each of the learning objectives:

1 Explain the nature, characteristics and audiences for public relations

Public relations is a management activity used to convey messages about the organisation or its products and services, in order to build and maintain relationships with significant stakeholders. These relationships are noteworthy and they should be mutually beneficial.

The main characteristics of public relations are that it represents a very cost-effective means of carrying messages with a high degree of credibility. However, the degree of control that management is able to exert over the transmission of these types of messages can be limited.

Public relations can be used to communicate with a range of publics (or stakeholders). These vary from employees (internal public relations), financial groups (financial or investor relations), customers (media relations) and organisations and communities (corporate public relations).

2 Consider the issues relating to corporate responsibility and cause-related marketing

Organisations are under increasing pressure to act and be perceived as credible, transparent, responsible and ethically sound. Being able to present corporate brands as contributors to the wider social framework, a role beyond that of simple profit generators, has enabled many organisations to achieve stronger, more positive market positions. One of the avenues available to organisations to express their values and attitudes towards their need to be responsible is cause-related marketing.

3 Provide an overview of some of the main tools used by public relations, including media relations, lobbying, corporate advertising and crisis management

Public relations consists of a range of communication activities, of which media relations, publicity and event management appear to be the main ones used by practitioners. However, in addition, lobbying, corporate advertising and crisis communications form an important aspect of public relations activities.

4 Consider reasons for the use of sponsorship and the types of objectives that might be set

Sponsorship permits one party an opportunity to exploit an association with a target audience of another organisation, in return for funds, services or resources. Sponsorship can create awareness for an organisation (or brand), provide associations delivered indirectly and so avoid the issues associated with direct persuasion as well as use of resources effectively and efficiently.

The primary reasons are to build awareness, develop customer loyalty and improve the perception (image) held of the brand or organisation. Secondary reasons include attracting new users, supporting intermediaries and providing a form of staff motivation and morale building.

5 Appreciate the variety and different forms of sponsorship activities

Sponsorship is used in three key areas. These are sports, programme/broadcast, and the arts. There is also growing interest in other activities such as wildlife/conservation and education. Of all of these, sport has attracted most attention and sponsorship money.

6 Understand the role of sponsorship in the communication mix

Sponsorship has become an important part of the mix as it allows brands to be communicated without the clutter and noise associated with advertising. At the same time sponsorship enables associations and linkages to be made that add value for all the participants to the communication process.

There seems little doubt that the introduction of new products and brands can be assisted by the use of appropriate sponsorships. Indeed, it appears that sponsorship, in certain contexts, can be used to prepare markets for the arrival and penetration of new brands. It is perhaps more natural and comfortable to align sponsorship with advertising but it has also been associated with sales promotion and public relations. Since awareness is regarded as the principal objective of using sponsorship, advertising is a more complementary and accommodating part of the mix.

Review questions

1. Define public relations and set out its principal characteristics.
2. Using an organisation of your choice, identify the main stakeholders and comment on why it is important to communicate with each of them.
3. Highlight the main objectives of using public relations.
4. Select an industry of your choice, and consider the possible topics that might cause organisations in the industry to actively lobby the regulators.
5. Identify the main phases associated with crisis management.
6. Why do you think an increasing number of organisations are using sponsorship as a part of their marketing communications mix?
7. Name four types of sponsorship.
8. If the objective of using sponsorship is to build awareness (among other things), then there is little point in using advertising. Discuss this view.
9. Consider three television programmes that are sponsored and evaluate how viewers might perceive the relationship between the programme content and the sponsor.
10. Explain the role of sponsorship within the communications mix.

References

Anon (2007) KittenAid hits hard to save unwanted cats. Retrieved 16 January 2008 from http://www.prweek/uk/thisweek/campaigns/article/766679/CAMPAIGN-KittenAid

Anon (2009) The Work: Robinsons, *Revolution*, December, 56–57.

Bartlett, M. (2007) Glowing at Glastonbury, *theMarketer* (September), 20–23.

Bokaie, J. (2007) Coke commits to global water conservation drive, *Marketing*, 6 June, 1.

Borremans, P. (2010) Ready for anything: Support and enhance your crisis communication plan with social media, *Communication World*, (July–August), 31–33.

Brownsell, A. (2009) Getting back on track, *Marketing*, 8 July, 26–27.

Brownsell, A. (2010) HSBC launches Brazilian cultural sponsorship programme, *Marketing*, 13 June. Retrieved 13 July from www.brandrepublic.co/news

Bruning, S.D. and Ledingham, J.A. (2000) Perceptions of relationships and evaluations of satisfaction: an exploration of interaction, *Public Relations Review*, 26(1), 85–95.

Coombs, W.T. (2007) Protecting organization reputations during a crisis: The development and application of situational crisis communication theory, *Corporate Reputation Review* 10(3), 163–176.

Coppetti, C., Wentzel, D., Tomczak, T. and Henkel, S. (2009) Improving incongruent sponsorships and audience participation, *Journal of Marketing Communications*, 15(1) (February), 17–34.

Cornwell, B.T., Humphreys, M.S., Maguire, A.M., Weeks, C.S. and Tellegen, C.L. (2006) Sponsorship-Linked Marketing: The Role of Articulation in Memory, *Journal of Consumer Research*, 33(3), 312–321.

Crimmins, J. and Horn, M. (1996) Sponsorship: from management ego trip to marketing success, *Journal of Advertising Research* (July/August), 11–21.

Cropp, F. and Pincus, J.D. (2001) The mystery of public relations: Unravelling its past, unmasking its future, in R.L. Heath (ed.), *Handbook of public relations*. Thousand Oaks, CA: Sage, 189–203.

Ehrenberg, A.S.C. (1974) Repetitive advertising and the consumer, *Journal of Advertising Research*, 14 (April), 25–34.

Fink, S. (2000) *Crisis Management Planning for the Inevitable*. New York: AMACON.

Gregory, A. (2004) Scope and structure of public relations: a technology driven view, *Public Relations Review*, 30(3) (September), 245–254.

Grimes, E. and Meenaghan, T. (1998) Focusing commercial sponsorship on the internal corporate audience, *International Journal of Advertising*, 17(1), 51–74.

Grunig, J.E. (1992) Models of public relations and communication, in *Excellence in Public Relations and Communications Management* (eds J.E. Grunig, D.M. Dozier, P. Ehling, L.A. Grunig, F.C. Repper and J. Whits). Hillsdale, NJ: Lawrence Erlbaum, 285–325.

Grunig, J.E. (1997) A situational theory of publics: Conceptual history, recent challenges and new research, in *Public Relations Research: An International Perspective* (eds D. Moss, T. MacManus and D. Vercic). London: International Thomson Business, 3–48.

Grunig, J. and Hunt, T. (1984) *Managing Public Relations*. New York: Holt, Rineholt & Winston.

Harverson, P. (1998) Why IT companies take the risk, *Financial Times*, 2 June, 12.

Hastings, G. (1984) Sponsorship works differently from advertising, *International Journal of Advertising*, 3, 171–176.

Hedburg, A. (2000) Bumper crop, *Marketing Week*, 19 October, 28–32.

Hoek, J., Gendall, P., Jeffcoat, M. and Orsman, D. (1997) Sponsorship and advertising: a comparison of their effects, *Journal of Marketing Communications*, 3, 21–32.

Jaques, T. (2007) Issue management and crisis management: An integrated, non-linear, relational construct, *Public Relations Review* 33(2), 147–157.

Jaques, T. (2009) Issue and crisis management: Quicksand in the definitional landscape *Public Relations Review*, 35(3) (September), 280–286.

Kimberley, S. (2010) Pre-emptive strike, *Marketing*, 31 March, 15.

Kleinman, M. (2007) Coca-Cola commits $20m for water aid. *Daily Telegraph*, 5 June. Retrieved 5 December 2007 from http://www.telegraph.co.uk/money/main.jhtml?xml=/money/2007/06/05/cncola05.xml

Lacey, R., Sneath, J.Z., Finney, R.Z. and Close, A.G. (2007) The impact of repeat attendance on event sponsorship effects, *Journal of Marketing Communications*, 13(4) (December), 243–255.

Magee, K. (2009) Prime-time TV wars: Entertainment PR, *PR Week*, 27 November, 20–25.

Marshall, D.W. and Cook, G. (1992) The corporate (sports) sponsor, *International Journal of Advertising*, 11, 307–324.

McDonald, C. (1991) Sponsorship and the image of the sponsor, *European Journal of Marketing*, 25, 11, 31–38.

Meenaghan, T. (1998) Current developments and future directions in sponsorship, *International Journal of Advertising*, 17(1), 3–28.

Miller, G. (1989) Persuasion and public relations: two 'Ps' in a pod, in *Public Relations Theory* (eds C. Botan and V. Hazelton). Hillsdale, NJ: Lawrence Erlbaum.

Mitroff, I. (2004) *Crisis leadership: Planning for the unthinkable*, Hoboken, NJ: Wiley.

Moloney, K. (1997) Government and lobbying activities, in *Public Relations: Principles and Practice* (ed. P.J. Kitchen). London: International Thomson Press.

Murphy, D. (2007) Lost in the crowd, *Marketing*, 29, August, 36–37.

Olson, E.L. and Thjomoe, H.M (2009) Sponsorship effect metric: assessing the financial value of sponsoring by comparisons to television advertising, *Journal of the Academy of Marketing Science*, 37, 504–515.

O'Reilly. G. (2009) BBC hires Headstream to promote latest series of Strictly Come Dancing online, prweek.com. Retrieved 05 January 2009 from www.prweek.com/uk/news/929883/BBC-hires-Headstream-promote-latest-series-Strictly-Dancing-online/

Poon, D.T.Y and Prendergast, G. (2006) A new framework for evaluating sponsorship opportunities, *International Journal of Advertising*, 25(4), 471–487.

Reed, D. (1994) Sponsorship, *Campaign*, 20 May, 37–38.

Schumann, D.W., Hathcote, J.M. and West, S. (1991) Corporate advertising in America: a review of published studies on use, measurement and effectiveness, *Journal of Advertising*, 20(3), 35–56.

Smolianov, P. and Aiyeku, J.F. (2009) Corporate Marketing Objectives and Evaluation Measures of Integrated Television Advertising and Sports Event Sponsorships, *Journal of Promotion Management*, 15(1&2), (January), 74–89.

Thomas, J. (2009) Sony Pictures in school science tie, *Marketing*, 23 September, 10.

Thomas, J. (2010) Climate Week signs up key sponsors for event, *Marketing*, 20 June, 9.

Thorncroft, A. (1996) Business arts sponsorship: arts face a harsh set of realities, *Financial Times*, 4 July, 1.

Thwaites, D. (1994) Corporate sponsorship by the financial services industry, *Journal of Marketing Management*, 10, 743–763.

Tripodi, J.A. (2001) Sponsorship: a confirmed weapon in the promotional armoury. *International Journal of Sports Marketing and Sponsorship*, 3(1) (March/April), 1–20.

Utalk (2010) Nestle KitKat comes under attack with new Greenpeace viral. Retrieved 23 March 2010, from www.utalkmarketing.com

Witcher, B., Craigen, G., Culligan, D. and Harvey, A. (1991) The links between objectives and functions in organisational sponsorship, *International Journal of Advertising*, 10, 13–33.

Yun, S.-H. (2006) Toward public relations theory-based study of public diplomacy: testing the applicability of the excellence study, *Journal of Public Relations Research*, 18(4), 287–312.

Chapter 11
Direct marketing and personal selling

Direct marketing is a strategy used to create a personal and intermediary-free dialogue with customers. This should be a measurable activity and it is very often media-based, with a view to creating and sustaining a mutually rewarding relationship. Personal selling involves a face-to-face dialogue between two persons or by one person and a group. Message flexibility is an important attribute, as is the immediate feedback that often flows from use of this promotional tool.

Aims and learning objectives

The aims of this chapter are to first consider the characteristics of direct marketing and second to explore some of the principal issues and concepts associated with personal selling.

The learning objectives are to enable readers to:

1. define direct marketing and set out its key characteristics;

2. describe the different methods used to implement direct marketing;

3. explain the significance of the database in direct marketing and consider different direct response media;

4. discuss the different types, roles and tasks of personal selling;

5. consider the strengths and weaknesses of personal selling as a form of marketing communication;

6. explain the concept of multiple sales channels;

7. consider how direct marketing and personal selling might best be integrated with the other tools of the marketing communications mix.

Introduction

This chapter explores both direct marketing and personal selling. In many ways these topics complement each other in that they are both characterised by their personal and relatively transparent direct nature. Direct marketing is a term used to refer to all media activities that generate a series of communications and responses with an existing or potential customer. Direct marketing is mainly concerned with the management of customer behaviour and is used to complement the strengths and weaknesses of the other communication disciplines. To put this another way, advertising and public relations provide information and develop brand values but sales promotion, direct marketing and personal selling drive response, most notably behaviour. Both direct marketing and personal selling have the potential to engage customers directly, explicitly and can provide both an intellectual as well as emotional basis upon which interaction and dialogue can be developed.

The role of direct marketing

Direct marketing is concerned with the management of customer behaviour and is used to complement the strengths and weaknesses of the other communication disciplines. To put it another way, advertising and public relations provide information and develop brand values but sales promotion and direct marketing drive response, most notably behaviour.

Direct marketing is a tool of marketing communications used to create and sustain a personal and intermediary free communication with customers, potential customers and other significant stakeholders. In most cases this is a media based activity and offers great scope for the collection and utilisation of pertinent and measurable data. There are a number of important issues associated with this definition. The first is that the activity should be measurable. That is, any response(s) must be associated with a particular individual, a particular media activity and a particular outcome, such as a sale or enquiry for further information. The second issue concerns the rewards that each party perceives through participation in the relationship. The customer receives a variety of tangible and intangible satisfactions. These include shopping convenience, time utility and the satisfaction and trust that can develop between customers and a provider of quality products and services when the customers realise and appreciate the personal attention they appear to be receiving.

The direct marketer derives benefits associated with precision target marketing and minimised waste, increased profits and the opportunities to provide established customers with other related products, without the huge costs of continually having to find new customers. In addition, direct marketing represents a strategic approach to the market. It actively seeks to remove channel intermediaries, at least from the initial communication, reduce costs, and improve the quality and speed of service for customers, and through this bundle of attributes presents a new offering for the market, which in itself may provide competitive advantage. First Direct, Churchill and the pioneer, Direct Line, all provide these advantages, which have enabled them to secure strong positions in the market.

Viewpoint 11.1	Everyone likes the direct approach

Direct marketing, in all of its different formats, is used by a great many organisations, some to a greater extent than others. In the Autumn of 2010 the prestige car brand Lexus launched its hybrid range and used direct marketing as the principal tool to deliver the communication strategy. Using the concept of evolution and natural selection, the direct and digital campaign was built around email and a direct mail pack. The goals were to generate awareness and interest among current Lexus customers and 'warm' prospects, with a view of stimulating brochure requests and test drives.

In contrast The National Trust launched a direct marketing campaign to help secure funding for the acquisition of a stretch of coast on the Llŷn Peninsula in North West Wales. Using direct mail, the campaign directed people to a bespoke microsite which contained information about the ecological importance, the threats facing the peninsula and an opportunity to make donations.

President Obama's election campaign was rooted in the use of direct and digital marketing, as he targeted swing voters, non-voters and others. Using database and email communications Obama generated so much in donations online that he was able to outspend the Republicans by 4:1 in TV advertising, and spend millions on a 30 minute ad that was then dissected by the media for 24 hours, dominating the media in the last days of the campaign.

Financial services companies such as Santander, Axa, Aviva, Barclays, Direct Line all use direct marketing as a core element of their communications programmes. LoveFilm, the video rental company, charities such as Barnardos and Oxfam, and numerous B2B companies all invest heavily in direct marketing.

Source: Based on Fernandez (2010a); Fernandez (2010b); Cooke (2008)

Question

If an organisation does not want to compete using advertising or direct marketing, what other methods could they use?

Task

Find two examples of companies using direct marketing and list the tools and media used.

Underpinning the direct marketing approach are the principles of trust and commitment, just as they support the validity of the other communication mix tools. If a meaningful relationship is to be developed over the long term and direct marketing is an instrumental part of the interaction, then the promises that the parties make to develop commitment and stability are of immense importance (Ganesan, 1994).

Types of direct brand

Direct marketing is assumed to refer to direct communication mix activity, but this is only part of the marketing picture. Using direct response media in this way is an increasingly common activity used to augment the communication activities surrounding a brand and to provide a new dimension to the context in which brands are perceived. However, direct marketing can be used by organisations in a number of different ways, very often reflecting the business strategy of the organisation. Four types can be identified and they should not be regarded as hierarchical, in the sense that there has to be progression from one type to another. They are reflections of the way different organisations use direct marketing and the degree to which the tool is used strategically.

Type 1: complementary tool

At this level, direct response media are used to complement the other communication mix activities used to support a brand. Their main use is to generate leads and to some extent awareness, information and reinforcement. For example, financial services companies, tour operators and travel agents use DRTV to stimulate enquiries, loans and bookings, respectively.

Type 2: primary differentiator

Rather than be one of a number of communication mix tools, at this level direct response media are the primary form of communication. They are used to provide a distinct point of differentiation from competitor offerings. They are the principal form of communication. In addition to the Type 1 advantages they are used to cut costs, avoid the use of intermediaries and reach finely targeted audiences (for example, book, music and wine clubs).

Type 3: sales channel

A third use for direct marketing and telemarketing in particular, concerns its use as a means of developing greater efficiency and as a means of augmenting current services. By utilising direct marketing as a sales tool, multiple sales channels can be used to meet the needs of different customer segments and so release resources to be deployed elsewhere and more effectively.

Type 4: brand vehicle

At this final level, brands are developed to exploit market space opportunities. The strategic element is most clearly evident at this level. Indeed, the entire organisation and its culture are normally oriented to the development of customer relationships through direct marketing activities. Prime examples are Lastminute.com and Amazon.

The growth of direct marketing

There can be little doubt that, of all the tools in the marketing communications mix, direct marketing has experienced the most growth in the past 15 years. The reasons for this growth are many and varied, but there have been three essential drivers behind the surge in direct marketing: technological advances; changing buyer lifestyles and expectations; and organisational expectations (see Figure 11.1). These forces for change demonstrate quite dramatically how a change in the context can impact on marketing communications.

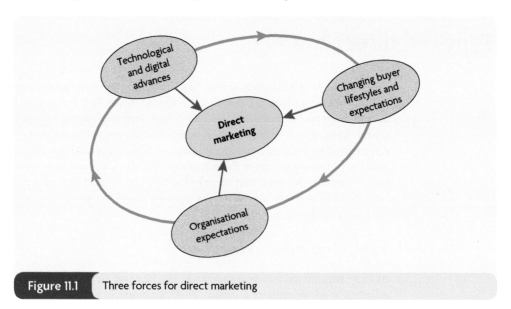

Figure 11.1   Three forces for direct marketing

Growth driver 1: technology

Rapid advances in technology have heralded the arrival of new sources and forms of information. Technology has enabled the collection, storage and analysis of customer data to become relatively simple, cost effective and straightforward. Furthermore, the management of this information is increasingly available to small businesses as well as the major blue chip multinational organisations. Computing costs have plummeted, while there has been a correspondingly enormous increase in the power that technology can deliver.

The technological surge has in turn stimulated three major developments. The first concerns the ability to capture information, the second to process and analyse it and the third to represent part or all of the information as a form of communication to stimulate interaction and perhaps dialogue to collect further information.

Growth driver 2: changing market context

The lifestyles of people in industrialised economies in particular, have evolved and will continue to do so. Generally, the brash phase of *selfishness* in the 1980s gave way to a more caring, society-oriented *selflessness* in the 1990s. The first decade of the twenty-first century suggests that a *self-oriented* lifestyle was prominent, reflected in short-term brand purchase behaviour and self-centred brand values and society behaviour. Perhaps the second decade will see further change as the global economy and forces for environmental adaptation bring about change to the way societies interact and individuals perceive their role within any one society. However, it seems as if there will be continued fragmentation of the media and finely tuned segmentation and communication devices will be necessary to communicate with discrete audiences.

Direct marketing offers a solution to this splintering and micro market scenario and addresses some of the changing needs of customers such as personalised, permission-based and informed communications. Management also benefits as direct marketing enables improved speed of response, lower waste and justification for the use and allocation of resources.

Growth driver 3: changing organisational expectations

Organisations can expect to continue experiencing performance pressures. These vary from the expectations of shareholders as they demand short-term returns on their investments to the impact this can have on managers. They are having to cope with an increasing cost base caused by demands on fuel and other resources by developing economies and a downward pressure on prices due to intense competition. This pressure on margins requires new routes to markets to reduce costs. Direct marketing addresses some of these changing management needs as there are no intermediary costs, there is fast access to markets (and withdrawal) plus opportunities to respond quickly to market developments and also justify their use and allocation of resources.

The impact of these drivers can be seen within the emergence of ideas about integrated marketing communications and an overall emphasis on relationship marketing principles. The enhanced ability of organisations to collect, store and manage customer lifestyle and transactional data, to generate personalised communications and their general enthusiasm for retention and loyalty schemes have combined to provide a huge movement towards an increased use of direct and interactive marketing initiatives.

The role of the database

At the hub of successful direct marketing and CRM activities is the database. A database is a collection of files held on a computer that contain data that can be related to one another and which can reproduce information in a variety of formats. Normally the data consist of information collected about prospects and customers that are used to determine appropriate segments and target markets and to record responses to communications conveyed by the organisation. A database therefore plays a role as a storage, sorting and administrative device to assist direct and personalised communications.

Age and lifestyle data are important signals of product usage. However, there will be attitudinal variances between people in similar groups demanding further analysis. This can, according to Reed (2000), uncover clues concerning what a direct mail piece should look like. So, older customers do not like soft colours and small type and sentences should not begin with 'and' or 'but'.

Increasingly, the information stored is gathered from transactions undertaken with customers, but on its own this information is not enough and further layering of data is required. The recency/frequency/monetary (RFM) model provides a base upon which lifestyle data, often bought in from a list agency, can be used to further refine the information held. Response analysis requires the identification of an organisation's best customers, and then another layer of data can be introduced which points to those that are particularly responsive to direct-response marketing activity (Fletcher, 1997). It is the increasing sophistication of the information held in databases that is enabling more effective targeting and communications.

Viewpoint 11.2   Tesco watches your trolleys

Tesco announced in the Spring of 2008 that they were going to monitor and record the shopping habits of over 60 million people in nine of the countries in which it operates.

Tesco Clubcard has 13.5 million current users in the UK, and versions of the card are available in South Korea, China and Malaysia. Each day an analysis is undertaken of their purchases. This data are then used to target discount coupons and promotions based on an individual's purchase patterns. The Clubcard is to be made available in Thailand, Hungary, Turkey, Slovakia, the Czech Republic and Poland.

Dunnhumby, who operate the database, have identified different types of shoppers:

- price sensitive shoppers – uses reward vouchers, few fresh foods, value lager;
- traditional shoppers – oldest group, buys small number of items from a list;
- mainstream shoppers – prefers easy-to-prepare family meals, saves Clubcard points for deals;
- healthy shoppers – any age but buys wholesome food, counts calories and fat;
- convenience shoppers – buys quick meals, often ready meals, prepared salads;
- finer foods shopper – affluent, older adults who prefer to cook with organic foods, exotic fruits and ovenware.

Source: Based on Hawkes (2008)

Question

To what extent does database information of this type provide Tesco with a competitive advantage?

Task

Visit dunnhumby.com and find out what they call relevance marketing.

Databases provide the means by which organisations, large and small, can monitor changes in customer lifestyles and attitudes or, in the business-to-business sector, the changing form of the interorganisational relationships and their impact on other members in the network as well as the market structure and level of competitive activity (Gundach and Murphy, 1993). It is through the use of the database that relationships with participants can be tracked, analysed and developed. Very importantly, database systems can be used not only to identify strategically important customers and segments but also to ascertain opportunities to cross-sell products (Kamakura *et al.*, 2003).

However, the merging of data generated through transactions with attitudinal and lifestyle data poses a further problem. In essence, this paints a picture of what has been achieved, it describes behaviour. What it does not do is explain why the behaviour occurred. It may be possible to track back through a campaign to examine the inputs, isolate variables and make a judgement, but the problem remains that the data itself, what has been collected, does not provide insight into what underpins the behaviour. Pearson (2003) suggests that direct marketing and market research data sets should be brought together into what has been referred to as 'consilience' (Wilson, 1998) or a unity of knowledge. This data-rich information should then be capable of providing organisations with data intelligence and an opportunity to predict behaviour and offer a new form of data value.

Permissions marketing

There are a number of tensions associated with the use of databases. These tensions can be related to concerns about privacy and the need to communicate sensitively with audiences who experience varying needs for privacy (Dolnicar and Jordaan, 2007). For example, customers have varying tolerances regarding the level of privacy that a database can exploit. These tolerances or thresholds (Goodwin, 1991) vary according to the nature of the information itself, how it was collected and even who collected it.

The information on a database very often exists simply because a customer entered into a transaction. The business entity that received the information as part of a transaction has a duty to acknowledge the confidential nature of the information and the context in which it was collected before selling the details to a third party or exploiting the information to the detriment of the individual who provided it in the first place. Breaking privacy codes and making unauthorised disclosures of personal details lays open the tenuous relationship an organisation thinks it has with its 'loyal' customers. These tensions have given rise to regulations requiring customers to provide organisations with their formal, express permission to use their personal data in particular ways.

It is commonly agreed that Godin (1999) is the pioneer of permission marketing (PM) (Krishnamurthy, 2001; Gomez and Hlavinka, 2007) and that the aim of PM is to 'initiate, sustain and develop a dialogue with customers, building trust and over time lifting the levels of permission, making it a more valuable asset' (Kent and Brandal, 2003: 491). To put it another way, PM is about 'getting the okay from individuals to market to them' (Smith, 2004: 52).

PM occurs when consumers give their explicit permission for marketers to send them various types of promotional messages (Krishnamurthy, 2001). Essentially customers authorise a marketer to transmit promotional messages in certain 'interest' categories. This is usually obtained when a customer registers to enter a website or completes a survey indicating their interests when registering for a service. Marketers are then able to target advertising messages more closely with the interests and needs of their registered customers. Definitions of PM vary according to the focus of the researchers, but they range from education, trust and share of wallet, to enticement and clutter.

Customers benefit from using PM through:

- a reduction in search costs and clutter;
- better organisation of the information search processes;
- improved message relevance through personalisation, customisation and recognition.

For organisations the benefits of using PM are related to:

- improved segmentation and targeting precision the acquisition of new customers, an increase of sales and the development of long-term, loyal customers;
- flexibility, resulting in improved interactivity, lower sales costs, enhanced direct communication with customers and increased profitability.

Direct response media

The choice of media for direct marketing can be very different from those selected for general advertising purposes. The main reason for using direct response media is that direct contact is made with prospects and customers in order that a direct response is solicited and a dialogue stimulated or maintained. In reality, a wide variety of media can be used, simply by attaching a telephone number, website address or response card.

Previously, broadcast media such as television and radio were the champions of the general advertiser. Now their adoption by direct marketers in the UK has changed the way these media operate. In terms of engagement, explored in Chapter 1, the broad cast format generated engagement through thinking and feeling. The use as a direct response implement changes the engagement to a behavioural orientation.

Direct mail, telemarketing and door-to-door activities are the main offline forms of direct response media, as they allow more personal, direct and evaluative means of reaching precisely targeted customers. Internet based direct work encompasses email, mobile and affiliate marketing as forms of direct linking.

Direct mail

Direct mail refers to personally addressed advertising that is delivered through the postal system. It can be personalised and targeted with great accuracy, and its results are capable of precise measurement.

The generation of enquiries and leads together with the intention of building a personal relationship with customers are the most important factors contributing to the growth of direct mail. Management should decide whether to target direct mail at current customers with the intention of building loyalty and retention rates, or whether they should chase new customers. The decision, acquisition or retention, should be part of the marketing plan but often this aspect of direct marketing lacks clarity, resulting in wastage and inefficiency. Direct mail can be expensive, at anything between £250 and £500 per 1,000 items dispatched. It should, therefore, be used selectively and for purposes other than creating awareness.

Organisations in the financial services sectors are the main users of this medium and the financial health of the sector is dependent to a large extent on some of the major financial services companies maintaining their spend on direct mail. However, an increasing number of other organisations are experimenting with this approach, as they try to improve the effectiveness of their investment in the communication mix and seek to reduce television advertising costs. The growth in consumer-based direct mail activities has outstripped that of the business-to-business sector. The number of direct mail items sent to consumers has increased considerably in comparison with the b2b sector.

Telemarketing

The prime qualities of the telephone are that it provides for interaction, is flexible and permits immediate feedback and the opportunity to overcome objections, all within the same communication event. Other dimensions of telemarketing include the development and maintenance of customer goodwill, allied to which is the increasing need to provide high levels of customer service. Telemarketing also allows organisations to undertake marketing research which is both highly measurable and accountable in that the effectiveness can be verified continuously and call rates, contacts reached and the number and quality of positive and negative responses are easily recorded and monitored.

Growth in telemarketing activity in the business-to-business sector has been largely at the expense of personal selling. The objectives have been to reduce costs and to utilise the expensive sales force and their skills to build on the openings and leads created by telemarketing and other lead generation activities. Some of the advantages of using the telephone as part of the media mix are that it allows for interaction between participants, it enables immediate feedback and sets up opportunities to overcome objections, all within the same communication event when both the sender and the receiver are geographically distant.

All of these activities can be executed by personal selling, but the speed, cost, accuracy and consistency of the information solicited through personal visits can often be improved upon by telemarketing. The complexity of the product will influence the degree to which this medium can be used successfully. However, if properly trained professional telemarketers are used, the sales results, if measured on a call basis, can outperform those produced by personal selling.

Contact centres use a variety of digital applications with the prime goals of reducing costs, improving efficiency and improving the client's reputation through quality of customer interaction. Automatic call distribution systems, call recording systems, computer–telephone integration, customer interaction management, predictive diallers and interactive voice response systems are just some of the ways in which technology is used in these environments.

Operator contact with customers can be also be supported by technology. Computer-assisted telephone interviewing (CATI) can provide varying degrees of technical support. The degree to which this is used depends on the task, the product and the nature of the target audience. The behaviour of call centre employees, however much they are regulated or controlled by various software applications, is a function of service quality, as perceived by callers. Referred to as customer orientation behaviours (COBs), Rafaeli *et al.* (2008) identify five COBs that are related to service quality. These are:

- anticipating customer requests;
- offering explanations and justifications;
- educating customers;
- providing emotional support;
- offering personalised information.

When these five COBs are used by call centre employees, customers perceive a high level of service quality. The implication of this, as pointed out by the researchers, is that as call centre managers invariably seek to minimise call length in order to reduce costs and increase the number of transactions, their actions appear to endanger service quality.

The costs of telemarketing are high. It is estimated for example, that is costs £15–£20 to reach a decision-maker in an organisation. When this is compared with £5 for a piece of direct mail or £150+ for a personal sales call to the same individual, it is the effectiveness of the call and the return on the investment that determines whether the costs are really high.

Carelines

Another reason to use telemarketing concerns the role which carelines can play within consumer/brand relationships. Manufacturers use contact centres to enable customers to:

- complain about a product performance and related experiences;
- seek product related advice;
- make suggestions regarding product or packaging development;
- comment about an action or development concerning the brand as a whole.

What binds these together is the potential all of these people have for repurchasing the brand, even those who complain bitterly about product performance and experience. If these people have their complaints dealt with properly then there is a reasonable probability that they will repurchase.

The majority of careline calls are not about complaints but seek advice or help about products. Food manufacturers can provide cooking and recipe advice, cosmetic and toiletries companies can provide healthcare advice and application guidelines while white goods and service-based organisations can provide technical and operational support.

Carelines are essentially a post-purchase support mechanism that facilities market feedback and intelligence gathering. They can warn of imminent problems (product defects), provide ideas for new products or variants and of course provide a valuable method to reassure customers and improve customer retention levels. Call operators, or agents as many of them are now being called, have to handle calls from a variety of new sources – web, email, interactive TV and mobile devices – and it is appreciated that many are more effective if they have direct product experience. Instant messaging channels enable online shoppers to ask questions that are routed to a call centre for response. Sales conversion ratios can be up by 40–50 per cent and costs are about £1 to answer an inbound question, compared with £3.50 by phone (Murphy, 2000). Kellogg's reports that its careline makes a 13:1 return on investment (Bashford, 2004).

While the Internet has provided further growth opportunities, it will also take on a number of the tasks currently the preserve of telemarketing bureaux. Websites enable product information and certain support advice to be accessed without the call centre costs and focus attention on other matters that are of concern to the customer. Chat room discussions, collaborative browsing and real-time text conversations are options to help care for customers in the future. However, it is probably the one-to-one telephone dialogue between customer and agent that will continue to provide satisfaction and benefits for both parties.

Inserts

Inserts are media materials that are placed in magazines or direct mail letters. These not only provide factual information about the product or service but also enable the recipient to respond to the request of the direct marketer. This request might be to place an order or post back a card for more information, such as a brochure.

Inserts have become more popular, but their cost is substantially higher than a four-colour advertisement in the magazine in which the insert is carried. Their popularity is based on their effectiveness as a lead generator, and new methods of delivering inserts to the home will become important to direct mailing houses in the future. Other vehicles, such as packages rather than letter mail, will become important.

Print

There are two main forms of direct response advertising through the printed media: first, catalogues and, secondly, magazines and newspapers.

Catalogues mailed direct to consumers have been an established method of selling products for a long time. Mail order organisations such as Freeman's, GUS and Littlewoods have successfully exploited this form of direct marketing. Organisations such as Tchibo and Kaleidoscope have successfully used mini-catalogues, but instead of providing account facilities and the appointment of specific freelance agents, their business transactions are on a cash-with-order basis.

Business-to-business marketers have begun to exploit this medium, and organisations such as Dell and IBM now use online and offline catalogues, partly to save costs and partly to free valuable sales personnel so that they can concentrate their time selling into larger accounts. Direct response advertising through the press is similar to general press advertising except that the advertiser provides a mechanism for the reader to take further action. The mechanism may be a telephone number (call free) or a coupon or cut-out reply slip requesting further information. Dell has transformed its marketing strategy to one that is based around building customised products for both consumers and business customers. Consumer direct print ads which offer an incentive, are designed explicitly to drive customers to the Dell website, where transactions are completed without reference to retailers, dealers or other intermediaries.

Exhibit 11.1	Direct response print ad from Dell
	Image courtesy of Dell

Door-to-door

This delivery method can be much cheaper than direct mail as there are no postage charges to
be accounted for. However, if the costs are much lower, so are the response rates. Responses
are lower because door-to-door drops cannot be personally addressed, as can direct mail, even
though the content and quality can be controlled in the same way.

Viewpoint 11.3	Onwards and upwards, direct to the sky

In the grip of the recession Sky television made great use of direct marketing. In the year to June 2009 Sky invested £31.8 million on direct mail, a substantial 80 per cent increase on the previous year. However, this represents a mere 10 per cent of Sky's investment in direct marketing. Press advertising, media inserts and door-drop work accounts for the majority of its direct work. The result of this activity was that direct marketing accounted for 40 per cent of Sky's new customers in the period.

Plans to continue this level of direct marketing are limited as the marketing strategy refocuses on the capabilities and facilities and in particular, subscriptions to Sky+ boxes and High Definition (HD) pictures. These benefits are not easily communicated through direct response and standard media. The need for face-to-face communication in order to demonstrate the benefits becomes more acute. As a result resources were reallocated to experiential marketing, such as shopping centre stands, consumer exhibitions and events, the field sales force and relationships with major high street retailers such as Dixons, Tesco and Comet.

Source: Based on Murphy (2009)

Question

Why might you recommend Sky use direct marketing to launch an extension into radio?

Task

Buy a daily tabloid newspaper, cut out the direct response ads and consider what is similar about them.

Avon (Cosmetics) and Betterware are traditionally recognised as professional practitioners of door-to-door direct marketing. Other organisations, such as the utility companies (gas, electricity and water), and domestic cleaning company, Molly Maid, are using door-to-door to create higher levels of market penetration.

Radio and television

Of the two main forms discussed earlier, radio and television, the former is used as a support medium for other advertising, often by providing enquiry numbers. Television has greater potential because it can provide the important visual dimension, but its use in the UK for direct marketing purposes has been limited. One of the main reasons for this has been the television contractors' attitude to pricing. However, the industry has experienced a period of great change and has introduced greater pricing flexibility, and a small but increasing number of direct marketers have used the small screen successfully, mainly by providing freephone numbers for customers. Direct Line, originally a motor insurance organisation, has been outstanding in its use of television not only to launch but also to help propel the phenomenal growth of a range of related products.

The Internet and digital media

The explosion of activity around digital media, the Internet and email communications has been quite astonishing in recent years and now represents a major new form of interactive marketing communications. The establishment of digital television services and the imminent withdrawal of analogue services, has driven new forms of interactivity. Initially home shopping and banking facilities were attractive to those whose lifestyles complement the benefits offered by the new technology but fully interactive services now bring increased leisure and entertainment opportunities. For more information on interactive marketing communications see Chapter 14.

Personal selling

In an era where relationship marketing has become increasingly understood and accepted as the contemporary approach to marketing theory and practice, so personal selling characterises the importance of strong relationships between vendor and buyer. The traditional image of personal selling is one that embraces the hard sell, with a brash and persistent salesperson delivering a volley of unrelenting, persuasive messages at a confused and reluctant consumer. Fortunately this image has receded as the professionalism and breadth of personal selling become more widely recognised and as the role of personal selling becomes even more important in the communications mix.

Personal selling activities can be observed at various stages in the buying process of both the consumer and business-to-business markets. This is because the potency of personal communications is very high, and messages can be adapted on the spot to meet the requirements of both parties. This flexibility, as we shall see later, enables objections to be overcome, information to be provided in the context of the buyer's environment and the conviction and power of demonstration to be brought to the buyer when the buyer requests it.

Personal selling is different from other forms of communication in that the transmitted messages represent, mainly, dyadic communications. This means that there are two persons involved in the communication process. Feedback and evaluation of transmitted messages are possible, more or less instantaneously, so that these personal selling messages can be tailored and be made much more personal than any of the other methods of communication.

Using the spectrum of activities identified by the hierarchy of effects, we can see that personal selling is close enough to the prospective buyer to induce a change in behaviour. That is, it is close enough to overcome objections, to provide information quickly and to respond to the prospects' overall needs, all in the context of the transaction, and to encourage them directly to place orders.

The tasks of personal selling

The generic tasks to be undertaken by the sales force have been changing because the environment in which organisations operate is shifting dramatically. These changes, in particular those associated with the development and implementation of new technologies, have had repercussions on the activities of the sales force and are discussed later in this chapter.

The tasks of those who undertake personal selling vary from organisation to organisation and in accord with the type of selling activities on which they focus. It is normally assumed that they collect and bring into the organisation orders from customers wishing to purchase products and services. In this sense the order aspect of the personal selling tool can be seen as one of four order-related tasks:

1. *Order takers* are salespersons to whom customers are drawn at the place of supply. Reception clerks at hotels and ticket desk personnel at theatres and cinemas typify this role.

2. *Order getters* are sales personnel who operate away from the organisation and who attempt to gain orders, largely through the provision of information, the use of demonstration techniques and services and the art of persuasion.

3. *Order collectors* are those who attempt to gather orders without physically meeting their customers. This is completed electronically or over the telephone. The growth of telemarketing operations was discussed in the previous chapter, but the time saved by both the buyer and the seller using the telephone to gather repeat and low-value orders frees valuable sales personnel to seek new customers and build relationships with current customers.

4. *Order supporters* are all those people who are secondary salespersons in that they are involved with the order once it has been secured, or are involved with the act of ordering,

Table 11.1	Tasks of personal selling
Prospecting	Finding new customers
Communicating	Informing various stakeholders and feeding back information about the market
Selling	The art of leading a prospect to a successful close
Information gathering	Reporting information about the market and reporting on individual activities
Servicing	Consulting, arranging, counselling, fixing and solving a multitude of customer 'problems'
Allocating	Placing scarce products and resources at times of shortage
Shaping	Building and sustaining relationships with customers and other stakeholders

usually by supplying information. Order processing or financial advice services typify this role. In truly customer-oriented organisations all customer-facing employees will be an order supporter.

However, this perspective of personal selling is narrow because it fails to set out the broader range of activities that a sales force can be required to undertake. Salespeople do more than get or take orders. The tasks listed in Table 11.1 provide direction and purpose, and also help to establish the criteria by which the performance of members of the personal selling unit can be evaluated. The organisation should decide which tasks it expects its representatives to undertake.

Personal selling is the most expensive element of the communications mix. The average cost per contact can easily exceed £250 when all markets and types of businesses are considered. It is generally agreed that personal selling is most effective at the later stages of the hierarchy of effects or buying process, rather than at the earlier stage of awareness building. Therefore, each organisation should determine the precise role the sales force is to play within the communications mix.

The role of personal selling

Personal selling is often referred to as interpersonal communication and from this perspective Reid *et al.* (2002) determined three major sales behaviours, namely getting, giving and using information:

- Getting information refers to sales behaviours aimed at information acquisition, for example gathering information about customers, markets and competitors.

- Giving information refers to the dissemination of information to customers and other stakeholders, for example sales presentations and seminar meetings designed to provide information about products and an organisation's capabilities and reputation.

- Using information refers to the salesperson's use of information to help solve a customer's problem. Associated with this is the process of gaining buyer commitment through the generation of information (Thayer, 1968, cited by Reid *et al.*, 2002).

These last authors suggest that using the information dynamic appears to be constant across all types of purchase situations. However, as the complexity of a purchase situation increases so the amount of giving information behaviours decline and getting information behaviours increase. This finding supports the need for a salesperson to be able to recognise particular situations in the buying process and then to adapt their behaviour to meet the buyer's contextual needs.

However, salespeople undertake numerous tasks in association with communication activities. Guenzi (2002) determined that some sales activities are generic simply because they are performed by most salespeople across a large number of industries. These generic activities are selling, customer relationship management and communicating to customers. Other activities such as market analysis, pre-sales services and the transfer of information about competitors to the organisation are industry specific. Interestingly he found that information-gathering activities are more likely to be undertaken by organisations operating in consumer markets than in b2b, possibly a reflection of the strength of the market orientation in both arenas.

The role of personal selling is largely one of representation. In b2b markets sales personnel operate at the boundary of the organisation. They provide the link between the needs of their own organisation and the needs of their customers. This linkage, or boundary spanning role, is absolutely vital, for a number of reasons that will be discussed shortly, but without personal selling, communication with other organisations would occur through electronic or print media and would foster discrete closed systems. Representation in this sense therefore refers to face-to-face encounters between people from different organisations.

Many authors consider the development, organisation and completion of a sale in a market exchange-based transaction to be the key part of the role of personal selling. Sales personnel provide a source of information for buyers so that they can make the right purchase decisions. In that sense they provide a good level of credibility, but they are also perceived, understandably, as biased. The degree of expertise held by the salesperson may be high, but the degree of perceived trustworthiness will vary, especially during the formative period of the relationship, unless other transactions with the selling organisation have been satisfactory. Once a number of transactions have been completed and product quality established, trustworthiness may improve. As the costs associated with personal selling are high, it is vital that sales personnel are used effectively. To that end, some organisations are employing other methods to decrease the time that the sales force spends on administration, travel and office work and to maximise the time spent in front of customers, where they can use their specific selling skills.

The amount of control that can be exercised over the delivery of the messages through the sales force depends upon a number of factors. Essentially, the level of control must be regarded as low, because each salesperson has the freedom to adapt messages to meet changing circumstances as negotiations proceed. In practice, however, the professionalism and training that many members of the sales force receive and the increasing accent on measuring levels of customer satisfaction mean that the degree of control over the message can be regarded, in most circumstances, as very good, although it can never, for example, be as high as that of advertising.

This flexibility is framed within the context of the product strategy. Decisions that impact upon strategy are not allowed. There is freedom to adapt the manner in which products are presented, but there is no freedom for the sales representatives to decide the priority of the products to be detailed.

Viewpoint 11.4   Flexible sales teams

Personal selling can take many forms but the face-to-face form of communication can be a strong force for engagement and behaviour change. Emerging brands benefit when brand owners and entrepreneurs visit retailers in person, and start to establish a relationship. For example, when Sam Galsworthy launched Sipsmith, an alcohol based brand, he used his motorbike to visit high-end style bars in and around London to ensure that bottles of his brand were given a prominent position at the bar, and to persuade bar managers to promote and recommend the brand to customers. As a result the barmen get to know the face behind the brand, something that wholesalers are not able to do.

Many large organisations, especially those in the b2b sector, employ their own sales teams to visit customers to provide advice, technical support for the product line and to resolve any problems and difficulties. Grocery and

FMCG producers use their sales force teams to develop sales with the multiple supermarkets and independent grocers. Providing adequate coverage can be difficult and expensive so temporary sales force teams are often used for product launches and periods of high demand. Field marketing agencies can provide these facilities. When Kellogg's launched Rice Crispies Totally Chocolatey a field sales team was used to visit hundreds of outlets in the London area, to get the brand established.

Source: Based on Benady (2009)

Question

Why should organisations maintain an employed, and expensive sales force when they can rent a sales force at any time?

Task

Choose a brand that you would like to make, then consider the role a sales team might play in your communication strategy.

Strengths and weaknesses of personal selling

There are a number of strengths and weaknesses associated with personal selling. It is interesting to note that some of the strengths can in turn be seen as weaknesses, particularly when management control over the communication process is not as attentive or as rigorous as it might be.

Strengths

Dyadic communications allow for interaction that, unlike the other communication mix tools, provides for fast, direct feedback. In comparison with the mass media, personal selling allows for the receiver to focus attention on the salesperson, with a reduced likelihood of distraction or noise.

There is a greater level of participation in the decision process by the vendor than in the other tools. When this is combined with the power to tailor messages in response to the feedback provided by the buyer, the sales process has a huge potential to solve customer problems.

Weaknesses

One of the major disadvantages of personal selling is the cost. Costs per contact are extremely high, and this means that management must find alternative means of communicating particular messages and improve the amount of time that sales personnel spend with prospects and customers. Reach and frequency through personal selling are always going to be low, regardless of the amount of funds available. Control over message delivery is very often low and, while the flexibility is an advantage, there is also the disadvantage of message inconsistency. This in turn can lead to confusion (a misunderstanding perhaps with regard to a product specification), the ramifications of which can be enormous in terms of cost and time spent by a variety of individuals from both parties to the contract.

The quality of the relationship can, therefore, be jeopardised through poor and inconsistent communications.

When personal selling should be a major part of the communications mix

In view of the role and the advantages and disadvantages of personal selling, when should it be a major part of the communications mix? Table 11.2 indicates some key factors using advertising as a comparison.

Table 11.2	When personal selling is a major element of the communications mix	
	Advertising relatively important	Personal selling relatively important
Number of customers	Large	Small
Buyers' information needs	Low	High
Size and importance of purchase	Small	Large
Post-purchase service required	Little	A lot
Product complexity	Low	High
Distribution strategy	Pull	Push
Pricing policy	Set	Negotiate
Web-enabled communications and exchanges	High	Low
Resources available for promotion	Many	Few

Source: Adapted from Cravens (1987)

The following is not an exhaustive list, but is presented as a means of considering some of the important issues: complexity, network factors, buyer significance and communication effectiveness.

Complexity

Personal selling is very important when there is a medium to high level of relationship complexity. Such complexity may be associated either with the physical characteristics of the product, such as computer software design, or with the environment in which the negotiations are taking place. For example, decisions related to the installation of products designed to automate an assembly line may well be a sensitive issue. This may be due to management's attitude towards the operators currently undertaking the work that the automation is expected to replace.

When the complexity of the offering is high, advertising and public relations cannot always convey benefits in the same way as personal selling. Personal selling allows the product to be demonstrated so that buyers can see and, if necessary, touch and taste it for themselves. Personal selling also allows explanations to be made about particular points that are of concern to the buyer or about the environment in which the buyer wishes to use the product.

Buyer significance

The significance of the product to the buyers in the target market is a very important factor in the decision on whether to use personal selling. Significance can be measured as a form of risk, and risk is associated with benefits and costs.

The absolute cost to the buyer will vary from organisation to organisation and from consumer to consumer. The significance of the purchase of an extra photocopier for a major multinational organisation may be low, but for a new start-up organisation or for an established organisation experiencing a dramatic turnaround, an extra photocopying machine may be highly significant and subject to high levels of resistance by a number of different internal stakeholders.

Communication effectiveness

There may be a number of ways to satisfy the communication objectives of a campaign, other than by using personal selling. Each of the other communication tools has strengths and weaknesses; consequently differing mixes provide different benefits. Have they all been considered?

One of the main reasons for using personal selling occurs when advertising alone, or any other medium, provides insufficient communications. The main reason for this inadequacy surfaces when advertising media cannot provide buyers with the information they require to make their decision. For example, someone buying a new car may well observe and read various magazine and newspaper advertisements. The decision to buy, however, requires information and data upon which a rational decision can be made. This rationality and experience of the car, through a test drive perhaps, balances the former, more emotional, elements that contributed to the earlier decision.

The decision to buy a car normally evokes high involvement, therefore car manufacturers try to provide a rich balance of emotional and factual information in their literature. From this perspective buyers seek further information at the website and seek experience and reassurance at a dealership. Car buyers sign orders with the presence and encouragement of salespersons. Very few cars are bought on a mail order basis, although some are bought over the Internet.

Personal selling provides a number of characteristics that make it more effective than the other elements of the mix. As discussed, in business-to-business marketing the complexity of many products requires salespeople to be able to discuss with clients their specific needs; in other words, to be able to talk in the customer's own language, to build source credibility through expertise and hopefully trustworthiness, and build a relationship that corresponds with the psychographic profile of each member of the DMU. In this case, mass communications would be inappropriate.

Channel network factors

When the number of members in a network is limited, the use of a sales force is advisable, as advertising is inefficient. Furthermore, the opportunity to build a close collaborative relationship with members may enable the development of a sustainable competitive advantage.

There are two further factors that influence the decision to use personal selling as part of the communications mix. When the customer base is small and dispersed across a wide geographic area it makes economic sense to use salespersons, as advertising in this situation is inadequate and ineffective.

Personal selling is the most expensive element of the communications mix. It may be that other elements of the mix may provide a more cost-effective way of delivering the message.

Integration and supporting the sales force

In an effort to increase the productivity of the sales force and to use their expensive skills more effectively, direct marketing has provided organisations with an opportunity to improve levels of performance and customer satisfaction. In particular, the use of an inside telemarketing department is seen as a compatible sales channel to the field sales force. The telemarketing team can accomplish the following tasks: they can search for and qualify new customers, so saving the field force from cold calling; they can service existing customer accounts and prepare the field force should they be required to attend to the client personally; they can seek repeat orders from marginal or geographically remote customers, particularly if they are low-unit-value consumable items; finally, they can provide a link between network members that serves to maintain the relationship, especially through periods of difficulty and instability. Many organisations prefer to place orders online or through telesales teams, as it does not involve the time costs associated with personal sales calls. The routine of such orders gives greater efficiency for all concerned with the relational exchange and reduces costs.

Direct mail activities are also becoming more important in areas where personal contact is seen as unnecessary or where limited field sales resources are deployed to key accounts. As with telesales, direct mail is often used to supplement the activities of the field force. Catalogue and electronic communications such as fax can be used for accounts, which may be regarded as relatively unattractive.

In addition to this, use of the Internet and mobile-based communications have provided new opportunities to reach customers. The website itself symbolises the changing orientation of marketing communications. Whereas once the brochure, mass media advertising and perhaps a communication mix incentive represented the central channel of communication, now the website and the database serve to integrate directed, sometimes interactive, one-to-one communications. These are supported in many cases by more call-to-action messages channelled through a variety of coordinated offline and digital media.

All of these activities free the field sales force to increase their productivity and to spend more time with established customers, key accounts or those with high profit potential.

Multichannel selling

A number of different sales channels have been identified so far and many organisations, in their search to reduce costs, have restructured their operations in an attempt to better meet the 'touchpoints' of their different customers.

Restructuring has often taken the form of introducing multiple sales channels with the simple objective of using less expensive channels to complete selling tasks that do not require personal, face-to-face contact. Technology-enhanced channels, mainly in the form of web-based and email communications, have grown considerably, often at the expense of telephone and mail facilities. Payne and Frow (2004) have developed a categorisation of sales channels and these are depicted in the vertical column of Table 11.3.

In order to better meet the needs of customers, organisations need to evolve their mix of channels. Customers will then be able to interact with their supplying organisations using the mix of channels that they prefer to use. Therefore, marketing communications needs to be used in order to best complement the different audiences, channel facilities and characteristics. Through mixing channels and communications in a complementary way, higher levels of

Table 11.3	Comparison of channel characteristics		
Channel	Breadth	Dominant form of communication	Cost/contact
Field sales	Key account, service and personal representation	Dialogue	High
Outlets	Retail branches, stores, depots and kiosks	Interactive	Medium
Telephony	Traditional telephone, facsimile, telex and contact centres	One-way and two-way	Low to medium
Direct marketing	Direct mail, radio and traditional television	One-way and two-way	Low
ecommerce	Email, Internet, interactive television	Interactive	Very low
mcommerce	Mobile telephony, SMS, WAP and 3G	Interactive	Very low

customer service can be achieved. The proliferation of channels may, however, lead organisations to believe that the greater the number of channels the greater the chances of commercial success. In addition to the view that multichannel customers are known to spend up to 30 per cent more than single channel customers, the Internet and overseas call centres also offer substantial (short-term) cost savings (Myers *et al.*, 2004).

Categorising customers

One simple approach to managing channels is to categorise accounts (customers) according to their potential attractiveness and the current strength of the relationship between supplier and buyer (see Figure 11.2). A strong relationship, for example, is indicative of two organisations engaged in mutually satisfying relational exchanges. A weak relationship suggests that the two parties have no experience of each other or, if they have, that it is not particularly satisfying. If there have been transactions, it may be that these can be classified as market exchange experiences. Attractiveness refers to the opportunities a buying organisation represents to the vendor: how large or small the potential business is in an organisation.

For reasons of clarity, these scales are presented as either high or low, strong or weak. However, they should be considered as a continuum, and with the use of some relatively simple evaluative criteria accounts can be positioned on the matrix and strategies formulated to move accounts to different positions, which in turn necessitate the use of different sales channel mixes.

Based on the original approach developed by Cravens *et al.* (1991) appropriate sales channels are superimposed on the grid so that optimum efficiency in selling effort and costs can be managed (Figure 11.3). Accounts in Section 1 vary in attractiveness, as some will be

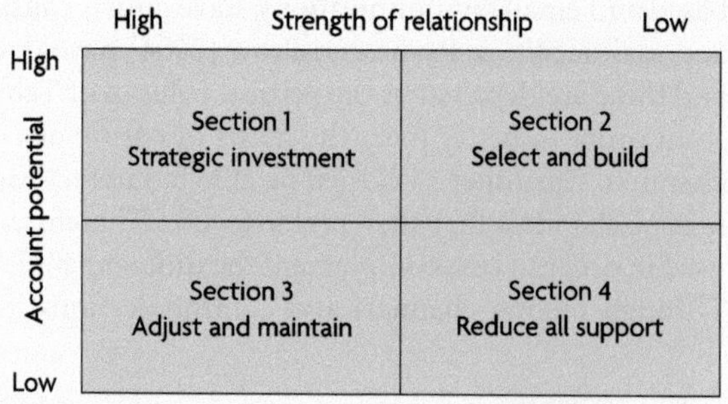

	Strength of relationship	
	High	**Low**
High (Account potential)	Section 1 Strategic investment	Section 2 Select and build
Low	Section 3 Adjust and maintain	Section 4 Reduce all support

Figure 11.2　Account investment grid

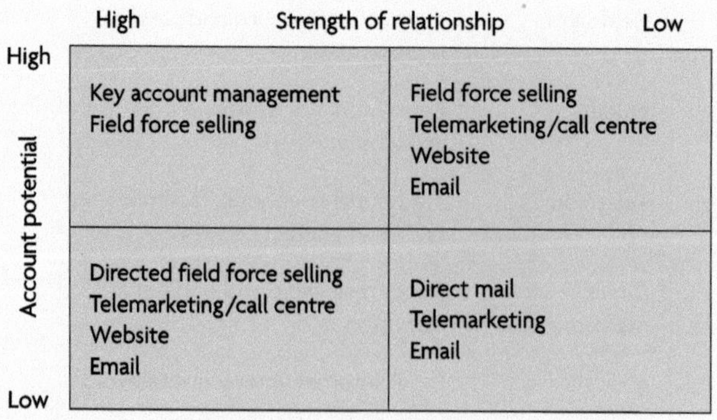

	Strength of relationship	
	High	**Low**
High (Account potential)	Key account management Field force selling	Field force selling Telemarketing/call centre Website Email
Low	Directed field force selling Telemarketing/call centre Website Email	Direct mail Telemarketing Email

Figure 11.3　Multichannel mix allocation
Source: After Cravens *et al.* (1991). Used with permission

assigned key account status. The others will be very important and will require a high level of selling effort (investment), which has to be delivered by the field sales force. Accounts in Section 2 are essentially prospects because of their weak relationship but high attractiveness. Selling effort should be proportional to the value of the prospects: high effort for good prospects and low for the others. Care should be given to allocating a time by which accounts in this section are moved to other parts of the grid, and in doing so save resources and maximise opportunities for growth. All the main sales channels should be used, commencing with direct and email to identify prospects, telesales for qualification purposes, field sales force selling directed at the strong prospects and telesales and website for the others. Website details provide support and information for those accounts that wish to remain distant. As the relationship becomes stronger, so field selling takes over from telemarketing and the coordinating activities of the contact or call centre. If the relationship weakens, then the account may be discontinued and selling redirected to other prospects.

Accounts in Section 3 do not offer strong potential and, although the relationship is strong, there are opportunities to switch the sales channel mix by reducing, but not eliminating, the level of field force activity and to give consideration to the introduction of telemarketing for particular accounts. Significant cost reductions can be achieved with these types of accounts by simply reviewing the means and reasoning behind the personal selling effort. Accounts in Section 4 should receive no field force calls, the prime sales channels being telesales, email, the website and perhaps catalogue selling depending upon the nature of the website.

Establishing a multiple sales channel strategy based on the grid suggested above may not be appropriate to all organisations. For example, the current level of performance may be considered as exceeding expectations, in which case there is no point in introducing change. It may be that the costs and revenues associated with redeployment are unfavourable and that the implications for the rest of the organisation of implementing the new sales channel approach are such that the transition should be either postponed or rejected. Payne and Frow (2004) suggest a range of channel options or strategies can be identified that relate to the channel needs of target segments. These range from a single dominant channel such as those used by Amazon and Egg, a customer segment approach designed for use with different channel types such as intermediaries, b2b end-user customers and consumers, one based on the different activity channels that customers prefer to use, such as a mix of online and offline resources to identify, see, demonstrate, select and pay for a computer and finally a truly integrated multi-channel strategy utilising CRM systems to integrate all customer information at whichever contact point the customer chooses to use. These strategies reflect some of the approaches that can be used and indeed various combinations can be used to meet customers' channel needs. However, experience has shown that costs can be reduced through the introduction of a multiple sales channel approach and that levels of customer satisfaction and the strength of the relationship between members of the network can be improved considerably. In addition, it is vital to remember that customers will move into and use new channel mixes over the customer lifecycle and that channel decisions should be regarded as fluid and developmental.

Summary

In order to help consolidate your understanding of direct marketing and personal selling, here are the key points summarised against each of the learning objectives:

1 Define direct marketing and set out its key characteristics

Direct marketing is a tool of marketing communications used to create and sustain a personal and intermediary free communication with customers, potential customers and other significant stakeholders. The key characteristic of direct marketing is that it has the capacity to provoke a behaviour response from the audience.

2 Describe the different methods used to implement direct marketing

Direct marketing can be used by organisations in a number of different ways, very often reflecting the business strategy of the organisation. Four types can be identified and they should not be regarded as hierarchical, in the sense that there has to be progression from one type to another. They are reflections of the way different organisations use direct marketing and the degree to which the tool is used strategically.

3 Explain the significance of the database in direct marketing and consider different direct response media

A database is a collection of files held on a computer that contain data that can be related to one another and which can reproduce information in a variety of formats. Normally the data consist of information collected about prospects and customers that are used to determine appropriate segments and target markets and to record responses to communications conveyed by the organisation. A database therefore plays a role as a storage, sorting and administrative device to assist direct and personalised communications.

Most media have a capacity of direct marketing applications, but television and radio, direct mail, telemarketing and the digital media are the most used.

4 Discuss the different types, roles and tasks of personal selling

There are four main ways of categorising personal selling. These are *order takers* who are salespersons to whom customers are drawn at the place of supply. *Order getters* are sales personnel who operate away from the organisation and who attempt to gain orders; *order collectors* attempt to gather orders over the telephone. Finally there are *order supporters* who are secondary salespersons in that they are involved with the order once it has been secured, or are involved with the act of ordering, usually by supplying information.

5 Consider the strengths and weaknesses of personal selling as a form of communication

Personal selling allows for interaction and dialogue, which entails both parties focusing on each other, with a reduced likelihood of distraction or noise. Both are able to tailor messages in response to the feedback provided by the other and solve customer problems. As a result there is a greater level of participation in the decision process by the vendor than in the other tools.

On the other hand the cost of personal selling is extremely high, and reach and frequency low. Control over message delivery can be low and message consistency variable.

6 Explain the concept of multiple sales channels

The introduction of multiple sales channels enables organisations the opportunity to complete some selling tasks without the expense or relative slowness of personal, face-to-face contact. Technology-enhanced channels, mainly in the form of web and email communications, have grown considerably, often at the expense of telephone and mail facilities.

In order to better meet the needs of customers, organisations need to evolve their mix of channels. Customers are better to interact with their supplying organisations using the mix of channels that they prefer to use.

7 Consider how direct marketing and personal selling might best be integrated with the other tools of the marketing communications mix

Advertising and public relations can play important roles creating awareness and shaping the attitudes and disposition of audiences. These help to drive web traffic where the complementary nature of direct marketing and personal selling enables organisations to improve levels of performance and customer satisfaction, through integration. By assigning each of them with roles within the overall decision-making process, efficiencies can be realised and costs slashed. Direct mail, telemarketing and web services have all served to improve the performance of organisations.

Review questions

1. Explain the different levels of direct marketing highlighting the key differences.
2. Write brief notes explaining the reasons why usage of direct marketing has grown in recent years.
3. Discuss the role of the database as the hub of marketing communications.
4. Why does direct mail continue to have a strong role to play in the direct marketing activities for many organisations?
5. Why might permission marketing be seen as an unnecessary cost and an infringement of civil liberties?
6. Which industries might use personal selling as a primary element of its marketing communications mix?
7. What are the different types of personal selling and what are the tasks that salespeople are normally expected to accomplish?
8. Describe the role of personal selling and highlight its main strengths and weaknesses.
9. Which factors need to be considered when determining the significance of personal selling in the communications mix?
10. Write brief notes outlining the way in which direct marketing might be used to assist personal selling activities.

References

Bashford, S. (2004) Telemarketing: customers calling, *Marketing*, 8 September. Retrieved 16 October 2004 from www.brandrepublic.com/news/

Benady, D. (2009) Field marketing comes into its own in the recession, *Marketing*. Retrieved 10 July 2010 from www.brandrepublic.com/features/

Cooke, C. (2008) Obama's Digital Campaign, *WPP*. Retrieved 12 August 2010 from www.wpp.com/wpp/marketing/digital/obamas-digital-campaign.htm

Cravens, D.W. (1987) *Strategic Marketing*. Homewood, IL: Irwin.

Cravens, D.W., Ingram, T.N. and LaForge, R.W. (1991) Evaluating multiple channel strategies, *Journal of Business and Industrial Marketing*, 6(3/4), 37–48.

Dolnicar, S. and Jordaan, Y. (2007) A market-orientated approach to responsibly managing information privacy concerns in direct marketing, *Journal of Advertising*, 36(2) (Summer) 123–149.

Fernandez, J. (2010a) Lexus unveils DM push for its hybrid range, *Marketing Week*, 10 August. Retrieved 12 August 2010 from www.marketingweek.co.uk/disciplines/direct-marketing/lexus-unveils-dm-push-for-its-hybrid-range/3016840.article

Fernandez, J. (2010b) National Trust uses DM for Welsh coastline appeal, *Marketing Week*, 10 August. Retrieved 12 August 2010 from www.marketingweek.co.uk/sectors/not-for-profit/national-trust-uses-dm-for-welsh-coastline-appeal/3016859.article

Fletcher, K. (1997) External drive, *Marketing*, 30 October, 39–42.

Ganesan, S. (1994) Determinants of long-term orientation in buyer–seller relationships. *Journal of Marketing*, 58 (April), 1–19.

Godin, S. (1999) *Permission Marketing: Turning Strangers into Friends, and Friends into Customers.* New York: Simon & Schuster.

Gomez, L. and Hlavinka, K. (2007) The total package: loyalty marketing in the world of consumer packaged goods (CPG), *Journal of Consumer Marketing*, 24(1), 48–56.

Goodwin, C. (1991) Privacy: recognition of a consumer right, *Journal of Public Policy and Marketing*, 10(1), 149–166.

Guenzi, P. (2002) Sales force activities and customer trust, *Journal of Marketing Management*, 18, 749–778.

Gundlach, G.T. and Murphy, P.E. (1993) Ethical and legal foundations of relational marketing exchanges, *Journal of Marketing*, 57 (October), 35–46.

Hawkes, S. (2008) Tesco rolls out trolley watch around the world, *The Times*, 12 April, 51.

Kent, R. and Brandal, H. (2003) Improving email response in a permission marketing context, *International Journal of Market Research*, 45(4), 489–503.

Krishnamurthy, S. (2001) A comprehensive analysis of permission marketing. *Journal of Computer-Mediated Communication*, 6(2) (January). Retrieved 8 March 2008 from www.jcmc.indiana.edu/vol6/issue2/krishnamurthy.html

Murphy, D. (2000) Call centres ponder price of technology, *Marketing*, 14 September, 43–44.

Murphy, D. (2009) Direct mail: finding its place in the mix, *Marketing: Top 100 Mailers*, 4 October, 4–9.

Myers, J.B., Pickersgill, A.D. and Metre van, E.S. (2004) Steering customers to the right channels, *McKinsey Quarterly*, 4, 16 November.

Payne, A. and Frow, P. (2004) The role of multichannel integration in customer relationship management, *Industrial Marketing Management*, 33(6) (August) 527–538.

Pearson, S. (2003) Data takes centre stage. Data 2003, *Marketing Direct*, sponsored supplement.

Rafaeli, A., Ziklik, L. and Doucet, L. (2008) The impact of call center employees' customer orientation behaviors on service quality, *Journal of Service Research*, 10(3) (February), 239–255.

Reid, A., Pullins, E.B. and Plank, R.E. (2002) The impact of purchase situation on sales-person communication behaviors in business markets, *Industrial Marketing Management*, 31(3), 205–213.

Reed, D. (2000) Too much, too often, *Marketing Week*, 12 October, 59–62.

Smith, J.W. (2004) Permission is not enough: empowerment and reciprocity must be included, too, *Marketing Management*, 13(3), 52.

Thayer, L. (1968) *Communication and Communication Systems.* Homewood, IL: Irwin.

Wilson, E.O. (1998) *Consilience: The Unity of Knowledge.* New York: Random House.

Chapter 12

Sales promotion, exhibitions and product placement

The additional value offered through sales promotions can form an important part of the communication mix and are often of strategic importance. By adding value to the offer and hoping to bring forward future sales, these techniques can be a source of competitive advantage, one that is invariably short-rather than long-run. Exhibitions and trade shows can be an integral and important component in the communications mix, especially in the b2b sector. Exhibitions are good at developing relationships with suppliers and customers. Product placement enables brands to be seen in the appropriate context and can help form brand associations for consumers. Product placement activities are growing as the regulations in many countries are becoming more relaxed.

Aims and learning objectives

The aims of this chapter are to consider the nature, role and characteristics associated with three important tools of marketing communications: namely sales promotion, exhibitions and product placement.

The learning objectives are to enable readers to:

1. discuss the nature, types and role of sales promotions;
2. explain how sales promotions can be used strategically in the communications mix;
3. describe the various sales promotion methods and techniques;
4. explain the characteristics and significance of exhibitions and trade shows;
5. consider the role of exhibitions in the marketing communications mix;
6. understand the concepts and issues associated with product placement.

Introduction

Three topics are explored in this chapter. The first part considers sales promotion and the tools and techniques used to incentivise customers. The middle part considers the characteristics of exhibitions, an important business-to-business tool. The final part of this chapter examines an interesting and developing tool, product placement.

If advertising is used to create brand values then the primary role of sales promotion is to engage audiences by delivering a call-to-action. These two tools complement each other as advertising seeks to work over the long term to create awareness and positive feelings, whereas sales promotion works in the shorter-term to encourage people to behave in particular ways and to create sales. Sales promotion offers buyers additional value, an inducement to generate an immediate sale. These inducements can be targeted at consumers, distributors, agents and members of the sales force. A whole range of network members can benefit from the use of sales promotion.

This promotional tool is traditionally referred to as a form of below-the-line communication because, unlike advertising, these agencies are not paid a commission by the media owners. The promotional costs are borne directly by the organisation initiating the activity, which in most cases is a manufacturer, producer or service provider.

Understanding the value of sales promotions

There are many sales promotion techniques, but they all offer a direct inducement or an incentive to encourage receivers of these messages to buy a product/service sooner rather than later. The inducement (for example, price deals, coupons, premiums) is presented as an added value to the basic product and is intended to encourage buyers to act 'now' rather than later. Sales promotion is used, therefore, principally as a means to accelerate sales. The acceleration represents the shortened period of time in which the transaction is completed relative to the time that would have elapsed had there not been a promotion. This action does not mean that an extra sale has been achieved, just that a potential future exchange is confirmed and transacted now.

Sales promotions consist of a wide range of tools and methods. These instruments are considered in more detail later but consideration of what constitutes sales promotion methods is important. In many cases price is the determinant variable and can be used to distinguish between instruments. Sales promotions are often perceived purely as a price discounting mechanism through price deals and the use of coupons. This, however, is not the whole picture, as there are many other ways in which incentives can be offered to buyers.

Reference has already been made to the idea that sales promotions are a way of providing value and it is this value orientation that should be used when considering the nature and essential characteristics of sales promotion. Peattie and Peattie (1994) established a useful way of discriminating between price and non-price sales promotion instruments. They refer to sales promotions that are value increasing and sales promotions that are value adding (see Table 12.1).

This demarcation is important because a large amount of research into sales promotion has been based on value-increasing approaches, most notably price deals and coupons (Gupta, 1988; Blattberg and Neslin, 1990; Krishna and Zhang, 1999). This tends to distort the way sales promotions are perceived and has led to some generalisations about the overall impact of this promotional discipline. There is a large range of other sales promotion instruments which add value and enhance the offering and which provide opportunities to derive longer-term benefits (see Table 12.2). However, research into these is limited (Gilbert and Jackaria, 2002).

As a result of this diversity of sales promotion instruments it should be of no surprise to learn that they are used for a wide range of reasons. Sales promotions can be targeted, with

Table 12.1	A value orientation of sales promotions
Value element	Explanation
Value-increasing	Value is increased by offering changes to the product quantity/quality or by lowering the price. Generally used and perceived as effective over the short term.
Value-adding	Value is added by offering something to augment the fundamental product/price offering. Premiums (gifts), information or opportunities can be offered as extras and the benefits realised over different periods of time: delayed (postal premiums), accumulated (loyalty programmes) or instant (scratch and win competitions). These have the potential to add value over the longer term.

Source: Based on Peattie and Peattie (1994)

Table 12.2	A typology of sales promotion
Value-increasing (alters price/quantity or price/quality equation)	Value-adding (offers 'something extra' while leaving core product and price unchanged)
Discount pricing	Samples
Money-off coupons	Special features (limited editions)
Payment terms (e.g. interest-free credit)	Valued packaging
Refunds	Product trial
Guarantees	In-pack gifts – premiums
Multipack or multi-buys	In-mail gifts – premiums
Quantity increases	Piggy back gifts – premiums
Buybacks	Gift coupons Information (e.g. brochure, catalogue) Clubs or loyalty programmes Competitions/prize draws

considerable precision, at particular audiences and there are three broad audiences to whom sales promotions can be targeted: consumers, members of the distribution network, and the sales forces of both manufacturers and resellers. It should be remembered that the accuracy of these promotional tools means that many subgroups within these broad groups can be reached quickly and accurately. However, sales promotions campaign can backfire. When KFC offered a downloadable coupon that was endorsed by Oprah Winfrey, franchises could not keep pace with demand, especially as KFC had not placed any control or limit on the number of coupons that could be downloaded.

The reasons why organisations use sales promotions are set out at Table 12.3.

Table 12.3	Reasons for the use of sales promotions
Reach new customers	They are useful in securing trials for new products and in defending shelf space against anticipated and existing competition.
Reduce distributor risk	The funds that manufacturers dedicate to them lower the distributor's risk in stocking new brands.
Reward behaviour	They can provide rewards for previous purchase behaviour.
Retention	They can provide interest and attract potential customers and in doing so encourage them to provide personal details for further communications activity.
Add value	They can encourage sampling and repeat purchase behaviour by providing extra value (superior to competitors' brands) and a reason to purchase.
Induce action	They can instil a sense of urgency among consumers to buy while a deal is available. They add excitement and interest at the point of purchase to the merchandising of mature and mundane products.
Preserve cash flow	Since sales promotion costs are incurred on a pay-as-you-go basis, they can spell survival for smaller, regional brands that cannot afford big advertising programmes.
Improve efficiency	Sales promotions allow manufacturers to use idle capacity and to adjust to demand and supply imbalances or softness in raw material prices and other input costs, while maintaining the same list prices.
Integration	They can provide a means of linking together other tools of the promotional mix.
Assist segmentation	They allow manufacturers to price discriminate among consumer segments that vary in price sensitivity. Most manufacturers believe that a high-list, high-deal policy is more profitable than offering a single price to all consumers. A portion of sales promotion expenditures, therefore, consists of reductions in list prices that are set for the least price-sensitive segment of the market.

As if in an attempt to categorise and manage this list, Lee (2002) suggests that the main reasons for the use of sales promotions can be reduced to four:

- as a reaction to competitor activities
- as a form of inertia – this is what we have always done
- as a way of meeting short-term sales objectives
- as a way of meeting long-term objectives.

The first three are used widely and Lee comments that many brand owners use sales promotion as a panic measure when competitors threaten to lure customers away. Cutting prices is undoubtedly a way of prompting a short-term sales response but it can also undermine a longer-term brand strategy.

| Viewpoint 12.1 | Participation in promotional programmes |

For the price of a tube of chewing gum, Trident offered music fans an opportunity to see Beyonce at the O₂ Arena. In order to promote awareness of the sales promotion event various stunts were staged. The first was in Piccadilly Circus, London, where 100 lookalike Beyonces performed a flash dance, and in doing so attracted extensive media coverage and over a million views of YouTube. Tickets were given to people donating to buskers who were hired to cover various Beyonce tracks, to people who sang Beyonce numbers in the Lucky Voice karaoke bar and to the winners in a an enormous game of musical chairs held in a shopping centre. As a result of this activity over 67,000 visited the Trident Unwrapped website.

Downloading discount vouchers is now commonplace for many people. To captialise on this the convenience store Spar ran an online game called Shelf Sniper. This involved shooting products on a moving conveyor using the mouse to control a barcode scanner. By reaching level two of the game, individuals won a £1 voucher redeemable against £10 worth of shopping.

Source: Based on Wallace (2010); Benady (2009)

Question

Why have these brands used games and events to run the promotion?

Task

What game might you use to support a sales promotion for a travel company?

Not too many years ago sales promotions were regarded as a key way of developing sales. However, the use of sales promotions, in particular the use of on-pack promotions, bonus packs, competitions and price deals have failed to maintain the growth of previous years. Reasons for the decline include changing consumer behaviour, the rise of digital media and a distinct lack of innovation in the industry. Another important factor has been the expectations and drive of resellers, and the main supermarket chains in particular. Most have followed low cost strategies (Porter, 1980) with an emphasis on reducing suppliers' costs to a minimum. Supermarkets also desire sales promotion programmes that are exclusive to them as this is seen as a major way of developing their retail brands. Supermarkets have become media owners and realise the value of their store space as a means of exposing others brands. Therefore, any form of sales promotion activity within their environments should be exclusive and tied into their brand. Providing on-pack promotions for individual stores is normally too expensive and uneconomic so this form of promotion has suffered a great deal.

New solutions have had to be found, and as Barrand (2004) suggests the use of digital media and the integration of sales promotion within other campaigns has been, and continues to be successful. The use of SMS, email, viral campaigns and the Internet are used increasingly to drive sales by providing the call-to-action, which for a long time was the province of sales promotion activities.

The use of sales promotion has soared during the recession as consumers trade down in search of economies. 'Bogofs' and twofers' were popular forms of promotion, as they represent quantity at low prices. Benady (2009) reports that today straight price discounts are valued most, exemplified by Tesco's 'buy one now, get one free later' campaign.

The role of sales promotion

The role of sales promotion has changed significantly over recent years. At one time, the largest proportion of communications budgets was normally allocated to advertising. In many cases advertising no longer dominates the communications budget and sales promotion has assumed the focus of the communications investment, for reasons that are described below. This is particularly evident in consumer markets that are mature, have reached a level of stagnation, and where price and promotion work are the few ways of inducing brand switching behaviour.

Short termism

The short-term financial focus of many industrialised economies has developed a managerial climate geared to short-term performance and evaluation, over periods as short as 12 weeks. To accomplish this, communications are required that work quickly and directly impact upon sales. Many see this as leading to an erosion of the brand franchise.

Managerial accountability

Following on from the previous reason is the increased pressure upon marketing managers to be accountable for their communications expenditure. The results of sales promotion activities are more easily justified and understood than those associated with advertising. The number of coupons returned for redemption and the number of bonus packs purchased can be calculated quickly and easily, with little room for error or misjudgement. Advertising, however, cannot be measured so easily, in either the short or the long term. The impact of this is that managers can relate this type of investment in communications to the bottom line much more comfortably than with advertising.

Brand performance

Technological advances have enabled retailers to track brand performance more effectively. This in turn means that manufacturers can be drawn into agreements that promulgate in-store promotional activity at the expense of other more traditional forms of mass media promotion. Barcode scanners, hand-held electronic shelf-checking equipment and computerised stock systems facilitate the tracking of merchandise. This means that brand managers can be held responsible much more quickly for below-par performance.

Brand expansion

As brand quality continues to improve and as brands proliferate on the shelves of increasingly larger supermarkets, so the number of decisions that a consumer has to make also increases. Faced with multiple-brand decisions and a reduced amount of time to complete the shopping expedition, the tension associated with the shopping experience has increased considerably over the last decade.

Promotions can make decision-making easier for consumers: they simplify a potentially difficult process. So, as brand choice increases, the level of shopping convenience falls. The conflict this causes can be resolved by the astute use of sales promotions. Some feel that the cognitive shopper selects brands that offer increased value, which makes decision-making easier and improves the level of convenience associated with the shopping experience. However, should there be promotions on two offerings from an individual's repertoire then the decision-making is not necessarily made easier.

Competition for shelf space

The continuing growth in the number of brands that are launched and the fragmentation of consumer markets mean that retailers have to be encouraged to make shelf space available. Sales promotions help manufacturers win valuable shelf space and assist retailers to attract increased levels of store traffic and higher utilisation of limited resources.

The credibility of this communication tool is low, as it is obvious to the receiver what the intention is of using sales promotion messages. However, because of the prominent and pervasive nature of the tool, consumers and members of the trade understand and largely accept the direct sales approach. Sales promotion is not a tool that hides its intentions, nor does it attempt to be devious (which is not allowed, by regulation).

The absolute costs of sales promotion are low, but the real costs need to be evaluated once a campaign has finished and all redemptions received and satisfied. The relative costs can be high, as not only do the costs of the premium or price discount need to be determined, but also the associated costs of additional transportation, lost profit, storage and additional time spent organising and administering a sales promotion campaign need to be accounted for.

In its favour, sales promotion allows for a high degree of control. Management is able to decide just when and where a sales promotion will occur and also estimate the sales effect. Sales promotions can be turned on and off quickly and adjusted to changed market conditions. The intended message is invariably the one that is received, as there is relatively little scope for it to be corrupted or damaged in transmission.

Sales promotion plans: the objectives

The objectives of using this tool are sales oriented and are geared to stimulating buyers either to use a product for the first time or to encourage use on a routine basis. One objective of sales promotion activity is to prompt buyers into action, to initiate a series of behaviours that result in long-run purchase activity. These actions can be seen to reflect high or low involvement and they occur in the conative stage of the attitudinal set. If the marketing objectives include the introduction of a new product or intention to enter a new market, then the key objective associated with low-involvement decisions is to stimulate trial use as soon as possible. When high-involvement decisions are present, then sales promotions need to be withheld until a suitable level of attitudinal development has been undertaken by public relations and advertising activities.

If a product is established in a market, then a key objective should be to use sales promotions to stimulate an increase in the number of purchases made by current customers and to attract users from competing products (see Figure 12.1). The objectives, therefore, are either

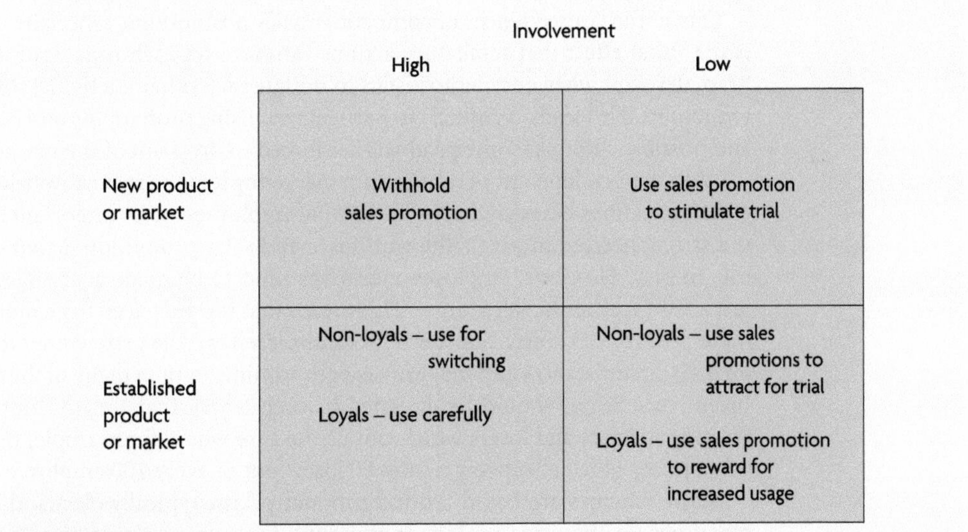

| | Involvement | |
	High	Low
New product or market	Withhold sales promotion	Use sales promotion to stimulate trial
Established product or market	Non-loyals – use for switching Loyals – use carefully	Non-loyals – use sales promotions to attract for trial Loyals – use sales promotion to reward for increased usage

Figure 12.1   A sales promotion objectives grid

to increase consumption for established products or to stimulate trial by encouraging new buyers to use a product. Once this has been agreed then the desired trial and usage levels need to be determined for each of the target audiences.

The strategic use of sales promotions

For a long time sales promotions have been regarded as a short-term tactical tool whose prime purpose is to encourage customers to try a brand or to switch brands (within their repertoire), attracted by the added value of the sales promotion. Indeed, Papatia and Krishnamurthi (1996) claim that coupons can actively promote switching behaviour and so reduce levels of loyalty. As discussed earlier what happens after a sales promotion activity finishes is debatable. Some claim that once a promotion is withdrawn satisfied customers will return to the brand unsupported by a sales promotion, but supported by other elements of the marketing communications mix: in particular advertising, to maintain awareness of the brand and its values; direct marketing, to provide personal attention and the opportunity to take immediate action; and public relations to sustain credibility and relevance.

By way of contrast it can be argued that sales promotion serves to discount a brand, either directly through price-based reductions or indirectly through coupons and premiums. Customer alignment is to the deal rather than to the brand itself. This serves to lower expectations of what a brand stands for and what it is capable of delivering. So, once a sales promotion is removed, the normal price is perceived as representing inferior value and so repeat purchase behaviour is deterred.

However, despite these less than positive views, some writers (Davis, 1992; O'Malley, 1998) argue that sales promotions have a strategic role to play in the communications mix. Traditionally they have been viewed as short-term tactical tools that can be used offensively to induce the trial of new products, or defensively for established products to retain shelf space and consumers. Sales promotions that do not work as intended may have been used to support inappropriate products or may have been devised without adequate planning. An example of the latter issue may be the Hoover free flights misjudgement and the associated over-subscription which followed the launch of that particular sales promotion activity. There can be no doubt that sales promotions oriented to consumer deals and Temporary Price Reductions (TPRs), in particular, do little to contribute to the overall strategy adopted for an organisation or even a product.

One of the consequences of competitive sales promotions, especially in consumer markets, is the spiral effect that retaliatory actions can have on each organisation. A sales promotion 'trap' develops when competitors start to imitate each other's activities, often based upon price reductions. This leads eventually to participants losing profitability and consumers losing value and possibly choice as some products are forced to drop out of the market.

With the development of relationship marketing and the move towards integrated marketing communications has been the realisation that employees are an important target audience. There is a strong need to motivate the workforce and sales promotion activities have an important role to play. However, employee incentives need to be made accessible to everyone and not just a few (such as the sales force). This means that rewards need to be more broadly spread and there needs to be choice. Vouchers, for example, enable the prizewinner to make a choice based on their circumstances and they are easier to administer than many of the other types of reward. Incentive schemes should be designed in such a way that they do not fall into the trap of creating winners and losers which can be the case when, for example, the top 20 in a scheme win a prize, which effectively creates 80 losers out of every 100 employees.

Many schemes are based around product prizes, typically electrical goods. However, for many people these are no longer attractive (or sufficiently motivating) as rewards. Virgin vouchers provide activity-based rewards where there is an experience that gives the recipient a memory. Activities such as hot-air ballooning, sky diving, visits to the theatre or to health farms appeal to a wide cross-section of people.

Viewpoint 12.2   Blitzing the independent stores

When Britvic Soft Drinks launched a key new product named Drench Juicy they needed quick penetration in the convenience and independent channels. This was because a planned summer tv ad would drive consumer demand so there had to be product availability.

To do this they used Reach, a field marketing team, in order to establish the 'water with a fruity taste' brand in the key retail outlets. A dedicated team of 100 people was appointed, with a goal of working across the top 17,000 outlets, selling three variants of Drench Juicy, merchandising them in chillers. They also sold price marked packs to ensure maximum rate of sale in stocking stores. In store sampling also took place, particularly at high footfall stores at peak times (e.g. lunch hours). The benefit of this was that not only did the brand get increased visibility but it also increased trial rates.

A direct mail campaign was used in the next best 6,000 independent stores. The blitz approach was repeated over three days, four weeks later. This drove increased volume and encouraged repeat purchase where the brand had sold through.

Using livewire technology the team was able to not only report results quickly but also react quickly to any issues that arose. The result of this activity was that the brand was sampled in over 600 stores, direct sales of over 40,000 cases was achieved and every new distribution point was supported with POS. Some 90 per cent distribution was achieved, with current listings in Boots, Morrisons, McColls, Sommerfield and WHSmith Travel, and over 15,000 independent stores.

Source: Based on Anon (2009)

Question

What other sales promotion techniques could have been used to support the launch?

Task

Go to www.promotion.com and read the advice about promotional activities.

The true strategic effect of sales promotion activities can only be achieved if they are coordinated with the other activities of the communications mix, and this requires planning. In particular, the complementary nature of sales promotion and advertising should be exploited through the use of common themes and messages, timing, targeting and allocation of resources (in particular budgets). Sales promotions that are planned as a sequence of predetermined activities, reflecting the promotional requirements of a product over the longer term, are more likely to be successful than those sales promotions that are simply reactions to competitors' moves and market developments.

The strategic impact of sales promotions is best observed when they are designed or built into a three- to four-year plan of promotional activities, coordinated with other elements of the communications mix, and integrated with the business strategy.

The manner in which many of the loyalty programmes are managed signals a move from pure sales promotion to direct marketing. The integration of these two approaches has become necessary in order that the advantages of both are realised. This does raise an interesting conflict, in that sales promotion is essentially a short-term tool, and direct marketing needs to work over the long term. The former is product oriented (albeit giving added value to consumers) and often oriented to mass audiences, whereas the latter is based upon developing a personal dialogue (Curtis, 1996).

Finally, the huge sums of money involved in some of the mainstream loyalty or reward-based programmes suggest that these should be seen as longer-term promotional investments. As the return will spread over many years, a medium-term perspective may be more appropriate rather than a short-term view based on a sales 'blip'.

Sales promotion methods

There are a variety of sales promotion methods or techniques. These vary in their characteristics but they are essentially incentives, which are rewards for buyers behaving in particular ways. There are some sales promotion activities run by brand owners that are targeted at the sales forces of the manufacturers and resellers. However, the two principal audiences for sales promotions are those targeted at distributors and those at consumers.

Manufacturers to distributors

Manufacturers and distributors, including retailers, see sales promotions as important devices to encourage trial among non-users and to stimulate repeat purchase among users. Retailers prefer in-store promotions (push) instead of promotions aimed at consumers (pull) strategies. This has implications for the communication mixes deployed by manufacturers. Essentially distributor-oriented promotions represent a business orientation and Table 12.4 sets out the main methods and techniques that can be used in this context.

Marketing communications between manufacturers and resellers are vitally important. Sales promotions play an increasingly important role in the coordination between the two parties. Resellers look for sales promotions to support their own marketing initiatives. Wheeler and Fermer (2009) estimate that the value of funding paid by consumer packaged goods manufacturers to grocery multiple retailers, to support promotional activities is approximately £8 billion per year, in the UK.

Supplier selection decisions depend in part upon the volume and value of the communications support. In other words, will supplier X or Y provide the necessary level of

Table 12.4	Distributor-oriented sales promotion techniques
Method	**Explanation**
Advertising allowance	A percentage allowance is given against a reseller's purchases during a specified campaign period. Instead of providing an allowance against product purchases, an allowance can be provided against the cost of an advertisement or campaign.
Buying allowance	In return for specific orders between certain dates, a reseller will be entitled to a refund or allowance of x per cent off the regular case or carton price.
Count and recount	Manufacturers may require resellers to clear old stock before a new or modified product is introduced. One way this can be achieved is to encourage resellers to move stock out of storage and into the store. The count and recount method provides an allowance for each case shifted into the store during a specified period of time.
Buy-back	Purchases made after the count and recount scheme (up to a maximum of the count and recount) are entitled to an allowance to encourage stores to replenish their stocks (with the manufacturer's product and not that of a competitor).
Dealer contests	Used to hold a reseller's attention by focusing them on a manufacturer's products not a competitor's.
Dealer conventions and meetings	These enable informal interaction between a manufacturer and its resellers and can aid the development and continuance of good relations between the two parties.
Training and support	This is an important communications function, especially when products are complex or subject to rapid change, as in IT markets. This can build stronger relationships and manufacturers have greater control over the messages that the resellers transmit.

communication support, either within the channel or direct to the consumer? Indeed, Wheeler and Fermer see trade based promotional support increasing and because of the balance of power in the marketing channels, this looks unlikely to change in the medium term. They see a move away from multibuy to price led activity, which all lead to a reduced ROI. In essence, suppliers are funding a disproportionate amount of the discounts demanded by consumers.

Manufacturers to consumers

Manufacturers use sales promotions to communicate with consumers mainly because they can be a cost-effective means of achieving short-term increases in sales. The objectives are twofold: first, to stimulate trial use by new users or second, to increase the amount of product used by current customers. Methods relating to these two main tasks are set out in Table 12.5.

These methods represent a pull-positioning strategy, as they are targeted at consumers. They can stimulate a shift in sales and they can be instigated and withdrawn at any time, subject to any contractual arrangements. Most brands outsource the design and implementation of sales promotion activities to specialist agencies. They in turn often employ fulfilment houses, organisations that manage the logistics associated with particular promotions. For example, premiums require the receipt and accountability of coupons or finance and then the dispatch of the designated product. Cadbury's ran a premium based promotion with their chocolate digestives brand of biscuit. Research shows that 90 per cent of biscuit consumption involves a drink, so a mug/biscuit combination is highly complementary. The promotion was based on people uploading a picture and personalising a mug, for just £7.99 (Wilde, 2009).

Finally, bonus packs and 2-4-1 offers in particular have been used by manufacturers to provide increased value to customers, move stock, reduce working capital and take customers out of the next purchase cycle by loading them with product and so disadvantage competitors. Whilst this works perfectly well for some, the offer does not work for all customers. Single person households are not always able to consume the extra product within the use by dates and therefore are unable to realise the value offered. In recognition of this situation, Tesco now

Table 12.5	Consumer-oriented sales promotion techniques
Method	**Explanation**
Sampling	Although very expensive, sampling is an effective way of getting people to try a product. Trial-size versions of the actual product are given away free. Sampling can also take the form of demonstrations, trial-size packs that have to be purchased or free use for a certain period of time.
Coupons	These are vouchers or certificates that entitle consumers to a price reduction on a particular product. The value of the reduction or discount is set and the coupon must be presented at purchase.
Price-offs	These are a direct reduction in the purchase price with the offer clearly labelled on the package or point of purchase display.
Bonus packs	These offer more product for the regular pack price, typically a 2 for 1 offer. They provide direct impact at the point of purchase and represent extra value.
Refunds and rebates	Used to invite consumers to send in a proof of purchase and in return receive a cash refund.
Premiums	Items of merchandise that are offered free or at a low cost in return for product purchase.
Contests and sweepstakes	A contest is a customer competition based on skill or ability. Entry requires a proof of purchase and winners are judged against a set of predetermined criteria. A sweepstake determines winners by chance and proof of purchase is not required. There is no judging and winners are drawn at random.

offer a deal based on 'buy one, get one free – later'. Customers can now reclaim their second item at a date that is convenient to them.

Trade shows and exhibitions

Trade shows and exhibitions fulfil a role for customers by enabling them to become familiar with new developments, new products and leading-edge brands. Very often these customers will be opinion leaders and use word-of-mouth communications to convey their feelings and both product and exhibition experiences to others. The role of trade fairs is to enable manufacturers, suppliers, and distributors to meet at a designated location. Drawn from a particular industry or related industries, the purpose is to exchange information about products and services and to build relationships. These events normally exclude consumers. Exhibitions are attended by consumers.

In the b2b market, trade shows are very often an integral and important component in the communications mix. Meeting friends, customers, suppliers, competitors and prospective customers is an important sociological and ritualistic event in the communication calendar for many companies. In the consumer sector, exhibitions provide a point of difference and offer continuity for those people who make the brand choice decisions at the point of purchase.

The idea of many suppliers joining together at a particular location in order to set out their products and services so that customers may meet, make comparisons and place orders is far from new. Indeed, not only does this form of promotional activity stretch back many centuries, it has also been used to explain the way the Internet works (Bertheron *et al.*, 1996).

At a basic level, trade shows can be oriented for industrial users and exhibitions for consumers and the content or purpose might be to consider general or specialised products/markets. According to Boukersi (2000), consumer-oriented general exhibitions tend to be larger and last longer than the more specialised industrial shows and it is clear that this more highly segmented and focused approach is proving more successful, based on the increasing number of these types of exhibitions.

Reasons to use exhibitions

There are many reasons to use exhibitions, but the primary reasons appear not to be 'to make sales' or 'because the competition is there' but because these events provide opportunities to meet potential and established customers and to create and sustain a series of relational exchanges. Li (2007) cited by Geigenmüller (2010) stresses that the impact of trade shows on the development of valuable long-term buyer-seller relationships is important.

The main aims therefore, are to develop long-term partnerships with customers, to build upon or develop the corporate identity and to gather up-to-date market intelligence (Shipley and Wong, 1993) and to exchange information about products, services and corporate developments. This implies that exhibitions should not be used as isolated events, but that they should be integrated into a series of activities, which serve to develop and sustain buyer relationships.

After a tentative start to the 1990s, the exhibition industry in this century has grown considerably. With managers increasingly accountable for their promotional spend, a greater number of budgets are now channelled into exhibitions and related events. In 1995, visitors attended 773 exhibitions in the UK, where venues exceeded 2,000 square feet. By 2005, the number had risen to 944 exhibitions (Advertising Association, 2008).

Costs can be reduced by using private exhibitions. The increased flexibility allows organisations to produce mini or private exhibitions for their clients at local venues (e.g. hotels). This can mean lower costs for the exhibitor and reduced time away from their businesses for those attending. The communication 'noise' and distraction associated with the larger public events can also be avoided by these private showings.

Viewpoint 12.3 Making an exhibit of cars in Beijing

The Beijing car show is a major event in a country where car sales increased 45 per cent in 2009. This rate growth should be considered against a background where only 50 out of a 1,000 people own a car. In Germany this figure is 500 in every 1,000. So, the potential for car manufacturers is huge and this is why the Beijing car show is well attended.

Some 80 per cent of the 1,000 cars on show are made locally and compete with American, European and Japanese brands. Car shows in Europe are largely about dealers and dealerships, the media and specialist journalists, and suppliers and parts equipment manufacturers. The emphasis is on relationships, news, and profiling each form of development. Very few orders are agreed at the shows, although many pre-show agreements are ceremoniously signed for photographers and the crowds.

The Chinese show is a sales extravaganza. The country's car network is relatively young and there are an insufficient number of dealerships. As a result, consumers having completed their Internet-based searches, arrive at the show armed with bags of cash, ready to secure their chosen vehicle.

Source: Based on Madden (2010); Bristow (2010)

Question

How would you use marketing communications to attract visitors to a car show?

Task

Make a list of the 10 critical activities associated with organising a trade show.

Exhibit 12.1 Scene from the Beijing Car Show . . . it's official

A security guard takes pictures of a Lamborghini Murciélago LP 670-4 Super Veloce China Limited Edition
Image courtesy of Getty Images/Feng Li

Characteristics of exhibitions and trade fairs

The main reasons for attending exhibitions and trade fairs are that they enable organisations to meet customers (and potential customers) in an agreeable environment, one where both have independently volunteered their time to attend; to place/take orders; to generate leads; and to gather market information. The reasons for attending exhibitions are set out in Table 12.6.

From this it is possible to distinguish the following strengths and weaknesses of using exhibitions as part of the marketing communications programme.

Strengths

The costs associated with exhibitions, if controlled properly, can mean that this is an effective and efficient means of communicating with customers. The costs per inquiry need to be calculated, but care needs to be taken over who is classified as an inquirer, as the quality of the audience varies considerably. Costs per order taken are usually the prime means of evaluating the success of an exhibition. This can paint a false picture, as the true success can never really be determined in terms of orders because of the variety of other factors that impinge upon the placement and timing of orders.

Viewpoint 12.4   Making an exhibition of Ireland

The development of Ireland's tourism market involves attracting both individuals for vacations and also the business market in terms of conferences, events and meetings. One thing that is common to both groups is the opportunity to visit and enjoy the breathtaking scenery and the warmth and friendliness of the people.

Some of Ireland's recent economic changes included an advantageous set of tax breaks designed to encourage investment in the construction industry. One of the results of this initiative has been the development of a huge number of recently completed high-quality hotels, many with conference centres. Thus, with a wealth of excellent suppliers, the challenge for Tourism Ireland at the International Confex 2007 exhibition was to stand out among the other 1,075 exhibitors and attract conference organisers to their exhibition platform.

To encourage visitors it was decided to send out mailers to key conference organisers prior to the exhibition and give them a reason to visit the Tourism Ireland stand. These mailers were designed to be personal invitations and included an invitation to experience some genuine Irish hospitality in the form of a Hot Irishman (coffee liqueur) or a Guinness. This was to be symbolic of the opportunities to relax away from a conference. Normally a return of 3 per cent might be expected for a mailer of this type. However, 2.9 per cent responded asking for more information because they were unable to attend the exhibition, while a further 7.1 per cent attended the stand. An overall response rate of 10 per cent was achieved.

Source: Based on UTalk (2007)

Question

Why was direct mail used to reach conference organisers?

Task

How would you attract business people to attend an exhibition on office equipment?

Products can be launched at exhibitions, and when integrated with a good PR campaign a powerful impact can be made. This can also be used to reinforce corporate identity. Exhibitions are an important means of gaining information about competitors, buyers and technical and political developments in the market, and they often serve to facilitate the recruitment process. Above all else, exhibitions provide an opportunity to meet customers on relatively neutral ground and, through personal interaction, develop relationships. Products can be demonstrated, prices agreed, technical problems discussed and trust and credibility enhanced.

Table 12.6	Reasons exhibitors choose to attend exhibitions

To meet existing customers
To take orders/make sales
To get leads and meet prospective new customers
To meet lapsed customers
To meet prospective members of the existing or new marketing channels
To provide market research opportunities and to collect marketing data

Weaknesses

One of the main drawbacks associated with exhibition work is the vast and disproportionate amount of management time that can be tied up with the planning and implementation of exhibitions. However, good planning is essential if the full potential benefits of exhibition work are to be realised.

Taking members of the sales force 'off the road' can also incur large costs. Depending on the nature of the business these opportunity costs can soar. Some pharmaceutical organisations estimate that it can cost approximately £5,000 per person per week to divert salespeople in this way.

The expected visitor profile must be analysed in order that the number of quality buyers visiting an exhibition can be determined. The variety of visitors attending an exhibition can be misleading, as the vast majority may not be serious buyers or, indeed, may not be directly related to the industry or the market in question. Research by Gopalakrishna *et al.* (2010) has found that approximately 40 per cent of first-time exhibitors, spanning a range of industries, do not return to the same show the following year. As Galea (2007) cited by Gopalakrishna *et al.* (2010) pointed out, a growing concern for managers is the ability to reach relevant decision-makers. The researchers response was to attempt an understanding of attendee behaviour, as this would help trade show organisers segment their audiences. From their research data they determined a typology of business show visitors. These are depicted at Table 12.7.

Exhibitions as a form of marketing communications

As a form of marketing communications, exhibitions enable products to be promoted, they can build brands and they can be an effective means of demonstrating products and building industry-wide credibility in a relatively short period of time. Attendance at exhibitions may also be regarded from a political standpoint, in that non-attendance by competitors may be taken as an opportunity by attendees to suggest weaknesses.

In the b2b sector new products and services are often introduced at exhibitions, especially if there are to be public relations activities and events that can be spun off the launch. In other words, exhibitions are not activities independent of the other communication tools. Exhibitions, if used effectively, can be part of an integrated communications campaign.

Advertising prior to, during and after a trade show can be dovetailed with public relations, sponsorship and personal selling. Sales promotions can also be incorporated through competitions among customers prior to the show to raise awareness, generate interest and to suggest customer involvement. Competitions during a show can be focused on the sales force to motivate and stimulate commercial activity and among visitors to generate interest in the stand, raise brand name awareness and encourage focus on particular products (new, revised or revolutionary) and generate sales leads and enquiries.

Table 12.7	A typology of trade show visitors

Segment name	Key characteristics
The basic shopper (40%)	Basic shoppers make about seven 'serious' visits to booths, 75 per cent are planned, and 70 per cent of visits are made to stand-alone booths which are accessible on all four sides.
The enthusiast (17%)	Enthusiasts make an average of 24 visits while at the trade show, more than three times that of the basic shopper. 80 per cent of their visits are planned and they prefer to be 'where the action is'.
The niche shopper (17%)	The niche shopper makes an average of 9.2 visits, which is greater than the basic shopper but lower than the enthusiast. The key characteristic of this type of shopper is that 40 per cent of their serious visits are made to small sized booths. The niche shopper prefers to work with specialty exhibitors who do not have a big presence at the show.
The brand shopper (17%)	Brand shoppers make about 10 serious visits and show the highest high preference for large booths. Their plan for the booths attended is also the highest, reflecting their need to plan and make their visit to the show as efficient as possible.
The apathetic shopper (11%)	Only 33 per cent of the apathetic shopper's booth visits are planned. They also prefer booths that are open on three sides, and which have a wide selection of products. The suggestion is that apathetic shoppers might represent 'newcomers' or attendees who are unfamiliar with the trade show.

Source: Gopalakrishna *et al.*, (2010). Used with permission

Perhaps above all else, trades shows and exhibitions play a major role in the development of relationships.

Digital media and trade shows

In many ways the use of a website as brochureware represented a first attempt at an online exhibition. In these situations, commercial organisations provided opportunities for people who physically could not get to see a product to gain some appreciation of its size, configuration and capability (through text).

Online trade shows are web-based platforms enabling manufacturers, suppliers and distributors an opportunity to exchange information, virtually. This facilitates speed, convenience and cost factors that influence small and medium sized organisations. As noted by Geigenmüller (2010), online show visitors can call on virtual halls and booths to obtain information about a firm's products and its services. Interaction between buyers and sellers occurs through chat rooms or video conferences, and forums. Online diaries or blogs are also used to discuss issues or leave messages for other participants.

However, the development of multimedia technologies has given not only commercial but also not-for-profit organisations the opportunity to showcase their wares on a global basis. One type of organisation to explore the use of this technology has been museums and art collections (static exhibits). Khoon *et al.* (2003) refer to the American History Documents (at www.indiana.edu/liblilly/histy/), Exploring Africa (at www.sc.edu/library/spcoll/sccoll/africa) and SCRAN (at www.scran.ac.uk) (which is a multimedia resource for Scottish history and culture) as examples of previous work and facilities in this area.

The use of multimedia technologies enables audiences across the world to access these collections and with the use of audio, video clips and streaming video, in addition to pictures and extensive text, these exhibitions can be brought to life, visited repeatedly, focus given to particular exhibits, materials updated quickly and unobtrusively, and links made to other similar facilities. The key difference between this development and previous brochureware-type facilities is the feeling of virtual reality, the sense that a digital visitor is actually in the exhibition, even though seated several thousand miles away.

The use of ecommerce and digital media in the management and presentation of exhibitions is increasing. It is unlikely that online exhibitions will ever replace the offline, real-world version, if only because of the need to form relationships and to network with industry members, to touch and feel products and to sense the atmosphere and vitality that exhibitions generate. However, there is huge scope to develop specialised exhibitions, online showcases that incorporate exhibits (products and services) from a variety of geographically dispersed locations.

Marketing management of exhibitions

Good management of exhibitions represents some key aspects of marketing communications in general. Successful events are driven by planning that takes place prior to the exhibition, with communications inviting a range of stakeholders, not just customers, in advance of the exhibition event. Stands should be designed to deliver key messages and press releases and press information packs should be prepared and distributed appropriately.

During the event itself staff should be well briefed, trained and knowledgeable about their role in terms of the brand and in the exhibition process. After the exhibition it is vital to follow up on contacts made and discussions or negotiations that have been held. In other words, the exhibition itself is a planned marketing communications activity, one where activities need to be planned prior to, during and after the event. What is key is that these activities are coordinated, themed and supported by brand-oriented staff.

Above all else, exhibitions are an important way of building relationships and signalling corporate identity. Trade shows are an important means of providing corporate hospitality and showing gratitude to all an organisation's customers, but in particular to its key account customers and others of strategic interest. Positive relationships with customers, competitors and suppliers are often reinforced through face-to-face dialogue that happens both formally in the exhibition hall and informally through the variety of social activities that surround and support these events.

Product placement

One way of overcoming the irritation factor associated with advertisements screened in cinemas prior to a film showing is to incorporate the product in the film that is shown. This practice is referred to as product placement, which is the inclusion of products and services in films (or media) for deliberate promotional exposure, often, but not always, in return for an agreed financial sum. It is regarded by some as a form of sales promotion, by others as sponsorship, but for the purposes of this text it is treated as an advertising medium because the 'advertiser' pays a third party for the opportunity to present the product in their channel.

A wide variety of products can be placed in this way, including drinks (both soft and alcoholic), cameras, laptops, confectionery, newspapers, cars, airlines, perfume and even holiday destinations and sports equipment. However, the development of product placement has inevitably led to new formats and fresh approaches, some of which only serve to muddy the waters.

Hudson and Hudson (2006) set out the development of product placement. Early forms of product placement concerned brand owners making deals with film producers and film stars to openly endorse the brand. The brand owner would fund props and facilities for the film in return for spoken and visual endorsement. Some of the first television programmes were named after the brands that sponsored them, for example, *The Colgate Comedy Hour* and the *Kraft Television Theatre* (Hudson and Hudson, 2006).

The establishment of product placement agencies in the 1980s helped formalise the process and removed much of the barter and haggling that had typified arrangements. The turning point occurred when the film *ET* depicted an alien being lured by Reese's Pieces. Hershey, the manufacturer, saw sales rise 65 per cent following the release of the film and since then product placement has grown year on year.

Two distinct forms of product placement-related activity have emerged, partly as a result of the proliferation of the media, the consequential surge in the production of entertainment programmes, and the media industry's need to generate income streams. Rather than place a product within a film, television or radio programme where it assumes a passive role, hoping to get noticed, a new approach sees entire entertainment programmes built around a single product. In contrast to the passivity of product placement, here a brand is actively woven into the theme or the plot of the programme. This latter approach has been labelled 'branded entertainment'. Hudson and Hudson (2006) depict this as a continuum, represented in Figure 12.2.

Hackley and Tiwsakul (2006) suggest the term 'entertainment marketing'. They believe the term reflects the diversity of ways in which brands are inserted into entertainment vehicles. This perspective subsumes product placement and incorporates celebrity endorsement and sponsorship, elements discussed elsewhere in this book.

Characteristics of product placement

Strengths

By presenting the product as part of the film, not only is it possible to build awareness, but source credibility can be improved significantly and brand images reinforced. The audience is assisted to identify and associate itself with the environment depicted in the film or with the celebrity who is using the product.

Levels of impact can be very high, as cinema audiences are very attentive to large-screen presentations. Rates of exposure can be high, particularly now that cinema films are being released through video outlets, satellite and various new regional cable and television organisations.

Perhaps the major advantage is that the majority of audiences appear to approve of this form of marketing communications, if only because it is unobtrusive and integral to the film (Nebenzahl and Secunda, 1993).

Weaknesses

Having achieved a placement in a film (video, television or radio programme) there is still a risk that the product will run unnoticed, especially if the placements coincide with distracting or action-oriented parts of the film. Associated with this is the lack of control the advertiser has over when, where and how the product will be presented. If the product is noticed, a small minority of audiences claim that this form of communication is unethical; it is even suggested that it is subliminal advertising, which is, of course, illegal. The absolute costs of product placement in films can be extremely high, counteracting the low relative costs or cost per contact. The final major drawback concerning this form of communication concerns its inability to provide explanation, detail, or indeed any substantive information about the product. The product is seen in use and is hopefully associated with an event, person(s) or objects that provide a source of pleasure, inspiration or aspiration for the individual viewer.

Viewpoint 12.5   Entertaining placement

Product placement originated in television shows, progressed into films and has now been utilised in other media and entertainment vehicles. The music industry for example has been looking for new income streams as illegal downloading fails to abate. Product placement in promotional videos is a partial solution. For example, Lady Gaga and Beyonce made a nine-minute long promotional video to support their collaborative single, 'Telephone'. Placements include state of the art LG handsets, the Virgin Mobile network, Diet Coke cans, an HP Envy laptop, and the website for dating agency 'PlentyofFish' is featured.

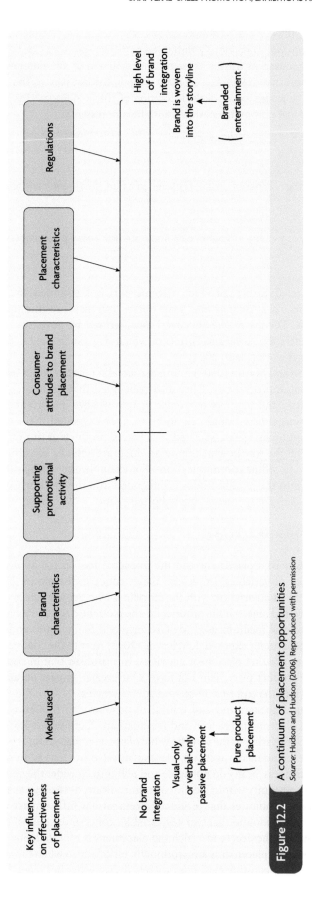

Figure 12.2   A continuum of placement opportunities
Source: Hudson and Hudson (2006). Reproduced with permission

The hit tv show, *American Idol* works closely with three particular sponsors, Coca Cola, Ford and AT&T. In 2009 Apple became the fourth sponsor. As a result these brands feature in or make maximum use of their association with the show. Nielsen report that Coke achieved 2,000 views in the last season. This was through the placement of Coke cups in front of the judges, plus Coke's decoration of the 'Red Room'. The show can only be accessed through iTunes, whilst Ford make promotional videos with the contestants.

Source: Based on various including Utalk (2010); Pemberton (2010); Dawn and Block (2009); Jones (2010)

Question

Should there be a limit on the number of products placed in a film, if so, how many and why?

Task

Watch a film or television programme of your choice and note how many placements have been made.

As indicated earlier, product placement is not confined to cinema films. Music videos, television plays, dramas and soap operas can also use this method to present advertisers' products. The novel *The Sweetest Taboo*, written by novelist Carole Matthews, includes frequent references to various Ford cars, which is not surprising as Ford paid her to mention their cars in her work (Plaut, 2004).

Pervan and Martin (2002) found that product placement in television soaps was an effective communications activity. They also concluded that the way a product is used in the soap, i.e. positive and negative outcomes, may well have important implications for the attitudes held towards these brands. In addition, they suggested that organisations should study the consumption imagery associated with placed products as this might yield significant information about the way in which these products are actually consumed. Product placement is not confined to offline communications. For example, the toothpaste brand Pearl Drops has been written into the plotline and was integrated into the social network Bebo's interactive drama called *Sofia's Diary*, a teen-targeted programme.

Placement Issues

The nature of a placement and the impact it has on the audience appear to be affected by a number of variables. Important issues concern: the nature of the placement (Sung *et al.*, 2009) and its association with the storyline; whether the actors use the product or it remains a background object; if the product fits the plot; the degree to which the product is prominently displayed; the medium used (de Gregorio and Sung, 2009) and the amount of time that the product is actually exposed. Karrh *et al.* (2003) refer to the relative lack of control that marketers have over product placement activities, but confirm that in comparison to advertising equivalents, product placement can have a far greater impact on audiences and in most cases at a fraction of the cost of a 30-second advertisement.

Cultural background and ethical disposition can influence an audience's perception of product placements (Nelson and Devanathan, 2006) whilst Russell and Belch (2005) refer to difficulties relating to the way the value of product placement is perceived. There is a view, held by creative and media agencies, that the 'number of seconds on screen' is a valid measurement of effectiveness. Many do not agree and prefer to consider the context of the placement and the level of continuity within a defined communications strategy as more meaningful measures.

Research indicates that product placement has little impact on changing brand attitudes. Homer (2009) found that two key variables concern the type of placement (subtle versus prominent) and the degree to which the placement is repeated. She finds that brand attitudes fall when product placements are prominent, especially so when they are repeated. When the placement is subtle consumer attitudes are relatively positive but repeated exposures have little impact.

Summary

In order to help consolidate your understanding of sales promotions, exhibitions and product placement, here are the key points summarised against each of the learning objectives:

1 Discuss the nature, types and role of sales promotions

Sales promotion offers buyers additional value, as an inducement to generate an immediate sale. These inducements can be targeted at consumers, distributors, agents and members of the sales force. Sales promotions used by resellers (largely retailers) to influence consumers are normally driven by manufacturers, although some price deals and other techniques are used to generate store traffic.

2 Explain how sales promotions can be used strategically in the communications mix

Sales promotions have a strategic role to play, particularly when they are used to complement the other activities in the promotional mix. By attempting to develop a consistent theme to a promotional plan, sales promotions can follow advertising's awareness-building activities with a series of messages that continue the theme already established.

3 Describe the various sales promotion methods and techniques

Sales promotions used by manufacturers to communicate with resellers are aimed at encouraging resellers to either try new products or purchase more of the ones they currently stock. To do this, trade allowances, in various guises, are the principal means. The majority of sales promotions are those used by manufacturers to influence consumers. Again, the main tasks are to encourage trial or increase product purchase. A range of techniques, from sampling and coupons to premiums, contests and sweepstakes, are all used with varying levels of success, but there has been a distinct shift away from traditional promotional instruments to the use of digital media in order to reflect consumer's preferences and media behaviour.

4 Explain the characteristics and significance of exhibitions and trade shows

The main reasons for attending exhibitions and trade fairs are that: it enables organisations to meet customers (and potential customers) in an agreeable environment, one where both have independently volunteered their time to attend; to place/take orders; to generate leads; and to gather market information.

5 Consider the role of exhibitions in the marketing communications mix

As a form of marketing communications, exhibitions enable products to be promoted, they can build brands and they can be an effective means of demonstrating products and building industry-wide credibility in a relatively short period of time. Positive relationships with customers, competitors and suppliers are often reinforced through face-to-face dialogue that happens both formally in the exhibition hall and informally through the variety of social activities that surround and support these events.

6 Understand the concepts and issues associated with product placement

Product placement is the inclusion of products and services in films (or media) for deliberate promotional exposure, often, but not always, in return for an agreed financial sum. It is regarded by some as a form of sales promotion, by others as sponsorship, but the most common linkage is with advertising, because the 'advertiser' pays a third party for the opportunity to present the product in their channel.

There are distinct forms of product placement. One involves the passive placement of a product within the media; the other sees whole entertainment programmes built around a single product, one where it is actively woven into the theme or the plot of the programme. This is known as 'branded entertainment'.

Review questions

1. Why do organisations use sales promotion and why has sales promotion assumed such a large share of promotional expenditure?

2. How might use of technology assist the development of loyalty and retention programmes?

3. List the main sales promotion methods used by manufacturers and targeted at consumers. How can coupons be used to reduce levels of buyer perceived risk?

4. Explain the objectives that manufacturers might have when encouraging resellers to take stock of more product.

5. How would you advise a newly appointed assistant brand manager on the expected outcomes of a sales promotion programme? (Choose any sector/industry of your choice.) Suggest four ways in which sales promotions can be evaluated.

6. Evaluate the differences between exhibitions and trade shows.

7. As sales manager for a company making plastic mouldings for use in the manufacture of consumer durables, set out the reasons for and against attendance at trade shows and exhibitions, as an exhibitor and as a visitor.

8. Write brief notes explaining the role exhibitions might play in a company's integrated marketing communications strategy.

9. Name two strengths and two weaknesses of product placement.

10. Identify four examples of product placement. Evaluate their effectiveness.

References

Advertising Association (2008) *Advertising Statistics YearBook 2008*. Henley on Thames: Advertising Association.

Anon (2009) Drench Juicy field marketing launch campaign, Utalk, 14 September. Retrieved 8 July 2010 from www.utalkmarketing.com/Pages/Article.aspx?

Barrand, D. (2004) Promoting change, *Marketing*, 6 October, 43–45.

Benady, D. (2009) Brands struggle to kick the sales promotion habit, *Marketing*, 11 December. Retrieved 13 July 2010 from www.brandrepublic.com/news

Bertheron, P., Pitt, L.F. and Watson, R.T. (1996) The World Wide Web as an advertising medium, *Journal of Advertising Research*, 6(1) (January/February), 43–54.

Blattberg, R.C. and Neslin, S.A. (1990) *Sales Promotion: Concepts, Methods and Strategies*. Englewood Cliffs, NJ: Prentice-Hall.

Boukersi, L. (2000) The role of trade fairs and exhibitions in international marketing communications, in *The Handbook of International Marketing Communications* (ed. S. Moyne). London: Blackwell, 117–135.

Bristow, M. (2010) Grand ambitions at Beijing car show, BBC News, 27 April 2010. Retrieved 14 July 2010 from www.news.bbc.co.uk/1/hi/8644730.stm

Curtis, J. (1996) Opposites attract, *Marketing*, 25 April, 28–29.

Davis, M. (1992) Sales promotions as a competitive strategy, *Management Decision*, 30(7), 5–10.

Dawn, R. and Block, A.B. (2009) Brands Take the 'American Idol' Stage, Billboard.com. Retrieved 31 March 2010 from www.adweek.com/aw/content_display/news/strategy/

de Gregorio, F. and Sung, Y. (2009) Giving a shout to Seagram's gin: extent of and attitudes towards brands in popular songs, *Journal of Brand Management*, 17(3), 218–235.

Galea, C. (2007) Show me the money: maximizing your trade show investment, available at: managesmarter.com. Accessed 20 September 2007.

Geigenmüller, A. (2010) The role of virtual trade fairs in relationship value creation, *Journal of Business and Industrial Marketing*, 25(4), 284–292.

Gopalakrishna, S., Roster, C.A. and Sridhar, S. (2010) An exploratory study of attendee activities at a business trade show, *Journal of Business & Industrial Marketing*, 25(4), 241–248.

Gilbert, D.C. and Jackaria, N. (2002) The efficacy of sales promotions in UK supermarkets: a consumer view, *International Journal of Retail & Distribution Management*, 30(6), 325–332.

Gupta, S. (1998) Impact of sales promotions on when, what and how much we buy, *Journal of Marketing Research*, 25(4), 342–355.

Hackley, C. and Tiwsakul, R. (2006) Entertainment marketing and experiential consumption 1, *Journal of Marketing Communications*, 12(1) (March), 63–75.

Homer, P.M. (2009) The Impact of Placement Type and Repetition on Attitude, *Journal of Advertising*, 38(3) (Fall), 21–31.

Hudson, S. and Hudson, D. (2006) Branded entertainment: a new advertising technique or product placement in disguise? *Journal of Marketing Management*, 22(5/6), 489–504.

Jones, L. (2010) Lady Gaga and Beyoncé's sexy music video 'Telephone' is trending on Twitter. What a surprise, *The Daily Telegraph*, 12 March. Retrieved 5 April 2010 from http://blogs. telegraph.co.uk/culture/lucyjones/100007056/lady-gaga-and-beyonce%E2%80%99s-sexy-music-video-telephone-is-trending-on-twitter-what-a-surprise/

Karrh, J.A., McKee, K.B., Britain, K. and Pardun, C.J. (2003) Practitioners' evolving views of product placement effectiveness, *Journal of Advertising Research*, 43(2) (June), 138–150.

Krishna, A. and Zhang, Z.J. (1999) Short or long duration coupons: the effect of the expiration date on the probability of coupon promotions. *Management Science*, 45(8), 1041–1057.

Lee, C.H. (2002) Sales promotions as strategic communication: the case of Singapore, *The Journal of Product and Brand Management*, 11(2), 103–114.

Li, L.Y. (2007) 'Marketing resources and performance of exhibitor firms in trade shows: a contingent resource perspective', *Industrial Marketing Management*, 36, 360–370.

Madden, N. (2010) Taking a spin around the China auto show, *Advertising Age*, 81(18), 17.

Nebenzahl, I.D. and Secunda, E. (1993) Consumer attitudes toward product placement in movies, *International Journal of Advertising*, 12, 1–11.

Nelson, M.R. and Devavathan, N. (2006) Brand placements, Bollywood style, *Journal of Consumer Behaviour*, 5(3), 211–221.

O'Malley, L. (1998) Can loyalty schemes really build loyalty? *Marketing Intelligence and Planning*, 16(1), 47–55.

Papatia, P. and Krishnamurthi, L. (1996) Measuring the dynamic effects of promotions on brand choice, *Journal of Marketing Research*, 33(1) (February), 20–35.

Peattie, S. and Peattie, K.J. (1994) Sales promotion, in *The Marketing Book* (ed. M.J. Baker), 3rd edn. London: Butterworth-Heinemann.

Pemberton, A. (2010) Is Lady Gaga's Video For 'Telephone' Just One Big Ad?, 23 March. Retrieved 30 March 2010 from www.new.music.yahoo.com/blogs/musictoob/

Pervan, S.J. and Martin, B.A.S. (2002) Product placement in US and New Zealand television soap operas: an exploratory study, *Journal of Marketing Communications*, 8, 101–113.

Plaut, M. (2004) Ford advertises the literary way, *BBC News/Business*. Retrieved 20 March 2008 from http://news.bbc.co.uk/1/hi/business/3522635.stm.

Porter, M.E. (1980) *Competitive Strategy: Techniques for Analyzing Industries and Companies*. New York: Free Press.

Russell, C.A. and Belch, M. (2005) A managerial investigation into the product placement industry, *Journal of Advertising Research*, 45(1) (March), 73–92.

Shipley, D. and Wong, K.S. (1993) Exhibiting strategy and implementation, *International Journal of Advertising*, 12(2), 117–130.

Sung, Y., de Gregorio, F. and Jung, J. (2009) Non-students consumer attitudes towards product placement: Implications for public policy and advertisers, *International Journal of Advertising*, 28(2), 257–285.

Utalk (2007) How direct mail boosted Tourism Ireland's conference market. Retrieved 4 January 2008 from www.utalkmarketing.com/pages/article.aspx?

Utalk (2010) Lady Gaga abnd Beyonce 'Telephone' video is a brand showcase. Retrieved 30 March 2010 from www.utalkmarketing.com

Wallace, C. (2010) Trident has Beyonce fans chewing up, *PR Week*, 15 April. Retrieved 13 July 2010 from www.brandrepublic.com/news

Wheeler, M. and Fermer, I. (2009) Who would be a sales director? *Warc Exclusive* (May). Retrieved 9 July 2010 from www.warc.com

Wilde, C. (2009) Cadbury Digestive's free personalised mug promotion, Promotions and Incentives, 2 October. Retrieved 13 July 2010 from www.brandrepublic.com/news/

Chapter 13
Media: conventional and digital

The use of media is required in order that content is delivered to, and conversations enabled, with specific audiences. The array of available media is continually growing. Each has strengths and weaknesses that impact the quality, effectiveness and the meaning attributed to a message by an audience. This chapter focuses on the nature and characteristics of both conventional, offline and contemporary, digital media.

Aims and learning objectives

The aim of this chapter is to establish the principal characteristics of each type of conventional and digital media. This will assist understanding of the management processes by which media are selected and scheduled to deliver advertiser's messages.

The learning objectives of this chapter are to:

1. determine the broad types of available media and classify them;
2. explain the main criteria used to evaluate media and their use;
3. examine the characteristics associated with each class of media;
4. describe the range of features available through the use of digital media;
5. explain the key differences between conventional and digital media;
6. explore some of the principles and issues associated with media planning.

Introduction

Organisations use a variety of media in order that they can deliver their planned messages and in many cases, listen to and interact with target audiences. This chapter considers the characteristics of both conventional and digital media and how they enable marketing communications. Although this chapter considers offline and digital media separately, in reality they should be used in an integrated way. It closes with a consideration of media planning concepts and approaches. The following chapter explores different digital media applications, as interactive marketing communications. Therefore, Chapters 13 and 14 contain a high level of complementary material and should be read together.

In order to understand the array of media it is helpful to categorise them. Six main *classes* of media can be identified. These are broadcast, print, outdoor, digital, in-store and other media classes. Within each of these classes there are particular *types* of media. For example, within the broadcast class there are television and radio, and within the print class there are newspapers and magazines.

Within each type of medium there are a huge number of independent media *vehicles* that can be selected to carry an advertiser's message. For example, within UK television there are the terrestrial networks (Independent Television Network, Channel 4 and Channel 5) and the satellite (BSkyB) and cable (e.g. Virgin Media) networks. In print, there are consumer and business-oriented magazines and the number of specialist magazines is expanding rapidly. These specialist magazines are targeted at particular activity and interest groups, such as *Amateur Photographer*, *Golf World* and the infamous *Sponge Divers Gazette*! This provides opportunities for advertisers to send messages to well-defined homogeneous groups, which improves effectiveness and reduces wastage in communication spend. Table 13.1 sets out the three categories of media – classes, types and vehicles – with a few examples.

Table 13.1	Summary chart of the main forms of media	
Class	**Type**	**Vehicles**
Broadcast	Television	*Coronation Street, X Factor*
	Radio	Virgin Radio, Classic FM
Print	Newspapers	The *Sunday Times, The Mirror, The Daily Telegraph,*
	Magazines: Consumer	*Cosmopolitan, Woman, The Grocer, Plumbing News*
	Business	
Outdoor	Billboards	96-, 48- and 6-sheet
	Street furniture	Adshel
	Transit	London Underground, airport buildings, taxis, hot-air balloons
Digital media	Internet	Websites, email, intranets
	Digital television	Teletext, SkyText
	CD-ROM	Various including music, educational, entertainment
In-store	Point-of-purchase	Bins, signs and displays
	Packaging	The Coca-Cola contour bottle
Other	Cinema	Pearl & Dean
	Exhibitions	Ideal Home, The Motor Show
	Product placement	Films, TV, books
	Ambient	Litter bins, golf tees, petrol pumps
	Guerrilla	Flyposting

Evaluative criteria

One of the key marketing tasks is to decide which combination of vehicles should be selected to carry the message to the target audience. First, however, it is necessary to consider the main characteristics of each type of media in order that media planning decisions can be based on some logic and rationale. The fundamental characteristics concern the costs, the richness of the communication, the interactive properties and audience profile associated with a communication event.

Costs

One of the important characteristics that need to be considered is the costs that are incurred using each type of medium. There are two types of cost: absolute and relative. Absolute costs are the costs of the time or space bought in a particular media vehicle. These costs have to be paid for and directly impact upon an organisation's cash flow. Relative costs are the costs of contacting each member of the target audience. Television, as will be seen later, has a high absolute cost but, because messages are delivered to a mass audience, when the absolute cost is divided by the total number of people receiving the message the relative cost is very low.

Communication richness

The way in which a message is delivered and understood by a target audience varies across types of media. Certain media, such as television, are able to use many communication dimensions, and through the use of sight, sound and movement can generate great impact with a message. Other types of media have only one dimension, such as the audio capacity of radio or the written word on a page of text. The number of communication dimensions that a media type has will influence the choice of media mix. This is because certain products, at particular points in their development, require the use of different media in order that the right message be conveyed and understood. A new product, for example, may require demonstration in order that the audience understands the product concept. The use of television may be a good way of achieving this. Once understood, the audience does not need to be educated in this way again and future messages need to convey different types of information that may not require demonstration, so radio, magazine or web-based advertising may suffice.

Interactive properties

Following on from the previous element is the important issue of interactive communications. The development of digital media has enabled interaction, which we know can lead to dialogue, and this in turn enables relationship development (Ballantyne, 2004). However, there are some circumstances in which interaction is not required due to the nature of the market, the product or the objectives of the campaign. In these circumstances the mix will need to consist of media that, primarily, deliver messages through one-way, mass communication.

Marketing communications that seek to engage audiences through behaviour, usually as a call-to-action, will need to use media that enable interaction and where support facilities are in place to facilitate interactive communications.

Audience profile

The profile of the target audience (male, female, young or old) and the number of people within each audience that a media type can reach are also significant factors in media decisions. For example, 30 per cent of adults in the socioeconomic grade A read the *Sunday Times*. Only 4 per cent of the C2 group also read this paper. Messages appropriate to the A group would be best placed in the *Sunday Times* and those for the C2 group transmitted through the *News of the World*, which 34 per cent of the C2 group read. The same approach applies to websites, television programmes and magazines. It is important that advertisers use media vehicles that convey their messages to their target markets with as little waste as possible.

Newspapers enable geographically dispersed audiences to be reached. The tone of their content can be controlled, but the cost per target reached is high. Each issue has a short lifespan, so for positive learning to occur in the target audience a number of insertions may be required.

A large number of magazines contain specialised material that appeals to particular target groups. These special-interest magazines (SIMs) enable certain sponsors to reach interested targets with reduced wastage. General-interest magazines (GIMs) appeal to a much wider cross-section of society, to larger generalised target groups. The life of these media vehicles is generally long and their 'pass along' readership high. It should not be forgotten, however, that noise levels can also be high owing to the intermittent manner in which magazines are often read and the number of competing messages from rival organisations.

Television reaches the greatest number of people, but although advertisers can reach general groups, such as men aged 16–24 or housewives, it is not capable of reaching specific interest groups and it incurs high levels of wastage. This blanket coverage offers opportunities for cable and satellite operators to offer more precise targeting, but for now television is a tool for those who wish to talk to mass audiences. Television is expensive from a cash-flow perspective but not in terms of the costs per target reached.

Radio offers a more reasonable costing structure than television and can be utilised to reach particular geographic audiences. For a long time, however, this was seen as its only real strength, particularly when its poor attention span and non-visual dimensions are considered. Although radio will never overtake television in terms of usage and overall popularity, radio has been shown to be capable of generating a much closer personal relationship with listeners, witnessed partly by the success of Classic FM and local radio stations, than is possible through posters, television or print.

The interesting point about outdoor and transit advertising is that exposure is only made by the interception of passing traffic. Many years ago Govoni *et al.* (1986) made the point that interception represents opportunistic coverage. Consequently the costs are low, at both investment and per contact levels.

The idea that messages implanted into media which then intercepts and interrupts the behaviour of an audience, is outdated. Although this represents the best use of old technology, today participation is key to engaging audiences. Digital media enables individuals to participate in conversations at times and places that are convenient to them, not the owners of brands.

Conventional media

Print media

Of the total amount spent on advertising, across all media, most is spent on the printed word. Newspapers and magazines are the two main types of media in this class. They attract advertisers for a variety of reasons, but the most important is that print media are very effective at delivering a message to a target audience.

Print media are most suitable for messages designed when high involvement is present in the target market. These readers not only control the pace at which they read (and reread) a magazine or newspaper, but also expend effort to read advertisements because they care about particular issues.

Magazines can be considered in terms of their intended markets, for example, consumer and business magazines. These can be refined to reach quite specialised audiences and tend to be selective in terms of the messages they carry. In contrast, newspapers reach a high percentage of the population and can be referred to as a mass medium. The messages that newspapers carry are usually for products and services that have a general appeal.

Customer magazines differ from consumer magazines because they are sent to customers direct, often without charge, and contain highly targeted and significant brand-related material. These have made a big impact in recent years and, partly because of high production values, have become a significant aspect of many direct marketing activities. In the summer of 2010, Virgin announced the launch of their new consumer magazine, *Maverick*. This is an interesting name in the light of Virgin's challenger brand strategy.

Viewpoint 13.1   Catalogues, magalogues and inspiration

When Bang & Olufsen, the leading edge design and production electronics brand, decided to publish a catalogue, a decision was made to split the biannual publication into two sections, half catalogue, and half branded content and editorial material.

Marks & Spencer's 'Home' catalogue and mini-books enable the company to present its entire range, something not possible in the limited space available in the retail stores. The 300+ page publication seeks to provide not only a visual list of all the products but it is also regarded as a means for providing inspiration and ideas.

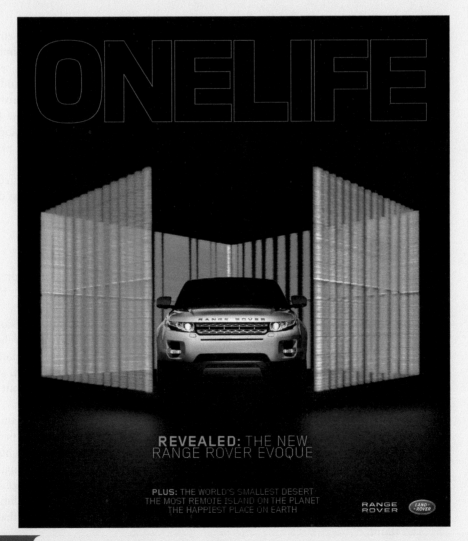

Exhibit 13.1   Land Rover's *OneLife* customer magazine
Image courtesy of Land Rover

Some organisations now use both print and e-magazines. For example, McLuhan (2010) refers to Mazda, who have been publishing *Zoom Zoom* since 2007. They have recently launched an e-zine, partly in response to the increasing number of pictures people are submitting of their own cars. The hard copy magazine does not have the capacity to accommodate them. The e-zines do, are relatively cost effective and are sent via email, containing embedded video material. These are updated regularly and are delivered at the same time as delivery of the print magazine.

Source: Based on Bashford (2010): McLuhan (2010)

Question

Why do you think print media are so effective in this context?

Task

Get a copy of any customer magazine sent direct to a household, and compare the content with a consumer magazine bought off the shelf of a retail store.

Catalogues continue to provide a route to market, despite online buying and environmental concerns. It appears that a printed catalogue can provide reassurance and imbue a brand with a sense of trust. Bashford (2010) reports research that shows that 45 per cent of people consult a printed catalogue prior to buying expensive and hence higher risk products, online. There is a trend to publish catalogues not just for product listing but also to provide branded content and editorial. These have been termed 'magalogues' and can increase the time the publication remains active in a household, referred to as dwell time. Magalogues provide a point of integration as the offline vehicle provides a point of group discussion prior to online purchase.

Directories are a form of print media and advertising expenditure has continued to increase. One of the largest consumer directories is Yell, and they have diversified across digital media formats, for example, Yell.com.

Broadcast media

Fundamentally, there are two main forms of broadcast media, television and radio. Advertisers use this class of media because it can reach mass audiences with their messages at a relatively low cost per target reached.

Approximately 99 per cent of the UK population has access to a television set and a similar number have a radio. The majority of viewers use television passively, as a form of entertainment. However, digitisation indicates that television has the potential to be used proactively for a range of services, such as banking and shopping as well as interactive advertising. Radio demands active participation, but can reach people who are out of the home environment.

Broadcast media allow advertisers to add visual and/or sound dimensions to their messages. The opportunity to demonstrate or to show the benefits or results that a particular product can bring gives life and energy to an advertiser's message. Television uses sight, sound and movement, whereas radio can only use its audio capacity to convey meaning, but it does stimulate a listener's imagination and thus can involve audiences in a message. Both media have the potential to tell stories and to appeal to people's emotions. These are dimensions that print media find difficulty in achieving effectively within the time allocations that advertisers can afford.

The costs associated with radio transmissions are relatively low when compared with television. This reflects the lack of prestige that radio has and the pervasiveness of television.

People are normally unable, and usually unwilling, to become actively involved with broadcast advertising messages. They cannot control the pace at which they consume such advertising and as time is expensive and short, so advertisers do not have the opportunity to present detailed information. The result is that this medium is most suitable for low-involvement messages. Where the need for elaboration is low and the peripheral processing route is preferred, messages transmitted through electronic media should seek to draw attention, create awareness and improve levels of interest.

As the television and radio industries become increasingly fragmented, so the ability to reach particular market segments has become more difficult, as the target audience is often dispersed across other media. This means that the potential effectiveness of advertising through these media decreases. These media are used a great deal in consumer markets, mainly because of their ability to reach large audiences, but there is often considerable wastage and inefficiency. The result is that advertisers are moving their advertising spend to other media, most notably, online.

Outdoor media

Outdoor media consist of three main formats: street furniture (such as bus shelters); billboards (consisting primarily of 96-, 48- and 6-sheet poster sites); and Transit (which covers the Underground, buses and taxis).

The range of outdoor media encompasses a large number of different media, each characterised by two elements. First, they can be observed at locations away from home. For this reason some refer to this medium as 'out-of-home'. Second, they are normally used to support messages that are transmitted through primary media: broadcast and print. Outdoor media can therefore, be seen to be a secondary but important support media for a complementary and effective communications mix.

Viewpoint 13.2   A laddering brand

The use of large or intriguing outdoor media simply to attract the attention of passers-by is a technique that has been employed by advertisers over the years. One of the more noticeable advertisers in recent years has been hosiery manufacturer Pretty Polly. In 2007, the brand wanted to stir a little bit of controversy and at the same time re-establish its credentials as a fashion brand for women.

Using an internationally recognised fashion photographer (Georges Antoni) they developed an eye-catching image of a model's long legs on a ladder. Referred to as 'Stairway to Heaven', the image was used in a variety of places: website, buses, billboards, in-store, through direct marketing and to support retailers.

In order to attract real media attention the image was placed on a temporary 64-ft high tower that was placed on the Chiswick Tower roundabout, a very busy traffic route to the west of London. The stunt achieved placement in several London newspapers, three national women's magazines, one national newspaper and several fashion websites.

Source: Based on Cowlett (2007)

Question

Is the use of this type of outdoor media likely to cause accidents rather than promote brand recall?

Task

Choose a brand and think of interesting ways in which outdoor media might be used to attract attention.

Exhibit 13.2 'Stairway to Heaven'
Image courtesy of Pretty Polly

Other reasons for the growth in outdoor expenditure are that it can reinforce messages transmitted through primary media, act as a substitute media when primary media are unavailable (e.g. tobacco organisations deprived of access to television and radio) and provide novelty and interest (electronic, inflatable and three-dimensional billboards), which can help avoid the clutter caused by the volume of advertising activity.

In-store media

As an increasing number of brand choice decisions are made during the shopping experience, advertisers have become aware of the need to provide suitable in-store communications. The primary objective of using in-store media is to direct the attention of shoppers and to stimulate them to make purchases. The content of messages can be easily controlled by either the retailer or the manufacturer. In addition, the timing and the exact placement of in-store messages can be equally well controlled.

As mentioned previously, both retailers and manufacturers make use of in-store media although, of the two main forms (point-of-purchase displays and packaging), retailers control the point-of-purchase displays and manufacturers the packaging. Increasingly, there is recognition of the huge potential of retail stores becoming an integrated media centre, with retailers selling and managing media space and time.

Decisions made at the point of purchase, especially those in the FMCG sector, often require buyers to build awareness through recognition. The design of packages and wrappers is important, as continuity of design, combined with the power to attract and hold the attention of prospective buyers, is a vital part of point-of-purchase activity.

There are a number of dimensions that can affect the power and utility of a package. Colour is influential, as the context of the product class can frame the purchase situation for a buyer. This means that colours should be appropriate to the product class, to the brand and to the prevailing culture if marketing overseas. The shape of the packaging can be a strong form of persuasion. Verebelyi (2000) suggests that this influence may be due to the decorative impact of some brands. The supreme example of this is the Coca-Cola contour bottle, with its unique shape and immediate power for brand recognition at the point of purchase (see Exhibit 13.3). The shape may also provide information about how to open and use the product, while some packages can be used after the product has been consumed for other purposes.

In certain markets packaging can be strategically important as it can affect positioning. Ampuero and Vial (2006) identify colour, typography, graphical forms and images as the key packaging variables from a design perspective. They then consider how these combine to

Exhibit 13.3	The Coca-Cola bottle
	The unique contours of the Coca-Cola bottle provide instant brand recognition.
	Image courtesy of Alamy Images

produce optimum positioning conditions. They conclude that dark-coloured cold packaging, which shows the product, is perceived to be associated with offerings that are elegant and expensive. The packaging for products targeted at customers for whom a low price is important should be light-coloured and show illustrations of people.

Retail media centres

Traditionally retailers allow their stores to be used in a variety of ways by a variety of organisations to communicate messages to their audiences. These audiences are jointly owned, not necessarily in equal proportion, by the branded food manufacturers that use stores for distribution purposes, and the retailers that try to build footfall or store traffic through retail branding approaches. As a result, the management of the media opportunities and the messages that are communicated are uncoordinated, inconsistent and the media potential, to a large extent, ignored. In the past, retailers will have argued that their core business rests with retailing, not selling and managing media. However, the media world has developed considerably in recent years, often in tandem with developments in technology. For a long time, retailers have built databases using customer information and developed sales promotion-based loyalty programmes as a result.

Cinema

The growth in cinema attendances in 2007 and 2009 has been linked to the increase in multiplex cinemas (multiple screens at each site) and, as Esposito reports, the appalling summer weather that drove many people into the cinema for their entertainment. Advertisers have followed the crowds but have also listened to the research that shows that cinema audiences remember more detail than television audiences and as a captive audience there are no distractions.

Advertising messages transmitted in a cinema have all the advantages of television-based messages. Audio and visual dimensions combine to provide high impact. However, the audience is more attentive because the main film has yet to be shown and there are fewer distractions or noise in the communication system. The implication is that cinema advertising has greater power than television advertisements. This power can be used to heighten levels of attention and, as the screen images are larger than life and because they appear in a darkened room that is largely unfamiliar to the audience, the potential to communicate effectively with the target audience is strong.

Viewpoint 13.3	Orange cinemas?

Orange are the only mobile operator to work with cinema (at the time of writing). In addition to their considerable £13.5 million spend on cinema advertising in 2007 they also sponsored the Bafta film awards. The reason for this activity is that the main cinema audience is the 16- to 34-year-old demographic and that matches Orange's target market. Interestingly they do not use cinema for product-based communications, but use the medium to develop a strong link between Orange and the cinema. Research indicates that Orange are perceived to be the number-one brand associated with film in the UK.

Mobile brand Orange has used a cinema campaign called 'The Film Board'. For several years 'The Film Board' has occupied the 'gold spot' – the last ad spot before the main feature film begins. The Board is a fictional panel, obsessed with product placement, who listen to famous people and celebrities pitch their ideas for movies. For example, John Cleese pitched his idea for a dramatic war film, but he is not taken seriously by the Board, who even get one of their executives to watch the pitch on their Orange 3G Mobile phone.

Source: Based on Esposito (2008); www.visit4info.com/details.cfm?adid 24648

Question

Although Orange have developed strong associations with cinema could it be said that they 'own the media' as they do not use the medium to promote products?

Task

Next time you visit the cinema make a note of the Film Board spot and consider how prominent Orange is.

Exhibit 13.4	A Vue Entertainment multiplex cinema
	Image courtesy of Vue Entertainment

Ambient media

Ambient media are a fairly recent innovation and represent a non-traditional alternative to outdoor media. Ambient media are regarded as out-of-home media that fail to fit any of the established outdoor categories. Ambient media can be classified according to a variety of factors, including standard posters, distribution, mobile posters, digital sponsorships and aerials. Of these, standard posters account for the vast majority of ambient activity (59 per cent) with distribution accounting for 24 per cent and the four remaining categories just 17 per cent.

Direct response media

The principal use of direct response media is to convey one of two types of message: one is oriented towards the development of brands and attitudes; the other is aimed at provoking a behavioural (and mental) response. It follows that attitude and response-based communications require different media.

Conventional media (television, print or radio) were once used just to develop brands and attitudes. Now they are used as a mechanism or device to provoke a response, through which consumers/buyers can follow up a message, enter into an immediate conversation and either request further information or purchase goods or services. The main difference with digital media is the time delay or response pause between receiving a message and acting on it. Through direct response mechanisms, the response may be delayed for as long as it takes to make a telephone call, press a button or fill out a reply coupon. However, the response pause and the use of a separate form of communication highlight the essential differences.

Estimates vary, but somewhere between 30 per cent and 40 per cent of all television advertisements now carry a telephone number or web address. Direct response television (DRTV) is attractive to those promoting service-based offerings and increasingly travel brands and some FMCG brands are using it. DRTV can be considered in terms of different levels of participation. Level 1 is viewing and engaging with a commercial message. Level 2 requires a respondent to phone or visit a website to collect more information and derive greater entertainment value. Only at Level 3 will there be an attempt to sell directly to the respondent. The main purpose for advertisers using this route is to extract personal information for the database in order to feed subsequent sales promotion and mailing activities.

One aspect that is crucial to the success of a direct response campaign is not the number of responses but the conversion of leads into sales. This means that the infrastructure to support these promotional activities must be thought through and put in place, otherwise the work and resources put into the visible level will be wasted if customers are unable to get the information they require – the provision of the infrastructure alone is not sufficient – the totality of the campaign should support the brand. Indeed, this is an opportunity to extend brand opportunities and provide increased brand experiences.

Digital media

The development of digital-based technologies and web-enabled communications has had a profound effect on marketing communications. However, the full potential of these new technologies has yet to be realised. This is due to two main reasons. One is because customers are still learning new ways of incorporating these facilities and adapting their behaviours. Second, the speed of technological change and development appears to be accelerating. Organisations are also learning how to use new technologies and observing changing customer behaviours. Interactivity and rapid two-way communications enabled by technology require the development of new communication strategies and a fresh understanding of how best to communicate with target audiences.

Enabling users to engage

The dramatic impact that digital technologies have had on people does not need amplification here. However, digitisation has provided marketers with the opportunity to develop new ways of communicating with a variety of audiences. This section explores some of the ways digital technology has enabled people and organisations to engage through marketing communications. The section closes with a comparison of some of the key characteristics of conventional and digital media.

The digital media now available has transformed the way in which consumers use the media, and has changed the way organisations communicate with audiences. The key characteristics of the main digital applications are considered in the following chapter. Here attention is given to how digital media can enhance communications with audiences.

Interactivity

Digital technology allows for true interactively based communications, where messages can be responded to more or less instantly. Technological advances have enabled organisations the opportunity to deploy a range of interactive communication opportunities, which ideally should be integrated in order to get the best effect. These include email, webpage interrogation and click-throughs from online ads, to blogs, microsites, communities, and mobile commerce.

Home shopping represents a significant change in buyer behaviour that may affect a range of ancillary activities. Several UK supermarket operators have invested heavily in shopping channels and they have had to learn new fulfilment operations and new processes and procedures to meet customer expectations. Although Tesco appears to have been particularly successful, there is little evidence to suggest that retailers will give up their high street presence, as predicted in the late 1990s. The physical shopping experience provides many consumers with significant entertainment and social interaction satisfactions and these are unlikely to be discarded for total virtual shopping.

The financial services sector can be expected to undergo further change as home banking in particular, has become a secure and more convenient transaction context. Entertainment possibilities will be even more attractive, as interactive games, advergaming, and interactive viewing through pay-per-view, video on demand and time shifting (which is, as Rosen pointed out as long ago as 1997, the option to view yesterday's programmes today), plus HD and 3D formats become easily accessible.

Multichannel marketing

Although not entirely responsible, digital technology has enabled organisations to reach new markets and different segments using more than a single marketing channel. Database-generated telemarketing, direct mail, email and Internet channels now complement field sales, retail and catalogue selling and have allowed organisations to determine which customers prefer which channels, and which are the most profitable. This in turn enables organisations to allocate resources far more effectively and to spread the customer base upon which profits are developed. A multichannel strategy should accommodate customers' account channel preferences, their usage patterns, needs, price sensitivities and preferred point of product and service access. So, as Stone and Shan (2002) put it, the goal is to manage each channel profitably while optimising the attributes of each channel so that they deliver value for each type of customer.

Multichannel strategies have added new marketing opportunities, and enabled audiences to access products and services in ways that best meet their own lifestyle and behavioural needs. For organisations this has reduced message wastage, used media more efficiently and, in doing so, reduced costs and improved communication effectiveness.

Viewpoint 13.4   Multichannel *NME*

NME is a long-term music brand launched in magazine format in 1953 (as *New Musical Express*). Among its claims are that it helped develop the careers of many bands and artists, including the Rolling Stones, Beatles, Bowie and the Sex Pistols. However, as the magazine market as whole continues to slide so *NME* was not immune especially as many of the readership are digital natives and generally averse to magazines.

Part of the remedy was to launch new media channels. The first of these was NME.com which now draws 1.8 million unique users. The website is used to complement the magazine, although it provides increased depth and covers content not always suitable for the print version and enables blogging from music events.

A further channel, NMETV, was launched in 2007. Available to 9 million homes, the programme content includes video and interviews, and can be used to enhance material in the magazine channel.

NME Radio was launched in the summer of 2008 and is available on a number of national digital broadcast platforms.

Each of the media channels offers different opportunities, but NME have been able to integrate them so that each one reinforces the other. The television channel draws a different audience to the magazine, the former claiming 25–34-year-olds and the latter 15–24-year-olds. The obvious remaining question is, which of these channels is the most profitable?

The answer is magazines, even though circulation fell 12 per cent in the second half of 2007.

Source: Based on Turner (2008)

Question

Is there an optimum number of channels that brands should use?

Task

Choose a grocery brand and find out how many channels are used to reach you.

Personalisation

For the first time, digital technology has empowered organisations to personalise messages and communicate with stakeholders on a one-to-one basis, on a scale that is commercially viable. This has driven the dramatic development of direct marketing, reshaped the basis on which organisations target and segment markets, stimulated dialogue, brought about a raft of new strategies and challenged the conventional approach to mass marketing and branding techniques.

The use of email communications is now extensive and viral marketing campaigns are commonplace. As with all forms of communication, the successful use of email requires an understanding of the recipient's behaviour. Email communication enables a high degree of personalisation, and, in order to personalise messages, it is necessary to understand the attitudinal and behavioural characteristics of each email audience (Chaffey, 2003). Chaffey suggests that the following need to be considered:

● How many recipients read their emails from home and at work?
● Which times of the day and days of the week do they read their email?
● How soon after receipt is email read?
● How do recipients configure their email readers?

Understanding the email behaviour of different audiences can be critical. By understanding online behaviour the level of personalisation given to email communications, and to homepage welcome messages, can be varied. However, email communication that is based on an understanding of the audience's email behaviour should influence the message content, the time when it should be sent and, most importantly, the keys to encouraging recipients to open the email and not delete it. These keys are the 'header' of the email, which contains the subject matter, and the 'from' address, which signifies whether the sender is known and hence strongly determines whether the email is perceived positively at the outset. If it is, then there is a stronger chance that the email will be opened and hence a greater opportunity for response and interactivity.

However, many people now expect a high level of personalisation and virtual recognition as opportunities arising through 'personalisation' reach beyond email communication. Personalisation is a sensitive area, often twinned with privacy issues.

Personalisation should be an integral aspect of relationship marketing, especially in b2b markets. The degree of personalisation will inevitably vary over the customer lifecycle and become more intimate as a relationship matures.

Mobility

Digital technologies now support a range of devices and applications that enable mobile communications. Mobile commerce (or mCommerce) refers to the use of wireless devices, such as mobile phones, for transactional activities. The wireless facility enables transactions to be undertaken in real time and at any location, a feature referred to as 'ubiquity'. The impact on marketing communications is significant. For example, there are increased opportunities to keep in touch with customers, improve communications convenience, develop localisation and personalisation strategies opportunities. All of these enable organisations to track people to particular locations. The delivery of personalised and pertinent information plus inducements and promotional offers in order to encourage specific purchase behaviour, can have greater impact.

SMS communications are used increasingly not just for brand awareness-based advertising but also as an effective way of delivering sales promotions, such as announcing special offers and prompting action. For example, BMW in Germany used MMS to prompt motorists to buy and fix snow tyres. As soon as the first flakes of snow started to fall an MMS message was sent to all BMW owners. Each message contained a picture of the owner's car, the tyres on offer, plus the contact details of the nearest dealer. The result was a conversion rate of 30 per cent.

Once again this reflects the increasing ubiquity of contemporary mobile communications. However, as with email, it is also important to consider the potential privacy concerns of customers, especially as the receipt of unwanted messages (i.e. spam) may well increase.

Speed

Digital technology has enabled aspects of marketing communications to be conducted at much faster, indeed electronic speeds. This impact is manifest in direct communications with end-users and in the production process itself. Draft documents, film and video clips, contracts, address lists and research and feedback reports, to name but a few, can all now be transmitted electronically, saving processing time and reducing the elapsed production time necessary to create and implement marketing communication activities and events.

Efficiency

Digital technology helps organisations to target their messages accurately to discrete groups or audiences. Indeed, one-to-one marketing is possible, and when compared with mass communications and broad audiences it is clear that digital technologies offer huge opportunities for narrow casting and reduced communication waste. Rather than shower audiences with messages that some of them do not wish to receive, direct marketing should, theoretically, enable each message to be received by all who are known to be favourably disposed to the communication.

This principle of narrow casting applies equally well to communication costs. Moving away from mass media to direct marketing and one-to-one communications reduces the absolute costs associated with campaigns. The relative costs may be higher but these richer communications facilitate interactive opportunities with a greater percentage of the target audience than previously experienced in the mass broadcast era.

A further type of efficiency can be seen in terms of the accuracy and precision of the messages that are delivered. Marketing communications delivers product information, specifications and service details, contracts, designs, drawings and development briefs when customising to meet customer needs. The use of IST can help organisations provide customers with precise information and reduce opportunities for information deviance.

Relationship development

As mentioned previously, digital technology is now used by organisations to gather and use information about customers in order to better meet their needs. Through the use of the database, organisations now seek to develop longer-term relationships with customers, with programmes and strategies that are dubiously termed as customer loyalty schemes. While there may be doubt about the term loyalty, there can be no doubt that digital technology has helped develop customer relationships. What should also be clear is that the existence of digital technology in an organisation or relationship is no guarantee that additional value will be created (Ryssel *et al.*, 2004).

Some customer service interface functions have been replaced with technology in the name of greater efficiency, cost savings and improved service. Financial services organisations are able to inform customers of their bank balances automatically without human intervention. Meyronin (2004: 222) refers to this as an 'infomediation' strategy and suggests that this neglect of the human interaction in the creation of joint value in service environments may be detrimental.

Key differences between conventional and digital media

Having considered the characteristics of both conventional and digital media, this appears to be the right point at which to bring the two together. In comparison with conventional media, the Internet and digital media facilities provide an interesting contrast (see Table 13.2).

Table 13.2	Comparison of digital and conventional media
Traditional media	**Digital media**
One-to-many	One-to-one and many-to-many
Greater monologue	Greater dialogue
Active provision	Passive provision
Mass marketing	Individualised marketing
General need	Personalised
Branding	Information
Segmentation	Communities

Space (or time) within conventional media is limited and costs rise as demand for the limited space/time increases. On the Internet, space is unlimited so absolute costs remain very low and static, while relative costs plummet as more visitors are recorded as having been to a site. Another aspect concerns the focus of advertising messages. Traditionally, advertisers tend to emphasise the emotional rather than information aspect, particularly where there is low involvement. Digital media allows focus on the provision of information and so the emotional aspect of advertising messages tends to have a lower significance. However, branding is becoming a more important aspect of Internet activity. There is evidence that there is greater use of emotions, especially when the goal is to keep people at a website, rather than driving them to it.

Viewpoint 13.5   Digital perception at Terminal 5

When Heathrow airport opened Terminal 5 in March 2008, a raft of new advertising technology was released. Over 200 digital screens have been built into the infrastructure of the airport, all with strategic placement. Here the advertising panels have been sited alongside the path that passengers take from check-in to their flight. Some giant displays are referred to as 'global gateways', some dominating the security area. Digital ads are incorporated into the flight-information screens.

The digital screens enable ad continuity so that a passenger may see a seemingly endless line of the same ads. This opportunity to reach a mass of people in this way is a first for this part of the advertising industry. Now the industry has the opportunity to use digital technology to deliver moving, interactive, responsive and time-specific advertising. This means that interactive ads can be changed for morning, noon and afternoon customers, unlike the traditional outdoor poster sites that need two weeks, several rolls of paper and a bucket of paste. Visa have taken four giant lightboxes that measure 29m × 36m and should be seen by all passengers as they move through to the departure areas.

Digital and interactive screens have been installed at other airports following the T5 launch, in the London Underground, in and around various new shopping centres and maybe even at a bus shelter near you.

Source: Based on Bainbridge (2008); Bokaie (2008)

Question

To what extent are these digital screens and their location likely to aid the exposure and perception opportunities (to reach travellers with effective messaging)?

Task

Next time you visit an air or rail terminal look out for digital screens and make a note of which brands are using them.

Table 13.3   Comparison of information content

Web sites/Internet	Traditional media
Good at providing rational, product-based information	Better at conveying emotional brand values
More efficient as costs do not increase in proportion to the size of the target audience	Costs are related to usage
Better at prompting customer action	Less effective for calling to action except point-of-purchase and telemarketing
Effective for short-term, product-oriented brand action goals and long-term corporate identity objectives	Normally associated with building long-term values
Poor at generating awareness and attention	Strong builders of awareness
Poor at managing attitudes	Capable of changing and monitoring attitudes
Measures of effectiveness weak and/or in the process of development	Established methodologies, if misleading or superficial (mass media); direct marketing techniques are superior
Dominant orientation – cognition	Dominant orientation – emotion

Apart from the obvious factor that digital media, and the Internet in particular, provide interactive opportunities that conventional media cannot provide, it is important to remember that opportunities-to-see are generally driven by customers rather than by the advertiser that interrupts viewing or reading activities. People drive the interaction at a speed that is convenient to them; they are not driven by others.

Management control over Internet-based marketing communications is relatively high, as not only are there greater opportunities to control the position and placement of advertisements, promotions and press releases, but it is also possible to change the content of these activities much more quickly than is possible with conventional media. The goals outlined above indicate the framework within which advertising needs to be managed.

In addition to considering the attributes of the two different forms of media, it is also worth considering the content of the information that each is capable of delivering. These are set out in Table 13.3.

As mentioned earlier, digital media are superior at providing rational, product-based information whereas conventional media are much better at conveying emotional brand values. The former have a dominant cognition orientation and the latter an emotional one. There are other differences, but the predominant message is that these types of media are, to a large extent, complementary, suggesting that they should be used together, not independently of the other.

Media planning

Once a message has been created a media plan should be determined. The aim of a media plan is to devise an optimum route for the delivery of the message to the target audience. This function is normally undertaken by specialists, either as part of a full service advertising agency or as a media house whose sole function is to buy air time or space from media owners (e.g. television contractors or magazine publishers) on behalf of their clients, the advertisers. This traditional role has changed since the mid-1990s, and many media independents now provide consultancy services, particularly at the strategic level, plus planning and media research and auditing services.

Traditionally, media departments have been responsible for two main functions. These are to 'plan' and to 'buy' time and space in appropriate media vehicles. There is a third task – to monitor a media schedule once it has been bought – but this is essentially a sub-function of buying. The planner identifies the target audience and the type of medium, while the buyer chooses programmes, frequency, spots and distribution, and assembles a multichannel schedule (Armstrong, 1993).

However, digital media requires a further function to be incorporated. This concerns the placement of messages at strategic locations. This serves to either drive traffic to a website, seed material in order to provoke word-of-mouth (viral) communication, or achieve higher search engine results.

Media planning is essentially a selection, scheduling and placement exercise. The selection refers to the choice of media vehicles to carry the message on behalf of the advertiser. Scheduling refers to the number of occasions, timing and duration that a message is exposed, in the selected vehicles, to the target audience. Placement concerns where and how messages can be found online.

However, there are several factors that complicate these seemingly straightforward tasks. First, the variety of available media is huge and rapidly increasing. This is referred to as media fragmentation. Secondly, the characteristics of the target audience are changing equally quickly. This is referred to as audience fragmentation. Third, search engine optimisation (see Chapter 14) is a dynamic activity because of the real-time activities of competitors and others working online. The job of the media planner is complicated by one further element: money. Advertisers have restricted financial resources and require the media planner to create a plan that delivers their messages not only effectively but also efficiently.

The task of the media planner, therefore, is to deliver advertising messages through a selection of media that match the viewing and/or reading habits of the target audience at the lowest possible cost. In order for these tasks to be accomplished, three sets of decisions need to be made about the choice of media, vehicles and schedules.

Decisions about the choice of media are complex. While choosing a single one is reasonably straightforward, choosing media in combination and attempting to generate synergistic effects is far from easy. Technological advances have made media planning for conventional media a much faster, more accurate process, one that is now more flexible and capable of adjusting to fast-changing market conditions.

Media planning concepts

Media planning involves certain key principles and concepts. These are set out in Table 13.4.

Table 13.4	Media planning concepts
Media concept	**Explanation**
Reach	The percentage of the target audience exposed to a message at least once during the relevant time period.
Coverage	Coverage refers to the size of a potential audience that might be exposed to a particular media vehicle.
Frequency	The number of times a member of the target audience is exposed to a media vehicle.
Ratings	A measure of the total number of exposures (OTS) generated within a particular period of time. The calculation itself is simply reach × frequency.
Duplication	The percentage of the target audience exposed to an advertisement in two or more media vehicles. Duplication provides an indication of the levels of frequency likely in a particular media schedule.
Effective frequency	The number of times an individual needs to be exposed to an advertisement before the communication is effective.

Reach

Building reach within a target audience is relatively easy as the planner needs to select a range of different media vehicles. This will enable different people in the target audience to have an opportunity to see the media vehicle. However, a point will be reached when it becomes more difficult to reach people who have not been exposed. As more vehicles are added, so repetition levels (the number of people who have seen the advertisement more than once) also increase.

Frequency

The number of times people are exposed to an ad should be a function of how many times planners believe targets need to see and learn about the ad before acting in particular ways. This frequency, essentially a repetition level, will always be greater than the advertisement exposure rate. However, a high opportunity-to-see (OTS) might be generated by either, a large number of the target audience being exposed once (high reach), or a small number being exposed several times (high frequency).

This then raises the first major issue. As all campaigns are restricted by limitations of time and budget, advertisers have to trade off reach against frequency. It is impossible to maximise both elements within a fixed budget and set period of time.

To launch a new product, it has been established that a wide number of people within the target audience need to become aware of the product's existence and its salient attributes or benefits. This means that reach is important but, as more and more people become aware, so more of them become exposed a second, third or fourth time, perhaps to different vehicles. At the outset, frequency is low and reach high, but as a campaign progresses so reach slows and frequency develops. Reach and frequency are inversely related within any period of time, and media planners must know what the objective of any campaign might be: to build reach or frequency.

Gross rating point

The term gross rating point (GRP) is used to express the relationship between reach and frequency and is a means of deciding which of the two concepts is important in a campaign. Reach × Frequency = GRPs.

Media plans are often determined on the number of GRPs generated during a certain time period. For example, the objective for a media plan could be to achieve 450 GRPs in a burst (usually four or five weeks). However, as suggested earlier, caution is required when interpreting a GRP, because 450 GRPs may be the result of 18 message exposures to just 25 per cent of the target market. It could also be an average of nine exposures to 50 per cent of the target market.

Effective frequency

Frequency refers to the number of times members of the target audience are exposed to the vehicle. Effective frequency refers to the number of times a message needs to be repeated for effective learning to occur. The level of effective frequency is generally unknown, but for a long time it was generally assumed to be 3, within any purchase period; the three-hit theory. The first exposure provokes a 'What is this?' reaction, the second reaction is 'What does this mean to me?' The reaction to the third is 'Oh I remember' (du Plessis, 1998).

Determining the average frequency partially solves the problem. This is the number of times a target reached by the schedule is exposed to the vehicle over a particular period of time. For example, a schedule may generate the following:

10 per cent of the audience is reached 10 times ($10 \times 10 = 100$)

25 per cent of the audience is reached 7 times ($25 \times 7 = 175$)

65 per cent of the audience is reached once ($65 \times 1 = 65$)

Total = 340 exposures

Average frequency = 340/100 = 3.4

This figure of average frequency is misleading because different groups of people have been reached with varying levels of frequency. In the example above, an average frequency of 3.4 is achieved but 65 per cent of the audience is reached only once. This means that the average frequency, in this example, may lead to an audience being underexposed.

The effective frequency model requires media to be purchased in blocks to provide intense communication. The problem is, how much should be bought and how intense should the media schedule be? An alternative approach dispenses with the block purchase and guesstimates of intensity and uses continuity as its base. Referred to as recency planning, that is recency of exposure, the proposition is that only a single message is required, once a decision to purchase has been made (Green, 2007). Any further exposures might be wasteful as they have no additional impact. Recency planning builds on the Weak Theory of advertising (Ehrenberg, 1974), namely that advertising works by reminding audiences of their preferred brands. There is also a growing general acceptance that advertising is not the all-powerful communication tool it was once thought to be, and that the timing and presentation of advertising messages needs to be reconsidered in the light of the way advertising is currently thought to work.

If it is accepted that consumer decision-making is more heavily influenced by 'running out' of particular products (opening empty fridges and store cupboards), than by exposure to advertising messages that are repeated remorselessly, then it follows that advertising needs to be directed at those people who are actually in the market and prepared to buy (Ephron, 1997).

Many fast-moving consumer goods products are purchased each week, and Jones (1995) argues that a single exposure to an advertising message in the week before a purchase is to be made is more important than adding further messages, thereby increasing frequency. Recency planning considers reach to be more important than frequency.

The goal of the recency approach is to reach those few consumers who are ready to buy (in the market). To do this the strategy requires reaching as many consumers as possible in as many weeks as possible (as far as the budget will extend). This requires a lower weekly weight and an extended number of weeks for a campaign. Advertising budgets are not cut; the fund is simply spread over a greater period of time. According to Ephron (1997), this approach is quite different from effective frequency models and quite revolutionary (see Table 13.5). The strategy requires reaching as many consumers as possible in as many weeks as possible.

This approach has been greeted with a number of objections. It has not been universally accepted, nor has it been widely implemented in the UK market. Gallucci (1997), among others, rejected the notion of recency planning because effectiveness will vary by brand, category and campaign. He claims that reaching 35 per cent of the Indonesian cola market once a week will not bring about the same result as reaching 65 per cent four times a week. However, as doubts increase about the reasoned approaches to how advertising works (Green,

Table 13.5	The key differences between effective frequency and recency planning
Recency planning model	**Effective frequency model**
Reach goal	Frequency goal
Continuity	Burst
One-week planning cycle	Four-week planning cycle
Lowest cost per reach point	Lowest cost per thousand
Low ratings	High ratings

Source: Adapted from Ephron (1997). Used by permission of WARC

2007; Heath and Feldwick, 2007)), the efficacy of recall and recognition tests (Heath, 2005), how brands are used by consumers as part of their own identity (Schembri *et al.*, 2010) and concern about the so the recency approach appears to be a more realistic and practical way of media planning.

The development of banner advertising on the Internet raises interesting questions concerning effective frequency in new media. Is the frequency rate different and, if so, how many times is exposure required in order to be effective? Research into this area is in its infancy and no single, accepted body of knowledge exists. Broussard (2000) reports that, in a limited study concerning the comparison of a direct-response and a branding-based campaign on the Internet, the lowest cost per lead in the direct-response campaign was achieved with low frequency levels. Results from the branding campaign suggest that up to seven exposures were necessary to improve brand awareness and knowledge of product attributes.

The debate concerning the development of recency planning and effective frequency will continue. What might be instrumental to the outcome of the debate will be a better understanding of how advertising works and the way buyers use advertising messages that are relevant to them.

Duplication

People do not buy and read just one magazine or watch a single television programme. Consumer media habits are complex, although distinct patterns can be observed, but it is likely that a certain percentage of the target audience will be exposed to an advertisement if it is placed in two or more media vehicles. Those who are exposed once constitute unduplicated reach. Those who are exposed to two or more advertisements carrying the same message are said to have been duplicated. Such overlapping of exposure, shown in Figure 13.1, is referred to as duplicated reach.

Duplication provides an indication of the levels of frequency likely in a particular schedule, so media plans need to specify levels of duplicated and unduplicated reach. Duplication also increases costs, so if the objective of the plan is unduplicated reach, duplication brings waste and inefficiency.

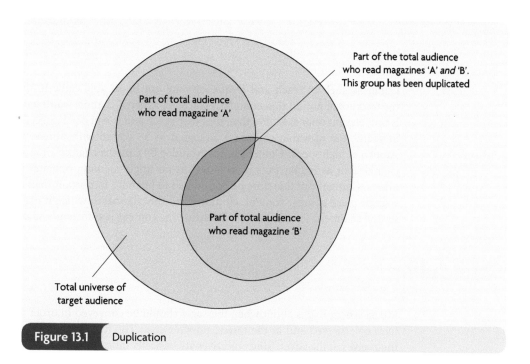

Figure 13.1   Duplication

Viewpoint 13.6   Media mix transparency at Anglian

The formulation and delivery of the right media mix has been a challenge for many organisations. Anglian, the home improvement company experimented with various combinations of media to determine which configuration of the media mix works best for them.

Anglian's traditional mix includes press, radio, DRTV, direct mail and door drops. With a campaign to promote its replacement windows, the company experimented with different combinations of three of these media.

Unsurprisingly they found that direct mail works best when implemented at the end of a television campaign, as awareness levels have been raised. Television worked best when used with press and door drops and direct mail worked best with current customers. As a result of the experiments, radio was removed from Anglian's media mix.

The company also reviewed the effectiveness of its website. One of its goals was to increase the number of leads generated from its paid search activities. Analysis found that there was an unusually high bounce rate (66 per cent) from the page visitors first encounter when clicking through from another site or sponsored link. This page is known as the landing page and bounce refers to a failure to click through the site from the landing page. It was found that the page did not contain the information or even products that visitors were looking for, despite clicking on a link that suggested a match.

Changes were made to the information provided about the products, prices and images were included, and they tested changes to the title to the form used by prospects when responding to 'Get a free quote' and 'Get a call back' to see which one worked best. Online price discounts, price matching promises and pick & mix sale offers were all incorporated.

One of the results of this landing page work was that the 'Get a call back' invitation generated a 108 per cent increase in conversions.

Source: Based on Anon (2009); Benjamin (2009)

Question

Why do you think Anglian did not incorporate the website in their experiment to determine the optimum media mix?

Task

Go to the Anglian website www.anglianhome.co.uk and make a list of the ways they prompt people into further action.

Concepts such as reach and frequency may not be so applicable in digital media. Indeed, the traditional notion that content is placed in a media channel waiting for audiences to see it, is not relevant online. Rather than deal with reach and frequency Franks (2010) refers to 'speed of share', the idea that content is intended to be shared with others, and that sharing can happen at high speed. Content is not bounded by a media channel, it crosses over to different channels, or as Franks puts it, 'it flows', as no single medium operates independently of the others. Content can therefore be considered to be more important than the media channel as a single piece of great content will transcend the channel in which it originated and populate several channels. The challenge is to ensure the content is sufficiently sticky and is memorable.

Scheduling

Media scheduling is about when messages should be conveyed in order that the media objectives be achieved and at the lowest possible cost. The first considerations are the objectives themselves. If the advertising objectives are basically short term, then the placements should be concentrated over a short period of time. Conversely, if awareness is to be built over a longer term, perhaps building a new brand, then the frequency of the placements need not be so intensive and can be spread over a period so that learning can occur incrementally.

The second consideration is the purchasing cycle. We have seen before that many feel that the optimum number of exposures is thought to be a minimum of three, and this should occur within each purchasing cycle. However, the counter argument to this is recency planning and so only one exposure is required immediately before purchase (Riebe *et al.*, 2008). This, of course, is only really applicable to packaged goods, and is not as applicable to the business-to-business sector. However, as a principle, the longer the cycle, the less frequency is required.

The third consideration is the level of involvement. If the objective of the plan is to create awareness, then when there is high involvement few repetitions will be required compared with low-involvement decisions. This is because people who are highly involved actively seek information and need little assistance to digest relevant information. Likewise, where there is low involvement, attitudes develop from use of the product, so frequency is important to maintain awareness and to prompt trial.

Finally, the placement of an advertisement is influenced by the characteristics of the target audience and their preferred activities. Selecting compatible *spots* can considerably improve the effectiveness of message delivery.

Summary

In order to help consolidate your understanding of the media, here are the key points summarised against each of the learning objectives:

1 Determine the broad types of available media and classify them

Of the many available media, six main classes can be identified. These are broadcast, print, outdoor, digital, in-store and other media classes. Within each of these classes there are particular types of media. For example, within the broadcast class there are television and radio, and within the print class there are newspapers and magazines. Within each type of medium there are a huge number of different individual media vehicles that can be selected to carry an advertiser's message.

2 Explain the main criteria used to evaluate media and their use

Understanding of the key characteristics of each type of media assists media selection and planning. The fundamental characteristics concern the costs, the richness of the communication, the interactive properties and audience profile associated with a communication event.

3 Examine the characteristics associated with each class of media

The rich array of characteristics that each class and type of media serve to engage audiences in different ways. Some media deliver content one way, others provide interactivity capability. Some work passively with an audience, others require audiences to be actively engaged with the media for the message to be communicated.

4 Describe the range of features available through the use of digital media

Digital media has a range of features that help distinguish it from conventional media. These include interactivity, multichannel marketing, speed, personalisation, mobility, efficiency and relationship development.

5 Explain the key differences between conventional and digital media

These two media work in different ways. In digital media opportunities-to-see are generally driven by customers. In conventional media it is the advertiser that interrupts the viewing or reading activities of the audience to communicate the message. There are differences in terms of time and space.

Digital media are superior at providing rational, product-based information whereas conventional media are generally stronger at conveying emotional brand values. The former have a dominant cognition orientation and the latter an emotional one. There are other differences, but the predominant message is that these types of media are, to a large extent, complementary, suggesting that they should be used together, not independently of the other.

6 Explore some of the principles and issues associated with media planning

Media planning is essentially a selection, scheduling and placement exercise. The selection refers to the choice of media vehicles to carry the message on behalf of the advertiser. Scheduling refers to the number of occasions, timing and duration that a message is exposed, in the selected vehicles, to the target audience. Placement concerns where and how messages can be found online. Concepts such as reach, frequency and gross ratings govern the way conventional media is planned and scheduled. The extent to which these concepts apply to digital media is debatable but issues concerning, speed of share, placement and response are key.

Review questions

1. Explain the differences between media classes, types and vehicles. Give two examples of each to support your answer.
2. Describe the main characteristics of the print media. Find examples to illustrate your points.
3. Compare and contrast newspapers and magazines as advertising media.
4. What do you think will be the impact on outdoor media of the growth in penetration. How will this affect advertisers?
5. If radio is unobtrusive, why should advertisers use it?
6. Why are the relative costs of each medium different?
7. Identify different ways in which multimedia applications might be configured.
8. Why is interactive media so important in contemporary marketing communications?
9. Examine each of the characteristics of digital media and find examples of each of them.
10. Explain each of the main concepts associated with media planning. How might these apply to digital media?

References

Ampuero, O. and Vial, N. (2006) Consumer perceptions of product packaging, *Journal of Consumer Marketing*, 23(2), 100–112.

Anon (2009) Latitude; Anglian, *Revolution; Success Stories 2009*, December, 4–5.

Armstrong, S. (1993) The business of buying: time, lads, please, *Media Week*, 3 September, 26–27.

Bainbridge, J. (2008) Now ad campaigns can take off, *The Independent*, 17 March, 10.

Ballantyne, D. (2004) Dialogue and its role in the development of relationship specific knowledge, *Journal of Business and Industrial Marketing*, 19(2), 114–123.

Bashford, S. (2010) Catalogues are order of the day, *Marketing*, 27 January, 33–36.

Benjamin, K. (2009) Harmonising mail with other media, *Marketing*, 14 October, 15–17.

Bokaie, J. (2008) Gateway to Britain, *Marketing*, 19 March, 16.

Broussard, G. (2000) How advertising frequency can work to build online effectiveness. *International Journal of Market Research*, 42(4), 439–457.

Chaffey, D. (2003) E-marketing insights: what's new in marketing. Retrieved 27 August 2004 from www.wnim.com/archive/issue1903/emarketing.htm

Cowlett, M. (2007) Pretty Polly replicates success of 'Hello Boys', *Campaign*, 14 March. Retrieved 25 January 2008 from www.prweek.com/uk/search/article/643525/

du Plessis, E. (1998) Memory and likeability: keys to understanding ad effects, *Admap* (July/August), 42–46.

Ehrenberg, A.S.C. (1974) Repetitive advertising and the consumer, *Journal of Advertising Research*, 14 (April), 25–34.

Ephron, E. (1997) Recency planning, *Admap* (February), 32–34.

Esposito, M. (2008) Cinema advertising: stars of the silver screen, *Marketing*, 9 January. Retrieved 19 January from www.brandrepublic.com/InDepth/Features/775594/Cinema-advertising-Stars-silver-screen/

Franks, J. (2010) Marketers, brace yourselves for the speed of share, Admap (January). Retrieved 2 June 2010 from www.warc.com/admap

Gallucci, P. (1997) There are no absolutes in media planning, *Admap* (July/August), 39–43.

Govoni, N., Eng, R. and Galper, M. (1986) *Promotional Management*. Englewood Cliffs, NJ: Prentice-Hall.

Green, A. (2007) How many times do people need to see my message before they buy? *Warc Media FAQ* (January). Retrieved 5 November 2010 from www.warc.com

Heath, R. (2005) Measuring the hidden power of emotive advertising, *International Journal of Market Research*, 47(5), 467–486.

Heath, R. and Feldwick, P. (2007) 50 years using the wrong model of TV advertising, *Admap*, (March), 36–38.

Jones, P. (1995) *When Ads Work: New Proof that Advertising Triggers Sales*. New York: Simon & Schuster, Free Press/Lexington Books.

McLuhan, R. (2010) Marketing's Customer Publishing Leagues 2010, *Marketing*. Retrieved 5 July 2010 from www.brandrepublic.com/league_tables/1009844/Marketings-Customer-Publishing-Leagues-2010/?DCMP=ILC-SEARCH

Meyronin, B. (2004) ICT: the creation of value and differentiation in services, *Managing Service Quality*, 14(2/3), 216–225.

Riebe, E., Dreesener, C. and Beal, V. (2008) The effect of recency of ad exposure on purchasing across categories and media, *ESOMAR*, June. Retrieved 2 June 2010 from www.warc.com/articlecentre/

Rosen, E.M. (1997) Digital TV will soon overtake the Internet, *Revolution* (July), 6–7.

Ryssel, R., Ritter, T. and Gemunden, H.G. (2004) The impact of information technology deployment on trust, commitment and value creation in business relationships, *Journal of Business and Industrial Marketing*, 19(3), 197–207.

Schembri, S., Merrilees, B. and Kristiansen, S. (2010) Brand consumption and narrative of the self, *Psychology and Marketing*, 27(6) (June) 623–638.

Stone, M. and Shan, P. (2002) Transforming the bank branch experience for customers, *What's New in Marketing*, 10 (September). Retrieved 23 August 2004 from http://www.wnim.com/archive/

Turner, C. (2008) How NME achieved multi-platform success, *Utalk Case Studies*. Retrieved 28 February 2008 from www.utalkmarketing.com/pages/

Verebelyi, N. (2000) The power of the pack, *Marketing*, 27 April, 37.

Chapter 14
Interactive marketing communications

For many organisations the use of digital, interactive marketing communications has become an important channel to reach and communicate effectively with specific audiences. Digital media based communications enable individual targeting, personalised messages, interactivity and opportunities to cultivate dialogue, share information and develop relationships.

Aims and learning objectives

The aims of this chapter are to explore the key tools and applications used by organisations in order that they communicate interactively with their audiences.

The learning objectives of this chapter are to:

1. appraise the nature and characteristics of interactive marketing communications;
2. consider some of the issues relating to the way in which each of the tools of the communications mix can be used interactively;
3. evaluate search engine marketing and distinguish the main features of both pay-per-click and search engine optimisation;
4. discuss the features of email marketing communications for both customer acquisition and retention;
5. evaluate the role of electronic word-of-mouth communications, and consider applications such as viral marketing communications, podcasting, Twitter, RSS feeds and web logs;
6. identify the characteristics of online communities and consider how social networks and affiliate marketing can be used to develop marketing communications opportunities.

Introduction

The title of this chapter is *interactive* marketing communications. The use of the word interactive is important as it denotes the key characteristic of this form of marketing communications. It is key because it signifies the functionality that is available, namely the ability of all participants in a communication network to respond to messages, share knowledge and create content. This is not a feature of most offline marketing communications media such as radio, billboards or magazines. It is also key because it indicates that this type of communication environment is open, that is, more democratic than conventional marketing communications. The latter tend to be one-sided and driven primarily by organisations and the satisfaction of their more overt needs. The word interactive suggests that all parties to a communication event are enabled to communicate. Finally, the word interactive is used to cover a wide spectrum of electronic environments, one that is not limited or defined by the Internet. For example, mobile communications do not operate online, yet can be used to reach people digitally wherever they are and engage them, potentially interactively.

Perhaps the strongest characteristic of interactive marketing communications is that it enables communications to move from one-way and simple two-way models to one that is literally 'interactive'. Interactivity normally precedes the establishment of dialogue between participants in the communication process. This in turn enables all participants to contribute to the content that is used in the communication process. This is referred to as user-generated-content, as demonstrated by people uploading videos to YouTube or even emailing comments to radio and television programmes. This symbolises a shift in the way in which marketing communications has developed, especially in the online environment. So, when the maintenance of 'relationships' is a central marketing activity it is possible to conclude that interactive marketing communications has an important role to play. Table 14.1 sets out some of the interactive properties associated with each of the primary tools of the marketing communications mix. The chapter then continues to consider some of the specific digital applications and facilities used by organisations to communicate with other organisations.

Search engine marketing

Websites need visitors and the higher the number of visitors the more effective the website is likely to be. Many people know of a particular site and simply type in the address or use a bookmark to access it. However, the majority of people arrive at sites following a search using particular key words and phrases to search for products, services, news, entertainment and the information they need. They do this through search engines and the results of each search are displayed in rank order. It is understandable therefore, that those ranked highest in the results lists are visited more often than those in lower positions.

Therefore, from a marketing perspective it is important to undertake marketing activities to attain the highest possible ranking position, and this is referred to as search engine marketing (SEM). There are two main search engine marketing techniques; search engine optimisation (SEO) and pay-per-click (PPC) with the latter outweighing the former quite substantially (Jarboe, 2005).

Search engine optimisation

Search engine optimisation (SEO), or as it used to be referred, organic search, is a process used to get a high ranking position on major search engines and directories. To achieve top-ranking positions, or least a first page listing, it is necessary to design webpages and create links with other quality websites, so that search engines can match closely a searcher's key words/phrases with the content of registered webpages.

Table 14.1 The interactive dimensions of the tools of the marketing communications mix

Marketing communications tool	Format	Comment
Interactive advertising	Banner ads	Over 50 per cent all web ads are banner ads, responsible for over 90 per cent of all Internet ad awareness. Although effective as a stand-alone ad, banner ads are linked through to an advertiser's chosen destination and therefore can act as a gateway to other websites. The aim of banner ads is to attract attention and stimulate interest, but the problem is that click-through rates are very low, at just 0.18 per cent (Mathews, 2007). Today, banners are not highly regarded but they continue to be used with many incorporating Flash, rich media, multipurpose units and sky-scrapers (very tall banner ads) as these formats generate better recall scores than the standard banner.
	Pop-ups	Also known as transitional online ads, pop-ups appear in separate browser windows, usually when webpages are being loaded or closed. With high speed loading, pop-ups are now generally regarded as intrusive.
	Microsites	This type of site is normally product or promotion-specific, and is often run as a joint promotion with other advertisers. Creating a separate site avoids the difficulty of directing traffic to either of the joint partners' sites. Microsites are much less expensive to set up than a traditional site and are particularly adept at building awareness as click-throughs to microsites are higher than through just banners.
	Online video	The development of YouTube has changed the perception of online video advertising. Online video ads can be used in a number of different ways apart from simply showing ads at the beginning or end of programmes. Online video content normally plays in an unstoppable loop, so the ads are unavoidable. In addition, advertisers are able to place ads within video streams, another reason preventing users from avoiding them. Also, video ads can be embedded within webpages and online articles, relating closely to the site content. A growth area.
	Advergames	The use of custom made online games designed to provide both entertainment and communicate a brand message, has grown considerably in recent years. Messages can be embedded as in integral part of the game, or they can be positioned passively, such as a billboard in Second Life. The messages may be designed to promote a brand or educate an audience. For example, banks have developed short games followed by messages about a new credit card. An alternative approach is to educate audiences as used in health campaigns to reach children to inform about diet and obesity issues. In all cases advergaming allows people to develop positive brand experiences through play.

Interactive sales promotions	Used to provoke a behavioural response, they can also be used in a mobile context, and not be restricted to an online context. The main aims of using interactive sales promotion are first, that they can either attract or retain customers, and second, that they provide interest and involvement with the brand by encouraging interaction and return visits. In reality, sampling, free gifts, e-coupons, price deals and competitions are the main incentives used interactively.
	The Internet enables sampling to occur very well. Music and software can be downloaded for trial purposes, while services such as photo processing can be tested risk-free through introductory offers. Another area experiencing growth is the rather oddly termed 'e-coupons'. Downloaded coupons can be redeemed online using a code at checkout, or printed off and used offline in-store.
Interactive direct marketing	Used to integrate a range of activities, but underpins the majority of communication activities in the online environment. There are some branding-based communications, but the majority of activity is wrapped up as direct marketing, whether that be in the form of direct response advertising (e.g. banners or rich media), sales promotion (e-coupons or sampling) or public relations (e.g. sponsorship, blogs and podcasts). Used to converge different media in order to convert warm prospects.
	Offline direct marketing is used to drive traffic to a website. This might be undertaken by branding or by providing incentives. For example, many insurance companies use direct response television ads to inform consumers of their low cost/high value insurance deals to be found at their website. Email and viral marketing are used extensively.
Interactive public relations	Used extensively to present the organisation (and its products and services) in a positive manner to a range of stakeholders. The goal is to create 'mentions' in both traditional media and online on other websites, which is important for establishing links and achieving higher search engine rankings. Newsletters and white papers are reputation-driven with a diverse range of content concerning organisational and/or technical-related material. These communications can be an essential part of the 'stickiness' that good websites seek to develop. Recipients who find these communications of value either anticipate their release or return to the host's website to search in archived files for past copies and items of interest.
	Statements concerning an organisation's position on an issue of public interest, corporate social responsibility or environmental matters can be published, while investor relations and public affairs issues are easily accommodated. Sponsorship activities are an important part of interactive online marketing communications, whether they be in the form of a partnership deal or direct sponsorship of a social networking site. Websites can also play an important role in terms of crisis management. In the event of an organisational crisis or disaster, up-to-date information can be posted quickly, either providing pertinent information or directing visitors to offline information and associated facilities.
Interactive personal selling	Face-to-face personal communications are, by definition, always interactive. However, the online application for the purposes of buying and selling remains the one part of the mix that cannot be easily addressed. Video conferencing does provide this facility but costs and logistics limit the practical application of this tool to conferencing and non-sales meetings. Although the Skype telephone software enables people to talk over the Internet using their PCs free of charge, using next-generation peer-to-peer software, the online environment is an impersonal medium and, as such, does not allow for direct personal communication.

Each search engine, such as Google, MSN Search and Yahoo, uses an algorithm to compare the content of relevant site pages with the key words/phrases used to initiate the search. Search engines use robotic electronic spiders to crawl around registered sites and from this compile an index of the words they find, placed there by the designer of each website. When a search is activated, it is the database housing these keyword/phrases that is searched, not the millions of world-wide webpages.

In order to get a high ranking it is important for a site to be registered, which is normally achieved by adding the URL of a site directly into a search engine. Some sites are automatically registered if there are links with another company that is already registered. Once registered, a high ranking is best achieved by attaining a match between the search words/phrases entered by the searcher and the words/phrases on the pages stored in the index. Achieving a good match can be helped by understanding, if not anticipating, the words and phrases that are likely to be used by individual searchers. Through web analytics, the study of website visitors' behaviour, it is possible to analyse the search terms used by current visitors. This can also help improve the matching process. However, there are some fundamental activities that can influence ranking positions.

The first important factor is referred to as 'keyphrase density', which refers to the number of times a key phrase is repeated in the text of a webpage. The next concerns the number of inbound links from what are regarded as good-quality sites. The greater the number of quality links, the higher the ranking is likely to be. Two further factors that affect a page's ranking concern the use of tags. The use of keywords in the *title tag* of a webpage and the *meta tags*, which signify the content and describe what searchers will find when they click on the site, are embedded by webpage designers and read by some search engine spiders. When key words and phrases used by searchers match those in these tags, it is likely that the site will have a higher ranking. For example, the airline easyJet, who sell more than 98 per cent of its seats via the www.easyjet.com website, use search engine optimisation to drive traffic to its websites across Europe. It is vital that easyJet appears when the search phrases associated with the discount airlines business are used.

Viewpoint 14.1   Searching the market for meerkats

Comparethemarket.com, a price comparison site for car insurance, was ranked fourth in the market and lacked the resources its main competitors could bring, especially in terms of advertising budgets, necessary to drive awareness, web visits and click through. Their name was instantly forgettable, their identity and name were very similar to their nearest competitor (gocompare), they had no single point of differentiation and they were last to the market. The task was to find a strong point of differentiation.

In this market it is easy to get people to remember 'compare'-led brand names but very difficult to get them to remember how one is different to the other. Fortunately the one element that distinguished this brand from the competition was the word 'market' in their name. It was reasoned that rather than use a rational attribute-based positioning like their competitors, who were perceived to be irritating and disliked, the key was to differentiate through entertainment.

In search terms the word market was expensive. At the time it was worth £5 per click so the task was to find a cheaper term or phrase that could be used by people as a substitute for 'market'.

The word 'meerkat' costs only 5p and so a campaign was built around a Russian meerkat called Aleksandr Orlov. He was portrayed as founder of www.comparethemeerkat.com, a site for comparing meerkats, and as someone who is frustrated by the confusion between Comparethemarket.com and Comparethemeerkat.com. The joke caught the imagination of the target audience and the site quickly assumed number one position. Orlov was an instant success, and quickly spawned tens of thousands of Facebook followers and instant recognition.

Source: Based on Jukes (2009); VCCP (2009); Ramsay (2009)

Question

To what extent is the success of SEO a function of second guessing the keywords people are likely to use?

Task

Identify three brands of coffee, submit the word coffee, and note the position of each of your brands in the listing.

Exhibit 14.1 Comparethemeerkat's Aleksandr Orlov from a Comparethemarket.com ad
Image courtesy of The Advertising Archives

Pay-per-click searches

Pay-per-click (PPC) is similar to display advertising found in offline print formats. Ads are displayed when particular search terms are entered into the search engine. These ads appear on the right-hand side of the results page and are often referred to as sponsored links. However, unlike offline display ads, where a fee is payable in order for the ad to be printed, here a fee is only payable once the display ad is clicked, and the searcher is taken through to the company's webpage. See Exhibit 14.2 for an example of these sponsored links displayed as a result of the keyphrase 'cheap airline tickets' input to Google.

It is important for organisations to maintain high visibility, especially in competitive markets, and they cannot rely on their search engine optimisation skills alone. PPC is a paid search list and once again, position in the listings (on the right-hand side of the page) is important. The position in the list is determined mainly through a bidding process. Each organisation bids an amount they are willing to pay for each searcher's click, against a particular key word or phrase. Unsurprisingly, the higher the bid the higher the position on a page. To place these bids, brokers (or PPC ad networks) are used and their role is to determine what a competitive cost per click should be for their client. They achieve this through market research to determine probable conversion rates, and from this deduce what the purchase and lifetime value of customers are likely to be. Consideration needs to be given to the quality of the landing page to which searchers are taken (not the home page), and whether the call-to-action is sufficiently strong.

Search engine marketing is important if only because of the relative ineffectiveness of other online marketing activities. The goal of SEM is to drive traffic to websites, and ranking on the search-results page is achieved in two fundamentally different ways. In SEO ranking searches are based on content while the PPC approach relies entirely on price as a ranking mechanism.

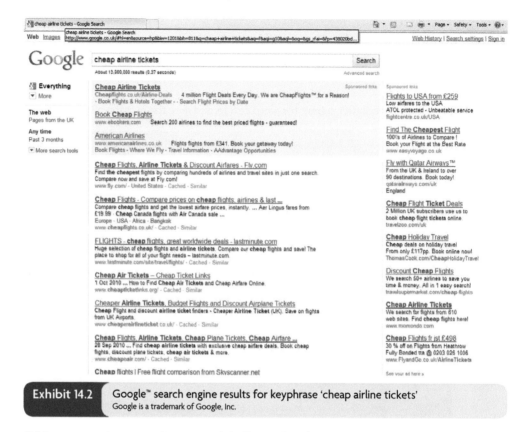

Exhibit 14.2	Google™ search engine results for keyphrase 'cheap airline tickets'
	Google is a trademark of Google, Inc.

Of these two main approaches, research indicates that the PPC model attracts far more investment (by advertisers) than the SEO model. This indicates that paid ads or sponsored links have low credibility and do not carry high levels of trust. Added to this is the overwhelming research that shows that SEO is more effective in terms of recall and driving site traffic (Jansen and Molina, 2006). However, Kimberley (2010) reports that research undertaken by IAB has found that brands are failing to exploit the potential offered by search engine marketing.

Viewpoint 14.2   Searching for quality chocolate

Luxury chocolate retailer Hotel Chocolat began as a mail-order business. However, the company's marketing strategy involved the development of a multichannel approach. This was realised through the launch of an online store and then through the opening of various offline stores.

The design and opening of its online store required that the company consider its search engine marketing and in particular SEO. In order to determine the key search words and phrases that customers for high quality chocolates would use, rather than just chocolate, they used a mind mapping process. Phrases such as 'Gifts for Christmas' and 'Gifts for Valentines' emerged, complementing their peak sales periods.

The company has bought a cocoa plantation in the West Indies and both text and video content was added to the site. This material was reflected in the site's tags so that a range of related ethical key phrases was built into its SEO work and Hotel Chocolat's search ratings improved.

Question

Why do people search for chocolate – don't we know where to buy our preferred chocolate?

Task

Choose a product category you are interested in and list some of the keywords that should assist SEO.

Email marketing

There are two key characteristics associated with email communications. First, it can be directed at clearly defined target groups and individuals. Second, email messages can be personalised and refined to meet the needs of individuals. In this sense email is the antithesis of broadcast communications, which are scattered among a mass audience and lack any sense of individualisation, let alone provide an opportunity for recipients to respond. In addition, email can be used with varying levels of frequency and intensity, which is important when building awareness, reinforcing messages or when attempting to persuade someone into a trial or purchase.

Organisations need to manage two key dimensions of email communications; outbound and inbound email. Outbound email concerns messages sent by a company often as a part of a direct marketing campaign, designed to persuade recipients to visit a website, to take a trial or make a purchase. The inbound dimension concerns the management of email communications received from customers and other stakeholders. These may have been stimulated either by an individual's use of the website, exposure to a news item about the product or organisation, or through product experience, which often entails a complaint. Managing inbound email represents a huge opportunity not only to build email lists for use in outbound campaigns, but also to provide high levels of customer service interaction and satisfaction. If undertaken properly and promptly this can help to build trust and reputation, which in turn can stimulate word-of-mouth communication, all essential aspects of marketing communication. Activity-triggered email that incorporates the interests of the target audience and which follow up on audience behaviour are deemed to be more successful and good practice, if only because of the higher conversion rates and return on investment.

Viewpoint 14.3   Email haven

Email marketing can not only stimulate a response but can also be used to develop brand experiences. For example, Haven, the holiday company, embedded video in their emails. In order to capture attention, these were designed to play automatically when the email is opened, rather than require the recipient to click on a link.

The facility appealed to two main audiences. Previous visitors could relive the Haven experience and have their beliefs reinforced, key to securing another booking. Potential visitors could feel the Haven experience virtually, provide a point of differentiation and build anticipation. The email also linked to the main website enabling recipients to access further information, offers and booking online.

The campaign successfully raised the conversion rate by 50 per cent.

Source: Based on Fletcher (2009)

Question

What might be the reasons for declining levels of email marketing?

Task

Find an online source of business mailing lists. Review the website and make a list of the sorts of questions you might ask.

The use of email to attract and retain customers has become a main feature of many marketing communications campaigns. Using appropriate email lists is a fast, efficient and effective way to communicate regularly with a market. Email-based marketing communication enables organisations to send a variety of messages concerning public relations-based announcements, newsletters and sales promotions, to distribute online catalogues and to start and manage permission-based contact lists. Many organisations build their own lists using data collected from their CRM system. By acquiring email responses and other contact mechanisms, addresses and contact details can be captured for the database and then accessed by all customer support staff. The use of email to attract and retain customers has become a main feature of many organisations' marketing communications campaigns. Indeed, email can be used to deliver messages at all points in the customer relationship lifecycle.

Short message services (SMS)

Although different in format, short message services (SMS), or 'texting', can be regarded as an extension of email communication. SMS is a non-intrusive but timely way of delivering information and as Doyle (2003) points out, the Global System for Mobile Communication (GSM) has become a standard protocol, so that users can send and receive information across geographic boundaries. Apart from pure text, other simple applications consist of games, email notifications, and information-delivery services such as sports and stock market updates.

Yaobin *et al.* (2010) undertook a study into the reasons why consumers use SMS. The research was based in China, where SMS is used extensively and the results highlighted three main reasons for use. These concern the perceived utilitarian value of SMS, the level of intrinsic enjoyment and the satisfaction derived from the involvement in communication. The third reason was the relatively low costs of use.

For some time organisations were relatively slow at adopting SMS despite the low costs and high level of user control (target, content and time). However, as organisations recognise these benefits so SMS has become an integral part of the media mix for many organisations. However, marketers also need to consider the potential concerns of consumers, most notably security and privacy. Just as with email, there is the potential for unwanted messages (i.e. spam) and Internet service providers (ISP) need to manage the increasing numbers of unsolicited messages through improved security systems as SMS becomes more widespread. Given that most consumers pay for SMS functionality, marketers should realise that invading personal privacy greatly reduces the potential value and effectiveness of SMS.

Apps

An app is a mobile application, a piece of software that is downloaded and runs on mobile devices such as smartphones. Apps enable users to do things such as find a cinema, restaurant, bank or other destination, read news, update a grocery list, track a team's score, play games, remember where the car is parked, all on a mobile phone (Sullivan, 2010). Procter & Gamble launched an app to support its Pampers brand, called *Hello Baby*, which allows pregnant women to track the development of their baby.

From a marketing communication perspective, apps enable a brand to be connected with a user as they move around. Some apps can become an integral part of a user's life, some can strengthen brand awareness, and others offer opportunities for more frequent interaction and brand engagement.

Most of the 140,000 available apps have been developed for Apple's iPhone and iPod Touch. Unsurprisingly, people prefer free apps, which is significant in terms of the limited opportunities brands have to recover the approximately £55,000 to $65,000 necessary to develop a mainstream app.

Goddard (2010) suggests that apps can be categorised into four types:

- **Campaign based** apps have high brand value content but little everyday utility. This means they will attract attention in the short term but will not serve to retain users.
- **Popular gimmick** apps are characterised by having low brand value, and are not very useful. Their value lies in supporting short term campaigns or events, but can become obsolete

when the campaign finishes. A brewer launched an app resembling a pint of beer that poured out when the mobile device was tilted. Good for entertainment purposes but once seen there is little value in repeating.

- **Straight utilities** are apps that serve as everyday tools. Location finders, currency converters, and recipe and menu directories can be useful but competition is high and standout opportunities are rare.
- **Branded utilities** are both highly useful and develop the brand promise. These are considered to be the most powerful types of mobile apps, simply because engagement occurs through the functionality which is tied to the essential value of the brand.

Apps enable brands such as Chanel, Ford, Pepsi, Visa, Lynx and many others, opportunities to provide users with branded content, which as Yuill (2010) suggests, can be anywhere at anytime to suit the user.

Widgets

Widgets are stand-alone applications that enable users to interact with the owner of the widget. As Chaffey (2008) suggests, the applications can provide functionality such as a calculator or real-time information, as in travel updates or weather forecasts. Widgets sit on a desktop, are relatively cheap to develop, easy to manage and ideally are distributed virally.

The real benefit of widgets is that they provide a way of advertising a brand, delivering online public relations or even driving direct response sales via affiliate marketing.

Blythe (2008) sees the real potential of widgets as sponsored entities on social networking sites. To date, attempts by brands to derive commercial benefit from social networking sites have been thwarted by the prevailing network culture that is essentially one that rejects advertising and outright commercialism. Sponsored widgets might provide a means of overcoming these difficulties as widgets offer benefits that might appeal to social network users. For example, the group Jamiroquai use a widget that allows their fans to keep up-to-date on video releases, tour dates and tracks. Cadbury have created a game called 'Room with a Goo'. In it players are required to stop Creme Eggs being smashed, blended and splattered. A widget on the Bebo site enables users to destroy or rebuild others Cadbury's Creme Eggs by either hugging or karate-chopping the eggs, virtually. A whole range of widget applications can be seen at www.directory.snipperoo.com.

Affiliate marketing

Associated with the concepts of communities and networks, affiliate marketing has become an essential aspect of online marketing communications and ecommerce. Walmsley (2010) estimates that affiliate marketing is worth approximately £4 billion in sales in the UK. Affiliate schemes are based on a network of websites on which advertisements or text links are placed. Those who click on them are taken directly to the host site. If this results in a sale, only then will the affiliate receive a commission (payment for the ad). Cookies, information generated by a web server and stored in the user's computer, ready for future access (http://www.cookiecentral.com/c_concept.htm), are used to track, monitor and record transactions and pay commission plus any agreed charges. As with many online marketing schemes, management can be undertaken in-house or outsourced. If the latter approach is adopted then many of the relationship issues discussed earlier, need to be considered and managed.

Amazon is probably one of the best examples of affiliate marketing schemes. Amazon has thousands of affiliates who all drive visitors to the Amazon website. If a product is sold to the visitor as a result of the click-through, then the affiliate is rewarded with a commission payment. Affiliate schemes are popular because they are low-cost operations, paid on a results-only basis and generating very favourable returns on investment.

McCormick (2010) reports on the use of affiliate marketing by Lastminute.com. This organisation considers its affiliate network as a team and an integral part of its marketing programme. Affiliates receive emails twice a week advising about key performing products and offers in their key sales areas. Blogs are used to provide up to date information. Lastminute.com also provide their affiliates with advice and facilities to generate increased income. For example, these include bespoke banners for placement by the key affiliate partners and templates and designs for email newsletters. Even quiet or underperforming affiliates are reached with communications that flag relevant offers to get them operating once again.

Review sites constitute a large proportion of affiliate activity and so these are targeted with specific offers to be run against each relevant review. Feedback is encouraged and analysis shows that clicks through from affiliates rose in 2009 by 22.4 per cent.

Augmented reality

Glasses Direct enable customers to see online how they look with different frames. The 'online mirror' technologies behind this facility are referred to as augmented reality (AR). By mixing the real world with digitally generated information or images, AR opens opportunities for both business and consumer-oriented interactive marketing communications (Clawson, 2009). So, augmented reality will allow people to see what they look like in different clothes, without having to get changed into them and with developments in mobile technology, without a change of location.

At the time of writing AR based technologies are developing but they are increasingly used in mobile applications in connection with location facilities. For example, they can be used as virtual wardrobes, shop fronts, store layouts and as a means of locating shops, tube stations, restaurants, pubs and theatres with a mobile phone (Benady, 2009).

| Viewpoint 14.4 | E.On augment their sponsorship of the FA Cup |

E.On's sponsorship of the FA Cup involved two trophy tours. One was the conventional nationwide tour enabling fans to physically get close to the famous cup. The other was a virtual tour enabled through augmented reality (AR). Fans of the two finalists were able to go online and using a webcam and capture an image of themselves lifting the FA Cup.

Marketing communications used to support the activities involved a national print campaign and viral video seeded across a range of targeted websites. They were both intended to raise awareness and the former intended to drive traffic to the website where there were instructions on how to use the AR facility, and of course, register with E.On.

The press work included an augmented reality marker, so that people with enabled phones could access the virtual FA Cup online, straightaway.

The digital campaign lasted just one week and over 90,000 users visited the site in that period whilst the seeded content prompted three times the normal click-throughs.

Source: Based on Dundas (2010)

Question

How might augmented reality assist marketing communications?

Task

Identify two non-football activities that would benefit from the use of augmented reality technology.

Bring your family and The FA Cup together in 4 easy steps.

1. Visit familyfootball.co.uk and select The Virtual FA Cup.

2. Hold the black symbol in the centre up to your webcam.

3. Experience that moment of glory felt by Chelsea yesterday.

4. Email a video or picture of your celebrations to your friends and family.

Exhibit 14.3 | **Virtual entertainment with AR**
Image for this past campaign is used courtesy of E.ON UK plc

Word-of-mouth communication

It was established in Chapter 2 that people use word-of-mouth recommendations to provide information and to support and reinforce their purchasing decisions. The impact of personal influences on the offline communication process can be important if communication is to be successful. Opinion leaders and formers were identified as significant personal influencers, simply because organisations target these individuals with messages knowing that they will transmit messages onwards to the organisation's target audience. The same principle is true of digital communications where the popular term 'word-of-mouse' is used to reflect personal, electronic recommendation and endorsement. However, the role of opinion formers is much diminished in the online world, especially with the predominant 18–25-year-old user group. For them expert opinion, as represented by opinion formers, is rejected in favour of peer group recommendation. For example, www.last.fm, a social music platform, tracks individual music preferences based on what people play on their computers or iPods, locates individuals in neighbourhoods who share similar tastes and then wait for them to interact. People share views, interests and favourite music and then make recommendations to others in their neighbourhood, based on shared preferences (Crow, 2007). Although there is a hint of social engineering, the power of peer group and opinion leader recommendation has seen this model copied by others, including book libraries.

Five main aspects of electronic word-of-mouth communication are considered here: viral marketing, podcasts, web logs (or blogs), Twitter and RSS feeds.

Viral marketing

Viral marketing involves the use of email to convey messages to a small part of a target audience where the content is sufficiently humorous, interesting or persuasive that the receiver feels emotionally compelled to send it on to a friend or acquaintance. For example, football matches between teams from the same city are always full of tension, grit and passion, and that is just the fans. One such cup match was played between Everton and Liverpool in February 2009. The match was being screened live but there was a technical error with the automated advertising system, just as the match went into extra time. So as fans watched a Tic Tac ad interrupt the match, unknown to them the winning goal was scored by Everton.

Once the inevitable arguments died down, the agency WCRS, who developed the ad for Tic Tac, decided to use the event to make a 20-second viral for a little bit of fun. The aim was to re-create Dan Gosling's goal, but instead they used two teams dressed as orange and lime Tic Tac men. Filmed on a winter's day on the Hackney Marshes, the viral not only poked fun at the issue but also provided entertainment around the Tic Tac brand (Nettleton, 2009).

Viral can also be used to support product launches, as demonstrated by the launch of Google Wave. Essentially a collaboration tool which allows users to swap messages, pictures, video, and gadgets and merges them into a single, user friendly application, it was important to demonstrate the features of the new product. This was achieved using a viral based on a scene from the film *Pulp Fiction*. The visual effects are performed through a remote user clicking on Google Wave, and the audio was just the dialogue from the film. The viral was viewed 500,000 times in the first two weeks, posted on 335 blogs and featured in over 4,600 tweets (GoViral, 2009).

The term, 'viral marketing' was developed by a venture capital company, Draper Fisher Juvertson (Juvertson and Draper, 1997). It was used to describe the Hotmail email service, one of the first free email address services offered to the general public and one that has grown enormously. According to Juvertson (2000: 12) they defined the term simply as 'network-enhanced word-of-mouth'. However, although the literature contains a variety of terminology used to explain what viral marketing is, for example *stealth marketing* (Kaikati and Kaikati,

Exhibit 14.4	Old Spice ads prove to be viral hits
	Image courtesy of The Advertising Archives

2004), *interactive marketing* (Blattberg and Deighton, 1991) and *referral marketing* (de Bruyn and Lilien, 2004), viral marketing (communications) is the term used here.

Porter and Golan (2006: 33) suggest that viral advertising is 'unpaid peer-to-peer communication of provocative content originating from an identified sponsor using the Internet to persuade or influence an audience to pass along the content to others'. They argue that these materials are usually seeded through the Internet, are often distributed through independent third-party sites, are usually personal, more credible than traditional advertising and humour is almost unanimously employed in executions. Kirby, a leading viral marketing consultant, agrees indicating that there are three key elements associated with viral marketing (2003):

- *content*, which he refers to as the 'viral agent' is the quality of the creative material and whether it is communicated as text, image or video;

- *seeding*, which requires identifying websites or people to send email to in order to kick start the virus;

- *tracking*, or monitoring, the impact of the virus and in doing so provide feedback and a means of assessing the return on the investment.

However, although these qualities might be present, it is necessary that receivers of viral messages are predisposed to open the message, derive value from the message and be sufficiently engaged to become a part of the virus campaign by sending it on to others.

There is no doubt that viral marketing is difficult to control and can be very unpredictable, yet despite these characteristics organisations are incorporating this approach within their marketing communications in order to reach their target audiences. Increasingly organisations are using word-of-mouth communications to generate conversations before the official launch. Kellogg's used social media for six months before officially launching Special K Crackers with traditional media. Ford in America used social media to encourage word-of-mouth communication for a year before running tv ads for the latest edition Fiesta (Anon, 2010). The key reasons for this approach are that it helps identify interested communities and consumer groups and it also encourages feedback, in a similar way to test marketing.

Social media

The terms social media and social networks have become increasingly prevalent. Although similar, they do not mean the same yet are often used interchangeably, and mistakenly. Kaplan and Haenlein (2009: 61) define social media as 'a group of Internet based applications that build on the ideological and technological foundations of Web 2.0 and that allow the creation and exchange of User Generated Content'. In other words social media refers to a broad range of web based applications and social networking sites are one of the many applications that are available. Others include weblogs, content communities (e.g. YouTube), collaborative projects (e.g. Wikipedia), virtual game worlds (e.g. World of Warcraft) and virtual social worlds (e.g. Second Life).

Social networks

One particular interpretation of online communities is the rapid development of social networks. Social networks are about people using the Internet to share lifestyle and experiences. The participants in these networks not only share information and experiences, but they can also use the interactive capacity to build new relationships. The critical aspect of social networks is that the content is user-generated and this means users own, control and develop content according to their needs, not those of a third party.

Social networks concern the Internet's ability to enable people to share experiences. Typical sites include MySpace, Bebo, YouTube and Facebook, each of which has experienced rapid growth in recent years. These sites provide certain segments of the population, mainly the 16–25-year-old group, an opportunity to use online networks to reach their friends, generate new ones and share experiences, information and insights. The activity might also be regarded as a supplement to their offline social networks. Some sites encourage ranking and rating of content that has been added to the site by others, for example Digg and Flickr. What is happening is that social networks are helping to re-engineer the way in which parts of society link together and share information (Walmsley, 2007).

The results of a European-wide study undertaken by Forrester Research reveal that there are six key characteristics that typify the dominant usage by online consumers of social media (Pinkerfield, 2007). There are those whose core activity on these sites is to publish content (9 per cent); those who prefer to comment (18 per cent); networkers (1 per cent); those who gather information (12 per cent); people who prefer to listen and observe interaction (19 per cent); and finally a large group who ignore all these activities (41 per cent).

When these data are aggregated on a country by country basis, it is revealed that the Dutch are the most active users publishing the most blogs and webpages. The Spanish prefer to comment, while the Italians actively gather information. French users are most likely to read blogs and reviews (are listeners), while UK users prefer to visit social media sites and make comments, typical of networkers. The study found that the Germans tend to ignore most social media.

The growth of MySpace and Facebook is partly a reflection of the relative investment made in them. MySpace has seen little investment and has attracted widespread criticism, whereas Facebook is perceived to be innovative and eager to meet the needs of its target audience. For example, as part of its strategic development in 2007, Facebook allowed its users to build and install applications within the social network. The more obvious marketing strategy would have been to charge developers the opportunity to access Facebook's users. However, by opening the site up in this way, and free of charge, huge numbers of people switched to the site and within a couple of months over 1,700 new applications, such as SuperPoke, which encourages users to 'slap, chest-bump or headbutt', photo slideshows and online data storage, had been developed, integrated and accessed by site visitors.

The relative immaturity of the social networking arena and the way in which content is developed raises challenges about how organisations can best use social media as part of their marketing communications to reach their target audiences. It has been mentioned earlier that site users are less than loyal as many have own multiple sites, so the challenge is to persuade users to visit their sites as often as possible and to encourage them to attract new users. The key therefore, is to create sites that are 'sticky', that is, contain sufficient content and facilities that engage users and give them reason to stay on the site for longer periods of time and also give them reason to return on a regular basis. If this works and the number of users increases then this should attract advertisers who are willing to pay premium rates.

However, questions then arise about the effectiveness of online ads in a social networking environment. Many users do not like brand advertising and prefer to take advice from their online peers in these communities when deciding what to buy, rather than listen to advertisers. Social networking is becoming a media channel in its own right and it is one that is reflecting the voice of consumers instead of those of brand owners.

An understanding of social media reveals that brand communications should not be invasive, intrusive or interruptive. In order to work, marketing communications need to become part of the context in which site users interact. Online advertising will continue to form a major revenue stream for the owners of these social networking sites, but increasingly this needs to be supplemented with the use of a mixture of sponsorship, product placement and public relations. For example, sponsored groups, such as Apple's 'Apple Students' group, with 400,000 members, have been developed (Hicks, 2007).

Asda approached Mumsnet.com, a parenting online community, for advice about the extent to which its clothing products encouraged the sexualisation of children. This followed the well publicised outcry concerning Primark's sales of padded bikini tops for young children (Charles, 2010).

See also Viewpoint 14.5 for two examples of the way in which brands are beginning to be involved with social networks.

Viewpoint 14.5   Kodak snaps into social media

Although more companies are using social media as part of their consumer communications, the role of social media within the business market is less well established. Kodak is one of the more advanced organisations, placing social media as a central element of their b2b programme.

The head of marketing at Kodak started using Twitter within his family but soon gained a following of over 27,000 'Kodak families', a substantial proportion of whom were also working through Facebook. Among these were commercial photographers and printers with whom Kodak were able to communicate directly, without any filters. As a result Kodak are able to gauge which products are being discussed and in what context. Automated tweet responses are enabled in many cases, but perhaps the major point is that Kodak has set up a Chief Listener. This person listens to the social media conversations and helps shape and route the dialogue so that Kodak are in a better position to learn from their business customers and consumers and in doing so are able to develop products and services that meet the needs of their markets more accurately.

Source: Based on Turner (2010)

Question
What are the key difficulties faced by brands attempting to use social networks to reach their target markets?

Task
Ask your networked friends what they feel about brands using social networks to reach them.

Web logs

Web logs, or blogs as they are commonly known, are personal online diaries. Although personal issues are recorded and shared, a large proportion of blogs concern organisations and public issues, and they are virtually free. As Wood *et al.* (2006) conclude, blogging represents a simple, straightforward way of creating a web presence.

Even if the quality and content of some blogs varies considerably, their popularity has grown enormously. The informality of blogs enables information to be communicated in a much more relaxed manner than most other forms of marketing communication. This is typified by the use of podcasting and the downloading of blogs to be 'consumed' at a later, more convenient time or while multi-tasking. Blogs represent user-generated-content (for more on UGC see Chapter 15) and are often a key indicator of the presence of an opinion leader or former.

Blogs can be understood using a number of criteria, other than the basic consumer or corporate demarcation. Typically, the content and the type of media are the main criteria. A blog can be categorised by its content or the general material with which it is concerned. The breadth of content is only limited by the imagination, but some of the more mainstream blogs tend to cover topics such as sport, travel, music, film, fashion and politics. Blogs can also be categorised according to the type of media. For example, 'vlogs' contain video collections, whereas a 'photoblog' is a collection of photos and a 'sketchblog' contains sketches.

Nardi *et al.* (2004), as cited by Jansen *et al.* (2009) found five reasons why people choose to blog:

- documenting their lives;
- providing commentary and opinions;
- expressing deeply held emotions;
- articulating ideas through writing;
- forming and maintaining communities.

These appear to be a list of outward facing reasons. What is not mentioned here are inner directed reasons, such as the need for feedback or psychological issues relating to the need for self-esteem, reassurance and reinforcement of an individual's identity.

Business-related or corporate blogs represent huge potential as a form of marketing communications for organisations. This is because blogs reflect the attitudes of the author, and these attitudes can influence others. As consumers write about their experiences with brands, opportunities exist for organisations to identify emerging trends, needs and preferences, and to also understand how brands are perceived. Sony used blogging as an integral part of its campaign to establish the Handycam and Cybershot brands. When shooting the ad in Miami, dubbed as 'Sony Foam City', Sony invited 200 visitors, mainly bloggers. Each was equipped with a Sony camera and encouraged to capture the soapy event which involved covering parts of Miami with foam. Clips of the ad and the making of the ad were then leaked onto the Internet in advance of the launch of the ad being released and in doing so created a buzz around the brands.

Organisations can set up *external* corporate blogs to communicate with customers, channel partners and other stakeholders. Many major organisations use external blogs to provide information about company issues and other organisations use blogs to launch brands or attend to customer issues. The other form of corporate blog is the *internal* blog. Here the focus is on enabling employees to write about and discuss corporate policies, issues and developments. Some organisations encourage interaction between their employees and customers and the general public. Although problems can arise through inappropriate comments and observations, blogging is an informal communication device that can serve to counter the formality often associated with planned marketing communications.

Therefore, enabling people to blog, perhaps by creating dedicated web space, facilitates interaction and communication through people with similar interests. There is also an added attraction in that communities of bloggers can attract advertisers and form valuable revenue streams. Blogs can be used by organisations as a form of public relations in order to communicate with a range of stakeholders. For example, a blog on an intranet can be used to support internal communications, on an extranet to support distributors and on the Internet to reach and influence consumers.

Microblogging

Microblogging or nanoblogging as it is sometimes referred to, is a short format version of blogging. It is a form of eWoM and uses web social communication services (Jansen *et al.*, 2009) of which Twitter is probably the best known. A microblog, or tweet, consists of a short comment, a post of 140 characters, which is shared with a network of followers. This makes production and consumption relatively easy in comparison to blogs.

These posts can be distributed through instant messages, email, mobile phones or the web. Therefore, as Jansen *et al.*, put it, people can share brand-related thoughts at any time, and more or less anywhere, with people who are connected via web, cell phone or IM and email, on an unprecedented scale.

Viewpoint 14.6   All of a twitter

The longer term impact of twittering is debated by many but there are several examples where the effectiveness of microblogging is clearly demonstrated. When *Daily Mail* journalist Jan Moir published a controversial article about the death of Boyzone singer, Stephen Gately, Scott Pack tweeted about a 'vile piece of journalism'. Soon various people had led responses and a twitterstorm emerged. The huge volume of activity, within a few hours, led the # janmoir story (# a twitter method of uniting all related tweets) to become the top topic. The effect of this activity was to make the *Mail* change its website headline, Marks and Spencer withdrew their advertising on the webpage, whilst the Press Complaints Commission received a record number of 1,000 complaints, a figure that was to rise to 22,000.

Twitter announced in April 2010 that they were to enable advertisers to purchase 'promoted tweets'. These ads are intended to be compatible with the conversations they accompany.

Source: Based on Henley (2009); www.bbc.co.uk

Question

To what extent does twittering represent a marketing opportunity for organisations?

Task

Find two twitter conversations, one led by a politician and the other by a celebrity. How does the content differ?

It is already understood that WoM has a particularly significant impact on purchasing decisions, but eWoM can take place close to or even during a purchase process. Although eWoM may be less personal than face2face WoM, it has substantially greater reach and has greater credibility because it is in print and accessible by others (Hennig-Thurau *et al.*, 2004). The implication of this is that microblogging offers huge potential to marketers. Twitter recognise this potential and in April 2010 announced that they were to allow advertising on their site. However these are not conventional adverts. These ads are tweets, and are an integral part of the conversations, referred to as 'Promoted Tweets'. These messages, limited to 140 characters, appear at the top of the page when a user has searched for that word, and will only show up in search results (Steele, 2010).

Jansen *et al.* explore the commercial potential and find that of all microblogs (in their sample), 19 per cent mention an organisation, product or service. Of these, '20 per cent express a sentiment or opinion concerning that company, product or service' (2009: 2184). They also find that the ratio of positive to negative tweets is approximately 50 per cent to 35 per cent. This last point is interesting as it is generally accepted that in offline WoM a positive brand experience is likely to be shared with three people whereas a negative experience is usually shared with nine others.

Podcasting

Podcasting emerged as a major new form of communication in 2005 and has grown significantly since then. This is mainly because of the huge growth in the adoption of MP3 players and the desire for fresh, up-to-date or different content.

Podcasting is a process whereby audio content is delivered over the Internet to iPods, MP3 players and computers, on demand. A podcast is a collection of files located at a feed address, which people can subscribe to by submitting the address to an aggregator. When new content becomes available it is automatically downloaded using an aggregator or feed reader which recognises feed formats such as RSS (see below).

In many ways podcasting is similar to radio broadcasts, yet there are a couple of major differences. First, podcast material is pre-recorded and time-shifted so that material can be listened to at a user's convenience, that is, on demand. The second difference is that listeners can take the material they have chosen to listen to, and play it at times and locations that are convenient to them. They can listen to the content as many times as they wish simply because the audio files can be retained.

Podcasting is relatively inexpensive and simple to execute. It opens up publishing to a host of new people, organisations as well as individuals, and it represents a new media channel for audio content. Users have control over what they listen to, when they listen to it and how many times they listen to the content.

RSS

RSS stands for 'really simple syndication' and refers to the distribution of news content on the web. Rather than trawl all relevant webpages to find new content and updates, RSS allows for specific content to be brought together and made available to an individual without their always having to return to numerous sites. Just checking the RSS feed to see whether something new has been posted online can save huge amounts of time.

Originally email was the preferred way of notifying people of breaking news and information updates. The problem with email is that not only has the user to sort out and organise the separate strands of information, they also have to contend with increasing amounts of spam and unwanted material that accompanies it. In addition, RSS feeds allow content updates to be read in a reader, not online.

From a publisher's point of view RSS feeds enable information to reach a wide audience. This is because of syndication. Once content has been created, RSS feeds allow the content to be grouped (syndicated) with websites that publish similar content. These are referred to as aggregator websites. Each feed consists of brief information about headlines, a summary of the content and a link to the article on the requisite website.

From a marketing perspective RSS feeds act as a media channel delivering a variety of information about news stories, events, headlines, project updates and even corporate information, often as press releases. This information is delivered quickly and efficiently to audiences who have signed up and effectively given express permission to be sent the information.

Interactive online communities

Armstrong and Hagel (1996) were two of the first researchers to propose the benefits of virtual communities. They also saw that the development of these communities is one of the key elements that differentiate interactive from traditional media. Communities of people who share a common interest(s), who interact, share information, develop understanding and build relationships all add value, in varying degrees, through their contribution to others involved with the website. In a sense, user groups and special interest groups are similar facilities, but the key with all these variations is the opportunity to share information electronically, often in real time.

Chaffey *et al.* (2006) refer to Durlacher (1999), who argues that there are four main types of community defined by their purpose, position, interest and profession (see Table 14.2). Communities can be characterised by several determining elements. Muniz and O'Guinn (2001) identify three core components:

- consciousness of kind: an intrinsic connection that members feel towards one another;
- the presence of shared rituals and traditions that perpetuate the community's history, culture and consciousness;
- a sense of moral responsibility, duty or obligation to the community as a whole and its individual members.

Within these online or virtual communities five particular characteristics can be identified. The first concerns the model of communication, which is essentially visitor-to-visitor and in some cases customer-to-customer. Second, communities create an identity that arises from each individual's involvement and sense of membership and belonging. The more frequent and intense the interaction, the stronger the identity the participants feel towards the community. Third, relationships, even close friendships develop among members, which in turn can facilitate mutual help and support. The fourth characteristic concerns the language that the community adopts. Very often specialised languages or codes of (electronic) behaviour emerge that have particular meaning to members. The fifth and final characteristic refers to the methods

Table 14.2	Four types of virtual community
Type of community	**Explanation**
Purpose	Those attempting to achieve the same goal or who are experiencing a similar process
Position	Those experiencing particular circumstances. These might be to do with life-stage issues (the old or the young), health issues or perhaps career development opportunities
Interest	Those sharing a hobby, pastime or who are passionately involved with, for example, sport, music, dance, family trees, jigsaws, gardening, film, etc.
Profession	Those involved with the provision of b2b services. Often created by publishers these portals provide information about jobs, company news, industry issues and trading facilities (e.g. auctions).

Source: Durlacher (1999). Used with permission

used to regulate and control the behaviour and operations of the community. Self-regulation is important in order to establish acceptable modes of conduct and interaction among the membership.

The role that members assume within these communities and the degree to which they participate also varies. There are members who attend but contribute little, those who create topics, lead discussion, those who summarise and those who perform brokerage or intermediary roles among other members.

According to Jepsen (2006) the number of consumers undertaking product information search within virtual communities can be expected to develop simply because the number of experienced Internet users will grow. The provision and form of online communities will inevitably develop and frameworks will emerge in order that understanding about the way they operate (effectively) is disseminated. Szmigin and Reppel (2004) have offered their customer bonding triangle framework, which is built on interactivity, technical infrastructure and service value elements (see Figure 14.1). It is argued by the authors of this framework that it is the fit between the elements that determines the level of bonding between community members. Further work is required in this area, but this framework provides an interesting conceptualisation of the elements that characterise this approach.

The knowledge held in virtual communities can be expected to be of significant value when searching for product information. In 1999, Kozinets presented four segments related to virtual communities, based around two dimensions. The four segments identified by Kozinets, are referred to as insiders, devotees, minglers and tourists. Insiders have strong social ties to other members of the community and consumption is central to their self-image. Devotees only have ties to the product, minglers are tied to the members and tourists do not have ties to the product or other members. Jepsen speculates that information provided by the virtual community may be sufficiently strong for insiders that it replaces information from offline sources. This is probably not the case for any of the other three segments.

As a final comment, how should marketers manage all of this activity? Well apart from developing an integrated approach to marketing communications, strategy and tactics and learning to listen to social media rather than invade and interrupt it, Coca-Cola have developed a 4Rs model to assist their approach to this important issue. The 4Rs are regarded as pillars of their social media strategy; reviewing, responding, recording and redirecting.

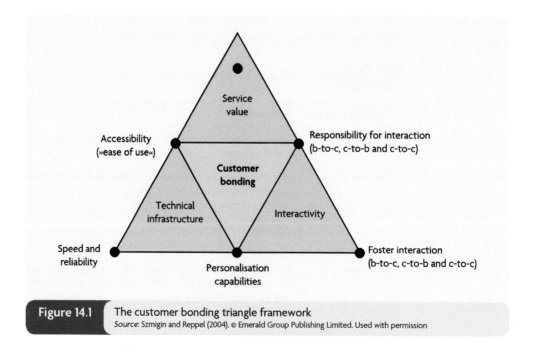

| Figure 14.1 | The customer bonding triangle framework |

Source: Szmigin and Reppel (2004). © Emerald Group Publishing Limited. Used with permission

Fawkes (2010) explains that conversations around the various Coke brands are tracked by specialist service companies. This review provides insight into the nature of the conversations and the overall sentiment being expressed about the brands. The response is enabled in two ways. Subject matter experts from a variety of departments inside the organisation respond to the specific or unusual queries and questions. A 'blog squad' of social media power users deal with the more general and orthodox questions posed by individuals.

The recording element refers to the development of blogs, podcasts and video material designed to entertain their audiences with compelling content. The redirecting pillar concerns the way Coca-Cola enables people to find and connect with the content that they create. This is achieved by interconnecting links through Google, Facebook and other major interfaces and search engines, through to MyCokeRewards. See also www.coca-cola.com.

Summary

In order to help consolidate your understanding of interactive marketing communications, here are the key points summarised against each of the learning objectives:

1 Appraise the nature and characteristics of interactive marketing communications

Interactive marketing communications allows participants in the communication process to interact with one another. Rather than passive one-way communication that characterises much of offline marketing communications, interactivity is inclusive, engages audiences and can lead to dialogue and the development of meaningful relationships.

2 Consider some of the issues relating to the way in which each of the tools of the communications mix can be used interactively

As offline revenues from television and print advertising decline, so money is being switched into interactive and online advertising. Direct response advertising is the primary approach used in this environment as advertisers seek to encourage users to click-through to destination webpages and microsites. Banner ads and sponsored link ads form the backbone of advertising in this fast-growing environment but online video advertising is set to grow.

Interactive based sales promotions, public relations and direct marketing all have key roles to play in a converging multimedia environment. Sales promotions and direct marketing provide incentives and motivation for people to become interactive and to become involved with a campaign or brand. Personal selling has the least application of all the traditional tools in an online environment.

3 Evaluate search engine marketing and distinguish the main features of both pay-per-click and search engine optimisation

There are two types of search engine marketing techniques: search engine optimisation (SEO) and pay-per-click (PPC). The latter outweighs the former quite substantially in terms of investment but the former is superior in terms of quality of results.

4 Discuss the features of email marketing communications for both customer acquisition and retention

Email communications can be directed at clearly defined target audiences, even individuals; they can be personalised and refined to meet the needs of individuals. In addition, email can be used with varying levels of frequency and intensity, which is important when building awareness, reinforcing messages or when attempting to persuade someone into a trial or purchase. It is a particularly useful way of provoking responses and can be used for customer acquisition and retention.

5 Evaluate the role of electronic word-of-mouth communications, and consider applications such as viral marketing communications, podcasting, RSS feeds, Twitter, and web logs

Word-of-mouth communications in an online environment is fast becoming a major form of communication. Viral marketing, podcasting, blogging and twittering are key ways in which word-of-mouth is being used.

6 Identify the characteristics of online communities and consider how social networks and affiliate marketing can be used to develop marketing communications opportunities

The development of online communities of people who share a common interest(s), interact, share information, develop understanding and build relationships has been a major characteristic of what is referred to as Web 2.0. In particular, social networks such as Facebook, MySpace and Bebo have millions of registered users and present major opportunities for communicating brands. The problem, however, is that conventional offline marketing communications, and advertising in particular, do not work in these environments. Alternative, more subtle and supportive communication strategies are required, such as sponsorship, product placement and public relations.

Review questions

1. Define interactive marketing communications and explain its key characteristics.
2. What might go wrong with the use of interactive marketing communications?
3. Identify reasons why organisations use interactive online advertising.
4. Name three types of online ad formats.
5. To what extent is online public relations just online advertising?
6. Explain the basic principles underpinning the way in which both search engine optimisation and pay-per-click systems operate.
7. Write a report examining the use of email as a form of marketing communications. Find examples to support the points you make.
8. Discuss the three key elements that Kirby associates with successful viral marketing.
9. Make brief notes concerning the ways in which marketing communications should be used within online communities.
10. Appraise the concept of word-of-mouth communication and consider its use within social networks.

References

Anon (2010) Brands use social media to drive pre-launch buzz, *Brand Week*. Retrieved 25 May 2010 from www.warc.com/news/

Armstrong, A. and Hagel III, J. (1996) The real value of on-line communities, *Harvard Business Review*, 74(3) (May/June), 134–141.

Benady, D. (2009) The future of shopping, *Revolution*, December, 48–51.

Blattberg, R.C. and Deighton, J. (1991) Interactive marketing: exploiting the age of address-ability, *Sloan Management Review*, 33(1), 5–14.

Blythe, A. (2008) How can brands exploit widgets? *Revolution* (April), 13.

de Bruyn, A. and Lilien, G.L. (2004) A multi-stage model of word-of-mouth through electronic referrals, *eBusiness Research Centre Working Paper*, February.

Chaffey, D., Ellis-Chadwick, F., Johnston, K. and Meyer, R. (2006) *Internet Marketing*. 3rd edn. Harlow: Pearson Education.

Chaffey, D. (2008) Using branded widgets, gadgets and buttons for web marketing. Retrieved 8 April 2008 from www.davechaffey.com/Internet-Marketing/C8-Communications/E-tools/Online-PR/Using-Widgets-Marketing

Charles, G. (2010) Asda calls in Mumsnet to approve kids clothes, *Marketing*, 21 April, 1.

Clawson, T. (2009) Don't believe the hype, *Revolution*, December, 44–47.

Crow, D. (2007) Talking about my generation, *The Business*, 28 July, 18–20.

Doyle, S. (2003) The big advantage of short messaging. Retrieved 16 May from www.sas.com/news

Dundas, C. (2010) Digital makes the brand connection, *Admap* (April). Retrieved 2 June 2010 from www.warc.com/ArticleCenter

Durlacher (1999) UK on-line community, *Durlacher Quarterly Internet Report*, Q3, 7–11, London.

Fawkes, F. (2010) Coca-Cola's Approach To Social Media, *FSFK*, 17 May. Retrieved 9 June 2010 from http://www.psfk.com/2010/05/brand-news-coca-cola%E2%80%99s-approach-to-social-media.html

Fletcher, M. (2009) Why data adds up, *Revolution – The Email Handbook*, September, 16–21.

Goddard, M. (2010) Sizing up a proposed app, *ABA Bank Marketing*, 42(4) (May) 20–23.

GoViral (2009) Viral View: Social Technographics: Are you keeping up with your online audience? Campaignlive, 6 November. Retrieved 14 June 2010 from http://www.brandrepublic.com/News/964382/Viral-View-Social-Technographics-keeping-online-audience/?DCMP=ILC-SEARCH

Henley, J. (2009) The power of tweets, *The Guardian*. Retrieved 3 November 2009 from www.guardian.co.uk

Hennig-Thurau, T., Gwinner, K.P. Walsh, G. and Gremle, D.D. (2004) Electronic word of mouth via consumer-opinion platforms: What motivates consumers to articulate themselves on the Internet?, *Journal of Interactive Marketing*, 18(1), 38–52.

Hicks, R. (2007) All About... Facebook, *Media Asia*, 3 August. Retrieved 13 August 2007 from http://www.brandrepublic.com/News/675228/About-Facebook/

Jansen, B.J. and Molina, P.R. (2006) The effectiveness of web search engines for retrieving relevant e-commerce links, *Information Processing and Management*, 42(4) (July), 1075–1098.

Jansen, B.J., Zhang, M., Sobel, K. and Chowdury, A. (2009) Twitter Power: Tweets as Electronic Word of Mouth, *Journal of the American Society for Information Science and Technology*, 60(11), 2169–2188.

Jarboe, G. (2005) Why does search engine marketing look like a penny-farthing bicycle?, *Internet Search Engine Database*, 11 January. Retrieved 27 July 2007, from www.isedb.com/news/article/1086/

Jepsen, A.L. (2006) Information search in virtual communities: is it replacing use of offline communication?, *Journal of Marketing Communications*, 12(4) (December), 247–261.

Jukes, M. (2009) Creative review: Comparethemarket.com, 26 February. Retrieved 20 September from www.brandrepublic.com/InDepth/Features/930643/APG-Creative-Strategy-Awards—Comparethemarketcom-meerkat-campaign-VCCP

Juvertson, S. (2000) *What is Viral Marketing?*, Draper Fisher Juvertson website. Retrieved 12 March 2006 from http://www.dfj.com/cgi-bin/artman/publish/printer_steve_may00.shtml

Juvertson, S. and Draper, T. (1997) *Viral marketing*, Draper Fisher Juvertson website. Retrieved 12 March 2006 from http://www.dfj.com/cgi-bin/artman/publish/printer_steve_tim_may97.html

Kaikati, A.M. and Kaikati, J.G. (2004) Stealth marketing: how to reach consumers surreptitiously, *California Management Review*, 46(4), 6–22.

Kaplan, A.M. and Haelein, M. (2010) Users of the world unite! The challenges and opportunities of social media, *Business Horizons*, 53, 59–68.

Kimberley, S. (2010) Search marketing fails to deliver full potential, *Marketing*, 30 June, 7.

Kirby, J. (2003) The message should be used as a means to an end, rather than just an end in itself, *VM-People*, 16 October. Retrieved 31 August 2007 from www.vm-people.de/en/vmknowledge/interviews/interviews_detail.php?id=15

Kozinets, R.V. (1999) E-tribalized marketing?: the strategic implications of virtual communities on consumption, *European Management Journal*, 17(3), 252–264.

Mathews, K. (2007) Is branding best and are click throughs through?, *Internet Advertising Bureau*. Retrieved 31 August 2007 from http://www.iabuk.net/en/1/isbrandingbestand areclickthroughsthrough.mxs

McCormick, A. (2010) Digital Report: Keep your affiliates onside, *Marketing*, 28 April, 41–43.

Muniz Jr, A.M. and O'Guinn, T.C. (2001) Brand community, *Journal of Consumer Research*, 27(4), 412–432.

Nardi, B.A., Schiano, D.J., Gumbrecht, M., and Swartz, L. (2004) Why we blog, *Communications of the ACM*, 47(12), 41–46.

Nettleton, K. (2009) Men dressed as Tic Tacs re-enact missed Everton goal, *Campaign*, 11 February. Retrieved 14 June 2010 from http://www.campaignlive.co.uk/news/880522/Men-dressed-Tic-Tacs-re-enact-missed-Everton-goal/?DCMP=ILC-SEARCH

Pinkerfield, H. (2007) New social media user types unveiled, *Revolution*, 28 June 2007. Retrieved 13 August 2007 from http://www.brandrepublic.com/News/667634/New-social-media-user-types-unveiled/

Porter, L. and Golan, G.J. (2006) From subservient chickens to brawny men: a comparison of viral advertising to television advertising, *Journal of Interactive Advertising*, 6(2), 30–38.

Ramsay, F. (2009) Building on Animal Magic, *Marketing*, 19 August, 20–21.

Steele, F. (2010) Twitter unveils advert Tweets in bid for profits, *Times Online*, 13 April. Retrieved 13 April 2010 from http://business.timesonline.co.uk/tol/business/industry_sectors/media/article7095914.ece

Sullivan, E.A. (2010) *Marketing App*-titude, *Marketing News*, 44(3), 15 March, 6.

Szmigin, I. and Reppel, A.E. (2004) Internet community bonding: the case of macnews.de, *European Journal of Marketing*, 38(5/6), 626–640.

Turner, C. (2010) How Kodak is using social media to convert users into consumers. Retrieved 20 March 2010 from www.utalkmarketing .com

VCCP (2009) Comparethemarket.com 'meerkat campaign', *campaignlive.co.uk*. Retrieved 17 September 2009 from http://www.brandrepublic.com/InDepth/Features/930643/APG-Creative-Strategy-Awards—Comparethemarketcom-meerkat-campaign-VCCP

Walmsley, A. (2007) Social networks are here to stay, *Marketing*, 27 June, 15.

Walmsley, A. (2010) Make your affiliations pay, *Marketing*, 5 May, 13.

Wood, W., Behling, R. and Haugen, S. (2006) Blogs and business: opportunities and headaches, *Issues in Information Systems*, V11(2), 312–316.

Yaobin, L., Deng, Z. and Bin, W. (2010) Exploring factors affecting Chinese consumers' usage of short message service for personal communication, *Information Systems Journal*, 20(2), 183–208.

Yuill, M. (2009) Smartphones and app stores driving mobile media, Admap, 503 (March). Retrieved 2 June 2010 from www.warc.com/articlecenter/

Chapter 15
Content: credibility, messages and creative approaches

The third element of the marketing communications mix is the content that is conveyed among audiences. It is therefore important to understand what organisations intend to say and how they say it. However, in an age of interaction, individual consumers also create and share content with others. In both cases, it is important that the presentation of the content is appropriate for the target audience so that they can assign meaning and respond appropriately.

Aims and learning objectives

The aim of this chapter is to consider some of the ways in which the content of marketing communication messages can be created, by focusing on some of the principal aspects of content believability, generation, message construction and presentation.

The learning objectives of this chapter are to:

1. examine the importance and characteristics of source credibility;

2. explore the advantages and disadvantages of using spokespersons in message presentation;

3. discuss the impact of user-generated content;

4. examine ideas concerning message framing and storytelling;

5. consider the characteristics of different types of message appeal;

6. indicate how informational and transformational motives can be used as tactical tools in advertising.

Introduction

Whether marketing communications converts people into becoming brand-loyal customers or acts as a defensive shield to reassure current buyers, there still remains a decision about the nature and form of the message to be conveyed: the content strategy. Traditionally, messages are considered to be either informational or emotional and conveyed from a company to customers. However, in addition to this messages can also be considered in terms of user-generated content, that is, messages conveyed from customers to companies and from customers to other customers. What is also of interest is that content can be placed inside entertainment vehicles, referred to as branded content. All of these are considered in this chapter.

In practice, the generation of suitable content is derived from a creative brief. For the sake of discussion and analysis, four elements will be considered. First, considerable attention is given to the source of a message and issues relating to *source credibility*. This is followed by a consideration of the *balance*, *structure* and *presentation* of the message itself to the target audience.

Message source

Messages are perceived in many different ways and are influenced by a variety of factors. However, a critical determinant concerns the credibility that is attributed to the source of the message itself. Kelman (1961) believed that the source of a message has three particular characteristics. These are: the level of perceived credibility as seen in terms of perceived objectivity and expertise; the degree to which the source is regarded as attractive and message recipients are motivated to develop a similar association or position; and the degree of power that the source is believed to possess. This is manifest in the ability of the source to reward or punish message recipients. The two former characteristics are evident in various forms of marketing communications, but the latter is directly observable in personal selling situations, and perhaps in the use of sales promotions.

Following this work on source characteristics three key components of source credibility can be distinguished:

- What is the level of perceived expertise (how much relevant knowledge the source is thought to hold)?
- What are the personal motives the source is believed to possess (what is the reason for the source to be involved)?
- What degree of trust can be placed in what the source says or does on behalf of the endorsement?

No matter what the level of expertise, if the level of trust is questionable, credibility will be adversely affected.

Establishing credibility

Credibility can be established in a number of ways. One simple approach is to list or display the key attributes of the product/service and then signal trustworthiness through the use of third-party endorsements and the comments of satisfied users. A more complex approach is to use referrals, suggestions and association.

Trustworthiness and expertise are the two principal elements of source credibility. One way of developing trust is to use spokespersons to speak on behalf of the sponsor of an advertisement and in effect, provide a testimonial for the product in question. Credibility, therefore, can be established by the initiator of the advertisement or by a spokesperson used by the initiator to convey the message.

Effectively, consumers trade off the validity of claims made by brands against the perceived trustworthiness (and expertise) of the individuals or organisations who deliver the message. The result is that a claim may have reduced impact if either of these two components is doubtful or not capable of verification but, if repeated enough times, will enable audiences to accept that the products are very effective and of sufficiently high performance for them to try.

Credibility established by the initiator

The credibility of the organisation initiating the communication process is important. An organisation should seek to enhance its reputation with its various stakeholders at every opportunity. However, organisational credibility is derived from the image, which in turn is a composite of many perceptions. Past decisions, current strategy and performance indicators, the level of perceived service and the type of channel members (e.g. high quality retail outlets) all influence the perception of an organisation and the level of credibility that follows.

One very important factor that influences credibility is branding. Private and family brands in particular, allow initiators to develop and launch new products more easily than those who do not have such brand strength. Brand extensions (such as Virgin into finance, lingerie and trains) have been launched with the credibility of the product firmly grounded in the strength of the parent brand name (Virgin). Consumers recognise the name and make associations that enable them to lower the perceived risk and in doing so provide a platform to try the new product.

The need to establish high levels of credibility, allows organisations to divert advertising spend away from a focus on brands to one that focuses on the organisation. Corporate advertising seeks to manage corporate image and to build reputation.

Viewpoint 15.1   Saucy make-up artists

Max Factor claims that its products are so good that they are used by the experts in their industry: 'The make-up of make-up artists'. Many of its recent campaigns feature expert make-up artists who work on blockbuster Hollywood movies. However, many of these experts are not known by the general public. The development of 'trustworthiness' therefore relies on the film's credentials.

As with all use of spokespersons, Max Factor needs to ensure that when using experts their target audiences perceive the messages to be genuinely believable. In this case, Max Factor uses these experts because they are perceived to be objective and independent simply because their job gives them freedom of choice with regard to the products they use.

Potential new customers seeing these advertisements are challenged on the grounds that if the brand is good enough for these experts then it should be good enough for them. If a viewer is already a Max Factor customer, then product experience will contribute to a support argument and these advertising messages are used to re-inforce previous brand choice decisions. Either way these Max Factor advertisements are extremely powerful.

Question

To what extent does the use of experts evade focus on product attributes and quality?

Task

Using various magazine ads for fragrances and cosmetics, make a list of the different ways source credibility is established.

Sarah Monzani. Make-up artist to Madonna.
'All a girl needs this season is a touch of gold.'

The New Gold Dust Collection

MAXFACTOR
the make-up of make-up artists

Gold Dust
Nail Varnish £5

Radiant Ruby
Lipstick £8

Bronze Shimmer
Panstik £7

Exhibit 15.1 A strong case of credibility with Max Factor
Image courtesy of The Advertising Archives

Credibility established by a spokesperson

People who deliver the message are often regarded as the source, when in reality they are only the messenger. These people carry the message and represent the true source or initiator of the message (e.g. manufacturer or retailer). Consequently, the testimonial they transmit must be credible. There are four main types of spokesperson: the expert, the celebrity, the chief executive officer and the consumer.

The expert has been used many times and was particularly popular when television advertising first established itself in the 1950s and 1960s. Experts are quickly recognisable because they wear white coats and round glasses, or dress and act like 'mad professors'. Through the use of symbolism, stereotypes and identification, these characters (and indeed others) can be established very quickly in the minds of receivers and a frame of reference generated that does not question the authenticity of the message being transmitted by such a person. Experts can also be users of products, for example professional photographers endorsing cameras, secretaries endorsing word processors and professional golfers endorsing golf equipment.

Exhibit 15.2	Nicole Kidman endorsing Chanel No 5
	Image courtesy of The Advertising Archives

Entertainment and sporting celebrities are used increasingly, not only to provide credibility for a range of high-involvement (e.g. Trinny and Susannah for Littlewoods, David Beckham for adidas, Michael Phelps for Speedo) and low-involvement decisions (e.g. Jamie Oliver for Sainsbury's, Cheryl Cole for L'Oréal Elvive shampoo) but also to grab the attention of people in markets where motivation to decide between competitive products may be low. The celebrity enables the message to stand out among the clutter and noise that typify many markets. It is also hoped that the celebrity and/or the voice-over will become a peripheral cue in the decision-making process: Peter Kaye for John Smith's (beer), Alan Hansen for Morrison's (supermarket) and as shown in Exhibit 15.2, Nicole Kidman for Chanel No. 5.

There are some potential problems that advertisers need to be aware of when considering the use of celebrities. First, does the celebrity fit the image of the brand and will the celebrity be acceptable to the target audience? Consideration also needs to be given to the longer-term relationship between the celebrity and the brand. Should the lifestyle of the celebrity change, what impact will this change have on the target audience and their attitude towards the brand?

The second problem concerns the impact that the celebrity makes relative to the brand. There is a danger that those receiving the message remember the celebrity but not the brand that is the focus of the advertising spend. The *celebrity* becomes the hero, rather than the product being advertised. Loveless (2007) reports on the financial services company First Plus who used celebrity mathematician Carol Vorderman to endorse their loan products. Some saw a discontinuity between this celebrity's values, and the possibility that the company she was endorsing might make some people worse off was highlighted. In these situations the endorser can overshadow the product to the extent that consumers might have trouble recalling the brand.

Celebrities are used because it is believed they provide a prompt for individuals to remember the brand and the message. In many ways they act as a peripheral cue, as in the elaboration likelihood model (Petty and Cacioppo, 1983). Agrawal and Kamakura (1995) argue that this cueing can also be associated with the development of brand personality. The celebrity/brand pairing enables the image and persona of the former to shape the perception of the brand. It is believed that this process works through transference theory (Andersen and Glassman, 1996), which is concerned with how a person interacts with others based upon past experiences and the influence of significant others in childhood (Sullivan 1953 cited by White *et al.* 2009). As a result of categorising people based on these experiences, individuals are able to replay their emotions and behaviour once they have classified new people who they encounter.

Using this in a marketing context, it is possible to predict how a person will form opinions of products and celebrity endorsers based on past experiences, which carry over into future experiences (Chen and Andersen, 1999). By linking products with celebrities who represent and signify particular meanings, advertisers can transfer the meaning a celebrity represents, to their product and then through various consumer rituals, the perceived image of a celebrity endorser can eventually transfer into an individual self-image (McCracken, 1989).

White *et al.* (2009) found that consumers who are exposed to negative information about a celebrity endorser, might transfer the negative perspective to the product. However, no such transference to the celebrity was found when there was negative information about the organisation.

Viewpoint 15.2   Kate Moss: winner or loser?

The sparkling career of superstar model Kate Moss was brought to an abrupt halt in 2005 when pictures of her were published in a national newspaper allegedly showing her taking drugs. This was followed shortly by another newspaper that published other lurid stories about her private life. The impact of the widespread publicity was devastating. First, H&M, at that time Europe's largest clothing chain, cancelled her £500,000 contract to be the brand's 'face'. After initially tolerating the tabloid attack the company decided that because of the close association with a charity dedicated to the prevention of drug abuse, the contract had to be cancelled. Consequently months of work and a £1 million advertising campaign, scheduled to be featured in glossy magazines, were abandoned.

Her contracts with the French fashion house Chanel, for whom she had been the face of Coco Mademoiselle perfume for four years, Rimmel and Burberry were all terminated.

However, her career was resurrected in 2006 when she first secured a lucrative contract to front a new campaign as the 'face' of Calvin Klein. This was followed by the announcement that she was to work with Topshop, not as a model and not as a conventional endorser. Her role was to be the designer for a new collection to be sold in all 309 branches of the High Street chain. This represented a significant shift for the superstar, from brand endorser to brand architect.

When the first collections went on sale there was a frenzy of activity. Some shoppers queued for eight hours to get first sight of the brand, the media gave the brand a mass of free publicity as they reported the opening event and Topshop themselves benefited through positive communications and sales and profits even though they had to limit individuals to buying just five items. This was to prevent exploitation of the Moss brand through sales on eBay.

Topshop appear to have struck gold with Kate Moss, and Moss herself has done nicely. As Armstrong (2006) commented, her earnings have been rumoured to have quadrupled since the allegations in 2005.

Source: Based on various including Alleyne (2005a, 2005b); Anon (2006); Armstrong (2006) and Rushton (2007)

Question

Use Transference theory to interpret the events depicted in this Viewpoint.

Task

Think of three brands and find out who is used to endorse them.

Exhibit 15.3	Supermodel Kate Moss
	Kate Moss has been the face of a number of brands during her career, stretching from the 1990s (left) to recent times (right).
	Getty Images/Leon Neal/AFP; Getty Images/Jim Smeal/WireImage

CEOs often relish the opportunity to sell their own products and there have been some notable business people who have 'fronted' their organisation. Richard Branson used to promote Virgin Financial products and Steve Jobs actively promotes the launch of new products, including the iPad, depicted at Exhibit 15.4. Here, the CEO openly promotes his company and its products. This form of testimonial is popular when the image of the CEO is positive and the photogenic and on-screen characteristics provide for enhanced credibility.

The use of consumers as a product endorser challenges audiences to recognise and identify with a 'typical consumer'. The identification of similar lifestyles, interests and opinions allows for better reception and understanding of the message.

Consumers are often depicted testing similar products, such as margarine and butter. The Pepsi Challenge required consumers to select Pepsi from Coca-Cola through blind taste tests. By showing someone using the product, someone who is similar to the receiver, the source is perceived as credible and the potential for successful persuasion is considerably enhanced.

Users are also stimulated to engage in word-of-mouth communication and to pass on positive comments and observations to their peers. WoM can be depicted in advertising but through the use of a variety of techniques (see Chapter 2) and social media, users can create content and share brand based information with others.

Exhibit 15.4	Steve Jobs promoting the iPad and Apple
	Image courtesy of Getty Images/Ryan Anson/AFP

User-generated content

Before considering ways in which messages are designed, framed and presented, it is important to consider that today, increasing numbers of messages are developed and communicated by ordinary individuals, just like you. Not only are these used to communicate with organisations of all types and sizes but they are also shared with peers, family, friends and others in communities such as social networks and specialist interest online communities (e.g. reunion and family history sites). This is referred to as user-generated content (UGC) and can be seen in action at Flickr, Twitter and Digg.

What is interesting is that although people understand the rules and norms associated with communicating across peer groups and social networks, organisations have yet to master these new marketing environments. Firms are not able to use traditional forms of free communication or with as much credibility and authority as individuals regularly do within these new environments. One of the reasons for this is the democratisation of the media and the language codes that have emerged. A simple example is SMS texting. Although used by millions everyday to great effect, mobile communications and text messaging are only now becoming commercially prominent, mainly as a result of smart phone technology.

In December 2006, *Time* named 'you' (the consumer) as its Person of the Year and in January 2007 *Advertising Age* followed suit when it named 'the consumer' as its Advertising Agency of the Year. Simms (2007a) reports that both awards were made on the basis that consumers are regarded as responsible for making and generating more engaging brand communications than any one agency, during the previous year. It has to be said that most of this content was online but this is changing as the offline world becomes a target for content generation. See Viewpoint 15.3 for an example of how brands are trying to generate UGC offline. UGC can appear in many ways and in a variety of formats. The original format for UGC can be seen in letters to newspapers. The letter becomes part of the content of the newspaper and sits alongside the editorial and journalist written copy. More recently however, digitisation has enabled faster, more immediate posting opportunities for UGC.

Viewpoint 15.3   UGC gets competitive

Traditionally, the Oxo brand has been positioned around families. For years the tv ad formula was to show a family eating a meal where the OXO gravy featured as part of the storyline. That model no longer works and to help the brand become more contemporary a new approach was adopted. This involved inviting families to develop and submit a script for their next TV campaign. The script had to be uploaded to the OXO Factor channel on YouTube. Five were selected by a panel of judges and shown on broadcast TV prime time slots. The public then voted for their favourite, which won £10,000 and was broadcast during the final of *The X Factor*.

Doritos sourced a user-generated ad using a competition supported by D&AD and Channel 4. Using an on-pack promotion and an online campaign, the public were invited to develop and shoot a 29-second TV ad, using a competition tool kit to be found on the Doritos website. Doritos ran a weekly TV show on its website, which screened a variety of content including industry tips and judges' comments.

The 'directors' of the top 15 spots were then invited to pitch their ad to a panel of judges, who chose the three best ads. These were then voted for by the public. The winner received £100,000, plus £1 for every vote cast for them.

Source: Based on Benady (2009); Williams (2010)

Question

Are there areas or subjects where user-generated content might not be helpful?

Task

If some of your friends offered to create online content for you, which three topics would you request?

Email enables viewers to interact with television and radio programmes, with presenters encouraging audiences to write and tell them 'what you think' about a topic. Discussion boards and online forums can only work through consumer participation and user-generated content. One of the more common forms of UGC is blogging. This involves individuals, sometimes in the name of organisations, but more often as independent consumers, posting information about topics of personal interest. Sometimes these people develop opinion leader status and organisations feed them information about the launch of new brands, so that they pass on the information to opinion followers.

Social network sites thrive on the shared views, opinions and beliefs, often brand-related, of networked friends. YouTube and Flickr provide opportunities for consumers to share video and photos respectively, with all material posted by users. Users post their content and respond to the work of others, often by rating the quality or entertainment value of content posted by others.

Muñiz and Schau (2007) refer to what they call vigilante marketing. In these circumstances, consumers create self-generated advertising content to promote brands with which they have a strong affiliation. They refer to a brand community site based on the Apple Newton. This was an early PDA launched in 1993 and discontinued by Apple in 1998 as Palm Pilot undercut on price and exceeded the Newton on quality, size and overall value. Many users at the time blamed Apple for poor communications and not explaining the Newton accurately enough to attract more customers. Approximately 3,000–4,000 Newton users still participate in online forums. They create what the authors label as *brand artefacts*, some of which closely resemble ads, all for a brand that ceased production nearly a decade earlier. Their actions serve to maintain a brand that has a special meaning for them.

Sourcing content

UGC can be derived through one of three main processes.

CrowdSource

Organisations can prompt the public into action, via the web community, to develop specific types of content and materials. Where organisations deliberately invite the entire web community to suggest material that can be used commercially, in return for a reward, the term crowdsourcing is used. In this circumstance the crowd may consist of amateurs or businesses. The difference between crowdsourcing and outsourcing is that the latter is directed at a predetermined, specific organisation.

OpenSource

The public may take the initiative themselves and communicate with a specific organisation or industry. Where a group of people voluntarily offer ideas and materials, without invitation, prompting or in search of a reward by an organisation, the term open-source materials is used.

FriendSource

The public may exchange information and ideas amongst themselves, without any direct communication with an organisation or brand owner. This occurs when friends and families communicate and share ideas and materials among themselves, for their own enjoyment, bonding and enrichment.

Some marketers are using the increasing occurrence of UGC as an opportunity to listen to and observe consumers and to find out what meanings they attribute to products, brands and company actions. Some companies invite consumers to offer content (ads), crowdsourcing. Unilever dissolved their 16-year-old relationship with their ad agency Lowe London, in order to embark on a crowdsourcing strategy. Focusing on their Peperami brand, they searched for material to support a tv and print campaign. The result was 1,185 ideas and the winner won £6,000 (Charles, 2009).

Ideas about co-creation and collaboration now pervade marketing communications. As noted in Chapter 2 on communication, there is an increasing role for messages to be shared with audiences, not sent to or at them (Earls, 2010). Understanding the relationships audiences prefer with product categories and brands enables the identification of opportunities to share and collaborate.

Message framing

The vast majority of messages are generated professionally, not by users, and various strategies and tactics are used to develop effective messages. One of these is message framing, a strategy to present brand messages. However, as Tsai (2007) indicates, it is controversial and empirically unproven. Message framing works on the hedonic principles of our motivation

Table 15.1	Factors associated with message framing	
Factor		**Explanation**
Self construal	Independent	Individuals (the self) seek to distinguish themselves from others. These individuals respond best to positive framing.
	Interdependent	Individuals (the self) try not to distinguish themselves from others. These individuals respond best to negative framing.
Consumer involvement	High involvement Low involvement	Refers to the extent to which personal relevance and perceived risk influences decision-making within a product category. When high, negative framing is preferred; when low, positive framing is preferred.
Product knowledge	High Low	Product knowledge consists of two elements: behavioural (usage) experience and mental (search, exposure and information). Message framing is more suitable where product knowledge is low.

Source: Based on Tsai (2007).

to seek happiness and to avoid pain. So messages can be framed to either focus a recipient's attention on positive outcomes (happiness) or take them away from the possible negative outcomes (pain). For example, a positively framed message might concern a brand of yoghurt presented as 'contains real fruit' or a car as 'a stylish design'. Conversely messages could be presented as 'contains only 5 per cent fat' and 'low carbon emissions' – these are regarded as negatively framed.

Many practitioners work on the basis that positive are better than negative messages whereas others believe negative framing promotes deeper thinking and consideration. However, there is little empirical evidence to support any of these views. Therefore, in an attempt to understand when it is better to use positive or negative framing Tsai argues that it is necessary to develop a holistic understanding of the target audience. This involves considering three factors: self-construal; consumer involvement; and product knowledge. These are explained in Table 15.1.

Tsai believes that these three factors moderate an individual's response when they are exposed to positively or negatively framed brand messages. In turn these influence the three main dimensions of a brand's communication. These are generally accepted by researchers such as Mackenzie and Lutz (1989) and Lafferty *et al.* (2002) to be attitude to the ad, attitude to the brand and purchase intention (see Chapter 3 for a consideration of these dimensions). Tsai develops a conceptual model to demonstrate this and argues that brand communication persuasiveness is moderated by these three factors.

His research concludes that positive message framing should be used when the following exists:

Independent self-construal × low consumer involvement × low product knowledge

Negative framing should be used when there is:

Interdependent self-construal × high consumer involvement × low product knowledge

While message framing may provide a strategic approach to the overall way in which messages should be presented, it is also necessary to consider how a message should be included in order to optimise effectiveness. Consideration is now given to storytelling, the different forms of message appeal and the balance of information and emotion in a message.

Storytelling

Stories are considered to be an integral part of the way we lead our lives as they enable us to make sense of our perceived world and our role within it. Stories are embedded in music, novels, fairytales, films, news, religion, politics and plays. They are the foundation of word-of-mouth communication and a significant dimension of brands, yet are often an understated aspect of marketing communications.

Stories are used to frame our understanding and to encourage individuals to want to become a part of the story itself and to identify with a brand and or its characters. Strong brands are built around a core theme or platform from which a series of linked stories can be developed. Cordiner (2009) refers to brands having a moral premise (platform); Honda's power of dreams, and Starbucks 'third space' about having somewhere for each of us between work and home. He suggests that the television programme *The Wire* has a platform based on broken America. The platform for Harley Davidson is to empower individuals to be free from the 'prison of suburban life'. Virgin's platform is to challenge the establishment, and Google's is to set information free.

Nike's platform is a will to win and from this stories about winning can be developed. One such story concerns an athletics coach who was annoyed about the quality of sports equipment and running shoes in particular. Inspiration arrived whilst eating his breakfast waffles. He then spent several months in the garage with a waffle iron and some rubber. What emerged was a new running shoe and a new company, Nike (Cordiner, 2009).

Stories can be understood in terms of four main categories. These are:

- **Myths and origins** can be used to recall how a company started and what its principles are, but very often the focus is on how it overcame early difficulties and achieved success. The current values can often be seen embedded in these stories. For example, the founders of HP started the company in a garage. As the company grew, so a stream of stories centred on the garage developed. These referred to the roots of the company, and became a central and controlling element in the culture of the company through time.

- **Corporate prophecies** are predictions about an organisation's future, which are often based on past stories or stories about other organisations.

- **Hero stories** recall people from the organisation who confronted and overcame a dilemma. The story provides a set of behaviours and values to be copied by others, especially during periods of crisis. These stories help people establish priorities and make decisions. This is a common approach as used by US Airways, with respect to their pilot C.B. Sullenberger, who landed his plane safely on the Hudson river in January 2009. He became the hero of 'the miracle on the Hudson'.

- **Archived narratives are an organisation's collection of** stories which trace its history and development. With organisations changing names, being merged, bought out and reconstituted there is an increasing need to access key stories from the past in order to provide a sense of history.

Microsoft developed a 'Storytelling Framework' to generate focused relevant communications. The framework acts as a filter so that key messages are constantly reinforced. Using a 'Master Narrative' which sets out the three key elements that all Microsoft stories must contain, the framework provides a means of simplifying stories and communications emerging from a complex environment. Rather than promote this approach as a communication device Microsoft has stressed the business significance of the storytelling framework (Love, 2006).

Viewpoint 15.4   Telling a story to sell a game

Halo is a hugely successful series of videogames about how the human race resists alien forces. The Xbox game from Microsoft has a strong and loyal fan base. However, in order to grow it was necessary to reach a mainstream audience. The problem was, depicting scenes of violence and aggression in the promotional material would only reinforce the mainstream audience's preconceptions.

The Master Chief is the central figure and lead character in the videogame series. Research found that Halo fans believed the Master Chief to be an heroic figure and it was his story that motivated them to play this game. The character Master Chief represents the classic heroic qualities, bravery, sacrifice, duty and selflessness.

Traditionally these games are promoted by featuring the continuous action, thrills, spills, violence and endeavour of the good overcoming the bad that is to be experienced playing the game. The goal for the launch of Halo 3 was to engage audiences emotionally so that they perceived the Master Chief as a hero and would be motivated to take part in the story itself.

A campaign called 'Believe' was created. This was based on drawing people into stories about the Master Chief. To do this a history of the Master Chief's feats, achievements and heroic deeds was created, and anchored in a virtual Museum of Humanity. A year before launch a teaser ad ('Starry Starry Night') ran just once on TV, throughout the region of Europe, Middle East and Africa (EMEA). This was preceded by promotion on the web, designed to make the ad an appointment to view.

A TV ad also called 'Starry, Starry Nights' featuring artefacts and a monument from an historic battle in which Master Chief heroically led his troops to victory, was used to introduce the museum and the whole campaign leading up to the launch. Further TV and viral films were used to depict different aspects of the Master Chief's past, supported by fictitious war veteran testimonials, which all served to develop folk lore and establish the concept of the museum.

All around Europe, statues were erected in honour of the hero Master Chief, murals were painted and street plaques created, all commemorating various fictional battleground sites. A war photography exhibition was held in UK cinemas, showing the work of fictional war photographer Jake Courage. A huge PR and events programme throughout mainstream and specialist press, ensured maximum exposure and excitement about the launch of Halo 3. On the day before the launch, celebrity film style premiere parties, linked over Xbox LIVE and streamed on xbox.com, were held.

The results of this integrated campaign broke all expectations. With a target of an additional 375,000 users, 600,000 were recruited. Opening day sales were £84 million, smashing the Spiderman 3 record. The 'Starry Starry Night' pre-launch campaign ad has been viewed over 10 million times at sites such as YouTube. The war veteran testimonial viral films were viewed over 7 million times in their first 24 hours of release. The Museum of Humanity centre piece television spot has been viewed over 2 million times online. Such is the power of storytelling.

Source: Based on Gallery *et al.* (2009); Cowen (2007)

Question

To what extent is storytelling applicable to all products, services, markets and organisations?

Task

Identify a brand within an interest, hobby or pastime and develop the outline of a story that could be used to promote it.

The following comment by Warlick (2009) was posted at the foot of the account of this tale:

'The "Believe" campaign catapulted Halo 3 from an ordinary video game into a worldwide cultural phenomenon due to its ability to build an emotional rapport with the audience. The innovative stream of interactive TV, Web and cinema advertisements was an inspired approach that successfully attracted an audience beyond the typical gamer.'

Message appeal

The presentation of a message and stories requires that an appeal be made to the target audience. The appeal is important, because unless the execution of the message appeal (the creative) is appropriate to the target audience's perception and expectations, the chances of successful communication are reduced.

There are two main factors associated with the presentation. Is the message to be dominated by the need to transmit product-oriented information or is there a need to transmit a message that appeals predominantly to the emotional senses of the receiver? The main choice of presentation style, therefore, concerns the degree of factual information transmitted in a message, an information-based appeal, against the level of imagery thought necessary to make sufficient impact for the message to command attention and then be processed, an emotional (or transformational) appeal. There are numerous presentational or executional techniques, associated with each of these two approaches, but the following are some of the more commonly used appeals.

Informational appeals

Factual

Sometimes referred to as the 'hard sell', the dominant objective of these appeals is to provide, often detailed, information. This type of appeal is commonly associated with high-involvement decisions where receivers are sufficiently motivated and able to process information. Persuasion, according to the ELM, is undertaken through the central processing route. This means that ads should be rational and contain logically reasoned arguments and information in order that receivers are able to complete their decision-making processes. Ads such as those for property improvements (e.g. Stannah Stairlifts), household cleaners (e.g. Cillit Bang) and some electronic devices (e.g. iPad) often present their key messages in a logical, factual and rational way.

Slice of life

As noted earlier, the establishment of credibility is vital if any message is to be accepted and processed. One of the ways in which this can be achieved is to present the message in such a way that the receiver can identify immediately with the scenario being presented. This process of creating similarity is used a great deal in advertising and is referred to as slice-of-life advertising. For example, many washing powder advertisers use a routine that depicts two ordinary women (assumed to be similar to the target receiver), invariably in a kitchen or garden, discussing the poor results achieved by one of their washing powders. Following the advice of one of the women the stubborn stains are seen to be overcome by the brand.

On successful decoding of this message the overall effect of this appeal is for the receiver to conclude the following: that person is like me; I have had the same problem as that person; they are satisfied using brand X, therefore I too, will use brand X. This technique is simple, well-tried, well-liked and successful, despite its sexist overtones. It is also interesting to note that a number of surveys have found that a majority of women feel that advertisers use inappropriate stereotyping to portray female roles, these being predominantly housewife and mother roles.

Demonstration

A similar technique is to present the problem to the audience as a demonstration. The focus brand is depicted as instrumental in the resolution of a problem. Headache remedies, floor cleaners and tyre commercials have traditionally demonstrated the pain, the dirt and the danger respectively, and then shown how the focus brand relieves the pain (Panadol), removes the stubborn dirt (Flash) or stops in the wet on a coin (or the edge of a rooftop – Continental tyres). Whether the execution is believable is a function of the credibility and the degree of life-like dialogue or copy that is used.

Comparative advertising

Comparative advertising is a popular means of positioning brands. Messages are based on the comparison of a brand with either a main competitor brand or all competing brands, with the aim of establishing and maintaining superiority. The comparison may centre on one or two key attributes and can be a good way of entering new markets. Entrants keen to establish a presence in a market have little to lose by comparing themselves with market leaders. However, market leaders have a great deal to lose and little to gain by comparing themselves with minor competitors.

Emotional and transformational appeals

Appeals based on logic and reason, are necessary in particular situations, especially where there is high involvement. However, as products become similar and as consumers become more aware of what is available in the category, so the need to differentiate becomes more important. Increasing numbers of advertisers are using messages that seek to appeal to the target's emotions and feelings, a 'soft sell'. Cars, toothpaste, toilet tissue and mineral water often use emotion-based messages to differentiate their products' position.

There are a number of appeals that can be used to elicit an emotional response from an individual receiver. Of the many techniques available, the main ones that can be observed to be used most are fear, humour, animation, sex, music and fantasy and surrealism.

Fear

Fear is used in one of two ways. The first type demonstrates the negative aspects or physical dangers associated with a particular behaviour or improper product usage. Drink driving, life assurance and toothpaste advertising typify this form of appeal. For example, Scottish Widows, a financial services brand belonging to Lloyds TSB has used a lady dressed in a black cape to symbolise the 'Widow'. The 'Widow' has become synonymous with the brand – even taking on iconic status – especially as research shows that four out of five people can link the image with the company.

The second approach is the threat of social rejection or disapproval if the brand is not used. This type of fear is used frequently in advertisements for such products as anti-dandruff shampoos and deodorants and is used to support consumers' needs for social acceptance and approval.

Fear appeals need to be constrained, if only to avoid being categorised as outrageous and socially unacceptable. There is a great deal of evidence that fear can facilitate attention and interest in a message and even motivate an individual to take a particular course of action: for example to stop smoking. Fear appeals are persuasive, according to Schiffman and Kanuk (1991), when low to moderate levels of fear are induced. Ray and Wilkie (1970), however, show that should the level of fear rise too much, inhibiting effects may prevent the desired action occurring. This inhibition is caused by the individual choosing to screen out, through perceptive selection, messages that conflict with current behaviour. The outcome may be that individuals deny the existence of a problem, claim there is no proof or say that it will not happen to them.

Humour

If receivers are in a positive mood they are more likely to process advertising messages with little cognitive elaboration (Batra and Stayman, 1990). The use of humour as an emotional appeal is attractive because it can attract attention, stimulate interest and foster a positive mood. This can occur because there is less effort involved with peripheral rather than central cognitive processing, and this helps to protect mood. In other words, the positive mood state is more likely to be maintained if cognitive effort is avoided. Both Yellow Pages and 118 118 have used humour to help convey the essence of their brand and to help differentiate it from the competition. Fosters has developed a communications strategy for the lager brand targeted at young men, based around humour. This involves television ads, sponsorship of the Edinburgh Comedy Awards and Channel4 comedy, and the remaking of classic British comedy, for distribution online (Charles, 2010).

Zhang and Zinkhan (2006) found that humour is more effective when there is low rather than high involvement. They also consider whether the media used also influences the humour. For example, television and radio demand less effort to process messages compared with print work. The choice of media used to deliver humorous content can therefore be critical.

It is also argued that humour is effective because argument quality is likely to be high. That is, the level of counter-argument can be substantially reduced. Arguments against the use of humour concern distraction from the focus brand, so that while attention is drawn, the message itself is lost. With the move to global branding and standardisation of advertising messages, humour does not travel well. While the level and type of humour are difficult to gauge in the context of the processing abilities of a domestic target audience, cultural differences seriously impede the transfer of jokes around the world.

Visual humour such as that generated by Catherine Tate, *Little Britain* and the older lavatorial humour that made Benny Hill so popular, is according to Archer (1994) more universally acceptable than word-based humour (e.g. Mock the Week and QI). This is partly because word-based humour can get lost in translation into meaning, without local references to provide the clues in order to decipher the joke. Humour, therefore, is a potentially powerful yet dangerous form of appeal. Haas (1997) reports that UK advertising executives have significantly higher confidence in the use of humour than their US counterparts, but concludes that 'humour is a vague concept and … its perception is influenced by many factors' (1997: 15). These factors shape the context in which messages are perceived and the humour conveyed.

Animation

Animation techniques have advanced considerably in recent years, with children as the prime target audience. However, animation has been successfully used in many adult-targeted advertisements, such as those by Schweppes, Compaq, Tetley Tea, Direct Line Insurance and British Gas. The main reason for using animation is that potentially boring and low interest/involvement products can be made visually interesting and provide a means of gaining attention and recognition. A further reason for the use of animation is that it is easier to convey complex products in a way that does not patronise the viewer.

Sex

Sexual innuendo and the use of sex as a means of promoting products and services are both common and controversial. Using sex as an appeal in messages is excellent for gaining the attention of buyers. Research shows, however, that it often achieves little else, particularly when the product is unrelated. Therefore, sex appeals normally work well for products such as perfume, clothing and jewellery but provide for poor effectiveness when the product is unrelated, such as cars, photocopiers and furniture.

The use of sex in advertising messages is mainly restricted to getting the attention of the audience and, in some circumstances, sustaining interest. It can be used openly, as in various lingerie, fragrance and perfume advertisements, such as WonderBra and Escape; sensually, as in the Häagen-Dazs and Cointreau campaigns; and humorously in some of the Specsaver's ads.

Music

Music can provide continuity between a series of advertisements and can also be a good peripheral cue. A jingle, melody or tune, if repeated sufficiently, can become associated with the advertisement. Processing and attitudes towards the advertisement may be directly influenced by the music. Music has the potential to gain attention and assist product differentiation. Braithwaite and Ware (1997) found that music in advertising messages is used primarily either to create a mood or to send a branded message. For example, the music *Frankie Goes to Hollywood – Relax* was used by Virgin Atlantic in their ad *Still Red Hot* to reinforce the brand's 25-year tenure, for impact and attention. In addition, music can also be used to signal a lifestyle and so communicate a brand identity through the style of music used. Advertisers have used music as a cue to trigger moods (Alpert *et al.*, 2005), influence an ad's attention-generating ability (Kellaris *et al.*, 1993) and influence attitudes to the brand and the ad (Lalwani *et al.*, 2009). For example, many advertisements for cars use music, partly because music is able to draw attention, generate mood and express brand personality (e.g. BMW, Peugeot, Renault).

The use of music is not restricted to advertising. Music can be an instrumental aspect of the overall atmosphere in retail and store environments, brand experience events, conferences as well as in entertainment venues and telemarketing environments. Oakes and North (2008) demonstrate that the use of slow-tempo music can heighten relaxation levels and reduce perceived waiting times. They even suggest this might be a more cost effective solution for supermarket managers than adding checkout clerks when the queues lengthen unexpectedly or at busy times.

Fantasy and surrealism

The use of fantasy and surrealism in advertising has grown partly as a result of the increased clutter and legal constraints imposed on some product classes. By using fantasy appeals, associations with certain images and symbols allow the advertiser to focus attention on the product. The receiver can engage in the distraction offered and become involved with the execution of the advertisement. If this is a rewarding experience it may be possible to affect the receiver's attitudes peripherally. Readers may notice that this links to the earlier discussion on 'liking the advertisement'.

Finally, an interesting contribution to the discussion of message appeals has been made by Lannon (1992). She reports that consumers' expectations of advertisements can be interpreted on the one hand as either literal or stylish and on the other as serious or entertaining, according to the tone of voice. This approach vindicates the view that consumers are active problem-solvers and willing and able to decode increasingly complex messages. They can become involved with the execution of the advertisement and the product attributes. The degree of involvement (she argues implicitly) is a function of the motivation each individual has at any one moment when exposed to a particular message.

Advertisers can challenge individuals by presenting questions and visual stimuli that demand attention and cognitive response. This can be achieved through the use of parody, mixing humour with a cognitive challenge. For example, Specsavers ran a campaign in 2010 that featured a multitude of bikini-clad women running with handbags and shopping bags, to get to a man on a beach who was spraying himself with deodorant. However, on reaching him, he put on a pair of 'ugly' glasses and the then disenchanted women dispersed. This was a parody of Lynx's infamous 'Billions' campaign (Thomas, 2010).

When individuals respond positively to a challenge, the advertiser can either provide closure (an answer) or, through surreal appeals, leave the receivers to answer the questions themselves in the context in which they perceive the message. One way of achieving this challenging position is to use an appeal that cognitively disorients the receiver (Parker and Churchill, 1986). If receivers are led to ask the question 'What is going on here?' their involvement in the message is likely to be very high.

The surrealist approach does not provide or allow for closure. The conformist approach, by contrast, does require closure in order to avoid any possible counter-arguing and message rejection. Parker and Churchill argue that, by leaving questions unanswered, receivers can become involved in both the product and the execution of the advertisement. Indeed, as most advertisements contain a measure of rational and emotional elements, it is the right blend of the two elements that is necessary according to the level of perceived risk and motivation that the target audience has at any one particular moment.

The content should be a balance of the informative and emotional dimensions. Furthermore, message quality is of paramount importance. Buzzell (1964) reported that, 'Advertising message quality is more important than the level of advertising expenditure' (1964: 30). Adams and Henderson Blair (1992) confirm that the weight of advertising is relatively unimportant, and that the quality of the appeal is the dominant factor. However, these may have been true at one time of conventional media when the correct blend of informative and emotional elements in any appeal is paramount for persuasive effectiveness. With so many different and varied media opportunities available today, the issue is not just the content but the speed at which it can be shared in digital channels.

Copycat messaging

There are certain occasions where the appeal used by a follower brand can be judged to mimic that of the brand leader. The reasoning for adopting a copycat approach may be that the category has been revolutionised by the brand leader. For example, Magners revitalised the stagnant UK cider market by demonstrating its refreshment property through television and poster ads that showed the drink being poured over ice. Sales boomed to £17 million in 2006 with the result that competitors are copycatting the approach. For example, Bulmers now claim their cider brand is 'Born for Ice' and a new brand, Maguires, has entered the market, also based on the over-ice proposition (Bowery, 2007).

Using a similar style of message can be used strategically, to diffuse the potency of the brand leader's marketing communications. Bowery refers to Matalan's use of four models that aped Marks & Spencer's iconic campaign based around Twiggy and three other models. Matalan did not reinforce their approach with a subsequent high-profile campaign but M&S have continued the message strategy to great effect.

Advertising tactics

The main creative elements of a message need to be brought together in order for an advertising plan to have substance. The processes used to develop message appeals need to be open but systematic.

The level of involvement and combination of the think/emotional dimensions that receivers bring to their decision-making processes are the core concepts to be considered when creating an advertising message. Rossiter and Percy (1997) claim that there are two broad types of motive that drive attitudes towards purchase behaviour. These are informational and transformational motives and are now considered in turn.

Informational motives

Individuals have a need for information to counter negative concerns about a purchase decision. These informational motives (see Table 15.2) are said to be negatively charged feelings. They can become positively charged, or the level of concern can be reduced considerably, by the acquisition of relevant information.

Table 15.2	Informational motives
Motive	**Possible emotional state**
Problem removal	Anger–relief
Problem avoidance	Fear–relaxation
Incomplete satisfaction	Disappointment–optimism
Mixed approach–avoidance	Guilt–peace of mind
Normal depletion	Mild annoyance–convenience

Transformational motives

Promises to enhance or to improve the user of a brand are referred to as transformational motives. These are related to the user's feelings and are capable of transforming a user's emotional state, hence they are positively charged. Three main transformational motives have been distinguished by Rossiter *et al.* (1991) (see Table 15.3). Various emotional states can be associated with each of these motives, and they should be used to portray an emotion that is appropriate to the needs of the target audience.

For example, Cancer Research UK changed the approach it used to communicate with donors. For a while, its campaigns were framed around messages about family loss and in that sense adopted a negative approach. The charity then adopted an 'All Clear' campaign. This frame conveyed messages about people diagnosed with cancer and their improved chances of recovery due to the benefits of the research. For many people this is low-involvement with transformational motives. This means that the use of an emotional-based claim in the message is important. The happy ending, based on people surviving, achieves this while the endline uses a voice-over that requests a donation so that the words 'all clear' can be heard by more people in the future.

One of the key communication objectives, identified earlier, is the need to create or improve levels of awareness regarding the product or organisation. This is achieved by determining whether awareness is required at the point of purchase or prior to purchase. Brand recognition (at the point of purchase) requires an emphasis upon visual stimuli, the package and the brand name, whereas brand recall (prior to purchase) requires an emphasis on a limited number of peripheral cues. These may be particular copy lines, the use of music or colours for continuity and attention-grabbing frequent use of the brand name in the context of the category need, or perhaps the use of strange or unexpected presentation formats.

Table 15.3	Transformational motives
Motive	**Possible emotional state**
Sensory gratification	Dull–elated
Intellectual stimulation	Bored–excited
Social approval	Apprehensive–flattered

Viewpoint 15.5   Messaging functional foods

Some food manufacturers have presented their products emphasising the functional benefits. These products claim to improve a person's health, by lowering their cholesterol level for example, or by improving their digestive systems, providing extra energy or even making people cleverer. Brands such as Tropicana juice drink contain extra calcium to build bone health and strength. Kingsmill make Head Start, a bread that contains Omega-3, designed to improve brain health. The success of Actimel yoghurt drinks is based on its probiotic content that provides immunity and eases the digestive tract. These and many other products are based on scientific developments and are proving to be popular.

One of the problems facing functional food manufacturers is how best to communicate the benefits. By providing too much scientific information audiences become confused and switch off. Providing too little information about the benefits can result in the message not getting through. When Kellogg's launched Rice Crispies Muddles, a prebiotic for children, the message failed to penetrate the market and the brand was altered to Rice Krispies Multigrain (Bashford, 2007).

There is an argument that in the future, specialist functional foods need to be targeted at specific niche, lifestage segments, middle-agers with high cholesterol, and older women with brittle bones. These need to be coupled with simplified messages that convey particular health benefits.

Source: Based on Bashford (2007); Simms (2007b)

Question

Should functional foods provide for transformational or informational messages?

Task

Select a grocery product of your choice, visit the website and determine whether the overall message is informational or transformational. Justify your response.

Exhibit 15.5   Functional foods

Brands such as Actimel and Branston Baked Beans need to communicate their key benefits clearly and in an unscientific manner.
Images courtesy of Danone; Alamy Images/Paul Mogford

Advertising tactics can be determined by the particular combination of involvement and motives that exist at a particular time within the target audience. If a high-involvement decision process is determined, with people using a central processing route, then the types of tactics shown in Figures 15.1 and 15.2 are recommended (Rossiter and Percy, 1997).

Option 1: An emotional claim

Correct emotional portrayal very important when brand is introduced

Getting the target to like the advertisement is not important

Option 2: A rational claim

If the target's initial attitude to the brand is favourable, then make benefit claims clear

If they are against the brand, use a refutational approach

If there is a clear brand leader, use a comparative approach

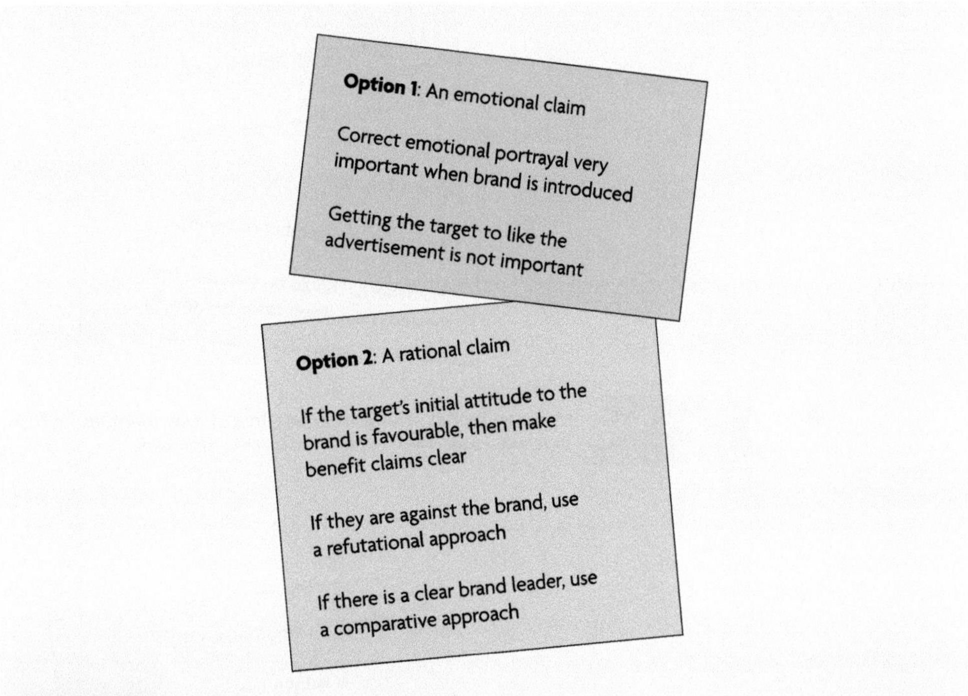

Figure 15.1 Message tactics where there are high involvement and informational motives
Source: After Rossiter and Percy (1997). Used with kind permission

Option 1: An emotional claim

Use emotion in the context of the prevailing lifestyle groups

Identification with the product is as important as liking the advertisement

Option 2: A rational claim

Include information as well

Overstate the benefits but do not understate them

Use repetition for reinforcement

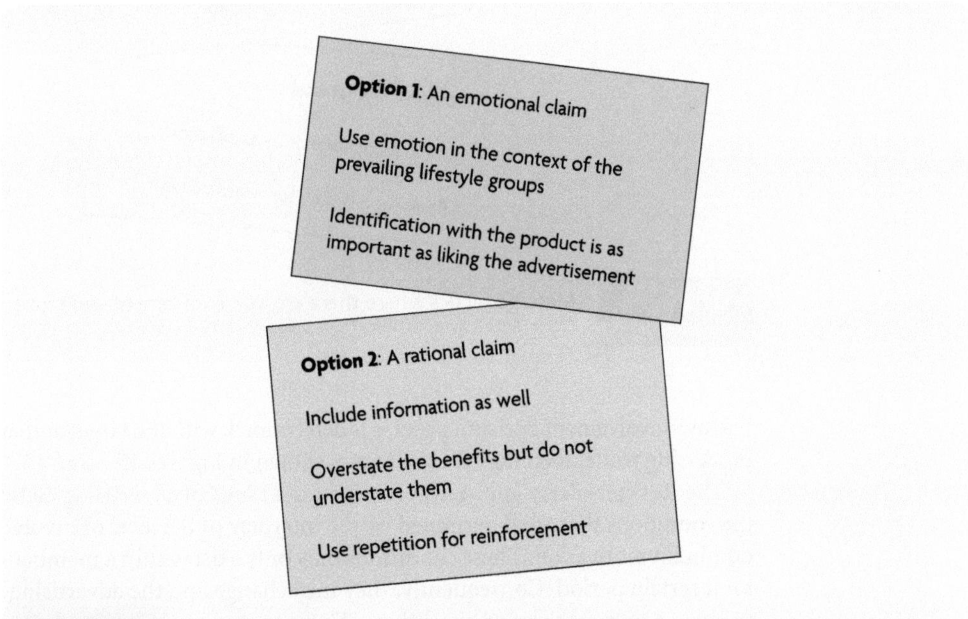

Figure 15.2 Message tactics where there are high involvement and transformational motives
Source: After Rossiter and Percy (1997). Used with kind permission

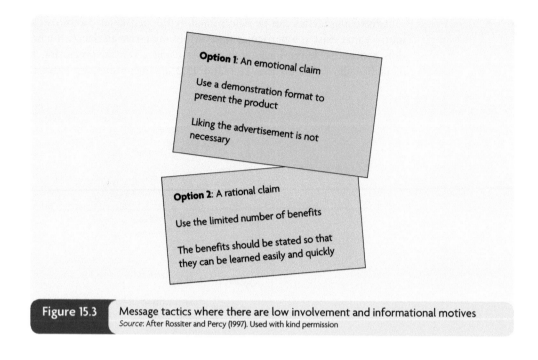

Figure 15.3   Message tactics where there are low involvement and informational motives
Source: After Rossiter and Percy (1997). Used with kind permission

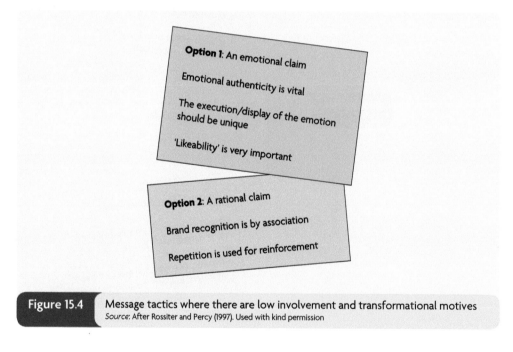

Figure 15.4   Message tactics where there are low involvement and transformational motives
Source: After Rossiter and Percy (1997). Used with kind permission

If a low-involvement decision process is determined, with the target audience using a peripheral processing route, then the types of tactics shown in Figures 15.3 and 15.4 are recommended.

The Rossiter–Percy approach provides for a range of advertising tactics that are oriented to the conditions that are determined by the interplay of the level of involvement and the type of dominant motivation. These conditions may only exist within a member of the target audience for a certain period. Consequently, they may change and the advertising tactics may also have to change to meet the new conditions. There are two main points that emerge from the work of Rossiter and Percy. The first is that all messages should be designed to carry both rational, logical information and emotional stimuli, but in varying degrees and forms.

Second, low-involvement conditions require the use of just one or two benefits in a message, whereas high-involvement conditions can sustain a number of different benefit claims. This is because persuasion through the central processing route is characterised by an evaluation of the alternatives within any one product category.

Summary

In order to help consolidate your understanding of messages and content, here are the key points summarised against each of the learning objectives.

1 Examine the importance and characteristics of source credibility

Source credibility consists of three key elements: the level of perceived expertise; the personal motives the source is believed to possess; and the degree of trust that can be placed in what the source says or does on behalf of the endorsement. Consumers trade off the validity of claims made by brands against the perceived trustworthiness (and expertise) of the individuals or organisations who deliver the message.

2 Explore the advantages and disadvantages of using spokespersons in message presentation

The use of spokespersons can draw attention and publicity to a brand, but should they fail to provide credibility or contravene a society's norms then the brand may be harmed. There are different types of spokesperson and each brings varying levels of effectiveness.

3 Discuss the impact of user-generated content

The use of user-generated content is increasing as communication becomes more democratised and technology advances. Information is increasingly being shared by consumers and content created in many different ways, including blogs, discussion boards and social networks.

4 Examine ideas concerning message framing and storytelling

Message framing works on the hedonic principles of our motivation to seek happiness and to avoid pain. Messages can be framed to either focus attention on positive outcomes (happiness) or take them away from the possible negative outcomes (pain).

Telling stories around a brand provides opportunities to frame our understanding and to encourage individuals to want to become a part of the story itself. Storytelling can also serve to help individuals identify with a brand and its characters. Strong brands are built around a core theme or platform from which a series of linked stories can be developed.

5 Consider the characteristics of different types of message appeal

Attention to message balance, structure and the form of the appeal is important if a message is to be successful and help achieve a campaign's goals. Increasing numbers of advertisers are using messages that seek to appeal to a target audience's emotions and feelings. This is necessary when products become similar and as consumers become more aware of what is available in the category. Of the many techniques available, the main ones used are fear, humour, animation, sex, music and fantasy and surrealism.

6 Indicate how informational and transformational motives can be used as tactical tools in advertising

It is claimed that there are two broad types of motive that drive attitudes towards purchase behaviour. These are informational and transformational motives. Individuals have a need for information to counter negative concerns about a purchase decision. These informational motives are said to be negatively charged feelings. They can become positively charged, or the level of concern can be reduced considerably, by the acquisition of relevant information.

Promises that a brand will enhance or improve a user are referred to as transformational motives. These are related to the user's feelings and are capable of transforming a user's emotional state, hence they are positively charged.

Review questions

1. Explain the three elements that constitute source credibility.
2. How can credibility be established?
3. Why do advertisers use spokespersons in their advertising? Find examples of each type of spokesperson.
4. Explain four forms of user-generated content.
5. Why is the use of user-generated content increasing?
6. Explain the principles upon which message framing is founded.
7. What are the four different categories of storytelling?
8. Find a brand that uses storytelling and identify the platform on which the stories are told.
9. Find examples of advertising messages for each of the main appeals identified.
10. Explain the difference between informational and transformational motivations.

References

Adams, A.J. and Henderson Blair, M. (1992) Persuasive advertising and sales accountability, *Journal of Advertising Research*, 32(2) (March/April), 20–25.

Agrawal, J. and Kamakura, W.A. (1995) 'The economic worth of celebrity endorsers: an event study analysis', *Journal of Marketing*, 59(3), 56–62.

Alleyne, R. (2005) Kate Moss apologises as Rimmel expresses 'shock and dismay', *Daily Telegraph*, 23 September. Retrieved 13 November 2007 from www.telegraph.co.uk/fashion/main.jhtml?xml=/fashion/2005/09/23/efkate23.xml

Alleyne, R. (2005) Kate Moss is dropped as the face of H&M, *Daily Telegraph*, 21 September. Retrieved 13 November 2007 from www.telegraph.co.uk/fashion/main.jhtml?xml=/fashion/2005/09/21/efkate21.xml

Alpert, M.I., Alpert, J.I. and Maltz, E.N. (2005) Purchase occasion influence on the role of music in advertising, *Journal of Business Research*, 58(3), 369–376.

Andersen, S. and Glassman, N. (1996), 'Responding to significant others when they are not there: effects on interpersonal inference, motivation and affect', in Sorretino, R.M. and Higgins, E.T. (eds) *Handbook of Motivation and Cognition*. New York: Guilford Press, 262–321.

Anon (2006) Kate Moss is the new face of Calvin Klein, *The Times*, 10 April. Retrieved 13 November from http://entertainment.timesonline.co.uk/tol/arts_and_entertainment/article703897.ece

Archer, B. (1994) Does humour cross borders?, *Campaign*, 17 June, 32–33.

Armstrong, L. (2006) Topshop deal keeps Kate Moss at the height of fashion, *The Times*, 21 September. Retrieved 13 November from http://women.timesonline.co.uk/tol/life_and_style/women/fashion/article646025.ece

Bashford, S. (2007) Functional foods: Now with added…, *Marketing*, 29 August, 26–29.

Batra, R. and Stayman, D.M. (1990) The role of mood in advertising effectiveness. *Journal of Consumer Research*, 17 (September), 203–214.

Benady, D. (2009) Advertising to the YouTube generation, *Marketing*, 25 November, 34–35.

Bowery, J. (2007) Haven't I seen you before?, *Marketing*, 6 June, 17.

Braithwaite, A. and Ware, R. (1997) The role of music in advertising, *Admap* (July/August), 44–47.

Buzzell, R. (1964) Predicting short-term changes in market share as a function of advertising strategy, *Journal of Marketing Research*, 1(3), 27–31.

Charles, G. (2009) Peperami ad will be test case for crowd-sourcing, *Marketing*, 4 November, 2.

Charles, G. (2010) Foster's set to remake British comedy shows, *Marketing*, 18 August, 1.

Chen, S. and Andersen, S.M. (1999) 'Relationships from the past in the present: significant other representations and transference in interpersonal life', *Advances in Experimental Social Psychology*, 31, 123–190.

Cordiner, R. (2009) Set free your core narrative: the brand as storyteller, *Admap*, October. Retrieved 8 July 2010 from www.warc.com

Cowen, N. (2007) Halo 3 review: Third time's the charm, *The Telegraph*, 26 September, retrieved 6 November 2010 from www.telegraph.co.uk/technology/3354551/Halo-3-review-Third-times-the-charm.html

Earls, M. (2010) The wisdom of crowds, *Admap* (May). Retrieved 10 May 2010 from www.warc.com/

Gallery, C., Rothenberg, T., Cohen, N. and Courage, J. (2009) Xbox Halo 3 – heroic storytelling, Account Planning Group – (UK), Gold & Grand Prix, Creative Strategy Awards. Retrieved 8 July 2010 from www.warc.com/

Haas, O. (1997) Humour in advertising, *Admap* (July/August), 14–15.

Kellaris, J.J., Cox, A.D. and Cox, D. (1993) The effect of background music on ad processing: A contingency explanation, *Journal of Marketing*, 57 (April), 114–125.

Kelman, H. (1961) Processes of opinion change, *Public Opinion Quarterly*, 25 (Spring), 57–78.

Lafferty, B.A., Goldsmith, R.E. and Newell, S.J. (2002) The dual credibility model: the influence of corporate and endorser credibility on attitudes and purchase intentions, *Journal of Marketing Theory and Practice*, 10(3), 1–12.

Lalwani, A.K., Lwin, M.O. and Ling, P.B. (2009) Does Audiovisual Congruency in Advertisements Increase Persuasion? The Role of Cultural Music and Products, *Journal of Global Marketing*, 22, 139–153.

Lannon, J. (1992) Asking the right questions – what do people do with advertising?, *Admap* (March), 11–16.

Love, M. (2006) Cutting through the clutter at Microsoft, *Strategic Communication Management*, 10(6), October/November, 18–21.

Loveless, H. (2007) Our Carol Vorderman loan nightmare, *Mail on Sunday*, 28 October. Retrieved 26 March 2008 from www.thisismoney.co.uk/campaigns/loansinsu/article

MacKenzie, S.B. and Lutz, R.L. (1989) An empirical examination of the structural antecedents of attitude toward the ad in an advertising pretesting context, *Journal of Marketing*, 53, 48–65.

McCracken, G. (1989) 'Who is the celebrity endorser? Cultural foundations of the endorsement process', *Journal of Consumer Research*, 16(3), 310–321.

Muñiz, A.M. and Schau, H.J. (2007) Vigilante marketing and consumer-created content communications, *Journal of Advertising*, 36(3) (Autumn), 35–50.

Oakes, S. and North, A.C. (2008) Using music to influence cognitive and affective responses in queues of low and high crowd density, *Journal of Marketing Management*, 24(5/6), 589–602.

Parker, R. and Churchill, L. (1986) Positioning by opening the consumer's mind, *International Journal of Advertising*, 5, 1–13.

Petty, R.E. and Cacioppo, J.T. (1983) Central and peripheral routes to persuasion: application to advertising. In *Advertising and Consumer Psychology* (eds L. Percy and A. Woodside), 3–23. Lexington, MA: Lexington Books.

Ray, M.L. and Wilkie, W.L. (1970) Fear: the potential of an appeal neglected by marketing, *Journal of Marketing*, 34 (January), 54–62.

Rossiter, J.R. and Percy, L. (1997) *Advertising and Promotion Management*, 2nd edn. New York: McGraw-Hill.

Rossiter, J.R., Percy, L. and Donovan, R.J. (1991) A better advertising planning grid, *Journal of Advertising Research* (October/November), 11–21.

Rushton, S. (2007) The big question: how did Topshop become the high street's dominant fashion brand?, *The Independent*, 1 May. Retrieved 13 November 2007 from http://news.independent.co.uk/uk/this_britain/article2499332.ece

Schiffman, L.G. and Kanuk, L. (1991) *Consumer Behavior*, 4th edn. Englewood Cliffs, NJ: Prentice-Hall.

Simms, J. (2007a) Advertising: and now a word from our customers, *Marketing*, 31 January. Retrieved 16 September 2007 from www.brandrepublic.com/News/629458/Advertising-word-customers/.

Simms, J. (2007b) Biggest brands, *Marketing*, 22 August 2007. Retrieved 6 November 2007 from www.brandrepublic.com/InDepth/Features/734340/Functional-foods-added/

Sullivan, H. (1953) *Interpersonal Theory of Psychiatry*, New York: NY Norton.

Thomas, J. (2010) Specsavers creates print campaign around England's World Cup exit, campaignlive.co.uk, 29 June 2010. Retrieved 20 July 2010 from www.brandrepublic.com/news/

Tsai, S.-P. (2007) Message framing strategy for brand communication. *Journal of Advertising Research*, 47(3) (September), 364–377.

Warlick, M. (2009) Xbox Halo 3 – heroic story telling, Creative Strategy Awards. Retrieved 8 July 2010 from www.warc.com/

White, D.W., Goddard, L. and Wilbur, N. (2009) The effects of negative information transference in the celebrity endorsement relationship, *International Journal of Retail & Distribution Management*, 37(4) 322–335.

Williams, M. (2010) Doritos ramps up prize fund for latest ad competition, campaignlive.co.uk, 16 February. Retrieved 6 April 2010 from www.campaignlive.co.uk/news/984073/Doritos-ramps-prize-fund-latest-ad-competition/

Zhang, Y. and Zinkhan, G.M. (2006) Responses to humorous ads: does audience involvement matter? *Journal of Advertising*, 35(4) (Winter), 113–127.

Minicase 3.1	Tapping into a new zeitgeist: women consumers, lifestyle trends and the *Red* Experience

Lorna Stevens: University of Ulster

In 1998, EMAP Elan launched a new woman's magazine called *Red* onto the already crowded UK women's monthly magazine market. The decision was based on the EMAP Elan's belief that there was an emerging sensibility in women in their thirties and forties that was not being catered for. This new 'zeitgeist' (spirit of the age) was the notion that age was a state of mind, and that contemporary women were taking youthful values and behaviours into their 30s and beyond. These 'middle-youth' women wanted a lively and vibrant magazine that helped them escape from their busy, day-to-day lives. EMAP Elan would offer women readers 'the precious experience of time to oneself' in a 'time poor world' (Rainey *et al.*, 1999).

The challenge for the *Red* team was to entice women in their 30s and 40s to buy the new magazine, and to do so they reckoned they would need to stress the pleasurable *experience* of consuming it. The advertising campaign revolved around three television ads, called 'Defining Moments', 'The Strip' and 'Me-Time'. Each of these advertisements made a direct appeal to the experiential aspects of consumption, namely the emotions and sensory feelings associated with the act of consumption (Holbrook and Hirschman, 1982).

Women's monthly magazines, while they are undeniably rich in information and advice for women, also have very strong experiential appeals for women. The editorial team at *Red* was convinced that women's magazines needed to provide an oasis of calm and pleasure in the midst of 'time-poor' everyday lives. Instead of addressing women in their 30s and 40s according to their numerous roles in life, then, the *Red* team decided that their unique proposition would be to focus on *Red* magazine as a self-indulgent, pleasurable *experience* that enabled women consumers to take time out from the demands of their daily, juggling lives. The name '*Red*' was chosen because it was considered 'quite sexy, quite glamorous, quite modern' (Anne-Marie Lavin, EMAP Elan). It also conjures up passion, warmth, feistiness, challenge, readability and simplicity. The focus of the marketing strategy would be on attitude and lifestyle, encapsulated by the core concept '*Red* Time is Me Time'.

The first television ad, 'Defining Moments' comprised a series of fleeting and evocative images, filmed in black-and-white, of a woman at work and at play, with soothing, classical music in the background. Its emphasis was on lifestyle rather than demographics. A female voiceover relates the following lines as the various scenes unfold:

> If you think life's too short for communal changing rooms/If you're madly in love with your garden/If you buy things and hide the receipts/If you're having an affair, or not/If you've grown up without growing old/ And you don't want to have it all, you just want to have what you want/Then it's probably time you saw *Red*.

The ad has an almost documentary quality as we see a quick succession of scenes from the woman's life. She is slim and attractive, dressed simply in a white shirt and dark trousers. We see her dining with friends, out of doors with her red setter dog; driving her car; dancing in a glamorous cocktail dress. We see her pensively looking out the window at bare winter branches, and a man leaving the house – an illicit lover or a devoted husband? Then we see her at a drawing board, talking on the phone; having her back scrubbed in a bath tub; on a bicycle with a child. The final image is the front cover of *Red*'s first issue, with the caption 'Go on, treat yourself.'

The advertisement's attractive and evocative cinematic style and its romantic images are clearly designed to appeal to women consumers' senses and emotions. By the end of the ad nothing is known about the magazine's contents, but the ad is designed to enable the target market to recognise aspects of themselves in the series of so-called 'defining moments'. Anne-Marie Lavin, the then marketing manager of *Red,* observes: 'I think you can launch a magazine quite easily, but it's more difficult to launch a brand, and everything that we do – and that's everything in the magazine used to market it – reflects those values.'

The second advertisement in the series is called 'The Strip', which was launched a year after 'Defining Moments'. This ad caused considerable debate at its inception stage, as it shows a woman doing a striptease. The *Red* team were somewhat anxious about this concept, and were worried that if the ad was too sexually suggestive it might alienate the target market. They therefore worked closely with the ad agency to ensure that the ad portrayed the woman in a humorous way, as a likeable, human subject, rather than an objectified sex object.

An attractive 30-something woman enters a dark room wearing a black coat and high-heeled shoes. She switches on a lamp, and picks up a red note from the console table.

Grinning, she tosses the note away from her, and her bag. Next she slowly removes her coat, shoulder by shoulder, and we realise she is doing a striptease. A woman's smoky voice sings *I dreamt that I was chasing – the monster out of me*. There are several cream sofas in the room, with scarlet cushions. The woman strikes various exaggerated, humorous poses as she gradually strips off to her underwear. At one point she kicks off one of her shoes, and it flies through the air, knocking over a tall vase of white lilies. She pulls a face, but continues to smile. We notice a bright green toy on the floor behind her. One of her stockings drifts onto a console table beside a framed photograph of a man, and she blows an exaggerated kiss at it. She walks over towards a sofa, tripping over the soft toy as she does so. She laughs and makes a face at herself in the mirror, and snatches some clothing from the back of the sofa. The next scene is of her reclining on the cream sofa, surrounded by rich red cushions, dressed in tracksuit bottoms and a fleecy top, smiling and reading a copy of *Red* magazine. A woman's voice now says '*Red* magazine – drop everything', underlining the humour that pervades the ad. Despite its somewhat risky and indeed risqué marketing strategy, the ad worked, and indeed sales of the magazine increased by 30,000 on the previous month.

The third advertisement, 'Me-Time', was launched a year after 'The Strip'. This ad was very different from the two previous ads, but once again there was a clear focus on the concept of 'me-time'. The ad focuses on ideal reading scenarios, and gives centre stage to a red sofa, which is used in every frame in the ad to symbolise the concept of 'me-time'. An elegant scarlet sofa is shown in a variety of idyllic places: a lush, flower-filled summer meadow, complete with butterflies; a sandy beach by moonlight; the sofa surrounded by a circle of candles; a sunny Mediterranean terrace; a rugged, mountain landscape overlooking a still lake, against a backdrop of a blue and white streaked sky. The final image is of a woman sitting on the sofa in an Italianate-style terrace, complete with elegant columns, urns and a water fountain. She sits, her bare feet drawn up beside her, absorbed in a copy of *Red* magazine, smiling. At the end of the ad a woman's voice says '*Red* magazine – your sofa awaits.' We are then shown the current issue of *Red*, against a luxurious red satin background, underlining its magical and precious qualities, and its associations with

sensuous pleasure and relaxation. 'Your sofa awaits' clearly recalls the famous line from the Cinderella fairytale 'Your carriage awaits'. And just as a pumpkin can become a glass carriage, a sofa can become a magic carpet when combined with a very special ingredient, *Red* magazine. In short, it can carry its readers off to better places!

The *Red* marketing campaign was a great success: against the odds, the magazine was able to squeeze its way into the crowded women's magazine market, and more importantly, hold its own there, a feat it has continued to perform in the 10 years since its launch. Much of *Red*'s success is down to the clear focus of EMAP Elan's marketing strategy, and its memorable TV ads, all of which were based on the concept of 'me-time'. The *Red* case is testimony to the fact that consumers are very receptive to ads that appeal to their emotions, feelings and senses. *Red* magazine's development team recognised that it was not just about getting the contents of the magazine right; it was about creating the right ambiance around the magazine, and developing a strong and appealing brand image and personality for *Red*. It was also about understanding its market, and positioning the brand in such a way as to reflect current lifestyle trends. By creating a brand that encapsulated the notion of me-time and self-indulgence, *Red* appealed to 'middle-youth' women in their 30s and 40s who wanted a lively and pleasurable read, *and* the chance to put their feet up and indulge in some 'me-time'!

Questions

1. Can you think of other marketing campaigns that have recognised a new consumer trend or 'zeitgeist' and developed their campaign around this?

2. Do you think that experiential appeals have become more commonplace than informational ones in advertising? If so, why do you think this is the case?

3. The women's magazine market is holding its own in the face of increased competition from the Internet, TV and newspapers, and in fact magazine readership is rising, with Keynote predicting that this trend will continue. Why do you think women's magazines continue to appeal to women?

Minicase 3.2   EasyPack, EasyComms

EasyPack was one the first furniture retailers in the UK to open large stores at out-of-town locations. Its initial success was founded on sales of flatpack kitchen and bedroom furniture, which it sold cheaply and discounted regularly. At the time it was a new retail concept whereby customers took home packs of furniture which they then assembled themselves. Trident, the name of the EasyPack kitchen brand is still a strong brand name, although many people do not associate the name as part of EasyPack. However, despite the company's success there were quality related problems typified by broken or missing parts. This association with poor quality has continued to tarnish the EasyPack brand.

Recently EasyPack's sales performance has declined and last year turnover fell by approximately 12 per cent. It is still the market leader as the market fell with the recession, but the fall in market share from 11.6 per cent to 9.4 per cent is of concern. More recent entrants to the market, Regents and ASF, are beginning to take market share from both ends of the market. Regents have strong design and quality attributes which are targeted at a niche market (of upwardly mobile professional people). Part of the strength of the ASF chain is its strong distribution and limited (flatpack) product range. Tougher competition combined with economic pressures and a series of strategy changes have served to confuse consumers' perception of EasyPack so that it is uncertain what the brand now offers customers.

Home owners are taking increased interest in their homes as home buying has become problematic with mortgages difficult to secure. Television programmes aimed at people interested in home decoration and design for all types of houses, attract large audiences. The housing boom in the 2004–07 saw the launch of a wave of new interior design, DIY and property based magazines to feed this market.

The style of communications used by EasyPack is largely fast paced, price oriented and features happy family couples with their new furniture. Television is the main media, used to promote its sales promotions activities. These are focused around the price-led sales at different times of the year (e.g. winter sales) and various discount initiatives used to boost store traffic. It has been said that too much reliance was placed on the company's market leadership position and little was done to communicate the EasyPack offer. Indeed, much has been done

to the product to correct the quality and missing parts problems but it is clear that these changes have not been communicated.

Whilst the EasyPack approach to marketing communications has been reasonably innovative, it has been designed to maintain the company's down market positioning. Some competitors however, have been quite radical, both in terms of the message, and the variety of media used. Some have featured celebrities to bring personality into their brand based advertising.

A new marketing team has been introduced and they plan to reverse the declining fortunes with a series of measures designed to change customer attitudes towards the EasyPack brand. The company will continue its focus on bedroom and kitchen furniture and instead of regular discounting, will move towards a value-for-money proposition. To accomplish this a range of other communication tools and media were considered. Rather than just change brand attitudes, some members of the team believe that EasyPack should increase their below-the-line spend, as this will help improve sales immediately and complement the value-for-money orientation. Others believe the campaign should be based on social media and want to see investment in the around-the-line spend.

Note: Some of the material has been amended and/or disguised to provide a suitable context for the minicase study and is not intended to imply good or bad management or current timescales.

Questions

1. Discuss the case for and against with regard to the three following possibilities:
   (a) the extent to which above-the-line activities should dominate EasyPack's marketing communications in order to change customer perceptions
   (b) the extent to which below-the-line activities should dominate EasyPack's marketing communications in order to change customer perceptions
   (c) the extent to which around-the-line activities should dominate EasyPack's marketing communications in order to change customer perceptions.
2. Select one and develop and justify a suitable marketing communications mix.

Minicase 3.3   ZipZap Channels

Over the years, ZipZap developed a twin channel approach to reach its customers. These channels consisted of their own sales force, which sold direct to business customers, and a dealer network. The dealer network had originally been created to cover particular geographic areas of the country that the sales force could not service economically. However, the dealers had subsequently expanded their areas, partly, they argued, to cope with market growth and the opportunities not satisfied by ZipZap's direct sales effort.

For a time these two channels coexisted reasonably comfortably, but eventually they began to compete with each other. This could be seen through heavy discounting of proposals to secure contracts, duplication of marketing and selling efforts, and customers becoming confused and uncertain about whom they should work with. The result was that an increasing number of leads were not being converted and business was lost to other, more effective competitors. Eventually many dealers started to become alienated and some even dropped ZipZap from their portfolio of suppliers.

By 2010, ZipZap recognised that the dealer conflict needed to be resolved. As a result of their research and by talking directly with the dealers, they began to understand that their dealers wanted to work with ZipZap more closely than was currently permitted, and they did not want to compete with the manufacturer's sales force.

ZipZap accepted that the dealer network was of the greatest importance, yet recognised that its size had to change. Of the original 117 dealers, 70 were released and the remaining 47 were designated as Professional Partners. These Partners were responsible for geographic areas, whilst ZipZap disbanded its direct sales force and a Key Account Management team was developed.

Once the structure was agreed, it was necessary to consider the mechanisms by which the marketing channel would function. Each Partner is allocated a Partner Manager who is directly responsible for the performance of their Professional Partners. In addition, a web-enabled customer relationship management (CRM) system was installed, designed to strengthen collaboration and assist with the development of relationships. This system provides, amongst other things, online support about stock availability, pricing, sales lead management, sales support, advertising, direct marketing, PR, training, plus finance and warranty.

Sales leads are often a sensitive issue with dealers, and ZipZap were aware that they had to install an effective and fair system to manage all sales leads, regardless of how they entered the company. As part of the overall CRM system, an outsourced Customer Contact Centre, utilising the ZipZap database, was developed. This is used to help generate leads through the website and email communications, and through telemarketing campaigns. All leads are channelled, vetted and qualified. The primary tasks are to ensure the accuracy of the data and to secure permission for future contact by whatever channel each lead was secured. These qualified leads are then posted onto the CRM system and accessed by the Partner Managers. They allocate each lead to the most appropriate Professional Partner, depending on factors such as location, resources and sales history, and an automatic email alert is sent to the Partner. By logging on to the site using a password, the Professional Partner can then access full details, including the equipment requirement, the channel preference and any relevant information. Whereas once it might have taken four or five days before the lead got through to the dealer, now it is less than 24 hours.

After the Partner has responded to the lead, all resulting activity is recorded on a tracking system, enabling the ZipZap Partner Manager to track progress and the outcome. If the lead does not generate a sale relatively quickly, the Professional Partner decides whether to hold onto it for future sales and marketing activity, or pass it back to ZipZap to follow up with online and telemarketing, to establish what further contact is appropriate.

In addition to product information, ZipZap understood that they needed to support their Professional Partners in other ways. They began to provide product and sales training, access to a bank of direct marketing mail packs, current price lists and brochures for their own marketing initiatives: all of these are available online through the system. ZipZap's own trade advertising schedules and marketing communication materials are also available in advance on the system, so Partners can plan any local marketing around the company's wider corporate effort. Assisting with recruitment, systems design and finance facilities are now an embedded aspect of the relationship. However, ZipZap refused to use trade promotions and the extent of their public relations activities was limited to press releases and some conference work. ZipZap attend the main exhibitions but discourage attendance at local events and trade shows believing it was up to the Professional Partners to invest where their customers were located.

ZipZap have high hopes for this targeted approach. This form of collaboration has led to a 23 per cent rise in sales, a 36 per cent market share and a conversion rate of 22 per cent.

Questions

Recently, some Professional Partners have expressed concern about the efficiency and role of ZipZap's marketing communications. They believe that the marketing communication mix used by ZipZap could be improved. As a member of the marketing team at ZipZap, prepare notes for your colleagues which respond to the following questions:

1. Explain how the marketing communications used by ZipZap should complement the preferred relationship style of the dealer or customer.

2. Using the ideas generated in response to the previous question, formulate a marketing communications mix for ZipZap.

3. Recommend and justify ways in which ZipZap could develop their web-based marketing communications.

Minicase 3.4 — Jol Yoghurt – keeping things in proportion

Yoghurt is a global food. All sorts of people, regardless of their demographics and geographic characteristics, consume it. Yoghurt consumption is increasing, partly because the food is convenient, portable, suitable for freezing and rich in nutrients. In recent years, however, new yoghurts based on scientific insights, such as the addition of probiotics, omega-3 and plant sterols, have proved extremely successful (particularly with people aged over 40). These products claim to improve a person's health, for example by lowering their cholesterol level, improving their digestive system, providing extra energy or even making them cleverer.

These products are typical of the new wave of 'functional foods'. These are ordinary products repositioned to provide 'clinically proven and claimable health benefits'. For example, Coca-Cola launched Diet Coke Plus, a vitamin-packed carbonated drink targeted at young women.

Research has found four distinct types of yoghurt consumer, and these are listed in Table 1.

The same study found that the use of scientific names and formulas in marketing communications messages, designed to support functional foods, was not entirely successful. This approach only worked when there was prior education and extensive exposure to the products.

Priority Foods is a major manufacturer and its research and development (R&D) programme has developed a new range of fruit yoghurts based on the functional food principle. Essentially, the new product is classified as a satiety product, that is, one that delivers a feeling of being full after eating. The technology associated with these products was developed to fight the obesity epidemic that has affected many western countries but is now also evident in other regions, including urban areas of China. The new product, code-named Jol, is to be positioned as a tasty, satisfying and healthy meal. It is to be used by people who want to manage their weight, yet who do not want to take part in a formal, controlled weight loss programme.

Table 1	Four Yoghurt Market Segments (Adapted from Luckow, 2005)	
Segment name	% of market	Yoghurt segment descriptors
Health seekers	33%	Consumers in this segment prefer rich, indulgent flavours but the yoghurt must have some health benefits as it is used as part of a low fat, low cholesterol diet. They trust messages from official endorsers and opinion formers.
Product lovers	24%	Consumers in this segment prefer to eat yoghurt as a quick and easy meal alternative. They like classic fruit flavours, trust endorsers and seek brands that contain omega-3 fatty acids to reduce the risk of heart disease.
Anti-health devotees	36%	Consumers in this segment use yoghurt as a quick and easy snack. They prefer brands with fruit at the bottom and trust some brand names. They are not interested in health related endorsements, as taste and colour are the critically important attributes.
Flavour cravers	7%	Consumers in this segment use natural yoghurt brands and avoid artificial flavours, colours or preservatives. They use yoghurt as part of a healthy diet and look specifically for brands containing functional ingredients. Endorsements and recommendations are important.

Formative ideas for a launch campaign include scheduling the media to run during the post festival months, for example January and February in Europe, when the Christmas and New Year celebrations are finished and resolutions to change behaviour are prominent in people's minds. The aim will be to give consumers a clear understanding of Jol and how it can fit into their own weight loss programme. In one country, the equivalent of a $750,000 sampling and sponsorship programme is planned, to enable people to taste *Jol* at various supermarkets and special events.

An initial strapline 'Are *you* feeling good?' is intended to highlight the satisfying effect of Jol and the emotional aspirations associated with weight loss.

Note: The above data is based on various publications and magazine articles, but details have been changed for assessment purposes and do not reflect current management practices.

Questions

As a marketing assistant at Priority you have been assigned to the Jol brand. You may choose any country or region on which to base your launch recommendations. The segmentation data applies to your country/region.

You are to prepare a report for your manager in which you should address the following tasks.

1. Determine and justify the range of marketing communications tools and media you believe are needed to support the Jol launch campaign in your chosen country or region.

2. Advise how marketing communications might be used effectively prior to and during the launch campaign for the Jol brand, in order to reach and motivate Priority's channel intermediaries.

Index